Asset Prices and Monetary Policy

A National Bureau
of Economic Research
Conference Report

Asset Prices and Monetary Policy

Edited by **John Y. Campbell**

The University of Chicago Press

Chicago and London

JOHN Y. CAMPBELL is Harvard College Professor and the Morton L.
and Carole S. Olshan Professor of Economics at Harvard University,
and a research associate of the National Bureau of Economic
Research.

The University of Chicago Press, Chicago 60637
The University of Chicago Press, Ltd., London
© 2008 by the National Bureau of Economic Research
No copyright is claimed for the contributions of Andrew Levin,
Monika Piazzesi, and Martin Schneider.
All rights reserved. Published 2008
Printed in the United States of America

17 16 15 14 13 12 11 10 09 08   1 2 3 4 5

ISBN-13: 978-0-226-09211-9 (cloth)
ISBN-10: 0-226-09211-9 (cloth)

Library of Congress Cataloging-in-Publication Data

Asset prices and monetary policy / edited by John Y. Campbell
       p. cm.
    Includes bibliographical references and index.
    ISBN-13: 978-0-226-09211-9 (cloth : alk. paper)
    ISBN-10: 0-226-09211-9 (cloth : alk. paper) 1. Monetary
  policy. 2. Securities—Prices. 3. Speculation. 4. Capital assets
  pricing model. 5. Investment analysis—Mathematics. 6. Capital
  investments. I. Campbell, John Y.
  HG230.3.A733 2008
  339.5'3—dc22

                                                    2007052628

⊗ The paper used in this publication meets the minimum requirements
of the American National Standard for Information Sciences—
Permanence of Paper for Printed Library Materials, ANSI Z39.48-1992.

Relation of the Directors to the Work and Publications of the National Bureau of Economic Research

1. The object of the NBER is to ascertain and present to the economics profession, and to the public more generally, important economic facts and their interpretation in a scientific manner without policy recommendations. The Board of Directors is charged with the responsibility of ensuring that the work of the NBER is carried on in strict conformity with this object.

2. The President shall establish an internal review process to ensure that book manuscripts proposed for publication DO NOT contain policy recommendations. This shall apply both to the proceedings of conferences and to manuscripts by a single author or by one or more co-authors but shall not apply to authors of comments at NBER conferences who are not NBER affiliates.

3. No book manuscript reporting research shall be published by the NBER until the President has sent to each member of the Board a notice that a manuscript is recommended for publication and that in the President's opinion it is suitable for publication in accordance with the above principles of the NBER. Such notification will include a table of contents and an abstract or summary of the manuscript's content, a list of contributors if applicable, and a response form for use by Directors who desire a copy of the manuscript for review. Each manuscript shall contain a summary drawing attention to the nature and treatment of the problem studied and the main conclusions reached.

4. No volume shall be published until forty-five days have elapsed from the above notification of intention to publish it. During this period a copy shall be sent to any Director requesting it, and if any Director objects to publication on the grounds that the manuscript contains policy recommendations, the objection will be presented to the author(s) or editor(s). In case of dispute, all members of the Board shall be notified, and the President shall appoint an ad hoc committee of the Board to decide the matter; thirty days additional shall be granted for this purpose.

5. The President shall present annually to the Board a report describing the internal manuscript review process, any objections made by Directors before publication or by anyone after publication, any disputes about such matters, and how they were handled.

6. Publications of the NBER issued for informational purposes concerning the work of the Bureau, or issued to inform the public of the activities at the Bureau, including but not limited to the NBER Digest and Reporter, shall be consistent with the object stated in paragraph 1. They shall contain a specific disclaimer noting that they have not passed through the review procedures required in this resolution. The Executive Committee of the Board is charged with the review of all such publications from time to time.

7. NBER working papers and manuscripts distributed on the Bureau's web site are not deemed to be publications for the purpose of this resolution, but they shall be consistent with the object stated in paragraph 1. Working papers shall contain a specific disclaimer noting that they have not passed through the review procedures required in this resolution. The NBER's web site shall contain a similar disclaimer. The President shall establish an internal review process to ensure that the working papers and the web site do not contain policy recommendations, and shall report annually to the Board on this process and any concerns raised in connection with it.

8. Unless otherwise determined by the Board or exempted by the terms of paragraphs 6 and 7, a copy of this resolution shall be printed in each NBER publication as described in paragraph 2 above.

Contents

Acknowledgments

It was an honor to be invited by Martin Feldstein to organize an NBER conference on asset prices and monetary policy. For the past thirty years, Marty Feldstein, in his role as president of the NBER, has encouraged lending economists to do high-quality empirical research, informed by economic theory, with relevance for policymakers. A key guarantor of the quality of this research is the NBER conference at which economists from academia, the public sector, and the private sector gather to discuss the work. The NBER conference volume is a lasting record of the conference and an influential outlet for the papers presented there. Its impact is enhanced by the publication of a group of related papers, together with informed discussion.

In this last year of Marty's tenure as president of the NBER, it is particularly appropriate to thank him for the opportunity to edit this conference volume on a key issue in monetary policy. Of course, the opportunity would not be nearly as tempting without the first-rate professional assistance of the NBER's conference and publication departments. Special thanks are due to Carl Beck, Lita Kimble, and Helena Fitz-Patrick from NBER and to Parker Smathers from the University of Chicago Press. In the early stages of the project, staff members at both the Bank of England and the Federal Reserve Board were particularly helpful in suggesting relevant topics. Finally, I would like to thank Ian Martin, a PhD student at Harvard, who served as rapporteur for the conference and made possible the publication of the general discussion.

Introduction

John Y. Campbell

During the past quarter century, monetary authorities in developed countries have been remarkably successful at reducing and stabilizing inflation. Fluctuations in output have also been less severe than they were in earlier decades, leading commentators to coin phrases such as "the great moderation" or "nice decade."[1] However, the same period has seen major fluctuations in asset markets, most obviously the sustained bull market in equities during the 1980s and 1990s, the boom and subsequent bust in technology stocks during the late 1990s and early 2000s, the dramatic increase in house prices in the first few years of this century, and, most recently, falling house prices and rising commodity prices.

Central bankers have always paid some attention to asset prices in connection with their mission of ensuring the soundness of the banking system. In the United States, for example, the Federal Reserve took measures to choke off the stock price boom of the late 1920s, provided liquidity after the stock market crash of 1987, and helped to engineer the bailout of the hedge fund Long-Term Capital Management in 1998. Recently, however, there has been increased interest in the relevance of asset prices for macroeconomic stability. The chapters in this volume, presented at a National Bureau of Economic Research (NBER) conference at the Wequassett Inn in Chatham, Massachusetts, on May 5–6, 2006, explore the relationship between asset prices and monetary policy from this point of view.

Several chapters in the volume ask what monetary authorities can learn

John Y. Campbell is Harvard College Professor and Morton L. and Carole S. Olshan Professor of Economics at Harvard University, and a research associate of the National Bureau of Economic Research.

1. "Nice" stands for noninflationary consistently expansionary, an acronym due to Governor Mervyn King of the Bank of England.

from asset markets. These chapters treat asset prices not as ultimate goals of monetary policy, nor as variables that can be directly controlled, but as indicators of macroeconomic conditions to which monetary authorities can respond.

Stephen G. Cecchetti opens the volume with an empirical analysis of equity markets in twenty-seven countries and housing markets in seventeen countries. He finds particularly strong linkages between housing markets and the macroeconomy. Housing booms predict strong economic growth in the near term, weak economic growth in the longer term, and relatively high inflation. Cecchetti argues that central bankers are and should be particularly concerned about extreme negative outcomes; they act as macroeconomic risk managers. Accordingly, Cecchetti evaluates the relation between equity and housing booms and extremely high inflation or low output. He finds that both types of booms worsen the distribution of worst outcomes (measured as the mean within the lower 25 percent tail of the output distribution or the upper 25 percent tail of the inflation distribution). There is some evidence that the equity market effects are stronger, and housing effects are weaker, in economies with market-based financial systems and high ratios of stock market capitalization to gross domestic product (GDP). Cecchetti uses these results to argue that traditional academic analysis, which looks at the first two moments of output and inflation, understates the importance of asset prices for the practice of central banking.

Central bankers will have greater confidence responding to asset prices if they understand what structural forces are driving them and how these forces affect output and inflation. One common view is that prices are driven by exogenous shocks to investor beliefs or preferences that have little or nothing to do with underlying macroeconomic fundamentals. In 1996, Alan Greenspan famously used the phrase "irrational exuberance" to describe a positive shock of this sort. An alternative view is that asset markets reflect evolving beliefs about the long-run prospects for the economy, particularly the trend rate of productivity growth.

The second chapter in this volume, by Simon Gilchrist and Masashi Saito, builds a model that embodies this alternative view. Their model contains a financial accelerator mechanism (Bernanke, Gertler, and Gilchrist 1999); that is, high asset prices increase the collateral of entrepreneurs and lower the cost of external funds for investment. Gilchrist and Saito evaluate several alternative monetary policies using a quadratic loss function in the output gap and inflation. They find that a policy of aggressive inflation targeting is less than ideal because, while it stabilizes inflation, it allows the financial accelerator to destabilize output. When expected productivity growth accelerates, asset prices rise, external funds become cheap, and investment and output increase by more than they would do in a frictionless economy. The monetary authority can offset this by calculating and responding to the "asset price gap," the difference between the level of asset prices and the level that would prevail in a frictionless economy. The benefits of such a policy are particularly large if the monetary authority has better information about long-run growth than does the private sector. However, Gilchrist and Saito caution that an uninformed central bank can do damage if it responds naively to the level of asset prices, because such a policy will tend to produce inflation when there is a productivity slowdown, and deflation when productivity growth accelerates.

Tommaso Monacelli's chapter also emphasizes the role of collateral in debt markets. Monacelli points out that in an economy in which some households are borrowing-constrained, welfare increases if the constraints are relaxed. The central bank should take this effect into account when formulating optimal monetary policy. Monacelli argues that it may be appropriate for a central bank to allow some surprise inflation when there is a temporary improvement in productivity. At such a time, borrowing constraints tend to bind more tightly, but if households have long-term nominal debt, inflation offsets the effect by eroding the real value of outstanding debt. However, Monacelli concedes the dominant importance of the standard argument for price stability in an economy where prices are costly to adjust. Monacelli goes on to consider the role of durable goods in providing collateral for household debt. He argues that constrained households tilt their consumption inefficiently toward durable goods, particularly when constraints are unusually tight, and that this increases the volatility of durable goods prices. Optimal monetary policy should have stability in the relative price of durable goods as an objective, balancing this against the objective of stability in nondurables price inflation.

Monika Piazzesi and Martin Schneider present a novel explanation for the volatility of house prices. They emphasize that house price booms occurred in many countries both in the 1970s, when inflation was high, and in the 2000s, when inflation was low. To explain this phenomenon, they suggest that some households are confused about the distinction between real and nominal interest rates, while other households understand it. This causes disagreement about the level of real interest rates at times when inflation is unusually high or low. In the 1970s, confused or "illusionary" households perceived high real rates, while rational households perceived low rates; in the 2000s, this pattern was reversed. Households that perceive low real rates wish to borrow, but Piazzesi and Schneider argue that in order to do so, they must invest in housing as collateral. Accordingly, disagreement about real interest rates drives up house prices. Shocks to inflation, whether positive or negative, have the potential to generate housing booms.

Asset prices can be informative not only about the state of the real economy, as emphasized by Gilchrist and Saito and Monacelli, and inflation, as emphasized by Piazzesi and Schneider, but also about the stance of monetary policy itself. This feedback from monetary policy to asset markets significantly complicates the task of central bankers who must decide how to respond to asset price movements. The chapter by Hans Dewachter and Marco Lyrio asks how the prices of long-term nominal government bonds respond to the macroeconomy and to the perceived stance of monetary policy. Dewachter and Lyrio point out that a standard structural macro model, in which investors are assumed to know the parameters of the model, is unable to explain the volatility of long-term interest rates. Because long rates are determined primarily by the long-run equilibrium real interest rate and the inflation target of the monetary authority, both of which are constant, the standard model implies that long rates are also close to constant. To generate realistic movements at the long end of the yield curve, Dewachter and Lyrio assume that bond market investors believe that the equilibrium real interest rate and long-run inflation target change over time and update their estimates of these variables using a Kalman filter. The authors fit their model to U.S. market data on nominal interest rates, together with survey data on inflation expectations. In an extended version of the model, they allow parameters to change when the chairmanship of the Federal Reserve changes. Dewachter and Lyrio find that learning about monetary policy is the main factor driving the prices of long-term nominal bonds.

If bond prices are determined by investors' beliefs about monetary policy, it is natural to ask how the monetary authority can shape those beliefs to improve its control over the yield curve. Glenn D. Rudebusch and John C. Williams discuss one approach that has been used recently by the central banks of New Zealand and Norway, the publication of a projected future path for the short-term interest rate that is directly controlled by the monetary authority. This approach goes significantly beyond the informal verbal discussion of the possible direction of policy that has been used recently by the Federal Reserve. Rudebusch and Williams analyze a simple New Keynesian structural model in which the public is uncertain about the central bank's inflation target or about the parameters of the policy rule that the bank uses to respond to macroeconomic shocks. They assume that the monetary authority cannot communicate these parameters directly but can release noisy forecasts of future short-term interest rates. They find that releasing interest rate projections generally improves the public's understanding of monetary policy, with beneficial results for macroeconomic stability. It is, however, possible that the policy can backfire, destabilizing the economy, if the public greatly overestimates the accuracy of the central bank's interest rate forecasts.

Recent increases in the price of oil and other mineral and agricultural commodities have renewed interest in the link between commodity prices and monetary policy. Jeffrey A. Frankel's chapter points out that, in theory, the world real interest rate is an important influence on commodity prices.

In equilibrium, the convenience yield of an inventory of commodities, plus the expected rate of real commodity price appreciation, must equal the real interest rate. Thus, a high real interest rate requires expected commodity price appreciation, which, in turn, requires a low commodity price today. Frankel presents evidence that this effect is important for many commodities. To the extent that the real interest rate is hard to measure directly because expected inflation is unobservable, commodity prices provide an important clue that should be used by monetary authorities.

Frankel goes on to argue that monetary policy should pay special attention to the prices of commodities that are exported or imported. He criticizes the policy of targeting consumer price inflation, which is currently used by many central banks around the world, on the ground that this policy does not properly handle shocks to the terms of trade. For example, a Consumer Price Index (CPI)-targeting oil importer facing an increase in the world price of oil is required to tighten monetary policy to offset the effect of the oil shock on domestic consumer prices, but Frankel argues that this policy worsens the real effect of the oil shock on the macroeconomy. Instead, Frankel suggests that monetary policy should stabilize an index of export prices or producer prices.

The last two chapters in this volume study the effects of macroeconomic announcements on asset prices. Empirically, this is an attractive strategy for identifying the reaction of asset prices to macroeconomic variables because other influences on asset prices have relatively small effects during the short periods of time around announcements. Roberto Rigobon and Brian Sack highlight a difficulty with the standard methodology for measuring announcement effects and propose a novel methodology to solve it. They point out that only the surprise component of a macroeconomic announcement should move asset markets, but this surprise component is measured with error because surveys of prior consensus forecasts are noisy and typically outdated. To correct for the effect of measurement error, they argue that other influences on asset prices should create equal asset-price variance in announcement periods and other equally short periods when announcements do not occur. If this is true, a comparison of variances provides additional information that can be used to identify the true announcement effect, even in the presence of announcement measurement error. Implementing their methodology, Rigobon and Sack find larger announcement effects than previous studies have done. The pattern of these effects is, however, familiar, with positive growth or inflation announcements driving up interest rates at all maturities and positive inflation announcements driving down stock prices.

Richard H. Clarida and Daniel Waldman ask how the exchange rate reacts to news about inflation. There are offsetting effects because inflation lowers the long-run equilibrium nominal exchange rate but may also lead the monetary authority to increase the short-run nominal interest rate, creating a wedge between the current exchange rate and its long-run value. Clarida and Waldman show that in a simple monetary policy model proposed by Clarida, Galí, and Gertler (2002), an optimizing central bank tightens aggressively in response to inflation news and thereby induces an exchange rate appreciation. Thus the announcement effect of inflation on the exchange rate can be used to learn about the stance of monetary policy, specifically, how close it is to an optimal policy. Empirically, Clarida and Waldman show that inflation announcements do tend to cause exchange rate appreciation, particularly in countries with explicit inflation targeting policies. In the United Kingdom and Norway, countries that moved in the direction of inflation targeting in 1997 and 2001, respectively, the authors find that the exchange rate response to inflation also changed in the direction predicted by their model.

Central bankers face the difficult task of integrating these and other insights into their decision-making process. The volume concludes with a fascinating panel discussion among three distinguished practitioners: Governor Donald L. Kohn of the Federal Reserve; former Governor Laurence H. Meyer, now vice chairman of Macroeconomic Advisers LLC; and William C. Dudley, advisory director of Goldman, Sachs & Co. Of course, all three panelists express their personal views and not those of their institutions.

The three panelists share the view that asset markets periodically develop "bubbles," upward price movements that cannot easily be justified by fundamentals and that often end in sharp declines. Governor Kohn contrasts the "conventional strategy" of responding to bubbles only insofar as they change expected output or inflation in the medium run, with a strategy of "extra action" that seeks to use monetary policy to dampen emerging bubbles. He characterizes extra action as a form of insurance against adverse consequences from the collapse of a bubble that is allowed to develop but argues that three conditions must be met for this insurance to be worth buying. First, the monetary authority must be able to identify an emerging bubble reliably and in real time. Second, contractionary monetary policy must reliably dampen the bubble. And, third, dampening the bubble must have substantial benefits for macroeconomic stability. Governor Kohn argues that these conditions have not been met in recent years in developed countries and are unlikely to be met in the future.[2]

Both Laurence H. Meyer and William C. Dudley are more sympathetic to policies of taking extra action against asset price bubbles.[3] Dudley argues that seasoned market observers can identify emerging bubbles in a timely manner. He agrees with Kohn that conventional monetary policy is

2. Governor Kohn's position appears to be close to those of the former and current Federal Reserve chairmen, Alan Greenspan (2002) and Ben Bernanke (2002).

3. In this respect, they are closer to the position expressed in a recent article published by the European Central Bank (2005).

ill-suited to dampen speculative activity in long-term asset markets but suggests that the monetary authority has alternative policies that may be more effective. Specifically, the central bank should regularly publish assessments of fair value in equity markets and should tighten margin requirements when a bubble appears to be developing. In addition, it would be helpful if the monetary authority had greater authority over capital adequacy and disclosure requirements for financial institutions. Meyer agrees that the central bank must regularly communicate its concerns about asset values with the public and argues that the monetary authority should at least err on the side of restraint when it perceives the emergence of an asset price bubble.

References

Bernanke, Ben. 2002. Asset-price "bubbles" and monetary policy. Remarks before the New York Chapter of the National Association for Business Economics, New York, NY.

Bernanke, Ben, Mark Gertler, and Simon Gilchrist. 1999. The Financial Accelerator in a Quantitative Business-Cycle Framework. In *Handbook of macroeconomics*. Vol. 1C, ed. John B. Taylor and Michael Woodford, 1341–93. Amsterdam: North-Holland.

Clarida, Richard, Jordi Galí, and Mark Gertler. 2002. A simple framework for international monetary policy analysis. *Journal of Monetary Economics* 49:879–904.

European Central Bank. 2005. Asset price bubbles and monetary policy. *Monthly Bulletin* (April):47–60.

Greenspan, Alan. 2002. Economic volatility. In *Rethinking stabilization policy*, 1–10. Kansas City, Mo: Federal Reserve Bank of Kansas City. 2002.

Measuring the Macroeconomic Risks Posed by Asset Price Booms

Stephen G. Cecchetti

1.1 Introduction

We pay central bankers to be paranoid. One of their primary responsibilities is to do extensive contingency planning, preparing for every possible calamity. And when they do their job well, most of us don't even notice. In the past decade, there are numerous examples of the central bank actions that were taken in response to an increase in the probability of disaster. These include the Federal Open Market Committee's interest rate reductions in the fall of 1998 that followed the Russian government's bond default, the preparations for the century date change, the enormous liquidity injections in the immediate aftermath of the September 11, 2001 terrorist attacks in the United States, as well as the discussions that occurred as nominal interest rates and inflation approached zero simultaneously. All of these episodes demonstrate policymakers' willingness to take actions in order to reduce the chance of disaster, acting as the risk mangers for the economic and financial system.

Then Federal Reserve Board Chairman Alan Greenspan put it best in

Stephen G. Cecchetti is the Rosenberg Professor of Global Finance, International Business School, Brandeis University, and a research associate of the National Bureau of Economic Research.

An earlier version of this chapter was distributed under the title "GDP at Risk: A Framework for Monetary Policy Response to Asset Price Movements." I would like to thank the discussant Andrew Levin as well as John Campbell, Blake LeBaron, Peter Phillips, Ritirupa Samanta, Jeremy Stein, and the participants at the conference for their numerous comments and suggestions. In addition, I owe an enormous debt to various collaborators over the years on related topics, especially Michael Bryan, Hans Genberg, Stefan Krause, Róisín O'Sullivan, and Sushil Wadhwani. Anne LePard and Damir Cosic provided research assistance. Finally, I would like to thank the Bank for International Settlements (BIS) for supplying some of the data. All of the views expressed here, as well as the errors, are my own.

2003 when he said that "A central bank seeking to maximize its probability of achieving its goals is driven, I believe, to a risk-management approach to policy. By this I mean that policymakers need to consider not only the most likely future path for the economy but also the distribution of possible outcomes about that path" (Greenspan 2003, 3). Importantly, the common practice of risk management requires controlling the probability of catastrophe. For a financial intermediary, the focus is on reducing the risk of significant monetary loss. For a central banker, it means acting to reduce the chances that output or the price level will be substantially below trend.

To control risk in financial institutions, risk managers employ the concept of *value-at-risk* (VaR). Value-at-risk measures the worst possible loss over a specific time horizon, at a given probability.[1] A commercial bank might say that the daily VaR for a trader controlling $100 million is $10 million at a 0.1 percent probability. That means that, given the historical data used in the bank's models, the trader cannot take a position that has more than one chance in 1,000 of losing 10 percent in one day.

In some circumstances, VaR is all you need. For example, if it is being used to measure the probability of institutional insolvency, it doesn't really matter how insolvent you are. But policymakers care not only about VaR, they are also concerned about the expected loss given that an event is in the lower tail—something called the *expected tail loss* (ETL). That is, not only where the 5th or 10th percentile of the distribution of gross domestic product (GDP) outcomes falls, but the expected value conditional on being in the lowest 5th or 10th percentile.

Risk-management measures like VaR and ETL are computed from the lower tail of the distribution of possible outcomes, examining the worst events that could occur. This requires moving beyond simple quadratic measures of risk like variance or standard deviation. It is fairly easy to imagine circumstances where the worst possible events have become worse, but the standard deviation of the distribution of all the possibilities is the same. This is one view of the case in the fall of 1998. The point forecasts for the aggregate price level and the GDP gap, and their standard deviation stayed roughly the same. But the lower tail shifted—the probability and size of a very bad outcome—rose. Policymakers acted in response to the perception that the GDP at risk and ETL had gone up.[2]

A risk-management approach comes naturally to central bankers. It is the basis for the creation and maintenance of the lender of last resort: the policy of providing loans to private financial intermediaries that are illiquid but not insolvent helps to ensure that the payments system continues

1. See Jorion (2001).
2. Formally, this means that the central bank's loss function is not quadratic. For a recent discussion, see Surico (forthcoming).

to operate smoothly. Together with deposit insurance, central bank lending is designed to reduce the probability of bank runs to a negligible level. (The implementation of prudential regulation and supervision is the response to the moral hazard created by these policies.)

All of this makes it surprising that many central bankers are hesitant to address the potential risks created by asset price booms and crashes—what are commonly referred to as *bubbles.* The evidence is not in dispute. Bubbles increase the volatility of growth and inflation and threaten the stability of the financial system. The 2003 IMF *World Economic Outlook* estimates that the average equity price bust lasts for 2.5 years and is associated with a 4 percent GDP loss that affects both consumption and investment. While less frequent, property (or housing) busts are twice as long and are associated with output losses that are twice as large.[3]

Asset price bubbles distort decisions throughout the economy. Wealth effects cause consumption to expand rapidly and then collapse. Increases in equity prices make it easier for firms to finance new projects, causing investment to boom and then bust. The collateral used to back loans is overvalued, so when prices collapse, it impairs the balance sheets of financial intermediaries that did the lending. It is the job of central bankers to eliminate the sort of economic distress caused by asset price bubbles. Although the rhetoric has been changing slowly, especially in the case of the responses to Australian and British housing market booms several years ago, most monetary policymakers remain reluctant to act directly to manage these risks.

Any discussion of bubbles must distinguish between equity and property prices. This is true for several reasons. First, the efficient markets hypothesis is more likely to apply to equity than to property. Arbitrage in stocks, which requires the ability to short sell, is at least possible. In housing and property, it is not. Second, even in the few countries with sizeable equity markets, ownership tends to be highly concentrated among the wealthy—people whose consumption decisions are well insulated from the vicissitudes of the stock market. By contrast, home ownership is spread much further down the income and wealth distribution. Finally, in many countries, housing purchases are highly leveraged, leaving the balance sheets of both households and financial intermediaries exposed to large price declines. This suggests that the macroeconomic impact of a boom and crash cycle in property prices might be larger in countries that have more credit outstanding.[4]

In this chapter, I examine equity and housing price booms and crashes from a risk management perspective. Using equity price data from twenty-

---

3. See the excellent essays in Chapter II of IMF (2003) for a summary of the evidence.
4. For a somewhat more detailed discussion of the issues and the debate, see Cecchetti (2003).

seven countries and housing price data from seventeen countries, I will look at the various consequences of rising equity and housing prices for growth and inflation. I begin by examining how asset price booms influence the mean and variance of deviations in (log) output and (log) price level from their (time-varying) trends. I then proceed to measure both the GDP at risk and the price level at risk that these booms create.

The scarcity of booms and crashes, especially in property prices, means that I must pool data across countries. From what data there are, I come to the following conclusions: housing booms are bad in virtually every way imaginable; they drive the output gap down, increase its volatility, increase GDP at risk, and push the lower tail of outcomes (ETL) even lower (decreasing the expected value of the GDP gap conditional on being in the lower tail of the distribution). By contrast, equity booms have little impact on either the level or volatility of the output and price-level gaps at horizons of three years; do not change GDP at risk, but increase the risk of prices falling dramatically below trend; and drive the lower tail (ETL) even lower.

Before continuing, it is worth noting the relationship between the use of risk management and robust control in the context of monetary policy. Robust control examines policy making in the presence of model uncertainty.[5] Instead of choosing optimal policy based on the most likely economic model, it ignores the probability that any particular model of the economy is true and selects the policy that delivers the best result even when the worst model is true. That is, it computes the policy path or instrument rule that minimizes the maximum loss, regardless of how likely or unlikely that case might be. As Onatski and Stock (2002) show, in contrast to the standard case in which uncertainty breeds caution, this has the potential to yield aggressive policy responses—aggressive enough to ensure that the worst outcomes are avoided.[6]

While the risk management and robust-control approaches to policy making both go beyond simple quadratic measures of loss, they are quite different. Rather than focusing on model uncertainty ignoring the probability of particular cases, concepts like VaR and ETL are designed to help control both the size and likelihood of bad outcomes. In the case of asset price booms, that means first computing the probability distribution associated with growth and inflation outcomes conditional on seeing equity or property prices rise suddenly and then looking for ways in which policymakers can mitigate the worst possible outcome.

---

5. See Svensson (2007) and Dennis, Leitemo, and Söderström (2006) for discussions.
6. The simplest example involves the case of inflation control. Imagine that policymakers are unsure whether inflation follows a random walk or not—the largest root of the autoregressive representation of the inflation rate is estimated to be less than one, but there is some finite probability that it actually equals one. Because it is the worst possible, the robust control solution is for policymakers to react to shocks as if inflation were nonstationary. In most environments, that means aggressively countering virtually anything that would force inflation up.

The remainder of this chapter proceeds as follows. Section 1.2 provides overwhelming evidence that the distribution of output and price-level deviations from their trends have fat tails, implying that methods based on quadratic loss and normal approximations could be misleading. Then, in section 1.3, I characterize the distribution of output and price-level conditional on housing and equity booms. That is, I look at the mean, variance, value-at-risk, and expected lower tail of output and price level conditional on asset price booms. Overall, the results suggest that normal approximations are inadequate. Section 1.4 expands the discussion contrasting housing and equity booms.

There is a growing consensus that traditional interest rate policy is not very useful in the battle to combat the deleterious macroeconomic effects of asset price bubbles.[7] At the same time, it is clear that policymakers cannot ignore the threat that equity and housing booms and busts pose for central bankers' stabilization goals. Adopting a risk management perspective means asking whether there are institutional solutions to the problem. That is, are there ways to structure the financial system that will then inoculate the real economy from the adverse effects of bubbles? With this question in mind, I examine the relative impact of asset price booms in economies with market- versus bank-based financial systems. The results, reported in section 1.5, suggest that market-based systems have a somewhat higher GDP at risk in the aftermath of equity booms, but those systems weather housing booms equally poorly.

1.2   GDP and Prices: General Considerations

Financial economists employ concepts like value-at-risk in order to address the problems created by fat tails. That is, cases in which a normal (Gaussian) distribution provides an overly optimistic picture of the likelihood of extreme events. Equity returns are notorious for exhibiting high probabilities of extreme events in their lower tail. Because these "bad" outcomes are so important for controlling the risk of large losses, modeling them has attracted substantial attention.[8]

Aggregate output and prices share some of the properties exhibited by equity returns. The distribution of deviations of (log) output and the (log) price level from their respective trend exhibit fat tails. That is, the probability of observing a large negative realization is substantially higher than one would infer from a Gaussian distribution. To see this, I have calculated the 5th percentile of the distribution of log output and log price-level deviations from their Hodrick-Prescott (Hodrick and Prescott 1997) trends,

---

7. See Cecchetti (2006) for a discussion.
8. See LeBaron and Samanta (2005) for a discussion of the issues surrounding modeling fat-tailed distributions.

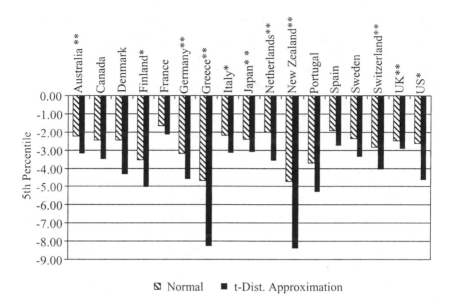

Fig. 1.1   GDP at risk, normal versus *t*-distribution approximation. GDP at risk: Normal versus fat-tailed

Notes: The *s refer to the significance level of the Jacque-Bera test for normality. A single * is for countries with a *p*-value of 0.10 or less, while ** signifies a *p*-value of 0.05 or less. The test statistic equals $(n/6)[\mu_3^2 + (\mu_4 - 3)/4]$, where μ_3 and μ_4 are the sample third and fourth moments, and n is the sample size. The statistic is distributed as χ-squared with 2 degrees of freedom. Test results are reported for the deviations of quarterly log GDP and log prices from a Hodrick-Prescott filtered trend with parameter equal to 1,600. The sample is from 1970 to 2003.

with smoothing parameter set to 1,600, for a series of countries using quarterly data from 1970 to 2003.[9] These results are plotted in figures 1.1 and 1.2. (The appendix provides a more detailed description of the data.) The figures also include results for a Jacque-Bera test for normality—these are the *s next to the country names. Normality is rejected for eleven of seventeen cases using the output gap and ten of seventeen using the price-level gap.

The figures show the results for the following calculation. For the normal distribution, this is just 1.645 times the standard deviation of the series. The alternative, which takes the fatness of the tails of the distribution into

9. I have also computed results for a shorter sample beginning in 1985 that verify the inaccuracies of the normal approximation reported in the following. In addition, the results throughout the chapter are robust to using a smoothing parameter of 9,600, rather than 1,600; to using the residuals from a four-order autoregression; and to using the residuals from the estimation of a two-equation aggregate demand—aggregate supply model based on Rudebusch and Svensson (1999) as implemented in Cecchetti, Flores-Lagunes, and Krause (2006) that includes interest rates.

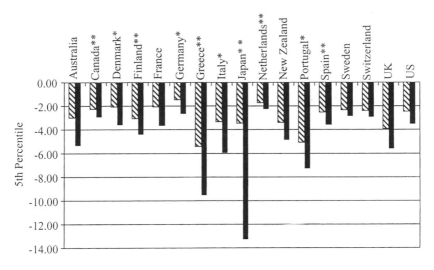

Fig. 1.2   Price level at risk, normal versus *t*-distribution approximation. Price level at risk: Normal versus fat-tailed

Note: See explanatory note for figure 1.1.

account, begins by the computation of a Hill index. As described in LeBaron and Samanta (2005), the Hill index is an estimate of the number of moments of a distribution that exists. For a normal distribution, the index is infinity. After computing the index, the tail is approximately distributed as a Student *t* with degrees of freedom equal to the Hill index value. So the *t*-distribution approximation to the 5th percentile of the deviations of log GDP or the log price level from their trend is equal to the standard deviation of the series times the 5 percent level of the *t*-distribution with degrees of freedom equal to the series' Hill index.[10]

As one would expect, in some countries the deviations of output and prices from trend—their output and price-level gaps—have fatter tails than others. But if one were to use the normal distribution, the errors would be large—averaging roughly 50 percent. For the United States, the 5th percentile of the normal distribution implies a deviation of output from trend of slightly more than –2.5 percent. Taking the fatness of the lower tail of the actual data into account yields an estimate of more than 4.5 percent. That is, the 5 percent GDP at risk for the United States (without conditioning on anything). For the price level, the estimates diverge by

10. Computation of the Hill index requires a decision about where the tail of the distribution starts. I take LeBaron and Samanta's (2005) advice and use the bottom 10 percent of the observations.

less with the normal distribution, giving a 5 percent price-level at risk equal to –2.5 percent and the t-distribution approximation yielding an estimate of –3.5 percent.

It is important to keep in mind that standard statistical and econometric procedures are designed to characterize behavior near the mean of the data, so they are particularly ill-suited to the examination of tail events. This means that when extreme events are more likely than the normal distribution implies, and we care about them, it is important to adopt techniques that explicitly account for fat tails.

1.3   Risks Created by Asset Price Bubbles

Managing risk means having information about the entire distribution of possible outcomes. That is, one needs to know not only the mean and variance, but tail probabilities as well. With that in mind, I now compute the mean, variance, value-at-risk, and expected lower tail for output and price-level deviations from their trends, all conditional on the asset price booms.

1.3.1   The Mean

How do asset price booms change the mean and volatility of output and price-level gaps? I examine this question using a series of regression, which allow straightforward statistical inference. Throughout this exercise, I treat asset price booms and busts as events that are exogenous with respect to the behavior of output and price paths several years into the future.[11]

To study the conditional mean, consider the following regression:

$$(1) \qquad x_{it} = a + b\, d_{it-k}(\alpha) + \varepsilon_{it},$$

where x_{it} is the level of the output (or price-level) gap; $d_{it-k}(\alpha)$ is a dummy variable that takes on the value 1 if k periods earlier the filtered asset price data exceeds the threshold α. The coefficient b measures the impact of the asset price boom on the distribution of the gap variable.

Before continuing, let me pause to describe the procedure used to construct the data.[12] First, for each country, I take the deviation of the log of each series—real GDP, the aggregate price level, the real equity price index, and the real housing price index—from its Hodrick-Prescott filtered trend with a smoothing parameter equal to 1,600 (the results are robust to using a parameter of 9,600). All data are quarterly, and most samples are

11. The fact that the results are robust to various changes in the filtering of the data, including the use of residuals from a simple model in place of the simple filtered data as described in footnote 7, suggests that this assumption is relatively innocuous.

12. The seventeen countries in the housing price sample are Australia, Belgium, Canada, Denmark, Finland, Greece, Ireland, Israel, the Netherlands, New Zealand, Norway, Portugal, Spain, Sweden, Switzerland, the United Kingdom, and the United States. The twenty-seven countries in the equity price data sample add Austria, Chile, France, Germany, Italy, Japan, Korea, Mexico, Peru, and South Africa.

from 1970 to 2003.[13] To construct the dummy variable d_{it-k}, I filter the log equity and housing price data using a Hodrick-Prescott filter with smoothing parameter equal to 3,200 (again, this is robust to increasing the parameter value). It is important to note that the use of a two-sided filter means that large positive deviations of asset prices from trend—these are the booms—must be followed by crashes. Put another way, the booms I locate cannot continue indefinitely.

Finally, taking deviations from country-specific (and time-varying) trends has the advantage in that it removes country-fixed effects. While there are surely numerous conditions that vary in these countries over the sample, this is at least a minimum condition for pooling.[14]

Returning to the results, table 1.1 reports estimates for equation (1). To read the table, take the example of the last entry in the third column under housing. That's the one where the threshold α equals 10 percent, and the lag k is twelve quarters. For this case, the estimate of b is –1.42 with a p-value of 0.00. This means that, conditional on seeing a housing boom that is 10 percent above trend, the mean of the output gap twelve quarters later is, on average, 1.42 percent. That seems like a big number, and it is precisely estimated.[15]

Overall, these results allow a number of conclusions. First, in the near term, at horizons of four quarters, both equity and housing booms lead to positive output gaps. This is for the simple reason that at a four-quarter horizon, an asset-market boom is likely to continue, adding fuel to the general economic growth. Second, housing booms create future declines in output and increases in prices while equity booms do not. And third, the bigger the housing boom, the bigger the expected drop in output and the expected increase in the price level.

1.3.2   Volatility

Next, I examine the impact of asset price booms on the volatility of output and price deviation from trend. To do this, I regress the square of the gap, that is $(x_{it})^2$ on the dummy variable $d_{it-k}(\alpha)$. That is,

$$(2) \qquad (x_{it})^2 = a' + b'd_{it-k}(\alpha) + v_{it}.$$

To simplify interpretation, I standardize the data, dividing by the variance of the entire sample. This means that the coefficient is a measure of the percentage increase in the volatility. So, for example, a number like 5.28

13. While it would be interesting to look at shorter samples, there is simply not enough data to do it.

14. As in section 1.2, the results in section 1.3 are robust to use of residuals from a fourth-order autoregression and to use of residuals from a model that includes interest rates and external prices.

15. To address problems of heteroskedasiticity (throughout) and serial correlation (within each country), I have estimated the standard errors and resulting p-values using a panel version the Newey-West (Newey and West 1987) procedure with lags equal to 1.5k.

Table 1.1   Impact of asset price booms on the levels (lag of asset price [k])

Threshold (α)	Level of the output gap			Price level		
	4	8	12	4	8	12
			Equity			
Data	*0.03*	*0.01*	0.00	−0.07	0.00	0.04
	1.00	*0.96*	0.25	0.03	0.50	0.92
4	*1.05*	*0.28*	−0.21	−0.61	0.10	0.99
	1.00	*0.99*	0.10	0.30	0.58	0.94
12	*0.92*	*0.32*	−0.15	0.04	0.54	1.32
	1.00	*0.99*	0.23	0.51	0.71	0.92
20	*0.85*	0.16	−0.07	−0.65	0.71	1.58
	1.00	0.81	0.38	0.39	0.69	0.88
			Housing			
Data	*0.06*	**−0.04**	**−0.09**	*0.04*	*0.08*	*0.07*
	1.00	**0.00**	**0.00**	*0.99*	*1.00*	*1.00*
2	*0.46*	**−0.53**	**−0.92**	*0.62*	*0.96*	*0.70*
	1.00	**0.00**	**0.00**	*1.00*	*1.00*	*1.00*
6	*0.85*	**−0.50**	**−1.28**	*0.55*	*1.14*	*0.95*
	1.00	**0.01**	**0.00**	*0.98*	*1.00*	*1.00*
10	*1.10*	−0.42	**−1.42**	*0.52*	*1.19*	*1.04*
	1.00	0.12	**0.00**	*0.92*	*1.00*	*1.00*

Notes: Table 1.1 reports the coefficient b in the regression $x_{it} = a + bd_{it-k}(\alpha) + \varepsilon_{it}$, where x is the deviation of either log GDP or the log price from a Hodrick-Prescott filtered trend, with parameter 1,600; and d is either a dummy variable equal to 1 if the filtered asset price exceeds the threshold (in percent), or the filtered asset price data itself. In each case, the first row of numbers is the coefficient itself, while the second row is a p-value for the test that b is strictly less than 0, computed using Newey-West standard errors with lags equal to 1.5 times k. *Italicized* values are significantly greater than 0, while **bold** values are significantly less than 0, both at the 5 percent level. Samples are described in the data appendix.

(that's the estimate for a 10 percent housing price boom at a horizon of four quarters) means a 5.28 percent increase in volatility. The results are reported in table 1.2, and they are quite stark. Housing booms increase the volatility of growth at all horizons, and that's it. Interestingly, neither housing nor equity booms have a measurable impact on the volatility of prices. And equity booms do not affect the volatility of growth—the estimates are both economically tiny and statistically irrelevant.

Focusing on the bottom-left panel of the table 1.2—the impact of housing booms on GDP volatility—we see that the bigger the boom, the bigger the impact on volatility. But the bigger impact is at short horizons where we know from table 1.1 that, on average, growth rises. So, while housing booms increase volatility, it seems to do it primarily on the upside.

1.3.3   GDP and Price Level at Risk

Next, I turn to an examination of the tails of the distribution of output and price-level outcomes, conditional on asset price booms. Are GDP at

Table 1.2   **Impact of asset price booms on volatility (lag of asset price [*k*])**

	Volatility of the output gap			Price level volatility		
Threshold (α)	4	8	12	4	8	12
			Equity			
Data	0.00	0.01	0.00	0.00	0.00	0.00
	0.14	0.07	0.30	0.38	0.08	0.18
4	0.03	0.33	0.24	0.00	0.00	0.00
	0.43	0.08	0.14	0.15	0.54	0.46
12	0.15	0.05	0.19	0.00	0.00	0.00
	0.26	0.41	0.15	0.13	0.13	0.12
20	0.39	0.20	0.11	0.00	0.00	0.01
	0.12	0.27	0.34	0.16	0.11	0.06
			Housing			
Data	**0.22**	0.12	0.05	−0.02	0.00	0.02
	0.04	0.18	0.35	0.64	0.53	0.34
2	**2.46**	**2.84**	1.43	−0.09	0.50	0.66
	0.02	**0.01**	0.12	0.57	0.12	0.17
6	**4.39**	**4.75**	1.93	0.55	0.60	0.87
	0.01	**0.01**	0.12	0.18	0.10	0.16
10	**5.48**	2.46	**5.28**	0.88	0.38	0.80
	0.04	0.07	**0.04**	0.16	0.23	0.19

Notes: Table 1.2 reports the coefficient b_2 in the regression $(x_{it})^2 = a_2 + b_2\, d_{it-k}(\alpha) + \eta_{it}$, where x is the deviation of either log GDP or the log price from a Hodrick-Prescott filtered trend, with parameter 1,600; and d is either a dummy variable equal to 1 if the filtered asset price exceeds the threshold α (in percent), or the filtered asset price data itself (those are the rows labeled "data"). In each case, the first row of numbers is the coefficient itself, while the second row is a *p*-value for the test that b_2 is strictly greater than 0, computed using Newey-West standard errors with lags equal to 1.5 times k. **Bold** values are significantly greater than 1 at the 5 percent level.

risk and price level at risk affected by the equity or housing booms or busts? If, for example, there is a dramatic increase in equity prices, should this change our view of the possibility of bad events? And, importantly, are normal approximations likely to give the wrong signal?

Equity Bubbles

For equity booms, the answer to this question is reported in figure 1.3. The horizontal axis in the figure plots the minimum size of the equity price deviation, and the vertical axis plots the 5th percentile of the distribution of future outcomes for the GDP gap—the 5 percent GDP at risk. The two lines show the 5 percent GDP at risk four quarters ahead and twelve quarters ahead. So, for example, if equity prices are at least 10 percent above trend, the 5th percentile of the distribution of the GDP gap twelve quarters into the future is −3.6. As it turns out, this is only slight below the 5th percentile of the unconditional distribution for deviations of GDP from trend, which is 3.44, so it isn't very troubling. In other words, the GDP at risk from

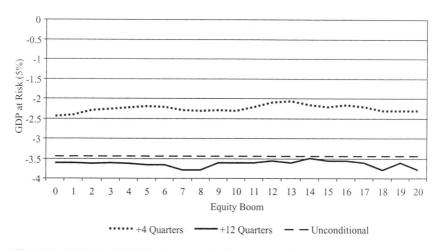

Fig. 1.3   GDP at risk following an equity boom

a 10 percent equity boom is only very slightly below the unconditional GDP at risk. The upper line in the figure, the 5 percent GDP at risk four quarters ahead, is always significantly *above* the unconditional 5th percentile of the GDP gap distribution. The reason for this is that all booms are likely to continue, so the horizon for the collapse of equity prices and GDP both is beyond four quarters.

Figure 1.4 reports the results for price level at risk following an equity boom. The price level at risk results differ quite a bit from the GDP at risk results. Since some central banks will care about prices rising while others may care more about prices falling, I report the risk results for both tails of the distribution. These are referred to as the 95 percent price level at risk. As the equity boom grows, the risk of the price level falling below trend (shown in panel A of figure 1.4) grows substantially. When real equity prices are 15 percent or more above trend, the 5th percentile of the distribution of price-level gap four quarters out is more than –9 percent. Depending on the current level of inflation, that could be a significant risk. By contrast, the risk of the extreme positive price-level gaps (in panel B of figure 1.4) goes down. Conditional on an equity boom, the distribution of price-level deviations from trend shifts down.

Housing Bubbles

Turning to housing bubbles, figures 1.5 and 1.6 report computations analogous to those reported in figure 1.3 and 1.4. The results in these two figures suggest that housing booms are followed by an increased risk of a large decline in GDP in four to twelve quarters and a decreased risk of prices falling below trend. Note from the scale that the GDP at risk is quite large. When real house prices are 5 percent or more above trend, there is a

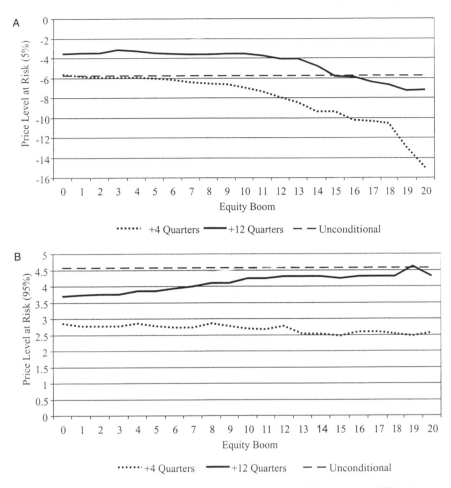

Fig. 1.4   Price level at risk following an equity boom: *A,* **Risk of prices** *falling* **significantly** *below* **trend;** *B,* **Risk of prices** *rising* **significantly** *above* **trend**

5 percent probability that twelve quarters later GDP will be at least 3.44 percent below trend—substantially below the unconditional 5th percentile of 2.86 percent.[16]

Housing booms affect the price level at risk as well. The information in figure 1.6 suggests that a housing boom has very little impact on the upper tail of the price-level distribution, but dramatically eliminates the lower tail—at least at a twelve-quarter horizon. Unconditionally, the upper tail 5 percent price level at risk twelve quarters following a 10 percent housing

16. Note that because the countries in the sample differ, the unconditional distributions for the price-level and GDP gaps are different between the equity and housing booms.

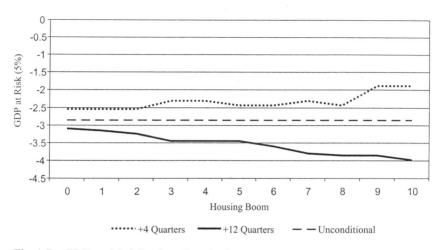

Fig. 1.5   GDP at risk following a housing boom

price boom is roughly one-quarter the unconditional 5th percentile—that is, it—1 percent as compared with –4 percent.

Comparing the Normal Approximation and the Empirical Density

It is important to ask whether there is any difference between the results in figures 1.3 and 1.5 and those from a simple normal approximation. That is, if a central banker had been looking at the –1.645 times the standard deviation of the distribution of output and price-level gaps, conditional on an equity market boom, would they have done anything differently? The results suggest that the answer to this is yes.

Figure 1.7 compares the 5th percentile for the GDP gap computed using a normal approximation with one from the empirical density. For equity booms, the normal approximation gives an overly pessimistic view of the size of the lower tail. The average distance between the two estimates of the 5th percentile of the distribution is roughly three-quarters of 1 percentage point. This particular example suggests that a policymaker using a quadratic loss would likely overestimate the importance of an equity boom.

Housing is another story. Here the normal distribution gives an overly optimistic view of the true size of the lower tail. The 5th percentile of the empirical density is, on average, 1.25 percentage points below what is implied by the normal approximation. Because the probability of extreme negative outcomes for the GDP gap is higher than suggested by a Gaussian distribution, policymakers focusing on quadratic loss will underestimate the importance of a housing boom.

In the case of price-level outcomes, normal approximations are also misleading. For example, twelve quarters following a housing boom, the 5th percentile of the upper tail of outcomes is 2.5 percentage points *smaller*

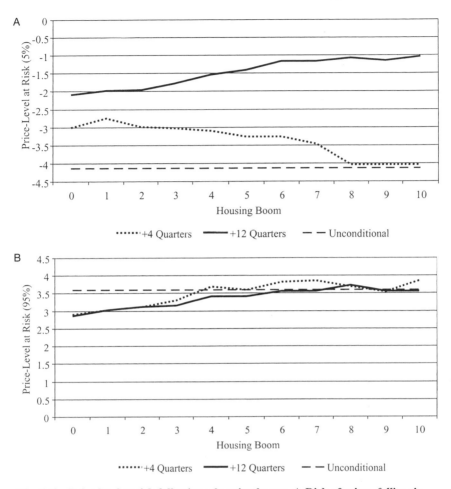

Fig. 1.6   Price level at risk following a housing boom: *A,* **Risk of prices** *falling* **significantly** *below* **trend;** *B,* **Risk of prices** *rising* **significantly** *above* **trend**

than would be implied by simply multiplying the standard deviation of the observed outcomes by 1.64.

1.3.4.   Expected Lower Tail Loss

Direct statistical inference for a number like GDP at risk is difficult.[17] Instead of constructing Monte Carlo experiments that might allow confi-

17. Quantile regression, pioneered by Koenker (2005), is an alternative to the figures in section 1.3.3 and the regressions in section 1.3.4. Rather sorting the data based on arbitrarily chosen thresholds for the right-hand-side variables, quantile regression examines changes in the relationship based on the quantile of the regression residuals. Such a technique has the distinct advantage of allowing for the additional control variable in the regression. Future research will examine the robustness of these results to these alternative statistical methods.

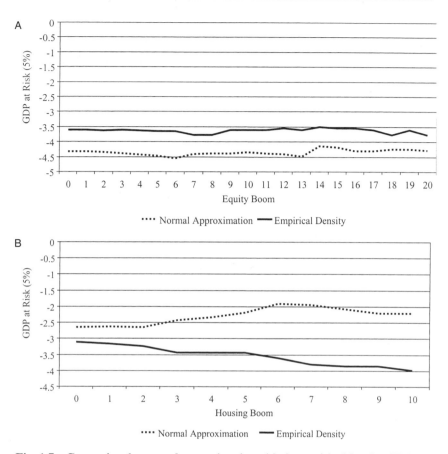

Fig. 1.7   Comparing the normal approximation with the empirical density GDP at risk at + twelve quarter horizon: *A*, Conditional on an equity boom; *B*, Conditional on a housing boom

dence interval estimation, I turn to the examination of the ETL. This is the expected value, conditional on being in the tail of the distribution. As in the case of the GDP at risk and price level at risk, here I ask whether the ETL changes when asset prices boom. In order to do inference, I run a regression similar to equation (1):

$$(3) \quad x_{it} = a + b_0 d_{it-k}(\alpha) + b_1 \text{tail}(\beta)_{it} + b_3 \, d_{it-k}(\alpha) x \text{tail}(\beta)_{it} + \eta_{it},$$

where x_{it} is the output or price-level gap; $d_{it-k}(\alpha)$ is a dummy variable equal to 1 if k periods earlier the filtered asset price data exceeds the threshold α; and $\text{tail}(\beta)_{it}$ is a dummy variable that equals 1 if x_{it} is in the β percent lower tail of the distribution of all x_{it}.

The coefficient b_3 on the interaction term in equation (3) provides an estimate of the impact of an asset price boom of size α on the ETL in the lowest β percent of the distribution of the output or price-level gap. Because of the structure of the regression, it is possible to compute standard errors that are robust to both serial correlation and heteroskedasiticity in the error term η_{it}.[18]

The results of this regression are reported in table 1.3, and they are quite striking. Asset price booms—both equity and housing—result in a fall in the expected lower tail loss. The decline is both economically and statistically significant. Put another way, equity and housing booms make it more likely that something bad will happen.

1.3.5 Summary of the Results

Table 1.4 summarizes the results of this section. The conclusion is that housing booms dramatically change the distribution of outcomes in virtually every way. By contrast, equity booms have little impact on the mean and variance of deviation from trend, but do affect the lower tail of the distribution.

1.4 The Difference between Equity and Housing Bubbles

To understand the differential impact of equity and housing bubbles, it is useful to focus on their consumption effects. Booms in either equity or property prices drive up the wealth of individuals. The natural response to an increase in wealth is to raise consumption. If you are rich, you can buy a fancy car, purchase a bigger and flatter television, go on nicer vacations, eat in expensive restaurants, and the like. And the data show that this is exactly what happens.

A useful rule of thumb is that a $1 increase in U.S. wealth generates between two and five cents of additional consumption by American households.[19] That is, the marginal propensity to consume for wealth is in the range of 0.02 to 0.05.

As Norman, Sebastia-Barriel, and Weeken (2002) note, the marginal propensity to consume is of somewhat less interest than the elasticity of consumption with respect to wealth.[20] They emphasize that we care more about the impact of a 10 percent increase in the value of wealth than we do about the number of cents or pence that consumption rises per dollar or pound of additional wealth. This is especially true of equity wealth because the size of equity markets vary so widely across countries. Bertaut (2002) reports that, at the end of 2001, total equity market capitalization

---

18. The estimation method is an adaptation of the Newey-West estimator to a panel in which there is serial correlation and heteroskedasiticity within a country, but no dependence between countries.

19. See, for example, Norman, Sebastia-Barriel, and Weeken (2002).

20. The elasticity of consumption with respect to wealth is equal to the marginal propensity to consume out of wealth times the ratio of wealth to consumption.

Table 1.3   Impact of asset price booms on the lowest quartile (lag of asset price [k])

Threshold (α)	Output gap			Price-level gap		
	4	8	12	4	8	12
		Equity				
Data	−0.03	−0.02	0.01	**−0.26**	**−0.21**	0.03
	0.10	0.12	0.63	**0.02**	0.06	0.59
4	**−3.81**	**−2.50**	**−1.87**	−14.05	−16.12	−13.88
	0.00	**0.00**	**0.00**	**0.00**	**0.00**	**0.00**
12	**−4.63**	**−1.75**	**−1.70**	−16.38	−19.20	−16.35
	0.00	**0.01**	**0.01**	**0.00**	**0.00**	**0.00**
20	**−5.37**	**−2.05**	**−0.85**	−18.06	−20.73	−17.36
	0.00	**0.02**	**0.05**	**0.00**	**0.00**	**0.00**
		Housing				
Data	−0.01	−0.03	−0.01	0.06	0.10	0.09
	0.35	0.11	0.35	0.67	0.84	0.76
2	**−1.53**	**−1.08**	**−0.69**	−2.47	−4.03	−5.01
	0.00	**0.00**	**0.00**	**0.00**	**0.00**	**0.01**
6	**−1.42**	**−1.15**	**−0.28**	−2.89	−4.83	−9.22
	0.00	**0.00**	0.18	**0.00**	**0.00**	**0.00**
10	**−1.16**	**−0.34**	**−0.59**	−3.28	−3.91	−12.29
	0.00	0.12	0.08	**0.00**	**0.00**	**0.00**

Notes: Table 1.3 reports the coefficient b_3 in the regression $x_{it} = a + b_1 d_{it-k}(\alpha) + b_2 tail(\beta)_{it} + b_3 d_{it-k}(\alpha)x\ tail_{it}(\beta) + \upsilon_{it}$, where x_{it} is the deviation of either log GDP or the log price from a Hodrick-Prescott filtered trend, with parameter 1,600; $tail_{it}(\beta)$ is a dummy variable that equals 1 if x_{it} in the lower β-percent tail; and d is either a dummy variable equal to 1 if the filtered asset price exceeds the threshold α (in percent), or the filtered asset price data itself (those are the rows labeled "data"). In each case, the first row of numbers is the coefficient itself, while the second row is a *p*-value for the test that b_3 (the coefficient on the interaction term) is strictly less than 0, computed using Newey-West standard errors with lags equal to 1.5 times k. **Bold** values are significantly greater than 1 at the 5 percent level.

equaled 153 percent of GDP in the United Kingdom, but only 59 percent of GDP in Germany. To understand the importance of this, consider the impact of a 10 percent increase in equity prices on consumption in each country, assuming that the marginal propensity to consume is the same. The estimated impact in the United Kingdom the impact would be roughly three times as large as that in Germany.[21]

This highlights the importance of thinking about bubbles in housing and equity prices separately. There are two reasons for this. First, equity prices are substantially more volatile than housing prices, so the former is much less likely to be permanent than the latter. Reasonably, households respond more aggressively to changes in wealth that they perceive to be perma-

21. Careful econometric estimates show an even larger disparity. Bertuat (2002) reports that 10 percent increase in stock market creates 0.5 to 1.0 percent increase in consumption in the long run in the United States and United Kingdom, but only 0.07 in Germany where the equity is less than 60 percent of GDP.

Table 1.4   **Summary of the impact of asset price booms on the distribution of macroeconomic outcomes (lag of asset price)**

	Output gap		Price-level gap	
Moment	$k=4$	$k=12$	$k=4$	$k=12$
Equity				
Mean	Higher	None	None	None
Variance	None	None	None	None
5% VaR	Better	None	None	Worse
25% Expected Tail Loss	Lower	Lower	Lower	Lower
Housing				
Mean	Higher	Lower	Higher	Higher
Variance	Higher	Higher	None	None
5% VaR	Better	Worse	Better	None
25% Expected Tail Loss	Lower	Lower	Lower	Lower

Note: Table 1.4 summarizes the results in tables 1.1, 1.2, and 1.3 and figures 1.3 to 1.6.

nent.[22] Second, equity ownership tends to be concentrated among the wealthy—people who are much less likely to adjust their consumption levels. Housing ownership, by contrast, is distributed more broadly. And while the quality of housing and the concentration of ownership vary across countries, the differences are far less dramatic.

Returning to the evidence, using data from fourteen developed countries, Case, Quigley, and Shiller (2005) discuss how a 1 percent increase in housing wealth raises consumption by between 0.11 and 0.17 percent. By contrast, they find that the stock market wealth elasticity of consumption is substantially smaller, only 0.02. It is natural that the housing booms would have more of an impact on the distribution of macroeconomic outcomes than equity booms do.

1.5   Policy Responses: Risk Management and Financial Structure

Is there anything to be done about all of this? Can we provide any useful guidance on how to avoid the risks bubbles pose? Researchers have investigated myriad possible responses, including, but not restricted to, reacting only to bubbles insofar as they influence inflation forecasts; reacting only to the fallout of a bubble after it bursts; leaning against a bubble as it develops; including asset prices in the price index central bankers target; and examining various regulator solutions involving margin and lending requirements. In Cecchetti (2006), I summarize the traditional debate in

22. Kishor (2005) estimates that while 98 percent of the change in housing wealth is permanent, only 55 percent of the change in financial wealth is. This suggests that the housing wealth effect should be roughly twice the stock market wealth effect.

each of these cases. Briefly, there is a consensus building against the purely activist view. As Gruen, Plumb, and Stone (2005) discuss, the information requirements for the activism are fairly high, and there are significant risks of costly missteps. The conclusion is that interest rates should play only a modest role in combating the destabilizing effects of asset price bubbles

From a risk management perspective, the discussion of central bank responses to asset price bubbles is unnecessarily restrictive. Why focus only on traditional monetary policy tools? Risk managers do more than simply monitor and react to developments; they build institutional structures that are unlikely to collapse when hit by large shocks. The regulators and supervisors of the financial system have built mechanisms exactly like this. Are there similar responses to bubbles? When subjected to equity and property price bubbles, are some financial systems more resilient than others?

Recent work by Dynan, Elmendorf and Sichel (2006) and Cecchetti, Flores-Lagunes, and Krause (2006) suggests that changes in the financial system have been an important source of stabilization over the past several decades. Their results suggest that enhanced household access to credit allows for increased consumption smoothing that has been a major factor in reducing the volatility of aggregate real growth.[23] This brings up the natural question: does the impact of housing and equity bubbles on GDP at risk or price level at risk depend on financial structure?

To examine this, I begin with data on financial structure taken from Demirguc-Kunt and Levine (2001). Briefly, Demirguc-Kunt and Levine have constructed a data set on financial indicators during the 1990s covering a broad cross section of countries. Included are measures of the relative size of a country's stock market and banking sector, as well as a measure of the relative efficiency of the two. Countries with "market-based financial systems" are those with bigger more efficient stock markets. I examine the relationship of this composite financial structure index and the behavior of an economy following booms in equity or housing prices.

As a first step, I reproduce figures 1.3 and 1.5 with the data for GDP at risk dividing the data based on whether it comes from a country with a predominantly market-based or bank-based financial system. The results, reported in figure 1.8, show that for countries where equity markets are important, equity booms increase GDP at risk. By contrast, GDP at risk following a housing boom is not sensitive to financial structure as characterized by this index.

To examine this a bit further, and to try to get a grasp on whether any of it is precise in a statistical sense, I add the financial structure variable to re-

23. The argument is that there is a linkage not only between financial system development and the *level* of real growth, as described in Ross Levine's (1997) survey, but also between financial development and the stability of real growth.

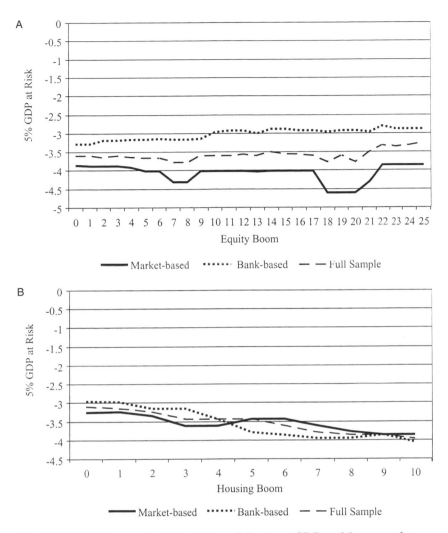

Fig. 1.8   Market- versus bank-based financial systems GDP at risk at + twelve quarter horizon: *A*, Equity booms; *B*, Housing booms

gressions (1), (2) and (3)—both as a level and interacted with the asset price boom dummy. Here's an example:

(1′) $x_{it} = a + b\mathrm{d}_{it-k}(\alpha) + cf_i + df_i\mathrm{d}_{it-k}(\alpha) + \varepsilon_{it},$

(2′) $(x_{it})^2 = a' + b'\mathrm{d}_{it-k}(\alpha) + c'f_i + d'f_i\mathrm{d}_{it-k}(\alpha) + \upsilon_{it}.$

(3′) $x_{it} = a + b_0\mathrm{d}_{it-k}(\alpha) + b_1\mathrm{tail}(\beta)_{it} + b_3\mathrm{d}_{it-k}(\alpha)x\mathrm{tail}(\beta)_{it}$

$\qquad\quad b_4 f_i + b_5 f_i\mathrm{d}_{it-k}(\alpha) + b_6 f_i\mathrm{tail}(\beta)_{it} + b_7 f_i\mathrm{d}_{it-k}(\alpha)x\mathrm{tail}(\beta)_{it} + \eta_{it},$

where f_i is the composite structure index from the CD-ROM that is distributed with Demirguc-Kunt and Levine (2001).[24]

Table 1.5 reports the estimated coefficients on the interactions terms in each of these: $f_i d_{it-k}(\alpha)$ in equations (1′) and (2′), and $f_i d_{it-k}(\alpha)x$ tail$(\beta)_{it}$ in equation (3′). These tell us whether differences in financial structure change the impact of an asset price boom on the mean, variance, or lower tail events in the distribution of the output gap. I report the results for a lag of four and twelve quarters. The financial structure index is positive for market-based economies and negative for bank-based ones. For example, it takes on a value of +0.17 for the United States and –0.18 for Greece.

Unsurprisingly, the strongest results are those for the mean. In countries with market-based financial systems, which is to say places where equity markets are important, the first and second column of the top panel in table 1.5 shows that equity price increases lead to bigger short-horizon booms and bigger long-horizon crashes (although the latter are imprecisely estimated). Analogously, for bank-based economies, housing booms lead to bigger short-horizon GDP booms, but smaller long-horizon crashes. (These are the results in the first and second column of the bottom panel of the table.)

Turning to the volatility, there is no measurable impact on financial structure. The point estimates reported in the fourth and fifth columns of table 1.5 are all small and the p-values are never below 0.2 or above 0.8.

Finally, looking at the far right columns of table 1.5, the results from estimating equation (3′), there is some weak evidence that market-based economies fare somewhat worse at longer horizons when hit with equity price booms. Again, this is really no surprise.

In the end, these results are disappointing. While we may believe that financial structure plays role in the real economic impact of asset price booms, the data available do not show much evidence of it.

1.6   Conclusion

Stability is the watchword for central bankers. Listen to most modern monetary policymakers speak about their goals, and you are likely to hear about the desire for low, stable inflation and high, stable growth. They will explain how they raise and lower their short-term interest rate target in order to meet their stability-oriented objectives. But listen closely, and you

24. The index average of deviations from the mean of (1) stock market capitalization divided by deposit money bank assets (relative size of stock market compared to banking sector), (2) total value traded in stock market divided by claims on private sector by deposit money banks (relative activity of stock market compared to banking sector), and (3) total value traded in stock market as a share of GDP divided by banking overhead costs as a share of total assets (relative efficiency of stock market compared to banking sector). The actual data are column EQ in the file called "request8095.xls." These data are the same as those.

Table 1.5   **Financial structure and the impact of asset price booms (lag of asset price in quarters)**

	Mean		Variance		Lowest Quartile	
Threshold (α)	4	12	4	12	4	12
			Equity			
Data	*0.07*	−0.03	0.00	0.00	0.06	**−0.07**
	1.00	0.15	0.62	0.32	0.84	**0.10**
8	*1.50*	−0.60	0.01	−0.01	1.41	−1.20
	0.95	0.31	0.31	0.65	0.69	0.25
16	2.31	−0.87	0.01	0.00	3.68	−2.03
	0.97	0.26	0.30	0.45	0.74	0.11
20	2.88	−1.82	0.00	0.02	5.25	**−3.57**
	0.98	0.12	0.42	0.19	0.78	**0.06**
			Housing			
	4	12	4	12	4	12
Data	**−0.14**	−0.04	0.00	0.00	−0.02	0.05
	0.07	0.36	0.65	0.54	0.44	0.64
4	−1.40	−1.60	0.03	−0.03	−1.06	0.59
	0.16	0.14	0.37	0.63	0.21	0.65
8	−1.90	−0.02	−0.09	−0.03	−0.50	0.19
	0.21	0.50	0.71	0.59	0.40	0.54
10	−0.83	0.04	−0.20	−0.04	−0.10	0.89
	0.38	0.51	0.77	0.58	0.49	0.61

Notes: Table 1.5 reports the regression coefficients from the interaction of the financial structure measure with the asset price boom dummy variable in equations (1'), (2'), and (3'). The more positive financial structure, the more market-based a country's financial system; the more negative, the more bank-based it is. In each case, the first row of numbers is the coefficient itself, while the second row is a p-value for the test that is strictly less than zero, computed using Newey-West standard errors with lags equal to 1.5 times k. *Italicized* values are significantly greater than zero at the 5 percent level and boldfaced values are significantly less than zero at the 10 percent level.

will realize that the statements are more nuanced. While stability is the ultimate objective, it is the possibility of catastrophe that keeps central bankers awake at night. They want to ensure that nothing really bad happens, and to do this, they are looking at the entire distribution of possible outcomes.

In analyzing the macroeconomic impact of asset price booms and crashes, it is the disasters that are the true concern. This suggests a different approach to risk, one based on keeping the probability of output deviating from its trend (or price level deviations from its target trend) over some time horizon below some fixed threshold. Policy responses should be built in order to keep the lower tail of the distribution—as measured by value-at-risk or the ETL—sufficiently small.

In this chapter, I use data from a broad cross section of countries to examine the mean, variance, and lower tail risks arising from booms and crashes in equity and housing markets. The conclusion is that housing bubbles change the entire distribution of macroeconomic outcomes. By contrast, equity bubbles tend to make the worst events even worse, leaving the mean and variance of the distributions roughly unchanged. The strong conclusion is that approximations that use the normal distribution, and analyses based on quadratic loss functions, have the potential to be extremely misleading. Looking further, I present weak evidence suggesting that those countries with market-based financial systems, where stock market capitalization is relatively large, weather housing booms somewhat better and equity booms somewhat worse than countries with bank-based financial systems.

In closing, it is important to emphasize one critical implication of adopting a risk management view. As mentioned earlier, econometric modeling tends to provide characterizations of what happens near the mean of the data. In fact, in order to improve the quality of estimates, researchers have a tendency to remove outliers. This is sometimes done in the guise of sensitivity analysis and other times using limited-influence estimation that explicitly truncates tail observations. This means that standard modeling strategies provide virtually no information about the behavior of the economy when it is under stress. As a result, evaluating the problems posed by extreme events, which is at the core of risk management, necessarily requires judgment. And to quote Chairman Greenspan (2004) one final time: "Such judgments, by their nature, are based on bits and pieces of history that cannot formally be associated with an analysis of variance."

Appendix

Data Appendix

Price Data

Price data computed for consumer price inflation data was obtained from the *International Financial Statistics* online and the OECD Economic Outlook no. 76, December 2004.

GDP

Gross domestic product data was obtained from the *International Financial Statistics* CD-ROM (December 2004) and the OECD Economic Outlook no. 76, December 2004.

Equity Prices

Equity prices are from the *International Financial Statistics* online.

Housing Prices

Data for Australia, Belgium, Canada, Denmark, Finland, Ireland, the Netherlands, Norway, Portugal, Spain, Sweden, Switzerland, the United Kingdom, and United States are all from the BIS. Data for Hong Kong are from the Hong Kong Monetary Authority, Census and Statistics Department, Monthly Digest of Statistics, table 5.9, column (6). Data for Israel are from the Israel Central Bureau of Statistics, online. Data for Japan are from Goldman Sachs. Data for New Zealand are from the Reserve Bank of New Zealand.

References

Bertaut, Carol. 2002. Equity prices, household wealth, and consumption growth in foreign industrial countries. International Finance Discussion Paper no. 724. Washington: Board of Governors of the Federal Reserve System.

Case, Karl E., John M. Quigley, and Robert J. Shiller. 2005. Comparing wealth effects: The stock market versus the housing market. *Advances in Macroeconomics* 5 (1). Article 1.

Cecchetti, Stephen G. 2003. What the FOMC says and does when the stock market booms. In *Asset prices and monetary policy*, ed. A. Richards and T. Robinson, 77–96. Proceedings of the Research Conference of the Reserve Bank of Australia. Canberra: McMillan.

———. 2006. The brave new world of central banking: Policy challenges posed by asset price booms and busts. *Economic Review of the National Institute of Economic and Social Research* 196 (May): 107–19.

Cecchetti, Stephen G., Alfonso Flores-Lagunes, and Stefan Krause. 2006. Assessing the sources of changes in the volatility of real output. *The Economics Journal* 116 (4): 408–33.

Demirguc-Kunt, Asli, and Ross Levine. 2001. Bank-based and market-based financial systems: Cross-country comparisons. In *Financial structure and economic growth,* ed. A. Demirguc-Kunt and R. Levine, 81–140. Cambridge, MA: MIT Press.

Dennis, Richard, Kai Leitemo, and Ulf Söderström. 2006. Methods for robust control. IGIER-Università Bocconi Working Paper no. 307. Milan: Innocenzo Gasparini Institute for Economic Research.

Dynan, Karen E., Douglas W. Elmendorf, and Daniel E. Sichel. 2006. Can financial innovation explain the reduced volatility of economic activity? *Journal of Monetary Economics* 53 (1): 123–50.

Greenspan, Alan. 2003. Opening remarks. In *Monetary policy and uncertainty: Adapting to a changing economy,* ed. Gordon H. Sellon, Jr.: 1–7. Proceedings of the Federal Reserve Bank of Kansas City Symposium. Kansas City, MO: Federal Reserve Bank of Kansas City.

———. 2004. Risk and uncertainty in monetary policy. *American Economic Review* 94 (2): 33–40.

Gruen, David, Michael Plumb, and Andrew Stone. 2005. How should monetary policy respond to asset price bubbles. *International Journal of Central Banking* 1 (3): 1–31.

Hodrick, Robert J., and Edward C. Prescott. 1997. Postwar U.S. business cycles: An empirical investigation. *Journal of Money, Credit, and Banking* 29 (1): 1–16.

International Monetary Fund (IMF). 2003. *World economic outlook.* Washington, DC: IMF, April.

Jorion, Phillipe. 2001. *Value at risk.* 2nd edition. New York: McGraw-Hill.

Kishor, N. Kundan. 2005. Does consumption respond more to housing wealth than to financial wealth? If so, why? University of Washington, Department of Economics. Unpublished Manuscript.

Koenker, Roger. 2005. *Quantile regression.* Cambridge, UK: Cambridge University Press.

LeBaron, Blake, and Ritirupa Samanta. 2005. Extreme value theory and fat tails in equity markets. Brandeis University, International Business School. Unpublished Manuscript.

Levine, Ross. 1997. Financial development and economic growth: Views and agenda. *Journal of Economic Literature* 35 (2): 688–726.

Newey, Whitney K., and Kenneth D. West. 1987. A simple, positive definite, heteroskedasticity and autocorrelation consistent covariance matrix. *Econometrica* 55 (3): 703–8.

Norman, Ben, Maria Sebastia-Barriel, and Olaf Weeken. 2002. Equity wealth and consumption—The experience of Germany, France and Italy in an international context. *Bank of England Quarterly Review* 42 (Spring): 78–85.

Onatski, Alexei, and James H. Stock. 2002. Robust monetary policy under model uncertainty in a small model of the U.S. economy. *Macroeconomic Dynamics* 6 (1): 85–110.

Rudebusch, Glenn D., and Lars E.O. Svensson. 1999. Policy rules for inflation targeting. In *Monetary policy rules,* ed. J. B. Taylor, 203–46. Chicago: University of Chicago Press.

Surico, Paolo. Forthcoming. U.S. monetary policy rules: The case for asymmetric preferences. *Journal of Economic Dynamics and Control.*

Svensson, Lars E.O. 2007. Robust control made simple: Lecture notes. Princeton University. Unpublished Manuscript.

Comment   Andrew Levin

This chapter addresses a crucial topic for monetary policymakers, namely, does an asset price boom substantially raise the likelihood of a subsequent macroeconomic crisis? In this context, the chapter introduces the terms *gross domestic product (GDP) at risk* and *price level at risk* to characterize the lower tail of the distribution of each variable and then seeks to quantify

Andrew Levin is assistant director of the Division of Monetary Affairs and chief of the Monetary Studies Section at the Board of Governors of the Federal Reserve System.

I am grateful to Steve Cecchetti for providing me with the data set used in his analysis. I also appreciate helpful discussions with Morris Davis, Benson Durham, and Roberto Perli and outstanding research assistance provided by Arshia Burney and Ben Johannsen. The views expressed in this comment are solely those of the author and should not be interpreted as representing the views of the Board of Governors of the Federal Reserve System nor of anyone else associated with the Federal Reserve System.

the extent to which these risks are exacerbated by booms in either equity prices or house prices. While it would be ideal if one could consider the marginal impact on truly extreme events (such as the U.S. Great Depression of the 1930s), broad indexes of asset prices are only available for a substantial cross section of industrial economies over the post-1970 period; thus, the results reported here reflect the incidence and severity of the various recessions that actually occurred within the sample. Despite these statistical challenges, the chapter obtains significant evidence that a boom in house prices is associated with a subsequent reduction in real economic activity.

Measuring GDP at Risk

The analysis of the chapter begins by presenting evidence that output fluctuations exhibit a heavy lower tail, similar to the distribution commonly observed for equity prices. In particular, for eleven of the seventeen countries under consideration, the Jarque-Bera (J-B) test rejects the null hypothesis of a Gaussian distribution at a confidence level of 95 percent, and density approximations based on a t-distribution imply a distinctly larger magnitude of output contractions at the bottom 5th percentile of the distribution. Nevertheless, several important issues should be considered in interpreting these results.

Positive versus Negative Outliers

The J-B test is designed to detect skewness or excess kurtosis but does not necessarily indicate a heavy *lower* tail of the distribution. Indeed, as shown by the histograms in figure 1C.1 of this comment, positive outliers account for six cases in which the J-B test rejects the Gaussian null hypothesis. These outliers are concentrated in the early 1970s for four countries (namely, Italy, Japan, Switzerland, and the United Kingdom), while the Finnish outliers are associated with the 1989 to 1990 boom, and the German outliers correspond to the postreunification period of 1991 to 1992. The incidence of positive outliers also underscores the challenges in constructing measures of the output gap in the absence of any structural model; for example, a sequence of positive outliers in Hodrick-Prescott (HP)-detrended GDP could reflect either a cyclical boom or a spurt in potential output.

Transitory versus Persistent Outliers

Figure 1C.2 of this comment depicts histograms for the remaining five countries for which the J-B test rejects the null hypothesis of a Gaussian distribution for detrended output. Even in these cases, it is important to distinguish instances of deep recession—that is, lasting several quarters or more—from transitory fluctuations that might reflect a brief period of political turmoil or natural disaster. For example, the two outliers for

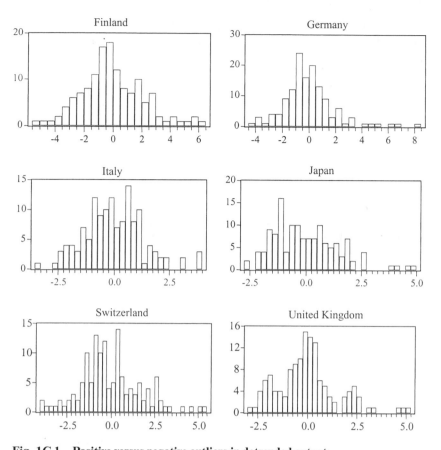

Fig. 1C.1   Positive versus negative outliers in detrended output

Note: For each country, the *x*-axis indicates the range of values of the HP-detrended output gap over the period 1970Q1 to 2003Q4, while the *y*-axis indicates the relative frequency of outcomes.

Australia reflect a single sharp recession that lasted from late 1982 through the end of 1983, whereas the data for Greece contains a single isolated outlier in the third quarter of 1974. The detrended output series for New Zealand also exhibits transitory outliers—both positive and negative— during 1973 to 1974, presumably reflecting the impact of highly volatile commodity prices. By contrast, the Netherlands's output trajectory has been remarkably stable over the past three decades, with a standard deviation of only 1.25 percent; in this case, one negative "outlier" reflects a single period in 1979, while the other two occurred during a more persistent contraction (lasting about a year) in 1982 to 1983. Finally, the cluster of negative outliers in the U.S. data correspond to the recession of 1981 to

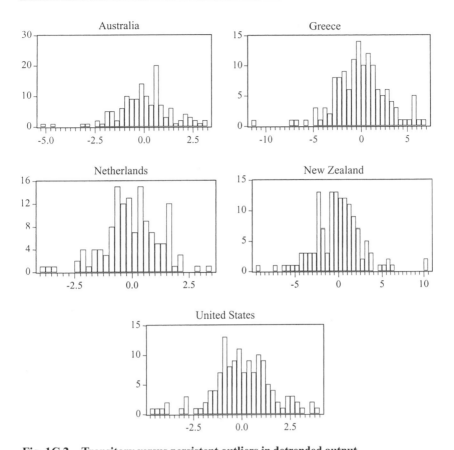

Fig. 1C.2   Transitory versus persistent outliers in detrended output

Note: For each country, the *x*-axis indicates the range of values of the HP-detrended output gap over the period 1970Q1 to 2003Q4, while the *y*-axis indicates the relative frequency of outcomes.

1983, which continues to be the largest contraction in U.S. economic activity since the Great Depression of the 1930s.

The Impact of House Price Booms

The chapter obtains substantial evidence that house price booms—measured by the deviation of each country's aggregate house price index from its HP-filtered trend—are associated with subsequent reductions in real economic activity. To shed further light on these results, it is helpful to focus on the specification that yields the highest level of statistical significance, namely, the extent to which a house price boom of at least 10 percentage points is associated with a substantial decline in the HP-detrended output gap twelve quarters later. The panel data set contains 103 observations (encompassing thirteen of the seventeen countries for which the relevant data is available) that satisfy this threshold for a house price boom, while the remaining control group of nearly 1,600 observations can be used to compute the distribution of output gaps that are *not* preceded by a house price boom at a twelve-quarter horizon.

Summary statistics regarding the distribution of output gaps—conditional on either the presence or absence of a house price boom twelve quarters earlier—are reported in table 1C.1 of this comment. Evidently, the occurrence of a house price boom systematically reduces the subsequent level of output: the mean of the conditional distribution is shifted downward by about 1.4 percent, a value that matches the regression estimate reported for this specification in table 1.1 of the chapter. The magnitude of this decline is also virtually identical to the impact shown in figure 1.5 of the chapter, which depicts the bottom 5th percentile of the unconditional distribution of output gaps in comparison with the same percentile conditional on the existence of a house price boom twelve quarters earlier.

Nevertheless, these results indicate that house price booms are *not* associated with substantially greater dispersion in the subsequent path of output. In particular, as shown in figure 1C.3 of this comment, the occurrence of a boom causes a downward shift in the entire distribution for detrended output but does not induce a heavier tail of adverse outcomes. This visual impression is confirmed by the summary statistics in the table: a house price boom has only modest effects on the standard deviation and the degree of skewness, while the degree of excess kurtosis is not affected at all. Thus, while house price booms do seem to generate some downside risk for the subsequent path of output, the magnitude of this risk appears to be fairly limited, relative to the effects of other macroeconomic disturbances.

Table 1C.1   **The distribution of detrended output conditional on a house-price boom twelve quarters earlier**

	No boom (1)	Boom (2)
No. of observations	1581	103
Mean	0.1	−1.3
Median	0.1	−1.2
Standard deviation	1.7	1.9
Skewness	0.4	−0.4
Excess Kurtosis	3.2	3.1

Notes: Table 1C.1 reports summary statistics regarding the conditional distribution of Hodrick-Prescott detrended output gaps for seventeen industrial countries over the period 1970Q1 to 2003Q4. Column (1) provides results for the set of observations that are preceded by a house-price boom twelve quarters earlier, while column (2) reflects all other observations.

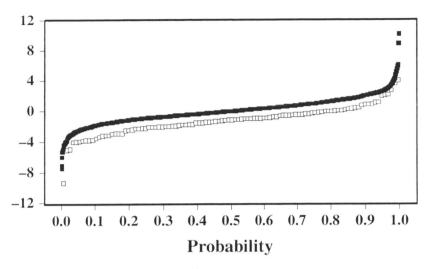

Fig. 1C.3   Housing booms and the distribution of output gaps

Note: This figure depicts the cumulative distribution of HP-detrended output gaps for seventeen industrial countries over the period 1970Q1 to 2003Q4. The hollow boxes denote this distribution for observations that are preceded by a house price boom twelve quarters earlier, while the solid boxes denote the distribution for all other observations.

Simulations of the Federal Reserve Board (FRB)/US Model

While these results reflect statistical patterns for a broad panel data set of industrial economies, simulations of the FRB/US model—which has been estimated using U.S. aggregate data and is used in ongoing policy analysis at the Federal Reserve Board—yield very similar implications regarding the macroeconomic effects of a sharp drop in house prices.[1] For example, figure 1C.4 of this comment depicts a scenario in which the aggregate house price index falls 10 percent during the second half of 2006 and by an additional 5 percent during 2007. As a result, U.S. real GDP declines to about 0.75 percent below baseline by the end of 2008.[2] The shaded regions in the figure indicate 70 and 90 percent confidence intervals obtained from stochastic simulations of the model, with shocks drawn from the set of estimated residuals over the period 1988 to 2004; these confidence intervals highlight the extent to which the model implies that even a steep drop in U.S. house prices would only have modest consequences for real GDP, at least in the absence of any other major disturbances.

1. See Brayton et al. (1997) for an overview of the specification and empirical properties of the FRB/US model.
2. Although not shown in the figure, the scenario assumes that movements in the federal funds rate are determined by Taylor's rule, which prescribes a gradual reduction to about 100 basis points below baseline by the end of 2008.

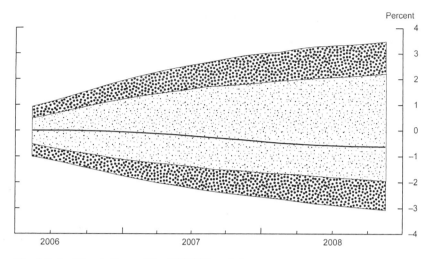

Percent

Fig. 1C.4   Simulations of the FRB/US model

Note: This figure depicts an FRB/US model simulation of a scenario in which the aggregate house price index declines by 10 percent during the second half of 2006 and an additional 5 percent during 2007; the response of U.S. real GDP (relative to baseline) is indicated by the solid line, while the shaded regions denote 70 and 90 percent confidence intervals obtained from stochastic simulations of the model, with shocks drawn from the set of estimated residuals over the period 1988 to 2004.

Real-Time Assessment of House Price Fluctuations

Finally, while the cross-country empirical analysis of this chapter has been conducted using HP-filtered aggregate house price indixes, it should be noted that financial market indicators may be useful for providing real-time information about market perceptions regarding the likelihood of a sharp decline in house prices.[3] For example, figure 1C.5 of this comment depicts the evolution of KMV-Moody measures of one-year-ahead expected default probabilities for twelve U.S. homebuilding firms over the period 1990 to 2006; while providing an early signal of downside risks to the residential construction industry prior to the onset of each of the past two recessions, this measure has not given any recent indications of a substantial near-term probability of a collapse in the housing market. This outlook is consistent with recently available information from housing futures and options, which began trading on the Chicago Mercantile Exchange in late May 2006 and suggested that market participants were anticipating a

3. Durham (2006) provides detailed analysis of asset prices related to the U.S. homebuilder industry along with an overview of Chicago Mercantile Exchange (CME) housing futures and options, while Campbell et al. (2006) analyze the extent to which recent trends in U.S. house prices can be interpreted in terms of movements in rents, real interest rates, and risk premia.

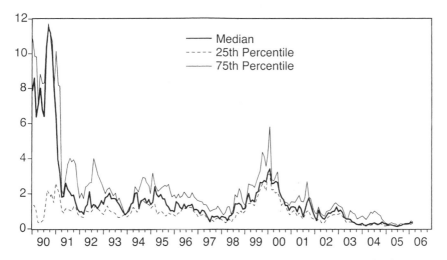

Fig. 1C.5   Expected default probabilities in the U.S. residential construction industry

Note: This figure depicts the quartiles of the distribution of one-year-ahead expected default probabilities (as estimated by KMV-Moodys) for twelve large publicly traded U.S. firms in the residential construction industry.

sharp slowing in the growth rate but apparently not a substantial decline in the level of U.S. house prices over the subsequent few quarters.

References

Brayton, F., A. Levin, R. Tryon, and J. Williams. 1997. The evolution of macro models at the Federal Reserve Board. *Carnegie-Rochester Conference Series on Public Policy* 42:115–67.

Campbell, S., M. Davis, J. Gallin, and R. Martin. 2006. What moves housing markets: A trend and variance decomposition of the rent-price ratio. Finance and Economics Discussion Series Paper no. 2006-29. Washington, DC: Board of Governors of the Federal Reserve System.

Durham, J. 2006. What do financial asset prices say about the housing market? Finance and Economics Discussion Series Paper no. 2006-32. Washington, DC: Board of Governors of the Federal Reserve System.

Discussion Summary

Lars E. O. Svensson questioned whether Alan Greenspan's "risk-management approach to policy" need be associated with special treatment of extreme events. Svensson suggested that everything Greenspan had said or written was consistent with Bayesian minimization of an expected loss function. In thinking about low-probability extreme events, it was not clear that you should ignore information from the rest of the distribution of events. Standard quadratic loss functions, for example, penalize bad outcomes. In fact, Charles Goodhart had even argued for an absolute-value loss function on the grounds that quadratic loss penalizes extreme outcomes too severely. For the same reason, Margaret Bray and Goodhart had argued for loss functions that are bounded from above.

John Williams said that he did think there was a useful distinction between risk management and minimizing expected loss and that he thought that Greenspan had distinguished between the two. He also argued that all central bankers adopt a risk management approach to some extent and that this causes econometric problems for the analysis of monetary policy because their adoption of such an approach means there are not many sharp economic downturns in the data. Levin suggests that it would be useful to look at periods of greater macroeconomic instability—such as the 1970s—to investigate the extent and causes of policy failures in these situations.

Jordi Galí asked why the analysis lumped together price run-ups that were followed by crashes with price run-ups that were not followed by crashes. He suggested that only the cases with collapses were interesting for the analysis. Cecchetti answered that he had wanted to condition only on the information that there was a price run-up. He did not want his analysis to have to rely on the knowledge that there was a subsequent collapse.

John Y. Campbell pointed out that the Hodrick-Prescott filter (used in the chapter to calculate deviations from trend) is two-sided. He suggested that this meant that the analysis was implicitly conditioning on a collapse because run-ups that were not followed by a collapse would be attributed to the trend.

Lars E. O. Svensson asked for clarification: what sorts of preferences imply an interest in risk management? What are the implications? Does the avoidance of extreme events act as a constraint, in the sense that the policymaker should minimize expected loss subject to some gross domestic product (GDP) at risk or price level at risk constraint? Cecchetti replied that he considered that he had observed policy actions that were driven by higher moment considerations. He believed that these actions were rational but could not be explained by minimization of a quadratic loss function. Svensson said that his prior was that these were, in fact, driven by quadratic loss. If not, he wondered whether Cecchetti thought that such actions were normatively sensible. Cecchetti answered that the central bank should care about extreme events although it was not clear that adjustment of interest rates would always be the appropriate policy response.

John Y. Campbell said that he thought that expected tail loss, discussed in section 1.3.4 of Cecchetti's chapter, was more relevant for policymakers than GDP at risk or price level at risk. Gross domestic product at risk is defined analogously to value at risk (VaR): that is, it specifies the loss that will be incurred over a given horizon at some chosen percentile of the distribution of outcomes. It does not consider the distribution of outcomes at still lower percentiles. Ignoring the distribution of extreme outcomes may make sense for financial institutions that become insolvent if extreme outcomes occur, but it is not appropriate for central banks conducting monetary policy.

Andrew Levin suggested that the discussion was relevant to the zero lower bound on nominal rates. Choosing higher inflation is like making an insurance payment against the possibility of hitting the zero lower bound and entering a liquidity trap. Taking out such insurance might or might not be worthwhile, depending on the size of the inflation cushion needed.

Expectations, Asset Prices, and Monetary Policy
The Role of Learning

Simon Gilchrist and Masashi Saito

2.1 Introduction

Recent studies on asset prices and monetary policy consider the benefits of allowing the monetary authority to respond to asset prices in a monetary policy rule.[1] These studies frequently rely on two key assumptions: (1) asset price movements create distortions in economic activity through their effect on the ability of managers to finance investment; and (2) there exist exogenous "bubbles" or nonfundamental asset price movements.[2] In such environments, nonfundamental increases in asset prices cause investment booms, an increase in output above potential, and rising rates of inflation. In this framework, a monetary policy that responds strongly to inflation is frequently found to be sufficient in suppressing the undesirable consequences of these asset price fluctuations. In other words, there is no

Simon Gilchrist is an associate professor of economics at Boston University and a research associate of the National Bureau of Economic Research. Masashi Saito is a researcher at the Institute for Monetary and Economic Studies, Bank of Japan.

We thank Michael Woodford; John Campbell; Andrea Pescatori; Martin Ellison; participants at the NBER Asset Prices and Monetary Policy Conference and the 7th Annual Bank of Finland/Center for Economic Policy Research (CEPR) Conference on Credit and the Macroeconomy; and seminar participants at the Bank of England, the Bank of Canada, the Bank of Japan, and the University of Tokyo for comments and suggestions. The views expressed in this chapter are those of the authors and do not necessarily reflect the official views of the Bank of Japan.

1. Bernanke and Gertler (1999, 2001), Cecchetti et al. (2000), Gilchrist and Leahy (2002), and Tetlow (2005) provide recent examples.

2. Mishkin and White (2003) provide recent discussions of the evidence on stock market bubbles and their role in monetary policy for the U.S. economy, while Okina, Shirakawa, and Shiratsuka (2001) describe the Japanese stock market boom of the late 1980s and assess the conduct of monetary policy during this episode. Borio and Lowe (2002) discuss the relationship between financial imbalances and monetary policy.

need to respond to asset prices above and beyond what is implied by their ability to forecast inflation.

The notion that adopting a policy of responding strongly to inflation is a sufficient response to bubbles rests in part on the assumption that bubbles distort the economy by increasing managers' ability to invest without distorting their perceptions of the value of new investment. As Dupor (2005) emphasizes, these conclusions are tempered to the extent that bubbles directly influence managerial valuations of capital. More generally, nonfundamental movements in asset prices cause distortions in aggregate demand through their influence on markups and, hence, inflation and distort the consumption/investment decision by influencing the cost of capital. A monetary policymaker with one instrument—the nominal interest rate— faces a trade-off between reducing distortions owing to variation in the markup and distortions owing to variations in the return on capital. In such an environment, the policymaker may find monetary policy rules that respond to asset prices to be beneficial.

While much of the literature has focused on nonfundamental movements in asset prices, it is often recognized that asset price booms occur in conjunction with changes in the underlying economic fundamentals (Beaudry and Portier 2004). A case in point is the late 1990s run-up in U.S. stock prices that was closely tied to perceived changes in trend productivity growth. Thus, a key question in the literature is whether the monetary authority can identify the source of movements in asset prices in an environment of technological change. As emphasized by Edge, Laubach, and Williams (2004), it is plausible to believe that the underlying trend growth in productivity is unknown and that both the private sector and the policymaker learn over time about the true state of the economy. In this case, the benefits of allowing the monetary authority to respond to asset prices may depend on both the information structure of the economy and the extent to which asset price movements distort economic activity through the financing mechanism described in the preceding.

To address these issues, we reconsider the design of monetary policy rules in an environment where asset prices reflect expectations about underlying changes in the trend growth rate of technology. Our economy is a standard New Keynesian framework augmented to include financial market imperfections through the financial accelerator mechanism described in Bernanke, Gertler, and Gilchrist (1999). In our framework, the private sector and the policymaker are uncertain about the trend growth rate of technology but gradually learn over time. This learning process is reflected in asset price movements. Revisions to expectations owing to learning influence asset prices and entrepreneurial net worth. Such revisions feed back into investment demand and are magnified through the financial accelerator mechanism.

Our findings reinforce previous results in the literature. In the absence of financial frictions, a policy of responding strongly to inflation is sufficient, even in situations where the private sector is uncertain about the true state of technology growth. In the absence of financial frictions, our economy shows essentially one distortion, owing to variations in the markup, which influences input choices. Suppressing inflation stabilizes the markup. Adding asset prices to the monetary policy rule is unlikely to provide further benefits, even in situations where the private sector is uninformed about the economy's true state of growth.

In the presence of financial market imperfections, a policy that responds strongly to inflation eliminates much of the distortionary effect of asset price movements on economic activity. Nonetheless, with inflation stabilized, the economy still exhibits significant deviations of output from potential. By giving weight to asset prices in the monetary policy rule, the monetary authority can improve upon these outcomes. Stabilizing output relative to potential comes at the cost of increased volatility of inflation, however. Thus, as in Dupor (2005), the monetary authority faces a trade-off owing to its desire to eliminate two distortions with one instrument.

Our policy analysis emphasizes the benefits to responding to an asset price gap—the gap between the observed asset prices and the potential level of asset prices that arises in a flexible-price economy without financial market imperfections. Computing such a gap requires the policymaker to make inferences regarding the true state of technology growth. We can thus distinguish between situations where the monetary authority has full information regarding the underlying state of technology growth and situations where the policymaker is learning about it over time. We can similarly distinguish between environments where the private sector is fully informed or is learning over time.

Our results imply that the benefits to responding to the asset price gap depend on the information structure of the economy. The benefits of responding to the asset price gap are greatest when the private sector is uninformed about the economy's true state of growth, but the policymaker is informed. At the other extreme, responding to the asset price gap may be detrimental when the private sector is informed and the policymaker is uninformed. In this case, the policymaker is responding to the "wrong" asset price gap.

We also consider alternative monetary policy rules that do not require the policymaker to infer the state of growth of the economy. These include responding to either asset price growth or output growth. Our findings suggest that both of these policies are likely to do well in our environment. On the other hand, we find that responding to the level of asset prices, as considered in much of the previous literature, is a particularly bad policy. Thus, the destabilizing effects of responding to asset price movements emphasized in previous studies may in part reflect the assumption that the monetary authority responds to the level of asset prices rather than their deviation from the potential level. If the latter is unobservable, responding to changes in asset prices is better than responding to the level itself.

2.1.1   Related Literature

Bernanke and Gertler (1999, 2001), Cecchetti et al. (2000), Gilchrist and Leahy (2002), and Tetlow (2005) introduce nonfundamental bubbles into an economy and study the benefits of allowing the monetary authority to respond to asset prices. According to Bernanke and Gertler (1999, 2001), a policy that implies a strong response to inflation stabilizes the economy, and asset prices are only useful to the extent that they provide information about inflation and the output gap. In this environment, bubbles are exogenous and affect the economy by increasing aggregate demand through a financial accelerator mechanism. A policy that responds strongly to inflation is sufficient to suppress this aggregate demand channel. Cecchetti et al. (2000) argue that there may be some benefit to responding to asset prices in such environments although it is likely to be small. This literature suggests that adopting a monetary policy rule that implies a strong policy response to inflation is sufficient even under two situations in which asset prices may contain a relatively large amount of information about the state of the economy: an economy with financial frictions and an economy with shocks that have a persistent impact on technology growth (Gilchrist and Leahy 2002).

Our framework differs from this analysis in two fundamental ways. First, in our economy, deviations between asset prices and underlying cash flows occur because agents do not know the true state of technology growth but instead are learning about it over time. Recent studies by French (2001), Roberts (2001), and Kahn and Rich (2003) emphasize the distinction between transitory and persistent movements in the growth rate of technology. Edge, Laubach, and Williams (2004) study the effect of learning about transitory and persistent movements in technology growth in a model-based environment. As an example of such learning, they document that the productivity growth forecasts of professional forecasters and policymakers did not change until 1999 although the trend had shifted in the mid-1990s. They also demonstrate that a constant-gain Kalman filter tracks well the actual forecasts of trend productivity in the 1970s and in the 1990s made by forecasters and policymakers. Pakko (2002) and Edge, Laubach, and Williams (2004) introduce learning with a Kalman filter to a real business cycle (RBC) model to understand the effect of changes in the trend growth rate of technology on economic activity. Our chapter is also related to Tambalotti (2003), who considers the role of learning in a dynamic stochastic general equilibrium model with price rigidities but no capital accumulation, and Dupor (2005), who considers an environment where agents learn about fundamental and nonfundamental shocks to the return on capital.

Our framework is closely related to Edge, Laubach, and Williams (2005), who allow for learning about the trend growth rate of technology in a dynamic stochastic general equilibrium model with price rigidities and capital accumulation. We extend their framework by allowing both the private sector and the policymaker to learn about the true state of technology growth. We do so in an environment where learning influences asset values, which feed back into real economic activity through the net worth channel emphasized by Bernanke, Gertler, and Gilchrist (1999). We show that this financial accelerator mechanism may be enhanced in the presence of learning. This stronger feedback mechanism raises the benefit to responding to asset prices, even in an environment where the policymaker is itself uninformed about the true state of technology growth.

Second, much of the previous literature focuses on the benefits of responding to the level of asset prices. In our framework, asset price movements would occur in the absence of frictions in either price-setting or financial markets. Thus, we emphasize the importance of the monetary authority's response to the asset price gap—the gap between the observed asset prices and the underlying potential level of asset prices. Our finding that responding to the growth rate of asset prices is also beneficial is related to Tetlow (2005), who compares the benefit of responding to the growth rate of asset prices relative to the level of asset prices in a robust control framework.

Our emphasis on asset price movements that are tied to fundamental changes in the underlying trend growth rate of the economy is related to the recent literature on the response of asset prices to news about future economic fundamentals. Barsky and DeLong (1993) and Kiyotaki (1990) study the effects of learning about the transitory and persistent components of dividend growth on asset prices in a partial equilibrium model. When the transitory and persistent shocks to dividend growth are not observed separately, investors extrapolate a transitory movement in dividend growth into the future, generating a large response in asset prices. The interest rate is fixed in these partial equilibrium models, which helps to generate large movements in asset prices. Kiley (2000) provides a comparison of the asset pricing implications of partial and general equilibrium models. Asset prices may fall in response to increases in the growth rate of technology, as real interest rates rise in general equilibrium.

In an RBC framework that allows for capital accumulation, a persistent increase in the growth rate of technology leads to a rise in the real interest rate and decreases in investment and asset prices. Consumption rises by a large amount due to a large wealth effect of expectations of future technology improvements (Barro and King 1984; Campbell 1994; Cochrane 1994). Using a New Keynesian model, Gilchrist and Leahy (2002) show that asset prices may rise rather than fall in response to a persistent increase in the growth rate of technology. This positive response in asset prices relies on an accommodative monetary policy that responds weakly to inflation. More recently, Christiano, Motto, and Rostagno (2005) emphasize the role of monetary policy in generating an asset price boom in a model with habit formation and adjustment costs to investment growth. In their model, favorable news about future technology tends to lower current inflation. As the monetary authority responds by lowering interest rates, asset prices rise. Jaimovich and Rebelo (2006) consider RBC environments that may produce asset price booms following favorable news about future technology. In our framework, as in Gilchrist and Leahy (2002), asset prices are more likely to rise in response to favorable news about future technology in the presence of accommodative monetary policy, and movements in asset prices are amplified in the presence of the financial accelerator mechanism.

Finally, there is a rich literature emphasizing the welfare benefits of monetary policy rules in environments with imperfect information and environments that allow for financial frictions. Dupor (2005) and Edge, Laubach, and Williams (2005) solve a Ramsey problem to study the characteristics of the optimal monetary policy, while Tambalotti (2003) uses a second-order approximation to the utility function in a model without capital. More closely related to our work, Faia and Monacelli (2006) use a second-order approximation to the policy function in the Bernanke, Gertler, and Gilchrist (1999) framework and find that including the level of asset prices in the interest rate rule with a modest coefficient is beneficial to welfare when the coefficient on inflation is relatively small. When the coefficient on inflation is sufficiently large, including asset prices in the policy rule does not improve welfare. Although we focus on a quadratic loss function rather than formal welfare analysis, our results imply modest benefits of allowing the monetary authority to respond to the asset price gap, even when the monetary authority is responding strongly to inflation. This difference in results may be partially attributable to our emphasis on asset price gaps rather than asset price levels as the variable in the policy rule.[3]

2.2   Model

The model is a dynamic stochastic general equilibrium model with a financial accelerator mechanism (Bernanke, Gertler, and Gilchrist 1999).[4]

---

3. Our finding that a policy that responds to the growth rate of asset prices or the growth rate of output performs well when the policymaker has imperfect information about the state of technology growth is related to Orphanides and Williams (2002), who find that in environments where the natural rates are unobservable, an interest rate rule that includes changes in economic activity (which does not require information on the natural rates) performs well.

4. The description of the model closely follows Bernanke, Gertler, and Gilchrist (1999) and Gertler, Gilchrist, and Natalucci (2006).

The financial accelerator mechanism links the relative price of capital (interpretable as asset prices), balance-sheet conditions of borrowers, the external finance premium defined as the cost of external funds relative to the cost of internal funds, and investment spending. Specifically, an unexpected increase in asset prices—as a result of a favorable shock to productivity of the economy, for example—increases the net worth of borrowers, decreases the external finance premium, and increases the capital expenditures of these borrowers. In general equilibrium, the increase in capital expenditures leads to a further increase in asset prices and magnifies the mechanism just described. To clarify the role of the financial accelerator mechanism in the relationship between asset prices and monetary policy, the following sections also consider a model in which the financial accelerator mechanism is absent.

2.2.1 Structure of the Economy

We first describe the structure of the economy, including the specification of monetary policy rules and the information structure. We consider the problems of households, entrepreneurs, capital producers, and retailers in turn.

Households

Households consume, hold money, save in the form of a one-period riskless bond whose nominal rate of return is known at the time of the purchase, and supply labor to the entrepreneurs who manage the production of wholesale goods.

Preferences are given by

$$E_0 \sum_{t=0}^{\infty} \beta^t u \left(C_t, H_t, \frac{M_t}{P_t} \right),$$

with

$$u \left(C_t, H_t, \frac{M_t}{P_t} \right) = \ln C_t - \theta \frac{H_t^{1+\gamma}}{t+\gamma} + \xi \ln \frac{M_t}{P_t},$$

where C_t is consumption, H_t is hours worked, M_t/P_t is real balances acquired in period t and carried into period $t + 1$, and γ, θ, and ξ are positive parameters.

The budget constraint is given by

$$C_t = \frac{W_t}{P_t} H_t + \Pi_t - T_t - \frac{M_t - M_{t-1}}{P_t} - \frac{B_{t+1} - R_t^n B_t}{P_t},$$

where W_t is the nominal wage for the household labor, Π_t is the real dividends from ownership of retail firms, T_t is lump-sum taxes, B_{t+1} is a riskless bond held between period t and period $t + 1$, and R_t^n is the nominal rate of return on the riskless bond held between period $t - 1$ and period t.

The first-order conditions for the household's optimization problem include

(1)
$$\frac{1}{C_t} = \beta E_t \left(\frac{1}{C_{t+1}} R_{t+1}^n \frac{P_t}{P_{t+1}} \right),$$

and

(2)
$$\frac{1}{C_t} \frac{W_t}{P_t} = \theta H_t^\gamma.$$

Entrepreneurs

Entrepreneurs manage the production of wholesale goods. The production of wholesale goods uses capital constructed by capital producers and labor supplied by both households and entrepreneurs. Entrepreneurs purchase capital from capital goods producers and finance the expenditures on capital with both entrepreneurial net worth (internal finance) and debt (external finance). We introduce financial market imperfections that make the cost of external funds depend on the entrepreneur's balance-sheet condition.

Entrepreneurs are risk neutral. To ensure that entrepreneurs do not accumulate enough funds to finance their expenditures on capital entirely with net worth, we assume that they have a finite lifetime. In particular, we assume that each entrepreneur survives until the next period with probability η. New entrepreneurs enter to replace those who exit. To ensure that new entrepreneurs have some funds available when starting out, each entrepreneur is endowed with H_t^e units of labor that are supplied inelastically as a managerial input to the wholesale-good production at nominal entrepreneurial wage W_t^e.

The entrepreneur starts any period t with capital K_t purchased from capital producers at the end of period $t - 1$ and produces wholesale goods Y_t with labor and capital. Labor L_t is a composite of household labor H_t and entrepreneurial labor H_t^e:

$$L_t = H_t^{1-\Omega}(H_t^e)^\Omega.$$

The entrepreneur's project is subject to an idiosyncratic shock ω_t, which affects both the production of wholesale goods and the effective quantity of capital held by the entrepreneur. We assume that ω_t is independently and identically distributed (*i.i.d.*) across entrepreneurs and time, satisfying $E(\omega_t) = 1$. The production function for the wholesale goods is given by

(3)
$$Y_t = \omega_t(A_t L_t)^\alpha K_t^{1-\alpha},$$

where A_t is exogenous technology common to all the entrepreneurs. Let $P_{W,t}$ denote the nominal price of wholesale goods, Q_t the price of capital relative to the aggregate price P_t to be defined later, and δ the depreciation rate. The entrepreneur's real revenue in period t is the sum of the production revenues and the real value of the undepreciated capital:

$$\omega_t \left[\frac{P_{W,t}}{P_t}(A_t L)^\alpha K_t^{1-\alpha} + Q_t(1 - \delta)K_t \right].$$

In any period t, the entrepreneur chooses the demand for both household labor and entrepreneurial labor to maximize profits given capital K_t acquired in the previous period. The first-order conditions are

(4)
$$\alpha(1 - \Omega)\frac{Y_t}{H_t} = \frac{W_t}{P_{W,t}},$$

and

(5)
$$\alpha\Omega\frac{Y_t}{H_t^e} = \frac{W_t^e}{P_{W,t}}.$$

At the end of period t, after the production of wholesale goods, the entrepreneur purchases capital K_{t+1} from capital producers at price Q_t. The capital is used as an input to the production of wholesale goods in period $t + 1$. The entrepreneur finances the purchase of capital $Q_t K_{t+1}$ partly with net worth N_{t+1} and partly by issuing nominal debt B_{t+1}:

$$Q_t K_{t+1} = N_{t+1} + \frac{B_{t+1}}{P_t}.$$

The entrepreneur's capital purchase decision depends on the expected rate of return on capital and the expected marginal cost of finance. The real rate of return on capital between period t and period $t + 1$, R_{t+1}^k, depends on the marginal profit from the production of wholesale goods and the capital gain:

(6)
$$R_{t+1}^k = \frac{\omega_{t+1} \left[\dfrac{P_{W,t+1}}{P_{t+1}}(1 - \alpha)\dfrac{\overline{Y}_{t+1}}{K_{t+1}} + (1 - \delta)Q_{t+1} \right]}{Q_t},$$

where $\overline{Y}_{t+1}$ is the average wholesale good production per entrepreneur ($Y_{t+1} = \omega_{t+1}\overline{Y}_{t+1}$). Under our assumption of $E_t\omega_{t+1} = 1$, the expected real rate of return on capital, $E_t R_{t+1}^k$, is given by

(7)
$$E_t R_{t+1}^k = E_t \left[\frac{\dfrac{P_{W,t+1}}{P_{t+1}}(1 - \alpha)\dfrac{\overline{Y}_{t+1}}{K_{t+1}} + (1 - \delta)Q_{t+1}}{Q_t} \right].$$

In the presence of financial market imperfections, the marginal cost of external funds depends on the entrepreneur's balance-sheet condition. As in Bernanke, Gertler, and Gilchrist (1999), we assume asymmetric information between borrowers (entrepreneurs) and lenders and a costly state verification. Specifically, the idiosyncratic shock to entrepreneurs, ω_t, is private information for the entrepreneur. To observe this, the lender must pay an auditing cost that is a fixed proportion μ_b of the realized gross return to capital held by the entrepreneur: $\mu_b R_{t+1}^k Q_t K_{t+1}$. The entrepreneur and the lender negotiate a financial contract that induces the entrepreneur to not misrepresent her earnings and minimizes the expected auditing costs incurred by the lender. We restrict attention to financial contracts that are negotiated one period at a time and offer lenders a payoff that is independent of aggregate risk. Under these assumptions, the optimal contract is a standard debt with costly bankruptcy: if the entrepreneur does not default, the lender receives a fixed payment independent of the realization of the idiosyncratic shock ω_t; and if the entrepreneur defaults, the lender audits and seizes whatever it finds.

In equilibrium, the cost of external funds between period t and period $t + 1$ is equated to the expected real rate of return on capital (7). We define the external finance premium s_t as the ratio of the entrepreneur's cost of external funds to the cost of internal funds, where the latter is equated to the cost of funds in the absence of financial market imperfections $E_t[R_{t+1}^n (P_t/P_{t+1})]$:

$$(8) \qquad s_t \equiv \frac{E_t R_{t+1}^k}{E_t \left(R_{t+1}^n \dfrac{P_t}{P_{t+1}} \right)}.$$

In the absence of financial market imperfections, there is no external finance premium ($s_t = 1$).

The agency problem implies that the cost of external funds depends on the financial position of the borrowers. In particular, the external finance premium increases when a smaller fraction of capital expenditures is financed by the entrepreneur's net worth:

$$(9) \qquad s_t = s\left(\frac{Q_t K_{t+1}}{N_{t+1}} \right),$$

where $s(\cdot)$ is an increasing function for $N_{t+1} < Q_t K_{t+1}$. The specific form of the function $s(\cdot)$ depends on the primitive parameters of the costly state verification problem, including the bankruptcy cost parameter μ_b and the distribution of the idiosyncratic shock ω_t. We specify a parametric form for the function $s(\cdot)$ in the next section.

The aggregate net worth of entrepreneurs at the end of period t is the sum of the equity held by entrepreneurs who survive from period $t - 1$ and the aggregate entrepreneurial wage, which consists of the wage earned by the entrepreneurs surviving from period $t - 1$ and the wage earned by newly emerged entrepreneurs in period t:

(10) $\quad N_{t+1} = \eta \left(R_t^k Q_{t-1} K_t - E_{t-1} R_t^k \cdot \dfrac{B_t}{P_{t-1}} \right) + \dfrac{W_t^e}{P_t}$

$\qquad = \eta [R_t^k Q_{t-1} K_t - E_{t-1} R_t^k (Q_{t-1} K_t - N_t)] + \dfrac{W_t^e}{P_t},$

where the second line used the relation $Q_{t-1} K_t = N_t + B_t/P_{t-1}$.

Unexpected changes in asset prices are the main source of changes in the entrepreneurial net worth and, hence, the external finance premium. Equations (6) and (7) suggest that unexpected changes in asset prices are the main source of unexpected changes in the real rate of return on capital— the difference between the realized rate of return on capital in period t, R_t^k, and the rate of return on capital anticipated in the previous period, $E_{t-1} R_t^k$, where the latter is the marginal cost of external funds between period $t-1$ and t. Equation (10), in turn, suggests that the main source of changes in the entrepreneurial net worth is unexpected movements in the real rate of return on capital, under the calibration that the entrepreneurial wage is small.[5] Finally, equation (9) implies that changes in the entrepreneurial net worth are the main source of changes in the external finance premium. Thus, movements in asset prices play a key role in the financial accelerator mechanism.

Entrepreneurs going out of business in period t consume the residual equity:

(11) $\qquad C_t^e = (1 - \eta) \left(R_t^k Q_{t-1} K_t - E_{t-1} R_t^k \cdot \dfrac{B_t}{P_{t-1}} \right),$

where C_t^e is the aggregate consumption of the entrepreneurs who exit in period t.

Overall, the financial accelerator mechanism implies that an unexpected increase in asset prices increases the net worth of entrepreneurs and improves their balance-sheet conditions. This, in turn, reduces the external finance premium and increases the demand for capital by these entrepreneurs. In equilibrium, the price of capital increases further, and capital producers increase the production of new capital. This additional increase in asset prices strengthens the mechanism just described. Thus, the countercyclical movement in the external finance premium implied by the financial market imperfections magnifies the effects of shocks to the economy.

Capital Producers

Capital producers use both final goods I_t and existing capital K_t to construct new capital K_{t+1}. They lease existing capital from the entrepreneurs.

---

5. In the calibration below, we set $\Omega = 0$, which makes the effects of changes in the entrepreneurial wage on net worth negligible.

Each capital producer operates a constant returns-to-scale technology for capital production $\phi(I_t/K_t)K_t$, where the function $\phi(\cdot)$ is increasing and concave, capturing the increasing marginal costs of capital production. The aggregate capital accumulation equation is given by

$$(12) \qquad K_{t+1} = (1 - \delta)K_t + \phi\left(\frac{I_t}{K_t}\right)K_t.$$

Taking the relative price of capital Q_t as given, capital producers choose inputs I_t and K_t to maximize profits from the formation of new capital. The following first-order condition for the capital producer's problem implies that investment (the demand for final goods by capital producers) and the quantity of new capital increase as the relative price of capital—interpretable as asset prices—increases:

$$(13) \qquad Q_t = \frac{1}{\phi'\left(\dfrac{I_t}{K_t}\right)}.$$

Retailers

There is a continuum of monopolistically competitive retailers of measure unity. Retailers buy wholesale goods from entrepreneurs in a competitive manner and then differentiate the product slightly at zero resource cost.

Let $Y_t(z)$ be the retail goods sold by retailer z, and let $P_t(z)$ be its nominal price. Final goods, Y_t, are the composite of individual retail goods

$$Y_t = \left[\int_0^1 Y_t(z)^{(\varepsilon-1)/\varepsilon}\,dz\right]^{\varepsilon/(\varepsilon-1)},$$

and the corresponding price index, P_t, is given by

$$P_t = \left[\int_0^1 P_t(z)^{1-\varepsilon}\,dz\right]^{1/(1-\varepsilon)}.$$

Households, capital producers, and the government demand the final goods.

Each retailer faces an isoelastic demand curve given by

$$(14) \qquad Y_t(z) = \left[\frac{P_t(z)}{P_t}\right]^{-\varepsilon} Y_t.$$

As in Calvo (1983), each retailer resets price with probability $(1 - \upsilon)$, independently of the time elapsed since the last price adjustment. Thus, in each period, a fraction $(1 - \upsilon)$ of retailers reset their prices, while the remaining fraction υ keeps their prices unchanged. The real marginal cost to the retailers of producing a unit of retail goods is the price of wholesale goods, relative to the price of final goods ($P_{W,t}/P_t$). Each retailer takes the demand curve in equation (14) and the price of wholesale goods as given and sets the retail price $P_t(z)$. All retailers given a chance to reset their prices in period t choose the same price P_t^* given by

$$(15) \qquad P_t^* = \frac{\varepsilon}{\varepsilon - 1} \frac{E_t \sum_{i=0}^{\infty} \upsilon^i \Lambda_{t,i} P_{t+i}^W Y_{t+i} \left(\dfrac{1}{P_{t+i}}\right)^{1-\varepsilon}}{E_t \sum_{i=0}^{\infty} \upsilon^i \Lambda_{t,i} Y_{t+i} \left(\dfrac{1}{P_{t+i}}\right)^{1-\varepsilon}},$$

where $\Lambda_{t,i} \equiv \beta^i C_t/C_{t+i}$ is the stochastic discount factor that the retailers take as given.

The aggregate price evolves according to

$$(16) \qquad P_t = [\upsilon P_{t-1}^{1-\varepsilon} + (1 - \upsilon)(P_t^*)^{1-\varepsilon}]^{1/(1-\varepsilon)}.$$

Combining equations (15) and (16) yields an expression that relates the current inflation to the current real marginal cost and the expected inflation, as described in the appendix.

Aggregate Resource Constraint

The aggregate resource constraint for final goods is

$$(17) \qquad Y_t = C_t + C_t^e + I_t + G_t,$$

where G_t is the government expenditures that we assume to be exogenous.[6]

Government

Exogenous government expenditures G_t are financed by lump-sum taxes T_t and money creation:

$$(18) \qquad G_t = \frac{M_t - M_{t-1}}{P_t} + T_t.$$

The money stock is adjusted to support the interest rate rule specified in the following. Lump-sum taxes adjust to satisfy the government budget constraint.

Technology Shock Process

The growth rate of technology has both transitory and persistent components:

$$(19) \qquad \ln A_t - \ln A_{t-1} = \mu_t + \varepsilon_t.$$

---

6. In the following calibration, we assume that actual resource costs to bankruptcy are negligible.

The persistent component of technology growth in deviation from the mean growth rate of technology, $(\mu_t - \mu)$, follows an AR(1) process:

$$(20) \qquad (\mu_t - \mu) = \rho_d(\mu_{t-1} - \mu) + \upsilon_t.$$

Shocks to the transitory and persistent components of technology growth are

$$(21) \qquad \varepsilon_t \sim i.i.d. N(0, \sigma_\varepsilon^2),$$

and

$$(22) \qquad \upsilon_t \sim i.i.d. N(0, \sigma_\upsilon^2).$$

Information Structure

Our technology process allows for two sources of variation: shocks to the transitory and persistent components of technology growth. We consider both the case of full information where agents observe both shocks separately and the case of imperfect information where agents observe the technology series, A_t, but cannot decompose movements in technology growth into their respective sources.

Monetary Policy Rules

The monetary authority conducts monetary policy using interest rate rules. We consider the following types of interest rate rules.

Policy Rule with Inflation Only. The first rule we consider is the one with current inflation only:

$$(23) \qquad R_{t+1}^n = R^n \pi_t^{\phi_\pi},$$

where $\pi_t \equiv P_t/P_{t-1}$ is inflation, and R^n is the steady-state nominal interest rate on the one-period bond. We assume that the policymaker targets 0 percent inflation. Bernanke and Gertler (1999, 2001) show that this rule with a large coefficient ϕ_π performs well in the economy with shocks to the bubble component of asset prices as well as shocks to technology.

Policy Rule with the Asset Price Gap. In the second rule that we consider, the monetary authority adjusts interest rates based on current inflation and the gap between the observed asset prices Q_t and the inferred potential level of asset prices Q_t^*:

$$(24) \qquad R_{t+1}^n = R^n \pi_t^{\phi_\pi} \left(\frac{Q_t}{Q_t^*} \right)^{\phi_Q},$$

where Q_t^* is the equilibrium level of asset prices in the economy without pricing and financial frictions.

The potential level of asset prices is computed under the information available to the policymaker. When the policymaker has full information, we use $Q^*_{\text{full},t}$, which is obtained by solving a flexible-price model without financial frictions under full information. When the policymaker has imperfect information, we use $Q^*_{\text{imp},t}$, which is obtained by solving a flexible-price model without financial frictions under imperfect information.

There are two ways to construct Q^*_t from the model. In the first, one could use the hypothetical levels of the state variables in the frictionless economy to compute Q^*_t. In the second, one may use the levels of the state variables in the model with both pricing and financial market frictions combined with the decision rule for the frictionless economy to compute Q^*_t. Neiss and Nelson (2003) follow the first approach, and Woodford (2003) argues that the second approach is more realistic. We adopt the first procedure because it is somewhat easier to work with.

Policy Rule with the Natural Rate and the Asset Price Gap. We also consider a policy rule that allows the policymaker to respond to movements in the natural rate of interest:

$$(25) \qquad R^n_{t+1} = R^*_{t+1}\, \pi_t^{\phi_\pi} \left(\frac{Q_t}{Q^*_t} \right)^{\phi_Q},$$

where R^*_{t+1} is the natural rate of interest that prevails between period t and period $t + 1$. We define the natural rate of interest as the real interest rate that supports the efficient allocation in the economy without pricing and financial frictions. It is computed based on the information available to the policymaker.

Policy Rule with Asset Price Growth or Output Growth. The policy rule with the asset price gap requires the policymaker to compute Q^*_t—the level of asset prices in the flexible-price economy without financial frictions. An alternative would be to allow the policymaker to respond to the growth rate of observed asset prices:

$$(26) \qquad R^n_{t+1} = R^n \pi_t^{\phi_\pi} \left(\frac{Q_t}{Q_{t-1}} \right)^{\phi_Q}.$$

This rule is considered in Tetlow (2005).

For comparison purposes, we also consider a monetary policy rule that includes a policy response to the growth rate of output:

$$(27) \qquad R^n_{t+1} = R^n \pi_t^{\phi_\pi} \left[\frac{Y_t}{\exp(\mu) Y_{t-1}} \right]^{\phi_Y},$$

where μ is the mean growth rate of technology.

Policy Rule with the Level of Asset Prices. As another rule that does not require the policymaker to infer the unobserved shocks and thus the potential level of asset prices, we consider a policy rule that includes a response to the level of asset prices in deviation from the nonstochastic steady-state level:

$$(28) \qquad R_{t+1}^n = R^n \, \pi_t^{\phi_\pi} \left(\frac{Q_t}{Q} \right)^{\phi_Q},$$

where Q is the nonstochastic steady-state level of asset prices. This rule is considered in Bernanke and Gertler (1999, 2001) and in Faia and Monacelli (2006). This rule does not take into account variation in the potential level of asset prices.

2.2.2 Filtering under Imperfect Information

Let $Z_t \equiv A_t/A_{t-1}$ denote technology growth, $\tilde{z}_t \equiv (\ln Z_t - \mu)$ the percentage deviation of technology growth from the mean, and $\tilde{d}_t \equiv (\mu_t - \mu)$ the percentage deviation of the persistent component of technology growth from the mean. Then we can write the technology process in equations (19) and (20) as

$$(29) \qquad \tilde{z} = \tilde{d}_t + \varepsilon_t,$$

and

$$(30) \qquad \tilde{d}_t = \rho_d \tilde{d}_{t-1} + v_t.$$

Under full information, agents observe both the shock to the transitory component of technology growth, ε_t, and the shock to the persistent component of technology growth, v_t. Under imperfect information, agents observe $\tilde{z}_t$, or the sum of two components, $(\tilde{d}_t + \varepsilon_t)$ but do not observe the two shocks separately.

Let $E[\tilde{d}_t | \tilde{z}_t, \tilde{z}_{t-1}, \ldots] \equiv \tilde{d}_{t|t}$ denote the inference of agents about the current state of the persistent component of technology growth based on the observations of current and past technology growth. We assume that agents update inferences based on the steady-state Kalman filter:

$$(31) \qquad \tilde{d}_{t|t} = \lambda \tilde{z}_t + (1 - \lambda) \, \rho_d \tilde{d}_{t-1|t-1},$$

where the gain, λ, is given by

$$(32) \qquad \lambda \equiv \frac{\phi - (1 - \rho_d^2) + \phi \sqrt{(1 - \rho_d^2)^2 \dfrac{1}{\phi^2} + 1 + \dfrac{2}{\phi} + 2\rho_d^2 \dfrac{1}{\phi}}}{2 + \phi - (1 - \rho_d^2) + \phi \sqrt{(1 - \rho_d^2)^2 \dfrac{1}{\phi^2} + 1 + \dfrac{2}{\phi} + 2\rho_d^2 \dfrac{1}{\phi}}},$$

and ϕ measures the signal-to-noise ratio:

$$(33) \qquad \phi \equiv \frac{\sigma_v^2}{\sigma_\varepsilon^2}.$$

It is straightforward to show that the gain, λ, is monotonically increasing in both the signal-to-noise ratio, ϕ, and the AR(1) coefficient on the persistent component of technology growth, ρ_d.

Given $\tilde{d}_{t|t}$, the inference about the shock to the transitory component of technology growth, $\varepsilon_{t|t} \equiv E[\varepsilon_t | \tilde{z}_t, \tilde{z}_{t-1}, \ldots]$, is given by

(34)
$$\varepsilon_{t|t} = \tilde{z}_t - \tilde{d}_{t|t},$$

and the inference about the shock to the persistent component of technology growth, $\upsilon_{t|t} \equiv E[\upsilon_t | \tilde{z}_t, \tilde{z}_{t-1}, \ldots]$, is given by

(35)
$$\upsilon_{t|t} = \tilde{d}_{t|t} - \rho_d \tilde{d}_{t-1|t-1}.$$

Properties of the Inference under Imperfect Information

We now illustrate the properties of the inference of agents about the state of technology growth. We consider how each of the shocks to the transitory and persistent components of technology growth affects the inference of agents.[7]

Figure 2.1 presents the response to a 1 percent increase in the transitory component of technology growth. The dashed line is the actual persistent component of technology growth in deviation from the mean technology growth rate, $\tilde{d}_t \equiv (\mu_t - \mu)$. The solid line is the inferred persistent component of technology growth in deviation from the mean growth rate, $\tilde{d}_{t|t}$. Although the shock considered here has no impact on the persistent component of technology growth, agents initially interpret part of the observed changes in technology growth to be persistent. Over time, they gradually learn that the shock was to the transitory component of technology growth.

Figure 2.2 presents the effect of a 1 percent increase in the persistent component of technology growth on both the actual and the inferred persistent component of technology growth, $\tilde{d}_t$ and $\tilde{d}_{t|t}$. Although the shock considered here changes the persistent component of technology growth, agents initially interpret most of the observed increase in technology growth to be transitory. Over time, as agents accumulate more observations of technology growth, they gradually revise their inferences.

Difference in Information between the Private Sector and the Policymaker

Our framework allows us to consider the case where the policymaker has different information from the private sector. The case where the policymaker and the private sector have the same information about the aggregate shocks to the economy is arguably more realistic than the case where

---

7. The parameter values related to the shock process used in these experiments are described in the following section.

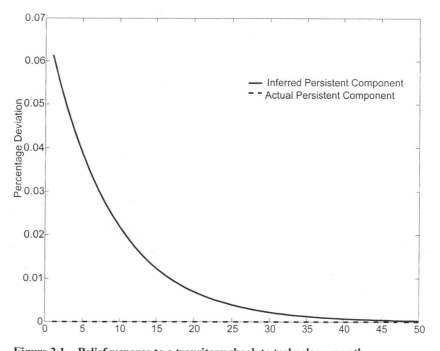

Figure 2.1   Belief response to a transitory shock to technology growth

Note: The dashed line is the realization of the persistent component of technology growth in percentage deviation from the mean technology growth rate: $\tilde{d}_t \equiv (\mu_t - \mu)$. The straight line is the inference about the persistent component of technology growth in percentage deviation from the mean technology growth rate: $E[\tilde{d}_t | \tilde{z}_t, \tilde{z}_{t-1}, ...] \equiv \tilde{d}_{t|t}$.

they have different information. Considering the cases where they have different information is useful for our analysis because in these cases the benefits or the losses from allowing a policy response to the asset price gap or the natural rate of interest are the greatest. Specifically, as we see in later sections, the gains from allowing the policymaker to respond to movements in the natural rate of interest or the asset price gap are greatest when the policymaker has full information and the private sector has imperfect information.[8] Allowing the policymaker to respond to the natural rate of interest or the asset price gap is most harmful when the policymaker has imperfect information and the private sector has full information.

In the case where the policymaker has full information and the private sector has imperfect information, we preclude the possibility that the latter learns more about the realizations of the shocks to the transitory and persistent components of technology growth by observing the former's be-

---

8. As described in the following, we assess the benefits of adopting various interest rate rules based on the variance of inflation and the output gap.

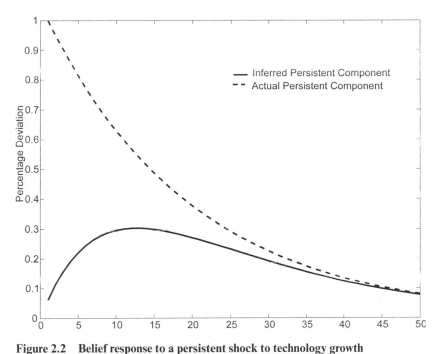

Figure 2.2   Belief response to a persistent shock to technology growth

Note: The dashed line is the realization of the persistent component of technology growth in percentage deviation from the mean technology growth rate: $\tilde{d}_t \equiv (\mu_t - \mu)$. The straight line is the inference about the persistent component of technology growth in percentage deviation from the mean technology growth rate: $E[\tilde{d}_t | \tilde{z}_t, \tilde{z}_{t-1}, ...] \equiv \tilde{d}_{t|t}$.

havior.[9] Because the policymaker's setting of the interest rate is affected by the information it possesses, the policymaker's information indirectly affects the behavior of the private sector through movements in the interest rate that is set, however. Thus, the policymaker's information affects the private sector's incentives but not the inferences regarding the state of technology growth. Likewise, in the case where the policymaker has imperfect information and the private sector has full information, we preclude the possibility that the former learns about the unobserved shocks to technology growth from the latter's behavior. Thus, when considering the case of different information between the private sector and the policymaker, we

9. Specifically, we assume that, when the private sector solves its optimization problem, it does not internalize the fact that the potential level of asset prices Q_t^* in the policy rule in equations (24) and (25) and the natural rate of interest R_{t+1}^* in the policy rule in equations (25) are functions of the realizations of the shocks μ_t and ε_t and capital stock, where those functions are obtained by solving for the efficient allocation in the frictionless economy. Note also that the variables about which the private sector learns—the realizations of the shocks to the transitory and persistent components of technology growth—are exogenous and independent of the policymaker's behavior.

view our results as providing a useful benchmark to assess the best- and worst-case scenarios relative to the more realistic situation where the private sector and the policymaker have the same information or may learn from each other's actions. Allowing for learning between the private sector and the policymaker is an interesting avenue for future research.

2.3 Calibration

We adopt a fairly standard calibration of preferences, technology, and the price-setting structure. The financial sector is calibrated to conform to a simplified version of Bernanke, Gertler, and Gilchrist (1999). These simplifications allow us to focus on the main distortion that is introduced by financial market imperfections—the introduction of a countercyclical premium on external funds that drives a wedge between the cost of external funds and the cost of internal funds.

2.3.1 Preferences, Technology, and Price-Setting

A period in the model is a quarter. The discount factor is $\beta = 0.984$. The labor share of income is $\alpha = 2/3$. Setting $\gamma = 0.8$ implies that the labor supply elasticity is $1/\gamma = 1.25$. The depreciation rate is $\delta = 0.025$. The elasticity of asset prices with respect to the investment-capital ratio is $\eta_k \equiv -[\phi''(i/k)Z(i/k)Z]/\phi'[(i/k)Z] = 0.25$, the same as in Bernanke, Gertler, and Gilchrist (1999) and Bernanke and Gertler (1999).[10] For the price setting, the steady-state markup is $\varepsilon/(\varepsilon - 1) = 1.1$, while the probability that a producer does not adjust prices in a given quarter is $\upsilon = 0.75$.

2.3.2 Financial Market Imperfections

When log-linearizing the model, we adopt a number of simplifications to the original financial sector specified in Bernanke, Gertler, and Gilchrist (1999). These simplifications allow us to focus on the primary distortion associated with financial market imperfections—namely, that it introduces a time-varying countercyclical wedge between the rate of return on capital and the rate of return on the riskless bond held by households. We assume that variations in entrepreneurial consumption and the entrepreneurial wage are negligible and can be ignored. We further assume that actual resource costs to bankruptcy are also negligible. Model simulations conducted under the original Bernanke, Gertler, and Gilchrist (1999) framework imply that these simplifications are reasonable.

The log-linearized model then implies that there are two key financial parameters to choose—the steady-state leverage ratio and the elasticity of the external finance premium with respect to leverage. The steady-state ratio of

---

10. Tetlow (2005) uses a value of 0.5641, and Faia and Monacelli (2005) use a value of 0.5 for the parameter η_k.

the real value of the capital stock to the entrepreneur's net worth is chosen so that the steady-state leverage ratio is 80 percent or $(QK - N)/N = 0.8$, which implies $(QK)/N = 1.8$. We also adopt a simplified functional form for the determination of the external finance premium in equation (9):

$$(36) \qquad s_t = \left(\frac{Q_t K_{t+1}}{N_{t+1}} \right)^x.$$

Financial market imperfections imply that the external finance premium increases when the leverage of the borrowers increases ($\chi > 0$). In line with the calibration adopted by Bernanke, Gertler, and Gilchrist (1999), the elasticity of the external finance premium with respect to leverage is set to 5 percent: $\chi = 0.05$. These parameterizations imply that the nonstochastic steady-state level of the external finance premium is $s = (QK/N)^x = 1.0298$. Increasing the level of the steady-state leverage ratio or the size of the sensitivity parameter χ strengthens the financial accelerator mechanism. In the case of no financial market imperfections, $\chi = 0$. In this case, balance-sheet conditions of the entrepreneurs are irrelevant for the cost of external funds and thus for their capital expenditure decisions.

2.3.3 Shock Process and Filtering

We set the mean technology growth rate at the average quarterly growth rate of total factor productivity in the United States between 1959 and 2002: $\mu = 0.00427$. We set the standard deviation of the shock to the transitory component of technology growth at $\sigma_\varepsilon = 0.01$, the standard deviation of the shock to the persistent component of technology growth at $\sigma_v = 0.001$, and the AR(1) coefficient on the persistent component of technology growth at $\rho_d = 0.95$. These parameter choices imply that the signal-to-noise ratio in equation (33) is

$$\phi = 0.01.$$

The Kalman gain parameter in equation (32) consistent with these shock parameters is[11]

$$\lambda = 0.06138.$$

2.4 Impulse Responses

In this section, we report impulse response functions to technology shocks to explore the roles of imperfect information and financial market imperfections and their effects on output, inflation, asset prices, and the ex-

---

11. This is within the range of values used in the literature. Edge, Laubach, and Williams (2005) use $\lambda = 0.025$ together with $\rho_d = 0.95$. Erceg, Guerrieri, and Gust (2005) use $\lambda = 0.1$ together with $\rho_d = 0.975$. Tambalotti (2003) uses $\rho_d = 0.93$ together with $\sigma_v/\sigma_\varepsilon = 0.08$ or $\phi \equiv \sigma_v^2/\sigma_\varepsilon^2 = 0.0064$, implying $\lambda = 0.0369$.

ternal finance premium. We explore the potential benefits of various monetary policy rules within this framework.

2.4.1   Transitory Shock to Technology Growth

We begin by examining the response of output, inflation, asset prices, and the external finance premium to a transitory increase in the growth rate of technology. We consider the model with and without the financial accelerator and also report the response of the flexible-price economy without the financial accelerator. This economy is undistorted and corresponds to our notion of the potential. We first consider a situation where both the private sector and the policymaker are fully informed regarding the state of technology growth. We then consider a situation where they both have imperfect information but learn over time according to the Kalman filter specified in the preceding.

For each model, we consider three monetary policy rules: a policy of responding weakly to inflation ($\ln R_{t+1}^n = \ln R^n + 1.1 \ln \pi_t$), a policy of responding strongly to inflation ($\ln R_{t+1}^n = \ln R^n + 2.0 \ln \pi_t$), and a policy rule that allows a policy response to the asset price gap in addition to a strong response to inflation [$\ln R_{t+1}^n = \ln R^n + 2.0 \ln \pi_t + 1.5(\ln Q_t - \ln Q_t^*)$]. In the case of imperfect information for the private sector, we assume that the monetary authority also has imperfect information so that the interest rate rule with the asset price gap is now $\ln R_{t+1}^n = \ln R^n + 2.0 \ln \pi_t + 1.5(\ln Q_t - \ln Q_{\text{imp},t}^*)$, where $Q_{\text{imp},t}^*$ is the level of asset prices in the frictionless economy under imperfect information.

Full Information for Both the Private Sector and the Policymaker

Figure 2.3 plots the response of the economy without the financial accelerator to a transitory increase in the growth rate of technology, when both the private sector and the policymaker have full information. The transitory shock to technology growth causes immediate increases in output, asset prices, and inflation. Along the path, output continues to rise owing to capital accumulation, while inflation and asset prices return to their initial steady-state levels. With no financial frictions, the external finance premium is constant at zero.

The strength of the response of output, inflation, and asset prices depends on the conduct of monetary policy. Under the policy of responding weakly to inflation, expected real interest rates are low relative to those implied by the flexible-price economy. As a result, asset prices are high, and output is above potential. In addition, inflation is above its target level of zero. The policy of responding strongly to inflation provides substantial improvement. Expected real interest rates rise sufficiently so that asset prices and output track their potential levels implied by the frictionless economy. In addition, the inflation response is dampened considerably. Because the asset price gap is essentially zero under the policy of responding

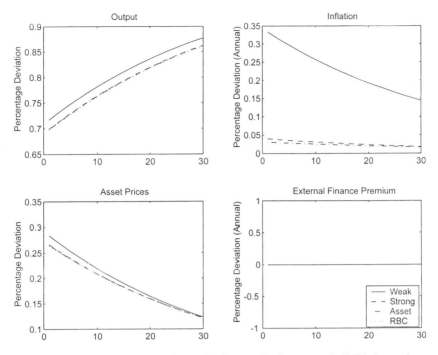

Figure 2.3   Response to a transitory shock to technology growth (full information, no financial accelerator

Note: Weak: $\ln R^n_{t+1} = \ln R^n + 1.1 \ln \pi_t$, Strong: $\ln R^n_{t+1} = \ln R^n + 2.0 \ln \pi_t$, Asset: $\ln R^n_{t+1} = \ln R^n + 2.0 \ln \pi_t = 1.5(\ln Q_t - \ln Q^*_t)$, RBC: Flexible-price model with full information and no financial market imperfections.

strongly to inflation, adding the asset price gap to the monetary policy rule produces no change in the path of output and has a negligible effect on inflation. Thus, with full information and no financial accelerator, there is little, if any, gain to allowing the monetary authority to respond to the asset price gap.

Figure 2.4 plots the response of the economy with the financial accelerator to the same transitory shock to technology growth. The financial accelerator mechanism amplifies the response of output and inflation because a favorable shock to technology raises asset prices and reduces the external finance premium. This amplified response represents distortions in the resource allocation induced by financial market imperfections. Asset prices and investment—variables that are closely linked to the financial accelerator mechanism—deviate from their efficient levels by a larger amount in the presence of financial market imperfections.

In the economy with the financial accelerator, adopting a policy rule that implies a strong response to inflation brings the path of inflation close to the target. It also reduces the response of the external finance premium and

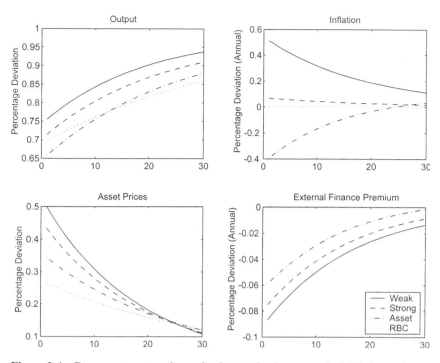

Figure 2.4   Response to a transitory shock to technology growth (full information, financial accelerator)

Note: Weak: $\ln R^n_{t+1} = \ln R^n + 1.1 \ln \pi_t$, Strong: $\ln R^n_{t+1} = \ln R^n + 2.0 \ln \pi_t$, Asset: $\ln R^n_{t+1} = \ln R^n + 2.0 \ln \pi_t$, $1.5(\ln Q_t - \ln Q^*_t)$, RBC: Flexible-price model with full information and no financial market imperfections.

reduces the amount of overinvestment that occurs. Nonetheless, there are still large deviations in output, asset prices, and investment from their potential levels. A policy of responding strongly to inflation is successful in decreasing the distortions arising from price rigidities, but is not sufficient to eliminate the distortions arising from financial market imperfections. Allowing the policymaker to respond to the asset price gap further reduces the investment distortion owing to the financial accelerator. As a result, output tracks potential more closely. This comes at the cost of producing deflation and increasing inflation variability, however.

Imperfect Information for Both the Private Sector and the Policymaker

Figure 2.5 plots the response of the economy without the financial accelerator to a transitory shock to technology growth, when both the private sector and the policymaker have imperfect information. For comparison purposes, the figure also shows the path of the frictionless economy under full information (the path labeled "RBC"). With imperfect information,

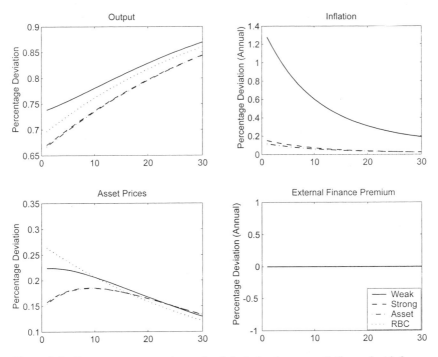

Figure 2.5   Response to a transitory shock to technology growth (imperfect information, no financial accelerator)

Note: Weak: $\ln R_{t+1}^n = \ln R^n + 1.1 \ln \pi_t$, Strong: $\ln R_{t+1}^n = \ln R^n + 2.0 \ln \pi_t$, Asset: $\ln R_{t+1}^n = \ln R^n + 2.0 \ln \pi_t + 1.5(\ln Q_t - \ln Q_t^*)$, RBC: Flexible-price model with full information and no financial market imperfections.

agents initially give some weight to the possibility that the observed increase in technology growth is persistent. An additional wealth effect owning to a perception of future technology improvements raises desired level of current consumption relative to the case of full information. Also, such a perception steepens the desired consumption profile. In the frictionless economy with imperfect information (not shown in the figure), this change in the desired consumption profile is supported by a higher expected real interest rate, and we observe a smaller response of asset prices and investment relative to the case of full information.

With the policy that implies a weak response to inflation, the rise in expected real interest rates is smaller than that in the frictionless economy, and consumption rises sharply without inducing an offsetting fall in investment. These combined effects imply a larger increase in output than what is observed in the case of full information. The inflation response is also much larger in the case of imperfect information. A policy of responding strongly to inflation implies an output path below the potential under full information, but substantially smaller response in inflation.[12] In the model with imperfect information but no financial accelerator, adding the asset price gap to the monetary policy rule again has no effect on the output path and only a negligible effect on inflation.

In the economy with the financial accelerator (figure 2.6), the policy of responding strongly to inflation is again beneficial, leading to reductions in the response of both the markup and the external finance premium. The model still implies distortions owing to the financial accelerator, however, and as a result, there are benefits to responding to the asset price gap. Allowing the monetary authority to respond to the asset price gap stabilizes the external finance premium and largely eliminates the overinvestment that occurs due to the financial accelerator. Output tracks potential more closely, but this once again occurs at the cost of increasing inflation variability.

Overall, the financial accelerator has effects on the external finance premium under imperfect information that are similar to those under full information. In response to a transitory shock, the primary effect of imperfect information is to cause a consumption boom that leads to increases in output and inflation. Although such a consumption boom can also influence asset prices and investment demand, imperfect information leads to an offsetting impulse to wait to invest in response to a perceived persistent increase in the growth rate of technology. As a result, with a policy that responds weakly to inflation, the investment distortions owing to the financial accelerator are only slightly larger under imperfect information than under full information.[13] Under both full and imperfect information, we find that there are benefits to adopting a policy rule that implies a strong response to inflation. In both cases, allowing the monetary authority to respond to the asset price gap reduces the overinvestment that occurs because of the decline in the external finance premium. Because responding to the asset price gap also produces deflation, the overall benefits will depend on the relative importance of output gap stability and inflation stability.

2.4.2   Persistent Shock to Technology Growth

We now consider the effect of a persistent increase in the growth rate of technology. We begin with the case in which both the private sector and the policymaker have full information and then report the results obtained un-

---

12. With imperfect information, a policy of responding strongly to inflation implies an output path that tracks the "potential output" path consistent with the policymaker's belief under imperfect information rather than that consistent with the true state of technology growth. The former (not shown in the figure) is below the latter (the path labeled "RBC") in this case.

13. This can be seen by comparing the movements in asset prices and the external finance premium labeled "Weak" in figure 2.4 and figure 2.6.

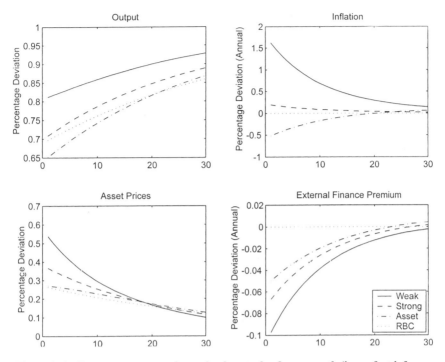

Figure 2.6   Response to a transitory shock to technology growth (imperfect information, financial accelerator)

Note: Weak: $\ln R_{t+1}^n = \ln R^n + 1.1 \ln \pi_t$, Strong: $\ln R_{t+1}^n = \ln R^n + 2.0 \ln \pi_t$, Asset: $\ln R_{t+1}^n = \ln R^n + 2.0 \ln \pi_t$, $1.5(\ln Q_t - \ln Q_t^*)$, RBC: Flexible-price model with full information and no financial market imperfections.

der imperfect information. We again consider policy rules that include a weak response to inflation, a strong response to inflation, and a rule that allows the monetary authority to respond to the asset price gap. We also report the response of the frictionless economy under full information, which corresponds to our notion of potential when we assess economic outcomes under alternative monetary policy rules.

Full Information for Both the Private Sector and the Policymaker

Figure 2.7 plots the response of the economy without the financial accelerator to a persistent increase in technology growth, when both the private sector and the policymaker have full information. With no distortions (the path labeled "RBC"), a persistent increase in technology growth implies a boom in consumption, but an initial fall in investment and asset prices. Over time, investment and asset prices rise as the process of capital accumulation takes place.

In the sticky-price model, the response of the economy again depends on

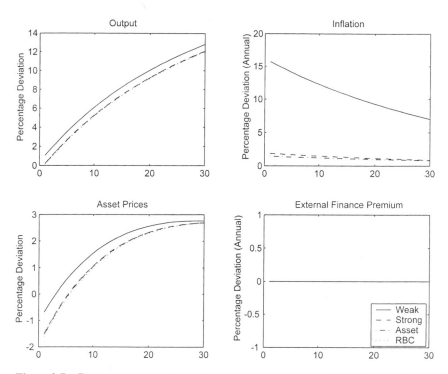

Figure 2.7   Response to a persistent shock to technology growth (full information, no financial accelerator)

Note: Weak: $\ln R^n_{t+1} = \ln R^n + 1.1 \ln \pi_t$, Strong: $\ln R^n_{t+1} = \ln R^n + 2.0 \ln \pi_t$, Asset: $\ln R^n_{t+1} = \ln R^n + 2.0 \ln \pi_t$, $1.5(\ln Q_t - \ln Q^*_t)$, RBC: Flexible-price model with full information and no financial market imperfections.

the conduct of monetary policy. Under the policy of responding weakly to inflation, the model generates less of an initial reduction in investment and a stronger output response. Inflation rises by 16 percentage points in this case. The policy of responding strongly to inflation succeeds in dampening inflation and brings output in line with potential. Investment and asset prices now fall upon impact, which eliminates the asset price gap. Without the financial accelerator, there is essentially no difference between the economy's response with and without the asset price gap in the monetary policy rule.

In the economy with the financial accelerator (figure 2.8), the persistent increase in technology growth combined with the policy of responding weakly to inflation causes a sharp drop in the external finance premium, a positive response of investment, and a substantial increase in asset prices. Asset prices rise rather than fall at the onset of a persistent increase in technology growth in the presence of the financial accelerator and accommodative monetary policy. The initial inflation response is also larger

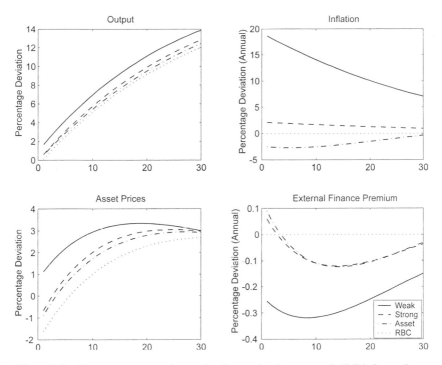

Figure 2.8   Response to a persistent shock to technology growth (full information, financial accelerator)

Note: Weak: $\ln R^n_{t+1} = \ln R^n + 1.1 \ln \pi_t$, Strong: $\ln R^n_{t+1} = \ln R^n + 2.0 \ln \pi_t$, Asset: $\ln R^n_{t+1} = \ln R^n + 2.0 \ln \pi_t\, 1.5(\ln Q_t - \ln Q^*_t)$, RBC: Flexible-price model with full information and no financial market imperfections.

now—on the order of 20 percentage points. The policy of responding strongly to inflation provides substantial benefits in terms of the output gap and inflation stabilization. We still observe movements in the external finance premium and, hence, some distortions in asset prices and investment, however. Allowing the monetary authority to respond to the asset price gap provides modest benefits in terms of further reducing the distortion in investment spending owing to the financial accelerator. This policy once again produces deflation.

Imperfect Information for Both the Private Sector and the Policymaker

Under imperfect information, the private sector initially gives a relatively large weight to the possibility that the observed increase in technology growth is transitory. The initial response is thus closer to what we would observe in the case of a transitory shock to technology growth under full information. Over time, the private sector learns that the increase in technology growth is persistent, and the economic outcomes become more similar to those obtained in the case of a persistent shock to technology growth under full information.

In the economy without the financial accelerator (figure 2.9), the persistent increase in technology growth combined with the policy of responding weakly to inflation again implies a large, albeit delayed, increase in inflation. In addition, output is more procyclical with sticky prices than would be the case under flexible prices. A policy of responding strongly to inflation dampens movements in the markup and eliminates most of the movements in inflation. In this case, output is above true potential but tracks the output level that would occur in the frictionless economy with imperfect information.[14]

With the financial accelerator (figure 2.10), the persistent increase in technology growth again produces a countercyclical movement in the external finance premium that implies a large distortion in investment spending relative to the frictionless RBC outcome. A policy of responding strongly to inflation reduces the size of asset price movements and reduces but does not eliminate movements in the external finance premium. Allowing the monetary authority to respond to the asset price gap is again beneficial. Such a policy further dampens asset price movements as well as the movements in the external finance premium. Once again, such a policy produces benefits in terms of stabilizing output gap but comes at the cost of destabilizing inflation.

Imperfect information magnifies the movements in the external finance premium in response to persistent shocks to the growth rate of technology. These magnification effects are sizeable. For example, with a policy that responds strongly to inflation, the movement in the external finance premium is twice as large in the case of imperfect information (figure 2.10), relative to the case of full information (figure 2.8). Because the private sector gives a relatively low initial weight to the probability that the increase in technology growth is persistent, imperfect information implies a series of positive shocks to expectations regarding future economic fundamentals. Such positive surprises raise the *ex post* realized rate of return on capital, relative to the anticipated rate of return, and enhance entrepreneurial net worth. These procyclical movements in net worth imply a strong humpshaped countercyclical response in the external finance premium as well as a greater degree of procyclicality in asset prices than would be the case under full information. Because the financial accelerator mechanism is strengthened by imperfect information and learning on the part of the private sector, we expect that the benefits of allowing the monetary authority to respond to asset prices, particularly in the form of reduction in the volatility of the output gap, to be greater in the case of imperfect infor-

14. The path labeled "RBC" in figure 2.9 is computed under full information.

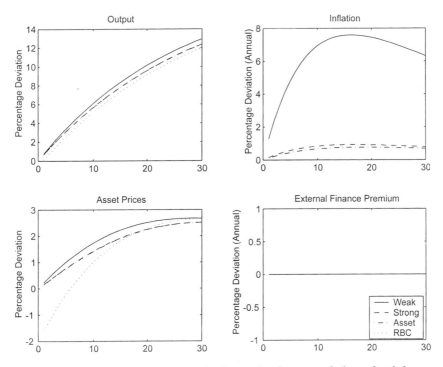

Figure 2.9   Response to a persistent shock to technology growth (imperfect information, no financial accelerator)

Note: Weak: $\ln R^n_{t+1} = \ln R^n + 1.1 \ln \pi_t$, Strong: $\ln R^n_{t+1} = \ln R^n + 2.0 \ln \pi_t$, Asset: $\ln R^n_{t+1} = \ln R^n + 2.0 \ln \pi_t, 1.5(\ln Q_t - \ln Q^*_t)$, RBC: Flexible-price model with full information and no financial market imperfections.

mation than in the case of full information.[15] We now turn to stochastic simulations to explore this issue further.

2.5   Stochastic Simulations

The previous section computed impulse response functions to technology shocks under alternative monetary policy rules. These results suggest potential benefits to adopting a policy that implies a strong response to inflation as well as to allowing the monetary authority to respond to the asset price gap—the gap between the observed asset prices and the potential

---

15. To be precise, the validity of this statement depends on the relative importance of the two types of shocks to technology growth. As we saw in this section, in response to a persistent shock to technology growth, the financial accelerator mechanism is strengthened by imperfect information on the part of the private sector. As we saw in the second subsection of section 2.4.1, in response to a transitory shock to technology growth, the effect of information structures on the strength of the financial accelerator mechanism is relatively small.

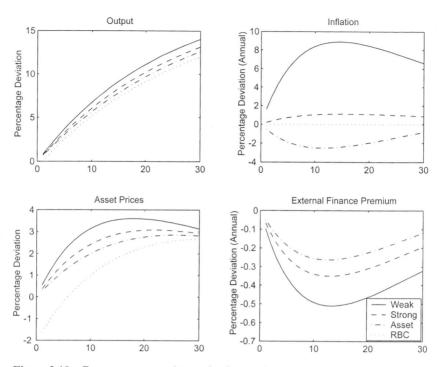

Figure 2.10   Response to a persistent shock to technology growth (imperfect information, financial accelerator)

Note: Weak: $\ln R^n_{t+1} = \ln R^n + 1.1 \ln \pi_t$, Strong: $\ln R^n_{t+1} = \ln R^n + 2.0 \ln \pi_t$, Asset: $\ln R^n_{t+1} = \ln R^n + 2.0 \ln \pi_t, 1.5(\ln Q_t - \ln Q^*_t)$, RBC: Flexible-price model with full information and no financial market imperfections.

level of asset prices that would occur in the flexible-price economy without financial market imperfections. The extent of these benefits depends on the degree of financial market imperfections and the information structure of the economy. To further explore these issues, we now conduct stochastic simulations of the various models considered. The stochastic simulations depend on the combined effect of both transitory and persistent shocks to technology growth. When conducting such simulations, we parameterize the technology shock process in the manner described in our calibration.

2.5.1   Benefits of Responding Strongly to Inflation

We first consider the benefits to adopting a policy that responds strongly to inflation. As Bernanke and Gertler (1999, 2001) and Gilchrist and Leahy (2002) have emphasized, most of the destabilizing effects of asset price fluctuations on the aggregate activity can be eliminated using such a rule. The results emphasized in Bernanke and Gertler (1999, 2001) are derived in an environment where exogenous movements in asset prices (bubbles) provide an additional source of fluctuations in net worth. These bubbles do not alter entrepreneurs' perceptions regarding the value of new investment in their framework, however.

In our environment, misperceptions regarding the future technology growth cause fluctuations in asset values. These misperceptions also influence investment demand. We wish to consider whether the policy prescription of responding strongly to inflation is robust to the information environment that we consider. To do so, we compare economic outcomes under the two alternative monetary policy rules—a policy rule that implies a weak response to inflation:

$$(37) \qquad \ln R^n_{t+1} = \ln R^n + 1.1 \ln \pi_t,$$

and a policy rule that implies a strong response to inflation:

$$(38) \qquad \ln R^n_{t+1} = \ln R^n + 2.0 \ln \pi_t.$$

To compute the benefits of various policy rules, we use stochastic model simulations to compute the variance of both the output gap and inflation, where the potential level of output, Y^*_{full}, is defined as the level of output that would prevail in the flexible-price economy without financial market imperfections but with full information about the shocks to technology growth. We also compute a loss function based on a weighted average of the variance of the output gap and the variance of inflation:[16]

$$(39) \qquad \text{Loss} = 0.5\text{var}(\ln Y - \ln Y^*_{full}) + 0.5\text{var}(\pi).$$

We report the results of these simulations in table 2.1.

The first two rows of table 2.1 consider an environment where the private sector has full information regarding the state of technology growth. For comparison purposes, we provide results for the model without the financial accelerator as well as the model with the financial accelerator. The variance of the output gap and inflation are reported in percentage points on a quarterly basis.

Responding strongly to inflation provides substantial benefits in both the economy with and without the financial accelerator. Without the financial accelerator, moving from a weak to strong response to inflation implies large reductions in the variance of both the output gap and inflation. In fact, under the policy of responding strongly to inflation, the variance of the output gap is very close to zero (0.006). The variance of inflation is also very small (0.044). This result is consistent with our observation from the impulse response experiments that, in the absence of the financial accelerator, the sticky-price model under the policy of responding strongly to inflation comes very close to reproducing the frictionless RBC outcome.

In the economy with the financial accelerator, we also see substantial

16. For simplicity, we report the results only for the equal-weighted loss.

Table 2.1   Benefits of responding strongly to inflation

	No financial accelerator			Financial accelerator		
	var(Y gap)	var(ln π)	Loss	var(Y gap)	var(ln π)	Loss
	Full information for the private sector					
$\phi_\pi = 1.1$	0.431	2.811	1.621	1.923	3.022	2.473
$\phi_\pi = 2.0$	0.006	0.044	0.025	0.470	0.056	0.263
	Imperfect information for the private sector					
$\phi_\pi = 1.1$	0.579	2.103	1.341	2.247	2.265	2.256
$\phi_\pi = 2.0$	0.099	0.028	0.063	0.870	0.045	0.458

Notes: The policy rule is ln $R^n_{t+1} = \ln R^n + \phi_\pi \ln \pi_t$. Y gap is defined as (ln Y − ln Y^*_{full}), where Y^*_{full} is the flexible-price equilibrium level of output in the absence of financial frictions and under full information. The loss is defined as 0.5var(Y gap) + 0.5var(ln π).

benefits to a policy that responds strongly to inflation. Both the output gap and inflation volatility are reduced with such a policy. Nonetheless, with the financial accelerator, output gap volatility is still significant (0.470) relative to the baseline sticky-price model (0.006). This finding reinforces the intuition that the model with the financial accelerator has two distortions—one on the markup and one on the return on capital. A policy of responding strongly to inflation does well at reducing the distortion owing to variation in the markup, but does not eliminate the distortion on the return on capital. The presence of this distortion causes an increase in output gap volatility.

We now consider the role of imperfect information regarding the state of technology growth. These results are reported in the second two rows of table 2.1. Imperfect information implies an increase in the variance of the output gap and a reduction in the variance of inflation.[17] Under the policy of responding weakly to inflation, the equal-weighted loss is actually lower with imperfect information than under full information. Because the pol-

17. The result that the variance of the output gap is larger under imperfect information than under full information on the part of the private sector can be explained by the fact that, when computing the variance of the output gap, we define the potential level of output as the level of output in the frictionless economy with full information. Under imperfect information on the part of the private sector, the equilibrium level of output deviates from such a full-information level. The result that the variance of inflation is smaller under imperfect information can be understood by considering the strength of the wealth effect of shocks to technology growth on consumption, which constitutes a large component of the aggregate demand. Under full information, wealth effect on consumption is larger when a movement in technology growth is persistent than when it is transitory. Under imperfect information, our calibration of the Kalman gain parameter ($\lambda = 0.06138$) implies that the private sector initially infers that observed movements in technology growth is mostly transitory, even when these movements are, in fact, generated by a shock to the persistent component of technology growth. The overall wealth effect of technology growth movements on consumption, including the effects of both transitory and persistent shocks (which occur with the same frequency), is thus smaller under imperfect information than under full information.

icy of responding strongly to inflation is clearly the dominant policy, it provides the more relevant comparison, however.

With the monetary policy that responds strongly to inflation, in the model without the financial accelerator, the presence of imperfect information has only a small effect on the variance of the output gap and inflation. In the model with the financial accelerator, imperfect information leads to a large increase in output gap volatility with very little reduction in the variance of inflation. As a result, with the financial accelerator, the loss is substantially higher under imperfect information (0.458) than under full information (0.263).

2.5.2   Benefits of Responding to the Asset Price Gap

We now consider whether a monetary policy that allows the nominal interest rate to respond to the asset price gap can improve upon a policy that responds to inflation only.[18]

Because we have already shown that a policy of responding strongly to inflation is beneficial, we restrict our attention to the case where the monetary authority responds strongly to inflation and then consider the additional gains from responding to the asset price gap:

(40) $$\ln R_{t+1}^n = \ln R^n + 2.0\ln \pi_t + \phi_Q(\ln Q_t - \ln Q_t^*).$$

We report results varying the coefficient on the asset price gap, ϕ_Q, from 0.1 to 2.0.

An important question in this analysis is how to gauge the benefits of one policy relative to another. Because there is a consensus in the literature that there are substantial gains to conducting a policy that responds strongly to inflation, we use these gains as the relevant benchmark. In particular, table 2.2 reports the difference between outcomes obtained from pursuing policy in equation (40) versus the policy of responding weakly to inflation in equation (37), divided by the difference between outcomes obtained from pursuing the policy of responding strongly to inflation in equation (38) versus the policy of responding weakly to inflation. For example, when computing the relative gain of adopting Policy Rule x in terms of the equal-weighted loss, we compute

(41)   Relative gain(Policy Rule x)

$$= \frac{\text{Loss(weak inflation response)} - \text{Loss(Policy Rule } x)}{\text{Loss(weak inflation response)} - \text{Loss(strong inflation response)}}.$$

18. Although not reported here, the output gap serves a similar role as the asset price gap: in the presence of financial market imperfections, allowing the monetary authority to respond to changes in the output gap in addition to responding strongly to inflation is beneficial, especially when the policymaker has full information. An interesting future direction of this line of research is to study economic environments in which the asset price gap plays a different role from the output gap.

Table 2.2   **Benefits of responding to the asset price gap (full information for the private sector)**

	No financial accelerator			Financial accelerator		
	var(Y gap)	var(ln π)	Loss	var(Y gap)	var(ln π)	Loss
	Full information for the policymaker					
$\phi_Q = 0.1$	1.00	1.00	1.00	1.03	1.01	1.01
$\phi_Q = 0.5$	1.00	1.00	1.00	1.10	1.01	1.04
$\phi_Q = 1.0$	1.00	1.00	1.00	1.13	0.98	1.03
$\phi_Q = 1.5$	1.01	1.00	1.00	1.17	0.95	1.02
$\phi_Q = 2.0$	1.01	1.00	1.00	1.22	0.92	1.02
	Imperfect information for the policymaker					
$\phi_Q = 0.1$	0.98	1.00	1.00	1.02	1.01	1.01
$\phi_Q = 0.5$	0.85	1.00	0.98	0.97	1.00	0.99
$\phi_Q = 1.0$	0.59	0.99	0.94	0.93	0.98	0.97
$\phi_Q = 1.5$	0.31	1.00	0.91	0.94	0.94	0.94
$\phi_Q = 2.0$	0.21	1.00	0.90	0.79	0.88	0.85

Notes: The policy rule is $\ln R_{t+1}^n = \ln R^n + 2.0 \ln \pi_t + \phi_Q(\ln Q_t - \ln Q_t^*)$. Y gap is defined as $(\ln Y - \ln Y_{full}^*)$, where Y_{full}^* is the flexible-price equilibrium level of output in the absence of financial frictions and under full information. The loss is defined as $0.5\text{var}(Y \text{ gap}) + 0.5\text{var}(\ln \pi)$. A value of larger than one implies that the policy is better than the policy that responds strongly to inflation. A negative value implies that the policy is worse than the policy that responds weakly to inflation.

We compute the relative gain for the reduction in output gap variance and inflation variance in an analogous manner. Doing so enables us to easily summarize the results: if the relative gain is above one, the policy in question provides gains relative to the policy of responding strongly to inflation. If the relative gain is negative, the policy in question provides outcomes that are strictly worse than those under the policy of responding weakly to inflation.[19]

In imperfect information environments, the policymaker may not have sufficient information to correctly compute the potential level of asset prices Q_t^*. We thus distinguish between cases where the policymaker can correctly assess the state of technology growth ($Q_t^* = Q_{full,t}^*$) and the case where the policymaker infers it based on current and past observations of technology growth ($Q_t^* = Q_{imp,t}^*$).

When considering the benefits of such rules, we distinguish between environments where the private sector has full and imperfect information.

19. Note that we cannot directly compare the numbers for the relative gain in the case of imperfect information for the private sector and in the case of full information for the private sector because the gain from moving from the policy of responding weakly to inflation to the policy of responding strongly to inflation (the denominator in the formula to calculate the relative gain in equation [41]) differs depending on the information structure for the private sector.

Thus, our information structure allows for four cases: (1) full information on the part of both the private sector and the policymaker; (2) full information for the private sector but imperfect information for the policymaker; (3) imperfect information for the private sector and full information for the policymaker; and (4) imperfect information for both. Within these four cases, we report results for the model with and without the financial accelerator.

Full Information for the Private Sector

We first consider the case of full information on the part of the private sector (table 2.2). The top rows of table 2.2 consider the case where the policymaker also has full information. In the sticky-price model without the financial accelerator, the relative gain is approximately unity.[20] Thus, there are almost no gains to allowing the monetary authority to respond to the asset price gap relative to the policy that responds strongly to inflation. By responding strongly to inflation, the monetary authority succeeds in stabilizing the markup, which is the only distortion in the economy. With the markup stabilized, the actual path for asset prices is nearly identical to the path under flexible prices, so giving weight to the asset price gap provides almost no gain.

In contrast, in the model with the financial accelerator, responding to the asset price gap provides clear gains in terms of output gap stabilization—on the order of 22 percent when the coefficient on the asset price gap is relatively large, with $\phi_Q = 2.0$. Although the policy that responds strongly to inflation stabilizes the markup, it does not eliminate the distortion due to financial market imperfections, which is reflected in the deviations of asset prices from the potential level that arises in the economy without pricing and financial frictions. Thus, responding to the asset price gap helps reduce distortions due to financial market imperfections. As the coefficient on the asset price gap is increased, the variance of the output gap falls but the variance of inflation rises. Based on the loss function in equation (39), which gives equal weight on the output gap and inflation, our parameterization implies a modest gain to responding to the asset price gap, with a coefficient on the asset price gap $0.1 < \phi_Q < 1.0$ minimizing this loss.

We now consider the case where the private sector has full information, but the policymaker has imperfect information. These results are reported

---

20. To deemphasize small differences in simulation results that may reflect sensitivity to a numerical solution or a simulation error, we report the relative gains rounded to the second decimal place. Our actual results suggest that the model exhibits an extremely small but positive gain to allowing the monetary authority to respond to the asset price gap in the case of full information and no financial accelerator. The relative gains are always less than 1.005, however, implying that to a first approximation the absolute gains to allowing the policymaker to respond to the asset price gap are zero.

in the bottom rows of table 2.2. In the sticky-price model without the financial accelerator, responding to the asset price gap is a strictly inferior policy, which leads to large increases in the variance of the output gap and inflation. In this environment, the potential level of asset prices measured by the monetary authority is no longer correct, and putting weight on the asset price gap pushes the economy away from the frictionless RBC outcome that is attainable under the policy of responding strongly to inflation. With the financial accelerator, there is a small gain to allowing a very weak policy response to the asset price gap ($\phi_Q = 0.1$), but a deterioration in terms of the variance of output gap and inflation for larger coefficients. When the monetary authority has imperfect information, it responds to the wrong measure of the asset price gap, which offsets any potential gains to be achieved relative to the policy that responds strongly to inflation only.

Imperfect Information for the Private Sector

We now consider the case where the private sector has imperfect information (table 2.3). We again begin with the case where the policymaker has full information. In the sticky-price model without the financial accelerator, allowing the monetary authority to respond to the asset price gap produces a small gain in terms of reducing the variance of the output gap. These gains are no longer present when the monetary authority also has imperfect information, however. In the absence of financial frictions, there are unlikely to be significant gains to allowing the monetary authority to respond to the asset price gap, even in the case where the private sector has imperfect information.

In the model with the financial accelerator, the gains to responding to the asset price gap are substantial. If the policymaker has full information, adopting a rule that responds to the asset price gap produces an incremental reduction in the variance of the output gap of 50 percent when $\phi_Q = 1.0$. Allowing the monetary authority to respond to the asset price gap reduces the variance of the output gap, but increases the variance of inflation. Overall, we see an improvement as measured by the equal-weighted loss, however.

When the policymaker has imperfect information, the gains obtained from responding to the asset price gap are somewhat smaller than the case where it has full information. Nonetheless, the gains are still positive and economically interesting. When the private sector has imperfect information, output gap volatility is increased relative to the case of full information (table 2.1). Because allowing the monetary authority to respond to the asset price gap reduces distortions arising from financial market imperfections and thus reduces the output variability, the overall gains from responding to the asset price gap are larger when the private sector has imperfect information relative to the case where it has full information. These larger gains offset the loss associated with the fact that the policymaker is

Table 2.3   **Benefits of responding to the asset price gap (imperfect information for the private sector)**

	No financial accelerator			Financial accelerator		
	var(Y gap)	var(ln π)	Loss	var(Y gap)	var(ln π)	Loss
	Full information for the policymaker					
$\phi_Q = 0.1$	1.02	1.00	1.00	1.09	1.00	1.04
$\phi_Q = 0.5$	1.11	0.99	1.01	1.36	1.00	1.14
$\phi_Q = 1.0$	1.12	0.99	1.01	1.50	0.98	1.18
$\phi_Q = 1.5$	1.06	0.99	1.00	1.51	0.93	1.16
$\phi_Q = 2.0$	0.97	0.99	0.99	1.53	0.86	1.12
	Imperfect information for the policymaker					
$\phi_Q = 0.1$	0.92	1.00	0.98	1.20	1.01	1.08
$\phi_Q = 0.5$	0.94	1.00	0.99	1.22	1.01	1.09
$\phi_Q = 1.0$	0.96	1.00	0.99	1.38	0.97	1.12
$\phi_Q = 1.5$	0.98	1.00	1.00	1.44	0.93	1.12
$\phi_Q = 2.0$	0.96	1.00	1.00	1.42	0.87	1.08

Notes: See table 2.2 notes.

responding to the "wrong" asset price gap. As a result, when the private sector has imperfect information, allowing the policymaker to respond to the asset price gap can be beneficial even when the policymaker also has imperfect information.

In summary, the results from tables 2.2 and 2.3 imply that there are gains associated with responding to the asset price gap in the presence of distortions in the return on capital caused by financial market imperfections. These gains are greatest when the private sector has imperfect information and the policymaker is fully informed about future economic fundamentals. Nonetheless, there are also gains from responding to the asset price gap when both the private sector and the policymaker have imperfect information. Finally, when choosing how to respond, the policymaker faces a trade off—increasing the coefficient on the asset price gap in the monetary policy rule reduces output gap volatility but increases inflation volatility.

2.5.3   Effects of Allowing a Policy Response to the Natural Rate

We now consider the robustness of the results in the previous subsection to allowing the policymaker to respond to movements in the natural rate of interest.[21] We consider the following interest rate rule:

$$(42) \qquad \ln R_{t+1}^n = \ln R_{t+1}^* + 2.0 \ln \pi_t + \phi_Q(\ln Q_t - \ln Q_t^*),$$

where R_{t+1}^* is the natural rate of interest that prevails between period t and period $t + 1$. The natural rate of interest is defined here as the real interest

21. We thank Michael Woodford for suggesting this line of extension.

rate that supports the efficient allocation in the economy in the absence of both the pricing and financial frictions. It is computed based on the information available to the policymaker. We fix the coefficient on inflation in the policy rule at 2.0 and consider various values for the coefficient on the asset price gap, ϕ_Q.

Tables 2.4 and 2.5 summarize the results. Table 2.4 considers the case of full information for the private sector, and table 2.5 considers the case of imperfect information for the private sector. As in tables 2.2 and 2.3, we report the gains from adopting a policy that implies a response to the natural rate of interest and the asset price gap as well as a strong response to inflation, relative to the gains from adopting a policy of responding strongly to inflation only.

When the policymaker has full information, allowing the policymaker to respond to movements in the natural rate of interest reduces the variability of both inflation and the output gap because the policymaker in this case computes the natural rate of interest correctly.

The effects of allowing the monetary authority to respond to movements in the natural rate of interest differ greatly depending on whether the financial accelerator is present. Without financial market imperfections, al-

Table 2.4   **Effects of allowing a policy response to the natural rate (full information for the private sector)**

	No financial accelerator			Financial accelerator		
	var(Y gap)	var(ln π)	Loss	var(Y gap)	var(ln π)	Loss
Full information for the policymaker						
$\phi_Q = 0$	1.02	1.02	1.02	1.09	1.02	1.04
$\phi_Q = 0.1$	1.02	1.02	1.02	1.11	1.02	1.05
$\phi_Q = 0.5$	1.02	1.02	1.02	1.16	1.01	1.05
$\phi_Q = 1.0$	1.02	1.02	1.02	1.20	0.98	1.05
$\phi_Q = 1.5$	1.02	1.02	1.02	1.23	0.94	1.03
$\phi_Q = 2.0$	1.02	1.02	1.02	1.25	0.88	1.00
Imperfect information for the policymaker						
$\phi_Q = 0$	1.01	1.01	1.01	1.08	0.97	1.03
$\phi_Q = 0.1$	1.00	1.01	1.01	1.05	1.01	1.02
$\phi_Q = 0.5$	0.87	1.00	0.98	1.04	1.00	1.01
$\phi_Q = 1.0$	0.61	1.00	0.95	1.00	0.97	0.98
$\phi_Q = 1.5$	0.40	1.00	0.92	0.96	0.93	0.94
$\phi_Q = 2.0$	0.12	1.01	0.89	0.88	0.86	0.87

Notes: The policy rule is ln $R_{t+1}^n = $ ln $R_{t+1}^* + 2.0$ ln $\pi_t + \phi_Q$(ln $Q_t - $ ln Q_t^*). Y gap is defined as (ln $Y - $ ln Y_{full}^*), where Y_{full}^* is the flexible-price equilibrium level of output in the absence of financial frictions and under full information. The loss is defined as 0.5var(Y gap) + 0.5var(ln π). A value of larger than one implies that the policy is better than the policy that responds strongly to inflation. A negative value implies that the policy is worse than the policy that responds weakly to inflation.

Table 2.5   **Effects of allowing a policy response to the natural rate (imperfect information for the private sector)**

	No financial accelerator			Financial accelerator		
	var(Y gap)	var($\ln \pi$)	Loss	var(Y gap)	var($\ln \pi$)	Loss
	Full information for the policymaker					
$\phi_Q = 0$	1.04	1.01	1.01	1.27	1.01	1.11
$\phi_Q = 0.1$	1.10	1.00	1.02	1.32	1.01	1.13
$\phi_Q = 0.5$	1.16	0.99	1.03	1.44	0.99	1.16
$\phi_Q = 1.0$	1.13	0.99	1.02	1.49	0.95	1.16
$\phi_Q = 1.5$	1.04	0.99	1.00	1.51	0.89	1.13
$\phi_Q = 2.0$	0.96	1.00	1.00	1.51	0.83	1.09
	Imperfect information for the policymaker					
$\phi_Q = 0$	1.01	1.01	1.01	1.19	1.02	1.09
$\phi_Q = 0.1$	1.03	1.01	1.02	1.26	1.02	1.11
$\phi_Q = 0.5$	0.98	1.01	1.01	1.39	1.00	1.15
$\phi_Q = 1.0$	0.98	1.01	1.01	1.39	0.95	1.12
$\phi_Q = 1.5$	0.99	1.01	1.01	1.42	0.90	1.10
$\phi_Q = 2.0$	0.99	1.01	1.01	1.43	0.86	1.08

Notes: See table 2.4 notes.

lowing the monetary authority with full information to respond to movements in the natural rate of interest almost completely eliminates the only distortion in the economy arising from the pricing frictions. In this situation, allowing the policymaker to respond to the asset price gap provides little gain. In the presence of the financial accelerator, allowing the monetary authority to respond to movements in the natural rate of interest tends to reduce distortions arising from both pricing and financial frictions. This is because the natural rate of interest is defined as the rate of interest that arises in the absence of both pricing and financial frictions.[22] In this situation, we still observe gains from allowing the monetary authority to respond to the asset price gap, but those gains are smaller relative to the case where the policy rule does not include a response to the natural rate of interest.

2.5.4   Policy Rules That Do Not Require Inferences

Monetary policy rules that allow the policymaker to respond to the asset price gap require inferences regarding the true state of technology growth. Because these policies are not necessarily robust to incorrect inference on the part of the policymaker, it is also useful to consider mone-

22. A different definition of the natural rate of interest would lead to somewhat different conclusions. For instance, if one defines the natural rate of interest as the interest rate in the absence of pricing frictions but in the presence financial frictions, allowing the monetary authority to respond to movements in the natural rate would have a smaller impact on the distortions arising from financial frictions.

tary policy rules that do not require the monetary authority to make inferences. We consider three such rules:

1. Policy rule with output growth:

(43) $\ln R^n_{t+1} = \ln R^n + 2.0 \ln \pi_t + \phi_Y(\ln Y_t - \ln Y_{t-1} - \mu).$

2. Policy rule with asset price growth:

(44) $\ln R^n_{t+1} = \ln R^n + 2.0 \ln \pi_t + \phi_Q(\ln Q_t - \ln Q_{t-1}).$

3. Policy rule with the level of asset prices:

(45) $\ln R^n_{t+1} = \ln R^n + 2.0 \ln \pi_t + \phi_Q(\ln Q_t - \ln Q),$

where Q is the nonstochastic steady-state level of asset prices ($Q = 1$ under our specification of the capital adjustment cost function).

Table 2.6 and table 2.7 report the relative gains from adopting these policy rules in the case where the private sector has full and imperfect information, respectively.

Table 2.6   **Policy rules that do not require inferences (full information for the private sector)**

	No financial accelerator			Financial accelerator		
	var(Y gap)	var($\ln \pi$)	Loss	var(Y gap)	var($\ln \pi$)	Loss
Policy with output growth: $\ln R^n_{t+1} = \ln R^n + 2.0 \ln \pi_t + \phi_Y(\ln Y_t - \ln Y_{t-1} - \mu)$						
$\phi_Y = 0.1$	0.99	1.00	1.00	1.03	1.01	1.01
$\phi_Y = 0.5$	0.85	1.01	0.99	1.04	1.01	1.02
$\phi_Y = 1.0$	0.57	1.00	0.95	1.04	1.01	1.02
$\phi_Y = 1.5$	0.23	0.98	0.88	0.97	0.99	0.98
$\phi_Y = 2.0$	−0.05	0.94	0.81	0.83	0.95	0.91
Policy with asset price growth: $\ln R^n_{t+1} = \ln R^n + 2.0 \ln \pi_t + \phi_Q(\ln Q_t - \ln Q_{t-1})$						
$\phi_Q = 0.1$	1.00	1.00	1.00	1.07	1.00	1.02
$\phi_Q = 0.5$	0.96	1.00	1.00	1.05	1.00	1.02
$\phi_Q = 1.0$	0.87	1.00	0.99	1.04	1.00	1.02
$\phi_Q = 1.5$	0.78	1.00	0.97	1.02	1.00	1.01
$\phi_Q = 2.0$	0.69	1.00	0.96	0.96	1.00	0.99
Policy with the level of asset prices: $\ln R^n_{t+1} = \ln R^n + 2.0 \ln \pi_t + \phi_Q(\ln Q_t - \ln Q)$						
$\phi_Q = 0.1$	0.99	1.01	1.00	1.01	1.01	1.01
$\phi_Q = 0.5$	0.71	0.70	0.70	1.10	0.73	0.85
$\phi_Q = 1.0$	0.13	−0.01	0.00	1.05	−0.31	0.13
$\phi_Q = 1.5$	−0.78	−1.57	−1.46	0.91	−1.98	−1.03
$\phi_Q = 2.0$	−2.16	−3.60	−3.41	0.71	−4.18	−2.57

Notes: Y gap is defined as $(\ln Y - \ln Y^*_{full})$, where Y^*_{full} is the flexible-price equilibrium level of output in the absence of financial frictions and under full information. The loss is defined as $0.5 \text{var}(Y \text{ gap}) + 0.5 \text{var}(\ln \pi)$. A value of larger than one implies that the policy is better than the policy that responds strongly to inflation. A negative value implies that the policy is worse than the policy that responds weakly to inflation.

Table 2.7   **Policy rules that do not require inferences (imperfect information for the private sector)**

	No financial accelerator			Financial accelerator		
	var(Y gap)	var(ln π)	Loss	var(Y gap)	var(ln π)	Loss
Policy with output growth: $\ln R^n_{t+1} = \ln R^n + 2.0 \ln \pi_t + \phi_Y(\ln Y_{t-1} - \ln Y_{t-1} - \mu)$						
$\phi_Y = 0.1$	0.97	1.00	1.00	1.20	1.01	1.08
$\phi_Y = 0.5$	0.90	1.01	0.99	1.40	1.02	1.16
$\phi_Y = 1.0$	0.74	1.00	0.95	1.40	1.01	1.16
$\phi_Y = 1.5$	0.54	0.96	0.88	1.40	0.98	1.14
$\phi_Y = 2.0$	0.33	0.90	0.79	1.37	0.92	1.24
Policy with asset price growth: $\ln R^n_{t+1} = \ln R^n + 2.0 \ln \pi_t + \phi_Q(\ln Q_t - \ln Q_{t-1})$						
$\phi_Q = 0.1$	0.95	1.00	0.99	1.11	1.00	1.05
$\phi_Q = 0.5$	0.93	1.00	0.99	1.15	1.00	1.06
$\phi_Q = 1.0$	0.96	1.00	0.99	1.33	1.00	1.13
$\phi_Q = 1.5$	0.92	1.00	0.99	1.31	1.00	1.12
$\phi_Q = 2.0$	0.98	1.00	0.99	1.39	1.00	1.15
Policy with the level of asset prices: $\ln R^n_{t+1} = \ln R^n + 2.0 \ln \pi_t + \phi_Q(\ln Q_t - \ln Q)$						
$\phi_Q = 0.1$	0.96	1.01	1.00	1.21	1.02	1.09
$\phi_Q = 0.5$	0.91	0.61	0.66	1.44	0.61	0.93
$\phi_Q = 1.0$	0.49	−0.65	−0.44	1.52	−0.80	0.09
$\phi_Q = 1.5$	0.13	−1.86	−1.49	1.48	−2.49	−0.97
$\phi_Q = 2.0$	−0.78	−4.54	−3.83	1.30	−5.42	−2.85

Notes: See table 2.6 notes.

In the absence of financial market imperfections, none of these policies provide substantial gains relative to the policy of responding strongly to inflation. Policies that respond to either output growth or asset price growth lead to an increase in the variance of the output gap, but have little impact on the variance of inflation. This is true under either full or imperfect information on the part of the private sector. In the absence of financial frictions, the policy of responding strongly to inflation does well at reducing variation in the markup, which is the only source of distortions. As a consequence, there is little to be gained from adding additional variables to interest rate rules.

In the presence of financial market imperfections, policies based on either output growth or asset price growth provide benefits relative to the policy of responding strongly to inflation. In relative terms, these benefits are much larger when the private sector has imperfect information regarding the state of technology growth. Depending on the coefficient values, these policies can do as well as policies based on the asset price gap. Because these policies do not require the policymaker to make inferences regarding the underlying potential of the economy, they are arguably more robust than policies based on the asset price gap.

Finally, we consider the policy rule that includes the level of the asset prices. This policy rule has been considered in the previous literature, but studies such as Bernanke and Gertler (1999, 2001) and Gilchrist and Leahy (2002) have argued against it. Here we confirm their results, albeit for somewhat different reasons. When the private sector has imperfect information, allowing a policy response to the level of asset prices provides clear benefits in terms of reducing output gap volatility in the model with the financial accelerator. It also leads, however, to a large increase in inflation volatility. For coefficients on the level of asset prices above 0.5, the inflation outcome is actually worse than what is obtained under the policy of responding weakly to inflation. This policy does not allow the monetary authority to adjust its policy owing to movements in asset prices that reflect changes in the desired level of investment spending in the frictionless economy. Because asset prices are procyclical on average in the frictionless economy, responding to the observed level of asset prices itself implies a strongly countercyclical policy that leads to significant deflation in expansionary environments. This deflationary response can be limited by adopting a policy that responds to either the asset price gap or the growth rate of asset prices.

2.6   Conclusion

This chapter considers the design of monetary policy rule in an environment where both the private sector and the monetary authority learn about the trend growth rate of technology. In the presence of financial market imperfections resulting from asymmetric information between lenders and borrowers, shocks to the economy that cause increases in asset prices improve the balance-sheet conditions of borrowers, reduce the external finance premium, and amplify the response of real economic activity. This amplification mechanism—the financial accelerator mechanism—represents a distortion in underlying economic activity that can only partially be eliminated by a policy of responding strongly to inflation. Such a policy stabilizes inflation but leaves a relatively large variability in the output gap. In this environment, because fluctuations in asset prices are closely linked to the financial accelerator mechanism, allowing the monetary authority to respond to the asset price gap—the gap between the observed asset prices and the potential level of asset prices that arises in the frictionless economy with flexible prices and no financial market imperfections—stabilizes the output gap but tends to increase the variability in inflation.

We also show that the overall gains from allowing the monetary authority to respond to the asset price gap are greatest when the monetary authority can correctly identify the true state of technology growth, while the private sector must infer it from past observations of technology growth. These gains are reduced to the extent that the monetary authority is also imperfectly informed about the state of technology growth. We further show that policy rules that respond to either the growth rate of asset prices or the growth rate of output provide most of the benefits associated with including the asset price gap in the monetary policy rule. Because it is efficient that asset prices fluctuate in the presence of shocks to technology growth, monetary policies that respond to the observed level of asset prices itself, and hence do not take into account changes in the potential level of asset prices, are particularly detrimental, however.

This chapter focuses on a quadratic loss function rather than formal welfare analysis in evaluating economic outcomes under different monetary policy rules. Thus, future work should be oriented toward assessing the robustness of our conclusions for welfare calculations. In addition, although learning combined with the financial accelerator mechanism increases the procyclicality in asset prices as well as the extent to which asset prices deviate from the potential level, our underlying frictionless economy implies a fall in asset prices in response to a persistent increase in technology growth. We are, therefore, also interested in exploring the robustness of our conclusions to alternative mechanisms that may provide a more realistic characterization of the link between asset prices and changes in expectations or news regarding future economic fundamentals.

Appendix

Equilibrium Conditions in Normalized Variables

This section lists the equilibrium conditions for the model in terms of the normalized, stationary variables.

We normalize the levels of consumption, investment, output, capital stock, and net worth by the level of technology so that these real quantities are stationary:

$$c_t \equiv \frac{C_t}{A_t}, i_t \equiv \frac{I_t}{A_t}, y_t \equiv \frac{Y_t}{A_t}, k_t \equiv \frac{K_t}{A_{t-1}}, \text{ and } n_t \equiv \frac{N_t}{A_{t-1}}.$$

K_t and N_t are determined in period t 1, and we normalize these variables by the level of technology in period $t - 1$. Also, let

$$Z_t \equiv \frac{A_t}{A_{t-1}}$$

denote technology growth.

The equilibrium conditions in terms of the normalized variables are as follows.

Consumption savings:

(A1) $$\frac{1}{c_t} = \beta E_t \left(\frac{1}{c_{t+1}} \frac{1}{Z_{t+1}} R_{t+1}^n \frac{P_t}{P_{t+1}} \right).$$

Expected real rate of return on capital:

(A2) $\quad E_t R_{t+1}^k \equiv \dfrac{E_t\left[(1-\alpha)\dfrac{y_{t+1}}{k_{t+1}}Z_{t+1}mc_{t+1} + (1-\delta)Q_{t+1}\right]}{Q_t},$

where $mc_t \equiv P_t^W/P_t$ is the real marginal cost.

Definition of the external finance premium:

The external finance premium is defined as the ratio of the expected real rate of return on capital (which is equal to the cost of external funds in equilibrium) to the expected real rate of return on the riskless bond (which is interpreted as the cost of internal funds):

(A3) $\quad s_t \equiv \dfrac{E_t R_{t+1}^k}{E_t\left(R_{t+1}^n \dfrac{P_t}{P_{t+1}}\right)}.$

Determination of the external finance premium:

(A4) $\quad s_t = \left(\dfrac{Q_t k_{t+1}}{n_{t+1}}\right)^x.$

Evolution of net worth:

Under our calibration of $\Omega = 0$,

$$n_{t+1} = \eta\left[R_t^k Q_{t-1} k_t \frac{1}{Z_t} - E_{t-1}R_t^k\left(Q_{t-1}k_t\frac{1}{Z_t} - n_t\frac{1}{Z_t}\right)\right].$$

Or, using the definition of the external finance premium $E_{t-1}R_t^k = s_{t-1}E_{t-1}[R_t^n(P_{t-1}/P_t),$

(A5) $\quad n_{t+1} = \eta\left[R_t^k Q_{t-1}k_t\frac{1}{Z_t} - s_{t-1}E_{t-1}\left(R_t^n\frac{P_{t-1}}{P_t}\right)\left(Q_{t-1}k_t\frac{1}{Z_t} - n_t\frac{1}{Z_t}\right)\right].$

Investment-Q relationship:

(A6) $\quad Q_t = \dfrac{1}{\phi'\left(\dfrac{i_t}{k_t Z_t}\right)}.$

Aggregate resource constraint:

Under our calibration of $C_t^e = 0$ and $G_t = 0$,

(A7) $\quad y_t = c_t + i_t.$

Production function:

Under our calibration of $\Omega = 0$,

(A8) $\quad y_t = H_t^\alpha k_t^{1-\alpha}\dfrac{1}{Z_t^{1-\alpha}}.$

Labor market equilibrium condition:

(A9)
$$\theta H_t^\gamma = \frac{1}{c_t} \alpha \frac{y_t}{H_t} mc_t.$$

Price setting:

(A10)
$$P_t^* = \frac{\varepsilon}{\varepsilon - 1} \frac{E_t \sum_{i=0}^\infty \upsilon^i \beta^i \left(\frac{c_{t+i}}{c_t}\frac{1}{A_t}\right)^{-1} MC_{t+i} y_{t+i} \left(\frac{1}{P_{t+i}}\right)^{1-\varepsilon}}{E_t \sum_{i=0}^\infty \upsilon^i \beta^i \left(\frac{c_{t+i}}{c_t}\frac{1}{A_t}\right)^{-1} y_{t+i} \left(\frac{1}{P_{t+i}}\right)^{1-\varepsilon}},$$

where $MC_t \equiv P_t mc_t = P_t^W$ is the nominal marginal cost of retail goods production.

Price index:

(A11)
$$P_t = [\upsilon P_{t-1}^{1-\varepsilon} + (1 - \upsilon)(P_t^*)^{1-\varepsilon}]^{1/(1-\varepsilon)}.$$

Capital accumulation:

(A12)
$$k_{t+1} = k_t \frac{1}{Z_t}(1 - \delta) + \phi\left(\frac{i_t}{k_t}Z_t\right)k_t\frac{1}{Z_t}.$$

Policy rule with inflation only:

$$R_{t+1}^n = R^n \pi_t^{\phi_\pi}.$$

Policy rule with the asset price gap:

$$R_{t+1}^n = R^n \pi_t^{\phi_\pi} \left(\frac{Q_t}{Q_t^*}\right)^{\phi_Q},$$

where Q_t^* is the flexible-price equilibrium level of asset prices in the absence of financial frictions. Q_t^* is computed under the information available to the policymaker.

Policy rule with the natural rate of interest and the asset price gap:

$$R_{t+1}^n = R_{t+1}^* \pi_t^{\phi_\pi} \left(\frac{Q_t}{Q_t^*}\right)^{\phi_Q},$$

where R_{t+1}^* is the natural rate of interest that is defined as the real interest rate that supports the efficient allocation in the economy without pricing and financial frictions. R_{t+1}^* is computed under the information available to the policymaker.

Policy rule with output growth:

$$R_{t+1}^n = R^n \pi_t^{\phi_\pi} \left(\frac{\frac{y_t}{y_{t-1}}Z_t}{\exp(\mu)}\right)^{\phi_Y}.$$

Policy rule with asset price growth:

$$R_{t+1}^n = R^n \pi_t^{\phi_\pi} \left(\frac{Q_t}{Q_{t-1}} \right)^{\phi_Q}.$$

Policy rule with the level of asset prices:

$$R_{t+1}^n = R^n \pi_t^{\phi_\pi} \left(\frac{Q_t}{Q} \right)^{\phi_Q},$$

where Q is the nonstochastic steady-state level of asset prices.

Technology shock process:

$$\ln Z_t = \mu_t + \varepsilon_t,$$

and

$$(\mu_t - \mu) = \rho_d(\mu_{t-1} - \mu) + \upsilon_t,$$

with $\varepsilon_t \sim i.i.d.\, N(0, \sigma_\varepsilon^2)$ and $\upsilon_t \sim i.i.d.\, N(0, \sigma_\upsilon^2)$.

Nonstochastic Steady State

This section lists the conditions for the nonstochastic steady state of the economy in terms of the normalized variables.

Let

$$\pi_t \equiv \frac{P_t}{P_{t-1}}$$

denote inflation.

Normalize the steady-state inflation at 0 percent.

$$\pi = 1.$$

We specify the capital adjustment cost function such that in the nonstochastic steady state, we have

$$Q = 1.$$

From equation (A10),

$$m_c = \frac{\varepsilon - 1}{\varepsilon}.$$

From equation (A1) and $\pi = 1$,

$$R^n = \frac{Z}{\beta}.$$

Using equations (A3) and (A4) and $Q = 1$, the nonstochastic steady-state level of the external finance premium, s, is given by

$$s = \frac{R^k}{R^n} = \left(\frac{k}{n}\right)^\chi,$$

where the parameter χ and the steady-state ratio of capital to net worth, k/n, are calibrated as described in the text.

From equation (A5),

$$\eta R^k \frac{1}{Z} = 1.$$

Note that R^k must also satisfy the preceding condition, $R^k/R^n = (k/n)^\chi$.

From equation (A2),

$$\frac{y}{k} = \frac{1}{(1-\alpha) Z \cdot mc} [R^k - (1-\delta)].$$

From equation (A12),

$$\frac{i}{k} = 1 - \frac{1}{Z}(1-\delta).$$

From equation (A7),

$$\frac{c}{k} = \frac{y}{k} - \frac{i}{k}.$$

We also have

$$\frac{y}{c} = \frac{\dfrac{y}{k}}{\dfrac{c}{k}}.$$

From equation (A9),

$$H = \left[\frac{\alpha}{\theta} \frac{y}{c} mc\right]^{1/(1+\gamma)}.$$

From equation (A8),

$$k = \frac{H}{\left(\dfrac{y}{k}\right)^{1/\alpha} Z^{(1-\alpha)/\alpha}}.$$

Then,

$$c = \frac{c}{k}k, \quad i = \frac{i}{k}k, \quad y = \frac{y}{k}k.$$

Log-Linearized Equilibrium Conditions

This section lists the equilibrium conditions in terms of log deviations in the normalized variables from the nonstochastic steady state.

Let $\tilde{z}_t$ denote the percentage deviation in technology growth from the mean:

$$\tilde{z}_t \equiv \ln Z_t - \mu.$$

Consumption-savings:

$$-\tilde{c}_t = -E_t\tilde{c}_{t+1} - E_t\tilde{z}_{t+1} + \tilde{r}^n_{t+1} - E_t\tilde{\pi}_{t+1}.$$

Expected real rate of return on capital:

$$E_t\tilde{r}^k_{t+1} \equiv \frac{mc(1-\alpha)\dfrac{y}{k}Z}{mc(1-\alpha)\dfrac{y}{k}Z + (1-\delta)}(E_t\tilde{y}_{t+1} - \tilde{k}_{t+1} + E_t\tilde{z}_{t+1} + E_t\widetilde{mc}_{t+1})$$

$$+ \frac{1-\delta}{mc(1-\alpha)\dfrac{y}{k}Z + (1-\delta)}E_t\tilde{q}_{t+1} - \tilde{q}_t.$$

Definition of the external finance premium:

$$\tilde{s}_t \equiv E_t\tilde{r}^k_{t+1} - (\tilde{r}^n_{t+1} - E_t\tilde{\pi}_{t+1}).$$

Determination of the external finance premium:

$$\tilde{s}_t = \chi(\tilde{q}_t + \tilde{k}_{t+1} - \tilde{n}_{t+1}).$$

Evolution of net worth:
Using the steady-state condition $\eta R^k/Z = 1$, net worth evolves according to

$$\tilde{n}_{t+1} = \frac{k}{n}\tilde{r}^k_t - \left(\frac{k}{n} - 1\right)E_{t-1}\tilde{r}^k_t + \tilde{n}_t - \tilde{z}_t.$$

Or, using the definition of the external finance premium, $E_{t-1}\tilde{r}^k_t \equiv \tilde{s}_{t-1} + (\tilde{r}^n_t - E_{t-1}\tilde{\pi}_t)$, we have

$$\tilde{n}_{t+1} = \frac{k}{n}\tilde{r}^k_t - \left(\frac{k}{n} - 1\right)(\tilde{s}_{t-1} + \tilde{r}^n_t - E_{t-1}\tilde{\pi}_t) + \tilde{n}_t - \tilde{z}_t.$$

Investment-Q relationship:

$$\tilde{q}_t = \eta_k(\tilde{i}_t - \tilde{k}_t + \tilde{z}_t),$$

where

$$\eta_k \equiv \frac{-\left[\Phi''\!\left(\frac{i}{k}Z\right)\frac{i}{k}Z\right]}{\Phi'\!\left(\frac{i}{k}Z\right)} = \frac{-\{\Phi''[Z - (1 - \delta)] \cdot [Z - (1 - \delta)]\}}{\Phi'[Z - (1 - \delta)]}.$$

Aggregate resource constraint:

$$\tilde{y}_t = \frac{c}{y}\tilde{c}_t + \frac{i}{y}\tilde{i}_t.$$

Production function:

$$\tilde{y}_t = \alpha\tilde{h}_t + (1 - \alpha)\tilde{k}_t - (1 - \alpha)\tilde{z}_t.$$

Labor market equilibrium condition:

$$\tilde{y}_t + \widetilde{mc}_t - \tilde{c}_t = (1 + \gamma)\tilde{h}_t.$$

Inflation:

$$\tilde{\pi}_t = \kappa\widetilde{mc}_t + \beta E_t\tilde{\pi}_{t+1},$$

where $\kappa \equiv (1 - \upsilon)(1 - \beta\upsilon)/\upsilon$.

Capital accumulation:

$$\tilde{k}_{t+1} = \frac{1 - \delta}{Z}(\tilde{k}_t - \tilde{z}_t) + \left(1 - \frac{1 - \delta}{Z}\right)\tilde{i}_t.$$

Policy rule with inflation only:

$$\tilde{r}^n_{t+1} = \phi_\pi\tilde{\pi}_t.$$

Policy rule with the asset price gap:

$$\tilde{r}^n_{t+1} = \phi_\pi\tilde{\pi}_t + \phi_Q(\tilde{q}_t - \tilde{q}^*_t).$$

Policy rule with the natural rate of interest and the asset price gap:

$$\tilde{r}^n_{t+1} = \tilde{r}^*_{t+1} + \phi_\pi\tilde{\pi}_t + \phi_Q(\tilde{q}_t - \tilde{q}^*_t).$$

Policy rule with output growth:

$$\tilde{r}^n_{t+1} = \phi_\pi\tilde{\pi}_t + \phi_Y(\tilde{y}_t - \tilde{y}_{t-1} + \tilde{z}_t).$$

Policy rule with asset price growth:

$$\tilde{r}^n_{t+1} = \phi_\pi\tilde{\pi}_t + \phi_Q(\tilde{q}_t - \tilde{q}_{t-1}).$$

Policy rule with the level of asset prices:

$$\tilde{r}^n_{t+1} = \phi_\pi\tilde{\pi}_t + \phi_Q\tilde{q}_t.$$

Technology shock process:

$$\tilde{z}_t = \tilde{d}_t + \varepsilon_t,$$

and

$$\tilde{d}_t = \rho_d \tilde{d}_{t-1} + v_t,$$

where $\tilde{d}_t$ is defined as

$$\tilde{d}_t \equiv (\mu_t - \mu).$$

Solution to the Model

This section describes the solution to the model.

When the Monetary Policy Rule Does Not Include the Asset Price Gap and the Natural Rate of Interest

When the interest rate rule does not include the asset price gap and the natural rate of interest, we do not need to compute the equilibrium in the frictionless economy to characterize the equilibrium in the economy with both pricing and financial frictions.

When the Private Sector Has Full Information

The solution to the model takes the form:

(A13) $X_t = B_1 X_{t-1} + B_2 u_t,$

where

$$X_t \equiv [\tilde{c}_t; \tilde{y}_t; \tilde{h}_t; \tilde{i}_t; \tilde{k}_{t+1}; \tilde{n}_{t+1}; \tilde{r}_t^k; \tilde{s}_t; \tilde{r}_{t+1}^n; \tilde{q}_t; \widetilde{mc}_t; \tilde{\pi}_t; \tilde{d}_t],$$

and

$$u_t \equiv [v_t; \varepsilon_t].$$

When the Private Sector Has Imperfect Information

We assume certainty equivalence. The solution under imperfect information is characterized by the same coefficients, B_1 and B_2, as in the case of full information. We replace the unobserved variables $(\tilde{d}_{t-1}, v_t, \varepsilon_t)$ on the right-hand side of the solution system in equation (A13) with inferences $(\tilde{d}_{t-1|t-1}, v_{t|t}, \varepsilon_{t|t})$ that are determined by the following four equations. The first specifies the process of the persistent component of technology growth:

(A14) $\tilde{d}_t = \rho_d \tilde{d}_{t-1} + v_t.$

The second links the observed technology growth, $\tilde{z}_t = (\tilde{d}_t + \varepsilon_t)$, to the inference about the persistent component of technology growth, $\tilde{d}_{t|t}$:

(A15) $\tilde{d}_{t|t} = \lambda_1 \tilde{z}_t + (1 - \lambda_1) \rho_d \tilde{d}_{t-1|t-1}$

$$= \lambda_1 (\tilde{d}_t + \varepsilon_t) + (1 - \lambda_1) \rho_d \tilde{d}_{t-1|t-1},$$

where λ_1 is the Kalman gain that the private sector uses.

The third defines the inference of the private sector about the realization of the shock to the persistent component of technology growth, $v_{t|t}$:

(A16) $v_{t|t} = \tilde{d}_{t|t} - \rho_d \tilde{d}_{t-1|t-1}.$

The fourth defines the inference of the private sector about the realization of the shock to the transitory component of technology growth, $\varepsilon_{t|t}$:

(A17) $\varepsilon_{t|t} = \tilde{z}_t - \tilde{d}_{t|t}$

$$= (\tilde{d}_t + \varepsilon_t) - \tilde{d}_{t|t}.$$

When the Monetary Policy Rule Includes the Asset Price Gap Or the Natural Rate of Interest

The solution described in the following concerns the case where the interest rate rule includes the natural rate of interest or the asset price gap.

When Both the Private Sector and the Policymaker Have Full Information

The solution to the model takes the form:

(A18) $X_t = B_3 X_{t-1} + B_4 u_t,$

where

$$X_t \equiv [\tilde{c}_t; \tilde{y}_t; \tilde{h}_t; \tilde{i}_t; \tilde{k}_{t+1}; \tilde{n}_{t+1}; \tilde{r}^k_t; \tilde{s}_t; \tilde{r}^n_{t+1}; \tilde{q}_t; \widetilde{mc}_t; \tilde{\pi}_t; \tilde{d}_t;$$
$$\tilde{c}^*_t; \tilde{y}^*_t; \tilde{h}^*_t; \tilde{i}^*_t; \tilde{k}^*_{t+1}; \tilde{n}^*_{t+1}; \tilde{r}^{k*}_t; \tilde{s}^*_t; \tilde{r}^{n*}_{t+1}; \tilde{q}^*_t; \widetilde{mc}^*_t; \tilde{\pi}^*_t; \tilde{d}^*_t],$$

and

$$u_t \equiv [v_t; \varepsilon_t; v^*_t; \varepsilon^*_t].$$

The variables with * denote those in the model without pricing and financial frictions, and the variables without * denote those in the model with both frictions.[23]

When the Private Sector Has Full Information and the Policymaker Has Imperfect Information

The solution is characterized by the same coefficients, B_3 and B_4, as in the case where both the private sector and the policymaker have full information. We replace the unobserved variables $(\tilde{d}^*_{t-1}, v^*_t, \varepsilon^*_t)$ on the right-hand side of the solution system with the inferences of the policymaker $(\tilde{d}^*_{t-1|t-1}, v^*_{t|t}, \varepsilon^*_{t|t})$ that are determined by the following four equations:

---

23. When we compute the impulse response or conduct stochastic simulations, the shocks are common across the model with frictions and the model without frictions: $v_t = v^*_t$ and $\varepsilon_t = \varepsilon^*_t$ for any period t.

(A19)
$$\tilde{d}_t^* = \rho_d \tilde{d}_{t-1}^* + v_t^*,$$

and

(A20)
$$\tilde{d}_{t|t}^* = \lambda_2 \tilde{z}_t + (1 - \lambda_2)\rho_d \tilde{d}_{t-1|t-1}^*$$
$$= \lambda_2(\tilde{d}_t^* + \varepsilon_t^*) + (1 - \lambda_2)\rho_d \tilde{d}_{t-1|t-1}^*,$$

where λ_2 is the Kalman gain that the policymaker uses, and

(A21)
$$v_{t|t}^* = \tilde{d}_{t|t}^* - \rho_d \tilde{d}_{t-1|t-1}^*,$$

and

(A22)
$$\varepsilon_{t|t}^* = \tilde{z}_t - \tilde{d}_{t|t}^*$$
$$= (\tilde{d}_t^* + \varepsilon_t^*) - \tilde{d}_{t|t}^*.$$

When Both the Private Sector and the Policymaker Have Imperfect Information

The solution is characterized by the same coefficients, B_3 and B_4, as in the case where both the private sector and the policymaker have full information. We replace the unobserved variables ($\tilde{d}_{t-1}$, v_t, ε_t, $\tilde{d}_{t-1}^*$, v_t^*, ε_t^*) on the right-hand side of the solution system in equation (A18) with the inferences of the private sector and the policymaker ($\tilde{d}_{t-1|t-1}$, $v_{t|t}$, $\varepsilon_{t|t}$, $\tilde{d}_{t-1|t-1}^*$, $v_{t|t}^*$, $\varepsilon_{t|t}^*$) that are determined by the eight equations (A14) to (A17) and (A19) to (A22). We assume that the private sector and the policymaker use the same Kalman gain ($\lambda_1 = \lambda_2$).

When the Private Sector Has Imperfect Information and the Policymaker Has Full Information

The solution is characterized by the same coefficients (B_3, B_4) as in the case where both the private sector and the policymaker have full information. We replace the unobserved variables ($\tilde{d}_{t-1}$, v_t, ε_t) on the right-hand side of the solution system in equation (A18) with the inferences of the private sector ($\tilde{d}_{t-1|t-1}$, $v_{t|t}$, $\varepsilon_{t|t}$) that are determined by the four equations (A14) to (A17).

References

Barro, Robert J., and Robert G. King. 1984. Time-separable preferences and intertemporal-substitution models of business cycles. *Quarterly Journal of Economics* 99 (4): 817–39.

Barsky, Robert B., and J. Bradford DeLong. 1993. Why does the stock market fluctuate? *Quarterly Journal of Economics* 108 (2): 291–311.

Beaudry, Paul, and Franck Portier. 2004. An exploration into Pigou's theory of cycles. *Journal of Monetary Economics* 51 (6): 1183–1216.

Bernanke, Ben, and Mark Gertler. 1999. Monetary policy and asset price volatility. *Federal Reserve Bank of Kansas City Economic Review,* 4th Quarter 1999, 17–51.
———. 2001. Should central banks respond to movements in asset prices? *American Economic Review* 91 (2): 253–57.
Bernanke, Ben, Mark Gertler, and Simon Gilchrist. 1999. The financial accelerator in a quantitative business cycle framework. In *Handbook of macroeconomics.* Vol. 1C, ed. John B. Taylor and Michael Woodford, 253–57. Amsterdam: Elsevier Science, North-Holland.
Borio, Claudio, and Phillip Lowe. 2002. Asset prices, financial, and monetary stability: Exploring the nexus. BIS Working Paper no. 114. Basel, Switzerland: Bank for International Settlements.
Calvo, Guillermo. 1983. Staggered prices in a utility-maximizing framework. *Journal of Monetary Economics* 12:383–98.
Campbell, John Y. 1994. Inspecting the mechanism: An analytical approach to the stochastic growth model. *Journal of Monetary Economics* 33:463–506.
Cecchetti, Stephen G., Hans Genberg, John Lipsky, and Sushil Wadhwani. 2000. *Asset prices and central bank policy.* Geneva Report on the World Economy 2. Geneva: International Center for Monetary and Banking Studies and Center for Economic Policy Research.
Christiano, Lawrence, Roberto Motto, and Massimo Rostagno. 2005. Monetary policy and a stock market boom-bust cycle. Northwestern University and the European Central Bank. Unpublished Manuscript.
Cochrane, John H. 1994. Shocks. *Carnegie-Rochester Conference Series on Public Policy* 41:295–364.
Dupor, Bill. 2005. Stabilizing non-fundamental asset price movements under discretion and limited information. *Journal of Monetary Economics* 52:727–47.
Edge, Rochelle M., Thomas Laubach, and John C. Williams. 2004. Learning and shifts in long-run productivity growth. Board of Governors of the Federal Reserve System, Finance and Economics Discussion Series no. 2004–21. Washington, DC: Board of Governors of the Federal Reserve System.
———. 2005. Monetary policy and shifts in long-run productivity growth. Board of Governors of the Federal Reserve System. Unpublished Manuscript.
Erceg, Christopher J., Luca Guerrieri, and Christopher Gust. 2005. SIGMA: A new open economy model for policy analysis. Board of Governors of the Federal Reserve System, International Finance Discussion Papers no. 835. Washington, DC: Board of Governors of the Federal Reserve System.
Faia, Ester, and Tomasso Monacelli. 2006. Optimal interest rate rules, asset prices and credit frictions. Universitat Pompeu Fabra and Università Bocconi. Unpublished Manuscript.
French, Mark. 2001. Estimating changes in trend growth of total factor productivity: Kalman and H-P filters versus a Markov-switching framework. Board of Governors of the Federal Reserve System, Finance and Economics Discussion Paper Series no. 2001–44. Washington, DC: Board of Governors of the Federal Reserve System.
Gertler, Mark, Simon Gilchrist, and Fabio M. Natalucci. 2006. External constraints on monetary policy and the financial accelerator. *Journal of Money, Credit and Banking,* forthcoming.
Gilchrist, Simon, and John V. Leahy. 2002. Monetary policy and asset prices. *Journal of Monetary Economics* 49:75–97.
Jaimovich, Nir, and Sergio Rebelo. 2006. Can news about the future drive the business cycle? University of California, San Diego, and Northwestern University. Unpublished Manuscript.

Kahn, James, and Robert W. Rich. 2003. Do business cycles really have permanent effects? Using growth theory to distinguish trends from cycles. Federal Reserve Bank of New York Staff Reports no. 159. New York: Federal Reserve Bank of New York.

Kiley, Michael T. 2000. Stock prices and fundamentals in a production economy. Board of Governors of the Federal Reserve System. Unpublished Manuscript.

Kiyotaki, Nobuhiro. 1990. Learning and the value of the firm. NBER Working Paper no. 3480. Cambridge, MA: National Bureau of Economic Research.

Mishkin, Frederic S., and Eugene N. White. 2003. U.S. stock market crashes and their aftermath: Implications for monetary policy. In *Asset price bubbles: Implications for monetary, regulatory, and international policies,* ed. William C. Hunter, George G. Kaufman, and Michael Pomerleano, 53–79. Cambridge, MA: MIT Press.

Neiss, Katharine S., and Edward Nelson. 2003. The real-interest-rate gap as an inflation indicator. *Macroeconomic Dynamics* 7:239–62.

Okina, Kunio, Masaaki Shirakawa, and Shigenori Shiratsuka. 2001. The asset price bubble and monetary policy: Japan's experience in the late 1980s and the lessons. *Bank of Japan Monetary and Economic Studies* 19 (S-1): 395–450.

Orphanides, Athanasios, and John C. Williams. 2002. Robust monetary policy rules with unknown natural rates. *Brookings Papers on Economic Activity* Issue no. 2:63–118. Washington, DC: Brookings Institution.

Pakko, Michael R. 2002. What happens when the technology growth trend changes? *Review of Economic Dynamics* 5:376–407.

Roberts, John M. 2001. Estimates of the productivity trend using time-varying parameter techniques. *Contributions to Macroeconomics* 1 (1): 1–30.

Tambalotti, Andrea. 2003. Optimal monetary policy and productivity growth. Federal Reserve Bank of New York. Unpublished Manuscript.

Tetlow, Robert J. 2005. Monetary policy, asset prices and misspecification: The robust approach to bubbles with model uncertainty. Board of Governors of the Federal Reserve System. Unpublished Manuscript.

Woodford, Michael. 2003. *Interest and prices: Foundation of a theory of monetary policy.* Princeton, NJ: Princeton University Press.

Discussion Summary

Lars E. O. Svensson suggested that as a general methodological point, it would be natural to specify a loss function, and then to solve for the optimal policy, resulting in an optimal reaction function. He argued that this should be feasible because the model had a linear-quadratic structure. The next question would then be how one could implement this optimal policy. Starting from ad hoc rules, without checking whether they are close to optimal, approaches the problem from the wrong direction. Gilchrist responded that the authors appreciated the merits of this approach, but had sought to work within the context of the previous literature, in particular, the influential work of Bernanke and Gertler.

Stephen G. Cecchetti emphasized the importance of distinguishing between the loss function, which defines the target variables, and the reaction function, which defines the response of the policy interest rate in terms of variables that need not themselves be target variables. For example, if asset prices were included in the reaction function, this did not necessarily imply that "asset price targeting" was taking place. Rather, it could reflect the fact that responding to asset prices helped in targeting other variables that entered the loss function.

Martin Schneider pointed out that in a linear model, one could always solve for asset prices as a linear function of state variables. In principle, therefore, the reaction function could be rewritten in terms of asset prices. Although this was legitimate if the model was correctly specified, he said it would be interesting to know the costs of doing so if the model was misspecified. Gilchrist responded that ideally one would have a model in which asset prices were forward-looking and, therefore, captured information that was not available elsewhere.

Tommaso Monacelli said that he had investigated the possibility of targeting the leverage ratio with a coauthor. It did not matter whether the reaction function was defined in terms of the leverage ratio, or asset prices, or inflation. The best outcome was obtained in all cases because the measures were all positively correlated. Gilchrist responded that in the framework of his chapter with Saito, the objective function includes both stability of inflation and stability of output. Because the model has two distortions, to the markup and the return on capital, two instruments are helpful to maximize the objective function. Inflation targeting enables policymakers to stabilize the markup, but targeting asset prices allows them to stabilize the return on capital and, hence, to reduce the variance of output.

Donald L. Kohn said that informational assumptions are critical and that policymakers learn about technological change from private-sector behavior. In the 1990s, he pointed out, models of the economy used by Federal Reserve Bank (FRB) staff had failed and predicted inflation; he was, therefore, skeptical that central banks have an informational advantage over the private sector. He said that the Fed would have been wrong to act on the claim that there was "irrational exuberance" in the stock market in 1996 and that it was extremely hard to measure the potential asset price Q^*.

Kohn also suggested that the role of leverage in the economy is complicated. It was popularly suggested that central banks should look at credit, but there had been a huge amount of financial innovation and, hence, credit expansion over the last twenty-five years. It would have been wrong to respond to this. As a general point, he argued that financial frictions are diminishing over time and that asymmetric information is, therefore, becoming less of a problem. Gilchrist responded that although he agreed that financial markets are handling information asymmetries in a more sophisticated fashion, the fact that people are taking on more leverage means that there could be severe consequences if the financial system were placed under strain.

Andrew Levin was also skeptical about the assumption that central bankers had more information than the private sector. He said that it was extremely hard to project total factor productivity and that his view was that the Fed's task was to try to infer total factor productivity (TFP) from information produced in the private sector. It was people in the private sector who saw TFP in their own sector of the economy—in the form, say, of patents that had just been obtained or the latest marketing information on a new product. Gilchrist said that he and Saito did not intend to promote the view that the Fed knows more than the private sector.

Jordi Galí commented that it was important to find variables that would indicate the state of the economy in a manner that did not depend on the details of the assumed model or the nature and dynamic properties of the underlying shocks hitting the economy. It would be appropriate for policymakers to respond to variables of this sort, whereas no consistently welfare-improving response would be possible if it required detailed knowledge of the economy's structure and the dynamic process of shocks to the economy.

Optimal Monetary Policy with Collateralized Household Debt and Borrowing Constraints

Tommaso Monacelli

Debt leverage of all types is often troublesome when one judges the stability of the economy. Should home prices fall, we would have reason to be concerned about mortgage debt.[1]

3.1 Introduction

The sizeable increase in house prices combined with an unprecedented rise in household debt have been among the most important facts observed in several Organization for Economic Cooperation and Development (OECD) countries in the last decade. In addition, the two facts are usually perceived as mutually reinforcing phenomena. The rise in house prices has induced households to increasingly extract equity from their accumulated assets, thereby encouraging further borrowing against the realized capital gains. Dynamics of this sort have been considered important in sustaining the level of private spending in several countries, especially during the business-cycle downturn of 2001. Figure 3.1 displays the dynamics of total private consumption and household mortgage debt in the United States. Figure 3.2 displays the joint behavior of private consumption and of (a harmonized index of) house prices. It is clear that these three variables display a significant degree of comovement at the business-cycle frequency.

A large part of the observed increase in household borrowing has been in the form of collateralized debt. Hence, the role of durable goods—especially housing—as an instrument of collateralization has also increased over time. Figure 3.3 displays the evolution of mortgage debt (as a prototype form of secured debt) as a share of total outstanding household debt. This share has increased from about 60 percent in 1952 to about 75 percent

Tommaso Monacelli is an associate professor of economics at Università Bocconi.

I would like to thank John Campbell and Hanno Lustig for very useful comments.

1. Former Federal Reserve Chairman Greenspan's remarks at America's Community Bankers Annual Convention, Washington, D.C., October 19, 2004.

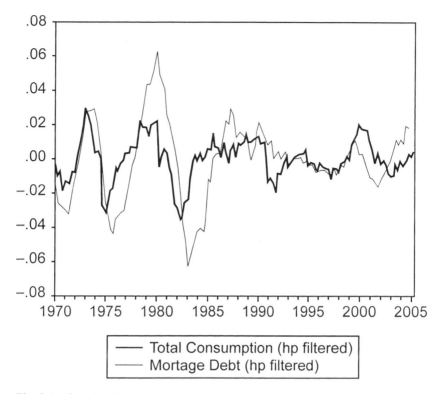

Fig. 3.1   Consumption and mortgage debt

in 2005. If one were to consider also vehicles loans, the share of collateralized debt in the United States would rise to about 90 percent.[2]

While developments in the housing sector and institutional features in mortgage markets (e.g., prevalence of fixed versus variable mortgage contracts, importance of equity withdrawal, down payment and refinancing rates) have become common vocabulary for monetary policymakers around the world, the same issues have received very scant attention in the recent normative analysis of monetary policy.

The monetary policy literature has soared in the last few years within the framework of the so-called New Neoclassical Synthesis (NNS). The NNS builds on microfounded models with imperfect competition and nominal rigidities and has currently emerged as a workhorse paradigm for the normative analysis of monetary policy.[3] However, in the NNS, the transmission mechanism of monetary policy remains limited to a typical real interest rate channel on aggregate demand. The latter channel ignores issues

2. See Campbell and Hercowitz (2005) and Aizcorbe, Kennickell, and Moore (2003).

3. See, among many others, Goodfriend and King (1997), Woodford (2003), Clarida, Galí, and Gertler (1999), King and Wolman (1999), Khan, King, and Wolman (2003).

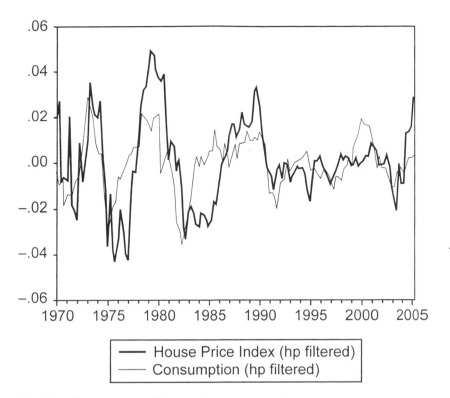

Fig. 3.2   Consumption and house prices

related to credit market imperfections, wealth effects linked to the evolution of asset prices, households' heterogeneity in saving rates, and determinants of collateralized debt.

Principles of optimal monetary policy within the NNS revolve around the polar star of price stability.[4] Consider the basic efficiency argument for price stability. Suppose, for the sake of exposition, that the economy experiences a positive productivity shock and that prices are completely rigid. Firms are constrained to comply with demand at that given price. Hence, they react by raising markups and reducing labor demand. The stickiness of prices generates room for a procyclical monetary intervention to boost aggregate demand in line with the higher desired production. In turn, this validates the strict stability of prices as an equilibrium choice by firms. In practice, this monetary policy intervention manages in eliminating the distortion induced by price stickiness.

Matters are different in our framework, characterized by two main fea-

---

4. In fact, much of the existing literature can be interpreted as studying the conditions under which deviating from the price stability paradigm can be consistent with efficiency. See Woodford (2003) for a complete analysis.

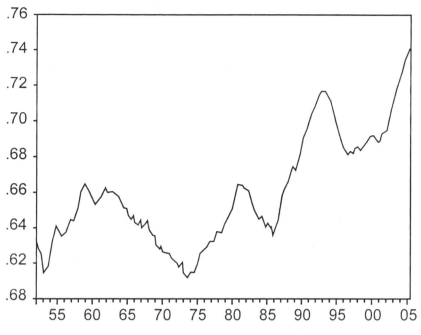

Fig. 3.3   Mortgage debt as a share of total outstanding household debt

tures. First, households display heterogenous patience rates and, therefore, different marginal utilities of consumption (saving). Second, the more impatient agents face a collateral constraint on nominal borrowing. Both elements constitute a deviation from the standard representative agent model with free borrowing, which is typical of the NNS. In that framework, by construction, debt is always zero in equilibrium.

To understand why these features may alter the baseline normative implication of price stability that emerges in the NNS, we emphasize two distinct dimensions: first, the role of nominal private debt per se; second, the role of durable prices in affecting the ability of borrowing by endogenously altering the value of the assets that act as collateral.

Consider the role of debt first. If debt contracts are predetermined in nominal terms, inflation can directly affect household's net worth by reducing the real value of outstanding debt service. Thus, inflation can have redistributive effects (from savers to borrowers). The key issue, then, is the extent to which a Ramsey-optimal policy would like to resort to this redistributive margin in equilibrium. Once again, consider a temporary rise in productivity. A constrained household (the borrower), whose marginal utility of current consumption exceeds the marginal utility of saving, would like to increase spending and do so disproportionately more than an unconstrained agent (the saver), who engages in consumption smoothing.

At the same time, in a model with collateral requirements, the borrower faces a wealth effect on labor supply. In fact, in order to sustain the surge in consumption, the borrower needs to optimally balance the purchasing of new debt with an increase in labor supply required to finance new collateral. The tighter the borrowing constraint, the more stringent the necessity of increasing labor supply. Importantly, monetary policy can exert an influence on this margin. By generating inflation, the monetary authority can positively affect the borrower's net worth, thereby allowing the constrained household to increase consumption for any given level of work effort.

Thus, the presence of nominal debt per se may constitute a motivation for deviating from a price stability prescription. In fact, and already previewing some of our key results, our analysis indicates that the optimal volatility of inflation is increasing in two parameters symbolizing heterogeneity: (1) the borrower's weight in the planner's objective function; (2) the borrower's impatience rate (relative to the saver).

However, and due to the presence of price stickiness, inflation variability is costly. Hence, monetary policy will have to optimally balance the incentive to offset the price stickiness distortion with the one of marginally affecting borrower's collateral constraint. Our results point out that, quantitatively, the incentive to offset the price stickiness distortion is predominant and that, already for a small degree of price stickiness, equilibrium deviations from price stability are small.[5]

Next consider the role of durable (asset) prices. In a way similar to the credit cycle effects exposed in Kiyotaki and Moore (1997) and Iacoviello (2005), movements in the real price of durables endogenously affect the borrowing limit and, in turn, consumption. The mechanism is simple. A rise in the price of durables induces, ceteris paribus, a fall in the marginal value of borrowing (i.e., a softening of the borrowing constraint). This implies, for the borrower, a fall in the marginal utility of current (nondurable) consumption relative to the option of shifting consumption intertemporally (in other words, a violation of the Euler equation), which can be validated only by a rise in current consumption. In turn, the increased demand for borrowing further stimulates the demand for durables and its relative price, inducing a cycle effect that further boosts (nondurable) spending.

In an efficient equilibrium with free borrowing and lending, the borrower would indeed like (given his impatience) to expand borrowing to finance current consumption. Yet he or she would do so *without* resorting to

---

5. In this context with incomplete markets (in fact, one-period nominal debt is the only traded asset), there is an even more fundamental motive for inflation volatility, namely the incentive of the planner to "complete the markets" by rendering nominal debt state contingent. This motive, however, is strictly intertwined with the redistributive motive we emphasize here. In fact, no debt would be traded in the absence of heterogeneity, which in turn is the essential feature justifying redistribution.

an increase in demand for durables. Hence, collateral limits per se induce inefficient movements in the relative price of durables. On the other hand, though, a strict stabilization of durable prices is largely detrimental for the borrower and would be inconsistent with the need of realizing sectoral relative price movements. As a result, the optimal policy balances the incentive to partially stabilize relative durable prices with the one of offsetting the stickiness in nondurable prices. In fact, in our simulations, a Ramsey-type policy emerges as an intermediate case between two extreme forms of Taylor-type interest rate rules: a rule that strictly stabilizes nondurable price inflation and a rule that strictly stabilizes the relative price of durables.

The existing literature related to this chapter originates from the seminal work of Bernanke and Gertler (1989), who emphasize the role of collateral requirements in affecting aggregate fluctuations. In Bernanke and Gertler (1989), collateral constraints are motivated by the presence of private information and limited liability. More recently, Kiyotaki and Moore (1997) build a general equilibrium model in which two categories of agents (borrowers and savers) trade private debt. Heterogeneity is introduced in the form of different patience rates. In Kiyotaki and Moore (1997), collateral requirements are motivated by the presence of limited enforcement, in a way similar to the approach followed here. Both Bernanke and Gertler (1989) and Kiyotaki and Moore (1997), despite some differences, share the central implication that the wealth of the borrower influences private spending. Iacoviello (2005) extends the work of Kiyotaki and Moore (1997) to build a bridge with the recent New Keynesian monetary policy framework. In his analysis, the role of nominal debt and asset prices are central for the propagation of monetary policy shocks, but no normative aspect is analyzed. Campbell and Hercowitz (2005) analyze the implications for macroeconomic volatility of the relaxation of collateral requirements in the United States (dated around 1980) in a general equilibrium environment. However, their real business-cycle framework is not suitable for a study of monetary policy, and it abstracts from any role of asset prices. Recently, Erceg and Levin (2006) study optimal monetary policy in an economy with two sectors (durable and nondurables) and similar to the one employed here. Their analysis, though, abstracts from any form of credit market imperfection.

3.2   The Model

The model builds on Iacoviello (2005) and Campbell and Hercowitz (2005). The economy is composed of two types of households, *borrowers* and *savers,* and two sectors—producing durable and nondurable goods, respectively—each populated by a large number of monopolistic competitive firms and by a perfectly competitive final-goods producer. The borrowers differ from the savers in that they exhibit a *lower patience rate* and, therefore, a higher propensity to consume.[6] Complementary to this assumption is the one that the borrowers face a *collateral constraint*. In fact, if agents were free to borrow and lend at the market interest rate, the borrowers would exhibit a tendency to accumulate debt indefinitely, rendering the steady state of the economy indeterminate. Peculiar to the borrowers is that their preferences are tilted toward current consumption. Formally, their marginal utility of current consumption exceeds the marginal utility of saving. As a result, in the face of a temporary positive shock to income, they do not act as consumption smoothers but tend instead to reduce saving. In this vein, the presence of household debt reflects equilibrium intertemporal trading between the two types of agents, with the savers acting as standard consumption-smoothers.[7]

3.2.1 Final-Good Producers

In each sector ($j = c, d$) a perfectly competitive final-good producer purchases $Y_{j,t}(i)$ units of intermediate good i. The final-good producer in sector j operates the production function:

$$(1) \qquad Y_{j,t} \equiv \left(\int_0^1 Y_{j,t}(i)^{(\varepsilon_j - 1)/\varepsilon_j} di \right)^{\varepsilon_j/(\varepsilon_j - 1)},$$

where $Y_{j,t}(i)$ is quantity demanded of the intermediate good i by final-good producer j, and ε_j is the elasticity of substitution between differentiated varieties in sector j. Notice, in particular, that in the durable good sector, $Y_{d,t}(i)$ refers to expenditure in the *new* durable intermediate good i (rather than services). Maximization of profits yields demand functions for the typical intermediate good i in sector j:

$$(2) \qquad Y_{j,t}(i) = \left[\frac{P_{j,t}(i)}{P_{j,t}} \right]^{-\varepsilon_j} Y_{j,t} \quad j = c, d$$

for all i. In particular, $P_{j,t} \equiv [\int_0^1 P_{j,t}(i)^{1-\varepsilon_j} di]^{1/(1-\varepsilon_j)}$ is the price index consistent with the final-good producer in sector j earning zero profits.[8]

6. For early general equilibrium models with heterogenous impatience rates, see Becker (1980), Woodford (1986), Becker and Foias (1987), Krusell and Smith (1998). More recently, see Kiyotaki and Moore (1997), Iacoviello (2005), and Campbell and Hercowitz (2005). Here we use the categories borrower/saver as synonymous of impatient and patient household, respectively. Notice, however, that the fact that the relatively more impatient (patient) agent emerges as a borrower (saver) is an equilibrium phenomenon.

7. Galí, Lopez-Salido, and Valles (2007) also construct a model in which agents are heterogenous along the consumption-smoothing dimension and use it to analyze the effects of government spending shocks. In their framework, the nonsmoothers are agents that are completely excluded from the possibility of borrowing (following Campbell and Mankiw [1989], those agents are named *rule-of-thumb* consumers). Hence, in that framework, private debt cannot emerge as an equilibrium phenomenon.

8. Hence, the problem of the final-good producer j is max $P_{j,t} Y_{j,t} - \int_0^1 P_{j,t}(i) Y_{j,t}(i) di$ subject to equation (1).

3.2.2 Borrowers/Workers

The representative borrower consumes an index of consumption *services* of durable and *nondurable* final goods, defined as:

$$(3) \qquad X_t \equiv [(1 - \alpha)^{1/\eta}(C_t)^{(\eta-1)/\eta} + \alpha^{1/\eta}(D_t)^{(\eta-1)/\eta}]^{\eta/(\eta-1)},$$

where C_t denotes consumption services of the final nondurable good, D_t denotes services from the stock of the final durable good at the end of period t, $\alpha > 0$ is the share of durable goods in the composite consumption index, and $\eta \geq 0$ is the elasticity of substitution between services of nondurable and durable goods. In the case $\eta \to 0$, nondurable consumption and durable services are perfect complements, whereas if $\eta \to \infty$, the two services are perfect substitutes.

The borrower maximizes the following utility program

$$(4) \qquad W_0 \equiv E_0 \left\{ \sum_{t=0}^{\infty} \beta^t U(X_t, N_t) \right\}$$

subject to the sequence of budget constraints (in *nominal* terms):

$$(5) \qquad P_{c,t}C_t + P_{d,t}[D_t - (1 - \delta)D_{t-1}] + R_{t-1}B_{t-1} = B_t + W_t N_t + T_t,$$

where B_t is end-of-period t nominal debt, and R_{t-1} is the nominal lending rate on loan contracts stipulated at time $t - 1$. Furthermore, W_t is the nominal wage, N_t is labor supply, and T_t are net government transfers. Labor is assumed to be perfectly mobile across sectors, implying that the nominal wage rate is common across sectors.

In real terms (units of nondurable consumption), equation (5) reads:

$$(6) \qquad C_t + q_t[D_t - (1 - \delta)D_{t-1}] + \frac{R_{t-1}b_{t-1}}{\pi_{c,t}} = b_t + \frac{W_t}{P_{c,t}}N_t + \frac{T_t}{P_{c,t}}$$

where $q_t \equiv P_{d,t}/P_{c,t}$ is the relative price of the durable good, and $b_t \equiv B_t/P_{c,t}$ is real debt. The left-hand side of equation (6) denotes uses of funds (durable and nondurable spending plus real debt service), while the right-hand side denotes available resources (new debt, real labor income, and transfers). An important feature of equation (6), which follows from debt contracts being predetermined in nominal terms, is that (nondurable) inflation can affect the borrower's net worth. Hence, for given outstanding debt, a rise in inflation lowers the current real burden of debt repayments.

Later we will work with the following specification of the utility function

$$U(X_t, N_t) = \log(X_t) - \frac{\upsilon}{1 + \varphi} N_t^{1+\varphi},$$

where φ is the inverse elasticity of labor supply and υ is a scale parameter.[9]

---

9. Notice that we abstract from an explicit role for money. Along the lines of Woodford (2003, ch. 2), one can think of the present economy as a cashless limit of a money-in-the-

Collateral Constraint

Private borrowing is subject to a limit. We assume that the whole stock of debt is collateralized. The borrowing limit is tied to the value of the durable good stock:

(7) $$B_t \leq (1 - \chi) D_t P_{d,t},$$

where χ is the fraction of the durable stock value that cannot be used as a collateral.

In general, one can broadly think of χ as the down payment rate, or the inverse of the *loan-to-value ratio,* and, therefore, an indirect measure of the tightness of the borrowing constraint.[10] Jappelli and Pagano (1989) provide evidence on the presence of liquidity constrained agents by linking their share to more structural features of the credit markets. In particular, they find that the share of liquidity-constrained agents is larger in countries in which a measure of the loan-to-value ratio is lower.[11]

Notice that movements in the durable good price directly affect the ability of borrowing. It is widely believed that the recent rise in house prices in the United States has induced households to increasingly extract equity from their accumulated assets, thereby encouraging further borrowing against their realized capital gains. This link between asset price fluctuations and ability of borrowing has presumably played an important role in determining households' spending patterns during the recent business-cycle evolution.[12]

We assume that, in a neighborhood of the deterministic steady state, equation (5) is always satisfied with equality.[13] We can then rewrite the col-

---

utility model, in which the weight of real money balances in utility is negligible. Our maintained assumption is that the monetary authority can directly control the short-run nominal interest rate. This allows us to abstract from any monetary transaction friction driving the optimal policy prescription toward the Friedman rule.

10. Notice, though, that $\chi = 0$ does not correspond to a situation in which the borrowing constraint is absent. That situation would obtain only in the case in which heterogeneity in patience rates were assumed away. See more on this point in the following.

11. The form of the collateral constraint has been deliberately kept simple to facilitate the analysis. However, there are at least two important dimensions that are neglected here. First is incorporating an explicit mortgage refinancing choice. In the United States, in the last few years, the ability of extract equity has worked primarily through refinancing decisions linked to the downward trend in nominal interest rates. Second is a distinction between fixed and variable rate mortgage contracts. For a positive analysis of these issues, see Calza, Monacelli, and Stracca (2006).

12. For instance, Alan Greenspan's view is summarized by the following excerpt:

Among the factors contributing to the strength of spending and the decline in saving have been developments in housing markets and home finance that have spurred rising household wealth and allowed greater access to that wealth. The rapid rise in home prices over the past several years has provided households with considerable capital gains. (House Committee on Banking, Housing, and Urban Affairs, *Federal Reserve's First Monetary Policy Report for 2005,* 109th Cong., 1st sess., February 16, 2005)

13. This assumption is obviously not uncontroversial. Ideally, one would like a model in which the borrowers may be free to choose to hit the borrowing limit only occasionally.

lateral constraint in real terms (i.e., in units of nondurable consumption) as follows:

(8) $$b_t = (1 - \chi)q_t D_t$$

Given $\{b_{-1}, D_{-1}\}$, the borrower chooses $\{N_t, b_t, D_t, C_t\}$ to maximize equation (4) subject to equations (6) and (8). By defining λ_t and $\lambda_t \psi_t$ as the multipliers on constraints (6) and (8), respectively, and $U_{x,t}$ as the marginal utility of a generic variable x, efficiency conditions read:

(9) $$\frac{-U_{n,t}}{U_{c,t}} = \frac{W_t}{P_{c,t}}$$

(10) $$U_{c,t} = \lambda_t$$

(11) $$U_{c,t}q_t = U_{d,t} + \beta(1 - \delta)E_t\{U_{c,t+1}q_{t+1}\} + U_{c,t}(1 - \chi)\psi_t q_t$$

(12) $$\psi_t = 1 - \beta E_t \left\{ \frac{U_{c,t+1}}{U_{c,t}} \frac{R_t}{\pi_{c,t+1}} \right\}$$

Equations (9) and (10) are standard. Respectively, they state that the marginal rate of substitution between consumption and leisure is equalized to the real wage (in units of nondurable [ND] consumption) and that the marginal utility of income is equalized to the marginal utility of consumption. Equation (11) is an intertemporal condition on durable demand. It requires the borrower to equate the marginal utility of current (nondurable) consumption to the marginal gain of durable services. The latter depends on three components: (1) the direct utility gain of an additional unit of durable $U_{d,t}$; (2) the expected utility stemming from the possibility of expanding future consumption by means of the realized resale value of the durable purchased in the previous period, $\beta(1 - \delta)E_t\{U_{c,t+1}q_{t+1}\}$; and (3) the marginal utility of relaxing the borrowing constraint $U_{c,t}(1 - \chi)\psi_t q_t$. Notice that, in the absence of borrowing constraints (i.e., $\psi_t = 0$), the latter component drops out. Intuitively, if ψ_t rises, the borrowing constraint binds more tightly (i.e., the marginal gain of relaxing the constraint is larger), and, therefore, the marginal gain of acquiring an additional unit of durable (which, once used as collateral, allows to expand borrowing) is higher.

The interpretation of ψ_t is more transparent from equation (12), which is a modified version of an Euler consumption condition. Indeed, it reduces to a standard intertemporal condition in the case of $\psi_t = 0$ for all t.

Hence, our assumption remains valid only to the extent that we consider small fluctuations around the relevant deterministic steady state (see more on this in the following) so that standard log-linearization techniques may still be applied. This can be assured by specifying disturbance processes of sufficiently small amplitude.

Alternatively, it has the interpretation of an asset price condition. In fact, the marginal value of additional borrowing (the left-hand side ψ_t) is tied to a payoff (right-hand side) that captures the deviation from a standard Euler equation. Consider, for the sake of argument, ψ_t rising from zero to a positive value. This implies, from equation (12), that $U_{c,t} > \beta E_t\{U_{c,t+1}(R/\pi_{c,t+1})\}$. In other words, the marginal utility of current consumption exceeds the marginal utility of saving, that is, the marginal gain of shifting one unit of consumption intertemporally. The higher ψ_t, the higher the net marginal benefit of purchasing the durable asset, which allows, by marginally relaxing the borrowing constraint, to purchase additional *current* consumption.

3.2.3   Savers

The economy is composed of a second category of consumers, labeled savers. They differ from the borrowers in the fact that they have a *higher patience rate*. In addition, we assume that the representative saver is the owner of the monopolistic firms in each sector. The saver does not supply labor. Saver's utility can be written:

$$(13) \qquad E_0\left\{\sum_{t=0}^{\infty}\gamma^t\,\tilde{U}(\tilde{X}_t,\tilde{D}_t)\right\}.$$

Importantly, preferences are such that the saver discounts the future more heavily than the borrower, hence $\gamma > \beta$. The saver's sequence of budget constraints reads (in nominal terms):

$$(14) \qquad P_{c,t}\tilde{C}_t + P_{d,t}[\tilde{D}_t - (1-\delta)\tilde{D}_{t-1}] + R_{t-1}\tilde{B}_{t-1} = \tilde{B}_t + \tilde{T}_t + \sum_j \tilde{\Gamma}_{j,t},$$

where $\tilde{C}_t$ is the saver's nondurable consumption, $\tilde{D}_t$ is the saver's utility services from the stock of durable goods, $\tilde{B}_t$ is end-of-period t nominal debt (credit), $\tilde{T}_t$ are net government transfers, and $\tilde{\Gamma}_{j,t}$ are nominal profits from the holding of monopolistic competitive firms in sector j.

The efficiency conditions for this program are a standard Euler equation:

$$(15) \qquad \tilde{U}_{c,t} = \gamma E_t\left\{\tilde{U}_{c,t+1}\frac{R_t}{\pi_{c,t+1}}\right\}$$

and a durable demand condition (in the absence of borrowing constraints)

$$(16) \qquad q_t\tilde{U}_{c,t} = \tilde{U}_{d,t} + \gamma(1-\delta)E_t\{\tilde{U}_{c,t+1}q_{t+1}\}.$$

In this case, being a permanent-income consumer, the saver will equate the marginal rate of substitution between durable and nondurable consumption exactly to the standard user cost expression prevailing in the absence of borrowing constraints.

3.2.4   Production and Pricing of Intermediate Goods

A typical intermediate good firm i in sector j hires labor (supplied by the borrowers) to operate a linear production function:

$$(17) \qquad Y_{j,t}(i) = A_{j,t} N_{j,t}(i),$$

where $A_{j,t}$ is a productivity shifter common to all firms in sector j. Each firm i has monopolistic power in the production of its own variety and, therefore, has leverage in setting the price. In so doing, it faces a quadratic cost equal to $(\vartheta_j/2)\{[P_{j,t}(i)]/[P_{j,t-1(i)}] - 1\}^2$, where the parameter ϑ_j measures the degree of sectoral nominal price rigidity. The higher ϑ_j, the more sluggish is the adjustment of nominal prices in sector j. In the particular case of $\vartheta_j = 0$, prices are flexible.

The problem of each monopolistic firm is to choose the sequence $\{N_{j,t}(i), P_{j,t}(i)\}_{t=0}^{\infty}$ in order to maximize expected discounted nominal profits:

$$(18) \qquad E_0\left\{\sum_{t=0}^{\infty} \Lambda_{j,t}\left\{P_{j,t}(i)Y_{j,t}(i) - W_t N_{j,t}(i) - \frac{\vartheta_j}{2}\left[\frac{P_{j,t}(i)}{P_{j,t-1}(i)} - 1\right]^2 P_{j,t}\right\}\right\}$$

subject to equations (1) and (17). In equation (18), $\Lambda_{j,t} \equiv \gamma E_t\{\tilde{\lambda}_{t+1}/\lambda_t\}$ is the saver's stochastic discount factor, and $\tilde{\lambda}_t$ is the saver's marginal utility of nominal income. Let's denote by $P_{j,t}(i)/P_{j,t}$ the relative price of variety i in sector j. In a *symmetric* equilibrium in which $P_{j,t}(i)/P_{j,t} = 1$ for all i and j, and all firms employ the same amount of labor in each sector, the first order condition of the preceding problem reads:

$$(19) \quad [(1 - \varepsilon_j) + \varepsilon_j mc_{j,t}]Y_{j,t} = \vartheta_j(\pi_{j,t} - 1)\pi_{j,t}$$

$$- \vartheta_j E_t\left\{\frac{\Lambda_{t+1}}{\Lambda_t}\frac{P_{j,t+1}}{P_{j,t}}(\pi_{j,t+1} - 1)\pi_{j,t+1}\right\} \quad (j = c, d),$$

where $\pi_{j,t} \equiv P_{j,t}/P_{j,t-1}$ is the gross inflation rate in sector j, and

$$(20) \qquad mc_{j,t} \equiv \frac{W_t}{P_{j,t}A_{j,t}}$$

is the real marginal cost in sector j. Recall that, due to labor being perfectly mobile, the nominal wage is common across sectors.

Rearranging equation (19), one can obtain the following sector-specific price setting constraint, assuming the form of a forward-looking Phillips curve

$$(21) \qquad \pi_{j,t}(\pi_{j,t} - 1) = \gamma E_t\left\{\frac{\Lambda_{t+1}}{\Lambda_t}\frac{P_{j,t+1}}{P_{j,t}}\pi_{j,t+1}(\pi_{j,t+1} - 1)\right\}$$

$$+ \frac{\varepsilon_j A_{j,t}N_{j,t}}{\vartheta_j}\left(mc_{j,t} - \frac{\varepsilon_j - 1}{\varepsilon_j}\right)$$

for $j = c, d,$ and where

$$\frac{\Lambda_{t+1}}{\Lambda_t} \frac{P_{j,t+1}}{P_{j,t}} = \frac{U_{\tilde{c},t+1}}{U_{\tilde{c},t}} \quad (\text{if } j = c)$$

$$\frac{\Lambda_{t+1}}{\Lambda_t} \frac{P_{j,t+1}}{P_{j,t}} = \frac{U_{\tilde{c},t+1}}{U_{\tilde{c},t}} \frac{q_{t+1}}{q_t} \quad (\text{if } j = d)$$

and

(22) $$mc_{j,t} = \frac{-U_{n,t}}{U_{c,t} A_{c,t}} \quad (\text{if } j = c)$$

(23) $$mc_{j,t} = \frac{-U_{n,t}}{U_{c,t} A_{d,t}} q_t^{-1} \quad (\text{if } j = d).$$

Equation (21) constraints the evolution of sectoral prices when the price-setting problem is inherently dynamic as in equation (18). It has the form of a so-called New Keynesian Phillips curve in that current inflation depends on future expected inflation and on the deviation of the real marginal cost from its flexible-price constant value. An equation such as (21) is a fundamental building block of the recent stream of models of the NNS.[14]

In the particular case of *flexible prices,* the real marginal cost must be constant and equal to the inverse steady-state markup $(\varepsilon_j - 1)/\varepsilon_j,$ for $j = c, d.$ Notice that, in the durable sector, variations in the relative price of durables (possibly due to sectoral asymmetric shocks) drive a wedge between the marginal rate of substitution between consumption and leisure on the one hand and the marginal product of labor on the other. Hence, the real marginal cost is directly affected by movements in the relative price. This aspect is important because it points to a typical inefficiency that constrains monetary policy in models with two sectors. Namely, in the presence of sectoral asymmetric disturbances, if prices in either sector are sticky, simultaneous stabilization of real marginal costs in both sectors becomes unfeasible. In fact, asymmetric shocks will necessarily require equilibrium movements in the relative price.

3.2.5   Market Clearing

Equilibrium in the goods market of sector j requires that the production of the final good be allocated to expenditure and to resource costs originating from the adjustment of prices

(24) $$Y_{c,t} = C_t + \tilde{C}_t + \frac{\vartheta_c}{2} (\pi_{c,t} - 1)^2$$

(25) $$Y_{d,t} = D_t - (1 - \delta)D_{t-1} + \tilde{D}_t - (1 - \delta)\tilde{D}_{t-1} + \frac{\vartheta_d}{2}(\pi_{d,t} - 1)^2.$$

---

14. See Galí and Gertler (1999) and Woodford (2003).

Equilibrium in the debt and labor market requires, respectively:

(26) $$B_t + \tilde{B}_t = 0$$

(27) $$\sum_j N_{j,t} = N_t.$$

3.2.6   Equilibrium

For any specified policy process $\{R_t\}$ and exogenous state vector $\{A_{c,t}, A_{d,t}\}$, an (imperfectly) *competitive allocation* is a sequence for $\{N_t, N_{c,t}, N_{d,t}, b_t, D_t, \tilde{D}_t, C_t, \tilde{C}_t, \pi_{c,t}, \pi_{d,t}, \psi_t, q_t\}$ satisfying equations (6) and (8) with equality, and equations (9) to (12), (15), (16), (21), (24), (25), and (27).

3.3   Steady State of the Competitive Equilibrium

In this section, we analyze the features of the deterministic steady state associated to the competitive equilibrium. We emphasize two results. First, the borrower is always constrained in the steady state (and, hence, will remain such forever). This is assured by the assumption that the borrower is more impatient than the saver, hence the marginal utility of saving if the former is lower than the one of the latter. Second, the steady-state level of debt is unique and positive. It is a general result of models with heterogenous discount rates and borrowing constraints that the patient agent will end up owning all available assets. This has been pointed out in earlier work by Becker (1980) and Becker and Foias (1987). In the context of our framework, this translates into the borrower holding a positive amount of debt in the steady state.

We proceed as follows. In the steady state, the saver's discount rate pins down the real rate of return. Hence, by combining the steady-state version of equation (15), which implies $R = \pi_c/\gamma$, with equation (12), we obtain

(28) $$\psi = 1 - \frac{\beta}{\gamma} > 0,$$

where π_c is the steady-state rate of inflation in nondurables. Notice that $\beta = \gamma$ implies $\psi = 0$. In other words, absence of heterogeneity entails that the borrowing constraint does not bind. That would correspond to the standard scenario in a representative agent economy.

A corollary of equation (28) is

(29) $$\frac{1}{\beta} > RR = \frac{1}{\gamma},$$

where RR is the steady-state real interest rate. Hence, the borrower's discount rate exceeds the steady-state real interest rate.

In a flexible price steady state for both sectors, taking the ratio of equations (22) and (23), the relative price of durables reads

$$(30) \qquad q = \frac{(\varepsilon_d - 1)/\varepsilon_d}{(\varepsilon_c - 1)/\varepsilon_c}.$$

Assuming equal price elasticity of demand in both sectors ($\varepsilon_d = \varepsilon_c$), we have $q = 1$. By evaluating equation (11) in the steady state (and given our preference specification), we obtain the relative consumption of durables by the borrower:

$$(31) \qquad \frac{D}{C} = \frac{\alpha}{1 - \alpha}[1 - \beta(1 - \delta) - (1 - \chi)\psi]^{-\eta}$$

Notice that the relative demand for durables is increasing in the shadow value of borrowing ψ. Intuitively, acquiring more durables allows to marginally relax the borrowing constraint.

The steady-state leverage ratio, defined as the ratio between steady-state debt and durable assets owned, can be written:

$$(32) \qquad \frac{b}{D} = (1 - \chi)$$

To pin down the level of debt we proceed as follows. We choose parameter υ in order to set a given level of hours worked in the steady state[15] ($N = \overline{N}$). By combining (6), (8), (32) we can write:

$$(33) \qquad D = \frac{\overline{N}}{\mu^c \Phi}$$

where $\mu^c \equiv \varepsilon^c/(\varepsilon^c - 1)$ is the (steady-state) markup in the nondurable sector and

$$\Phi \equiv \left\{ \frac{1 - \alpha}{\alpha}[1 - \beta(1 - \delta) - \psi(1 - \chi)]^\eta + \delta + \frac{(1 - \gamma)(1 - \chi)}{\gamma} \right\}.$$

Once D is obtained from equation (33), it is straightforward, using equation (32), to solve for the unique level of the borrower's debt in the steady state. This steady-state level of debt would be indeterminate in the special case in which agents did not exhibit heterogeneity in preference rates (see Becker 1980).

3.4   Optimal Monetary Policy

Having laid out our framework, we next proceed to study the optimal conduct of monetary policy. The optimal monetary policy literature in the context of dynamic stochastic general equilibrium (DSGE) models with

---

15. In particular, we will require that the borrower devotes to work one-third of the time unit.

nominal rigidities has soared in the last few years.[16] However, these developments have neglected a number of features that are central to the present analysis: (1) the presence of nominal private debt and heterogeneity; (2) the role of collateral constraints; and (3) the role of durable prices in affecting the ability of borrowing endogenously.

3.4.1   The Ramsey Problem

We assume that ex-ante *commitment* is feasible. In the classic approach to the study of optimal policy in dynamic economies (Ramsey 1927; Atkinson and Stiglitz 1980; Lucas and Stokey 1983; Chari, Christiano, and Kehoe 1991) and in a typical public finance spirit, a Ramsey planner maximizes the household's welfare subject to a resource constraint, to the constraints describing the equilibrium in the private-sector economy, via an explicit consideration of all the distortions that characterize both the long-run and the cyclical behavior of the economy.

Recently, there has been a resurgence of interest for a Ramsey-type approach in dynamic general equilibrium models with nominal rigidities. Khan, King, and Wolman (2003) analyze optimal monetary policy in an economy where the relevant distortions are imperfect competition, staggered price setting, and monetary transaction frictions. Schmitt-Grohe and Uribe (2004) and Siu (2004) focus on the joint optimal determination of monetary and fiscal policy. However, the issue of optimal policy in the face of households' credit constraints has been largely neglected.

A point of particular concern in defining the planner's problem in an economy with heterogeneity is the specification of the relevant objective function. Let's define by ω the weight assigned to the saver's utility in the planner's objective function. Then we assume that the planner maximizes the following weighted utility function:

$$(34) \qquad W_0 \equiv (1 - \omega) \sum_{t=0}^{\infty} \beta^t U(C_t, D_t, N_t) + \omega \sum_{t=0}^{\infty} \gamma^t U(\tilde{C}_t, \tilde{D}_t)$$

The Ramsey problem under commitment can be described as follows. Let $\{\lambda_{k,t}\}_{t=0}^{\infty}$ $(k = 1, 2, ..)$ represent sequences of Lagrange multipliers on the constraints (6), (8), (9) to (12), (15), (16), (21), (24), (25), and (27), respectively. For given stochastic processes $\{A_{c,t}, A_{d,t}\}_{t=0}^{\infty}$, plans for the control variables $\{N_t, N_{c,t}, N_{d,t}, b_t, D_t, \tilde{D}_t, C_t, \tilde{C}_t, \pi_{c,t}, \pi_{d,t}, \psi_t, q_t, R_t\}_{t=0}^{\infty}$ and for the costate variables $\{\lambda_{k,t}\}_{t=0}^{\infty}$ represent a first-best constrained allocation if they solve the following maximization problem:

$$(35) \qquad\qquad\qquad \max E_0 \{W_0\},$$

subject to equations (6), (8), (9) to (12), (15), (16), (21), (24), (25), and (27).

---

16. To name a few, see Adao, Correia, and Teles (2003), Khan, King, and Wolman (2003), Schmitt-Grohe and Uribe (2005), Woodford (2003), King and Wolman (1999), Clarida, Galí, and Gertler (1999), Benigno and Woodford (2005).

(Non-) Recursivity and Solution Approach

As a result of (some of) the constraints in problem (35) exhibiting future expectations of control variables, the maximization problem as spelled out in equation (35) is intrinsically nonrecursive.[17] As first emphasized in Kydland and Prescott (1980) and then developed by Marcet and Marimon (1999), a formal way to rewrite the same problem in a recursive stationary form is to enlarge the planner's state space with additional (pseudo) costate variables. Such variables bear the crucial meaning of tracking, along the dynamics, the value to the planner of committing to the preannounced policy plan. In appendix B and C, we show how to formulate the optimal plan in an equivalent recursive lagrangian form.

We then proceed in the following way. First, we compute the stationary allocations that characterize the deterministic steady state of the efficiency conditions of problem (35) for $t > 0$. We label this as deterministic Ramsey steady state. We then compute a log-linear approximation of the respective policy functions in the neighborhood of the Ramsey steady state.

The spirit of this exercise deserves some further comments. In concentrating on the (log-linear) dynamics in the neighborhood of the Ramsey steady state, we are in practice implicitly assuming that the economy has been evolving and policy has been conducted around such a steady state for a long period of time. Technically speaking, this amounts to assuming that the initial values of the lagged multipliers involved in problem (35) are set equal to their initial steady-state values. Khan, King, and Wolman (2003) apply this strategy to an optimal monetary policy problem in a closed economy. Under certain conditions, one can show that this approach is equivalent to evaluating policy as invariant from a "timeless perspective," as described in Woodford (2003) and Benigno and Woodford (2005).

3.4.2   Calibration

In this section, we describe our benchmark parameterization of the model. This will be useful for the quantitative analysis conducted in the following. We set the saver's and borrower's discount factors, respectively, to $\gamma - 0.99$ and $\beta = 0.98$. This implies an annual real interest rate (which is pinned down by the saver's degree of time preference) of $(1/\gamma)^4 = 1.04$.

Throughout, we are going to assume that the Ramsey planner sets the preference weight $\omega = 1/2$, although we will report sensitivity results on the value of this parameter.

We wish to work under the assumption that all outstanding debt is collateralized (hence, we ignore the role of unsecured debt, e.g., credit cards) and that durables are long-lived. Thus, in this context, durables mainly

---

17. See Kydland and Prescott (1980). As such, the system does not satisfy per se the principle of optimality, according to which the optimal decision at time t is a time invariant function only of a small set of state variables.

capture the role of housing. The depreciation rate for houses is much lower than the one usually assumed for physical capital and comprises between 1.5 percent and 3 percent per year. Because our model is parameterized on a quarterly basis, we set $\delta = 0.025^{\wedge}(1/4)$.

The annual average loan-to-value (LTV) ratio on home mortgages is roughly 0.75. This is the average value over the 1952 to 2005 period. This number has increased over time, as a consequence of financial liberalization, from about 72 percent at the beginning of the sample to a peak of 78 percent around the year 2000. The same parameter is only slightly higher when considering mortgages on new houses.[18] Hence, we set the LTV ratio as $(1 - \chi) = 0.75$, which yields $\chi = 0.25$.

The share of durable consumption in the aggregate spending index, defined by α, is set in such a way that $\delta(D + \tilde{D})$, the steady-state share of durable spending in total spending, is 0.2. This number is consistent with the combined share of durable consumption and residential investment in the National Income and Product Accounts (NIPA) tables. The elasticity of substitution between varieties in the nondurable sector ε_c is set equal to 8, which yields a steady state markup of about 15 percent. As a benchmark case, we set the elasticity of substitution between durable and nondurable consumption $\eta = 1$, implying a Cobb-Douglas specification of the consumption aggregator in equation (3).

In order to parameterize the degree of price stickiness in *nondurables*, we observe that, by log-linearizing equation (21) around a zero-inflation steady state, we can obtain an elasticity of inflation to real marginal cost (normalized by the steady-state level of output)[19] that takes the form $(\varepsilon_c - 1)/\vartheta$. This allows a direct comparison with empirical studies on the New Keynesian Phillips curve, such as in Galí and Gertler (1999) and Sbordone (2002) using a Calvo-Yun approach. In those studies, the slope coefficient of the log-linear Phillips curve can be expressed as $(1 - \hat{\vartheta})(1 - \beta\hat{\vartheta})/\hat{\vartheta}$, where $\hat{\vartheta}$ is the probability of not resetting the price in any given period in the Calvo-Yun model. For any given values of ε_c, which entails a choice on the steady-state level of the markup, we can thus build a mapping between the frequency of price adjustment in the Calvo-Yun model $1/(1 - \hat{\vartheta})$ and the degree of price stickiness ϑ in the Rotemberg setup. Traditionally, the sticky price literature has been considering a frequency of four quarters as a realistic value. Recently, Bils and Klenow (2004) argue that the observed frequency of price adjustment in the United States is higher and in the order of two quarters. As a benchmark, we parameterize $1/(1 - \hat{\vartheta}) = 4$, which implies $\hat{\vartheta} = 0.75$. Given $\varepsilon_c = 8$, the resulting stickiness parameter satisfies

---

18. The source for these numbers is the Federal Housing Finance Board (http://www .fhfb.gov).

19. To produce a slope coefficient directly comparable to the empirical literature on the New Keynesian Phillips curve, this elasticity needs to be normalized by the level of output when the price adjustment cost factor is not explicitly proportional to output, as assumed here.

$\vartheta = Y\hat{\vartheta}(\varepsilon - 1)/[(1 - \hat{\vartheta})(1 - \beta\hat{\vartheta})] \sim 17.5$, where Y is steady-state output. In general, however, we will conduct sensitivity experiments on the role of nondurable price stickiness.

A critical issue concerns the assumed degree of price stickiness in *durables*. The comprehensive study by Bils and Klenow (2004) does not report any direct evidence on the degree of stickiness of long-lived durables, housing in particular. It may appear reasonable to assume that house prices are in general more flexible than nondurable goods prices. Barsky, House, and Kimball (2007) argue that sales prices of new houses are flexible. One reason may be that, as the price of new houses can be negotiated, the role of fixed components such as menu costs can be more easily neutralized. In addition, figure 3.2 shows that house prices feature a pronounced business-cycle component.

To simplify matters, we will then work under the extreme assumption that durable prices are flexible. This assumption is not immaterial. Barsky, House, and Kimball (2007) argue that the assumption of flexible durable prices dramatically affect the ability of standard sticky price models to reproduce the empirical effects of monetary policy shocks on durable and nondurable spending. In particular, if durable prices are flexible, and against the observed vector autoregression (VAR)-based evidence, durable spending contracts during expansions. In addition, and regardless of the assumed degree of stickiness in nondurables, flexible durable prices tend to impart a form of neutrality to policy shocks to the entire economy. However, in Monacelli (2005), we argue that the introduction of borrowing constraints and the consideration of durables as collateral assets help in reconciling the model with the observed empirical evidence. In this vein, borrowing constraints act as a substitute of nominal rigidity in durable prices. In an extreme case, when nondurable prices are also assumed to be flexible, borrowing constraints can even partially act as a substitute of nominal rigidity altogether in generating nonneutral effects of monetary policy.

Table 3.1 summarizes the details of our baseline calibration:

3.5   The Role of Nominal Debt

We begin our analysis by focusing on the role of durable goods and nominal private debt in shaping the optimal policy problem. To that goal, we first analyze the optimal policy problem in a simplified version of our model featuring no borrowing constraints. Here we wish to understand whether the mere introduction of durable consumption can alter the basic prescription of price stability of the baseline New Keynesian sticky price model. We conclude that durability per se is not sufficient to alter that prescription. We then proceed by introducing household heterogeneity and a role for private debt. We show that the presence of nominal debt generates a redistributive margin for monetary policy that induces the policy

Table 3.1   **Baseline calibration**

Parameter	Description	Value
β	Borrower's discount rate	0.98
γ	Saver's discount rate	0.99
δ	Durable depreciation rate	$0.025^{1/4}$
χ	Inverse LTV ratio	0.25
ω	Ramsey preference weight	0.5
ϑ_d	Price stickiness in D sector	0
ϑ_c	Price stickiness in ND sector	17.5
ε_c	Price elasticity of demand in D sector	8
ε_d	Price elasticity of demand in ND sector	8
η	Elasticity of substitution between D and ND	1

Notes: LTV = loan-to-value; D = durable goods; ND = nondurable goods.

authority to optimally generate deviations from price stability. In equilibrium, though, we find that those deviations are small.

In both cases, we work with a simpler goods market structure, featuring only *one final-good sector.* In particular, the competitive final-good producer assembles intermediate goods purchased from a continuum of monopolistic competitive producers who run a linear production function as in equation (17) and set prices optimally, subject to quadratic adjustment costs. In this simpler economy, the final good can be costlessly transformed into both nondurable and durable consumption. Hence, the relative price between durable and nondurable goods is always $q_t = 1$. As a result, movements in the relative price of durables do not affect the ability of borrowing directly.

The reason for first concentrating on this simpler case is twofold. First, it allows us to study the role of nominal debt per se in shaping the normative conclusions of a standard New Keynesian model. Second, it allows to abstract from an additional distortion inherent to the two-sector economy and stemming from fluctuations in the relative price of durables. In fact, with two sectors, asymmetric sectoral shocks necessarily require, as already illustrated in the preceding, an adjustment in relative prices that cannot be brought about efficiently if prices are sticky in one or both sectors.[20]

3.5.1 Benchmark: Price Stability with Durable Goods and Free Borrowing

In order to understand the role of durable goods in the monetary policy problem, we begin by assuming that agents can borrow and lend freely at the market interest rate. This amounts to assuming away heterogeneity in

20. See Aoki (2001) and Woodford (2003) for an analysis of optimal monetary policy in the face of sectoral asymmetric shocks.

patience rates. To obtain such a benchmark version of our model, it suffices to evaluate the system of first-order conditions in equations (9) to (12) in the particular case of $\psi_t = 0$. This version of the model corresponds to a standard representative agent sticky price model simply augmented by the introduction of durable goods. In appendix A, we describe the structure of the competitive equilibrium in this case and the corresponding simplified form of the optimal policy problem.

Figure 3.4 displays impulse responses to a productivity shock in the benchmark economy with sticky prices, durable goods, and free borrowing under the Ramsey equilibrium.

We compare two cases: (1) $\delta = 1$ (full depreciation), which amounts to assuming away durability; and (2) $\delta = 0.025^{1/4}$, which is the value for the physical depreciation rate assumed in our baseline parameterization. It is evident that the benchmark result of price stability under the Ramsey policy is robust to the introduction of durable goods. With higher productivity (and income), the household would like to increase both durable and nondurable spending. Because durables can only be accumulated slowly

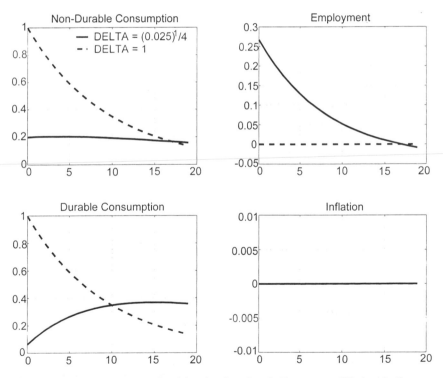

Fig. 3.4   Responses to a productivity shock under the Ramsey equilibrium in the model with *no* borrowing constraints: *With* durability (solid line) and *without* durability ($\delta = 1$, dashed line)

(recall that the household wishes to smooth the end-of-period stock D_t and *not* the flow of durable spending) and because efficiency requires the marginal utility of current consumption to be equated to the expected discounted marginal value of acquiring a new durable, nondurable consumption also moves more gradually, relative to the case $\delta = 1$. Inflation, however, is completely stabilized in both cases. The intuition is simple. The presence of durables does not introduce per se any additional distortion that the planner wishes to neutralize. Hence, as it is well understood in the standard case, the planner induces the economy to behave as if prices were completely flexible. This is obtained via monetary policy generating an expansion in demand, which induces firms to smooth markup fluctuations completely, thereby validating unchanged prices (zero inflation) as an equilibrium outcome.[21]

3.5.2   Optimal Inflation Volatility with Nominal Debt

Next we wish to consider the role of nominal private debt. In this version of the model, we reintroduce two critical features: (1) heterogeneity (in patience rates); (2) a collateral constraint (on the impatient household). Still, we continue to work within the one-final-good sector model (whose details are reported in appendix B). In this context, we wish to understand whether the possibility of using inflation to affect borrower's net worth, and, therefore, to marginally redistribute wealth from the saver to the borrower, may induce the planner to deviate from a strict price stability policy.

Figure 3.5 illustrates how the introduction of borrowing constraints affects the equilibrium dynamics. Once again, we show impulse responses to a rise in productivity. We compare two alternative cases, corresponding to two values of parameter χ (solid line for low χ and dashed line for high χ). A higher value of χ implies a lower LTV ratio and, therefore, a reduced ability to collateralize the purchase of durables (hence, broadly speaking, a tighter borrowing constraint). Unlike a standard permanent-income consumer, the borrower has preferences tilted toward current consumption. Hence, in the face of higher productivity (income), the borrower wishes to increase current consumption (reduce saving) and do so to a larger extent than the saver. In equilibrium, the two agents find it optimal to trade debt, with the saver ending up lending resources to the borrower, thereby financing the surge in consumption of the latter.

Notice that the presence of a collateral requirement (whose strength is indexed by χ) induces a wealth effect on the borrower's labor supply. In or-

---

21. The implication of durability in response to productivity shocks are relevant for another dimension, namely the equilibrium response of employment. One can show that whereas employment tends typically to fall in sticky price models in response to a rise in productivity (as a result of a downward shift in labor demand; see Galí 1999), the introduction of durables reverses the sign of that response (see Monacelli [2006] on this particular point). This is also evident in figure 3.4.

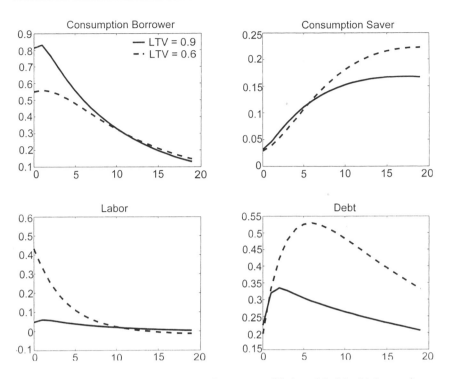

Fig. 3.5 Productivity shock under the Ramsey equilibrium: Model with borrowing constraint (*low* versus *high* loan-to-value ratio 1 – χ)

der to expand consumption, the borrower needs to optimally balance the purchasing of new debt with an increase in labor supply necessary to fi nance new collateral. The tighter the borrowing constraint (i.e., the higher χ), the more stringent the necessity of increasing labor supply. This debt-labor supply margin is indeed a general feature of models with collateral re-quirements.[22]

In principle, because debt is predetermined in nominal terms, monetary policy can affect borrower's net worth by altering the real value of the out-standing debt service. Hence, it is interesting to understand whether move-ments in inflation are part of the Ramsey equilibrium. In figure 3.6, we show impulse responses of inflation to the same productivity shock. We re-port paths for inflation under alternative values of ω, the weight attributed to the saver's utility in the Ramsey optimization problem. It is clear that the introduction of nominal debt alters the conclusions of the benchmark

22. For instance, Campbell and Hercowitz (2005) emphasize this channel as a vehicle for business-cycle expansions/contractions. In their analysis, the reduction in equity require-ments brought about by the financial reforms of the early eighties is a candidate theory of the so-called great moderation (Stock and Watson 2002).

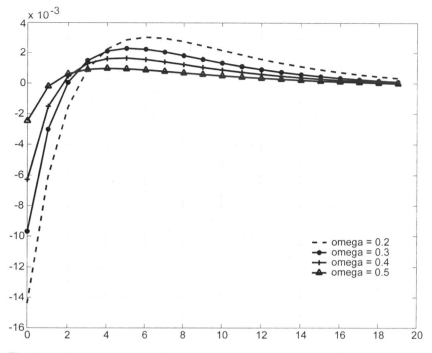

Fig. 3.6   Optimal response of inflation to a productivity shock: Effect of varying saver's weight ω in planner's objective

model in that it constitutes a motivation for deviating from a price stability prescription.

3.5.3   Heterogeneity

Notice that the amplitude of the inflation movements is decreasing in the saver's weight ω. Intuitively, the larger the Ramsey weight on saver's utility, the smaller the inflation redistributive motive and, supposedly, the smaller the variability in inflation. This conjecture is confirmed in figure 3.7, which plots the volatility of inflation as a function of ω. Under the Ramsey equilibrium, larger values of ω correspond to a smaller volatility of inflation.

Analyzing the effects of alternative values of ω is one way to address the role of heterogeneity. Another way is to look at the effect on inflation variability of different values of the borrower's patience rate β. For values of β approaching γ, we should observe a vanishing of the role of heterogeneous patience rates, which is key in driving the consumption-saving preferences of the two agents over the business cycle. Figure 3.8 plots optimal inflation volatility as a function of β.

The support of β is limited to the right by γ, which corresponds to the

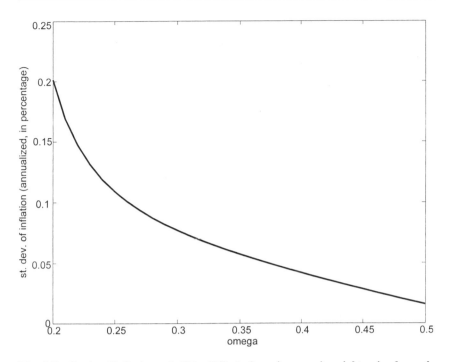

Fig. 3.7 Optimal inflation volatility: Effect of varying saver's weight ω in planner's objective function

saver's patience rate. Thus, we see that inflation variability falls for larger values of β. In particular, as the borrower's patience rate converges to the one of the saver, inflation volatility approaches the benchmark value of zero. In other words, when heterogeneity in patience rates vanishes, the borrowing constraint ceases to be binding (in, and in the vicinity of, the steady state), and the Ramsey equilibrium tends to mimic the optimal dynamics of a representative agent economy with price stickiness represented in the previous section. In that environment, we have already shown that reproducing the flexible price allocation corresponds to the constrained optimum.

3.5.4 Price Rigidity

It is important to emphasize that movements in inflation in the Ramsey equilibrium are overall very small. Due to the presence of price stickiness, in fact, inflation is costly. Hence, monetary policy has to optimally balance the incentive to offset the price stickiness distortion with the one of marginally relaxing borrower's collateral constraint via the redistributive effect of inflation. To explore how this trade-off is resolved, in figure 3.9 we plot

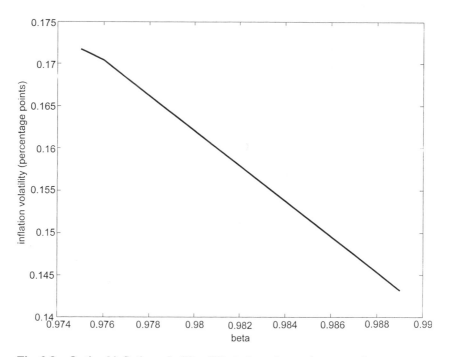

Fig. 3.8   Optimal inflation volatility: Effect of varying patience rate β

the volatility of inflation in the Ramsey equilibrium against the degree of nominal price stickiness ϑ. The extreme case of ϑ approaching zero corresponds to full price flexibility. Hence, we see that changes in the price stickiness parameter have a dramatic effect on the equilibrium volatility of inflation. In the case of flexible prices, inflation volatility (on an annualized basis) is around 2.5 percent. Yet already for small values of ϑ, the volatility of inflation drops significantly and remains barely positive.

This result points to a general feature shared with a large array of equilibrium business-cycle models recently employed for optimal monetary policy analysis: namely, the important quantitative role played by the price stickiness distortion in driving the optimal monetary policy prescription toward stable inflation. One may notice the resemblance of this result (despite the very different environment) with the one of Schmitt-Grohe and Uribe (2004) and Siu (2004), who analyze a joint problem of optimal monetary and fiscal policy. In that case, and in the presence of nominal nonstate contingent government debt, the planner balances the incentive to generate inflation variability, in order to reduce the finance cost of debt, with the cost of price variability due to price stickiness. Like here, optimal monetary policy points to resolving the trade-off in favor of minimizing the price stickiness distortion.

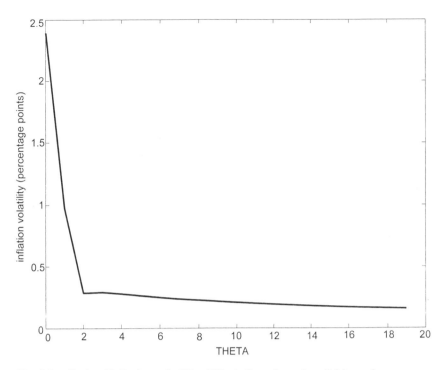

Fig. 3.9   **Optimal inflation volatility: Effect of varying price stickiness** ϑ

3.6   Durable Prices and Collateral

So far we have worked with a specialized version of our model featuring only one final-good sector. In so doing, we have neglected any role for endogenous fluctuations in the relative price of durables in directly affecting the ability of borrowing. Our normative analysis has so far highlighted the role of two distortions. On the one hand, the planner tries to minimize the cost of price variability due to the presence of price adjustment costs. At the same time, with nominal debt, the presence of a collateral requirement induces the planner to resort to inflation variability in order to marginally affect the borrowing constraint. However, the specification of a two-sector model introduces further distortions. With sectoral asymmetric shocks, the equilibrium dynamics require an adjustment in the relative price of durables. In the presence of price frictions or borrowing constraints, these relative price movements may be brought about in a way nonconsistent with efficiency. We investigate this point in the following.

3.6.1   Inefficient Movements in Relative Prices

Let us define the *natural* relative price of durables as the relative price prevailing with full price flexibility *and* free borrowing. In addition, we can define the relative price *gap* as the deviation of the relative price from that natural benchmark.

Figure 3.10 illustrates how the introduction of price stickiness or borrowing constraints alters the equilibrium dynamics. We plot-selected variables in response to a rise in productivity in the nondurable sector for three alternative cases: (1) the solid lines report responses in the *natural* case, that is, an economy with fully flexible prices and free borrowing; (2) the dashed lines display the equilibrium in the presence of collateral requirements only (therefore, with full price flexibility in both sectors); and (3) the dotted lines display the dynamics when the two-sector model with borrowing constraints is augmented with price stickiness in nondurables.

Consider the behavior in the natural case, which constitutes our benchmark. In the absence of borrowing frictions and with price flexibility in both sectors, the rise in productivity in nondurables is completely absorbed

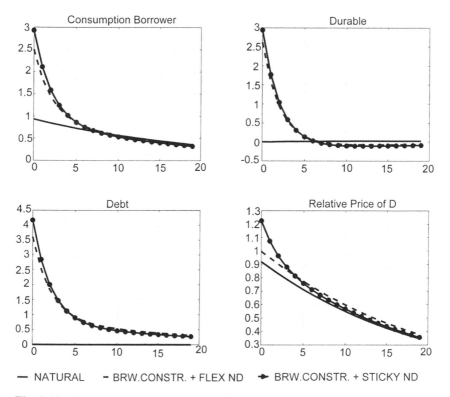

— NATURAL   – BRW.CONSTR. + FLEX ND   •— BRW.CONSTR. + STICKY ND

Fig. 3.10   Responses to a productivity shock in the two-sector model: (1) Natural versus (2) borrowing constraints with *flexible* nondurable prices versus (3) borrowing constraints with *sticky* nondurable prices

Note: In these simulations, monetary policy is described by a simple Taylor rule $R_t = 1.5\pi_{c,t}$.

via a rise in the relative price of durables and an expenditure switching toward nondurables. Consistently, equilibrium demand for durables is unchanged, and a rise in consumption is observed only in the nondurable sector.

Matters are different when a borrowing constraint is added (although still under the assumption of full price flexibility in both sectors). In this case (dashed line), the demand for durables must rise due to the need of financing further borrowing, with this expansion in durable demand being amplified for larger values of the inverse loan-to-value parameter χ. Importantly, in an efficient equilibrium with free borrowing and lending, the borrower would indeed like (given his impatience) to expand borrowing to finance current consumption, but in that case there would be no need to resort to an increase in demand for durables. Hence, we observe that the relative price of durables rises above its natural level in the presence of collateral constraints, with this effect being driven by a collateral motive on durable demand.

Figure 3.10 also illustrates that the adding of stickiness in nondurable prices introduces a further source of deviation from the natural relative price. With sticky nondurable prices, the demand for debt rises more and so does the demand for durables, inducing a larger increase in the relative price gap. Overall, the results indicate that both frictions contribute to generate inefficient movements in the relative price q_t from its natural level.

3.6.2   Collateral Effects

In the two-sector model, movements in the relative price of durables are important, for they exert an endogenous effect on the ability of borrowing. In this section, we highlight the importance of the transmission channel linking durable (asset) price variations to consumption. We define as *collateral effect* the acceleration on borrowing and consumption that derives from the price of durables directly affecting the right-hand side of equation (8). The intuition is akin to the "credit-cycle" phenomenon emphasized in Kiyotaki and Moore (1997) and Iacoviello (2005). The mechanism is simple. The rise in productivity in the nondurable sector boosts the relative price of durables and, therefore, the value of the asset that can be used as a collateral (the term $q_t D_t$ in equation ([8]). The resulting increase in borrower's net worth rises the demand for borrowing, which is necessary to finance a surge in consumption. In turn, the higher demand for collateral boosts durable prices even further, feeding back on the value of available collateral in a self-sustained cycle.

To illustrate this effect on borrowing and consumption, we compare responses to a productivity shock (in the nondurable sector) in two cases: with and without collateral effect. The absence of a collateral effect is obtained by specifying the borrowing constraint in the slightly modified form:

(36)
$$b_t = (1 - \chi) D_t q_t^\xi,$$

where $\xi \in [0, 1]$. We can broadly define ξ as a parameter measuring the ability of the constrained household to convert a rise in his net worth in ability of borrowing. The case with full collateral effect corresponds to $\xi = 1$, while the case without collateral effect corresponds to ξ small and close to zero. Figure 3.11 suggests that movements in durable prices are crucial for the amplification of the joint dynamics of borrowing and consumption. With a collateral effect at work, the rise in durable consumption and debt is much larger relative to the case in which the collateral effect is artificially shut down.

Importantly, the collateral effect produces also an acceleration in borrower's nondurable consumption. The intuition works as follows. The rise in the real price of durables, via its direct effect on the collateral value, induces a *fall* in the marginal value of borrowing (ψ_t in our model). In other words, the rise in asset prices boosts the ability of borrowing and induces a marginal relaxation of the borrowing constraint. This implies, for the borrower, a fall in the marginal utility of current (nondurable) consumption relative to the option of shifting consumption intertemporally (in other words, a violation of the Euler equation; see equation [12]), which can be validated only by a *rise* in current consumption. In turn, the increased demand for borrowing further boosts durable demand and in turn the real price of durables, inducing a circle that positively feedbacks on nondurable consumption.

3.6.3   Durable Prices: Ramsey versus Taylor

In this section, we investigate the behavior of the relative price of durables in the Ramsey equilibrium. To that goal, we proceed by solving the more general version of the Ramsey problem, as outlined in equation (35). In particular, we wish to understand whether dampening the volatility of durable (asset) prices should be of any concern for monetary policy in this context. It is important to recall, as suggested in the preceding, that there are two reasons for why the relative price of durables fluctuates in deviation from its natural benchmark: (1) the presence of a collateral requirement; (2) price stickiness in the nondurable sector.

To this goal, we compare the dynamics in the Ramsey equilibrium with a simple generalized Taylor type rule of the following form:

(37)
$$\frac{R_t}{R} = \left(\frac{\pi_{c,t}}{\pi_c} \right)^{\phi_\pi} \left(\frac{q_t}{q} \right)^{\phi_q} \qquad \phi_\pi > 1, \quad \phi_q \geq 0,$$

where R, π_c, q correspond, respectively, to the steady-state values of R_t, $\pi_{c,t}$, q_t. A rule such as equation (37) encompasses several alternative policy regimes, including the extreme cases of (1) strict nondurable inflation tar-

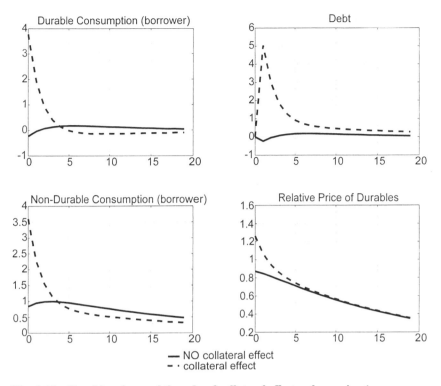

Fig. 3.11   Durable prices and the role of collateral effect on borrowing (responses to a productivity shock in ND sector)

Note: In these simulations, monetary policy is described by a simple Taylor rule $R_t = 1.5\pi_{c,t}$.

geting ($\phi_\pi \to \infty$, henceforth ND-targeting); and (2) strict durable price targeting ($\phi_q \to \infty$, henceforth q-targeting).

In figure 3.12, we compare the effects of a productivity rise in the nondurable sector under the Ramsey equilibrium with both the extreme cases of ND targeting and q-targeting. One central finding is immediately worth noticing: the amplitude of the response of the relative price of durables in the Ramsey equilibrium is intermediate between the extreme cases of ND targeting and q-targeting. In general, this feature of the Ramsey allocation is common to the equilibrium behavior of the entire set of variables displayed.

Consider a strict q-targeting rule first, and compare it with the outcome under the Ramsey equilibrium. Evidently, this type of policy rule is largely detrimental for the borrower. Not only it does induce a shut-off of the collateral effect on borrowing outlined in the preceding, but it also hinders the necessary relative sectoral adjustment, thereby generating a sizeable drop

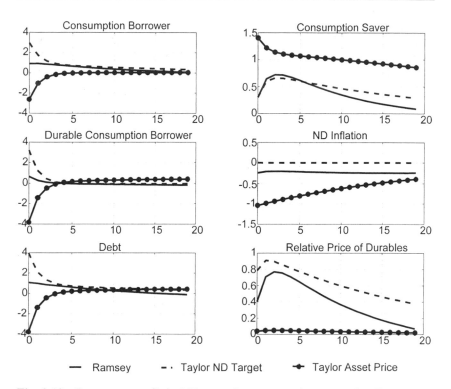

Fig. 3.12   Ramsey versus Strict ND-targeting versus strict q-targeting: Responses to a productivity shock in ND sector

in the demand for collateral and borrowing, and, therefore, in turn, for nondurable consumption by the borrower. At the same time, because debt falls in equilibrium, this reduces the consumption-smoothing possibilities by the saver, whose consumption volatility is in fact amplified relative to the Ramsey-optimal allocation.

Consider next a ND-targeting rule. In that case, the effect is somewhat symmetric. Relative to a Ramsey equilibrium, strict stabilization of nondurable inflation induces an acceleration in the relative price of durables and in turn an amplified rise in borrowing and durable demand. This, in turn, is also reflected in an amplified surge in consumption by the borrower.

Interestingly, the Ramsey-optimal policy emerges as an intermediate case between the two extreme targeting cases outlined in the preceding.[23] In fact, the planner wishes to optimally balance two margins. On the one

---

23. Notice that the behavior of the relative price of durables q_t is exactly symmetric in the case of a productivity shock in the *durable* sector. In that case (not displayed here), q_t tends to fall under ND-targeting, while it falls less in the Ramsey equilibrium.

hand is the incentive to partially stabilize inefficient movements in the relative price of durables due to the presence of a collateral constraint. On the other hand, the planner also has the objective to stabilize nondurable inflation due to the presence of a sticky price distortion in that sector. Hence, a monetary policy that aimed at strictly targeting nondurable inflation would lead to an excess volatility in real durable prices and to an excess volatility in the borrower's consumption and debt.

3.7 Conclusions

We have laid out a framework for the analysis of optimal monetary in the presence of nominal private debt and of a collateral constraint on borrowing. The emergence of a borrowing-lending decision in the equilibrium of our economy requires heterogencity between a patient and an impatient agent. At the margin, and relative to a standard representative agent economy with price stickiness, optimal policy in this context requires a partial use of inflation volatility with a redistributive motive. However, the fact that, due to the presence of price stickiness, inflation movements are costly heavily biases the optimal policy prescription toward low inflation volatility. When durable prices have the additional effect of altering the value of the collateral and in turn the ability of borrowing, optimal policy has a motive for partially stabilizing the relative price of durables. This is due to the fact that the model incorporates a motive for durable goods demand (and, therefore, a pressure on prices) that is strictly linked to the presence of an inefficient collateral requirement.

There are several other features that have remained unexplored in the current context and that would deserve a more thorough normative analysis. First, detailed institutional characteristics of mortgage markets should be more adequately incorporated, for instance, the presence of an equity withdrawal margin, the possibility of resorting to mortgage refinancing, as well as the decision of opting for a flexible versus fixed rate mortgage structure. Second, the analysis should contemplate the possibility that borrowing constraints may be only occasionally binding, and that, in the presence of uncertainty, the borrower's decisions may be driven by a precautionary saving motive. Third, one may wish to extend this framework to the presence of collateral requirements on other forms of spending, such as business investment. Fourth, one may think of extending the present context to comprise the interaction between monetary and fiscal policy. The analysis of the latter, in particular, may fruitfully take advantage of the implications of the assumed heterogeneity and of the presence of a collateral constraint, in order to emphasize, in particular, transmission channels of fiscal policy alternative to the typical ones embedded in the standard neoclassical growth model.

Appendix A

Competitive Equilibrium with Durable Goods and Free Borrowing

The (symmetric) equilibrium in the one-sector economy with free borrowing, durable goods, and sticky prices can be described (in compact form) by the following set of equations:

Efficiency condition on nondurable and durable consumption:

$$(38) \qquad 1 = \frac{U_{d,t}}{U_{c,t}} + \beta(1-\delta)E_t\left\{\frac{U_{c,t+1}}{U_{c,t}}\right\}$$

Standard Euler equation:

$$(39) \qquad 1 = \beta\,E_t\left\{\frac{U_{c,t+1}}{U_{c,t}}\,\frac{R_t}{\pi_{t+1}}\right\}$$

Phillips curve:

$$(40) \qquad (\pi_t - 1)\pi_t = \gamma E_t\left\{\frac{U_{c,t+1}}{U_{c,t}}\,(\pi_{t+1} - 1)\,\pi_{t+1}\right\}$$

$$+ A_t N_t \frac{\varepsilon}{\vartheta}\left(-\frac{U_{n,t}}{A_t U_{c,t}} - \frac{\varepsilon - 1}{\varepsilon}\right)$$

Resource constraint:

$$(41) \qquad A_t N_t = C_t + D_t - (1-\delta)D_{t-1} + \frac{\vartheta}{2}(\pi_t - 1)^2,$$

where π_t is Consumer Price Index (CPI) (final-goods) inflation. For any policy sequence $\{R_t\}_{t=0}^{\infty}$ and stochastic process $\{A_t\}_{t=0}^{\infty}$, an (imperfectly) competitive equilibrium in the one-sector economy with sticky prices and durable consumption is a sequence $\{N_t, D_t, C_t, \pi_t\}_{t=0}^{\infty}$, solving equations (38) to (41). A Ramsey equilibrium in this economy can be obtained by maximizing $E_0\{\sum_{t=0}^{\infty}\beta^t U(C_t, D_t, N_t)\}$, subject to equations (38), (40) and (41).

Appendix B

One (Final-Good) Sector Economy

Here we briefly describe the competitive equilibrium in the one-sector economy, featuring sticky prices, heterogenous patience rates, and borrowing constraints:

Borrower's efficiency condition on nondurable and durable consumption:

$$(42) \qquad U_{c,t} = U_{d,t} + \beta(1 - \delta)E_t\{U_{c,t+1}\} + U_{c,t}(1 - \chi)\psi_t$$

Deviation from Euler equation:

$$(43) \qquad \psi_t = 1 - \beta E_t\left\{\frac{U_{c,t+1}}{U_{c,t}}\frac{R_t}{\pi_{t+1}}\right\}$$

Phillips curve:

$$(44) \qquad (\pi_t - 1)\pi_t = \gamma E_t\left\{\frac{\tilde{U}_{c,t+1}}{\tilde{U}_{c,t}}(\pi_{t+1} - 1)\pi_{t+1}\right\}$$

$$+ A_t N_t \frac{\varepsilon}{\vartheta}\left(-\frac{U_{n,t}}{A_t U_{c,t}} - \frac{\varepsilon - 1}{\varepsilon}\right)$$

Resource constraint:

$$(45) \qquad A_t N_t = C_t + D_t - (1 - \delta)D_{t-1} + \frac{\vartheta}{2}(\pi_t - 1)^2$$

Borrower's flow budget constraint (with $T_t = 0$):

$$(46) \qquad C_t + q_t[D_t - (1 - \delta)D_{t-1}] + \frac{R_{t-1}b_{t-1}}{\pi_{c,t}} = b_t + \frac{-U_{n,t}}{A_t U_{c,t}}N_t$$

Saver's efficiency conditions:

$$(47) \qquad \tilde{U}_{c,t} = \gamma E_t\left\{\tilde{U}_{c,t+1}\frac{R_t}{\pi_{t+1}}\right\}$$

$$(48) \qquad \tilde{U}_{c,t} = \tilde{U}_{d,t} + \gamma(1 - \delta)E_t\{\tilde{U}_{c,t+1}\}$$

For any policy sequence $\{R_t\}_{t=0}^{\infty}$ and stochastic process $\{A_t\}_{t=0}^{\infty}$, an (imperfectly) competitive equilibrium in the one-sector economy with sticky prices and borrowing constraints in a sequence $\{N_t, b_t, D_t, \tilde{D}_t, C_t, \tilde{C}_t, \pi_t\}$, solving equations (42) to (48).

Recursive Ramsey Problem in the One-Sector Economy

Let's define by $\Delta \equiv \beta^{\omega}\gamma^{1-\omega}$ the discount factor relevant from the viewpoint of the Ramsey planner problem, where ω is the weight attached on the saver's utility. In the following, we describe the form of the optimal policy program in recursive form. This is necessary because the original problem is not time-invariant due to the fact that some constraints (such as equation [21]) exhibit future expectations of control variables. The recursive lagrangian problem in the economy with one final-good sector can be written as follows:

$$\max E_0 \sum_{t=0}^{\infty} \Bigg[[(1 - \omega)\beta^t U(C_t, D_t, N_t) + \omega\gamma^t U(\tilde{C}_t, \tilde{D}_t)]$$

$$+ \Delta^t\lambda_{1,t}(\{U_{c,t}[1 - (1 - \chi)\psi_t]\} - U_{d,t}) - \Delta^{t-1}\lambda_{1,t-1}\beta(1 - \delta)U_{c,t}$$

$$+ \Delta^t\lambda_{2,t}\left[(\psi_t - 1)\frac{U_{c,t}}{R_t}\right] + \Delta^t\lambda_{2,t-1}\frac{U_{c,t}}{\pi_t}$$

$$+ \Delta^t\lambda_{3,t}\left(\frac{U_{\tilde{c},t}}{R_t}\right) - \gamma\Delta^{t-1}\lambda_{3,t-1}\frac{U_{\tilde{c},t}}{\pi_t}$$

$$+ \Delta^t\lambda_{4,t}\left[A_tN_t - C_t - \tilde{C}_t - D_t - \tilde{D}_t - \frac{\vartheta}{2}(\pi_t - 1)^2\right] + \Delta^{t+1}\lambda_{4,t+1}(1 - \delta)(D_t + \tilde{D}_t)$$

$$+ \Delta^t\lambda_{5,t}[b_t - (1 - \chi)D_t]$$

$$+ \Delta^t\lambda_{6,t}\left(C_t + D_t + \frac{R_{t-1}b_{t-1}}{\pi_t} - b_t + \frac{U_{n,t}}{U_{c,t}}N_t\right) - \Delta^t\lambda_{6,t+1}\left[(1 - \delta)D_t + \frac{R_tb_t}{\pi_{t+1}}\right]$$

$$+ \Delta^t\lambda_{7,t}(\tilde{U}_{c,t} - \tilde{U}_{d,t}) - \gamma\Delta^{t-1}\lambda_{7,t-1}(1 - \delta)\tilde{U}_{c,t}$$

$$+ (\Delta^t\lambda_{8,t} - \gamma\Delta^{t-1}\lambda_{8,t-1})[\tilde{U}_{c,t}(\pi_t - 1)\pi_t] - \Delta^t\lambda_{8,t}\frac{\varepsilon A_tN_t}{\vartheta}\left(\frac{-U_{n,t}}{A_tU_{c,t}} - \mu^{-1}\right)\Bigg],$$

where $\mu \equiv \varepsilon/(\varepsilon - 1)$ is the steady state markup, and π_t is final good inflation. This maximization program is recursive saddle-point stationary in the amplified state space $\{A_t, Z_t\}$, where $Z_t \equiv \{\lambda_{1,t-1}, \lambda_{2,t-1}, \lambda_{3,t-1}, \lambda_{7,t-1}, \lambda_{8,t-1}\}$. The corresponding (log-linearized) set of first-order conditions describe a time-invariant system of difference equations to the extent that the initial condition $Z_0 = \bar{Z} \equiv [\bar{\lambda}_1, \bar{\lambda}_2, \bar{\lambda}_3, \bar{\lambda}_7, \bar{\lambda}_8]$ is added, where $\bar{\lambda}_j$ denotes the steady-state value of multiplier λ_j, for $j = 1, 2, 3, 7, 8$.

Appendix C
Recursive Ramsey Problem in the Two-Sector Economy

The recursive lagrangian for the Ramsey problem in the two sector economy can be written

$$\max E_0 \sum_{t=0}^{\infty} \left[\left[(1 - \omega)\beta^t U(C_t, D_t, N_t) + \omega\gamma^t U(\tilde{C}_t) \right] \right.$$

$$+ \Delta^t\lambda_{1,t}(\{q_t U_{c,t}[1 - (1 - \chi)\psi_t]\} - U_{d,t}) - \Delta^{t-1}\lambda_{1,t-1}\beta(1 - \delta)q_t U_{c,t}$$

$$+ \Delta^t\lambda_{2,t}\left[(\psi_t - 1)\frac{U_{c,t}}{R_t}\right] + \Delta^t\lambda_{2,t-1}\frac{U_{c,t}}{\pi_{c,t}}$$

$$+ \Delta^t\lambda_{3,t}\left(\frac{U_{\tilde{c},t}}{R_t}\right) - \gamma\Delta^{t-1}\lambda_{3,t-1}\frac{U_{\tilde{c},t}}{\pi_{c,t}}$$

$$+ \Delta^t\lambda_{4,t}[A_{c,t}N_{c,t} - C_t - \tilde{C}_t - \frac{\vartheta_c}{2}(\pi_{c,t} - 1)^2]$$

$$+ \Delta^t\lambda_{5,t}[b_t - (1 - \chi)D_t q_t]$$

$$+ \Delta^t\lambda_{6,t}\left(C_t + q_t D_t + \frac{R_{t-1}b_{t-1}}{\pi_{c,t}} - b_t + \frac{U_{n,t}}{U_{c,t}}N_t\right) - \Delta^t\lambda_{6,t+1}\left[(1 - \delta)D_t q_{t+1} + \frac{R_t b_t}{\pi_{c,t+1}}\right]$$

$$+ \Delta^t\lambda_{7,t}(q_t \tilde{U}_{c,t} - \tilde{U}_{d,t}) - \Delta^{t-1}\lambda_{7,t-1}[-\gamma(1 - \delta)\tilde{U}_{c,t}q_t]$$

$$+ (\Delta^t\lambda_{8,t} - \gamma\Delta^{t-1}\lambda_{8,t-1})[\tilde{U}_{c,t}(\pi_{c,t} - 1)\pi_{c,t}] - \Delta^t\lambda_{8,t}\frac{\varepsilon_c A_{c,t}N_{c,t}}{\vartheta_c}\left(\frac{-U_{n,t}}{A_{c,t}U_{c,t}} - \mu_c^{-1}\right)$$

$$+ (\Delta^t\lambda_{9,t} - \gamma\Delta^{t-1}\lambda_{9,t-1})[q_t\tilde{U}_{c,t}(\pi_{d,t} - 1)\pi_{d,t}] - \Delta^t\lambda_{9,t}\frac{\varepsilon_d A_{d,t}N_{d,t}}{\vartheta_d}\left(\frac{-U_{n,t}}{A_{d,t}U_{c,t}q_t} - \mu_d^{-1}\right)$$

$$+ \Delta^t\lambda_{10,t}\left[A_{d,t}N_{d,t} - D_t - \tilde{D}_t - \frac{\vartheta_d}{2}(\pi_{d,t} - 1)^2\right] + \Delta^{t+1}\lambda_{10,t+1}(1 - \delta)(D_t + \tilde{D}_t)$$

$$+ \Delta^t\lambda_{11,t}(N_t - N_{c,t} - N_{d,t})$$

$$+ \Delta^t\lambda_{12,t}\left(\frac{\pi_{d,t}}{\pi_{c,t}q_t}\right) - \Delta^{t+1}\lambda_{12,t+1}q_{t+1}^{-1}\right]$$

This maximization program is recursive saddle-point stationary in the amplified state space $\{\mathbf{A}_{c,t}, \mathbf{A}_{d,t}, Z'_t\}$, where $Z'_t \equiv \{\lambda_{1,t-1}, \lambda_{2,t-1}, \lambda_{3,t-1}, \lambda_{7,t-1}, \lambda_{8,t-1}, \lambda_{9,t-1}\}$ and with the initial condition $Z'_0 = \bar{Z}'$.

References

Adao, B., Correia, I., and P. Teles. 2003. Gaps and triangles. *Review of Economic Studies* 60:4.

Aoki, A. 2001. Optimal monetary policy responses to relative price changes. *Journal of Monetary Economics* 48:55–80.

Aizcorbe, A., A. Kennickell, and K. Moore. 2003. Recent changes in U.S. family finances: Evidence from the 1998 and 2001 Survey of Consumer Finances. *Federal Reserve Bulletin* 89:1–32.

Atkinson, A. B., and J. Stiglitz. 1980. The design of tax structure: Direct versus indirect taxation. *Lectures on public economics.* New York: McGraw-Hill.

Barsky, R., C. House, and M. Kimball. 2007. Sticky price models and durable goods. *American Economic Review* 97 (3): 984–98.

Becker, R. 1980. On the long-run steady state in a simple dynamic model of equilibrium with heterogenous agents. *Quarterly Journal of Economics* 95(2):375–82.

Becker, R., and C. Foias. 1987. A characterization of Ramsey equilibrium. *Journal of Economic Theory* 41:173–84.

Benigno, P., and M. Woodford. 2005. Inflation stabilization and welfare: The case of a distorted steady state. *Journal of the European Economic Association,* 3:1185–1236.

Bernanke, B., and M. Gertler. 1989. Agency costs, net worth and business fluctuations. *American Economic Review* 79 (March): 14–31.

Bils, M., and P. Klenow. 2004. Some evidence on the importance of sticky prices. *Journal of Political Economy* 112 (October): 947–85.

Calza, A., T. Monacelli, and L. Stracca. 2006. Mortgage markets, collateral constraints and monetary policy: Do institutional factors matter? European Central Bank and Università Bocconi. Mimeograph.

Campbell, J. Y., and Z. Hercowitz. 2005. The role of collateralized household debt in macroeconomic stabilization. NBER Working Paper no. 11330. Cambridge, MA: National Bureau of Economic Research.

Campbell, J. Y., and G. Mankiw. 1989. Consumption, income and interest rates: Reinterpreting the time series evidence. *NBER Macroeconomics Annual 1989,* ed. O. J. Blanchard and S. Fischer, 234–44. Cambridge, MA: MIT Press.

Chari, V. V., L. J. Christiano, and P. J. Kehoe. 1991. Optimal fiscal and monetary policy: Some recent results. *Journal of Money, Credit and Banking* 23:519–39.

Clarida, R., J. Galí, and M. Gertler. 1999. The science of monetary policy: A New Keynesian perspective. *Journal of Economic Literature* 37:1661–1707.

Erceg, C., and A. Levin. 2005. Optimal monetary policy with durable consumption goods. *Journal of Monetary Economics* 53 (7): 134–59.

Galí, J. 1999. Technology, employment, and the business cycle: Do technology shocks explain aggregate fluctuations? *American Economic Review* 249:271.

Galí, J., and M. Gertler. 1999. Inflation dynamics: A structural econometric analysis. *Journal of Monetary Economics* 44 (2): 195–222.

Galí, J., D. Lopez-Salido, and J. Valles. 2007. Understanding the effects of government spending on consumption. *Journal of the European Economic Association* 5 (1): 227–70.

Goodfriend, M., and R. King. 1997. The new neoclassical synthesis and the role of monetary policy. *NBER Macroeconomics Annual 1997,* ed. B. Bernanke and J. Rotemberg, 231–83. Cambridge, MA: MIT Press.

Iacoviello, M. 2005. House prices, borrowing constraints and monetary policy in the business cycle. *American Economic Review* 95 (3): 739–64.

Jappelli, T., and M. Pagano. 1989. Consumption and capital markets imperfections: An international comparison. *American Economic Review* 79:1088–1105.

Khan, A., R. King, and A. L. Wolman. 2003. Optimal monetary policy. *Review of Economic Studies* 60:4.

King, R., and A. L. Wolman. 1999. What should the monetary authority do when prices are sticky. In *Monetary policy rules,* ed. J. B. Taylor, 349–98. Chicago: University of Chicago Press.

Kiyotaki, N., and J. Moore. 1997. Credit cycles. *Journal of Political Economy* 105 (April):211–48.

Krusell, P., and A. Smith. 1998. Income and wealth heterogeneity in the macroeconomy. *Journal of Political Economy* 106:867–96.

Kydland, F., and E. C. Prescott. 1980. Dynamic optimal taxation, rational expectations and optimal control. *Journal of Economic Dynamics and Control* 2:79–91.

Lucas, R. E., and N. Stokey. 1983. Optimal fiscal and monetary policy in an economy without capital. *Journal of Monetary Economics* 12:55–93.

Marcet, A., and R. Marimon. 1999. Recursive contracts. Universitat Pompeu Fabra. Unpublished Manuscript.

Monacelli, T. 2005. New Keynesian models, durable goods and borrowing constraints. Unpublished Manuscript.

———. 2006. Productivity shocks, employment and durable goods. Unpublished Manuscript.

Ramsey, F. P. 1927. A contribution to the theory of taxation. *Economic Journal* 37:47–61.

Schmitt-Grohe, S., and M. Uribe. 2004. Optimal fiscal and monetary policy under sticky prices. *Journal of Economic Theory* 114:198–230.

———. 2005. Optimal inflation stabilization in a medium-scale macroeconomic model. Duke University. Mimeograph.

Siu, H. 2004. Optimal fiscal and monetary policy with sticky prices. *Journal of Monetary Economics* 51 (3): 575–607.

Stock, J., and M. Watson. 2002. Has the business cycle changed and why? *NBER Macroeconomics Annual 2002,* ed. M. Gertler and K. Rogoff, 159–218. Cambridge, MA: MIT Press.

Woodford, M. 1986. Stationary sunspot equilibria in a finance contrained economy. *Journal of Economic Theory* 40:128–37.

———. 2003. *Interest and prices: Foundations of a theory of monetary policy.* Princeton, NJ: Princeton University Press.

Comment   Hanno Lustig

Introduction

Inflation has significant distributional effects when households issue and invest in nominal securities. In recent work, Doepke and Schneider (2007) carefully document large distributional effects from the rise in inflation in the United States in the seventies. The surge in inflation transferred real resources from the old to the young, who borrow in nominal terms, mainly to finance the house purchase. There may be some welfare benefits from this type of redistribution if these borrowers are financially constrained. In the context of an overlapping generations model, Doepke and Schneider (2007) argue that the large inflation episodes in the seventies improved the welfare of the average U.S. household. These distributional

Hanno Lustig is an assistant professor of economics at the University of California, Los Angeles, and a faculty research fellow of the National Bureau of Economic Research.

effects are at the heart of Monacelli's chapter. Monacelli wants an answer to the following normative question: how does a benevolent planner who is in charge of monetary policy trade off the potential redistribution benefits of inflation against the costs?

Model Ingredients

There are three key ingredients of the model: (1) household heterogeneity in time discount rates, (2) sticky prices, and (3) nominal noncontingent debt backed by housing collateral. Monacelli's Ramsey planner trades off the benefits of surprise inflation on the household side of the economy against the costs on the producer side.

Environment

The model builds on recent work by Iacoviello (2005) and Kiyotaki and Moore (1997). The model has two types of households, borrowers and savers. The borrowers are more impatient, and they run into binding borrowing constraints. These households issue nominal one-period, risk-free debt that is collateralized by their equity in their house. On the producer side, firms incur an adjustment cost when changing the nominal price of a commodity. Monacelli's work fits in the Ramsey tradition. By setting monetary policy, the planner in fact chooses the optimal equilibrium prices and allocations to maximize the weighted utilities of the borrower and the saver, subject to the constraints imposed by the environment. On the household side, the planner faces two types of frictions. These frictions impede the planner in equalizing the intertemporal marginal rate of substitution of these two different types of households.

The first friction is the *market incompleteness*. Agents only trade nominal one-period, risk-free debt. This implies that, when the planner chooses consumption streams, he has to make sure that the "nominal" present discounted value of these consumption streams less the labor income streams is measurable with respect to (w.r.t) the history of shocks at $t-1$ at each node, simply because the market structure does not allow for any state contingency in the nominal value of net financial wealth. The planner faces what Aiyagari et al. (2002) refer to as *measurability constraints*.

The second friction is the *borrowing constraint*. The planner has to make sure that the "nominal" present discounted value of these consumption streams less the labor income streams satisfies the borrowing constraint at each node.

Of course, the planner can use unanticipated inflation to create some state contingency in the real value of the household's liabilities, thus partially completing the market. But the Ramsey planner needs to trade off these benefits from surprise inflation against the costs. On the production side, firms incur adjustment costs when changing the nominal prices. This is the third friction in the model: nominal *prices are sticky.* Hence, surprise inflation distorts the firm's production decisions.

Inflation: Not a Bad Thing after All?

The Ramsey planner chooses a monetary policy that gets the economy as close as possible to the first-best, given these constraints and costs.

Completing the Market with Inflation

In the absence of sticky price frictions, the planner would simply create enough inflation volatility—and, hence, state contingency in the real value of the borrower's outstanding liabilities—to equalize the intertemporal marginal rate of substitution (IMRS) of both households in each state of the world. In this case, the measurability constraint does not bind. However, once we add sticky prices to the picture, the incentives of the planner change.

Sticky Prices

In Monacelli's model, all of the state contingency in real returns comes from unexpected inflation because the nominal debt has a maturity of just one period. Hence, the only way to change its real value by 10 percent is through surprise inflation of 10 percent. And, perhaps not surprisingly, the planner decides not to use this channel very much at all when prices are sticky. But let us consider the case in which the borrower issues *n*-period debt. Well, in this case, the planner could commit to spreading out the increase in inflation and the short rate over the next *n* periods, instead of bunching all of it in this period. This reduces the size of the distortion of allocations. Instead of creating 10 percent inflation today, the government could raise the price level by a bit more than 10 percent, but spread out over a longer period—shorter than the maturity of the debt. This strategy delivers the same percent drop in the real value of outstanding debt. The quantitative conclusion of Monacelli's chapter might be quite different if there were was nominal debt of longer maturities available to households. The average maturity of outstanding mortgages for U.S. households is probably well in excess of ten years because most new contracts have a thirty-year maturity. So this seems like an important issue.

Fiscal Policy

Similar issues arise in the fiscal policy debate. Governments issue mostly nominal non-contingent debt, and, hence, they have to resort to inflation to create some optimal state contingency in the returns. For example, in case of a bad fiscal shock, the government would like to lower the real value of outstanding debt to avoid large increases in marginal tax rates (Lucas and Stokey 1983). However, if the government cannot issue real, contingent securities but instead only issues nominal debt, it could create inflation instead (to complete the market). Siu (2004) studies optimal monetary and fiscal policy in an environment where the government only issues one-period nominal debt, and he finds the costs of inflation outweigh the benefits, just like Monacelli. The government sticks to the Friedman rule. However, Lustig, Sleet, and Yeltekin (2006) show that this conclusion changes when the government can issue nominal debt of longer maturities. They show it is optimal for the government to issue nominal debt of longer maturities because this allows the government to spread out the costs of distortions associated with inflation over the maturity of the debt. The government willingly pays the risk premium on longer bonds because of its superior hedging properties.

Suggestions for Future Work

As pointed out by the author as well, it seems of key importance to have agents in the model trade securities that look more like mortgage contracts. Real-world mortgage contracts come with fixed rates (FRM) or floating rates (ARM). Of course, this inflation channel is much less effective when a large fraction of households have adjustable rate mortgages. The fraction of fixed rate mortgages varies substantially over time. In fact, it varied between 30 percent and 80 percent over the last twenty years (Campbell 2006). This variation would have first-order effects on how much leverage monetary policy has in redistributing wealth by creating inflation. The slope of the yield curve is a key determinant of the fixed-floating ratio in the United States.[1] When the slope of the yield curve increases and this causes more households to chooses ARMs, the Fed actually loses much of its ability to redistribute wealth across households.

Interestingly, Campbell (2006) argues that households seem to act as if long-term interest rates are strongly mean-reverting because they tend to lock in the low interest rates by choosing an FRM when interest rates are low. Perhaps households choose the FRMs because they provide some hedging. When interest rates are low to begin with, households may think the monetary authorities are more likely to bail them out by creating inflation when a bad aggregate shock hits the economy.

Conclusion

Monetary policymakers have a powerful redistribution tool at their disposal. Inflation redistributes wealth from those who hold nominal debt to

---

1. Hemert, Kojien, and Nieuwerburgh (2006) argue that a lot of the variation can be attributed to variation in the inflation risk premium. In most of the models used for analyzing normative questions on monetary policy, risk premiums are small and constant. In the data, there is plenty of evidence of large and time-varying risk premiums in bond markets.

those who have issued it. This chapter begins to provide some answers in a stylized model to the question of whether this motive would cause a benevolent planner to deviate from the Friedman rule in a significant way. The provisional answer is no, but more work is needed to obtain precise, quantitative answers.

References

Aiyagari, S. R., A. Marcet, T. J. Sargent, and J. Seppala. 2002. Optimal taxation without state-contingent debt. *Journal of Political Economy* 110 (6): 1220–54.

Campbell, J. Y. 2006. Household finance. *Journal of Finance* 61 (4): 1553–1607.

Doepke, M., and M. Schneider. 2007. Inflation as a redistribution shock: Effects on aggregates and welfare. *Journal of Political Economy,* forthcoming.

Hemert, O. V., R. Kojien, and S. V. Nieuwerburgh. 2006. Mortgage timing. New York University, Working Paper.

Iacoviello, M. 2005. House prices, borrowing constraints, and monetary policy in the business cycle. *American Economic Review* 95:739–61.

Kiyotaki, N., and J. Moore. 1997. Credit cycles. *Journal of Political Economy* 105 (2): 211–48.

Lucas, R. J., and N. L. Stokey. 1983. Optimal fiscal and monetary policy in an economy without capital. *Journal of Monetary Economics* 12 (1): 55–93.

Lustig, H., C. Sleet, and S. Yeltekin. 2006. Fiscal hedging and the yield curve. Carnegie Mellon University, Working Paper.

Siu, H. 2004. Optimal fiscal and monetary policy with sticky prices. *Journal of Monetary Economics* 51: 547–607.

Discussion Summary

Tommaso Monacelli emphasized that the assumption of noncontingent debt was both realistic and a general feature of the literature. Making debt state contingent was an obvious policy implication, but would be hard to implement.

Richard H. Clarida said that steady states in models with heterogeneous agents and borrowing constraints were complicated and asked whether it was obvious that there was such a steady state in this model. Monacelli replied that in fact it was the existence of the binding borrowing constraint that ensured a unique steady state.

As a matter of practical relevance, Clarida commented on the increasing importance of securitized debt as opposed to bank lending and drew attention to how the two forms of credit intermediation have differing implications for the financial system's response to stress.

Marvin Goodfriend said that he liked the way the chapter combined macroeconomics and finance. The only way to decide which frictions were important was to put them all in the same model and to have a horse race.

In this case, it appeared that the goal of stabilizing prices was most important.

Andrew Levin suggested that life-cycle considerations could be a significant source of heterogeneity; for example, older households might choose to consume their housing wealth in a model with overlapping generations. In a similar vein to Goodfriend's comment about the blend of macroeconomics and finance, Levin also pointed to the benefit of integrating political economy issues into the analysis. For example, in the late 1800s, some farmers favored a higher rate of inflation as a means of diminishing the real value of their debts.

4

Inflation Illusion, Credit, and Asset Prices

Monika Piazzesi and Martin Schneider

4.1 Introduction

Modigliani and Cohn (1979) argue that investors who suffer from inflation illusion price assets as if real payoffs are discounted at the nominal interest rate. They use this idea to rationalize the stock market slump of the 1970s, which coincided with high inflation and high nominal interest rates. More recently, inflation illusion has again become a prominent theme in the financial press because the 2000s housing boom coincides with low inflation and low nominal interest rates.[1] However, an early critique of the inflation illusion hypothesis (Summers 1983) points out that the 1970s saw a housing boom coincide with *high* nominal interest rates. International evidence presented in the following points to a more general stylized fact: in many countries, house-price booms occurred in the high-inflation 1970s and further—typically stronger—booms occurred in the more recent low-inflation environment.

Monika Piazzesi is a professor of finance and the John Huizinga Faculty Fellow at the Graduate School of Business, University of Chicago, and a research associate of the National Bureau of Economic Research. Martin Schneider is an assistant professor of economics at New York University, and a faculty research fellow of the National Bureau of Economic Research.

For comments and suggestions, we thank Olivier Blanchard, Markus Brunnermeier, John Campbell, Martin Feldstein, and participants at the NBER Asset Pricing and Monetary Policy Preconference in November 2005 and the Conference in May 2006. We also thank Pedro Gete for excellent research assistance. The views expressed herein are those of the authors and not necessarily those of the Federal Reserve Bank of Minneapolis or the Federal Reserve System.

1. For example, see Pam Woodall's survey on world property markets in the *Economist* on March 29, 2003. The article "Castles in Hot Air" in this report and an earlier article, "Going through the Roof" in the *Economist* on March 28, 2002, argue that inflation illusion fuels the recent house-price boom.

In this chapter, we consider the effect of inflation illusion on asset prices in a general equilibrium model with heterogeneous agents. The key assumptions are that (1) agents who suffer from inflation illusion interact with "smart" agents in markets for nominal credit instruments, and (2) borrowing must be backed by real estate. We show under these assumptions that nominal interest rates move with smart agents' inflation expectations, and housing booms occur whenever these expectations are either especially high or low. Moreover, the housing boom is stronger when credit markets are more developed, which suggests that recent financial development may have increased the potential for inflation illusion to drive house prices.

We are led to consider investor heterogeneity because we want our model to account for movements in nominal interest rates. In the data, nominal rates comove with measures of expected inflation, which suggests that at least some investors are aware of the distinction between real and nominal rates. For example, even if stock prices were low in the high inflation 1970s because illusionary investors were discounting at high nominal rates, someone must have also priced high inflation expectations into nominal rates. In our model, there are smart investors who understand the Fisher equation: bond returns are given by the nominal interest rate minus expected inflation. At the same time, there are illusion investors who believe that all changes in nominal rates reflect changes in real interest rates. The equilibrium nominal interest rate then moves—typically less than one for one—with changes in smart investors' inflation expectations.

The key effect in the model is that illusionary and smart investors disagree about real interest rates when smart investors' inflation expectations are either especially high or low. In either case, disagreement generates increased borrowing and lending among households as well as a house-price boom. To see how disagreement about real rates obtains, assume first that smart investors' inflation expectations rise above the historical mean and thus drive up nominal interest rates. Illusionary investors attribute any increase in nominal rates to an increase in real rates. As a result, they end up perceiving higher real rates than smart investors. In contrast, if smart investors have unusually low inflation expectations and drive down nominal rates, illusionary investors perceive lower real rates than smart investors.

Disagreement about real interest rates generates house-price booms if borrowing must be backed by real estate. Indeed, increased credit market activity raises the demand for collateral, which in turn drives up house prices. More specifically, our model generates two scenarios for a housing boom, illustrated in figure 4.1. The scenarios differ in which group of households perceives lower real rates and thus drives up house prices. In a low inflation environment, such as the 2000s, the increased demand for housing and mortgages is due to illusionary agents, who mistake low nominal rates for low real rates, while smart investors are happy to invest in bonds. In times of high expected inflation, such as the 1970s, the roles of

	smart households	illusionary households
1970s	expect high inflation	
(high nominal rate)	perceive low real rate	perceive high real rate
	$\Longrightarrow$ borrow and buy houses	$\Longrightarrow$ lend
2000s	expect low inflation	
(low nominal rate)	perceive high real rate	perceive low real rate
	$\Longrightarrow$ lend	$\Longrightarrow$ borrow and buy houses

Fig. 4.1   Housing booms under different inflation scenarios

the two groups are reversed: smart investors borrow and shift their portfolio toward real estate, while illusion agents are deterred from mortgages and housing, by high nominal rates.

The mechanism we emphasize works only if housing serves as collateral. If borrowing was not possible, disagreement about real interest rates would lead some agents to rebalance their portfolios from housing toward bonds and other agents to shift funds in the opposite direction. It is then not obvious why house prices should increase; indeed, in our model, they remain unchanged. However, if agents who perceive low real rates can build leveraged portfolios, thus investing more than their own wealth in housing, disagreement raises the demand for housing sufficiently to generate a boom. Moreover, the effect is stronger the more borrowers can leverage their portfolios: in the model, the equilibrium house price is increasing in the maximal loan-to-value ratio. More generally, broader access to credit and lower transaction costs in the credit market can be expected to work in the same direction.

While our model is motivated by disagreement about real interest rates that emerges because some investors suffer from inflation illusion, our formal analysis only assumes that investors disagree about the real payoff on nominal bonds. The theoretical effect we highlight is thus more general and could apply in situations where disagreement derives from other sources of heterogeneity. One example is differences in tax rates: investors in high tax brackets perceive a lower real return on bonds—and, if interest is tax deductible, a lower cost of borrowing—than investors in lower brackets. Another source of disagreement about real rates is differences in inflation expectations. This is considered in Piazzesi and Schneider (2006), where we use inflation surveys to document differences in expected inflation rates across age cohorts in the 1970s and quantify the effect of such differences for house and stock price movements at that time.

We have described illusionary investors as investors who mistake changes in nominal interest rates for changes in real rates. This mistake does not require investors to be unaware of inflation or to be wrong about the inflation rate. All that matters is that investors confuse real and nominal returns when making portfolio choice decisions. For example, consider an illusionary investor who compares the utility he obtains from buying a home to the nominal cost of borrowing. This investor agrees with his smart neighbor about expected inflation. However, the difference between the two neighbors is that the smart neighbor actually uses the expected inflation rate to compute the real cost of his mortgage. Indeed, disagreement about real interest rates does not require disagreement about inflation— differences in agents' understanding of the impact of inflation on returns is enough.[2]

Recently, there has been renewed interest in the empirical implications of inflation illusion in equity and real estate markets. Campbell and Vuolteenaho (2004) decompose the dividend yield on stocks into three components: expected dividend growth, a subjective risk premium (identified from a cross-sectional regression), and a "mispricing term." They show that positive correlation of dividend yields with inflation is mostly due to the mispricing term. This indicates that stocks are undervalued by conventional measures when inflation is high.[3] Brunnermeier and Julliard (2006) examine the relationship between house prices and inflation. They derive a decomposition for the price-rent ratio, that is, the price-dividend ratio on housing. Using data from the U.K. housing market, they construct a mispricing component of the price-rent ratio that is negatively related to inflation. By their measure, houses thus appear overvalued when inflation is low.

There are few formal models of inflation illusion. The so-called Fed model, widely used by practitioners, is sometimes used to motivate a monotonic relationship between asset prices and inflation. According to the Fed model, inflation illusion leads investors to apply a modified Gordon growth formula to determine the price-dividend ratio on long-lived assets:

---

2. This observation implies that we cannot derive evidence about illusion or the fraction of illusionary agents in the population from inflation surveys. In particular, many investors may suffer from inflation illusion today, even though the Michigan inflation survey does not indicate much inflation disagreement during the 2000s. It is an open and interesting question how we can design surveys (e.g., about mortgage planning) that are able to distinguish between illusion and disagreement.

3. Cohen, Polk, and Vuolteenaho (2005) study the cross section of stock returns and show that capital asset pricing model (CAPM) betas decrease with the inflation rate. This finding is also consistent with inflation illusion; when inflation is high, the compensation for each unit of market beta is lower than what the overall difference in stock returns and riskless securities would suggest.

instead of using the real interest rate to discount future (real) cash flows as in the usual formula, investors discount at the nominal rate. The modified formula is useful for thinking about stocks that appear undervalued in the 1970s and overvalued in the 1990s.[4] Its application to the housing market, however, runs into Summers's critique—house prices should be low together with stock prices in the 1970s.

The Fed model does not deliver a complete account of asset prices under inflation illusion because it takes the nominal interest rate as exogenous. It, therefore, sidesteps the question why nominal rates comove with expected inflation. In contrast, our general equilibrium model of inflation illusion determines the nominal rate endogenously and links it to smart investors' inflation expectations. In addition, our model is not subject to the Summers's critique. Indeed, inflation illusion matters in our model when inflation is far from its historical mean in either direction, and it induces a nonmonotonic relationship between mispricing in the housing market and inflation. The inflation illusion hypothesis is thus consistent with housing booms not only in the low-interest 2000s but also in the high-interest 1970s.

Basak and Yan (2005) also consider a general equilibrium model in which preferences of illusion investors are defined over nominal consumption. With power utility, investors who expect high inflation thus effectively discount the future at a lower (higher) rate if the intertemporal elasticity of substitution is larger (smaller) than one and interest rates reflect these preferences. Our approach differs in its emphasis on heterogeneity and housing as collateral (as in Kiyotaki and Moore 1997). Moreover, the preferences of illusion investors in our model do not depend on expected inflation.

The purpose of this chapter is to isolate the effects of inflation illusion on house prices and interest rates in general equilibrium; we thus abstract from many other factors that matter for asset prices. In particular, we do not consider other possible links between inflation and house-price booms. Feldstein (1980) has shown that the tax treatment of houses and mortgages makes housing a more attractive asset when expected inflation is high. On the one hand, inflation increases taxable nominal capital gains, which are more easily sheltered from tax for housing than for, say, equity. On the other hand, the inflation increases tax-deductible nominal mortgage interest and thus lowers the effective cost of borrowing.[5]

The chapter is organized as follows. Section 4.2 presents cross-country

---

4. Ritter and Warr (2002), Sharpe (2002), and Asness (2003) document that dividend yields on stocks are indeed highly correlated with nominal interest rates.

5. There is an interesting connection between this second effect and our analysis. When smart investors are in different tax brackets, an increase in expected inflation will make the effective costs of borrowing computed by Feldstein more different across households. Agents thus disagree more about (after-tax) real rates when inflation is high. Through the mechanism described in the preceding, this should generate further upward pressure on house prices: agents in high tax brackets would find it cheaper to take out a mortgage and drive up house prices, while agents in low tax brackets would be happy to lend.

evidence on price-rent ratios, using various house-price measures. Section 4.3 presents our heterogeneous agent model with inflation illusion. Section 4.4 describes equilibrium housing booms in high and low inflation environments. Section 4.5 explains how these equilibria capture the historical experience of the 1970s and 2000s. Section 4.6 concludes and discusses future research. Proofs are collected in the appendix.

4.2   Cross-Country Evidence

We construct an annual cross-country data set for the period 1970 to 2004. This sample period is dictated by the availability of house-price data. The data set covers twelve countries: Australia, Canada, France, Germany, Ireland, Italy, Japan, the Netherlands, Spain, Sweden, United Kingdom, and United States.

4.2.1   Price-Dividend Ratios for Stocks

To measure the price-dividend ratio for stocks, we rely on Morgan-Stanley Country Indexes available from the Web site www.msci.com. For each country, we obtain two annual series, labeled "price index" (PI) and "gross index" (GI), and compute the dividend yield as $(GI_t/G_{t-1})/(PI_t/PI_{t-1}) - 1$. This procedure recovers a price-dividend ratio with interpretable units. For example, the average PD-ratios in the United States and the United Kingdom were 35.9 and 26, respectively, over the 1970 to 2004 period.

4.2.2   Price-Rent Ratios for Houses

The measurement of price-dividend ratios for housing, or price-rent ratios, is more difficult because houses do not trade on exchanges like stocks. We have two options—data from national accounts or data on price indexes constructed by the national central banks available through the Bank of International Settlements (BIS). For the national accounts, we follow the methodology in Piazzesi, Schneider, and Tuzel (2007). We measure the numerator as the value of the aggregate residential housing stock and the denominator as aggregate expenditures on housing services, including owner-estimated rents. We have data from national accounts for the United States and the United Kingdom. Based on price indexes constructed by the national central banks, we measure the national residential price index divided by the consumer price index for each country. These data are available from the BIS. To measure real rents, we use the rent component of each country's consumer price index available from Datastream and divide by the consumer price index.[6]

---

6. There are two missing observations in the BIS data set. First, we interpolate the 2004 observation for Ireland using data from the *Annual Housing Statistics Bulletin* published by the

National account data have several advantages. First, the resulting price-rent ratios have meaningful units because the numerator and denominator are measured in dollars. For example, the average price-rent ratios in the United States and the United Kingdom over the 1970 to 2004 period were 17.6 and 26.5, respectively. In contrast, the units of PD-ratios based on house price and rent indexes are not meaningful; the ratios are normalized to 1 in some base year (which is 1985 in fig. 4.2). The ratios are only useful for looking at percentage changes over time.

Second, the price-rent ratios from national accounts do not involve any quality judgements. Again, the reason is that they are measured in dollars. In contrast, an index construction tracks the evolution of the purchase or rental value of an appropriately defined "unit of housing." The definition of "one unit" of housing does not only involve the square footage of living space but also quality changes of that space over time. The quality judgements are especially problematic for price-rent ratios because the numerator and denominator are constructed by different agencies that may use different definitions.

We can correct for quality changes at low frequencies by taking out linear time trends from real rents in the denominator. We will plot the resulting corrected ratios as dotted lines in our figures. Examples of such low-frequency changes in quality are modern amenities—such as air conditioning, central heating, and electricity—which were absent from homes a century ago. Today's homes also benefit from infrastructure in cities—such as roads, sidewalks, and public transportation—which has improved slowly over time. However, correcting linear time trends does not take into account high-frequency changes in quality such as quality variations of homes traded over the business cycle or shifting neighborhood effects.

Finally, price-rent ratios from national accounts are available for a long time period, while most house price indexes start in the 1970s. In this chapter, we do not exploit this advantage of the national accounts data, because we focus on stock and house price movements around the high-inflation episode in the 1970s and the recent low-inflation episode.

4.2.3   Inflation and Real Interest Rates

For each country, we obtain annual consumer-price inflation and the three-month nominal interest rate on government bonds from the International Monetary Fund's (IMF) International Financial Statistics database. We construct the ex post real rate as the difference between the nominal rate and the inflation rate.

Irish Department of the Environment, Heritage, and Local Government. Second, we interpolate the 1970 observation for Spain, assuming that real house price growth is equal to real rent growth for that year.

4.2.4   Cross-Country Empirical Facts

Figures 4.2 and 4.3 show the price-dividend ratios of houses and stocks together with inflation and the real rate for each country. The PD-ratios of houses in figure 4.2 are measured with BIS data, while those in figure 4.3 are from national accounts. We focus on two episodes. During the inflation episode of the late 1970s and early 1980s, the PD-ratio of housing was relatively high, while the PD-ratio of stocks was relatively low. During the disinflation episode of the 2000s, the same situation emerges. Moreover, ex post real rates were low, or even negative, during both episodes.

4.3   The Model

Our model describes heterogeneous households, some of whom may suffer from inflation illusion. Households trade real estate and nominal assets (bonds) with each other as well as a "rest of the economy" sector. Real estate is an asset that cannot be sold short but that can be used as collateral. Bonds are special because they promise nominal payoffs and because they can be held in negative quantities.

4.3.1   Setup

There are two dates, 0 and 1, and one consumption good. There is a unit mass of risk-neutral households who discount date 1 consumption by the factor β. Households can invest in nominal bonds and real estate. A unit of real estate (or "houses") trades at the price p at date 0 and is expected to pay off p' at date 1. This payoff equals the resale price of the house plus any dividend from housing (which may include utility from ownership, etc.) Real estate cannot be sold short. Households can buy or sell one-period nominal bonds. If they choose to borrow by issuing bonds, they must respect a collateral constraint: the value of the bonds issued must be less than ϕ times the value of their house. The parameter ϕ is the maximal loan-to-value (LTV) ratio.

Nominal bonds trade at a price $1/R$ at date 0, where R is the (gross) nominal interest rate from date 0 to date 1. Households expect the nominal bond to pay off x goods at date 1. The expected payoff x is subjective and may be different for smart investors and illusionary households. For smart households who understand the Fisher equation and expect inflation π, the expected payoff of a nominal bond is $x = 1/\pi$.[7] Households who suffer

7. To see why, consider a nominal bond that costs $1/R$ dollars today and pays \$1 tomorrow, or $1/q'$ units of consumption, where q' is the price of consumption tomorrow. Now consider a portfolio of q nominal bonds. The price of the portfolio is $1/R$ units of numeraire and its payoff is $q/q' = 1/\pi$ units of consumption tomorrow. The model thus determines the price $1/R$ of a nominal bond in \$.

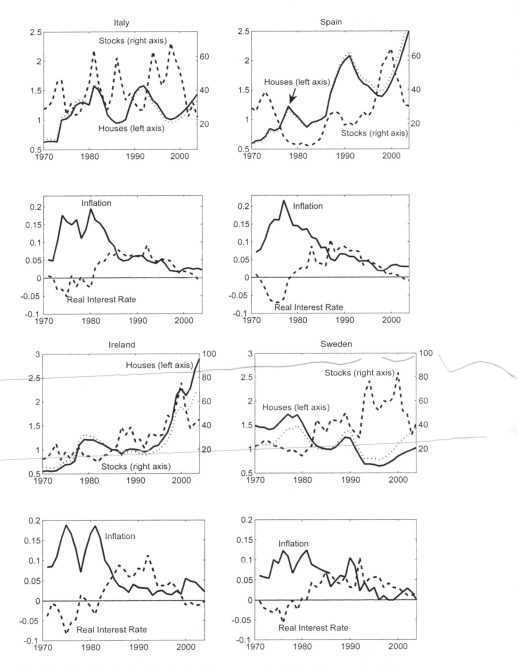

Fig. 4.2 Price-dividend ratios for housing measured with BIS house price indexes (left scale) and stocks (right scale), together with inflation and ex post real rates

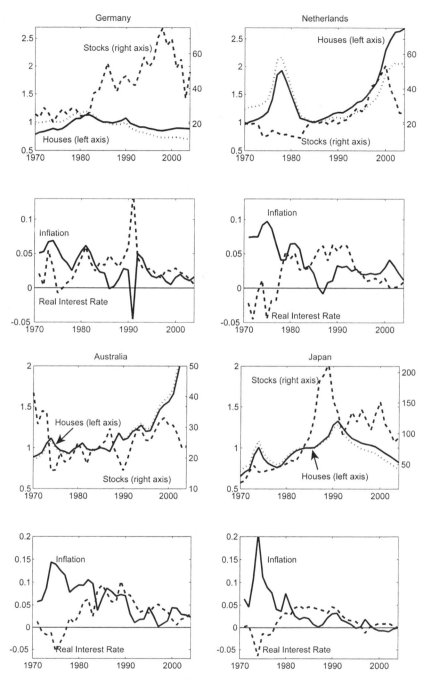

Fig. 4.2 **(cont.) Price-dividend ratios for housing measured with BIS house price indexes (left scale) and stocks (right scale), together with inflation and ex post real rates**

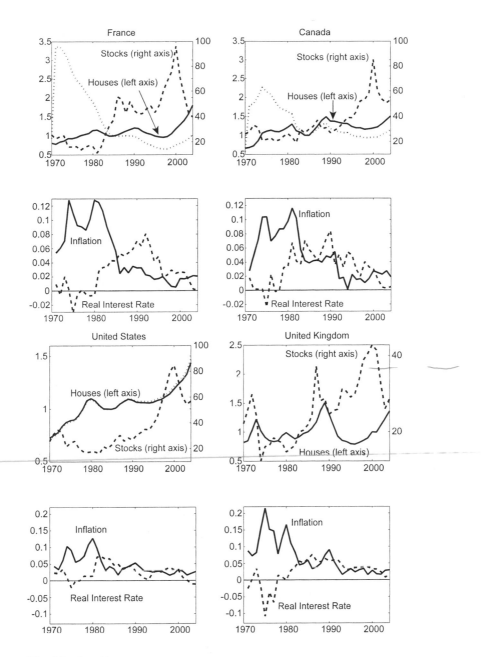

Fig. 4.2 (cont.)

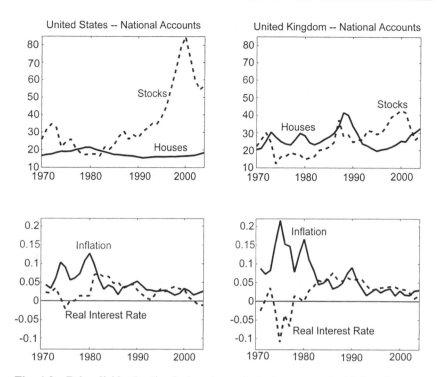

Fig. 4.3   Price-dividend ratios for housing and stocks measured with data from national accounts (on the same scale)

from inflation illusion do not necessarily associate x with their expected inflation rate.

Every household enters the period with an endowment of goods y, an endowment of houses $\bar{h}_0$, and an amount of goods $\bar{b}_0$ from past bond market activity. For given market prices p and $1/R$, as well as expected payoffs p' and x, a household chooses consumption c and c', the quantity of houses h, and the amount of goods invested in bonds b to solve

(1)
$$\max c + \beta c'$$
$$c + b + ph = \bar{w}(p) := \bar{b}_0 + p\bar{h}_0 + y$$
$$c' = (Rx)b + p'h,$$
$$c, c', h \geq 0,$$
$$-b \leq \phi ph.$$

This simple setup does not make explicit the utility agents obtain from housing. One way to interpret it is that housing services and other consumption are perfect substitutes, that the dividend from houses owned prior to trading at date 0 is contained in y, and that the date 1 dividend per unit of house is contained in p'. Our analysis holds fixed the dividend from housing so that changes in the house price p' represent changes in the price-rent ratio. We normalize the aggregate quantity of houses to 1. The initial endowment of housing units $\bar{h}_0$ thus represents the share of the total housing stock that is not acquired by households at date 0. We assume that households must own all houses after trading at date 0. In particular, the household sector cannot, on aggregate, sell houses to the rest of the economy. We thus assume $\bar{h}_0 < 1$.

The "rest of the economy" (ROE) sector consolidates the government, foreign, and business sectors. It may also contain "old" households who do not plan for the future because date 0 is the last period of their life. The ROE sells $1 - \bar{h}_0 > 0$ units of real estate in the housing market and $\bar{b} \geq 0$ worth of bonds in the credit market. It also redeems all bonds that households enter date 0 with (worth $\bar{b}_0$). It consumes the proceeds from these trades:

$$C^{\text{ROE}} = p(1 - \bar{h}_0) + \bar{b} - \bar{b}_0.$$

The value of new housing units $p(1 - \bar{h}_0)$ corresponds to gross residential investment plus the value of houses sold by "old" households to households planning for the future at date 0. This interpretation justifies our assumption that $\bar{h}_0 < 1$.

The bond endowment $\bar{b}_0$ consists of all payments households receive from past credit market activity, including interest on bonds held in the previous period. Household income y comprises labor income and dividends on real estate the household owns before trading at date 0. We assume throughout that the sum of this initial nonhousing wealth is large enough that the household sector can afford to buy all bonds supplied by the rest of the economy:

(2) $$\bar{b} < \bar{b}_0 + y.$$

We view this assumption as mild because changes in aggregate household sector asset positions tend to be small relative to aggregate income, as documented in Piazzesi and Schneider (2006).

We assume that expectations about payoffs on bonds and houses at date 1 are given exogenously. Households agree on the expected payoff from houses p'. However, the perceived payoff x of a nominal bond depends on households' understanding of real interest rates. To accommodate these differences in perceived bond payoffs, we work with a finite number of household types, indexed by i. There are α_i households of type i, with $\sum_i \alpha_i = 1$. The market prices of bonds and houses at date 0 are determined endogenously: $1/R$ and p, respectively. When choosing portfolios, households thus agree on the expected real housing return p'/p, but they disagree on the expected real bond return Rx^i, the ex ante real rate.

We consider temporary equilibria in which date 0 prices are endogenous but expectations about future payoffs are exogenously given (as in Grandmont 1977). A temporary equilibrium consists of a house price p and an interest rate R together with date 0 consumption and asset choices for the various types (c^i, b^i, h^i) such that (1) households optimize given their (subjective) expected payoffs (p', x^i), and (2) markets for goods and assets clear at date 0:

$$1 = \sum_i \alpha_i h^i,$$

$$\bar{b} = \sum_i \alpha_i b^i,$$

$$\sum_i \alpha_i c^i + C^{\text{ROE}} = y.$$

The market clearing condition for goods illustrates how ROE consumption accommodates deviations of household consumption from household income.

4.3.2   Modeling Inflation Illusion

Differences in the subjective bond payoffs x^i capture how illusionary and smart investors differ in their perceptions of real rates. We always assume that smart agents expect nominal bonds to pay off $x = 1/\pi$. In other words, smart agents understand the Fisher equation that says that the (ex ante) real interest rate equals the nominal interest rate—quoted in the market—minus the expected inflation rate:

$$(3) \qquad \text{real rate} = \log R - \log \pi.$$

In contrast, agents who suffer from inflation illusion believe that the payoff of nominal bonds x is constant. As a result, they view real interest rates as equal to nominal interest rates up to a constant:

$$(4) \qquad \text{real rate} = \log R - \text{constant}.$$

In particular, they interpret positive deviations of the nominal interest rates from its long-run average as an instance of high real rates, and they interpret unusually low nominal rates as unusually low real rates.

To generate time series predictions, we perform comparative statics exercises with respect to the distribution of nominal bond payoffs x^i. In particular, we compute equilibria for three versions of the model. Our benchmark exercise assumes that all agents agree on the same moderate, expected bond payoff. Intuitively, it captures a time period where expected inflation and the nominal rate are at their long-run averages. While agents in the model act as if they agree, they do think about interest rates in very different terms. Smart agents observe the nominal rate and believe that it reflects moderate inflation because of the Fisher equation (3). In contrast, illusion investors believe that it reflects a normal level of the real rate because of equation (4).

While this difference in thinking about interest rates does not matter in normal times, it matters when expected inflation and nominal rates deviate from their long-run average. We consider two scenarios where expected bond payoffs differ across agents. Under the 1970s scenario, smart investors expect high inflation and thus believe that bond payoffs are lower than average. However, illusion investors continue to believe that real interest rates are equal to nominal rates up to a constant. Formally, illusion investors thus behave as if bond payoffs are unchanged from the benchmark. Under the 2000s scenarios, smart investors expect low inflation and thus believe that bond payoffs are higher than average. As before, illusion investors act as if bond payoffs have not moved. In both cases, what matters in terms of the model is disagreement about ex ante real rates. It is thus helpful to first analyze a generic case, where some agents expect high bond payoffs and others expect low bond payoffs. This is what we do in the following. We then use the formal results to discuss the 1970s and 2000s scenarios.

4.4   Equilibrium House Prices and Interest Rates

In this section, we characterize equilibrium prices, first for a benchmark case with identical subjective real rates and then for the case of heterogeneous subjective real rates. The latter case is used in the following to argue that inflation illusion induces house price booms when smart investors have subjective real rates that are either very high or very low.

4.4.1   Solution to the Household Problem

The collateral constraint implies that households cannot borrow against future income. Instead, borrowing is useful only to set up leveraged portfolio strategies that increase the return on wealth. To solve problem (1), a household must, therefore, first determine the best portfolio strategy. If the return on the optimal portfolio is higher than the discount rate β^{-1}, then it is optimal to invest all date 0 wealth $\overline{w}$. If the best portfolio return is lower than the discount rate, it is instead optimal to save nothing and simply consume $\overline{w}$ at date 0.

Two polar portfolio strategies are available. If the subjective expected return on bonds, Rx^i, is higher than the return on housing, p'/p, then the optimal portfolio is 100 percent invested in bonds. If the expected bond return, or equivalently, the expected cost of borrowing, is lower than the housing return, the best portfolio strategy is to borrow up to the collateral constraint and invest in housing. For every unit invested in housing, only $1 - \phi$ units must come out of initial wealth because ϕ units can be borrowed. Therefore, the expected return on wealth invested in the leveraged portfolio—equivalently, the expected return on housing equity—is

$$\frac{1}{1 - \phi}\left(\frac{p'}{p} - \phi Rx^i\right).$$

In the following, we focus on equilibria in which the return on housing is less than or equal to the discount rate: $p'/p \leq \beta^{-1}$. For this case, the optimal consumption-savings and portfolio decisions can be summarized as follows, using two cutoff points for the real rate Rx^i. If $Rx^i > \beta^{-1}$, the household invests all wealth in bonds; he consumes nothing at date 0 and buys no houses. If $Rx^i < \phi^{-1}[p'/p - (1 - \phi)\beta^{-1}]$, the household borrows up to the collateral constraint, invests his own wealth plus all borrowed funds in housing, and again consumes nothing. Finally, if Rx^i is in between the two cutoffs (this is possible whenever $p'/p < \beta^{-1}$), then the household consumes all wealth at date 0 and does not invest. Finally, at the cutoff points themselves, the household is indifferent between neighboring strategies.

4.4.2   Identical Subjective Real Rates

As a benchmark, we consider an equilibrium in which all households agree on the same ex ante real rate Rx^*. In this case, the expected bond payoff $x^* = 1/\pi^*$ is determined by the inflation expectations of smart agents π^*. Because both houses and bonds are in positive net supply, the expected returns on the two assets must be equal and also greater than or equal to the discount rate. We consider an equilibrium in which there is some consumption at date t. To make households indifferent between consumption and saving, both returns must equal the discount rate:

$$(5) \qquad Rx^* = \beta^{-1} = \frac{p'}{p}.$$

Here the first equality is again the Fisher equation: the nominal interest rate equals the ex ante real rate—here the discount rate—multiplied by the expected rate of inflation π^*. The second equality says that the house price is the present discounted value of future payoffs, discounted at the real interest rate. In the benchmark equilibrium, the house price is independent of expected inflation.

We assume that initial endowments and asset supplies are such that markets can clear at these prices. In particular, the supply of assets, with houses evaluated at the prices $p = \beta p'$ implied by equation (5), must be smaller than the initial wealth of the household sector:

$$(6) \qquad \overline{b} + \beta p' < \overline{b}_0 + \beta p' \overline{h}_0 + y.$$

Similarly to equation (2), this assumption is also satisfied if changes in aggregate household asset positions are small relative to income.

4.4.3   Heterogeneous Subjective Real Rates

We assume that a fraction α of households expects nominal bonds to have low payoffs $\underline{x}$, while a fraction $1 - \alpha$ of households expects high payoffs $\overline{x} > \underline{x}$. We refer to these two groups as low-interest and high-interest households, respectively. To again ensure the existence of equilibria in which some consumption takes place at date 0, we modify equation (6) to

(7)
$$\bar{b} + \beta p' \frac{x}{\bar{x}} < \bar{b}_0 + \beta p' \frac{x}{\bar{x}} \bar{h}_0 + y.$$

If some new housing units are bought by households planning for the future at date 0 ($\bar{h}_0 < 1$), this condition is stronger than equation (6). In the following equilibria, $\beta p'^{(\underline{x}/\bar{x})}$ is an upper bound for the house price. The condition is thus still satisfied provided changes in asset positions—including investment on housing—are small relative to income.

Proposition 1 characterizes equilibrium prices as a function of the share α of low-interest households. We know from the benchmark equilibrium that when households agree on their subjective real rates (that is, $\alpha = 0$ or $\alpha = 1$), the Fisher equation holds and the house price is at its benchmark level $p = \beta p'$. When households disagree, the nominal rate reflects a weighted average of their payoff expectations. Moreover, sufficient disagreement in the population generates a house-price boom ($p > \beta p'$). The proposition formally states this result for the case where the maximal loan-to-value ratio ϕ is sufficiently large relative to the supply of bonds from the rest of the economy $\bar{b}$. For low ϕ or high $\bar{b}$, the same type of equilibrium continues to exist, but it need not be unique. We relegate the analysis of the latter case to the appendix.

PROPOSITION 1: *Prices and the Distribution of Views on Ex Ante Real Rates*

Suppose $\phi (\bar{b}_0 + y) > \bar{h}_0 \bar{b}$. There is a unique equilibrium in which

(a) the nominal interest rate is continuous and nondecreasing in the fraction α of low-interest agents; there exist cutoffs $\bar{\alpha}_R$ and $\underline{\alpha}_R$ such that $1 > \bar{\alpha}_R \geq \underline{\alpha}_R > 0$ and

$$R = \beta^{-1}/\underline{x} \qquad \text{if } \alpha \geq \bar{\alpha}_R,$$
$$R = \beta^{-1}/\bar{x} \qquad \text{if } \alpha \leq \underline{\alpha}_R,$$
$$R \in [\beta^{-1}/\bar{x}, \beta^{-1}/\underline{x}] \qquad \text{otherwise.}$$

(b) the house price is hump-shaped in α; there exists $\underline{\alpha}_p \in (0, \underline{\alpha}_R)$ such that

$$p = \beta p' \qquad \text{if } \alpha \notin (\underline{\alpha}_p, \alpha_R),$$
$$p > \beta p' \qquad \text{otherwise.}$$

PROOF: See the appendix.

The pattern of interest rates and house prices is shown in figure 4.4. To obtain some intuition, consider first an economy where all agents agree on real interest rates ($\alpha = 0$). This economy is in a benchmark equilibrium,

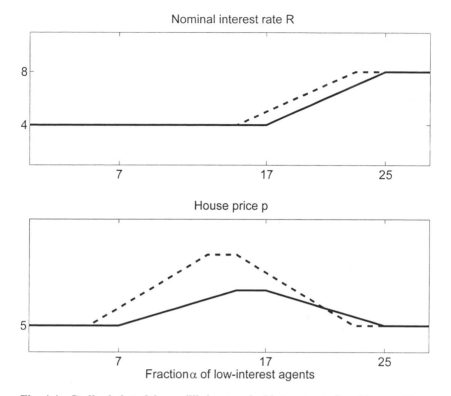

Fig. 4.4   Stylized plot of the equilibrium nominal interest rate R and house price p, both as functions of the fraction α of low-interest agents who believe that nominal bonds have low payoffs, $\underline{x}$.

Notes: Solid lines are for an initial equilibrium; dotted lines are for an equilibrium with a higher maximal LTV ratio ϕ.

where households are indifferent between consumption and savings as well as between different portfolios. Consider now what happens when some high-interest agents are replaced by low-interest agents, that is, α rises. At the original prices, the subjective real interest rate of low-interest agents is below the discount rate and also below the return on housing. Consumption and bonds become unattractive for the low-interest agents: they prefer to invest in housing and also take on mortgages to exploit the low (subjective) cost of borrowing. For small α, this makes little difference in the credit market: the high-interest agents, who are indifferent between consumption and bonds, are happy to fund a few more mortgages at the original interest rate. Similarly, the house price need not change as long as there are enough high-interest agents who are willing to sell houses.

The situation changes once there is a critical mass of low-interest agents. As these agents become more numerous, their total wealth—which they invest in housing equity—goes up. Their demand for houses at the original benchmark price $\beta p'$ eventually outpaces the available supply. For markets to clear, building leveraged portfolios must become less attractive. There are two ways in which this can happen: the cost of borrowing can rise or the return on housing can fall. Part (a) of the proposition shows that the former occurs: the nominal interest rate rises to reflect, at least in part, the low expected bond payoff. Part (b) shows that the house price also reacts: it goes up in order to lower the expected return on housing. Put differently, with sufficient disagreement about ex ante real rates, higher housing demand due to cheap mortgages drives up house prices. This occurs even though everyone agrees that the expected future payoff from houses has not changed.

To see what happens for high α, consider an economy where all agents agree on low bond payoffs. This economy is again in a benchmark equilibrium, but now with a high nominal interest rate reflecting the low payoff expectations. Assume next that some low-interest agents are replaced by high-interest agents, that is, α falls. At the original benchmark prices, the subjective real bond return of the high-interest agents now rises above the discount rate and the housing return. High-interest agents thus prefer to invest all wealth in bonds. As long as there are not too many of them, this does not affect prices: they can easily sell houses and buy bonds at the benchmark prices. However, once the high-interest agents reach a critical mass, the nominal interest rate must fall. A lower nominal interest rate not only reduces the bond demand of the high-interest agents, but it also encourages the low-interest agents to take on mortgages, which increases the supply of bonds. The availability of cheap borrowing in turn increases the demand for houses from the low-interest agents: we are back in the region where disagreement increases house prices.

Our finding that disagreement about ex ante real rates leads to house-price booms is related to the classic result that, in a market with short sale constraints and heterogeneous beliefs, assets are valued by the most optimistic investor (Miller 1977).[8] The key difference between our setup and Miller's is that we do not assume disagreement about payoffs to the booming asset—in our case, housing—itself. Instead, there is disagreement about subjective real interest rates. The similarity arises because mortgages and housing together can be used to form the composite asset *housing equity*, defined as housing net of mortgage debt. The collateral constraint implies that housing equity cannot be sold short. Moreover, there is disagreement about its expected payoff $p' - bRx$. In equilibrium, the value of housing equity is driven by investors who are most optimistic about its

8. In the simplest version of Miller's argument, risk-neutral investors disagree about stock payoffs. If borrowing is allowed, the stock price must make the most optimistic investor indifferent between holding stocks and bonds—if this were not true, the most optimistic investor would run a leveraged strategy, creating excess demand for stocks. All other investors, who are prevented from shorting the stock, remain on the sidelines.

payoff, that is, the investors who believe in low real bond payoffs and, hence, a low cost of borrowing.

4.4.4   The Role of Collateral

Proposition 2 shows that the possibility of borrowing is critical for our results and that house-price booms driven by disagreement are stronger the higher is the leverage ratio.

PROPOSITION 2: *The Role of Collateral*

Suppose $\phi(\overline{b}_0 + y) > \overline{h}_0 \overline{b}$.

(a) If $\phi = 0$, the unique equilibrium has $p = \beta p'$.
(b) If $\phi > \phi^*$, the house price achieves a maximum at

$$\hat{p} := \beta p' \left(1 - \phi + \phi \frac{\overline{x}}{\underline{x}} \right)^{-1};$$

(c) If $\phi > \phi^*$, the cutoffs $\underline{\alpha}_p$, $\overline{\alpha}_p$, $\overline{\alpha}_R$, and $\underline{\alpha}_R$ that govern house price and interest rate behavior are decreasing in the maximal LTV value ϕ. In particular, we have

$$\underline{\alpha}_p(\phi) = (1 - \phi)\beta p' / \overline{w}(\beta p'),$$

$$\overline{\alpha}_p(\phi) = 1 - (\overline{b} + \phi\beta p') / \overline{w}(\beta p').$$

PROOF: See the appendix.

Part (a) of the proposition says that if the maximal LTV ratio ϕ is equal to zero—in other words, bond holdings are constrained to be nonnegative—then the house price is constant regardless of the extent of disagreement. In an economy without borrowing, disagreement about real rates will only be reflected in the portfolio positions: low-interest agents perceive a low return on bonds and hold only houses, while high-interest agents perceive a high return on bonds and hold only bonds. The possibility of leverage is thus necessary for disagreement to generate house-price booms. Part (b) says that when there is sufficient leverage—here we focus again on the case $\phi > \phi^*$ that is also considered in Proposition 1—the maximal price $\hat{p}$ that can occur in a house-price boom is increasing in the loan-to-value ratio ϕ. The comparative static of increasing ϕ is represented by the dotted lines in figure 4.4.

Part (c) characterizes the cutoff levels for the fraction of low-interest agents in terms of the maximal LTV ratio ϕ. It says that the cutoffs $\underline{\alpha}_p$ and $\overline{\alpha}_p$ for the house price are decreasing in the maximal leverage ratio ϕ that borrowers can achieve. At values of α in the interval $[\underline{\alpha}_p, \overline{\alpha}_p]$, there is sufficient disagreement such that a house-price boom must occur in any equilibrium. Higher ϕ means that an individual borrower can issue more bonds relative to his own wealth and can thus invest a larger multiple of his own wealth in housing. The effect on prices is best seen by starting from an equilibrium with agreement. Suppose first that everyone agrees on high real rates and replace a few agents with low-interest agents, who now become leverages. Higher demand for houses per individual borrower means that it takes fewer leveragers to upset the original equilibrium and force an increase in the house price. This explains why the lower bound $\underline{\alpha}_p$ is decreasing in ϕ.

For the converse thought experiment, suppose that initially everyone agrees on low real rates and then replace a few agents with high-interest types. At the original equilibrium prices, the high-interest agents invest exclusively in bonds. With higher ϕ, it takes more bond investors to upset the original equilibrium because low-interest investors can absorb more bond demand simply by issuing more mortgages, even without an increase in the house price. Therefore, it takes more bond investors to force a drop in interest rates that finally leads to an increase in the house price. This explains why the upper bound $\overline{\alpha}_p$ is also decreasing in ϕ. The upper bound is also decreasing in the supply of bonds from the rest of the economy. The more such bonds are outstanding, the less important it is for low-interest investors to supply additional bonds. It thus again takes more high-interest types to force a drop in the interest rate.

4.5   House-Price Booms and Inflation

To compare the behavior of house prices across decades, consider now three distinct environments. Let x^* denote bond payoff expectations in a normal environment with average inflation and nominal rates. As discussed in the preceding, illusion agents always expect a bond payoff x^* and do not relate it to their expected inflation rate. Let $x^{lo} < x^*$ denote a low payoff that was expected by smart investors during the 1970s when they expected inflation to be high, $x^{lo} = 1/\pi^{hi}$. Let $x^{hi} = 1/\pi^{lo} > x^*$ denote a high bond payoff that was expected by smart investors in the 2000s when they expected low inflation, $\pi^{lo} < \pi^{hi}$. In a normal year, smart investors also expect a payoff equal (or close) to $x^* = 1/\pi^*$. If the two investor types happen to agree, the economy is simply in a benchmark equilibrium, where the Fisher equation (for the smart investors) implies a nominal interest rate of $\beta^{-1}\pi^*$ and the house price is $\beta p'$.[9]

Now consider the 1970s scenario, where smart investors' inflation expectations jump to $\pi^{hi} > \pi^*$. The price reaction follows from Propositions 1 and 2, setting $\underline{x} = x^{lo} = 1/\pi^{hi}$ and $\overline{x} = x^*$. Suppose that at the relevant parameters (α, ϕ), the economy is in the region described in Proposition 2, where the nominal interest rate rises above $\beta^{-1}\pi^*$ but not all the way to

---

9. Even if the agreement is not perfect and the two payoffs are simply close, part (b) of Proposition 1 says that the house price will be close to its benchmark value.

$\beta^{-1}\pi^{hi}$, while the house price rises above $\beta p'$. We then obtain an equilibrium in which a house-price boom coincides with a high nominal interest rate. When smart investors see the nominal rate, they consider borrowing a good deal because the nominal rate does not fully reflect their high inflation expectations. Their demand for collateral drives up house prices. In contrast, illusion agents see the nominal rate and believe times are great for investing in bonds.

Under the 2000s scenario, smart investors' inflation expectations are below the long run average at $\pi^{lo} < \pi^*$. We again read off prices from Propositions 1 and 2, now setting $\bar{x} = x^{hi} = 1/\pi^{lo}$ and $\underline{x} = x^*$. If the economy is in the region where interest rates partially adjust, we obtain a house-price boom that goes along with low nominal interest rates. Moreover, the role of the two investor types is now reversed: under the 2000s scenario, it is illusion investors who are eager to borrow as they perceive low real rates. Illusion investors' demand for houses thus drives up house prices. In contrast, smart investors prefer to invest in bonds.

4.5.1 Structural Change and the Size of House-Price Booms

Changes in the maximal LTV ratio ϕ can be interpreted as the result of financial innovation—for example, in the screening technology available to intermediaries who originate mortgages. Proposition 2 suggests two ways in which financial development is conducive to housing booms in a low-inflation environment, as under the 2000s scenario. First, part (a) of the proposition says that higher leverage directly leads to higher house prices. Second, part (b) says that, with more opportunities for leverage, it takes fewer inflation illusion agents to generate enough disagreement for a house-price boom.[10] Taken together, these observations suggest that financial development may explain why the house-price booms of the 2000s were typically stronger than those of the 1970s.

Another consequence of financial development is that the fraction of households who participate in mortgage markets has increased recently, especially among lower income households (see, for example, Doepke and Schneider 2006). The model shows that an extreme increase in the participation rate is conducive to housing booms ($\phi = 0$ and $\phi > 0$ correspond to a zero and a 100 percent participation rate, respectively). More generally, one would expect that a smaller increase has similar effects. Moreover, an inflow of poor unsophisticated investors might generate more disagreement about real rates.

Another structural change that occurred between the 1970s and the

---

10. Interestingly, the same argument does not apply to illusion-induced booms in high-inflation environments. The discussion after Proposition 2 implies that, in high-inflation environments, higher leverage implies that it takes more illusion investors to generate a boom.

2000s is the increased opening of U.S. credit markets to foreigners. Doepke and Schneider (2006) show that the net nominal asset position of the U.S.-household sector has reached historical lows in recent years, while foreigners have become important net nominal lenders. In our model, this change is captured by a reduction in the supply of bonds $\bar{b}$ provided to the household sector by the rest of the economy. Proposition 2 shows that higher $\bar{b}$ increases the parameter region where housing booms can occur by keeping nominal interest rates low even if a lot of investors believe that real rates are low. Strong foreign demand for bonds thus facilitates housing booms due to illusion in both high- and low-inflation environments.

4.5.2 The Relationship between Inflation and Real Estate "Mispricing"

Consider an econometrician whose goal is to decompose house prices into a "fundamental" and a (residual) "mispricing" component. In the typical application, the fundamental component is taken to be a risk-adjusted present discounted value of profits to be made from the housing stock. If the data were generated by our (risk-neutral) model, correct measurement of rents and real interest rates would thus lead the econometrician to recover the benchmark price $\beta p'$ as the fundamental component. The mispricing is then simply $p - \beta p'$, a series with two peaks that occur during the 1970s and 2000s. It follows that the relationship between inflation and real estate mispricing is nonlinear: housing booms that push prices beyond fundamentals occur both at high inflation rates (during the 1970s) and at low inflation rates (during the 2000s).

If data were generated simply by repeatedly running our model with different inflation expectations, an econometrician who regresses his measure of mispricing on inflation should not detect a significant relationship. However, the coefficients in a linear regression could turn out to be (misleadingly) significant if there is another factor that changes over time. As one example, suppose that there is structural change in the credit market, so that ϕ increases over time, as discussed in the preceding. In this case, the first peak of the real estate mispricing series during the high 1970s inflation is smaller than its second peak during the low 2000s inflation. Thus, a linear regression of mispricing on inflation might uncover a significantly negative linear relationship between real estate mispricing and inflation. In this example, the omitted variable "credit market development" will be responsible for the finding, although the true relationship between inflation and mispricing is nonlinear.

The relationship between real estate mispricing and inflation is also sensitive to how the fundamental component is measured in the face of structural change. For example, suppose that deregulation of rental markets induces a trend in $\beta p'$—and, hence, house prices—that has nothing to do with inflation. Consider now an econometrician who determines the fundamental value of housing by estimating a stationary process with the same mean as the observed house price over his or her sample. Because he or she ignores the trend in fundamentals, this econometrician will tend to find negative mispricing early in his sample period and positive mispricing later in the sample period. If inflation also happened to decrease over the sample period, there will be a spurious negative relationship between mispricing and inflation that has nothing to do with inflation illusion.

4.6   Conclusion

This chapter has considered a stylized economy with heterogeneous agents, some of whom suffer from inflation illusion. Our model predicts a nonmonotonic relationship between house price-rent ratios and inflation: house prices are high whenever inflation is far away from its historical average. According to the model, a high-inflation environment—such as the 1970s—is a time when smart households drive up house prices because they are able to borrow cheaply from illusionary households. The latter do not realize that nominal rates are high only because expected inflation is high and thus perceive higher real rates than smart households. In contrast, in a low-inflation environment—such as the 2000s—the role of the two groups is reversed: illusionary households drive up house prices because they think they are borrowing cheaply from smart households. They do not realize that nominal interest rates are low only because of low expected inflation and thus perceive lower real rates than smart households. Recent financial market development has made borrowing easier, which might explain why the housing boom of the 2000s is more pronounced than the 1970s boom.

We emphasize that general equilibrium effects matter for thinking about the effect of inflation illusion on asset prices. While the Fed model consists of a relationship between endogenous variables, our model jointly determines both the nominal interest rate and house prices. We have shown that investor heterogeneity is one way to reconcile the comovement of nominal rates and inflation with real effects of inflation illusion and also to avoid Summers's critique. An important task for future research is to quantify the implications of inflation illusion and to compare the effect we have derived here to other candidate explanations for house-price booms.

Another interesting issue is the effect of inflation illusion on stock prices. The cross-country evidence in this chapter shows that the price-dividend ratios of housing and stocks often move in opposite directions. The mechanism we emphasize can help produce such negative comovement. Indeed, disagreement about real interest rates makes bonds more attractive to investors who perceive high real rates, while it makes real estate more attractive to investors who perceive low real rates. In relative terms, stocks thus become less attractive to both investor types. The resulting shift in portfolio demand away from stocks should thus lower stock prices while increasing house prices.

Appendix

This appendix characterizes the equilibriums of our model. We begin with three lemmas. Lemma 1 shows that, in any equilibrium, we must have $\beta^{-1}/\overline{x} \le R \le \beta^{-1}/\underline{x}$ and $p \ge \beta p'$. Lemma 2 derives conditions for the existence of equilibriums with $p = \beta p'$, while Lemma 3 does the same for the case $p > \beta p'$. Propositions 1* and 2* then provide a full description of the equilibriums that can occur. In particular, these propositions do not assume that $\phi(\overline{b}_0 + y) > \overline{h}_0 \overline{b}$, an assumption that was made in the text to ensure uniqueness. We provide a brief discussion of why multiplicity can occur—and why it is not particularly interesting from an economic perspective here—after Proposition 2*. Finally, we derive Propositions 1 and 2 stated in the text.

LEMMA 1: *In any equilibrium, $\beta^{-1}/\overline{x} \le R \le \beta^{-1}/\underline{x}$ and $p \ge \beta p'$.*

PROOF: If $R < \beta^{-1}/\overline{x}$, then no household invests in bonds, which cannot be an equilibrium because bonds are in positive net supply.

If $p < \beta p'$, then it is optimal for both household types to save all initial wealth because the real return on housing p'/p is higher than the discount rate. Summing up the market clearing conditions for bonds and houses, the house price must satisfy

$$(A1) \qquad p + \overline{b} = \overline{b}_0 + p\overline{h}_0 + y.$$

Because $\overline{h}_0 < 1$ and condition (2) holds, the solution for p is positive. But now condition (6) implies that

$$(A2) \qquad \frac{p'}{p} = \frac{p'(1 - \overline{h}_0)}{y + \overline{b}_0 - \overline{b}} < \beta^{-1},$$

a contradiction.

Finally, if $R > \beta^{-1}/\underline{x}$, the real rate on bonds perceived by both types is strictly higher than the discount rate, and, because $p \ge \beta p'$ (by the argument in the previous paragraph), the real bond return is also strictly higher than the return on housing. It follows that no agent wants to hold housing, which cannot be an equilibrium because houses are in positive net supply.■

LEMMA 2: *Define the cutoffs:*

$$\overline{\alpha}_p = 1 - (\overline{b} + \phi\beta p')/\overline{w}(\beta p'),$$

$$\underline{\alpha}_p = (1 - \phi)\,\beta p'/\overline{w}(\beta p').$$

An equilibrium with $p = \beta p'$ exists if and only if either

(a) $\alpha \geq \overline{\alpha}_p$, *in which case $R\underline{x} = \beta^{-1}$, or*
(b) $\alpha \leq \underline{\alpha}_p$, *in which case $R\overline{x} = \beta^{-1}$.*

PROOF: We assume first that $R\overline{x} > \beta^{-1}$, which leads to case (a) and in the following consider $R\overline{x} = \beta^{-1}$, which leads to case (b). If $R\overline{x} > \beta^{-1} = p'/p$, then high-interest agents hold only bonds. We must have $R\underline{x} \leq \beta^{-1}$ as otherwise nobody holds houses. We cannot have $R\underline{x} < \beta^{-1}$. If this were true, low-interest agents would want to invest all wealth in a leveraged portfolio strategy. All agents would then invest all wealth so that the value of the total asset supply would equal the total value of wealth, and the house price would be determined by equation (A1). As argued in the proof of Lemma 1, condition (6) would then imply $p'/p < \beta^{-1}$ (cf. equation [A2]), which contradicts our assumption that $p = \beta p'$.

We conclude that equilibria with $p = \beta p'$ and $R\overline{x} > \beta^{-1}$ must have $R\underline{x} = \beta^{-1}$. Low-interest agents are thus indifferent between bonds, houses, and consumption, while high-interest agents hold only bonds. Markets can clear at these prices as long as there are sufficiently many bonds available to satisfy the demand of the high-interest agents. Bond supply can come either from the ROE sector or because low-interest agents issue mortgages. We obtain the cutoff for case (a):

(A3) $$\overline{b} + \phi\beta p' \geq (1 - \alpha)\,(\beta p'\overline{h}_0 + \overline{b}_0 + y).$$

As long as this inequality holds, condition (6) guarantees that the remaining wealth (owned by the low-interest agents) is high enough such that the latter agents can afford to purchase the whole housing stock, that is,

$$(1 - \phi)\beta p' < \alpha\,(\beta p'\overline{h}_0 + \overline{b}_0 + y).$$

Because low-interest agents are indifferent between all portfolio strategies, a suitable number of them can be assigned to both markets to ensure market clearing. It follows that equilibriums with $p = \beta p'$ and $R\overline{x} > \beta^{-1}$ exist if and only if condition (A3) holds.

Suppose now that $R\overline{x} = \beta^{-1}$. Because $R\underline{x} < \beta^{-1} = p'/p$, low-interest agents will use the leveraged strategy and hold no bonds. For an equilibrium of this type to exist, we need the value of the housing stock to be large enough to satisfy the demand of the low-interest agents, which defines the cutoff for case (b):

(A4) $$(1 - \phi)\beta p' \geq \alpha\,(\beta p'\overline{h}_0 + \overline{b}_0 + y).$$

If this inequality is satisfied, condition (6) again ensures that the remaining wealth (owned by the high-interest agents) is large enough that the high-interest agents can absorb all bonds issued by the ROE and the low-interest agents, that is,

$$\overline{b} + \phi\beta p' < (1 - \alpha)(\beta p'\overline{h}_0 + \overline{b}_0 + y).$$

It follows that equilibria with $p = \beta p'$ and $R\overline{x} = \beta^{-1}$ exist if and only if condition (A4) holds.∎

LEMMA 3: *An equilibrium with $p > \beta p'$ exists only if $\phi > 0$ and at least one of four sets of conditions holds:*

(a) $\phi > \overline{h}_0\overline{b}/(\overline{b}_0 + y) := \phi^*$ and

$$\overline{\alpha}_p > \alpha > 1 - (\overline{b} + \phi\hat{p})/\overline{w}(\hat{p}),$$

(b) $\phi < \phi^*$ and

$$\overline{\alpha}_p < \alpha < 1 - (\overline{b} + \phi\hat{p})/\overline{w}(\hat{p}),$$

(c) $\underline{\alpha}_p < \alpha < (1 - \phi)\hat{p}/w(\hat{p}),$
(d) $\phi > 0$ and $(1 - \phi)\hat{p}/\overline{w}(\hat{p}) \le \alpha \le 1 - (\overline{b} + \phi\hat{p})/\overline{w}(\hat{p}).$

For all cases, there exist values of α that satisfy the conditions.

Conversely, assume $\phi > 0$. If cases (a) or (b) apply, the equilibrium house price and interest rate are given by

(A5)
$$p = \frac{(1 - \alpha)(\overline{b}_0 + y) - \overline{b}}{\phi - (1 - \alpha)\overline{h}_0},$$

(A6) $$R = \beta^{-1}\frac{1}{\phi\underline{x}}\left(\frac{\beta p'[\phi - \overline{h}_0(1 - \alpha)]}{(1 - \alpha)(y + \overline{b}_0) - \overline{b}} - (1 - \phi)\right).$$

In case (a), p is decreasing in α and R is increasing in α.
If case (c) applies, then $R\overline{x} = \beta^{-1}$ and

(A7)
$$p = \frac{\alpha(\overline{b}_0 + y)}{1 - \phi - \alpha\overline{h}_0},$$

and the price p is increasing in α.
If case (d) applies, $p = \hat{p}$ and $R\overline{x} = \beta^{-1}$.

PROOF: If $p'/p < \beta^{-1}$, high-interest agents do not own houses in equilibrium. Indeed, we know from Lemma 1 that we must have $R\overline{x} \ge \beta^{-1}$. Because $p'/p < \beta^{-1} \le R\overline{x}$, owning houses without leverage is worse than owning bonds for high-interest agents. More generally, even the return on a maximally leveraged strategy is strictly worse than the return on bonds for the high-interest agents:

$$\frac{1}{1-\phi}\left(\frac{p'}{p} - \phi R\overline{x}\right) \le \frac{1}{1-\phi}\left(\frac{p'}{p} - \phi\beta^{-1}\right) < \beta^{-1} \le R\overline{x}.$$

Because high-interest agents do not own houses, low-interest agents must be willing to do so, which requires

(A8) $$\frac{1}{1-\phi}\left(\frac{p'}{p} - \phi Rx\right) \ge \beta^{-1}.$$

It follows that we cannot have $\phi = 0$, as otherwise $p'/p = \beta^{-1}$. To derive the other conditions, we first consider $R\overline{x} > \beta^{-1}$, which corresponds to cases (a) and (b). We then consider $R\overline{x} = \beta^{-1}$, which corresponds to cases (c) and (d).

Cases (a) and (b). We first show that if there is an equilibrium with $p > \beta p'$ and $R\overline{x} > \beta^{-1}$, either case (a) or case (b) applies. If $R\overline{x} > \beta^{-1}$, high-interest agents invest all their wealth in bonds and hold no houses. We must then have equation (A8) hold with equality. Indeed, if equation (A8) were to hold strictly, then low-interest agents would invest all wealth in leveraged portfolios so that all agents would save all wealth and the house price would be pinned down by equation (A1). Substituting this price formula back into equation (A8), we obtain

(A9) $$\overline{b} + \tilde{p} > \tilde{p}\overline{h}_0 + y + \overline{b}_0,$$

where $\tilde{p} = \beta p'(1 - \phi + \phi\beta R\underline{x})^{-1}$. The last inequality contradicts our assumption (7). To see this, define the function

$$h(p) := \frac{\overline{b} + p}{p\overline{h}_0 + y + \overline{b}_0},$$

which is strictly increasing because $\overline{h}_0 < 1$ and $\overline{b} < \overline{b}_0 + y$. We can write equation (A9) as $h(\tilde{p}) > 1$ and equation (7) as $h(\beta p'\overline{x}/\underline{x}) < 1$ so that we would need $\tilde{p} > \beta p'\ \overline{x}/\underline{x}$. However, $R\overline{x} > \beta^{-1}$ implies $\tilde{p} < \hat{p} < \beta p'\overline{x}/\underline{x}$, a contradiction.

Because (A8) holds with equality, low-interest agents must be indifferent between consumption and holding leveraged portfolios. There must be a subset of low-interest agents that holds all houses and issues ϕp mortgages. These mortgages, together with the debt issued by the ROE, must in turn be held by high-interest agents. Because high-interest agents invest all wealth in bonds, the total outstanding debt must be equal to high-interest agents' wealth. For the bond market to clear, the equilibrium house price must satisfy

(A10) $$\overline{b} + \phi p = (1 - \alpha)(p\overline{h}_0 + \overline{b}_0 + y).$$

The solution for the house price is equation (A5). The interest rate R is then pinned down by equation (A8), which we have assumed to hold with equality. The solution for the interest rate is equation (A6).

The solutions (p, R) in equations (A5) to (A6) must satisfy $p > \beta p'$ and $R\bar{x} > \beta^{-1}$. Since they are equilibrium prices, they must also be positive, which gives rise to two possibilities. Assume first that

(A11) $$\phi/\bar{h}_0 > (1 - \alpha) > \frac{\bar{b}}{\bar{b}_0 + y}.$$

The conditions $p > \beta p'$ and $R\bar{x} > \beta^{-1}$ can now be written as

(A12) $$\bar{b} + \phi\beta p' < (1 - \alpha)(\beta p'\bar{h}_0 + \bar{b}_0 + y),$$

(A13) $$\bar{b} + \hat{p}\phi > (1 - \alpha)(\hat{p}\bar{h}_0 + \bar{b}_0 + y),$$

which defines the cutoffs for α in case (a).

A second set of parameters that leads to positive prices is

(A14) $$\bar{b}/(\bar{b}_0 + y) > (1 - \alpha) > \phi/\bar{h}_0.$$

The conditions $p > \beta p'$ and $R\bar{x} > \beta^{-1}$ now define the cutoffs for α in case (b):

(A15) $$\bar{b} + \phi\beta p' > (1 - \alpha)(\beta p'\bar{h}_0 + \bar{b}_0 + y),$$

(A16) $$\bar{b} + \hat{p}\phi < (1 - \alpha)(\hat{p}\bar{h}_0 + \bar{b}_0 + y).$$

It remains to define

$$\phi^* = \bar{h}_0 \frac{\bar{b}}{\bar{b}_0 + y}.$$

We have thus shown that existence of an equilibrium with $p > \beta p'$ and $R\bar{x} > \beta^{-1}$ implies either (a) or (b).

We now show that there exist values of α that satisfy these conditions. Begin with case (a), and consider the function

$$f(p) := \frac{\bar{b} + \phi p}{p\bar{h}_0 + \bar{b}_0 + y},$$

which is continuously differentiable with

$$f'(p) = \frac{\phi(\bar{b}_0 + y) - \bar{b}\bar{h}_0}{(p\bar{h}_0 + \bar{b}_0 + y)^2},$$

and is, therefore, strictly increasing if and only if $\phi > \phi^*$. Conditions (A12) and (A13) can be written as $f(\hat{p}) > 1 - \alpha > f(\beta p)$. If follows that, if $\phi > \phi^*$, there exist values of α that satisfy both conditions simultaneously. Any such value of α will also satisfy equation (A11) because

$$\lim_{p \to \infty} f(p) = \phi/\bar{h}_0 > f(\hat{p}) > 1 - \alpha > f(\beta p') > f(0) = \frac{\bar{b}}{\bar{b}_0 + y}.$$

A similar argument applies to case (b). Indeed, equations (A15) and (A16) can be written as $f(\hat{p}) < 1 - \alpha < f(\beta p)$. If $\phi < \phi^*$, then f is strictly decreasing, which implies that there are values of α that satisfy equations to (A14) to (A16).

Suppose now that we have a pair (ϕ, α) that satisfies the conditions of case (a) or (b), and suppose prices are given by equations (A5) and (A6). The bond market clears by construction of the house price. For the housing market to clear, the wealth of the low-interest agents evaluated at p must be high enough that these agents can afford to hold all houses:

$$(A17) \qquad (1 - \phi)p < \alpha(p\overline{h}_0 + \overline{b}_0 + y).$$

Because equation (A10) is assumed to hold, equation (A17) is equivalent to

$$\overline{b} + p \leq p\overline{h}_0 + \overline{b}_0 + y.$$

But this inequality is implied by equation (7) because $R\overline{x} > \beta^{-1}$ guarantees $p < \hat{p}$. If we are in case (a), equation (A11) holds and implies that the price (A-5) decreasing in α, while the interest rate (A6) is increasing in α.

To sum up, we have shown that an equilibrium with $p > \beta p'$ exists if either $\phi > \phi^*$ and conditions (A12) and (A13) hold or $\phi < \phi^*$ and conditions (A15) and (A16) hold. For either case, there are values of α that satisfy the conditions. Finally, if either pair of conditions holds, there is an equilibrium with prices (A5) and (A6) that satisfies $p > \beta p'$.

Case (c). We show that if there is an equilibrium such that $p > \beta p'$, $R\overline{x} = \beta^{-1}$ and equation (A8) holds with strict inequality, then case (c) applies. Under these conditions, low-interest agents invest all their wealth in a leveraged portfolio strategy. Because high-interest agents do not hold houses, housing equity in the entire housing stock must equal the wealth of low-interest agents:

$$(A18) \qquad (1 - \phi)p = \alpha(p\overline{h}_0 + \overline{b}_0 + y).$$

The solution for the house price is equation (A7).

The solution for p must be positive so that $\alpha \leq (1 - \phi)/\overline{h}_0$. In addition, it must satisfy $p > \beta p'$ as well as equation (A8) with strict inequality. This implies the cutoffs for case (c):

$$(A19) \qquad (1 - \phi)\beta p' < \alpha(\beta p'\overline{h}_0 + \overline{b}_0 + y),$$

$$(A20) \qquad (1 - \phi)\hat{p} > \alpha(\hat{p}\overline{h}_0 + \overline{b}_0 + y).$$

We now show that there exist values of α that satisfy the conditions of case (c). The function

$$g(p) := \frac{(1 - \phi)p}{p\overline{h}_0 + \overline{b}_0 + y}$$

is strictly increasing and continuous in p, with $\lim_{p\to\infty} g(p) = (1 - \phi)/\overline{h}_0$. It follows that there exist values of α that satisfy $g(\beta p') < \alpha < g(\hat{p})$, which is equivalent to equations (A19) and (A20).

Finally, suppose that there is an α such that equations (A19) and (A20) hold and that the house price is given by equation (A7). This price is positive because g is strictly increasing so that equation (A21) implies

$$\alpha < g(\hat{p}) < \lim_{p \to \infty} g(p) = (1 - \phi)/\overline{h}_0.$$

The house market clears by construction. For the bond market to clear, the wealth of the high-interest agents must be high enough at p to absorb all bonds, that is,

(A21) $$\overline{b} + \phi p < (1 - \alpha)(p\overline{h}_0 + \overline{b}_0 + y).$$

Because equation (A18) holds, equation (A21) is equivalent to

$$\overline{b} + p < p\overline{h}_0 + \overline{b}_0 + y.$$

This inequality is implied by equation (7) because equation (A8) guarantees $p < \hat{p}$. We have thus shown that an equilibrium with $p > \beta p'$ and $R\overline{x} = \beta^{-1}$ exists only if equations (A19) and (A20) hold. There are values of α that satisfy these conditions. Given the conditions, there is an equilibrium with $R\overline{x} = \beta^{-1}$ and house price (A7). The house price is also increasing in α.

Case (d). We show that if there is an equilibrium such that $p > \beta p'$, $R\overline{x} = \beta^{-1}$ and equation (A8) holds with equality, then case (d) applies. Substituting $R\overline{x} = \beta^{-1}$ into equation (A8) and solving for the house price, we obtain $p = \hat{p}$. Because $R\overline{x} = \beta^{-1} > p'/p$, high-interest agents do not hold houses. Because $R\underline{x} < \beta^{-1}$, low-interest agents do not hold bonds. For the house market to clear, the wealth of the low-interest agents—evaluated at the price $\hat{p}$—must be high enough so that these agents can afford the housing equity required to purchase the entire housing stock:

(A22) $$(1 - \phi)\hat{p} \le \alpha(\hat{p}\overline{h}_0 + \overline{b}_0 + y).$$

At the same time, bond market clearing requires that the wealth of the high-interest agents is high enough so that they can absorb all bonds:

(A23) $$\overline{b} + \phi\hat{p} \le (1 - \alpha)(\hat{p}\overline{h}_0 + \overline{b}_0 + y).$$

We have thus derived the conditions for case (d). Condition (7) implies that there exist values of α that satisfy both inequalities. Finally, if there is an α that falls under case (d), then equation (A22) says that we can pick a subset of the low-interest agents that holds all houses as part of leveraged portfolios, while equation (A23) says that we can pick a subset of the high-interest agents who hold all bonds.∎

PROPOSITION 1*:

(a) *For every maximal LTV ratio $\phi < 1$, there exist cutoffs $\overline{\alpha}_R$ and $\underline{\alpha}_R$ such that $1 > \overline{\alpha}_R \ge \underline{\alpha}_R > 0$, and the equilibrium nominal interest rate satisfies*

$$R = \beta^{-1}/\underline{x} \qquad \text{if } \alpha \geq \overline{\alpha}_R,$$

$$R = \beta^{-1}/\overline{x} \qquad \text{if } \alpha \leq \underline{\alpha}_R,$$

$$R \in [\beta^{-1}/\overline{x}, \beta^{-1}/\underline{x}] \quad \text{otherwise.}$$

(b) *For every maximal LTV ratio* $\phi \in (0, 1)$, *there exist cutoffs* $\overline{\alpha}_p$ *and* $\underline{\alpha}_p$ *such that* $\overline{\alpha}_R \geq \overline{\alpha}_p > \underline{\alpha}_p > 0$, *and the equilibrium house price satisfies*

$$p = \beta p' \qquad \text{if } \alpha \notin (\underline{\alpha}_p, \overline{\alpha}_R],$$

$$p > \beta p' \qquad \text{if } \alpha \in (\underline{\alpha}_p, \overline{\alpha}_p),$$

$$p \in [\beta p', \hat{p}] \qquad \text{otherwise.}$$

Moreover, there exists $\alpha \in (\underline{\alpha}_p, \alpha_R)$ *such that there is an equilibrium with* $p = \hat{p}$.

PROOF: We first define the cutoffs:

$$\overline{\alpha}_R = \begin{cases} 1 - (\overline{b} + \phi\hat{p})/\overline{w}(\hat{p}) & \text{if } \phi < \phi^*, \\ \overline{\alpha}_p & \text{if } \phi \geq \phi^*. \end{cases}$$

$$\underline{\alpha}_R = \begin{cases} \overline{\alpha}_p & \text{if } \phi < \phi^*, \\ 1 - (\overline{b} + \phi\hat{p})/\overline{w}(\hat{p}) & \text{if } \phi \geq \phi^*. \end{cases}$$

Part (a). If $\phi \geq \phi^*$, then there is an equilibrium with $Rx = \beta^{-1}$, by case (a) of Lemma 2. Lemmas 2 and 3 imply also that there cannot be any other type of equilibrium. If $\phi < \phi^*$, then case (b) of Lemma 3 says that

$$\overline{\alpha}_R = 1 - (\overline{b} + \phi\hat{p})/\overline{w}(\hat{p}) > 1 - (b + \phi\beta p')/\overline{w}(\beta p').$$

This means that for every $\alpha \geq \overline{\alpha}_R$, there is an equilibrium with $R\underline{x} = \beta^{-1}$, again by case (a) of Lemma 2. Inspection of the other case in Lemmas 2 and 3 again shows that this is the only equilibrium. Any $\alpha \leq \underline{\alpha}_R$ must satisfy the conditions of either case (b) of Lemma 2, or case (c) or case (d) of Lemma 3. It cannot satisfy the conditions of any other case. In all the relevant cases, the equilibrium interest rate is $R\overline{x} = \beta^{-1}$.

Part (b). For $\alpha > \overline{\alpha}_R$, the only equilibrium is that of case (a) of Lemma 2, which has $p = \beta p'$. If $\alpha \leq \underline{\alpha}_p$, the only type of equilibrium is case (b) of Lemma 2, which has $p = \beta p'$. If $\underline{\alpha}_p \leq \alpha \leq \overline{\alpha}_p$, then Lemma 2 does not apply. Comparing the cutoffs, one of the cases in Lemma 3 always applies so that $p > \beta p'$. Finally, for every $\phi > 0$, there exist values of α such that part (d) of Lemma 3 applies. In the latter equilibrium, $p = \hat{p}$.

PROPOSITION 2*:

(a) *If borrowing is not possible* $(\phi = 0)$, *then* $p = \beta p'$ *for all* α.

(b) *The cutoffs* $\underline{\alpha}_p, \overline{\alpha}_p, \overline{\alpha}_R$, *and* α_R *that govern house price and interest rate behavior are decreasing in the maximal LTV value* ϕ. *In particular, we have*

$$\underline{\alpha}_p(\phi) = (1 - \phi)\beta p'/\overline{w}(\beta p'),$$

$$\overline{\alpha}_p(\phi) = 1 - (\overline{b} + \phi\beta p')/\overline{w}(\beta p').$$

(c) *There is a threshold for the maximal LTV ratio $\phi^* := \overline{h}_0\overline{b}/(\overline{b}_0 + y) \in (0, 1)$ such that*

(i) *if $\phi \in (\phi^*, 1)$, equilibrium is unique for all α and*

$$\overline{\alpha}_p(\phi) = \overline{\alpha}_R(\phi) > \underline{\alpha}_R(\phi) > \underline{\alpha}_p(\phi).$$

The interest rate is continuous and nondecreasing in the fraction α, whereas the house price is continuous and hump-shaped in α, with a maximum of $p = \hat{p}$.

(ii) *if $\phi \in (0, \phi^*)$, then*

$$\overline{\alpha}_R(\phi) > \overline{\alpha}_p(\phi) = \underline{\alpha}_R(\phi) > \underline{\alpha}_p(\phi).$$

For $\alpha \le \overline{\alpha}_p(\phi)$, the interest rate and house price are continuous and nondecreasing in the fraction α. If $\alpha \ge \overline{\alpha}_R(\phi)$, then $R\underline{x} = \beta^{-1}$ and $p = \beta p'$. If $\alpha \in [\overline{\alpha}_p(\phi), \overline{\alpha}_R(\phi)]$, there can be up to three equilibriums with $R \in [\beta^{-1}/\overline{x}, \beta^{-1}/\underline{x}]$ and $p \in [\beta p', \hat{p}]$.

PROOF: Part (a). If $\phi = 0$, then Lemma 3 does not apply. The result follows directly from Lemma 2.

Part (b). The formulas for $\overline{\alpha}_p$ and $\underline{\alpha}_p$ follow directly from the proof of Proposition 1. These cutoffs are decreasing in ϕ because $\overline{w}$ is positive and does not depend on ϕ. To show that $\overline{\alpha}_p$ and $\underline{\alpha}_p$ are also decreasing in ϕ, it is sufficient to show that $(b + \phi\hat{p})/\overline{w}(\hat{p})$ is increasing in ϕ. The derivative

$$\frac{d\,[(b + \phi\hat{p})/\overline{w}(\hat{p})]}{d\phi} = \frac{\hat{p}}{\overline{w}(\hat{p})^2} \frac{\overline{w}(\hat{p}) - [1 - (\underline{x}/\overline{x})]\,\overline{h}_0\,(\overline{b} + \hat{p}\phi)}{1 - \phi + \phi(\underline{x}/\overline{x})}$$

is positive because equation (7) guarantees $\overline{w}(\hat{p}) > \overline{b} + \hat{p}$ and h_0, ϕ and $\underline{x}/\overline{x}$ are all smaller than one.

Part (c). Our assumption equation (2) can be written as

$$\overline{w}(\beta p') > \overline{b} + \beta p'\phi,$$

and, therefore, implies that $\overline{\alpha}_p > \underline{\alpha}_p$ for all ϕ. Case (c) of Lemma 3 implies that $\underline{\alpha}_R > \underline{\alpha}_p$ for all ϕ.

If $\phi > \phi^*$, the conditions of Lemmas 2 and 3 are mutually exclusive, and exactly one case of Lemma 3 can be relevant for a given value of α. Equilibrium is thus unique. Moreover, Lemma 3 implies that the price is increasing in α in case (c) and decreasing in case (a). Comparing the price formulas shows that the price is continuous and hump-shaped. Similarly, case (a) of Lemma 3 says that the interest rate is increasing, while it is constant in all other cases. Comparison of the formulas shows that the interest rate is also continuous.

If $\phi < \phi^*$, $\overline{\alpha}_R > \overline{\alpha}_p$ follows from case (b) of Lemma 3. Unless $\alpha \in [\overline{\alpha}_p, \overline{\alpha}_R]$, exactly one of the cases in Lemma 3 applies so that equilibrium is unique. If $\alpha \in [\overline{\alpha}_p, \overline{\alpha}_R]$, then case (a) of Lemma 2 as well as cases (b) and (c) of Lemma 3 can in principle all apply. Therefore, there can be up to three equilibriums.■

Remarks

If ϕ is low, multiple equilibria can obtain for some intermediate values of α (case [ii]). This happens because, with risk neutrality, portfolio choice reacts to prices only through discrete jumps, while the effect of prices on wealth is continuous. Consider again the thought experiment where initially all agents agree on real rates and then some are replaced by high-interest types. For high α, bond demand is due to high-interest agents, whose wealth is increasing in the house price. At the same time, the supply of bonds comes in part from borrowing by low-interest agents. Locally, the latter also increases with the house price, as the borrowing constraint is relaxed. Both supply and demand are locally not sensitive to the interest rate. Markets can then clear both at a high house price, which give rises to high supply and demand, and at a low house price, which gives rise to low supply and demand.[11] Because this multiplicity is due to auxiliary assumptions and does not affect the main effect we emphasize—house-price booms occur for intermediate values of α—we do not use it in our interpretation of the following model.

Proof of Proposition 1

Proposition 1 establishes the existence of cutoffs for price and interest rates in any equilibrium. Under the additional assumption $\phi > \phi^* = h_0 b/(b_0 + y)$, part (c, i) of Proposition 2* shows uniqueness, the special form of the cutoffs, as well as the monotonicity of the interest rate and the hump shape of the house price.■

Proof of Proposition 2

Part (a) is the same as part (a) of Proposition 2*. Part (b) follows from part (a) of Proposition 1*.

Part (c) follows from part (c, i) of Proposition 2*.■

---

11. If φ is higher, bond supply becomes more sensitive to the interest rate and equilibrium is unique. The same is true if the exogenous bond supply $\overline{b}$ is smaller; in fact, $\varphi^* = 0$ if $\overline{b} = 0$. In addition, equilibrium is unique if bond demand becomes less sensitive to the house price as $\overline{h}_0$ falls; we have $\varphi^* = 0$ also if $\overline{h}_0 = 0$.

References

Asness, Clifford. 2003. Fight the Fed model: The relationship between future returns and stock and bond market yields. *Journal of Portfolio Management* 30 (1): 11–24.
Basak, Suleyman, and Hongjun Yan. 2005. Equilibrium asset prices and investor behavior in the presence of money illusion. London Business School and Yale School of Management, Working Paper.
Brunnermeier, Markus, and Christian Julliard. 2006. Money illusion and housing frenzies. NBER Working Paper no. 12810. Cambridge, MA: National Bureau of Economic Research, December.
Campbell, John Y., and Tuomo Vuolteenaho. 2004. Inflation illusion and stock prices. *American Economic Review* 94 (2): 19–23.
Cohen, Randolph B., Christopher Polk, and Tuomo Vuolteenaho. 2005. Money illusion in the stock market: The Modigliani-Cohn hypothesis. *Quarterly Journal of Economics* 120 (2): 639–68.
Doepke, Matthias, and Martin Schneider. 2006. Inflation and the redistribution of nominal wealth. *Journal of Political Economy* 114 (6): 1069–97.
Feldstein, Martin. 1980. Inflation and the stock market. *American Economic Review* 70 (5): 839–47.
Grandmont, Jean-Michel. 1977. Temporary general equilibrium. *Econometrica* 45 (3): 535–72.
Kiyotaki, Nobuhiro, and John Moore. 1997. Credit cycles. *Journal of Political Economy* 105 (2): 211–48.
Miller, Edward M. 1977. Risk, uncertainty, and divergence of opinion. *Journal of Finance* 32 (4): 1151–68.
Modigliani, Franco, and Richard Cohn. 1979. Inflation, rational valuation, and the market. *Financial Analysts Journal* 35 (2): 24–44.
Piazzesi, Monika, and Martin Schneider. 2006. Inflation and the price of real assets. University of Chicago and New York University, Working Paper.
Piazzesi, Monika, Martin Schneider, and Selale Tuzel. 2007. Housing, consumption and asset pricing. *Journal of Financial Economics* 83 (3): 531–69.
Ritter, Jay R., and Richard S. Warr. 2002. The decline of inflation and the bull market of 1982–1999. *Journal of Financial and Quantitative Analysis* 37 (1): 29–61.
Sharpe, Steven A. 2002. Reexamining stock valuation and inflation: The implications of analysts' earnings forecasts. *Review of Economics and Statistics* 84 (4): 632–48.
Summers, Lawrence H. 1983. The nonadjustment of nominal interest rates: A study of the Fisher effect. In *Symposium in honor of Arthur Okun,* ed. James Tobin, 201–41. Washington, DC: Brookings Institution.

Comment   Markus K. Brunnermeier

The fact that the house price-rent ratio—a real measure of house price fundamentals—covaries with the nominal interest rate rather than the real in-

Markus K. Brunnermeier is a professor of economics at Princeton University, and a research associate of the National Bureau of Economic Research.

terest rate is one of the many puzzles in real estate economics. Increases in the nominal interest rate, which may be completely caused by increases in inflation, depress the house price-rent ratio.

A similar negative correlation between inflation and stock prices prompted Modigliani and Cohn (1979) to conjecture that investors are prone to money illusion: they confuse nominal and real interest rates. When that is the case, investors mistakenly discount real future cash flows with the nominal interest rate (or, alternatively, ignore the fact that cash flows tend to grow in nominal terms as inflation rises). Consequently, the price-earnings ratio of stocks negatively comoves with inflation.

Initially, Modigliani and Cohn's money illusion hypothesis did not seem to apply to the housing market since—as Summers (1983) pointed out—in the early 1970s, house prices were high even though inflation was rising. However, over a longer time series, there seems to be clear evidence that inflation depresses the house price-rent ratio even after controlling for fundamental factors that determine house prices (see Brunnermeier and Julliard 2008). This naturally leads to the question: what was different in the United States in the early 1970s.

The authors of this chapter provide a fresh perspective on this puzzle. They argue that money illusion can also explain house-price movements in the 1970s because it is not the level of inflation that matters, but the level of disagreement on inflation between rational investors and investors who suffer from money illusion. As inflation rises, rational households would like to short long-term nominal bonds, that is, borrow money (if the nominal rate does not adjust fully). However, in order to do so, they have to buy real estate as collateral. The authors argue that this mechanism led to an increase in housing demand by rational investors in the 1970s. This is in contrast to the late 1990s, when investors that were prone to money illusion boosted demand for housing.

To make this point precisely, the authors propose a very tractable two-period model. Agents derive utility from a single consumption good in both periods. Because agents' utility is linear, we can alternatively think of a model in which consumption only occurs in the last period, but households can "store" wealth for one period with a storage return of $1/\beta$. In addition to storage, agents can transfer wealth in two ways. They can buy a bond that pays a real interest rate of R/π or, alternatively, they can buy real estate. For simplicity, the authors consider housing as pure investment good and abstract from any service flow housing provides. House prices in period one are exogenously fixed to be the constant p'.

In summary, in a frictionless world, agents have three ways to transfer wealth from period zero to the consumption period one. (See table 4C.1.)

Of course, in a world without frictions and homogeneous beliefs, no-arbitrage guarantees that $R/\pi = 1/\beta$ and $p = \beta p'$.

To make the model interesting, the authors introduce heterogeneous be-

Table 4C.1   **Payoff matrix: Possible wealth transfers from time $t = 0$ to time $t = 1$.**

	$t = 0$	$t = 1$
Storage (analogy)	$-\beta$	$+1$
Bond	-1	$+R/\pi$
Housing	$-p$	$+p'$

liefs about the real bond return, R/π. Rational agents have correct beliefs, while agents that are prone to money illusion have a distorted view of the real interest rate. They believe that inflation is always at some benchmark level, for example, 4 percent.

The heterogeneity in beliefs about the real interest rate leads to trading activity in the bond market. Whenever investors with money illusion underestimate the real interest rate, they sell the bond, while rational investors buy it. Without any further assumptions, investors' risk-neutrality would imply that they trade an infinite amount of bonds, and the housing market would be a complete side show.

What makes the model interesting are two constraints: (1) a collateral constraint that implies that one can only short bonds (borrow money) if one owns a house as collateral and (2) a short-sale constraint for housing.[1] When inflation is low, money illusion investors underestimate the real interest rate and buy houses because they seem relatively cheap, while rational investors cannot short-sell houses. This is the standard effect of money illusion also studied in Brunnermeier and Julliard (2008). On the other hand, when inflation is high, investors that suffer from money illusion mistakenly think that the real interest is high and buy bonds. Rational investors realize that the bond price is too high and want to short it. In order to do so, they have to buy houses as a collateral. This, together with the shorting restrictions that irrational investors face, leads to excessively high house prices. The authors claim that this mechanism explains the increase in the house price-rent ratio in the 1970s. My comments are the following:

Inflation Disagreement or Violation of Fisher Equation

What makes this analysis different from earlier work on money illusion is that the effects are primarily driven by disagreement among rational investors and investors who are prone to money illusion. While an extreme form of money illusion in which agents never change their belief about inflation predicts a (downward sloping) monotonic relationship between inflation and the mispricing in the housing market, this chapter predicts a U-shaped pattern. Housing prices are excessively high whenever investors

---

1. While the plausibility of short-sale constraints is fiercely debated for the stock market (see, e.g., Battalio and Schultz 2006), it seems uncontroversial for the housing market.

disagree about future inflation forecasts. This occurs when inflation is either very low (late 1990s)—because irrational investors predict inflation to be too high—but also when inflation is very high (as in 1970s)—because the irrational investors' inflation forecast is too low. To check the plausibility of this assumption, it seems natural to look at inflation forecast survey data. There are three main surveys of inflation forecasts. The Survey of Professional Forecasters and the Livingston Survey elicit inflation expectations of professional forecasters working for the financial industry. Unlike the former two, the Michigan Survey of Consumer Attitudes and Behavior focuses on individual households and, hence, seems the most appropriate one as this model attempts to capture not only rational forecasters but also households that are prone to money illusion. Mankiw, Reis, and Wolfers (2004) provide an interesting analysis of inflation expectations. Their study shows, among other things, that disagreement—measured by the interquartile range—slightly leads the median inflation expectation and steadily declines from 1983 onward, with the exception of a blip in the early 1990s. Overlaying the plot with the house price-rent ratio shows that the disagreement explanation of this chapter does a very good job for the 1970s, but is less convincing for the house-price frenzy that started in the late 1990s (see fig. 4C.1).

However, simply looking at disagreement measures of inflation forecasts does not do full justice to this model because money illusion can take on very subtle forms. It might very well be that individuals—when asked—have a good estimate of inflation, but nevertheless fail to distinguish between nominal and real mortgage interest rates. Put differently, it is quite plausible that money illusion reflects a failure of the Fisher equation—agents may ignore that real interest rates are roughly equal nominal interest rates minus inflation—rather than a biased inflation forecast. Hence, with a slight reinterpretation, the authors' mechanism may still be compelling.

An Alternative Hypothesis for 1970s

Another unusual feature of the 1970s is that the house price-rent ratio—unlike in other periods—negatively comoves with the real mortgage interest rate. The price-rent ratio in the 1970s is above its trend when real mortgage rates are low (or even negative) and below its trend when real mortgage rates are high. This observation is consistent with the following alternative hypothesis: a sharp increase in inflation alerts households such that they subsequently correctly take inflation effect into account and focus on the real interest rate. On the other hand, a gradual change in inflation can easily go by unnoticed by a fraction of households. This alternative hypothesis suggests that, in the 1970s, the hedging aspect of housing against inflation risk and especially the tax-deductability of mortgage interest payments were driving housing demand. The fact that nominal

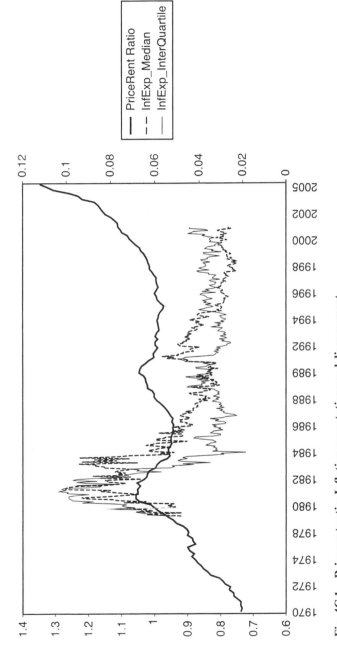

Fig. 4C.1 Price-rent ratio: Inflation expectations and disagreement

Notes: The thick solid line represents the house price-rent ratio (left scale). The thin dashed line depicts the median inflation expectations from the Michigan Survey of Consumer Attitudes and Behavior as provided by Mankiw et al. (2004). The thin solid line shows household disagreement measured as the interquartile range of inflation expectations.

mortgage interest payments are tax-deductible creates a huge incentive to buy a house and borrow money when inflation is high, an effect that was widely discussed at that time. It is, therefore, not surprising that house prices boomed (as emphasized in Poterba [1984] and Titman [1982]). Note also that this alternative hypothesis would also square nicely with Amihud's (1996) finding that the Modigliani-Cohn hypothesis does not hold for the Israeli stock market. High inflation in Israel may have alerted investors to the difference between nominal and real interest rates.

Loan-to-Value-Ratio

When disagreement is high, that is, when either inflation is very high or fairly low, agents would be willing to leverage their housing investment more. One might, therefore, guess that the loan-to-value ratio should be higher in the 1970s and late 1990s. However, Japelli and Pagano (1989, 1994) and Almeida, Campello, and Liu (2006) document an average loan-to-value ratio of 89 percent for the 1980s, which exceeds the 80 percent value registered in both the 1970s and 1990s. Because there are many caveats attached to these numbers, a more elaborate study of real estate leverage would be desirable. Of course, it might also be that banks act rationally and limit credit whenever real estate is overpriced, therefore reducing the average loan-to-value ratio.

Role of Intermediaries

There are no intermediaries in the model, even though they play a significant role in the mortgage market. Their importance was even more pronounced in the 1970s, before mortgages were securitized. While in the model irrational investors take the other side of the mortgage contract in a high inflation environment, in the 1970s, the banking sector, especially thrifts, took on a large part of the inflation risk. As inflation spiked, banks seemed to have lost a large fraction of their value because they issued mortgages that were partially financed by short-term demand deposits (see, e.g., White 1991). Even though some thrifts were arguably poorly managed, I find it more plausible that professional bank managers were surprised by the inflation spikes and inadequately hedged rather than prone to money illusion.

Possible Extensions

The model could be extended in a variety of ways to gain further insights into the mechanism. Departing from the linear utility function specification would enrich the model in two ways. First, it would give housing a role as a hedge against inflation risk. Second, varying the elasticity of intertemporal substitution can cause interesting wealth and feedback effects. Another possibility to augment the model is to allow for disagreement about future house prices. The authors abstract from this by assuming that the future house price is fixed at p'. If agents were to disagree about the future house price p', current house prices would also increase in this disagreement measure. The reasoning is analogous to Miller (1977): optimists push up house prices, while pessimists cannot push them back down because they face short-sale constraints.

Overall, the chapter provides a very interesting U-shaped relation between the price-rent ratio and inflation by combining money illusion and disagreement about inflation with realistic collateral constraints and short-sale constraint on housing. The authors' focus on disagreement about inflation forecasts provides a novel explanation of why we observed relatively high house prices in the 1970s when inflation was high.

References

Almeida, Heitor, Murillo Campello, and Crocker Liu. 2006. The financial accelerator: Evidence from international housing markets. *Review of Finance* 10 (3): 1–32.

Amihud, Yakov. 1996. Unexpected inflation and stock returns revisited—Evidence from Israel. *Journal of Money, Credit, and Banking* 28 (1): 22–33.

Battalio, Robert, and Paul Schultz. 2006. Options and bubbles. *Journal of Finance* 61 (5): 2071–2102.

Brunnermeier, Markus K., and Christian Julliard. 2008. Money illusion and housing frenzies. *Review of Financial Studies* 21 (8): 135–80.

Jappelli, Tullio, and Marco Pagano. 1989. Consumption and capital market imperfections: An international comparison. *American Economic Review* 79(5): 1088–1105.

———. 1994. Savings, growth, and liquidity constraints. *Quarterly Journal of Economics* 109 (1): 83–109.

Mankiw, N. Gregory, Ricardo Reis, and Justin Wolfers. 2004. Disagreement about inflation expectations. In *NBER macroeconomic annual 2003*, ed. Mark Gertler and Kenneth Rogoff, 209–48. Cambridge, MA: MIT Press.

Miller, Edward M. 1977. Risk, uncertainty, and divergence of opinion. *Journal of Finance* 32 (4): 1151–68.

Modigliani, Franco, and Richard Cohn. 1979. Inflation, rational valuation and the market. *Financial Analysis Journal* 37 (3): 24–44.

Poterba, James M. 1984. Tax subsidies to owner-occupied housing: An asset market approach. *Quarterly Journal of Economics* 99 (4): 729–52.

Summers, Lawrence H. The nonadjustment of nominal interest rates: A study of the Fisher effect. In *Symposium in honor of Arthur Okun*, ed. James Tobin, 201–41, Washington DC: Brookings Institution.

Titman, Sheridan. 1982. The effects of anticipated inflation on housing market equilibrium. *Journal of Finance* 37 (3): 827–42.

White, Lawrence. 1991. *The S&L debacle*. New York: Oxford University Press.

Discussion Summary

Martin Schneider responded to Brunnermeier's discussion by saying that the authors had wanted to incorporate heterogeneity because it appeared that nominal interest rates respond strongly to inflation. In a framework with a representative agent subject to inflation illusion, this would not be the case. Schneider also argued that it was not possible to identify the proportion of people subject to inflation illusion from surveys. Finally, he said that the results of the quantitative model were included in the chapter primarily to convince people that the effects highlighted in the chapter could be quantitatively important.

Stephen G. Cecchetti said that he was surprised that high nominal interest rates were associated with high house prices because mortgage qualifications related to nominal rates: that is, φ, the parameter that drives the results when people disagree, was decreasing in the nominal interest rate. Schneider replied that he thought that financial innovation had helped to amplify this effect.

Martin Feldstein said that he thought the tax treatment of mortgage interest payments is an important factor for house prices. The government focuses on nominal interest rates for the purpose of deductions, so when inflation is high, the after-tax real interest rate decreases. This, he suggested, drives much of the variation in house prices. Piazzesi agreed and said that the authors were addressing the issue in a companion paper.

Donald L. Kohn said that if inflation illusion were responsible for the housing-price boom, one might expect to see less of a boom in inflation-targeting countries than in the United States. But that was not the case. He suggested that this cast doubt on the chapter's hypothesis and that it might be instead that irrational investors in housing merely extrapolate past capital gains forward. If the argument of the chapter were correct, however, it would make it harder for monetary policymakers to respond to house-price bubbles because changes in interest rates and inflation would worsen disagreement among investors and increase housing demand.

Marvin Goodfriend responded to Kohn that there is an identification problem: central banks may choose to target inflation because they lack credibility. In this case, disagreement about inflation may be just as severe in inflation-targeting countries. Goodfriend also said that more flexible monetary policy, with multiple goals, may lead the central bank to lose control of investor beliefs about inflation and that the chapter provides an example of a real distortion that can arise from such a loss of control.

Simon Gilchrist said that it would be important to look for direct evidence for the increased dispersion of beliefs relied upon by this model and others like it.

John C. Williams pointed out that the house price-rent ratio had increased greatly in recent years and that this run-up was not uniform over the United States but rather was concentrated on the coasts. If so, the model asked us to believe that people on the coasts were most subject to illusion. Schneider replied that he thought that supply considerations could explain this fact: in the center of the country, supply expanded to meet demand, while on the coasts, supply was fixed.

Andrew Levin said that the reason that the original inflation illusion literature had not focused on housing prices was because the tax effect was so obvious: there was a huge benefit to housing investors from the fact that tax deductions were based on nominal rates. Schneider agreed that the tax effect was first-order. But he argued that the disagreement effect was also first-order; in the authors' other paper, they found that the two effects were of comparable magnitudes. Brunnermeier said that his paper with Julliard finds a substantial effect of money illusion on housing prices, and this effect can be rationalized through the tax channel because money illusion and interest rate deductability have opposite effects on housing prices.

Learning, Macroeconomic Dynamics, and the Term Structure of Interest Rates

Hans Dewachter and Marco Lyrio

5.1 Introduction

Since the seminal papers by Vasicek (1977) and Cox, Ingersoll, and Ross (1985), there is a consensus in the finance literature that term structure models should respond to three requirements: absence of arbitrage opportunities and both econometric and numerical tractability. Models designed to meet these criteria can be useful, for instance, in the pricing of fixed income derivatives and in the assessment of the risks implied by fixed income portfolios. More recently, however, a number of requirements have been added to the modeling of the yield curve dynamics. Satisfactory models should also (1) be able to identify the economic forces behind movements in the yield curve, (2) take into account the way central banks implement their monetary policies, and (3) have a macroeconomic framework consistent with the stochastic discount factor implied by the model. In this chapter, we present a model that fulfills all of the preceding requirements and, in addition, integrates learning dynamics within this macro-finance framework.

The model presented in this chapter builds on recent developments (phases) in the *affine term structure* literature. The first phase is character-

Hans Dewachter is a professor in international economics at the Catholic University of Leuven. Marco Lyrio is an assistant professor of finance at Warwick Business School.

We are grateful for financial support from the FWO-Vlaanderen (Project No. G.0332.01). We thank the discussant, Jordi Galí; the organizer, John Campbell; and the participants at the National Bureau of Economic Research (NBER) Conference on Asset Prices and Monetary Policy for very helpful comments. We also thank Konstantijn Maes; Raf Wouters; and seminar participants at the National Bank of Belgium; 2004 Conference on Computing in Economics and Finance; Heriot-Watt University; the Catholic University of Leuven; Tilburg University; the University of Amsterdam; the European Central Bank; and the University of Warwick for useful discussions and comments on a previous version of this chapter. The authors are responsible for remaining errors.

ized by the use of latent or unobservable factors, as defined in Duffie and Kan (1996) and summarized in Dai and Singleton (2000). Although this framework excludes arbitrage opportunities and is reasonably tractable, the factors derived from such models do not have a direct economic meaning and are simply labeled according to their effect on the yield curve (i.e., as a "level," a "slope," and a "curvature" factor).

The second phase involves the inclusion of macroeconomic variables as factors in the standard affine term structure model. Ang and Piazzesi (2003) show that such an inclusion improves the forecasting performance of vector autoregression (VAR) models in which no-arbitrage restrictions are imposed.[1] Their model, nevertheless, still includes unobservable factors without an explicit macroeconomic interpretation. Kozicki and Tinsley (2001, 2002) indicate the importance of long-run inflation expectations in modeling the yield curve and connect the level factor in affine term structure models to these long-run inflation expectations. This interpretation of the level factor is confirmed by Dewachter and Lyrio (2006), who estimate an affine term structure model based only on factors with a well-specified macroeconomic interpretation. The mentioned papers do not attempt, however, to propose a macroeconomic framework consistent with the pricing kernel implied by their models.

The third and most recent phase in this line of research is marked by the use of structural macro relations together with the standard affine term structure model. The structural macro model replaces the unrestricted VAR setup adopted in previous research and has commonly been based on a New Keynesian framework. Hördahl, Tristani, and Vestin (2006) find that the forecasting performance of such a model is comparable to that of standard latent factor models. They are also able to explain part of the empirical failure of the expectations hypothesis. A similar approach is adopted by Rudebusch and Wu (2003). Bekaert, Cho, and Moreno (2006) go one step further and impose consistency between the pricing kernel and the macro model.

The success of macro-finance models is remarkable given the well-documented dynamic inconsistencies between the long-run implications of the macroeconomic models and the term structure of interest rates.[2] In particular, standard macroeconomic models fail to generate sufficient persistence to account for the time variation at the long end of the yield curve. The success of macro-finance models in fitting jointly the term structure and the macroeconomic dynamics, in fact, crucially hinges on the introduction of additional inert and latent factors with a macroeconomic inter-

---

1. Other papers using this approach include Dewachter, Lyrio, and Maes (2006) and Diebold, Rudebusch, and Aruoba (2006).

2. For instance, Gürkaynak, Sack, and Swanson (2005) and Ellingsen and Söderström (2001) show that standard macroeconomic models cannot account for the sensitivity of long-run forward rates to standard macroeconomic shocks.

pretation. For instance, Bekaert, Cho, and Moreno (2006), Dewachter and Lyrio (2006), and Hördahl, Tristani, and Vestin (2006), among others, introduce a time-varying (partly) exogenous implicit inflation target of the central bank and show that it accounts for the time variation in long-maturity yields.

The main goal of this chapter is to build and estimate macro-finance models that generate these additional factors endogenously from a macroeconomic framework. To this end, we introduce learning into the framework of standard macro-finance models. Extending macro-finance models with learning dynamics seems a promising route to model jointly the macroeconomic and term structure dynamics for two reasons. First, learning generates endogenously additional and potentially persistent factors in the form of subjective expectations.[3] Second, learning, especially constant gain learning, introduces sufficient persistence in the perceived macroeconomic dynamics to generate a level factor in the term structure of interest rates. Such a level factor is crucial to account for the time variation in the long end of the yield curve.[4]

Our approach connects the macro-finance models of the term structure to the learning literature. Links between learning and the term structure of interest rates are also actively analyzed in the learning literature. For example, Cogley (2005) uses a time-varying Bayesian VAR to account for the joint dynamics of macroeconomic variables and the term structure of interest rates. Kozicki and Tinsley (2005) use a reduced-form VAR in macroeconomic and term structure variables and assume agents have imperfect information with respect to the inflation target. They find that subjective long-run inflation expectations are crucial in fitting movements in long-maturity yields and inflation expectations and report a substantial difference between the central bank's inflation target and the subjective expectations of the inflation target. Orphanides and Williams (2005a) introduce long-run inflation expectations in the structural macroeconomic models by substituting expectations by and calibrating the learning parameters on observed survey data.[5] This chapter complements this recent and rapidly growing literature. First, we do not rely on reduced-form VAR dynamics. Instead, we use a standard New Keynesian model to describe the macroeconomic dimension and impose consistency of the pricing kernel for the term structure and the macroeconomic dynamics. Second, following Sargent and Williams (2005), we generate the subjective expectations based on a learning technology that is optimal given the structural equations and the

---

3. Milani (2007) finds that the persistence in the learning dynamics is sufficiently strong to capture much of the inertia of the macroeconomic series.

4. Orphanides and Williams (2005a,b), using a calibrated learning model, show that learning affects the long end of the term structure.

5. Other papers using survey expectations as proxies for the theoretical expectations include Roberts (1997) and Rudebusch (2002).

priors of the agents. Third, we estimate jointly the deep parameters of the structural equations and the learning parameters. The term structure of interest rates and surveys of inflation expectations are included as additional information variables in the measurement equation. We find that the proposed model generates sufficiently volatile subjective long-run expectations of macroeconomic variables to account for most of the time variation in long-maturity yields and surveys of inflation expectations. This is achieved without reference to additional latent factors and, hence, offers an alternative approach to the current macro-finance literature.

The remainder of the chapter is divided in four sections. In section 5.2, we present the macroeconomic framework, which is based on a standard New Keynesian macro model. We introduce imperfect information with respect to the endpoints of macroeconomic variables, discuss the respective priors, and derive the optimal learning rule. The perceived and actual laws of motion are derived together with the conditions for stability of the macroeconomic dynamics. The perceived law of motion forms the basis to generate the implied term structures of interest rates and inflation expectations. The estimation methodology is presented in section 5.3. Both the yield curve and surveys of inflation expectations are used as additional information variables to identify subjective expectations. In section 5.4, we present the estimation results and compare the performance of the estimated models in fitting the term structure of interest rates. We show that macro-finance models, built on structural equations and learning, explain a substantial part of the time variation of long-maturity yields and inflation expectations. We conclude in section 5.5 by summarizing the main findings of the chapter.

5.2 Macroeconomic Dynamics

We use the standard monetary three-equation New Keynesian framework as presented in, for instance, Hördahl, Tristani, and Vestin (2006), Bekaert, Cho, and Moreno (2006), and Cho and Moreno (2006). These models can be considered as minimal versions of a fully structural model (e.g., Christiano, Eichenbaum, and Evans 2005; Smets and Wouters 2003) and commonly represent the benchmark model in the literature linking macroeconomic dynamics and the term structure. We follow the standard Euler equation procedure employed in the learning literature (Bullard and Mitra 2002; Evans and Honkapohja 2001) and replace the rational expectations operator by a subjective expectations operator.[6] In the following model, subjective expectations differ from rational expectations because we assume that agents do not observe the inflation target of the central

---

6. An alternative micro-founded approach to learning has been developed by Preston (2005). We leave this extension for future research.

bank nor the equilibrium output-neutral real interest rate. Finally, in section 5.2.3 we solve for the macroeconomic dynamics, that is, the actual law of motion. The solution is given in the form of a reduced VAR(I) model in an extended state space.

5.2.1   Structural Equations

The structural model used is a parsimonious three-equation representation of the underlying macroeconomic structure, containing aggregate supply (AS) and investment saving (IS) equations and a monetary policy rule identifying the riskless nominal interest rate. To account for the persistence in inflation, the output gap, and the policy rate, we add inflation indexation, habit formation, and interest rate smoothing to the standard model.

The design of the AS equation is motivated by the sticky price models based on Calvo (1983). In line with the standard Calvo price-setting theory, we assume a world where only a fraction of the firms updates prices at any given date, while the nonoptimizing firms are assumed to use some rule of thumb (indexation scheme) in adjusting their prices (e.g., Galí and Gertler 1999). This setting leads to a positive relation between (transitory) inflation on the one hand and real marginal costs on the other. Specific assumptions are made with respect to the marginal costs and the indexation scheme of the nonoptimizing agents. First, we assume that marginal costs are proportional to the output gap and an additional cost-push shock, ε_π. Second, nonoptimizing firms are assumed to adjust prices according to an indexation scheme based on past inflation rates. The degree of indexation is measured by the parameter δ_π, and the indexation scheme at time t is given by $\pi^* + \delta_\pi(\pi_{t-1} - \pi^*)$ with π^* the inflation target and π_{t-1} the previous period inflation rate. Following these assumptions, the standard AS curve is given by:

(1)
$$\pi_t = c_\pi + \mu_{\pi,1}E_t\pi_{t+1} + \mu_{\pi,2}\pi_{t-1} + \kappa_\pi y_t + \sigma_\pi\varepsilon_{\pi,t},$$

(2)
$$c_\pi = \left[1 - \frac{\delta_\pi}{(1 + \psi\delta_\pi)} - \frac{\psi}{(1 + \psi\delta_\pi)}\right]\pi^*,$$

$$\mu_{\pi,1} = \frac{\psi}{(1 + \psi\delta_\pi)}, \mu_{\pi,2} = \frac{\delta_\pi}{(1 + \psi\delta_\pi)},$$

where ψ represents the discount factor, and κ_π measures the sensitivity of inflation to the output gap. Given the assumed proportionality between marginal costs and output gap, κ_π is a rescaled parameter of the sensitivity of inflation to the real marginal cost. Endogenous inflation persistence, $\mu_{\pi,2} > 0$, arises as a consequence of the assumption that nonoptimizing agents use past inflation in their indexation scheme. Finally, we impose long-run neutrality of output with respect to inflation. Given the setup of the model, this amounts to setting the discount factor (ψ) to one. Long-run neutrality is characterized by inflation parameters in the AS equation adding up to one, implying that $\mu_{\pi,1} = (1 - \mu_{\pi,2})$.

The IS curve is recovered from the Euler equation on private consumption. Following the recent strand of literature incorporating external habit formation in the utility function (e.g., Cho and Moreno 2006), and imposing the standard market clearing condition, we obtain the following IS equation:

$$(3) \qquad y_t = \mu_y E_t y_{t+1} + (1 - \mu_y) y_{t-1} + \phi(i_t - E_t \pi_{t+1} - r) + \sigma_y \varepsilon_{y,\,t},$$

where the parameters μ_y and ϕ are functions of the utility parameters related to the agent's level of relative risk aversion, σ, and (external) habit formation, h:[7]

$$(4) \qquad \mu_y = \frac{\sigma}{\sigma + h(\sigma - 1)}, \quad \phi = -\frac{1}{\sigma + h(\sigma - 1)}.$$

Habit formation is introduced as a means to generate additional output gap persistence. Without habits, that is, $h = 0$, the purely forward-looking IS curve is recovered. The demand shock $\varepsilon_{y,\,t}$ refers to (independent) shocks in preferences.[8] Equation (3) establishes the interpretation of r as an output-neutral real interest rate. Other things equal, ex ante real interest rate levels ($i_t - E_t \pi_{t+1}$) above r reduce output (and inflation), while for ex ante real interest rates below r, output (and inflation) increases. Although we could allow for time variation in this output-neutral real interest rate, we restrain from doing so in order to avoid additional complexities in the estimation arising from the fact that this variable is unobservable.

We close the model by specifying a monetary policy in terms of a Taylor rule. Following Clarida, Galí, and Gertler (1999), we use a policy rule accounting for both interest rate smoothing and idiosyncratic policy shocks, $\varepsilon_{i,\,t}$. The monetary policy rate equation is given by:

$$(5) \qquad i_t = (1 - \gamma_{i-1})i_t^T + \gamma_{i-1} i_{t-1} + \sigma_i \varepsilon_{i,\,t}.$$

We model the central bank's targeted interest rate, i_t^T, by means of a Taylor rule in the output gap, y_t, and inflation gap, $\pi_t - \pi^*$:

---

7. We assume the following utility function:

$$U(C_t) = (1 - \sigma)^{-1} G_t \left(\frac{C_t}{H_t}\right)^{1-\sigma},$$

with G_t an independent stochastic preference factor and an external habit level, H_t, specified as $H_t = C_{t-1}^h$. Note that in order to have a well-defined steady state, the habit persistence needs to be restricted, $0 \leq h \leq 1$, as explained in Fuhrer (2000).

8. Note that only by linearly detrending output we obtain a one-to-one relation between the shock in the IS equation and preference (demand) shocks. In general, the interpretation of ε_y as a demand shock is at least partially flawed, given the fact that it might also contain shocks to permanent output.

(6) $$i_t^T = r + E_t\pi_{t+1} + \gamma_\pi(\pi_t - \pi^*) + \gamma_y y_t,$$

where π^* denotes the inflation target of the central bank. This policy rule differs from the standard formulation of Taylor rules as we assign a weight of one to the expected inflation term. By imposing this condition, we model explicitly the idea that the central bank is actually targeting an ex ante real interest rate in function of the macroeconomic state, that is, $\pi_t - \pi^*$ and y_t.

The model can be summarized in a standard matrix notation by defining the state space by a vector of macroeconomic variables, $X_t = [\pi_t, y_t, i_t]'$ and a vector of structural shocks, $\varepsilon_t = [\varepsilon_{\pi,t}, \varepsilon_{y,t}, \varepsilon_{i,t}]'$. Using a vector $\mathbf{C}$ and matrices $\mathbf{A}$, $\mathbf{B}$, $\mathbf{D}$, and $\mathbf{S}$ of appropriate dimensions, we write the structural equations as:

(7) $$\mathbf{A}X_t = \mathbf{C} + \mathbf{B}E_tX_{t+1} + \mathbf{D}X_{t-1} + \mathbf{S}\varepsilon_t.$$

5.2.2   Perceived Law of Motion

The structural model (eq. [7]) is solved under two sets of expectations operators. First, we solve the model under the assumption of rational expectations. The rational expectations solution builds on perfect information of agents with respect to the structural parameters and results in a time-invariant structural VAR representation for the perceived law of motion. Next, we relax the perfect information assumption and extend the perceived law of motion by introducing uncertainty with respect to the endpoints of the macroeconomic variables. This alternative implies a perceived law of motion described in terms of a VECM. Both versions can be seen as special cases of a generic model for expectations, composed of (1) a set of prior beliefs of the agents and (2) an optimal learning rule. In this section, we first describe the priors of the generic model; subsequently, we solve for the optimal learning rule under both rational expectations and the extended set of beliefs. Finally, we discuss the implications of the perceived law of motion for the term structure of interest rates and the term structure of inflation expectations.

Priors and Learning

The beliefs of agents are summarized in terms of a generic model for the macroeconomic dynamics. More specifically, denoting the perceived stochastic trends by ζ_t^P and observable macroeconomic variables by X_t the priors take the form:

(8) $$X_t = \xi_t^P + \Phi^P(X_{t-1} - \xi_t^P) + \Sigma^P \varepsilon_t$$

$$\xi_t^P = V^P\zeta_t^P$$

$$\zeta_t^P = \zeta_{t-1}^P + \Sigma_\zeta \upsilon_{\zeta,t}.$$

Macroeconomic dynamics can be decomposed into a transitory and permanent component. The permanent component of the dynamics is generated by a set of stochastic trends ζ_t^P. The stochastic trends are generated by a set of permanent shocks, $\upsilon_{\zeta,t}$ with standard deviation:

(9)
$$\Sigma_\zeta = \begin{bmatrix} \sigma_{\zeta,\pi} & 0 & 0 \\ 0 & \sigma_{\zeta,y} & 0 \\ 0 & 0 & \sigma_{\zeta,r} \end{bmatrix}.$$

The stochastic trends determine a set of perceived stochastic endpoints ξ_t^P, $\xi_t^P = V^P \zeta_t^P$, identifying the long-run expectations of the macroeconomic variables, X_t (see Kozicki and Tinsley 2001):

(10)
$$\xi_t^P = \lim_{s \to \infty} E_t^P X_{t+s}.$$

The perceived transitory dynamics, that is, dynamics relative to the long-run expectations, are modeled in terms of a standard VAR(I) model. More in particular, transitory dynamics are described by the matrix Φ^P, modeling the inertia and interaction in the transitory dynamics, and Σ^P the impact matrix of the transitory shocks, ε_t. Finally, the priors can be restated in extended state space $\tilde{X}_t = [X_t', \xi_t^{P'}]$ by defining $\eta_t = [\varepsilon_t', \upsilon_{\zeta,t}']'$ as:

(11)
$$\tilde{X}_t = \tilde{\Phi}^P \tilde{X}_{t-1} + \tilde{\Sigma}^P \eta_t$$

or equivalently:

(12)
$$\begin{bmatrix} X_t \\ \xi_t^P \end{bmatrix} = \begin{bmatrix} \Phi^P & (I - \Phi^P) \\ 0 & I \end{bmatrix} \begin{bmatrix} X_{t-1} \\ \xi_{t-1}^P \end{bmatrix} + \begin{bmatrix} \Sigma^P & (I - \Phi^P)V\Sigma_\zeta \\ 0 & V\Sigma_\zeta \end{bmatrix} \begin{bmatrix} \varepsilon_t \\ \upsilon_{\zeta,t} \end{bmatrix}.$$

In general, we assume that the stochastic endpoints are not observed. Agents, therefore, face an inference problem for the stochastic endpoints ξ_t^P, which is solved by means of a mean squared error (MSE) optimal Kalman filter learning rule. Denoting the inferred values for the stochastic endpoints by $\xi_{t|t}^P$, the learning algorithm becomes:

(13)
$$\xi_{t|t}^P = \xi_{t-1|t-1}^P + K(X_t - E_{t-1}^P X_t),$$

where K is obtained as the steady-state solution to the Kalman filtering equations:

(14)
$$K_t = P_{t|t-1}(I - \Phi^P)'F_t^{-1}$$
$$F_t = (I - \Phi^P)P_{t|t-1}(I - \Phi^P)' + \Sigma^P \Sigma^{P'}$$
$$P_{t+1|t} = P_{t|t-1} - P_{t|t-1}(I - \Phi^P)'F_t^{-1}(I - \Phi^P)P_{t|t-1} + \Sigma_\zeta \Sigma_\zeta'.$$

This perceived law of motion embeds various forms of expectational assumptions. We distinguish between rational expectations and models incorporating imperfect information or credibility with respect to the inflation target and output-neutral real interest rate.

Rational Expectations

Rational expectations are obtained as a specific case of the perceived law of motion. More in particular, rational expectations generated by the preceding structural equations are recovered by two sets of informational assumptions. First, agents believe in deterministic endpoints. Within the context of the preceding structural model endpoints are deterministic, that is, $\Sigma_\zeta = 0$, and are identified by solving the structural model for the steady state. Under the restriction that in the long run no trade-off exists between the output gap and the monetary policy, that is, $\mu_{\pi,1} = (1 - \mu_{\pi,2})$, the steady state of the model is determined by the level of the inflation target, π^*, the steady state of the output gap, y^* (fixed to zero), and the output-neutral real interest rate level, $r = r^*$:

$$(15) \qquad \xi_t^P = \lim_{s \to \infty} E_t \begin{bmatrix} \pi_{t+s} \\ y_{t+s} \\ i_{t+s} \end{bmatrix} = V \begin{bmatrix} \pi^* \\ y^* \\ r^* \end{bmatrix} = \begin{bmatrix} 1 & 0 & 0 \\ 0 & 1 & 0 \\ 1 & 0 & 1 \end{bmatrix} \begin{bmatrix} \pi^* \\ y^* \\ r^* \end{bmatrix},$$

where E_t denotes the rational expectations operator. The mapping V is determined by the structural equations. Under rational expectations, the inflation target determines the long-run inflation expectations. The long-run expectations for the output gap are fixed at $y^* = 0$, and the long-run expectations for the nominal interest rate are determined by the Fisher hypothesis, linking the endpoint of the interest rate to the sum of the real interest rate and inflation expectations. Next, rational expectations imply that agents know the structural parameters, such that transitory dynamics, that is, the matrices $\Phi^P = \Phi^{re}$ and $\Sigma^P = \Sigma^{re}$ are determined by the standard rational expectations conditions:

$$(16) \qquad \Phi^{re} = (A - B\Phi^{re})^{-1}\mathbf{D}$$

$$\Sigma^{re} = (A - B\Phi^{re})^{-1}\mathbf{S}.$$

The perceived law of motion under rational expectations can be restated in an extended state space as:[9]

$$(17) \qquad \begin{bmatrix} X_t \\ \xi_t^P \end{bmatrix} = \begin{bmatrix} \Phi^{re} & (I - \Phi^{re}) \\ 0 & I \end{bmatrix} \begin{bmatrix} X_{t-1} \\ \xi_{t-1}^P \end{bmatrix} + \begin{bmatrix} \Sigma^{re} \\ 0 \end{bmatrix} \varepsilon_t,$$

with initial condition ξ_{S0}^P

9. Note that the solution can also be written more concisely in structural VAR form as:

$$X_t = C^{re} + \Phi^{re} X_{t-1} + \Sigma^{re}\varepsilon_t,$$

with $C^{re} = (I - \Phi^{re})\xi_{St}^{re}$.

(18)
$$\xi_0^P = \begin{bmatrix} 1 & 0 & 0 \\ 0 & 1 & 0 \\ 1 & 0 & 1 \end{bmatrix} \begin{bmatrix} \pi^* \\ y^* \\ r^* \end{bmatrix}.$$

Finally, note that under rational expectations with deterministic endpoints and perfect information, agents do not face an inference problem. This perfect information assumption (i.e., $\Sigma_\zeta = 0$) generates a Kalman gain $K = 0$ (see eq. [14]). Rational expectations are, therefore, a limiting case of the learning model.

Stochastic Endpoints and Learning

Next to rational expectations, we introduce an alternative set of priors implying stochastic endpoints for the macroeconomic variables. Within the context of the preceding structural model, stochastic endpoints ξ_t^P arise as the consequence of perceived underlying stochastic trends in the economy, $\zeta_t^P = [\pi_t^{*P}, y_t^{*P}, r_t^{*P}]$, representing the vector containing the perceived inflation target, π_t^{*P}, the perceived long-run output gap, y_t^{*P} (fixed to zero), and the perceived long-run output-neutral real interest rate, r_t^{*P}. The size of the perceived time variation in the stochastic trends is measured by Σ_ζ. Denoting the expectations operator under this set of priors by E_t^P, it can be verified that:

(19)
$$\lim_{s \to \infty} E_t^P X_{t+s} = \xi_t^P = V\zeta_t^P$$

or equivalently

(20)
$$\lim_{s \to \infty} E_t^P \begin{bmatrix} \pi_{t+s} \\ y_{t+s} \\ i_{t+s} \end{bmatrix} = V \begin{bmatrix} \pi_t^{*P} \\ y_t^{*P} \\ r_t^{*P} \end{bmatrix} = \begin{bmatrix} 1 & 0 & 0 \\ 0 & 1 & 0 \\ 1 & 0 & 1 \end{bmatrix} \begin{bmatrix} \pi_t^{*P} \\ y_t^{*P} \\ r_t^{*P} \end{bmatrix}.$$

The priors about the transitory dynamics, that is, the dynamics relative to the stochastic endpoints, are assumed to coincide with the ones implied by the rational expectations model. This implies that the matrices Φ^P and Σ^P are identical to their rational expectations equivalents: $\Phi^P = \Phi^{re}$ and $\Sigma^P = \Sigma^{re}$. By equating the perceived transitory dynamics to those implied by the rational expectations model, we obtain a perceived law of motion that differs from the rational expectations solution only due to the introduction of stochastic endpoints. The final perceived law of motion (PLM) can be written in extended state space as:

(21)
$$\begin{bmatrix} X_t \\ \xi_t^P \end{bmatrix} = \begin{bmatrix} \Phi^P & (I - \Phi^P) \\ 0 & I \end{bmatrix} \begin{bmatrix} X_{t-1} \\ \xi_{t-1}^P \end{bmatrix} + \begin{bmatrix} \Sigma^P & (I - \Phi^P)V\Sigma_\zeta \\ 0 & V\Sigma_\zeta \end{bmatrix} \begin{bmatrix} \varepsilon_t \\ \upsilon_{\zeta,t} \end{bmatrix}.$$

Finally, under this prior, agents face an inference problem and, hence, resort to learning the stochastic endpoints by means of a Kalman filter. The optimal learning rule for this prior is within the class of stochastic gradient rules with the gain defined by the Kalman filter. This gain depends on the specificities of the prior, that is, the specific values for Σ_ζ, Σ^P, and Φ^P. As in Orphanides and Williams (2005a), we assume that agents substitute the unknown stochastic endpoints by the ones inferred by the learning rule.

The Term Structure of Interest Rates

Standard no-arbitrage conditions are used to generate bond prices consistent with the perceived law of motion. Imposing no-arbitrage under the PLM reflects the view that bond prices are set by the private sector and should, therefore, be consistent with the perceived dynamics and information set of these agents. Within the context of default-free, zero-coupon bonds, no-arbitrage implies a pricing equation of the form:

$$(22) \qquad P_t(\tau) = E_t^P [M_{t+1}P_{t+1}(\tau - 1)],$$

where E^P denotes the subjective expectations operator generated by the PLM (see eq. [11]), $P(\tau)$ denotes the price of a default-free, zero-coupon bond with maturity τ, and M_t denotes the pricing kernel consistent with the PLM. We follow Bekaert, Cho, and Moreno (2006) in using the utility function implied by the macroeconomic framework to identify the prices of risk. While this approach has the advantage of guaranteeing consistency of the pricing kernel, it comes at the cost of loss of flexibility in modeling the prices of risk.[10] The (log) pricing kernel consistent with the PLM is the homoskedastic (log) pricing kernel:

$$(23) \qquad m_{t+1} = -i_t - \frac{1}{2}\sigma_m^2 - \Lambda\eta_{t+1},$$

where the prices of risk, Λ, are determined by the structural parameters

$$(24) \qquad \Lambda = \sigma e_y \tilde{\Sigma}^P + e_\pi \tilde{\Sigma}^P - \sigma_y e_y,$$

where $\mathbf{e}_x$ denotes a vector selecting the elements of the x-equation, that is, e_y selects the row of $\tilde{\Sigma}^P$ related to the y-equation. No-arbitrage restrictions imposed on conditional Gaussian and linear state space dynamics generate exponentially affine bond pricing models (see, for instance, Ang and Piazzesi 2003):

$$(25) \qquad P(\tau) = \exp[a(\tau) + b(\tau)\tilde{\mathbf{X}}_{t|t}],$$

10. The standard approach in modeling the term structure is to assume a essentially affine term structure representation. As shown by Duffee (2002), such representations do not restrict the prices of risk to be constant.

where $\tilde{\mathbf{X}}_{t|t}$ denotes the inferred state vector, obtained by replacing ξ_t^P by its inferred value $\xi_{t|t}^P$, $\tilde{\mathbf{X}}_{t|t} = (X_t', \xi_{t|t}^{P'})'$. The factor loadings $a(\tau)$ and $b(\tau)$ can be obtained by solving difference equations representing the set of nonlinear restrictions imposed by the no-arbitrage conditions:

$$(26) \quad a(\tau) = -\delta_0 + a(\tau - 1) - [b(\tau - 1)]\tilde{\Sigma}^P\Lambda' + \frac{1}{2}b(\tau - 1)\tilde{\Sigma}^P\tilde{\Sigma}^{P'}b(\tau - 1)'$$

$$b(\tau) = b(\tau - 1)\tilde{\Phi}^P - \delta_1',$$

with $\delta_0 = 0$, and δ_1 implicitly defined by the identity $i_t = \delta_1'\tilde{\mathbf{X}}_{t|t}$. The system has a particular solution given the initial conditions $a(0) = 0$ and $b(0) = 0$.

Exponentially affine bond price models lead to affine yield curve models. Defining the yield of a bond with maturity τ_1 by $y(\tau_1) = -ln[P_t(\tau_1)]/\tau_1$ and the vector of yields spanning the term structure by $\mathbf{Y}_t = [y_t(\tau_1), \ldots, y_t(\tau_n)]'$, the term structure can be written as an affine function of the extended state space variables:

$$(27) \quad \mathbf{Y}_t = \mathbf{A}_y + \mathbf{B}_y\tilde{\mathbf{X}}_{t|t} + \upsilon_{y,t},$$

where $\mathbf{A}_y$ and $\mathbf{B}_y$ denote matrices containing the maturity-specific factor loadings for the yield curve $\{\mathbf{A}_y = [-a(\tau_1)/\tau_1, \ldots, -a(\tau_n)/\tau_n]'$ and $\mathbf{B}_y = [-b(\tau_1)'/\tau_1, \ldots, -b(\tau_n)'/\tau_n]'\}$, and $\upsilon_{y,t}$ contains maturity-specific measurement errors.

The Term Structure of Inflation Expectations

The representation of the term structure of inflation expectations is obtained by iterating the PLM (eq. [11]) forward. It is straightforward to show that the linearity of the PLM generates an affine representation for the term structure of inflation expectations in the extended state space, $\tilde{\mathbf{X}}_{t|t}$. The term structure of average inflation expectations is described by

$$(28) \quad E_t^P\bar{\pi}(\tau) = \frac{1}{\tau}\sum_{i=0}^{\tau-1}E_t^P(\pi_{t+i}) = e_\pi[a_s(\tau) + b_s(\tau)\tilde{\mathbf{X}}_{t|t}],$$

where $E_t^P\bar{\pi}(\tau)$ denotes the time t average inflation expectation over the horizon τ, e_π denotes a vector selecting π_t out of the vector $\tilde{\mathbf{X}}_{t|t}$, and $a_e(\tau)$, $b_e(\tau)$, $a_s(\tau)$ and $b_s(\tau)$ are maturity-dependent functions generated by the system:

$$(29) \quad a_e(\tau) = 0, b_e(\tau) = b_e(\tau - 1)\tilde{\Phi}^P$$

$$a_s(\tau) = \frac{1}{\tau}\sum_{i=0}^{\tau-1}a_e(i) = 0, \text{ and } b_s(\tau) = \frac{1}{\tau}\sum_{i=0}^{\tau-1}b_e(i)$$

solved under the initial conditions $a_e(0) = 0$ and $b_e(0) = I$. Equation (28), applied over varying horizons τ, forms the model-implied term structure of average inflation expectations. The term structure of inflation expectations, unlike the term structure of interest rates, is not observable. We use surveys of average inflation expectations for different maturities as a proxy for the term structure of inflation expectations. We relate these surveys,

$s(\tau)$, to the model-implied average inflation expectations by allowing for idiosyncratic measurement errors, $\upsilon_{s,t}(\tau)$, in the survey responses:

$$(30) \qquad s_t(\tau) = e_\pi a_s(\tau) + e_\pi b_s(\tau)\tilde{\mathbf{X}}_{t|t} + \upsilon_{s,t}(\tau),$$

where $s_t(\tau)$ denotes the time t survey response concerning the average inflation expectations over the horizon τ. Finally, denoting the vector containing a set of surveys of inflation expectations for different horizons by $\mathbf{S}_t = [s_t(\tau_1), \ldots, s_t(\tau_m)]'$, and defining $A_s = 0$ and $B_s = [[e_\pi b_s(\tau_1)]', \ldots, [e_\pi b_s(\tau_m)]']'$, equation (30) can be restated as:

$$(31) \qquad \mathbf{S}_t = A_s + B_s \tilde{\mathbf{X}}_{t|t} + \upsilon_{s,t}.$$

5.2.3   Actual Law of Motion

The actual law of motion (ALM), describing the observed dynamics of macroeconomic variables, is obtained by substituting the subjective expectations (eq. [11]) into the structural equations (eq. [7]). Because the subjective expectations are formed on the basis of the inferred stochastic endpoints, $\xi_{t|t}^P$ and on observable macroeconomic data, the relevant space of the ALM coincides with that of the PLM, that is, $\tilde{\mathbf{X}}_{t|t}$. Due to the simplicity of the learning algorithm, the ALM can be solved in closed form. In the appendix, we show that the ALM reduces to a standard VAR(I) in the extended state space:

$$(32) \qquad \tilde{\mathbf{X}}_{t|t} = \tilde{C}^A + \tilde{\Phi}^A \tilde{\mathbf{X}}_{t-1|t-1} + \tilde{\Sigma}^A \varepsilon_t,$$

with

$$(33) \qquad \tilde{C}^A = \left\{ \begin{array}{c} [A - B(\Phi^P + K_\Phi)]^{-1} C \\ K[A - B(\Phi^P + K_\Phi)]^{-1} C \end{array} \right\}$$

$$\tilde{\Phi}^A = \begin{pmatrix} \Phi^P & [A - B(\Phi^P + K_\Phi)]^{-1} B(I - K_\Phi)(I - \Phi^P) \\ 0 & I - K\{I - [A - B(\Phi^P + K_\Phi)]^{-1} B(I - K_\Phi)\}(I - \Phi^P) \end{pmatrix}$$

$$\tilde{\Sigma}^A = \left\{ \begin{array}{c} [A - B(\Phi^P + K_\Phi)]^{-1} S \\ K[A - B(\Phi^P + K_\Phi)]^{-1} S \end{array} \right\},$$

and $K_\Phi = (I - \Phi^P) K$, A, B and S and Φ^P determined by the parameters of the structural equations, and $\mathbf{K}$ the constant gain matrix implied by the agents' priors. The closed form solution can be used to highlight some of the properties of the ALM. First, subjective beliefs about the stochastic endpoints, $\xi_{t|t}^P$, only affect the actual macroeconomic dynamics if an expectation channel exists, that is, $B \neq 0$ in equation (7). One aspect in which macroeconomic dynamics may be affected by subjective beliefs concerns the modeling of persistence. Under rational expectations, persistence is driven by inflation indexation, habit persistence, and interest rate smoothing affecting the roots of the $\Phi^{re} = \Phi^P$ matrix. Learning introduces an additional source of persistence in the form of the persistence in the subjective expectations, $\xi^P_{t|t}$. Persistence in the beliefs follows itself from the inertia in the learning rule, that is, the updating procedure. Milani (2007) shows in a different context that persistence due to learning is important and (partly) takes over the role of inflation indexation and habit formation. In the empirical section, we find similar results, especially for inflation persistence and interest rate smoothing.

Second, the rational expectations model is nested within the learning framework. By imposing the priors consistent with rational expectations, that is, $\Sigma_\zeta = 0$ (implying $K_\Phi = 0$) and $\xi^P_{t|t} = V[\pi^*, 0, r]'$, it can be verified that the ALM simplifies to the rational expectations reduced form, equation (17). Third, the nonstationarity of the PLM does not necessarily carry over to the ALM. The eigenvalues of the matrix $\tilde{\Phi}^A$ depend both on the structural parameters contained in A, B, Φ^P and on the learning parameters K.[11] Finally, if the ALM is stationary, the unconditional distribution of the extended state space vector $\tilde{X}_{t|t}$ is identified. Conditional on the maintained assumption of normality of the structural shocks, ε_t, this distribution is given by:

(34) $$\tilde{X}_{t|t} \sim N(E\tilde{X}_{t|t}, \Omega_{\tilde{X}}),$$

with

$$E\tilde{X}_{t|t} = \begin{bmatrix} (I - \Phi^{re})^{-1}C^{re} \\ (I - \Phi^{re})^{-1}C^{re} \end{bmatrix}$$

$$\text{vec}\,(\Omega_X) = (I - \tilde{\Phi}^A \otimes \tilde{\Phi}^A)^{-1}\,\text{vec}\,(\tilde{\Sigma}^A\tilde{\Sigma}^{A\prime}).$$

Equation (34) represents the unconditional distribution for the extended state under learning. This distribution is characterized by two properties. First, as far as unconditional means are concerned, the ALM and the rational expectations model are observationally equivalent. The unconditional mean of the rational expectations model, that is, $(I - \Phi^{re})^{-1}C^{re}$, coincides with the unconditional mean under the ALM for both the observable macroeconomic variables (inflation, output gap, and policy rate) and the perceived long-run expectations of the agents. The rational expectations model thus serves as a benchmark in mean for the model under learning. Second, in line with the literature on constant gain learning (e.g., Evans

---

11. Note that the stationarity of the ALM is inconsistent with the nonstationarity of the PLM under learning. This inconsistency arises from the fact that the ALM is solved under the assumption of a time-invariant inflation target of the central bank. In the empirical section, we allow for time variation in the central bank inflation target. More specifically, we allow for the inflation target to be chairman-specific. This extension renders the ALM nonstationary and partially reconciles the ALM and the PLM dynamics.

and Honkapohja 2001), the unconditional variance of the stochastic end-points, $\xi_{t|t}^P$, is in general positive, implying nonconvergence of the stochastic endpoints to the true values implied by the rational expectations equilibrium, $[\pi^*, 0, r + \pi^*]'$.

5.3   Estimation Methodology

The actual law of motion for both macroeconomic variables and the inferred stochastic endpoints is used to estimate both the structural and the learning parameters. In order to identify the subjective beliefs, we use information variables directly related to the PLM, that is, the term structure of interest rates and inflation expectations. In section 5.3.1, we discuss the details of the estimation procedure. Subsequently, in section 5.3.2, we explain the different versions of the model that are estimated.

5.3.1   Maximum Likelihood Estimation

The model is estimated by means of log-likelihood in the extended state space with the ALM dynamics serving as the transition equation:

$$(35) \qquad \tilde{\mathbf{X}}_{t|t} = \tilde{C}^A + \tilde{\Phi}^A \tilde{X}_{t-1|t-1} + \tilde{\Sigma}^A \varepsilon_t$$

and a measurement equation, relating the extended state to observable economic variables. The observable variables included in the measurement equation consist of macroeconomic variables, X_t (inflation, output gap, and policy rate), a sample of yields spanning the term structure of interest rates, Y_t (one-, two-, three-, four-, five-, and ten-year yields), and a sample of the term structure of inflation expectations, proxied by survey data on inflation expectations, S_t (one- and ten-year average inflation expectations).[12] The observable variables are collected in the vector $Z_t = [X_t', Y_t', S_t']'$. Using the affine representation of each of these variables in the extended state space, as discussed in section 5.2.2, the measurement equation becomes:

$$(36) \qquad \mathbf{Z}_t = A_m + B_m \tilde{X}_{t|t} + \upsilon_{z,t},$$

where $\upsilon_{z,t}$ denotes idiosyncratic measurement errors with variance-covariance matrix Ψ, and A_m and B_m represent the derived affine representations of the respective subsets of observable variables X_t, Y_t and S_t (B_x is defined as $X_t = B_x \tilde{X}_{t|t}$, i.e., $B_x = [I_{3 \times 3}, 0_{3 \times 3}]$, A_y, A_s, B_y and B_s are defined in equations [27] and [31], respectively):

12. Survey expectations are increasingly used in the empirical literature. Roberts (1997) shows that models including survey expectations can account for some of the (unexplained) inflation inertia. Survey expectations are also starting to be used in the bond pricing literature. Kim and Orphanides (2005) use survey expectations on short-term interest rate movements as an additional input in a otherwise standard Vasicek model. Also, Chun (2005) uses several survey expectations as additional inputs in a two-factor term structure model. Finally, Bekaert, Cho, and Moreno (2006) show the empirical relevance of surveys (on inflation) by showing that surveys help to forecast inflation better than any rational expectations model.

$$A_m = \begin{bmatrix} 0 \\ A_y \\ A_s \end{bmatrix}, B_m = \begin{bmatrix} B_x \\ B_y \\ B_s \end{bmatrix} \text{ and } \Psi = \begin{bmatrix} 0 & 0 & 0 \\ 0 & \Psi_y & 0 \\ 0 & 0 & \Psi_s \end{bmatrix}.$$

Prediction errors, $\mathbf{Z}_t - E_{t-1}^A \mathbf{Z}_t$, and their corresponding log-likelihood value $l(\mathbf{Z}_t - E_{t-1}^A \mathbf{Z}_t; \theta)$, where E_{t-1}^A denotes the expectations operator based on the ALM, are functions of both the structural macroeconomic shocks and the measurement errors:

$$(37) \qquad \mathbf{Z}_t - E_{t-1}^A \mathbf{Z}_t = B_m(\tilde{\mathbf{X}}_{t|t} - E_{t-1}^A \tilde{\mathbf{X}}_{t|t}) + \upsilon_{z,t} = B_m(\tilde{\Sigma}^A \varepsilon_t) + \upsilon_{z,t}$$

$$l(\mathbf{Z}_t - E_{t-1}^A \mathbf{Z}_t; \theta) = -\frac{1}{2}|\Omega_Z| - \frac{1}{2}(\mathbf{Z}_t - E_{t-1}^A \mathbf{Z}_t)'\Omega_Z^{-1}(\mathbf{Z}_t - E_{t-1}^A \mathbf{Z}_t)$$

$$\Omega_Z = B_m \tilde{\Sigma}^A \tilde{\Sigma}^{A'} B_m' + \Psi.$$

One contribution of this chapter is that the deep parameters of the structural equations and the parameters of the learning procedure are estimated jointly based on a wide variety of information variables, that is, macroeconomic variables, term structure variables, and surveys of inflation expectations.[13] The parameters to be estimated are collected in the parameter vector θ, containing the deep parameters of the structural equations (δ_π, κ_π, σ, h, r, π^*, γ_π, γ_y, γ_{i-1}, σ_π, σ_y, σ_i), the learning parameters (priors on the volatility of the stochastic trends $\sigma_{\zeta,\pi}$, $\sigma_{\zeta,r}$, and initial values $\zeta_{0|0}$), and the variances of the measurement errors [$diag(\Psi)$]:

$$(38) \qquad \theta = [\delta_\pi, \kappa_\pi, \sigma, h, r, \pi^*, \gamma_\pi, \gamma_y, \gamma_{i-1}, \sigma_\pi,$$
$$\sigma_y, \sigma_i, \sigma_{\zeta,\pi}, \sigma_{\zeta,r}, \zeta_{0|0}, diag(\Psi)].$$

Not all deep parameters and learning parameters are estimated. We follow Hördahl, Tristani, and Vestin (2006) and Bekaert, Cho, and Moreno (2006) by fixing the discount factor to one, $\psi = 1$. Also, throughout the estimation the prior on the uncertainty of the long-run value for the output gap is restricted to zero, $\sigma_{\zeta,y} = 0$. This restriction guarantees that the long-run expected output gap is fixed to zero under the PLM. Furthermore, we impose the theoretical constraints $\sigma_{\zeta,\pi}$, $\sigma_{\zeta,r} \geq 0$ and $0 \leq h \leq 1$. Finally, parameter estimates are constrained to satisfy two conditions. First, parameter estimates must be consistent with the existence of a unique rational expectations solution. Second, under learning, parameter estimates should imply eigenvalues of $\tilde{\Phi}^A$ strictly smaller than one in absolute value in order

---

13. Other research estimating learning parameters include Orphanides and Williams (2005a) and Milani (2007). Orphanides and Williams (2005a) estimate the constant gain by minimizing the distance between the model-implied inflation expectations and those reported in the survey of professional forecasters. Milani (2007) estimates jointly, using Bayesian methods, the constant gain and the deep parameters of a structural macroeconomic model. We complement their analyses by including more information in the measurement equation, notably term structure of interest rates.

to guarantee stability of the ALM. The model is estimated using a Broyden-Fletcher-Goldfarb-Shanno (BFGS) algorithm.

5.3.2   Estimated Versions of the Model

We estimate a total of eight models. Model versions differ depending on (1) the type of information included in the measurement equation, (2) the assumptions concerning the learning procedure, (3) the time variation in the inflation target, and (4) the prices of risk. Four versions are based on the baseline model presented in the previous section, two versions are extensions allowing for heterogeneity in the monetary policy, and the final two versions allow for more flexibility in the prices of risk.

Regarding the information included in the measurement equation, we distinguish between the macro and the general versions of the model. In the macro version, we restrict the measurement equation to incorporate only macroeconomic information, while in the general version, we include all available information. The macro version of the model is motivated by the concern that including term structure and survey information in the measurement equation may bias the estimates of the deep and learning parameters in order to fit the term structure and the survey expectations. To avoid this problem, a two-step procedure is employed. In the first step, the deep and learning parameters are estimated while restricting the measurement equation to contain only macroeconomic variables. In the second step, we fix the parameter estimates for the deep and learning parameters obtained in the first step and optimize the likelihood based on the full measurement equation over the remaining parameters, $diag(\Psi)$. In the general versions of the model, the estimation of all parameters is performed in one step on the basis of the most general measurement equation.

We estimate both rational expectations and learning versions of the model. The learning versions of the model include four additional parameters describing the priors of the agents, $\sigma_{\zeta,\pi}$, $\sigma_{\zeta,r}$, and the starting values for the stochastic trends, $\zeta_{0|0}$. The distinction between rational expectations and learning models identifies the contribution of learning to the overall fit of the respective series. The four baseline models can be summarized as follows:

- Rational Expectations Macro: The rational expectations version is estimated using a two-step procedure ensuring that the deep parameters are based only on macroeconomic information.
- Rational Expectations I: The rational expectations version is estimated using a one-step procedure based on the general measurement equation.
- Learning Macro: The learning version is estimated using a two-step procedure ensuring that the deep parameters are based only on macroeconomic information.

• Learning I: The learning version is estimated using a one-step procedure based on the general measurement equation.

In addition to the four baseline models, we estimate two extensions to allow for heterogeneity in the monetary policy rule and in the agents' priors. The heterogeneity is modeled by means of chairman-specific policy rules and priors.[14] Specifically, the time-invariant policy rule parameters π^*, γ_π, γ_y and γ_{i-1} of the baseline models are replaced by chairman-specific parameters π_j^*, $\gamma_{\pi,j}$, $\gamma_{y,j}$ and $\gamma_{i-1,j}$, where j denotes the presiding chairman.[15] The heterogeneity in priors is modeled analogously by replacing the learning parameters $\sigma_{\zeta,\pi}$ and $\sigma_{\zeta,r}$ by their chairman-specific equivalents, $\sigma_{\zeta,\pi,j}$ and $\sigma_{\zeta,r,j}$. We estimate both the rational expectations version of this model, labeled Rational Expectations II, and the learning version of the model, labeled Learning II. The model versions Rational Expectations I and Learning I, implying time-invariant policy rules and beliefs, are nested in the respective extensions and, hence, identify the contribution of allowing for policy heterogeneity in the overall fit.[16] Finally, the last two models, Rational Expectations III and Learning III, extend the models Rational Expectations II and Learning II by allowing for time variation in the prices of risk. In these versions, we disregard consistency of the princing kernel with the IS curve and posit an affine function for the prices of risk: $\Lambda_t = \Lambda_0 + \Lambda_1 \tilde{X}_{t|t}$.[17]

5.4   Estimation Results

5.4.1   Data

We estimate the proposed models using quarterly data for the United States. The data covers the period from 1963:Q4 until 2003:Q4 (161 quarterly observations). The data set contains three series of macroeconomic

---

14. This procedure differs from other research that allows for time variation in the inflation target. For instance, Dewachter and Lyrio (2006), Kozicki and Tinsley (2005), and Hördahl, Tristani, and Vestin (2006) allow for variation in the inflation target of the central bank by modeling the inflation target as a inert autoregressive process. This approach results in quite variable inflation target dynamics. In contrast, this chapter allows for discrete jumps in the inflation target at prespecified dates. Beyond these dates, the inflation target is constant.

15. The chairmen included in the analysis are Martin (1951–1970), Burns (1970–1978), Miller (1978–1979), Volcker (1979–1987), and Greenspan (1987–2006). We divide the Volcker period in two subperiods in order to account for the well-documented change in monetary policy that took place during this term, that is, the change from monetary targeting to a more convential monetary policy. The first Volcker period ends in 1982:Q3.

16. For an analysis of regime changes on monetary policy, see Schorfheide (2005) or Sims and Zha (2006). Both papers make use of Markov switching techniques identifying the regime breaks endogenously. We, in contrast, fix the dates of the breaks to the moments of a change in the Fed chairman.

17. Note that allowing for time-varying prices of risk adds 42 parameters to be estimated. In order to keep the estimation tractable, we restrict Λ_1 to be diagonal.

observations: quarter-by-quarter inflation (based on the gross domestic product [GDP] deflator and collected from the National Income and Product Accounts), the output gap (constructed as the log of GDP minus the log of the natural output level, based on Congressional Budget Office data), and the Federal funds rate, representing the policy rate. Next to the macroeconomic variables, the data set includes six yields with maturities of one, two, three, four, five, and ten years. The data for yields up to five years are from the Center for Research in Security Prices (CRSP) database.[18] The ten-year yields were obtained from the Federal Reserve. Finally, we also use survey data on short- and long-run inflation expectations. More specifically, we include the one- and ten-year average inflation forecast, as reported by the Federal Reserve Bank of Philadelphia in the Survey of Professional Forecasters.

Table 5.1 presents descriptive statistics on the data set described in the preceding, which are depicted in figure 5.1. These statistics point to the usual observations: the average term structure is upward sloping; the volatility of yields decreases with maturity; normality is rejected for all series (based on Jarque-Bera [JB] statistics); and all variables display significant inertia, with a first-order autocorrelation coefficient typically higher than 0.90. Inflation displays a somewhat lower inertia, that is, an autocorrelation coefficient of 0.76.

Table 5.1 also presents the correlation structure of the data. Three data features can be highlighted. First, the yields are extremely correlated across the maturity spectrum. This points to the well-known fact that a limited number of factors account for the comovement of the yields. Second, there is a strong correlation between the term structure and the macroeconomic variables, with significant positive correlations between inflation and the term structure and significant negative correlations between the term structure and the output gap. These correlation patterns are an indication of common factors driving macroeconomic and yield curve dynamics. Finally, we observe a substantial and positive correlation between the surveys of inflation expectations and both the macroeconomic variables (especially inflation and the Federal funds rate) and the yield curve. Again, this suggests that the factors affecting the yield curve and macroeconomic variables also drive movements in the surveys of inflation expectations.

5.4.2   Parameter Estimates

Tables 5.2–5.4 report the estimation results for the rational expectations versions of the model. Our estimates for the macro model (table 5.2) are broadly in line with the literature. We observe a mild domination of the forward looking terms for both the AS and IS curves ($\mu_{\pi,1} = 0.524$ and

18. We thank Geert Bekaert, Seonghoon Cho, and Antonio Moreno for sharing the data set.

Table 5.1   Summary of data statistics (United States, 1963:Q4–2003:Q4, 161 observations)

	π	y	i	$\bar{y}_{1y}$	$\bar{y}_{2y}$	$\bar{y}_{3y}$	$\bar{y}_{4y}$	$\bar{y}_{5y}$	$\bar{y}_{10y}$	S_{1y}	S_{10y}
Mean (%)	4.49**	−1.11**	6.63**	6.52**	6.73**	6.90**	7.03**	7.11**	7.42**	4.18**	4.01**
SD (%)	2.83**	2.59**	3.28**	2.73**	2.67**	2.58**	2.53**	2.48**	2.47**	1.98**	1.49**
Auto	0.76**	0.95**	0.91**	0.93**	0.94**	0.95**	0.95**	0.96**	0.96**	0.98**	0.96**
Skew	1.49**	−0.47**	1.21**	0.78**	0.81**	0.85**	0.90**	0.88**	0.99**	0.83**	1.14**
Kurt	5.51**	3.51**	5.20**	4.06**	3.96**	3.92**	3.95**	3.67**	3.66**	2.79**	3.72**
JB	101.85	7.61	71.59	23.84	23.88	24.84	27.92	23.63	29.07	15.88	23.02
	(0.00)	(0.02)	(0.00)	(0.00)	(0.00)	(0.00)	(0.00)	(0.00)	(0.00)	(0.00)	(0.00)

Correlation matrix

	π	y	i	$\bar{y}_{1y}$	$\bar{y}_{2y}$	$\bar{y}_{3y}$	$\bar{y}_{4y}$	$\bar{y}_{5y}$	$\bar{y}_{10y}$	S_{1y}	S_{10y}
π	1.00										
y	−0.25**	1.00									
i	0.72**	−0.25**	1.00								
$\bar{y}_{1y}$	0.67**	−0.31**	0.95**	1.00							
$\bar{y}_{2y}$	0.65**	−0.39**	0.93**	0.99**	1.00						
$\bar{y}_{3y}$	0.62**	−0.44**	0.90**	0.98**	0.99**	1.00					
$\bar{y}_{4y}$	0.61**	−0.48**	0.89**	0.96**	0.99**	0.99**	1.00				
$\bar{y}_{5y}$	0.59**	−0.51**	0.87**	0.95**	0.98**	0.99**	0.99**	1.00			
$\bar{y}_{10y}$	0.59	−0.57	0.84	0.92**	0.96**	0.98**	0.99**	0.99**	1.00		
S_{1y}	0.83**	−0.46**	0.77**	0.77**	0.76**	0.74**	0.75**	0.73**	0.73**	1.00	
S_{10y}	0.80**	−0.63**	0.86**	0.86**	0.87**	0.870**	0.88**	0.88**	0.90**	0.98**	1.00

Notes: Inflation (π) is expressed in annual terms and is constructed by taking the quarterly percentage change in the GDP deflator (collected from the National Income and Product Accounts). The output gap (y) series is constructed from data provided by the Congressional Budget Office (CBO). The Fed rate is used as the short-term interest rate or the policy rate (i). Bond yield data concern month-end yields on zero-coupon U.S. Treasury bonds, expressed in annual terms. Data on yields up to five years are based on CRSP data and on ten-year yields based on the Federal Reserve. Mean = the sample arithmetic average in percentage p.a.; SD = standard deviation; Auto = the first order quarterly autocorrelation; Skew = skewness; Kurt = kurtosis; and JB = the Jarque-Bera normality test statistic with the significance level at which the null of normality may be rejected underneath it.

**Significant at the 5 percent confidence level.

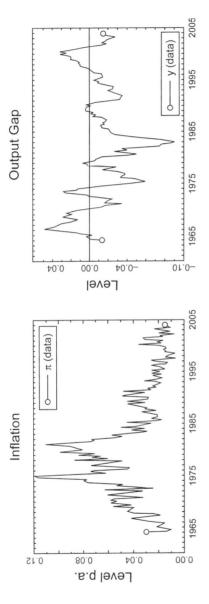

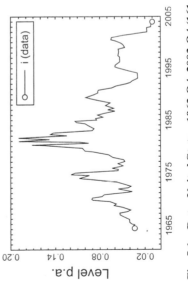

Fig. 5.1 Data, United States, 1963:Q4–2003:Q4 (161 observations)

Table 5.2   **Parameter estimates: Rational Expectations Macro and Rational Expectations I**

$$\pi_t = \mu_{\pi,1} E_t \pi_{t+1} + (1 - \mu_{\pi,1}) \pi_{t-1} + \kappa_\pi y_t + \sigma_\pi \varepsilon_{\pi,t}$$

$$y_t = \mu_y E_t y_{t+1} + (1 - \mu_y) y_{t-1} + \phi(i_t - E_t \pi_{t+1} - r) + \sigma_y \varepsilon_{y,t}$$

$$i_t = (1 - \gamma_{i-1})[r + E_t \pi_{t+1} + \gamma_\pi(\pi_t - \pi^*) + \gamma_y y_t] + \gamma_{i-1} i_{t-1} + \sigma_i \varepsilon_{i,t}$$

		Rat. Exp. Macro		Rat. Exp. I	
π-eq.	$\mu_{\pi,1}$	0.524**	(0.019)	0.527**	(0.007)
	$\kappa_\pi(\times 10^2)$	0.055	(0.278)	0.582**	(0.236)
y-eq.	μ_y	0.509**	(0.013)	0.580**	(0.018)
	ϕ	−0.019*	(0.011)	−0.012**	(0.005)
i-eq.	γ_{i-1}	0.862**	(0.036)	0.934**	(0.004)
	γ_π	0.674*	(0.356)	0.100	(0.165)
	γ_y	0.569	(0.504)	0.010	(0.172)
	r	0.025**	(0.010)	0.028**	(0.002)
	π^*	0.032**	(0.011)	0.044**	(0.002)
SD	σ_π	0.0063**	(0.0004)	0.0069**	(0.0004)
	σ_y	0.0043**	(0.0003)	0.0070**	(0.0009)
	σ_i	0.0133**	(0.0004)	0.0134**	(0.0005)
Struct	δ_π	0.908**	(0.069)	0.895**	(0.025)
	h	1.000	—	0.738**	(0.055)
	$\sigma(\times 10^{-2})$	0.274	(0.170)	0.496**	(0.201)

Notes: SD = standard deviation; Struct = structural parameters. Maximum likelihood estimates with standard errors in parentheses. Dash indicates standard deviation was not computed.

**Significant at the 5 percent level.
*Significant at the 10 percent level.

$\mu_y = 0.509$, respectively). The deviation from the purely forward-looking model ($\mu_{\pi,1} = 1$ and $\mu_y = 1$) is explained by the relatively high values for the inflation indexation parameter, δ_π, and the habit persistence, h, estimated at 0.908 and 1, respectively. Both estimates for the inflation sensitivity to the output gap, κ_π, and the output gap sensitivity to the real interest rate, ϕ, are small, 0.00055 and −0.019, respectively. Although these values are smaller than the ones typically used in calibration-based studies, they are commonly found in empirical studies using generalized method of moments (GMM) or full information maximum likelihood (FIMI) methods. Our estimates imply an active monetary policy rule. The ex ante real interest rate reacts positively to both inflation and the output gap, $\gamma_\pi = 0.674$ and $\gamma_y = 0.569$. Significant interest rate smoothing is also observed in the policy rule ($\gamma_{i-1} = 0.862$). As often found in the literature, some of the estimated parameters are not statistically significant. Similar results have been reported, for instance, by Cho and Moreno (2006).

Table 5.3   **Parameter estimates: Rational Expectations II**

$$\pi_t = \mu_{\pi,1}E_t\pi_{t+1} + (1 - \mu_{\pi,1})\pi_{t-1} + \kappa_\pi y_t + \sigma_\pi \varepsilon_{\pi,t}$$

$$y_t = \mu_y E_t y_{t+1} + (1 - \mu_y)y_{t-1} + \phi(i_t - E_t\pi_{t+1} - r) + \sigma_y \varepsilon_{y,t}$$

$$i_t = (1 - \gamma_{i-1})\left[r + E_t\pi_{t+1} + \gamma_\pi(\pi_t - \pi*) + \gamma_y y_t\right] + \gamma_{i-1}i_{t-1} + \sigma_i \varepsilon_{i,t}$$

		Rational Expectations II	
π-eq.	$\mu_{\pi,1}$	0.598**	(0.010)
	$\kappa_\pi(\times 10^2)$	0.627**	(0.256)
y-eq.	μ_y	0.589**	(0.018)
	ϕ	−0.020**	(0.008)
	r	0.029**	(0.002)

		Martins		Burns		Miller	
i-eq.	γ_{i-1}	0.863**	(0.033)	0.612**	(0.032)	0.782**	(0.515)
	γ_π	0.745	(0.537)	0.244**	(0.109)	0.374	(1.605)
	γ_y	0.397	(0.425)	0.735**	(0.181)	1.131	(2.044)
	$\pi*$	0.018**	(0.003)	0.038**	(0.002)	0.055**	(0.012)

		Volcker (a)		Volcker (b)		Greenspan	
i-eq.	γ_{i-1}	0.840**	(0.009)	0.959**	(0.022)	0.951**	(0.011)
	γ_π	0.541**	(0.212)	2.301	(2.091)	1.676**	(0.847)
	γ_y	0.531**	(0.222)	−1.189**	(0.505)	1.674**	(0.717)
	$\pi*$	0.082**	(0.002)	0.052**	(0.001)	0.032**	(0.001)
SD	σ_π	0.0071**	(0.0004)				
	σ_y	0.0069**	(0.0008)				
	σ_i	0.0194**	(0.0017)				
Struct	δ_π	0.673**	(0.029)				
	h	0.721**	(0.052)				
	$\sigma(\times 10^{-2})$	0.294**	(0.115)				

Note: See table 5.2 notes.

**Significant at the 5 percent level.

Extending the standard macro model by (1) including yield curve and inflation survey data in the measurement equation (Rational Expectations I, II, and III); (2) allowing for chairman-specific monetary policy (Rational Expectations II and III); and (3) introducing time variation in the prices of risk (Rational Expectations III) affects the parameter estimates significantly. First, the estimated persistence decreases, as shown by the decrease in the indexation parameter δ_π, which takes a value of 0.67 and 0.57 in the Rational Expectations II and III models, respectively, and by the decrease in the habit persistence, h, for the Rational Expectations I, II, and III models to 0.738, 0.721, and 0.750, respectively. As a result of the drop in the indexation or the habit persistence, the forward-looking components

Table 5.4 Parameter estimates: Rational Expectations III

$$\pi_t = \mu_{\pi,1}E_t\pi_{t+1} + (1 - \mu_{\pi,1})\pi_{t-1} + \kappa_\pi y_t + \sigma_\pi \varepsilon_{\pi,t}$$

$$y_t = \mu_y E_t y_{t+1} + (1 - \mu_y)y_{t-1} + \phi(i_t - E_t\pi_{t+1} - r) + \sigma_y \varepsilon_{y,t}$$

$$i_t = (1 - \gamma_{i-1})[r + E_t\pi_{t+1} + \gamma_\pi(\pi_t - \pi^*) + \gamma_y y_t] + \gamma_{i-1}i_{t-1} + \sigma_i \varepsilon_{i,t}$$

		Rational Expectations III	
π-eq.	$\mu_{\pi,1}$	0.638**	(0.017)
	$\kappa_\pi(\times 10^2)$	0.925*	(0.549)
y-eq.	μ_y	0.582**	(0.013)
	ϕ	−0.025**	(0.012)
	r	0.020**	(0.006)

		Martins		Burns		Miller	
i-eq.	γ_{i-1}	0.845**	(0.029)	0.482**	(0.041)	0.654**	(0.289)
	γ_π	0.511	(0.681)	0.176	(0.170)	0.233	(1.391)
	γ_y	0.363	(0.346)	0.516**	(0.248)	0.846	(0.991)
	π^*	0.018**	(0.005)	0.047**	(0.002)	0.060**	(0.006)

		Volcker (a)		Volcker (b)		Greenspan	
i-eq.	γ_{i-1}	0.779**	(0.029)	0.943**	(0.034)	0.928**	(0.026)
	γ_π	0.317	(0.308)	1.657	(1.759)	1.338	(0.949)
	γ_y	0.395*	(0.221)	−0.239	(0.396)	1.092	(0.692)
	π^*	0.078**	(0.003)	0.049**	(0.002)	0.032**	(0.001)
SD	σ_π	0.0081**	(0.0006)				
	σ_y	0.0053**	(0.0004)				
	σ_i	0.0136**	(0.0008)				
Struct	δ_π	0.567**	(0.042)				
	h	0.750**	(0.044)				
	$\sigma(\times 10^{-2})$	0.233**	(0.107)				
Prices of risk	$\Lambda_{0,\pi}$	−0.974	(0.612)				
	$\Lambda_{0,y}$	−0.271	(0.389)				
	$\Lambda_{0,i}$	0.045	(0.136)				
	$\Lambda_{1,\pi,\pi}$	0.067	(7.131)				
	$\Lambda_{1,y,y}$	−0.573	(14.905)				
	$\Lambda_{1,i,i}$	3.010	(2.152)				

Notes: See table 5.2 notes.
**Significant at the 5 percent level.
*Significant at the 10 percent level.

($\mu_{\pi,1}$ and μ_y) in the AS and IS equation increase. The estimates of monetary policy rule indicate for all versions of the model that (1) monetary policy is relatively inert, and (2) the Taylor principle is satisfied because the ex ante real interest rate tends to increase with both the inflation gap and the output gap. Nevertheless, the estimated inflation and output gap responses vary across the alternative versions of the model. Based on the results in table 5.3 and 5.4, we find, as do Clarida, Galí, and Gertler (2000), a strong increase in the responsiveness to the inflation gap during the Volcker and Greenspan periods.

Tables 5.5 to 5.7 report the estimation results for the versions where learning is introduced. The central parameters in the analysis, distinguishing learning models from rational expectations models, are the standard deviations of the perceived stochastic trends ζ_t^P, $\sigma_{\zeta,\pi}$, and $\sigma_{\zeta,r}$.[19] Our estimates for these parameters are statistically significant, indicating a rejection of rational expectations models. This finding holds irrespective of the version of the learning model and indicates the importance of the learning specification in modeling the joint dynamics of the macroeconomic variables, the yield curve, and the survey expectations. One interpretation of the parameters $\sigma_{\zeta,\pi}$ and $\sigma_{\zeta,r}$ is in terms of the perceived uncertainty with respect to the endpoints of the macroeconomic state. The estimates of the parameters $\sigma_{\zeta,\pi}$ and $\sigma_{\zeta,r}$ in the Learning II and III versions of the model indicate substantial time variation in the uncertainty with respect to the inflation and real interest rate endpoints. Interestingly, we find uncertainty for both inflation and real interest rate endpoint to be significantly lower during the Greenspan term than under previous chairmen. The introduction of learning dynamics affects significantly the estimates of the deep parameters relative to those obtained for the rational expectations counterparts. First, across learning models, we find that the forward-looking component in the AS equation ($\mu_{\pi,1}$) increases substantially and significantly relative to the rational expectations versions of the model. This increase is explained by the decrease in the inflation indexation parameter.[20] The interest rate smoothing parameter drops significantly to values on average around 0.8 in the learning cases, which are more in line with Rudebusch (2002). A second effect of learning is the increase in the inflation sensitivity to the output gap. We estimate κ_π levels of 0.05, 0.012, and 0.009 in the Learning I, II, and III models, respectively. Finally, note that one problematic feature of the estimation across learning specifications is the identification of the inflation targets, π_j^*, and the real interest rate r, which present large standard errors. This drop in significance can be attributed to the fact that the stochastic endpoints take over the role of these parameters in the expectation formation process.

Figures 5.2 to 5.4 plot the macro variables and their endpoints for each model. Endpoints, representing long-run (subjective) expectations, are de-

---

19. Note that the parameter $\sigma_{\zeta,y}$ was fixed to zero for consistency with the assumption of long-run neutrality of output (see section 5.2).

20. The decrease in the inflation indexation as a consequence of the introduction of learning is also found in other studies. For instance, Milani (2007), introducing constant gain learning in a New Keynesian macroeconomic model, finds an even stronger effect, with the inflation indexation parameter close to zero after the introduction of learning.

Table 5.5   Parameter estimates: Learning Macro and Learning I

$$\pi_t = \mu_{\pi,1}E_t\pi_{t+1} + (1 - \mu_{\pi,1})\pi_{t-1} + \kappa_\pi y_t + \sigma_\pi\varepsilon_{\pi,t}$$

$$y_t = \mu_y E_t y_{t+1} + (1 - \mu_y)y_{t-1} + \phi(i_t - E_t\pi_{t+1} - r) + \sigma_y\varepsilon_{y,t}$$

$$i_t = (1 - \gamma_{i-1})[r + E_t\pi_{t+1} + \gamma_\pi(\pi_t - \pi^*) + \gamma_y y_t] + \gamma_{i-1}i_{t-1} + \sigma_i\varepsilon_{i,t}$$

		Learning Macro		Learning I	
π-eq.	$\mu_{\pi,1}$	0.672**	(0.056)	0.759**	(0.023)
	$\kappa_\pi(\times 10^2)$	0.431	(0.504)	4.912	(3.184)
y-eq.	μ_y	0.504**	(0.028)	0.541**	(0.007)
	ϕ	−0.008	(0.023)	−0.038**	(0.016)
i-eq.	γ_{i-1}	0.833**	(0.039)	0.671**	(0.009)
	γ_π	0.401	(0.300)	0.149	(0.097)
	γ_y	0.504	(0.416)	0.363**	(0.046)
	r	0.028	(0.265)	0.030	(0.053)
	π^*	0.031	(0.669)	0.036	(0.360)
SD	σ_π	0.0062**	(0.0005)	0.0087**	(0.0006)
	σ_y	0.0043**	(0.0003)	0.0050**	(0.0003)
	σ_i	0.0132**	(0.0004)	0.0126**	(0.0004)
Struct	δ_π	0.489**	(0.123)	0.318**	(0.039)
	h	1.000	—	0.913**	(0.036)
	$\sigma(\times 10^{-2})$	0.618	(1.778)	0.142**	(0.058)
Learning	$\sigma_{\zeta,\pi}$	0.044**	(0.013)	0.015**	(0.001)
	$\sigma_{\zeta,y}$	0.000	—	0.000	—
	$\sigma_{\zeta,r}$	0.043	(0.141)	0.023**	(0.001)
Initial points	$\xi_{0,\pi}$	0.018	(0.022)	0.012**	(0.005)
	$\xi_{0,y}$	0.000	—	0.000	—
	$\xi_{0,i}$	0.014	(0.022)	0.042**	(0.004)

Notes: See table 5.2 notes.
**Significant at the 5 percent level.

terministic in the rational expectations models and stochastic in the learning cases. As figure 5.2 shows, in the presence of learning long-run inflation expectations are time varying and therefore different from the constant central bank's inflation target (around 3 to 4 percent per year). These endpoints are also remarkably similar across model specifications. Allowing for chairman-specific policy rules (models II and III) leads to significantly different inflation targets across rational expectations and learning models. In the Rational Expectations models II and III, the estimated inflation targets show a gradual increase over the seventies until the end of the Volcker experiment, subsequently decreasing over time (around 5 percent in the second Volcker period and 3.2 percent in the Greenspan term). This gradual decline in inflation targets seems unrealistic given the strong deflationary

Table 5.6 **Parameter estimates: Learning II**

$$\pi_t = \mu_{\pi,1}E_t\pi_{t+1} + (1 - \mu_{\pi,1})\pi_{t-1} + \kappa_\pi y_t + \sigma_\pi\varepsilon_{\pi,t}$$

$$y_t = \mu_y E_t y_{t+1} + (1 - \mu_y)y_{t-1} + \phi(i_t - E_t\pi_{t+1} - r) + \sigma_y\varepsilon_{y,t}$$

$$i_t = (1 - \gamma_{i-1})[r + E_t\pi_{t+1} + \gamma_\pi(\pi_t - \pi^*) + \gamma_y y_t] + \gamma_{i-1}i_{t-1} + \sigma_i\varepsilon_{i,t}$$

		Learning II					
π-eq.	$\mu_{\pi,1}$	0.728**	(0.027)				
	$\kappa_\pi(\times 10^2)$	1.182**	(0.323)				
y-eq.	μ_y	0.528**	(0.008)				
	ϕ	−0.022**	(0.008)				
	r	0.026	(0.100)				

		Martins		Burns		Miller	
i-eq.	γ_{t-1}	0.804**	(0.046)	0.268**	(0.047)	0.637**	(0.388)
	γ_π	0.406	(1.150)	0.161	(0.111)	0.244	(1.014)
	γ_y	0.012	(0.293)	0.513**	(0.060)	0.310	(0.315)
	π^*	0.028	(0.265)	0.087	(0.621)	0.053	(0.478)
Learning	$\sigma_{\zeta,\pi}$	0.018**	(0.003)	0.014**	(0.002)	0.019**	(0.006)
	$\sigma_{\zeta,y}$	0.000	—	0.000	—	0.000	—
	$\sigma_{\zeta,r}$	0.007	(0.008)	0.016**	(0.002)	0.019	(0.040)

		Volcker (a)		Volcker (b)		Greenspan	
i-eq.	γ_{i-1}	0.185**	(0.049)	0.795**	(0.022)	0.850**	(0.018)
	γ_π	0.564**	(0.095)	0.353	(0.290)	0.405	(0.630)
	γ_y	0.109	(0.079)	0.369**	(0.122)	0.224	(0.210)
	π^*	0.003	(0.177)	0.010	(0.285)	0.025	(0.266)
Learning	$\sigma_{\zeta,\pi}$	0.004	(0.004)	0.018**	(0.002)	0.008**	(0.002)
	$\sigma_{\zeta,y}$	0.000	—	0.000	—	0.000	—
	$\sigma_{\zeta,r}$	0.031**	(0.002)	0.049**	(0.003)	0.016**	(0.002)
SD	σ_π	0.0088**	(0.0006)				
	σ_y	0.0048**	(0.0004)				
	σ_i	0.0105**	(0.0006)				
Struct	δ_π	0.374**	(0.051)				
	h	0.935**	(0.035)				
	$\sigma(\times 10^{-2})$	0.235**	(0.079)				
Initial points	$\xi_{0,\pi}$	0.009	(0.008)				
	$\xi_{0,y}$	0.000	—				
	$\xi_{0,i}$	0.033**	(0.004)				

Notes: See table 5.2 notes.

**Significant at the 5 percent level.

Table 5.7 **Parameter estimates: Learning III**

		Learning III	
π-eq.	$\mu_{\pi,1}$	0.702**	(0.023)
	$\kappa_\pi(\times 10^2)$	0.883**	(0.417)
y-eq.	μ_y	0.523**	(0.016)
	ϕ	−0.023**	(0.010)
	r	0.016	(0.094)

		Martins		Burns		Miller	
i-eq.	γ_{i-1}	0.735**	(0.088)	0.198**	(0.077)	0.352	(0.932)
	γ_π	0.394	(0.628)	0.124	(0.129)	0.925	(0.765)
	γ_y	0.032	(0.239)	0.350**	(0.068)	0.223	(0.858)
	π^*	0.015	(0.258)	0.041	(0.753)	0.067	(0.106)
Learning	$\sigma_{\zeta,\pi}$	0.018**	(0.004)	0.013**	(0.002)	0.019**	(0.006)
	$\sigma_{\zeta,y}$	0.000	—	0.000	—	0.000	—
	$\sigma_{\zeta,r}$	0.005	(0.009)	0.013**	(0.003)	0.013	(0.074)

		Volcker (a)		Volcker (b)		Greenspan	
i-eq.	γ_{i-1}	0.284**	(0.047)	0.796**	(0.033)	0.846**	(0.024)
	γ_π	0.659**	(0.223)	0.275	(0.366)	0.558	(0.601)
	γ_y	0.042	(0.174)	0.198	(0.145)	0.040	(0.176)
	π^*	0.002	(0.148)	0.009	(0.376)	0.016	(0.189)
Learning	$\sigma_{\zeta,\pi}$	0.005	(0.005)	0.018**	(0.002)	0.009**	(0.002)
	$\sigma_{\zeta,y}$	0.000	—	0.000	—	0.000	—
	$\sigma_{\zeta,r}$	0.027**	(0.003)	0.054**	(0.006)	0.008**	(0.002)

SD	σ_π	0.0087**	(0.0007)
	σ_y	0.0045**	(0.0004)
	σ_i	0.0117**	(0.0010)
Struct	δ_π	0.424**	(0.047)
	h	0.956**	(0.073)
	$\sigma(\times 10^{-2})$	0.223**	(0.0947)
Initial points	$\xi_{0,\pi}$	0.009	(0.012)
	$\xi_{0,y}$	0.000	—
	$\xi_{0,i}$	0.033**	(0.007)
Prices of risk	$\Lambda_{0,\pi}$	0.156	(0.256)
	$\Lambda_{0,y}$	0.132	(0.227)
	$\Lambda_{0,i}$	−0.235**	(0.104)
	$\Lambda_{1,\pi,\pi}$	0.145	(3.750)
	$\Lambda_{1,y,y}$	−2.667	(5.194)
	$\Lambda_{1,i,i}$	2.197**	(0.972)
	$\Lambda_{1,\xi_\pi,\xi_\pi}$	−0.937	(4.538)
	Λ_{1,ξ_y,ξ_y}	0.000	—
	Λ_{1,ξ_i,ξ_i}	0.029	(1.068)

Notes: See table 5.2 notes.
**Significant at the 5 percent level.

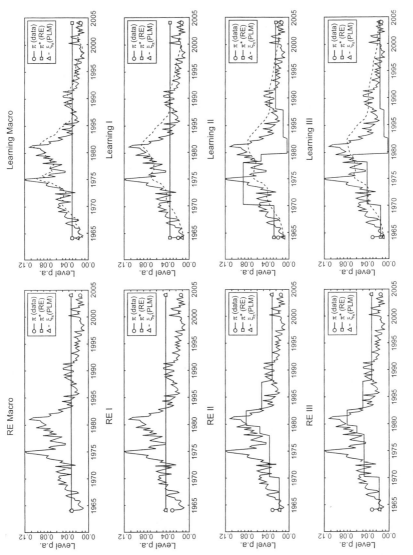

Fig. 5.2 Inflation

policy conducted by Volcker.[21] Under learning, the estimated chairman-specific inflation targets seem more in line with the historical record of U.S. monetary policy. Estimates of time-varying inflation targets, in line with our results, can be found in Kozicki and Tinsley (2005) and Milani (2007).

Figure 5.3 shows the differences between the long-run real interest rate expectations under learning and the values implied by rational expectations models. This difference is less pronounced than in the inflation case and is also similar across learning models. Figure 5.4 presents equivalent graphs for the long-run expectations regarding the short-run policy rate. We observe again sizable differences between the implied rational expectations endpoints and the subjective long-run expectations under learning. The variability in the long-run expectation for the nominal interest rate is dominated by variation in the inflation endpoint.

5.4.3   Comparing Learning and Rational Expectations Models

Bayesian Information Criterion (BIC) and Likelihood Decomposition

We use the Bayesian Information Criterion (BIC) for an overall evaluation of the performance across models. Although this criterion does not constitute a formal statistical test, it takes into account (1) the use of different procedures in the estimation of the models (i.e., Macro and general versions) and (2) the fact that, although rational expectations and learning models are nested, standard likelihood ratio tests are not appropriate as the parameter restrictions of the rational expectations models are on the boundary of the admissible parameter space, that is, $\sigma_{\zeta,\pi} = 0$ and $\sigma_{\zeta,r} = 0$. Next to the BIC, we also compare the performance of the different models through a likelihood decomposition, showing the contribution of the macro variables, the yield curve, and the surveys of inflation expectations.

The results are presented in table 5.8. According to the BIC, learning models outperform their rational expectations counterparts. More strongly, Learning I models outperform any of the estimated rational expectations models. According to this criterion, Learning III models present the best specification, incorporating learning dynamics, heterogeneity in monetary policy rules and priors, and time variation in the prices of

---

21. One explanation for the observed time series of inflation targets is that inflation targets adapt so as to fit the surveys of inflation expectations. Because under rational expectations long-run expectations coincide with the inflation targets, inflation targets need to track the survey of inflation expectations. Some evidence in favor of this interpretation can be found in table 5.8. Comparing the macro part of the likelihood, one observes a drop from the Rational Expectations I to the Rational Expectations II model, indicating that allowing for chairman-specific inflation targets worsened the macroeconomic fit. This drop in likelihood is more than compensated by the increase in likelihood in the term structure of interest rates and survey parts of the likelihood.

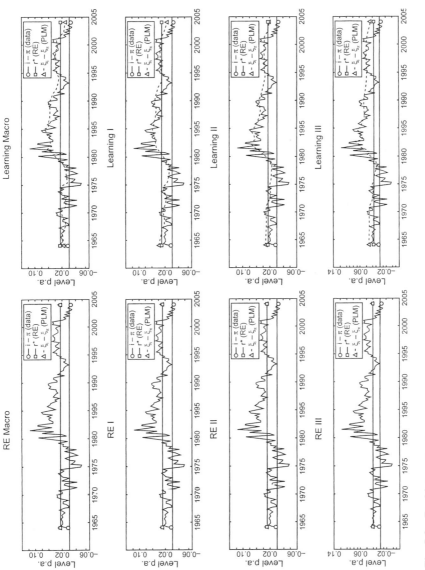

Fig. 5.3 Real interest rate

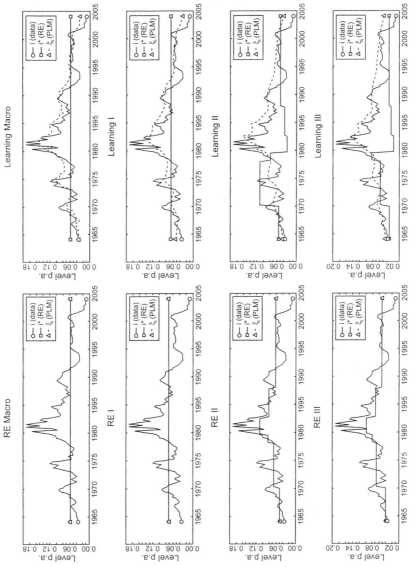

Fig. 5.4 Policy interest rate

Table 5.8   **Likelihood decomposition**

| | Components | | | | |
	Macroeconomy	Yield curve	Inflation expectation	Total	BIC
Rational Expectations Macro	12.07	20.98	5.61	38.66	−76.70
Rational Expectations I	11.75	23.23	5.55	40.53	−80.42
Rational Expectations II	11.57	25.07	6.21	42.85	−84.44
Rational Expectations III	11.71	25.25	6.22	43.18	−85.00
Learning Macro	12.08	22.08	6.07	40.23	−79.72
Learning I	11.81	26.05	6.50	44.36	−87.97
Learning II	12.03	27.74	6.74	46.51	−91.32
Learning III	12.02	27.93	6.78	46.73	−91.50

risk.[22] The likelihood decomposition shows that the superior performance of learning models is accounted for in each of its components. There seems to be, however, a trade off in fitting those components. From a macro perspective, the Learning Macro model presents the best performance (12.08 as average log-likelihood). From a yield curve and inflation expectations perspective, the Learning III model provides the best fit. The inclusion of this information in the measurement equation, therefore, slightly biases the model toward fitting yield curve and survey data at the expense of the macroeconomic part.

Prediction Errors

Table 5.9 presents summary statistics for the prediction errors of all variables in the alternative model specifications. In all cases, we find evidence of model misspecification due to the significant means and autocorrelation coefficients of the prediction errors. Therefore, none of the models is accepted as a completely satisfactory representation of the joint dynamics of the macroeconomy, the yield curve, and surveys of inflation expectations.[23] There is, however, a clear distinction between learning and rational expectations models. In most cases, learning models outperform their rational expectations counterpart. Introducing learning typically leads to an in-

22. The findings of the BIC are confirmed by approximative likelihood ratio tests. We reestimated the learning models fixing the learning parameters to small values, $\sigma_{\zeta,\pi} = \sigma_{\zeta,r} = 0.0001$, and $\zeta_{0|0} = [\pi^*, 0, r]$. Likelihood ratio (LR) tests performed using the latter models as the null hypothesis reject the proxy models at 1 percent significance levels. Also, note that the Rational Expectations I, II, and III and Learning I, II, and III are nested. Likelihood ratio tests indicate that both the Learning I and II and the Rational Expectations I and II models are rejected against the alternatives, Rational Expectations III and Learning III.

23. The rejection of the overall model is common in the macro-finance literature (e.g., Bekaert, Cho, and Moreno 2006 and Cho and Moreno 2006). In the pure finance literature, it has also been shown to be difficult to find affine term structure representations that are not rejected by the data.

Table 5.9　　**Summary statistics of prediction errors of macroeconomic variables, yield curve, and survey of inflation expectations**

	π	y	i	y_{1y}	y_{3y}	y_{5y}	y_{10y}	S_{1y}	S_{10y}
				A. Rational Expectations Macro					
R^2	0.77	0.91	0.83	0.71	0.49	0.35	0.21	0.75	0.36
Mean (%)	0.07	−0.04	0.05	0.02	0.66**	1.08**	1.64**	0.31**	0.51**
SD (%)	1.20	0.78	1.36	1.48	1.83	2.00	2.19	0.92	1.02
Auto	−0.25**	0.21**	−0.10	0.38**	0.75**	0.86**	0.93**	0.58**	0.97**
				B. Rational Expectations I					
R^2	0.76	0.87	0.82	0.76	0.74	0.68	0.50	0.65	−0.08
Mean (%)	−0.04	−0.35**	−0.03	−0.25**	−0.08	0.00	0.14	0.03	−0.10
SD (%)	1.21	0.94	1.38	1.34	1.32	1.41	1.74	1.08	1.22
Auto	−0.20**	0.53**	−0.12	0.19**	0.51**	0.72**	0.89**	0.74**	0.98**
				C. Rational Expectations II					
R^2	0.74	0.84	0.83	0.82	0.84	0.83	0.79	0.75	0.72
Mean (%)	0.05	−0.36**	−0.03	−0.25**	−0.03	0.07	0.25	0.01	−0.08
SD (%)	1.27	1.04	1.34	1.16	1.03	1.03	1.12	0.91	0.62
Auto	0.09	0.63**	−0.12	0.10	0.40**	0.59**	0.75**	0.80**	0.79**
				D. Rational Expectations III					
R^2	0.74	0.85	0.83	0.84	0.84	0.82	0.78	0.74	0.76
Mean (%)	0.06	−0.27**	0.13	−0.15	0.03	0.10	0.23**	−0.02	0.01
SD (%)	1.28	1.02	1.33	1.11	1.03	1.04	1.15	0.93	0.57
Auto	0.19	0.61**	−0.06	0.10	0.42**	0.59**	0.74**	0.85**	0.81**
				E. Learning Macro					
R^2	0.79	0.90	0.83	0.77	0.75	0.74	0.79	0.83	0.66
Mean (%)	0.00	−0.07	−0.01	−0.03	0.63**	1.20**	2.83**	−0.02	0.29**
SD (%)	1.15	0.82	1.34	1.30	1.30	1.26	1.14	0.74	0.72
Auto	−0.08	0.26**	−0.10	0.22**	0.48**	0.57**	0.58**	0.72**	0.88**
				F. Learning I					
R^2	0.70	0.89	0.83	0.84	0.86	0.88	0.88	0.88	0.66
Mean (%)	0.02	−0.22**	−0.03	−0.24**	−0.02	0.14**	0.52**	−0.11**	0.10
SD (%)	1.36	0.88	1.34	1.09	0.96	0.87	0.84	0.64	0.68
Auto	0.42**	0.43**	0.07	0.24**	0.46**	0.52**	0.59**	0.85**	0.97**
				G. Learning II					
R^2	0.72	0.89	0.87	0.88	0.90	0.91	0.92	0.90	0.81
Mean (%)	0.03	−0.19	0.04	−0.18**	−0.14**	−0.09	0.19**	−0.09	0.04
SD (%)	1.32	0.84	1.18	0.96	0.82	0.75	0.70	0.59	0.51
Auto	0.36**	0.34**	0.11	0.21**	0.32**	0.38**	0.41**	0.83**	0.94**
				H. Learning III					
R^2	0.72	0.90	0.86	0.87	0.90	0.91	0.91	0.89	0.83
Mean (%)	0.07	−0.16**	0.17	0.00	0.01	−0.03	0.05	−0.04	0.03
SD (%)	1.32	0.83	1.23	0.99	0.83	0.76	0.72	0.60	0.48
Auto	0.34**	0.31*	0.12	0.21**	0.30**	0.35**	0.38**	0.84**	0.94**

Notes: Mean = the sample average in percentage per year; SD = the standard deviation in percentage per year; and Auto = the first order quarterly autocorrelation.
**Significant at the 5 percent level.
*Significant at the 10 percent level.

crease in the in-sample predictive power of all variables, except inflation, and to a decrease in the standard deviation and the autocorrelation of the prediction errors. The inclusion of chairman-specific policies seems to have a considerable positive effect in the fit of the yield curve and surveys of inflation expectations. For learning models, although the inclusion of time-varying prices of risk decreases the mean of the forecast errors, overall, it does not seem to improve the results in a significant way.

5.4.4   Learning Dynamics, Inflation Expectations, and Bond Markets

Do macroeconomic models including learning fit the term structure of interest rates and inflation expectations? To answer this question, we analyze the fitting errors of the respective models. As shown in table 5.10, learning models with chairman-specific policy rules (Learning II and III) explain 95 percent of the variation in the yield curve and more than 85 percent of the variation in the surveys of inflation expectations. Furthermore, the mean fitting errors for the yield curve are low, ranging from 6 to 20 basis points for the Learning II model, and from 2 to 8 basis points for the Learning III model. These results are comparable to studies using latent factor models (e.g., de Jong 2000). This can also be seen in figures 5.5 and 5.6, which show the fit for the one- and the ten-year yields across models. The difference in performance across models is especially pronounced for the ten-year yield. The performance across models regarding the fit of survey of ten-year average inflation expectations can be seen in figure 5.7. In general terms, Learning II and III models fit both the yield curve and surveys of inflation expectations relatively well.

To identify the contribution of learning in the mentioned performance, we compare the Rational Expectations II and Learning II models (analogous results are obtained for Rational Expectations III and Learning III models). We observe an increase in fit due to learning between 4 percent (one-year yield) and 14 percent (ten-year yield). Furthermore, we observe a significant reduction in the remaining autocorrelation in the fitting errors. To identify the contribution of chairman-specific monetary policy rules and priors, we compare the Learning I and II models. Learning II models show an increase in the explained variation in the yield curve between 2 and 4 percent and in the survey of inflation expectations between 1 and 14 percent. We observe also a general decrease in the remaining autocorrelation in the fitting errors.

Why do learning models outperform their rational expectations counterparts? To answer this question, we analyze the affine term structure representations of rational expectations and learning models. More specifically, we look at the affine representations for the term structure of interest rates and inflation expectations in a transformed state space, decomposing the observed macroeconomic variables in perceived permanent and temporary components. This decomposition is achieved by the rotation matrix $\mathbf{T}$:

Table 5.10   **Summary statistics of fitting errors of yield curve and survey of inflation expectations**

	y_{1y}	y_{3y}	y_{5y}	y_{10y}	S_{1y}	S_{10y}
		A. Rational Expectations Macro				
R^2	0.84	0.54	0.38	0.23	0.70	0.38
Mean (%)	−0.04	0.61**	1.04**	1.62**	0.26**	0.52**
SD (%)	1.10	1.75	1.96	2.16	1.00	1.01
Auto	0.64**	0.85**	0.91**	0.95**	0.57**	0.97**
		B. Rational Expectations I				
R^2	0.87	0.78	0.70	0.52	0.65	−0.05
Mean (%)	−0.22	−0.05	0.02	0.16	0.06	−0.08
SD (%)	0.97	1.22	1.37	1.70	1.07	1.20
Auto	0.51**	0.72**	0.82**	0.94**	0.66**	0.97**
		C. Rational Expectations II				
R^2	0.91	0.88	0.85	0.81	0.82	0.73
Mean (%)	−0.23**	0.01	0.11	0.27**	0.02	−0.08
SD (%)	0.83	0.90	0.95	1.07	0.78	0.61
Auto	0.43**	0.62**	0.72**	0.82**	0.75**	0.82**
		D. Rational Expectations III				
R^2	0.92	0.89	0.86	0.81	0.79	0.77
Mean (%)	−0.24**	0.00	0.10	0.23**	0.00	0.02
SD (%)	0.78	0.86	0.92	1.07	0.83	0.56
Auto	0.40**	0.60**	0.70**	0.80**	0.83**	0.83**
		E. Learning Macro				
R^2	0.88	0.78	0.75	0.80	0.81	0.71
Mean (%)	−0.02	0.66**	1.22**	2.85**	0.01	0.33**
SD (%)	0.96	1.21	1.24	1.12	0.80	0.69
Auto	0.53**	0.70**	0.74**	0.79**	0.70**	0.85**
		F. Learning I				
R^2	0.93	0.91	0.91	0.91	0.91	0.71
Mean (%)	−0.20**	0.02	0.17**	0.53**	−0.07	0.14**
SD (%)	0.73	0.78	0.74	0.74	0.54	0.64
Auto	0.39**	0.56**	0.60**	0.71**	0.77**	0.96**
		G. Learning II				
R^2	0.95	0.95	0.95	0.95	0.92	0.85
Mean (%)	−0.16**	−0.10**	−0.06	0.20**	−0.05	0.09
SD (%)	0.59	0.59	0.57	0.55	0.51	0.46
Auto	0.23**	0.33**	0.39**	0.52**	0.71**	0.92**
		H. Learning III				
R^2	0.95	0.95	0.95	0.95	0.92	0.86
Mean (%)	−0.08	−0.02	−0.05	0.03	0.00	0.07*
SD (%)	0.60	0.58	0.56	0.54	0.51	0.44
Auto	0.22**	0.31**	0.35**	0.49**	0.69**	0.92**

Note: See table 5.9 note.

**Significant at the 5 percent level.

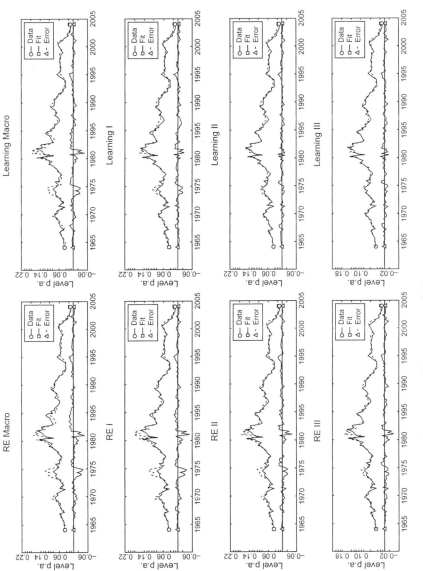

Fig. 5.5   Term structure fit across models, one-year yield

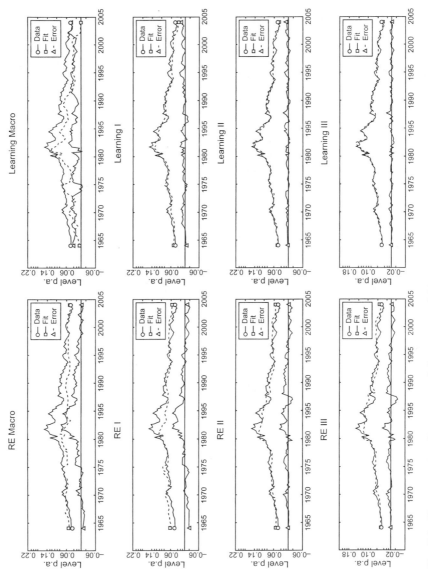

Fig. 5.6 Term structure fit across models, ten-year yield

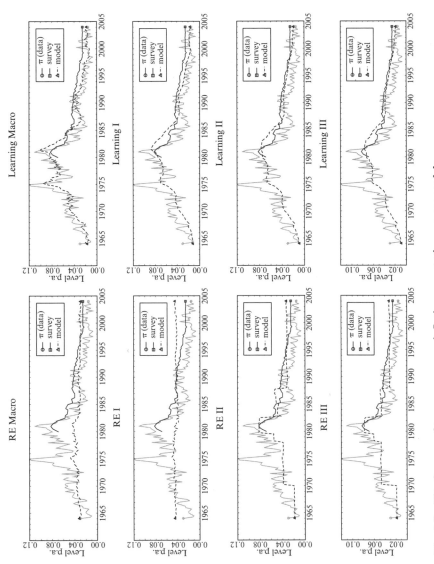

Fig. 5.7 Fit of survey of ten-year average inflation expectations across models

$$(39) \qquad \mathbf{T} = \begin{bmatrix} I_3 & -I_3 \\ 0 & I_3 \end{bmatrix},$$

which generates the decomposition:

$$(40) \qquad \tilde{\mathbf{X}}_{t|t}^T = \begin{bmatrix} \mathbf{X}_t - \xi_{t|t}^P \\ \xi_{t|t}^P \end{bmatrix} = T \begin{bmatrix} \mathbf{X}_t \\ \xi_{t|t}^P \end{bmatrix}.$$

The affine representation of the term structure of interest rates and inflation expectations can be restated in this state space as:

$$(41) \qquad Y_t = A_y + B_y \tilde{\mathbf{X}}_{t|t} + \upsilon_{y,t} = A_y + B_y T^{-1} T \tilde{\mathbf{X}}_{t|t} + \upsilon_{y,t}$$
$$= A_y + B_y^T \tilde{\mathbf{X}}_{t|t}^T + \upsilon_{y,t}$$

and

$$(42) \qquad S_t = A_s + B_s \tilde{\mathbf{X}}_{t|t} + \upsilon_{s,t} = A_s + B_s T^{-1} T \tilde{\mathbf{X}}_{t|t} + \upsilon_{s,t}$$
$$= A_s + B_s^T \tilde{\mathbf{X}}_{t|t}^T + \upsilon_{s,t}.$$

Figure 5.8 shows the transformed yield curve loadings for each of the models.[24] We identify one slope factor driving the yield spread, represented by the perceived transitory interest rate component, and two curvature factors, that is, the perceived output gap and the perceived inflation gap. The curvature factors affect primarily but marginally the intermediate maturity yields. We also obtain a level factor, exerting its influence equally over the entire yield curve. This factor is driven only by changes in the perceived stochastic endpoint for the policy rate. While both rational expectations and learning models share a level factor in the transformed state space, the implications of this factor differ across models. Rational expectations models imply a deterministic endpoint for the policy rate, that is, $\xi_{i,t} = r + \pi^*$.[25] The level factor is, therefore, constant and cannot explain the time variation in long-maturity yields. Learning models generate endogenous stochastic endpoints for the policy rate, which seem to be sufficiently volatile to account for the time variation in the long end of the yield curve.

---

24. Note that in the versions II and III of both rational expectations and learning models, yield curve and inflation expectations loadings also depend on the policy rule parameters. Given that we identify six policy regimes, we have six sets of loadings. For reasons of brevity, we only present the loadings implied by the Greenspan policy rules.

25. Note that to the extent that one allows for time-varying inflation targets within the rational expectations framework, one can generate exogenously volatility in the endpoints. This is the approach followed in the standard macro-finance literature. The Rational Expectations II and III panels in figures 5.2 and 5.4 are examples of this approach. The main advantage of learning is that there is no need to refer to exogenous shocks (i.e., in the inflation target) to account for the time variation in the long end of the yield curve. The stochastic endpoints are generated endogenously in the model.

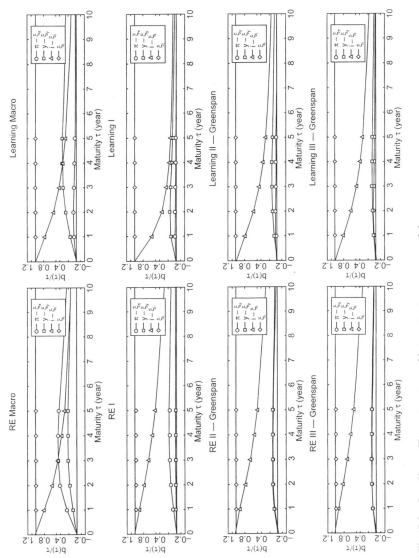

Fig. 5.8 Loading—Term structure of interest rates across models

5.5   Conclusions

In this chapter we built and estimated a macroeconomic model including learning. Learning was introduced in the model by assuming that agents do not believe in time-invariant inflation targets nor in constant equilibrium real rates. Given these priors, the optimal learning rule was derived in terms of a Kalman gain updating rule. We estimated the model including in the measurement equation, next to the standard macroeconomic variables, bond yields, and surveys of inflation expectations. The structural and learning parameters were estimated jointly. The findings of the chapter can be summarized as follows. First, including learning improves the fit of the model independently of the type of information included in the measurement equation. Although learning models improve on the rational expectations models, they are not fully satisfactory. Autocorrelation in the errors was found to be significant. Finally, we found that introducing learning in a standard New Keynesian model generated sufficiently volatile stochastic endpoints to fit the variation in long-maturity yields and in surveys of inflation expectations. The learning model, therefore, complements the current macro-finance literature linking macroeconomic and term structure dynamics.

Appendix

ALM Dynamics

In this appendix, we derive a closed form solution for the actual law of motion (ALM). The derivation follows the standard approach in the learning literature by substituting subjective expectations, that is, the PLM, into the structural equations. The structural equations are described in equation (7), which is repeated here as:

$$(43) \qquad AX_t = C + BE_t X_{t+1} + DX_{t-1} + S\varepsilon_t,$$

while the PLM is described by means of a vector error correction model (VECM) in the inferred stochastic endpoints:

$$(44) \qquad X_t = (I - \Phi^P)\xi^P_{t|t} + \Phi^P X_{t-1} + \Sigma^P \varepsilon_t$$

and a learning rule based on the Kalman filter updating rule:

$$(45) \qquad \xi^P_{t|t} = \xi^P_{t-1|t-1} + K(X_t - E^P_{t-1}X_t).$$

Deriving the Actual Law of Motion

A first step in obtaining the actual law of motion (ALM) consists of deriving the expectations implied by the PLM, equations (44) and (45). Under the PLM, the one-step ahead prediction, $E^P_t X_{t+1}$, is given by:

(46) $$E_t^P X_{t+1} = (I - \Phi^P) E_t^P \xi_{t+1|t+1}^P + \Phi^P X_t.$$

Under the PLM dynamics, the stochastic endpoints $\xi_{t|t}^P$ are random walks, that is, $E_{t-1}^P(X_t - E_{t-1}^P X_t) = 0$, such that $E_t^P \xi_{t+1|t+1}^P = \xi_{t|t}^P$. The one-step ahead expectations are given by:

(47) $$E_t^P X_{t+1} = (I - \Phi^P) \xi_{t|t}^P + \Phi^P X_t.$$

Substituting the learning rule, equation (45), for $\xi_{t|t}^P$, we obtain a description for the expectations as:

(48) $$E_t^P X_{t+1} = (I - \Phi^P)[\xi_{t-1|t-1}^P + K(X_t - E_{t-1}^P X_t)] + \Phi^P X_t$$

or equivalently, by lagging equation (47) one period giving a closed form expression for $E_{t-1}^P X_t = (I - \Phi^P) \xi_{t-1|t-1}^P + \Phi^P X_{t-1}$:

(49) $$E_t^P X_{t+1} = (I - \Phi^P)\{\xi_{t-1|t-1}^P + K[X_t - (I - \Phi^P)\xi_{t-1|t-1}^P - \Phi^P X_{t-1}]\}$$
$$+ \Phi^P X_t.$$

This expression can also be written as:

(50) $$E_t^P X_{t+1} = [I - (I - \Phi^P)K](I - \Phi^P)\xi_{t-1|t-1}^P$$
$$+ [\Phi^P + (I - \Phi^P)K]X_t - (I - \Phi^P)K\Phi^P X_{t-1}.$$

Denoting the matrix $(I - \Phi^P)K$ by $\mathbf{K}_\Phi$, we obtain the final expression for the one-step ahead expectation as:

(51) $$E_t^P X_{t+1} = (I - \mathbf{K}_\Phi)(I - \Phi^P)\xi_{t-1|t-1}^P + (\Phi^P + \mathbf{K}_\Phi)X_t - \mathbf{K}_\Phi \Phi^P X_{t-1}.$$

The second step in deriving the ALM dynamics consists of inserting the subjective expectations, equation (51), into the structural equations, that is, equation (43):

(52) $$AX_t = C + B[(I - \mathbf{K}_\Phi)(I - \Phi^P)\xi_{t-1|t-1}^P + (\Phi^P + \mathbf{K}_\Phi)X_t - \mathbf{K}_\Phi \Phi^P X_{t-1}]$$
$$+ DX_{t-1} + S\varepsilon_t.$$

Solving for X_t, we obtain:

(53) $$X_t = [A - B(\Phi^P + \mathbf{K}_\Phi)]^{-1}C + [A - B(\Phi^P + \mathbf{K}_\Phi)]^{-1}$$
$$\cdot B(I - \mathbf{K}_\Phi)(I - \Phi^P)\xi_{t-1|t-1}^P [A - B(\Phi^P + \mathbf{K}_\Phi)]^{-1}(D - B\mathbf{K}_\Phi \Phi^P)X_{t-1}$$
$$+ [A - B(\Phi^P + \mathbf{K}_\Phi)]^{-1}S\varepsilon_t.$$

Note that if the rational expectations solution is unique, and if $\Phi^P = \Phi^{re}$, the expression $[A - B(\Phi^P + \mathbf{K}_\Phi)]^{-1}(D - B\mathbf{K}_\Phi \Phi^P)$ equals Φ^P, which allows us to rewrite the preceding dynamics as:

(54) $$X_t = [A - B(\Phi^P + \mathbf{K}_\Phi)]^{-1}C + [A - B(\Phi^P + \mathbf{K}_\Phi)]^{-1}B(I - \mathbf{K}_\Phi)$$
$$\cdot (I - \Phi^P)\xi_{t-1|t-1}^P \Phi^P X_{t-1} + [A - B(\Phi^P + \mathbf{K}_\Phi)]^{-1}S\varepsilon_t.$$

Equation (54) describes the actual law of motion for the observable macro-economic variables as a function of the previous state, X_{t-1}, the inferred stochastic endpoints, $\xi^P_{t-1|t-1}$, and the structural shocks, ε_t. This description is only a partial description of the ALM because the dynamics of the stochastic endpoints are not taken into account. In order to obtain a complete characterization of the ALM, we add the learning rule, that is, equation (45). The joint dynamics of the observable macroeconomic variables, X_t, and the inferred stochastic endpoints, $\xi^P_{t|t}$ is given by:

$$
\begin{bmatrix} I & 0 \\ -K & I \end{bmatrix} \begin{bmatrix} X_t \\ \xi^P_{t|t} \end{bmatrix} = \left\{ \begin{array}{c} [A - B(\Phi^P + K_\Phi)]^{-1}C \\ 0 \end{array} \right\}
$$

$$
+ \left\{ \begin{array}{cc} \Phi^P & [A - B(\Phi^P + K_\Phi)]^{-1}B(I - K_\Phi)(I - \Phi^P) \\ -K\Phi^P & [I - K(I - \Phi^P)] \end{array} \right\} \begin{bmatrix} X_{t-1} \\ \xi^P_{t-1|t-1} \end{bmatrix}
$$

$$
+ \left\{ \begin{array}{c} [A - B(\Phi^P + K_\Phi)]^{-1}S \\ 0 \end{array} \right\} \varepsilon_t,
$$

where the dynamics for $\xi^P_{t|t}$ are given by equation (45). Finally, premultiplying by

(55)
$$
\begin{bmatrix} I & 0 \\ -K & I \end{bmatrix}^{-1} = \begin{bmatrix} I & 0 \\ K & I \end{bmatrix}
$$

yields a complete description of the ALM:

$$
\begin{bmatrix} X_t \\ \xi^P_{t|t} \end{bmatrix} = \left\{ \begin{array}{c} [A - B(\Phi^P + K_\Phi)]^{-1}C \\ K[A - B(\Phi^P + K_\Phi)]^{-1}C \end{array} \right\}
$$

$$
+ \begin{pmatrix} \Phi^P & [A - B(\Phi^P + K_\Phi)]^{-1}B(I - K_\Phi)(I - \Phi^P) \\ 0 & I - K\{I - [A - B(\Phi^P + K_\Phi)]^{-1}B(I - K_\Phi)\}(I - \Phi^P) \end{pmatrix} \begin{bmatrix} X_{t-1} \\ \xi^P_{t-1|t-1} \end{bmatrix}
$$

$$
+ \left\{ \begin{array}{c} [A - B(\Phi^P + K_\Phi)]^{-1}S \\ K[A - B(\Phi^P + K_\Phi)]^{-1}S \end{array} \right\} \varepsilon_t.
$$

This ALM is represented in extended state space, $\tilde{X}_{t|t} = [X'_t, \xi^{P'}_{t|t}]'$ by

(56)
$$
\tilde{X}_{t|t} = \tilde{C}^A + \tilde{\Phi}^A \tilde{X}_{t-1|t-1} + \tilde{\Sigma}^A \varepsilon_t,
$$

with

$$(57) \quad \tilde{C}^A = \begin{cases} [A - B(\Phi^P + K_\Phi)]^- C \\ K[A - B(\Phi^P + K_\Phi)]^{-1}C \end{cases}$$

$$\tilde{\Phi}^A = \begin{pmatrix} \Phi^P & [A - B(\Phi^P + K_\Phi)]^{-1}B(I - K_\Phi)(I - \Phi^P) \\ 0 & I - K\{I - [A - B(\Phi^P + K_\Phi)]^{-1}B(I - K_\Phi)\}(I - \Phi^P) \end{pmatrix}$$

$$\tilde{\Sigma}^A = \begin{cases} [A - B(\Phi^P + K_\Phi)]^{-1}S \\ K[A - B(\Phi^P + K_\Phi)]^{-1}S \end{cases}.$$

Properties of the Actual Law of Motion

Based on the final representation of the ALM as stated in equation (56), some properties of the ALM can be described in more detail. A first property is that the unconditional mean of the ALM coincides with the unconditional mean of the rational expectations model. Denoting the expectations operators under rational expectations and under the ALM by, respectively, E^{re} and E^A, the equivalence between unconditional expectations can be formalized as:

$$(58) \quad E^A X_t = E^{re} X_t = (I - \Phi^{re})^{-1} C^{re},$$

$$E^A \xi_{t|t}^P = E^{re} X_t = (I - \Phi^{re})^{-1} C^{re}.$$

We show this property by showing that $X_t = (I - \Phi^{re})^{-1} C^{re} = \xi_{t|t}$ is a steady state under the ALM. In the derivation we make extensive use of the properties of the rational expectations solution. More specifically, the unconditional mean for X_t based on the rational expectations model is given by:

$$(59) \quad E^{re}(X_t) = (I - \Phi^{re})^{-1} C^{re},$$

where the values for Φ^{re} and C^{re} satisfy the rational expectations conditions:

$$(60) \quad C^{re} = (A - B\Phi^{re})^{-1}C + (A - B\Phi^{re})^{-1}BC^{re}$$

$$\Phi^{re} = (A - B\Phi^{re})^{-1}D$$

$$\Sigma^{re} = (A - B\Phi^{re})^{-1}S.$$

We now show that the unconditional mean of X_t under the ALM, denoted by $E_t^A X_t$ coincides with the unconditional mean of the rational expectations model:

$$(61) \quad E_t^A X_t = E^{re} X_t = (I - \Phi^{re})^{-1} C^{re}.$$

In order to show this equivalence, we show that the point $X_t = (I - \Phi^{re})^{-1} C^{re}$ and $\xi_{t|t} = (I - \Phi^{re})^{-1} C^{re}$ are a steady state for the ALM. Substituting this particular point in the ALM, we obtain that this point is a steady state if it solves:

$$(I - \Phi^{re})^{-1}C^{re} = [A - B(\Phi^P + K_\Phi)]^{-1}C + \Phi^P(I - \Phi^{re})^{-1}C^{re}$$
$$+ [A - B(\Phi^P + K_\Phi)]^{-1}B(I - K_\Phi)(I - \Phi^P)(I - \Phi^{re})^{-1}C^{re}.$$

Noting that $\Phi^{re} = \Phi^P$ we can rewrite the equation by subtracting from both sides $\Phi^P(I - \Phi^{re})^{-1}C^{re}$, resulting in the equality:

$$(I - \Phi^P)(I - \Phi^{re})^{-1}C^{re} = [A - B(\Phi^P + K_\Phi)]^{-1}C$$
$$+ [A - B(\Phi^P + K_\Phi)]^{-1}B(I - K_\Phi)(I - \Phi^P)(I - \Phi^{re})^{-1}C^{re}.$$

Premultiplying by $[A - B(\Phi^P + K_\Phi)]^{-1}$,

$$[A - B(\Phi^P + K_\Phi)]C^{re} = C + B(I - K_\Phi)C^{re}.$$

Finally, this condition holds whenever a rational expectations equilibrium exists, that is, adding $BK_\Phi C^{re}$ to both sides, the preceding condition reduces to the rational expectations condition for C^{re}:

$$(A - B\Phi^P)C^{re} = C + BC^{re}.$$

The preceding derivation thus implies that if a rational expectations equilibrium exists, then the unconditional expectations of the rational expectations equilibrium coincides with the steady state of the ALM. If we assume, moreover, that all of the eigenvalues of $\tilde{\Phi}^A$ are strictly smaller than 1 in absolute value, the steady state of the ALM is attracting and defines the unconditional mean of the observable variables X_t. The second equality, that is, $E^A\xi_{t|t}^P = (I - \Phi^{re})^{-1}C^{re}$, can be shown analogously.

A second property is the unconditional normality of the extended state vector $\tilde{X}_{t|t}$ under the ALM. Assuming a standard normal distribution for the structural shocks, ε_t, it is well known that the linearity of the state space dynamics and the assumed stability of the ALM (all eigenvalues of $\tilde{\Phi}^A$ are assumed to be strictly smaller than 1) implies that the unconditional distribution for $\tilde{X}_{t|t}$ is:

$$\tilde{X}_{t|t} \sim N(E^A\tilde{X}_{t|t}, \Omega_{\tilde{X}}),$$

with

$$E^A\tilde{X}_{t|t} = \iota_{2\times1} \otimes (I - \Phi^{re})^{-1}C^{re}$$
$$\text{vec}(\Omega_{\tilde{X}}) = (I - \tilde{\Phi}^A \otimes \tilde{\Phi}^A)^{-1}\text{vec}(\tilde{\Sigma}^A\tilde{\Sigma}^{A\prime}).$$

References

Ang, A., and M. Piazzesi. 2003. A no-arbitrage vector autoregression of term structure dynamics with macroeconomic and latent variables. *Journal of Monetary Economics* 50:745–87.

Bekaert, G., S. Cho, and A. Moreno. 2006. New-Keynesian macroeconomics and the term structure. Columbia University, Working Paper.

Bullard, J., and K. Mitra. 2002. Learning about monetary policy rules. *Journal of Monetary Economics* 49 (6): 1105–29.

Calvo, G. 1983. Staggered prices in a utility-maximizing framework. *Journal of Monetary Economics* 12:383–98.

Cho, S., and A. Moreno. 2006. A small-sample study of the New-Keynesian macro model. *Journal of Money, Credit, and Banking* 38 (6): 1461–81.

Christiano, L., M. Eichenbaum, and C. Evans. 2005. Nominal rigidities and the dynamic effects of a shock to monetary policy. *Journal of Political Economy* 113 (1): 1–45.

Chun, A. 2005. Expectations, bond yields and monetary policy. Stanford University, Working Paper.

Clarida, R., J. Galí, and M. Gertler. 1999. The science of monetary policy: A New Keynesian perspective. *Journal of Economic Literature* 37:1661–1707.

———. 2000. Monetary policy rules and macroeconomic stability: Evidence and some theory. *Quarterly Journal of Economics* 115 (February): 147–80.

Cogley, T. 2005. Changing beliefs and the term structure of interest rates: Cross-equation restrictions with drifting parameters. *Review of Economic Dynamics* 8:420–51.

Cox, J., J. Ingersoll, and S. Ross. 1985. A theory of the term structure of interest rates. *Econometrica* 53:385–408.

Dai, Q., and K. Singleton. 2000. Specification analysis of affine term structure models. *Journal of Finance* 55 (5): 1943–78.

De Jong, F. 2000. Time series and cross-section information in affine term-structure models. *Journal of Business and Economic Statistics* 18 (3): 300–314.

Dewachter, H., and M. Lyrio. 2006. Macro factors and the term structure of interest rates. *Journal of Money, Credit, and Banking* 38 (1): 119–40.

Dewachter, H., M. Lyrio, and K. Maes. 2006. A joint model for the term structure of interest rates and the macroeconomy. *Journal of Applied Econometrics* 21 (4): 439–62.

Diebold, F., G. Rudebusch, and S. Aruoba. 2006. The macroeconomy and the yield curve: A dynamic latent factor approach. *Journal of Econometrics* 131 (1–2): 309–38.

Duffee, G. 2002. Term premia and interest rate forecasts in affine models. *Journal of Finance* 57:405–43.

Duffie, D., and R. Kan. 1996. A yield-factor model of interest rates. *Mathematical Finance* 6:379–406.

Ellingsen, T., and U. Söderström. 2001. Monetary policy and market interest rates. *American Economic Review* 91 (5): 1594–1607.

Evans, G., and S. Honkapohja. 2001. *Learning and expectations in macroeconomics*. Princeton, NJ: Princeton University Press.

Fuhrer, J. 2000. Habit formation in consumption and its implications for monetary-policy models. *American Economic Review* 90 (3): 367–90.

Galí, J., and M. Gertler. 1999. Inflation dynamics: A structural econometric analysis. *Journal of Monetary Economics* 44:195–222.

Gürkaynak, R., B. Sack, and E. Swanson. 2005. The sensitivity of long-term interest rates to economic news: Evidence and implications for macroeconomic models. *American Economic Review* 95 (1): 425–36.

Hördahl, P., O. Tristani, and D. Vestin. 2006. A joint econometric model of macroeconomic and term-structure dynamics. *Journal of Econometrics* 131 (1–2): 405–44.

Kim, D., and A. Orphanides. 2005. Term structure estimation with survey data on interest rate forecasts. CEPR Discussion Paper Series no. 5341. London: Center for Economic Policy Research.

Kozicki, S., and P. A. Tinsley. 2001. Shifting endpoints in the term structure of interest rates. *Journal of Monetary Economics* 47:613–52.

———. 2002. Dynamic specifications in optimizing trend-deviation macro models. *Journal of Economic Dynamics and Control* 26:1585–1611.

Kozicki, S., and P. A. Tinsley 2005. Permanent and transitory policy shocks in an empirical macro model with asymmetric information. *Journal of Economic Dynamics and Control* 29:1985–2015.

Milani, F. 2007. Expectations, learning and macroeconomic persistence. *Jounral of Monetary Economics* 54:2065–82.

Orphanides, A., and J. Williams. 2005a. The decline of activist stabilization policy: Natural rate misperceptions, learning, and expectations. *Journal of Economic Dynamics and Control* 29:1927–50.

———. 2005b. Inflation scares and forecast-based monetary policy. *Review of Economic Dynamics* 8:498–527.

Preston, B. 2005. Learning about monetary policy rules when long-horizon expectations matter. *Journal of Central Banking* 1 (2): 81–126.

Roberts, J. 1997. Is inflation sticky? *Journal of Monetary Economics* 39:173–96.

Rudebusch, G. 2002. Term structure evidence on interest rate smoothing and monetary policy inertia. *Journal of Monetary Economics* 49:1161–87.

Rudebusch, G., and T. Wu. 2003. A macro-finance model of the term structure, monetary policy, and the economy. *Economic Journal*, forthcoming.

Sargent, T., and N. Williams. 2005. Impacts of priors on convergence and escapes from Nash inflation. *Review of Economic Dynamics* 8:360–91.

Schorfheide, F. 2005. Learning and monetary policy shifts. *Review of Economic Dynamics* 8 (2): 392–419.

Sims, C., and T. Zha. 2006. Were there regime switches in U.S. monetary policy? *American Economic Review* 96 (1): 54–81.

Smets, F., and R. Wouters. 2003. Monetary policy in an estimated stochastic dynamic general equilibrium model of the euro area. *Journal of the European Economic Association* 1 (5): 1123–75.

Vasicek, O. 1977. An equilibrium characterization of the term structure. *Journal of Financial Economics* 5:177–88.

Comment   Jordi Galí

The present chapter by Dewachter and Lyrio is part of a small but growing literature that seeks to understand the yield curve and its evolution over time by combining two different modeling approaches: the arbitrage-free relations familiar from the finance literature and the dynamic general equilibrium approach of modern macroeconomic theory. Dewachter and

Jordi Galí is director and a senior researcher of the Centre de Recerca en Economia Internacional (CREI), and a professor of economics, all at the Universitat Pompeu Fabra, and a research associate of the National Bureau of Economic Research.

Lyrio's specific objective (and that of other recent papers cited by the authors) is to reconcile the observed behavior of the term structure with a fully articulated model of inflation, monetary policy, and economic activity. As discussed by Dewachter and Lyrio, an important requirement in order to achieve that objective is the introduction of a "level factor," that is, variations in long-term expectations of short-term rates, that can account for the high volatility of the long-term yield. The main novelty of the present Dewachter and Lyrio chapter lies in the endogenous modelling of that level factor, whose variations result from the evolving perceptions by private agents on the endpoint short-term rate (or, more precisely, its two components: the real rate and inflation), brought about by the assumed learning dynamics.

A Simple Model of the Term Structure

In order to illustrate the basic point of the Dewachter and Lyrio chapter, consider the following model of the term structure, generally referred to as the expectations hypothesis (EH) model

$$(1) \qquad i_t^{(n)} = \frac{1}{n} \sum_{k=0}^{n-1} E_t\{i_{t+k}\},$$

where $i_t^{(n)}$ is the yield on an n-period bond, and i_t denotes the short-term nominal rate on a (nominally) riskless one-period bond held between period t and $t + 1$. Let me assume the following exogenous stationary process for the short rate:

$$(2) \qquad i_t - i^* = \phi(i_{t-1} - i^*) + \varepsilon_t,$$

where i^* is the unconditional mean of the short term rate, and $\phi \in (0, 1)$. Then, under rational expectations we have

$$(3) \qquad i_t^{(n)} = (1 - \Theta_n)i^* + \Theta_n i_t,$$

where $\Theta_n \equiv (1/n)(1 - \phi^n)/(1 - \phi)$.

An Empirical Puzzle

As equation (3) makes clear, the EH model implies a very tight relation between short-term and long-term rates, one which is clearly violated in U.S. data. In particular, the EH model implies that long-term rates should be much less volatile than they actually are. To see this, note that applying ordinary least squares (OLS) to equation (2) using quarterly data on the three-month Treasury Bill (TB) rate over the sample period 1954:Q1 to 2005:Q4 yields an estimate $\hat{\phi} = 0.96$. The latter, in turn, implies a value $\Theta_{40} \approx 0.5$, where $n = 40$ corresponding to a ten-year maturity. Hence, the model predicts that the yield on a ten-year bond should have a standard deviation roughly half the size the standard deviation of the TB rate. That prediction is clearly rejected by the data: the ratio of standard deviations is approximately 0.9 rather than 0.5. In other words, the long-term rate appears to be excessively volatile relative to the predictions of the EH model.

A Proposed Solution: Endpoint Learning

Let me define, following Dewachter and Lyrio, the *perceived endpoint* for the short rate as the subjective long-run expectation

$$i_t^{*P} \equiv \lim_{k \to \infty} E_t^P \{i_{t+k}\},$$

where E_t^P is the subjective expectations operator. Agents' *perceived law of motion* for that endpoint is assumed to be given by the random walk model

(4) $$i_t^{*P} = i_{t-1}^{*P} + v_t.$$

Deviations from the endpoint are assumed to follow a stationary AR(1) process analogous to the rational expectations model described in the preceding:

$$i_t - i_t^{*P} = \phi(i_{t-1} - i_{t-1}^{*P}) + \varepsilon_t$$

given that the perceived endpoint is not observed, agents estimate it using the Kalman filter learning algorithm:

$$i_{t|t}^{*P} = i_{t-1|t-1}^{*P} + K[i_t - E_{t-1}^P(i_t)],$$

where $K \in (0, 1)$.

Note that, while agents in this economy believe the endpoint for the short-term rate to vary over time, we assume that the short-term rate fluctuates around a constant mean value i^* according to the process

$$i_t - i^* = \phi(i_{t-1} - i^*) + \varepsilon_t.$$

By combining the previous equations, one can show that, in equilibrium, agents' estimate of the endpoint follows the stationary AR(1) process

(5) $$i_{t|t}^{*P} - i^* = [1 - K(1 - \phi)](i_{t-1|t-1}^{*P} - i^*) + K\varepsilon_t,$$

Finally, one can combine the previous equation with the EH model of the term structure (1) to yield the following expression for the n-period bond yield under learning:

$$i_t^{(n)} = \frac{1}{n} \sum_{k=0}^{n-1} E_t^P \{i_{t+k}\}$$

$$= (1 - \Theta_n)i_{t|t}^{*P} + \Theta_n i_t.$$

A comparison of equation (6) to equation (3) makes clear that variations in the estimated endpoint $i^{*P}_{t|t}$ in the model under learning provide an additional source of volatility for long-term yields, and one whose relative importance rises with the maturity on the bond (as Θ_n is decreasing in n). Furthermore, because the time series properties of $i^{*P}_{t|t}$ depend on some unobservables (e.g., the variance of υ_t in the preceding model—which measures the extent of the departure from rational expectations), the model with learning gives the researcher some room to improve on the fit of its rational expectations counterpart.

Dewachter and Lyrio's Contribution

The simple learning model of the previous subsection conveys the essence of Dewachter and Lyrio's proposed framework for understanding the term structure dynamics. Needless to say, Dewachter and Lyrio's model is richer in several dimensions, some of which are likely to be important. First, and most noticeably, Dewachter and Lyrio's model is a general equilibrium one. Thus, and in contrast with the preceding framework, the short-term rate does not follow an exogenous process but instead is determined according to a Taylor-type rule that has the output gap and inflation as arguments. The output gap and inflation are, in turn, determined (simultaneously with the short-term rate) by a hybrid New Keynesian Phillips curve and a dynamic IS equation, which, in combination with the interest rate rule, constitute the macro block of Dewachter and Lyrio's model.

Secondly, Dewachter and Lyrio use a pricing kernel consistent with the macro model in order to derive an affine model for the yield curve. This is in contrast with the simple (though pedagogically useful) expectations hypothesis model shown in the preceding. As a result, the yields for different maturities are not only a function of the current short-term rate and its perceived endpoint, but also of inflation, the output gap, as well as agents' current estimates of all those variables' endpoints.

The different models estimated by Dewachter and Lyrio (four versions of the rational expectations model and four of the learning model) and their implied fit of the time series for bond yields of different maturities lead a number of interesting insights, many of which are discussed in detail in Dewachter and Lyrio's chapter. Most importantly, given the chapter's objectives, and as summarized graphically by figure 5.6 in that chapter, Dewachter and Lyrio's findings point to a potentially large explanatory role of learning dynamics as a source of the low frequency movement in long-term yields. While the estimated versions of the rational expectations (RE) model that allow for chairman-specific interest rate rules and time-varying price of risk (RE II and RE III) do a much better job than the simple bare-bones RE model (RE macro), they fall well short of the learning model once term structure data are used to estimate the latter (as in Learning I through III). Furthermore, much of the improvement in fit is due to a "level factor" generated by variations in the estimated inflation endpoint, which is reflected one for one in variations in the short-term rate endpoint. That feature of Dewachter and Lyrio's learning model is shown to be largely consistent with the observed evolution of survey-based long-term inflation expectations (which, in turn, display more variation than any model with chairman-specific inflation targets—but no learning about the latter—is bound to entail).

Of particular interest to monetary economists (even to those who may not care so much about the term structure) are the implications for the estimated deep parameters of Dewachter and Lyrio's "macro block" resulting from the need to fit the term structure data, as well as the allowance for learning dynamics. Two findings are worth emphasizing. First, the importance of the backward-looking component of the hybrid New Keynesian Phillips curve goes down substantially when learning dynamics are allowed for. Second, the variances of the innovations in the perceived inflation and real rate endpoints tend to be smaller under Greenspan than under previous Fed chairmen, possibly suggesting an enhanced transparency of monetary policy over the past two decades (because the true endpoints are indeed constant during each chairman's tenure).

Open Issues and Caveats

The present chapter by Dewachter and Lyrio constitutes an important contribution to the macro-finance literature on term structure dynamics. It is well written, and it contains a careful and extensive empirical analysis. Naturally, the chapter leaves a number of issues unexplained. It also relies on a number of assumptions that are not fully appealing. Let me turn to those briefly.

Do We Need a Full-Fledged DSGE Model to Explain the Term Structure Dynamics?

A simpler alternative to the full-fledged macro model developed and analyzed by Dewachter and Lyrio would consist of a partial equilibrium model of the term structure (e.g., the affine model used by Dewachter and Lyrio) that takes as given the joint process for the short-term rate i_t and the price kernel m_t. (e.g., a reduced form vector autoregression [VAR]). That process could be augmented with a perceived law of motion for the short-term endpoint, as well as with a learning algorithm similar to the one proposed by Dewachter and Lyrio. The use of a full-fledged model may impose unnecessary structure for the purpose at hand.

On the other hand, one can think of a possible justification for the dynamic stochastic general equilibrium (DSGE) approach pursued in the Dewachter and Lyrio chapter: to explore the macroeconomic implications of versions of a framework whose structure (including the embedded endpoint learning model) and estimated parameters are successful at fitting the term structure data. Among the questions one could ask based on that framework are the following: How does endpoint learning affect the transmission of monetary policy shocks? How does endpoint learning affect the desirability of alternative monetary policy rules? These are interesting and possibly important questions, but ones that fall beyond the scope of the Dewachter and Lyrio chapter.

A Strong Departure from Rational Expectations

A persistent gap between the perceived dynamics for some macro variables (or driving forces) and the actual equilibrium dynamics is a natural feature of models with constant-gain learning. Dewachter and Lyrio's framework is no exception in that regard. Yet, in Dewachter and Lyrio's model, the gap between the perceived law of motion and the actual law of motion is particularly large. In particular, Dewachter and Lyrio's assumptions imply that agents believe the law of motion for the inflation and real rate endpoints corresponds to two independent random walks. By contrast, in all the equilibriums considered by Dewachter and Lyrio, the estimated endpoints follow a stationary process, with an unconditional mean that corresponds to the deterministic steady state of the rational expectations equilibrium. A similar gap emerges in the simple model of the term structure analyzed in the preceding, as a comparison of equations (4) and (5) reveals. In my opinion, a perceived law of motion that shares with the actual law of motion the latter's order of integration would seem to be among the desiderata to be fulfilled by nonrational expectations models.

Two Competing Models

One can think of two alternative competing models that are likely to account for the observed behavior of bond yields equally well. The first class of models, exemplified by the present chapter, takes the "true" inflation and real rate endpoints to be constant, while letting agents learn about those endpoints using some constant-gain learning algorithm. The second class of models, exemplified by Hördahl, Tristani, and Vestin (2006), among others, assumes rational expectations, combined with time-varying endpoints for the real rate or inflation. The latter could, in turn, be justified by changes in the central bank's inflation target or changes in trend productivity growth. Sorting out the empirical merits of both families of models is likely to be nontrivial and is a task that also falls beyond the scope of Dewachter and Lyrio's present chapter. Yet the use of information on survey-based long-run expectations, as done in the present chapter, may be useful in achieving that objective.

Reference

Hördahl, P., O. Tristani, and D. Vestin. 2006. A joint econometric model of macro-economic and term-structure dynamics. *Journal of Econometrics* 131 (1–2): 405–44.

Discussion Summary

Hans Dewachter responded to Jordi Galí that the authors had estimated a model of rational expectations and time-varying endpoints, but had found their estimates to be implausible in several respects. For example, they had found a considerable degree of variation in the inflation target, on the order of 2 percent per year. One of the aims of this chapter was to avoid this.

John Y. Campbell suggested that it might be interesting to examine the endpoints for the real rate and inflation separately. He found it plausible that there was considerable variation in the case of inflation, but puzzling—although, in the light of long-term Treasury inflation-protected securities (TIPS) rates, perhaps empirically plausible—that there should be much variation in the case of the real rate. Second, he thought that allowing for regime changes when a new chairman was appointed was a nice idea, but that it seemed inconsistent with the assumption of constant gain learning. Plausibly, there was more uncertainty following the appointment of a new chairman. At such times, one might have expected to see more volatility and higher risk premiums.

Glenn D. Rudebusch said that the aim of this literature was to unify the macro and finance approaches. But he was unhappy at the assumption that the price of risk was constant. In combination with homoskedasticity, this assumption led to constant risk premiums in the model. He suggested that the finance literature attributed some of the variation in the long bond rate to changing risk premiums. In this sense, the chapter did not fall into the mainstream macro-finance literature. Peter Westaway agreed that the Bank of England had also found that much of the variation in long interest rates could be attributed to a changing risk premium.

In response to Galí's question of why a dynamic stochastic general equilibrium (DSGE) model was needed, *Thomas Laubach* suggested that one answer was that DGSE models offer the possibility of calibrating macro parameters.

Michael Woodford agreed with Galí that the benchmark model should assume rational expectations. Regarding the fact that the inflation target has to move "too much" in an estimated rational expectations model, he asked whether the authors were uncomfortable believing this themselves or believing that other people could believe it.

On the topic of different endpoints for the real rate and for inflation, *Brian Sack* pointed out that for much of the last thirty years, the "level" factor has been the dominant influence on movements of the yield curve (that is, the yield curve has moved mostly in parallel). Over the last five years, however, the "slope" factor has been much more important (that is, the short end of the curve has moved, while the long end has remained stable). A shift to more stable inflation expectations may explain this. Sack also argued that the authors' model should be confronted with the evidence that macroeconomic forecasts respond strongly to data announcements.

6

Revealing the Secrets of the Temple
The Value of Publishing Central Bank Interest Rate Projections

Glenn D. Rudebusch and John C. Williams

6.1 Introduction

The modern approach to monetary policy stresses the importance of guiding and influencing the public's expectations about future central bank actions. In this forward-looking view of monetary policy, the current setting of the policy interest rate, which is an overnight or very short-term rate, is *on its own* of little importance for private agents' decisions about consumption, investment, labor supply, and price setting. Instead, those decisions are more importantly driven by expectations of *future* short rates, especially as embodied in longer-term interest rates and other asset prices (along with the appropriate adjustments for risk). That is, the current policy rate is most relevant to the extent it conveys information about future policy settings and influences longer-maturity interest rates. Accordingly, at its core, monetary policy can be considered a process of shaping the entire yield curve of interest rates in order to achieve various macroeconomic objectives.

The crucial role that private-sector interest rate expectations play in macroeconomic stabilization naturally raises the question: how can central banks best guide private expectations of future monetary policy actions? In the past, central bankers typically assumed that the accumulated record of their past policy actions was the best means of such communi-

Glenn D. Rudebusch is a senior vice president and associate director of research at the Federal Reserve Bank of San Francisco. John C. Williams is a senior vice president and advisor at the Federal Reserve Bank of San Francisco.

For helpful comments, we thank Petra Geraats, Marvin Goodfriend, Øistein Røisland, Lars E.O. Svensson, and colleagues throughout the Federal Reserve System. Vuong Nguyen provided excellent research assistance. The views expressed in this chapter are our own and not necessarily those of others at the Federal Reserve Bank of San Francisco.

cation. In this view, actions spoke louder than words, and private agents, by examining past policy behavior, could uncover a systematic policy pattern or rule that would be useful in predicting future policy actions. Recently, however, there is a new appreciation of the value of good communication as an accompaniment to good policy actions, and, as a result, some central banks have started to place more importance on signaling their intentions for future policy. In practice, much of this central bank signaling of future policy intentions is implicit or indirect—essentially, a process of suggesting the future policy path by revealing information other than the future policy path. For example, some inflation-targeting central banks provide descriptions of their macroeconomic models and objectives as well as their current assessments of the state of the economy, but it is left to the public to infer the future policy path that is consistent with this information. A common such communication strategy is to publish an economic projection that is based on the assumption that the policy interest rate will not change in the future from its current setting. Private agents must then compare this constant interest rate projection to the announced economic objectives in order to back out the actual expected policy rate path. For example, if, at some future date, the published constant interest rate inflation projection is higher (lower) than the inflation target, then, in general, private agents should infer that the policy rate is likely to increase (decrease). This implicit signaling procedure has been criticized for supplying a circuitous, vague, and potentially confusing expression of the central bank's actual views of the likely path of policy.[1] Despite these criticisms, a published constant interest rate economic projection remains a key component of many central bank communication strategies.

Implicit signaling remains widespread among central banks because nearly all of them are extremely reluctant to directly reveal their views on likely future policy actions. Indeed, one of the strongest central banking taboos is the prohibition against talking publicly about future interest rates (Faust and Leeper 2005). This taboo largely arises from the belief that financial markets would tend to interpret any central bank statements about the likely future path of policy as commitments to future action, as opposed to projections based on existing information and subject to considerable change. Thus, many central banks will at best only give indirect hints or use coded language about policy inclinations in order to retain a plausible deniability in case markets are disappointed as the future unfolds.

Although the expected future path of the policy rate remains a closely guarded secret at most central banks, a few have recently provided some direct signals to the public about their policy intentions. Notably, in 2003, the

---

1. For discussion and critiques of this communication strategy, see Rudebusch and Svensson (1999), Goodhart (2001), Leitemo (2003), Svensson (2005b), Faust and Leeper (2005), and Woodford (2005).

U.S. Federal Reserve, or more specifically the Federal Open Market Committee (FOMC), started to issue statements commenting on the future path of its policy rate. These verbal forward-looking policy inclinations, including, for example, the famous phrase, "policy accommodation can be removed at a pace that is likely to be measured," have been considered in central banking circles unusually explicit statements about the future path of policy, even though the phrasing is far from unambiguous. A much bolder step than the FOMC's direct verbal signaling has been taken by the central banks of New Zealand and Norway (the RBNZ and the Norges Bank, respectively), which now publish *numerical* forecasts of the future path of the policy interest rate. These public quantitative policy rate projections represent a dramatic change from the past communication practices of central banks. However, while direct signaling of policy inclinations—whether verbal or quantitative—has been more prevalent in recent years, its future use remains quite contentious and uncertain. Indeed, as a practical matter, Federal Reserve Bank of St. Louis President William Poole (2005a) has stated that "the most important communications issue facing the FOMC currently is whether and how to continue to provide forward guidance on policy decisions."

More broadly, among central bank and academic researchers, there is an ongoing debate about the value of greater transparency and especially the provision of direct signals of the future interest rate path. There may be political benefits obtained from such transparency, such as greater accountability and legitimacy; however, the main argument in favor of directly communicating the central bank's view of the most likely future policy path is an economic one that is based on the benefits of sharing central bank information with private economic agents. As the current Federal Reserve Chairman Ben Bernanke (2004) has suggested, "FOMC communication can help inform the public's expectations of the future course of short-term interest rates, providing the Committee with increased influence over longer-term rates and hence a greater ability to achieve its macroeconomic objectives." This view is supported by research that argues that FOMC statements do affect financial markets and can alter expectations about the future course of policy (e.g., Kohn and Sack 2004; Bernanke, Reinhart, and Sack 2004; and Gürkaynak, Sack, and Swanson 2005a). However, the large research literature on transparency is only a partial buttress for this argument. The theoretical literature has obtained conflicting results on the value of transparency, depending on the exact details of the modeling specification.[2] In addition, this literature has not focused on the issue of the effectiveness of explicit future policy signals for enhancing macroeco-

---

2. The literature on central bank transparency is summarized in Geraats (2002), Carpenter (2004), and Woodford (2005). As discussed in the following, a key dissent on the value of transparency is Morris and Shin (2002, 2005) who argue that, in certain circumstances, greater central bank transparency may lead to less private-sector information gathering and reduced welfare.

nomic stabilization.[3] In the next section, we describe in more detail the real-world direct signaling of policy inclinations by central banks and outline some of the arguments for and against such transparency.

The unresolved debate among central bankers and researchers about the value of the direct signaling of policy intentions provides the key motivation for our formal analysis. In sections 6.3 and 6.4, we examine the macroeconomic effects of direct revelation of a central bank's expectations about the future path of the policy rate in a small theoretical model in which private agents have imperfect information about the determination of monetary policy. In particular, we focus on an issue that has received relatively little attention in the literature, namely, the desirability of central bank transparency about the expected path of policy when the public is uncertain about the central bank's preferences and, therefore, the future path of policy. We show that publication of interest rate projections better aligns the expectations of the public and the central bank in the spirit of Bernanke's quote in the preceding. Thus, publishing interest rate projections facilitates the management of expectations and the yield curve. We then show that, under reasonable conditions, improving the alignment of expectations also helps the central bank better meet its goals, providing support for full central bank transparency.

6.2   The Revelation of Policy Inclinations by Central Banks

As background for our formal analysis of direct central bank signaling of the likely future path of the policy interest rate, it will be useful to describe briefly some actual instances of such central bank communication and consider the arguments that have been made for and against the provision of these signals.

6.2.1   Recent Examples of Direct Policy Signaling by Central Banks

Some of the most intriguing direct signals of future policy inclinations have been contained in statements issued by the Federal Reserve following FOMC meetings, and it is useful to describe in detail some of this recent history. At times, the FOMC policy statements have provided direct verbal indications of the expected path of policy, which is quite unusual given the Fed's historical secrecy about the setting of the policy rate. Indeed, it was just over a decade ago, in July 1995, that the Fed first even announced a contemporaneous numerical level for the target federal funds rate.[4] An-

3. An important exception is Faust and Leeper (2005), who examine central bank interest rate projections. More generally, Svensson (1997) and Geraats (2005) discuss the value of central bank inflation and output forecasts.

4. The first policy announcement following an FOMC meeting occurred in February 1994 and only vaguely noted that "the FOMC decided to increase slightly the degree of pressure on reserve positions." In July 1995, the policy statement noted that the decrease in reserve pressures would also be reflected in "a 25 basis point decline in the federal funds rate." Rude-

other example of the Fed's reticence to reveal policy rate information is illustrated in its semiannual *Monetary Policy Report*. For over two decades, Fed policymakers have been surveyed internally about the economic outlook on a semiannual basis and have been asked to provide macroeconomic forecasts based on their individual views of an "appropriate" (presumably an optimal) future path for the policy interest rate.[5] The ranges and central tendencies of the resulting inflation, output, and unemployment forecasts are released to the public; however, the underlying conditioning policy paths are not published and, indeed, are not even collected from the survey participants. A similar secrecy applies to forecasts prepared by the staff of the Federal Reserve Board, which are distinct from the policymakers' own views. These detailed projections are circulated internally before each FOMC meeting in the so-called Greenbook and are made public with a five-year lag. Still, although over 100 economic series are projected, the underlying staff forecast for the policy rate (the federal funds rate) is not tabulated.[6]

In general, Fed policymakers' views on the future policy path have been so closely guarded that they were only rarely even discussed internally. One exception occurred from 1983 to 1999, when the FOMC voted not only on the current setting of the policy interest rate but also on the expected direction of future changes in the stance of policy over the very near term— strictly speaking, over the "intermeeting period," the approximately six-week interval until the next meeting.[7] These future policy inclinations were known as the policy "tilt" or "bias." An "asymmetric bias" meant that the FOMC judged that a policy move in one direction was more likely than in the other, while a "symmetric" judgment meant that the next policy move was equally likely to be up or down. Information about the policy bias was contained in the operational instructions or "domestic policy directive" sent to the trading desk at the New York Fed. Before May 1999, each directive was only released to the public after the next FOMC meeting, so, when released, the directive was, strictly speaking, outdated and of limited use to markets.[8] Following the FOMC meeting in May 1999, as well as af-

---

busch (1995) described some of the difficulties in inferring even the ex post level of the federal funds rate target before 1994. Of course, changes in the discount rate, which is an administered interest rate, have always been announced.

5. These economic forecasts are summarized in the Fed's *Monetary Policy Report* to Congress, which was originally required by the Full Employment and Balanced Growth Act of 1978.

6. Similarly, the research staff of the Federal Reserve Bank of San Francisco frequently publish their forecasts for various economic series but never for the federal funds rate.

7. Especially in the 1990s, the relevant horizon was often interpreted as a longer period, which, as noted in the following, led to some confusion. Thornton and Wheelock (2000) provide a fascinating history of the policy bias and its interpretation.

8. The secrecy of the directive was the subject of a famous Freedom of Information complaint that came before the U.S. Supreme Court. As described by Goodfriend (1986, p 71), one of the reasons given defending the need for the secrecy of the directive was, "The FOMC does not wish to precommit its future policy actions and current disclosure of the directive would tend to precommit the FOMC."

ter the subsequent five meetings that year, the post-meeting policy statement explicitly announced the expected future direction of policy as contained in the directive. The relevant forward-looking language from these 1999 statements is shown in the first several rows of table 6.1. For example, after the October 5, 1999, meeting, the policy statement noted that "the Committee adopted a directive that was biased toward a possible firming of policy going forward."

The Fed's first attempt at directly signaling the direction of future policy in 1999 was, in some sense, a straightforward and logical extension of the earlier transparency about the contemporaneous policy setting that was initiated in July 1995. Essentially, because the FOMC had been voting on both the current policy setting and a future policy inclination, it seemed natural to communicate both pieces of information to the public. At the FOMC meeting on July 1, 1998 (based on now-public transcripts), Donald L. Kohn, who was then a Fed research director, noted that an important rationale for releasing the directive stemmed "from a desire at times to warn markets that a change might be forthcoming in order to reduce the odds on an overreaction because of the surprise when policy tightening or easing actually occurred." Any such ability to shape market expectations of future policy by using the policy statement would seem to be quite attractive.

After the fact, however, the Fed policymakers were not pleased with the market reactions to the policy statements in 1999, and there was anguished discussion in FOMC meetings that year about the apparent confused reactions in financial markets to the release of the forward-looking language. At the start of 2000, given the FOMC's unhappiness with market responses, the direct signals of policy inclinations were replaced by implicit ones, specifically statements about the "balance of risks" to achieving the Fed's economic objectives. The formulaic balance of risks language in the policy statement went as follows, with only one of the three sets of alternative bracketed words to be used depending on the circumstances: "Against the background of its long-run goals of price stability and sustainable economic growth and of the information currently available, the Committee believes that the risks are [balanced with respect to prospects for both goals][weighted mainly toward conditions that may generate heightened inflation pressures][weighted mainly toward conditions that may generate economic weakness] in the foreseeable future" (Federal Reserve Board 2000, 2). Of course, the three alternative balance of risks options could be roughly mapped into the three earlier policy bias options of higher, unchanged, or lower future rates; however, the looser linkage obtained by avoiding any references to future policy actions appeared important. Fed Governor Laurence H. Meyer described the motivation for the balance of risks language at the December 21, 1999, FOMC meeting: "The majority [in the FOMC] also wants to change the language to focus on the

Table 6.1		Forward-looking language in policy statements issued after FOMC meetings (all FOMC meetings from May 1999 to June 2006)
Date of meeting	Funds rate	Forward-looking language in FOMC policy statement
05/18/1999	4.75	"...the Committee was concerned about the potential for a buildup of inflationary imbalances that could undermine the favorable performance of the economy and therefore adopted a directive that is tilted toward the possibility of a firming in the stance of monetary policy."
06/30/1999	5.00	"...the FOMC has chosen to adopt a directive that includes no predilection about near-term policy action."
08/24/1999	5.25	"...the directive the Federal Open Market Committee adopted is symmetrical with regard to the outlook for policy over the near term."
10/05/1999	5.25	"...the Committee adopted a directive that was biased toward a possible firming of policy going forward. Committee members emphasized that such a directive did not signify a commitment to near-term action."
11/16/1999	5.50	"...the directive the Federal Open Market Committee adopted is symmetrical with regard to the outlook for policy over the near term."
12/21/1999	5.50	"...the Committee decided to adopt a symmetric directive in order to indicate that the focus of policy in the intermeeting period must be ensuring a smooth transition into the Year 2000."
02/02/2000	5.75	"...the Committee believes the risks are weighted mainly toward conditions that may generate heightened inflation pressures in the foreseeable future."
03/21/2000	6.00	Same as 02/02/2000.
05/16/2000	6.50	Same as 02/02/2000.
06/28/2000	6.50	Same as 02/02/2000.
08/22/2000	6.50	Same as 02/02/2000.
10/03/2000	6.50	Same as 02/02/2000.
11/15/2000	6.50	Same as 02/02/2000.
12/19/2000	6.50	"...the Committee consequently believes the risks are weighted mainly toward conditions that may generate economic weakness in the foreseeable future."
01/03/2001	6.50	Same as 12/19/2000.
01/31/2001	5.50	Same as 12/19/2000.
03/20/2001	5.00	Same as 12/19/2000.
04/18/2001	4.50	Same as 12/19/2000.
05/15/2001	4.00	Same as 12/19/2000.
06/27/2001	3.75	Same as 12/19/2000.
08/21/2001	3.50	Same as 12/19/2000.
09/17/2001	3.00	Same as 12/19/2000.
10/02/2001	2.50	Same as 12/19/2000.
11/06/2001	2.00	Same as 12/19/2000.
12/11/2001	1.75	Same as 12/19/2000.
01/30/2002	1.75	Same as 12/19/2000.
03/19/2002	1.75	"...the Committee believes that, for the foreseeable future, ...the risks are balanced with respect to the prospects for both goals."
05/07/2002	1.75	Same as 03/19/2002.

(*continued*)

Table 6.1 (continued)

Date of meeting	Funds rate	Forward-looking language in FOMC policy statement
06/26/2002	1.75	Same as 03/19/2002.
08/13/2002	1.75	". . . the Committee believes that, for the foreseeable future, . . . the risks are weighted mainly toward conditions that may generate economic weakness."
09/24/2002	1.75	Same as 08/13/2002.
11/06/2002	1.25	". . . the Committee believes that . . . the risks are balanced with respect to the prospects for both goals for the foreseeable future."
12/10/2002	1.25	Same as 11/06/2002.
01/29/2003	1.25	Same as 11/06/2002.
03/18/2003	1.25	"In light of the unusually large uncertainties clouding the geopolitical situation . . . the Committee does not believe it can usefully characterize the current balance of risks . . ."
05/06/2003	1.25	". . . the Committee perceives that over the next few quarters the upside and downside risks to the attainment of sustainable growth are roughly equal. In contrast, over the same period, the probability of an unwelcome substantial fall in inflation, though minor, exceeds that of a pickup in inflation from its already low level. The Committee believes that, taken together, the balance of risks to achieving its goals is weighted toward weakness over the foreseeable future."
06/25/2003	1.00	Similar to 05/06/2003.
08/12/2003	1.00	". . . the Committee believes that policy accommodation can be maintained for a considerable period."
09/16/2003	1.00	Same as 08/12/2003.
10/28/2003	1.00	Same as 08/12/2003.
12/09/2003	1.00	Same as 08/12/2003.
01/28/2004	1.00	"With inflation quite low and resource use slack, the Committee believes that it can be patient in removing its policy accommodation."
03/16/2004	1.00	Same as 01/28/2004.
05/04/2004	1.00	". . . the Committee believes that policy accommodation can be removed at a pace that is likely to be measured."
06/30/2004	1.25	Same as 05/04/2004.
08/10/2004	1.50	Same as 05/04/2004.
09/21/2004	1.75	Same as 05/04/2004.
11/10/2004	2.00	Same as 05/04/2004.
12/14/2004	2.25	Same as 05/04/2004.
02/02/2005	2.50	Same as 05/04/2004.
03/22/2005	2.75	Same as 05/04/2004.
05/03/2005	3.00	Same as 05/04/2004.
06/30/2005	3.25	Same as 05/04/2004.
08/09/2005	3.50	Same as 05/04/2004.
09/20/2005	3.75	Same as 05/04/2004.
11/01/2005	4.00	Same as 05/04/2004.
12/13/2005	4.25	"The Committee judges that some further policy firming is likely to be needed to keep the risks to the attainment of both sustainable economic growth and price stability roughly in balance."

Table 6.1   (continued)

Date of meeting	Funds rate	Forward-looking language in FOMC policy statement
01/31/2006	4.50	"The Committee judges that some further policy firming may be needed to keep the risks to the attainment of both sustainable economic growth and price stability roughly in balance."
03/28/2006	4.75	Same as 01/31/2006.
05/10/2006	5.00	"The Committee judges that some further policy firming may yet be needed to address inflation risks…"
06/29/2006	5.25	"…the Committee judges that some inflation risks remain."

Notes: The date of each FOMC meeting or conference call (or the second day of a two-day meeting) is given along with the intended target level of the federal funds rate prevailing after the meeting and the salient forward-looking language in the postmeeting statement about the future policy inclination or the balance of economic risks.

balance of risks in the forecast in order to detach it from an explicit reference to policy." Indeed, at that meeting, there was a general agreement among the participants at the FOMC meeting to reestablish the taboo against any direct forward-looking signals about policy.

In the event, the implicit balance of risks language was also an imperfect and short-lived alternative. Its tight formulaic corset of a choice between "heightened inflation pressures" and "economic weakness" was not able to capture the Committee's worries in 2003 about a disinflationary economic slowdown and the possibility of inflation falling too low. Instead, the FOMC again decided that a direct statement about its future policy inclinations could be a useful means to guide market expectations. Therefore, as shown in table 6.1, in August 2003, the FOMC introduced the following language into its public statement: "the Committee believes that policy accommodation can be maintained for a considerable period" (Federal Reserve Board 2003). This was a direct, though not unambiguous, indication that the FOMC anticipated that the policy interest rate could be kept low for some time. The balance of risks language also remained in the statement in various forms, but it was essentially trumped by the direct forward-looking language. This initial direct signal was followed by "the Committee believes that it can be patient in removing its policy accommodation" in January 2004, and by "policy accommodation can be removed at a pace that is likely to be measured" in May 2004, and by "some further policy firming is likely to be needed" in December 2005, and by "further policy firming may be needed" in January 2006. Kohn (2005), as a member of the FOMC, described the underlying reasoning behind this return to an explicit signal of future policy:

> The unusual situation at that time [in 2003] shifted our assessment of the balance of costs and benefits in favor of a public statement about our ex-

pectations for the near-term path of policy. Markets appeared to be anticipating that inflation would pick up soon after the expansion gained traction, and therefore that interest rates would rise fairly steeply. This expectation was contrary to our own outlook. We saw economic slack and rapid productivity growth keeping inflation down for some time. Our expectations about policy also took account of the fact that the level of inflation was already low—lower than it had been for several decades. We thought that our reaction to a strengthening economy would be somewhat different this time than it had been in many past economic expansions and unlike what the markets seemed to anticipate.

Furthermore, unlike in 1999, the direct verbal policy signaling begun by the Fed in 2003 was viewed by many to have been useful in guiding financial markets (as discussed in the following). However, as noted in the introduction, its continued future use remains open to debate. Indeed, direct interest rate guidance was removed from the policy statement released after the FOMC meeting on June 29, 2006—the last entry in table 6.1. At that meeting, the Fed returned to an indirect indication of future policy inclinations by noting that "some inflation risks remain."

A few other central banks have also provided direct verbal signals about their future policy inclinations.[9] For example, in 1999, the Bank of Japan lowered its policy interest rate to zero and announced its intention to maintain the zero rate "until deflationary concerns are dispelled." This verbal signal to the public that the Bank of Japan would maintain a zero policy rate into the future—conditional on continued price deflation—was a key element of what was known as the "zero interest rate policy" and later as "quantitative easing." This signal, which tried to persuade financial market participants to lower their expectations of future short rates and, hence, lower long rates, was part of an attempt to stimulate the economy and escape from deflation. Just as in the United States, however, the continued future use of such direct signals appears in doubt. (See Bernanke, Reinhart, and Sack 2004; Oda and Ueda 2005.)

In contrast to the signals given in the United States and Japan, which were verbal and appeared to be transitory responses to special circumstances, two central banks—the RBNZ and the Norges Bank—have been providing quantitative and ongoing guidance on the future policy rate path.[10] Indeed, the RBNZ has provided numerical policy interest rate projections that reflect the policymaker's views to the public since 1997 (Archer 2005). For example, figure 6.1, which is from the March 2006 RBNZ *Monetary Policy Statement*, contrasts the RBNZ's expected path for future policy over the next two years with the path expected by finan-

9. In 2006, the Bank of Canada telegraphed its intentions in policy statements that noted "some modest further increase in the policy interest rate may be required to keep aggregate supply and demand in balance and inflation on target over the medium term."

10. The Central Bank of Colombia also published quantitative interest rate forecasts in four inflation reports from December 2003 to September 2004.

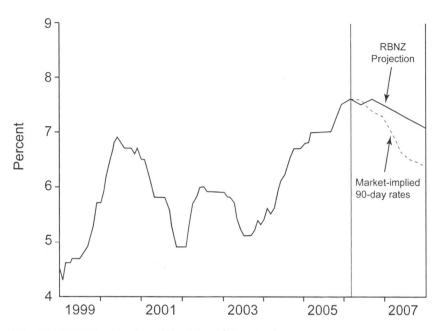

Fig. 6.1   RBNZ projection of short-term interest rate

Note: The solid line shows the historical data and the RBNZ's March 2006 baseline projection for the ninety-day interest rate (which is closely linked to the official policy interest rate). The dashed line shows expected rates in financial markets.

Source: RBNZ March 2006 *Monetary Policy Statement,* figure 2.6.

cial markets.[11] In this *Statement,* the Governor of the RBNZ describes the expected policy path as follows:

> As long as these inflation risks remain under control, we do not expect to raise interest rates again in this cycle. However given the time that it will take to bring inflation back towards the mid-point of the [inflation] target band, we do not expect to be in a position to ease policy this year. Any earlier easing would require a more rapid reduction in domestic inflation pressures than the substantial slowing already assumed in our projections. (Reserve Bank of New Zealand 2006, 2)

All in all, the RBNZ *Monetary Policy Statement* provides a remarkably clear judgment on the most likely future path of policy.

While the RBNZ has been a pioneer in the publication of quantitative projections of the policy interest rate (and other economic variables), the Norges Bank has recently gone even further, as described in Qvigstad (2005) and Svensson (2006b). Since 2005, the Norges Bank has been providing not only the numerical expected future path of the policy interest rate, but also confidence intervals around this projection and state-

11. The policy rate of the RBNZ is actually an overnight Official Cash Rate, but that is closely linked to the ninety-day interest rate, which is displayed.

contingent alternative scenarios. As shown in figure 6.2, which is from the November 2005 Norges Bank *Inflation Report* (Norges Bank 2005, 12), the baseline policy interest rate path rises steadily over the next three years. As described in the report, the projections "indicate that the interest rate will increase by about 1 percentage point in the course of next year, which is in line with expectations in the money and foreign exchange market. At the two to three year horizon, we expect a further, gradual rise in the interest rate. Our interest rate projections further out are somewhat higher than forward rates in the financial market" (Norges Bank 2005, 5). The Norges Bank also provides a probability distribution or fan chart around its baseline interest rate projection, as denoted by the shaded regions in figure 6.2. By outlining the range of possible monetary policy responses to unexpected macroeconomic disturbances, these confidence intervals highlight the conditional nature of the baseline projection. The conditionality of the interest rate projection is further reinforced by two specific alternative scenarios that are displayed in figure 6.2 and described in the *Inflation Report*.

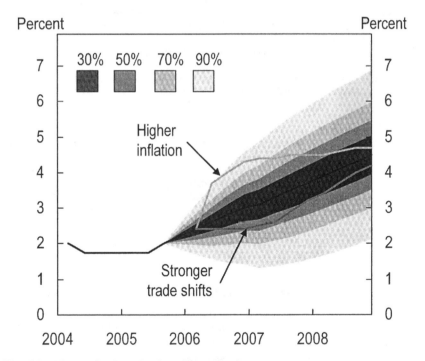

Fig. 6.2   Norges Bank projection of its policy interest rate

Note: The dark central line is the recent past and the Norges Bank's November 2005 baseline projection of the policy interest rate ("sight deposit rate") over the next three years. The surrounding bands represent 30, 50, 70, and 90 percent confidence intervals around the baseline projection. Projected policy rate paths under two separate alternate scenarios are also shown.

Source: Norges Bank November 2005 *Inflation Report,* chart 1.9a.

In one alternative, labeled "Stronger trade shifts," the greater pass-through of low import prices lowers inflation and the policy rate, while in the other, labeled "Higher inflation," a shock boosts inflation and the policy rate.

6.2.2   Assessments of Direct Signaling of Policy Inclinations

The preceding descriptions of various instances of direct policy rate signaling convey some of the variety of the recent historical experience. The range of practice—from complete silence to explicit quarter-by-quarter numerical guidance—is breathtakingly wide. Such signaling has elicited strong reactions, both pro and con, from central bankers and academic researchers. We will consider two common practical objections to direct signals and then survey some of the research on the effects of transparency.

The first objection is an institutional one. Many have argued that forward-looking policy signals are very difficult, if not impossible, for monetary policymakers to produce; that is, a committee of monetary policymakers may be unable to agree on a likely future path. This is the view of Goodhart (2001, 172–73), a former member of the Monetary Policy Committee (MPC) of the Bank of England, who notes:

> It is hard to see how a committee could ever reach a majority for any particular time path. A great advantage of restricting the choice to what to do now, this month, is that it makes the decision relatively simple, even stark. Given the difficulties involved already in achieving majority agreement in the MPC on this simple decision, the idea of trying to choose a complete time path by discretionary choice seems entirely fanciful and counterproductive.

Blinder (2004) and Mishkin (2004) essentially concur with Goodhart's pessimistic assessment. Of course, as Blinder (1998) earlier bemoaned, it seems quite unsatisfactory to ignore the fact that optimal policy in an economy with forward-looking agents will require at least an implicit time profile for future policy. Indeed, Svensson (2005b) has argued that conveying an understanding of the likely future path of the policy rate is crucial, and he suggests obtaining consensus on a quantitative path with a fairly straightforward voting mechanism. In this respect, the successful practical example of the Norges Bank, in which a seven-person executive board has been able to agree on and publish a quantitative future policy path, should alleviate some concerns about the impracticality of obtaining agreement on future policy rate signals.[12] In the following, in our formal modeling, we do not address the institutional dynamics of policy committees but simply

---

12. Alternatively, the diversity of opinion about the future on a policy committee could be informative, and Archer (2005) suggested publishing the "braid" of separate interest rate paths of individual committee members. As noted by Archer (2005), the New Zealand experience is not informative on this issue, as the RBNZ has a single monetary policymaker.

assume that the monetary authority can formulate a likely future path for the policy rate.

A second objection to direct signaling is that financial market participants will inevitably misinterpret the central bank's signals.[13] Policymakers often express the fear that financial markets will misconstrue statements of policy inclinations and, in particular, that the markets will interpret them as essentially guarantees of future policy action.[14] At the FOMC meeting on July 1, 1998, Kohn noted that a forward-looking policy announcement "could lock in market expectations and reduce flexibility because it would set up situations in which the market expected some action and the Committee would then have to worry about disappointing those expectations." In the event, of course, as noted in the preceding, such misunderstandings did occur. As described in *The Wall Street Journal* (Schlesinger 2000, A2):

> When the Fed started revealing its "bias" statements in May, financial markets tended to treat the directives as a virtual guarantee of the outcome of subsequent meetings—assuming a "bias" toward tightening likely meant a rate rise, and that a neutral bias likely meant no rate rise. That wasn't what the Fed intended. With markets ascribing greater clarity to Fed statements than the Fed did, officials at times felt boxed in by extreme market reactions.

A similar view of the confusion resulting from the direct signals was expressed in the official postmortem assessment of the 1999 policy statements, titled "Modifications to the FOMC's Disclosure Procedures" (released on January 19, 2000), which noted that the direct forward-looking policy language

> caused some unanticipated confusion. It became apparent that the public was uncertain about the interpretation of the language used to characterize possible future developments, about the time period to which it applied, and about the extent to which the announced changes in that language represented major shifts in the Committee's assessment. Perhaps partly as a result, the announcement of a directive biased toward tightening seemed to exaggerate the responses of financial markets to subsequent information bearing on the likely course of interest rates and monetary policy. (Federal Reserve Board 2000, 1)

Of course, part of the confusion in 1999 stemmed from the particular language that was used in the statement. In contrast, the direct verbal policy signals provided by the Fed in 2003 and thereafter have been generally viewed as successful. Kohn (2005), Bernanke (2004), and Woodford (2005), for example, all argue that the language was properly interpreted and that

---

13. A related objection is that the presence of forward-looking policy signals may change the behavior of financial market participants so that financial markets provide a less useful summary of private information for central banks.

14. The Governor of the Bank of England (King 2006) recently noted that "trying to give direct hints on the path of interest rates over the next few months risks deceiving financial markets into believing there are definite plans for the next few months when no such plans exist."

market rates were influenced in the right direction. This interpretation has garnered some support from empirical studies as well. Overall, for example, the incremental steps toward greater openness and transparency that the Fed took throughout the 1990s and early 2000s appear to have had important effects on financial markets. Indeed, as documented by Lange, Sack, and Whitesell (2003) and Swanson (2006), financial markets became much better at forecasting the future path of monetary policy than they were in the 1980s and early 1990s and more certain of their forecast ex ante, as measured by implied volatilities from options.[15] Other studies that have been more narrowly focused on the specific effects of recent forward-looking Fed policy statements, notably Bernanke, Reinhart, and Sack (2004) and Gürkaynak, Sack, and Swanson (2005a), have supported the notion that these statements have been useful in suggesting to the public a particular course of future action, although as described in Rudebusch (2006), any improvement has been at a horizon of only a couple of months. The experience of the RBNZ, which has given specific numerical policy guidance for over a decade, is generally positive. As discussed by Archer (2005), financial markets in New Zealand have reacted favorably to the central bank's interest rate forecasts and understood their conditionality. Although the Norges Bank has only a very brief track record of interest rate projections, the explicit confidence bands provided should reinforce forecast conditionality, and so far, its experience has been favorable.

Of course, the counterfactuals in these cases cannot be observed, so it is difficult to assess definitely the effectiveness of the recent direct interest rate communication. Indeed, some have judged the recent U.S. episode far less favorably. As noted in *Business Week Online* (Miller 2005):

> But what started out as a well-meaning attempt to give investors a clear sense of where monetary policy was headed has degenerated into a muddled message that has sown confusion in financial markets and helped fan fears of higher inflation among investors. That has raised questions inside and outside the Fed about whether the central bank's extraordinary strategy of mollycoddling the markets has done more harm than good.

And the president of the European Central Bank (ECB), Jean-Claude Trichet (2006), made it clear that the ECB would not be sending similar direct signals about the likely path of its policy interest rate.[16]

---

15. Of course, this greater certainty about future rates may be precisely the worry of those opposing direct guidance on interest rates, namely, that providing information about the first moment of future interest rates—the expected path—will distort the second moment of future rates, reducing the implied volatility or dispersion of expected future rates in an unwarranted fashion.

16. Trichet (2006) noted that

> The ECB does not embark on a particular multi-monthly pre-commitment on interest rates or on the path of future policy interest rates. As the Governing Council has decided to regularly consider the most up-to-date information, such an unconditional commitment

Even among those who judged the Fed's direct signaling to have been useful, many considered it a one-time solution for a transitory deflationary risk. Notably, the signaling could be considered a particular example of the strategy of stimulating the economy discussed by Reifschneider and Williams (2000) and Eggertsson and Woodford (2003), which provides assurances when the current policy rate is close to or at its lower bound that future rates will also be kept low. Indeed, as noted in the preceding, it appears unlikely that the Fed will employ an ongoing strategy of direct signaling. For example, in the United States, the minutes of the FOMC meeting of November 10, 2004, stated, "A few members felt that, because of greater uncertainties, it might become appropriate eventually to move away from the recent practice of providing guidance about the likely future path of policy, while others emphasized the desirability of continuing to be as informative as possible about the Committee's perceived outlook." And, as noted in the preceding, direct signals were discontinued in the June 2006 policy statement.[17]

For some, given the sophistication of the financial system, it is perhaps easy to dismiss at an abstract level concerns about the inevitable breakdown of communication between central banks and markets. However, there is still much unknown about the precise relationship between the revelation of information and market pricing, and this black box has long worried central bankers (Goodfriend 1986). Perhaps the most subtle rendering by a policymaker of the difficulties inherent in communicating with financial markets is provided by Kohn (2005):

> In fact, economists do not fully understand how markets incorporate information. Herding behavior, information cascades, multiple equilibria, and the amount of investment in financial research all pose puzzles about markets and information. The situation is complicated still more when an important participant is seen as having superior information owing to its investment in research or its understanding of its own be-

---

would limit the ability of the Governing Council to react to changes in the economic situation and therefore hamper our credibility and our capacity to preserve the solid anchoring of inflation expectations. This is, in particular, the reason why we refused to promise to maintain interest rates at 2 percent for a "considerable period of time."

17. Poole (2005b) appears to express the view of at least a few FOMC members when he notes that

most of the time the FOMC cannot provide accurate information to the market as to the probable course of the target fed funds rate, in terms of a specific path measured in basis points. The future path will be conditional on future information that cannot itself be predicted. Attempts to provide specific forward-looking guidance will prove inaccurate and even misleading to the market. Moreover, the Fed could create a credibility problem for itself if forward guidance is too specific. If the market acts on the guidance, and the Fed subsequently responds to new information in a way that departs from the guidance, then the market will naturally feel that it has been misled. But if the Fed fails to respond to new information that seems to demand a response, in the interest of doing what it said it was going to do, then failure to respond may also damage credibility.

havior. In such circumstances, certain types of central bank talk might actually impinge on welfare-enhancing market pricing by being misunderstood and receiving too much weight relative to private judgments.

Some of the research underlying this apprehension about transparency is by Morris and Shin (2002), who provided a simple theoretical model in which the public revelation of policy information can be bad for social welfare. This work has been widely cited and followed by a vigorous debate introducing new theoretical modifications. For example, Svensson (2006a) argues that the Morris and Shin result has been widely misinterpreted and that their antitransparency result is only obtained for a small set of unlikely parameter values, while various authors, including Roca (2005) and Hellwig (2005), show that transparency can increase welfare in more general models. Indeed, as is apparent in surveys by Geraats (2002), Carpenter (2004), and Woodford (2005), many conclusions about the value of transparency appear to hinge on the exact specification of the theoretical models. However, with just a few exceptions, the literature has not actually examined the effects of the release of forward-looking *policy* information for macroeconomic dynamics and stabilization. It is this line of reasoning that we pursue in the next two sections.

6.3   A Framework for Analyzing Central Bank Interest Rate Projections

In this section and the next, we analyze how publishing central bank interest rate projections can affect private expectations and macroeconomic performance in a simple model of the economy. In this section, we describe our framework, which is a standard New Keynesian structure modified to allow for asymmetric information sets for private agents and the central bank. In particular, in our model, as described in detail in the next section, the central bank may have an informational advantage over the public that reflects its better information regarding its policy intentions. At the outset, note that we abstract from two issues that have been widely discussed in the past literature on central bank transparency. First, we assume that the central bank is able to commit to future policy actions and therefore does not face a Barro-Gordon time inconsistency problem. Second, we assume that the central bank's provision of information does not affect a private agent's collection or use of idiosyncratic information; thus, we ignore the strategic complementarity highlighted in Morris and Shin (2002).

6.3.1   A Model of Interest Rates, Output, and Inflation

For our analysis, we use a standard log-linearized New Keynesian model (see Woodford [2003] for further discussion). The output gap, y_t, is determined by a forward-looking "IS curve" given by the intertemporal saving decision:

(1) $$y_t = -(i_t - E_t\pi_{t+1} - r_t^*) + E_t y_{t+1},$$

where i_t is the nominal interest rate, π_t is the inflation rate, r_t^* is the natural rate of interest (which is assumed to follow a known stationary process), and E_t denotes mathematical expectations conditional on the available time t information set. (Throughout our analysis, we abstract from intercepts.) We have implicitly assumed log preferences so that the coefficient on the interest rate is unity. Solving this equation forward $T-1$ periods, we can express the output gap in terms of the expected short-term real interest rate gaps over the next T periods and the output gap T periods in the future:

(2) $$y_t = -E_t \sum_{j=0}^{T-1} (i_{t+j} - \pi_{t+j+1} - r_{t+j}^*) + E_t y_{t+T}.$$

This version of the IS curve illustrates a basic insight of modern macroeconomic theory: monetary policy affects output through the expected future path of real interest rates. Generalizations of this model that incorporate a richer description of consumption, investment, and other components of output leave this basic insight intact (see Woodford [2003] and Fuhrer and Rudebusch [2004] for discussion).

It is useful to reformulate this condition in terms of bond yields. Denote the ex ante real T-period bond rate by $R_{T,t}$, which, abstracting from a term premium, equals the expected average real interest rate over the next T periods:

(3) $$R_{T,t} \equiv -E_t \frac{1}{T} \sum_{j=0}^{T-1} (i_{t+j} - \pi_{t+1+j}).$$

Let $R_{T,t}^*$ denote the expected average natural rate of interest over the next T periods:

(4) $$R_{T,t}^* = E_t \frac{1}{T} \sum_{j=0}^{T-1} r_{t+j}^*.$$

Given these definitions, the IS curve can be represented by the following simple equation relating the output gap to the real bond rate gap, which is the difference between the real bond rate and the corresponding natural rate, plus the output gap expected T periods in the future (which, for sufficiently large values of T is approximately zero):

(5) $$y_t = -T(R_{T,t} - R_{T,t}^*) + E_t y_{t+T}.$$

This formulation makes evident the central role of long-term real interest rates for the conduct of monetary policy (see McGough, Rudebusch, and Williams 2005).

The inflation rate, π_t, is given by the New Keynesian Phillips curve of the form:

(6) $$\pi_t = \beta E_t \pi_{t+1} + \kappa(y_t + u_t),$$

where u_t is a distortionary stationary shock to marginal cost, β is the rate of time preference, and κ measures the sensitivity of inflation to the output gap. Solving this equation forward yields the following equation for inflation in terms of expected real bond rates:

(7) $$\pi_t = -\kappa E_t \sum_{j=0}^{\infty} \beta^j (R_{T,t+j} - R^*_{T,t+j} + y_{t+T} - u_{t+j}).$$

As in the case of the output gap equation, this reformulation of the Phillips curve highlights the central role of expected real bond rate gaps in determining current inflation. It is clear from this representation that private agents, and by implication monetary policymakers who strive to ensure macroeconomic stabilization, are interested in the whole future path of the short-term policy interest rate.

For our following analysis, we assume $\kappa = 0.15$ and $\beta = 1$. The value of κ is consistent with Calvo price setting with one-quarter of all prices reoptimized each quarter, log utility from consumption, and a 0.8 elasticity of disutility from work.[18] We assume that the variance of the markup shocks equals unity; shocks to the natural rate of interest play no part in our analysis in the following. Our results are not qualitatively sensitive to these parameter assumptions.

6.3.2   Monetary Policy

As is standard in the literature, we assume that the central bank's objective is to minimize the weighted sum of the unconditional variance of the inflation gap, which is the difference between the inflation rate and a time-varying target inflation rate, π^*_t, and the unconditional variance of the output gap. Specifically, the central bank loss, $\mathscr{L}$, is given by:

(8) $$\mathscr{L} = \mathrm{VAR}\,(\pi_t - \pi^*_t) + \lambda \mathrm{VAR}\,(y_t),$$

where $\mathrm{VAR}(x)$ denotes the unconditional variance of a variable x and λ is the relative weight on output gap variability.

We allow for modest variation over time in the medium-term inflation rate that the central bank attempts to achieve. Specifically, we assume that the inflation target is a mean zero autoregressive process, subject to stochastic shocks:

(9) $$\pi^*_t = \delta \pi^*_{t-1} + \upsilon_t, \quad \delta \in (0, 1), \quad \upsilon_t \sim N(0, \sigma^2_\upsilon),$$

where the inflation target innovation, υ_t, is assumed to be an independently and identically distributed (i.i.d.) normally distributed random variable. Note that the unconditional, or long-run, inflation target is assumed to be

18. We assume $\beta = 1$, so monetary policies can be easily evaluated in terms of unconditional variances.

constant. We assume that π_t^* is persistent, with $\delta = 0.9$, but that its conditional variance is quite small, with $\sigma_\upsilon^2 = 0.01$. Persistent target shocks can be justified by time variation in the factors that influence the optimal choice of the inflation rate, including distortions to the economy, bias in inflation measures, and structural changes that affect the magnitude of the problems associated with the zero lower bound on interest rates. In addition, the optimal strategy in the vicinity of the lower bound is to implicitly target a higher rate of inflation than usual for a number of years, as discussed in Reifschneider and Williams (2000) and Eggertsson and Woodford (2003), providing justification for time variation in the medium-run inflation objective.[19] Note that the assumed implied unconditional standard deviation of the inflation target is only about 0.2 percentage point, which is plausibly modest. Indeed, much related recent macro-finance research finds that the inflation target embedded in bond yields does move significantly and persistently over time (e.g., Kozicki and Tinsley 2001; Rudebusch and Wu 2004, 2007; Gürkaynak, Sack, and Swanson 2005b; and Hördahl, Tristani, and Vestin 2006).[20] In any case, the resulting unconditional variation fits well inside the explicit inflation target ranges announced by many central banks, which are typically a percentage point in width.

As discussed in Woodford (2003), in this model optimal monetary policy under commitment with complete information is implicitly described by the condition:

$$\pi_t = \pi_t^* - \frac{\lambda}{\kappa}(y_t + y_{t-1}).$$

In the following, we append a transitory policy shock, w_t, to this optimality condition so that monetary policy is set according to:

$$(10) \qquad \pi_t = \pi_t^* + w_t - \frac{\lambda}{\kappa}(y_t - y_{t-1}),$$

where w_t is assumed to be an i.i.d. normally distributed random variable with variance $\sigma_w^2 = 1$. Throughout the following, we assume that policy is set according to this equation and is not recalibrated depending on the information assumptions that we make. We view the policy shocks as representing the central bank's response to transitory factors outside the model. Indeed, as stressed by Svensson (2005a, b), good monetary policy in prac-

---

19. For example, one could interpret the recent heightened concerns about the possibility of deflationary stagnation in the United States as an episode of implicitly targeting a somewhat higher rate of inflation than usual for a few years owing to concerns about the zero lower bound on interest rates.

20. More generally, in the United States, and in many other countries, there is considerable empirical evidence that persistent shocks to the inflation target have occurred, as exemplified by the disinflations of the early 1980s and again in the early 1990s, which suggest a gradual ratcheting down of the inflation target over time. See, for example, Bomfim and Rudebusch (2000), Erceg and Levin (2003), and Cogley and Sbordone (2005).

tice involves a vast amount of subtle knowledge and judgment. In part, such information may reflect policymakers' assessments about asymmetric risks to the outlook that are not directly connected to the mean forecast for inflation and output. For example, these asymmetric risks may reflect fears about fallout from financial instability, and the Fed has responded a number of times to threats to the financial system: in 1987, following the stock market crash, in 1998, when international financial markets threatened to freeze up, and in 2001, following the terrorist attacks on September 11. Finally, it should be stressed that in real time the policymaker may not have a clear read on the data and does not know the best way to minimize the loss function.

Although the policy equation is written in an implicit form in terms of the inflation gap and the change in output, it can be equivalently represented by an explicit interest rate reaction function where the policy instrument, the short-term interest rate, is determined by variables in the system. In such a formulation, the time-varying inflation target, π_t^*, and the policy shock, w_t, represent deviations by the central bank from its policy reaction function, similar to the residuals of an estimated monetary policy rule (as in Svensson 2003; Rudebusch 2002, 2006).

6.4   The Macroeconomic Effects of Publishing Interest Rate Projections

In this section, we use the theoretical framework outlined in the preceding to analyze how publishing central bank interest rate projections affects macroeconomic behavior and the central bank calculation of loss. A crucial aspect of our analysis is the structure of information: what the public knows and doesn't know. Because the focus of this chapter is on the effects of publishing interest rate projections, in the following we focus on the effects of incomplete knowledge on the part of the public regarding the future path of policy that is ultimately due to uncertainty about the future actions of the central bank. We abstract from information asymmetries regarding the state of the economy, a topic analyzed in a recent paper by Walsh (2005). In particular, we assume that the public and the central bank have identical and complete information about the parameters describing the model economy and both observe the current shocks to the natural rate of interest and the shock to marginal costs, r_t^* and u_t, respectively.[21] That is, the public and the central bank are both assumed to know the structure and parameters of

21. This assumption seems appropriate for analyzing inflation targeting central banks, the majority of which provide detailed information regarding their views on the economic outlook, conditional on some stipulated path of policy (e.g., constant nominal rate or market expectations). For non-inflation-targeting central banks, communication of interest rate projections likely conveys useful information both about the central bank's views on the economy and about the policy response to the outlook. See Geraats (2005) for a discussion and references to the literature on the effects of transparency when the central bank has asymmetric information regarding the economic outlook.

the equations describing output, inflation, and the inflation target, and the functional form of the equation describing monetary policy.

We consider two illustrative examples where the public is imperfectly informed regarding future policy actions and is uncertain how the central bank will respond in the future to economic conditions. First, we analyze the case, which we refer to as "policy rule uncertainty," in which the public does not know the parameters of the policy rule. In this case, private agents must estimate a policy rule using information from both past central bank actions and information contained in published interest rate projections. The publication of central bank interest rate projections may facilitate the public's understanding of the policy rule and so improve their predictions of the future course of the economy. In the second case, we examine an economy where the public has imperfect knowledge of the central bank's medium-run inflation target, π_t^*, which we refer to as "inflation target uncertainty." The public is assumed to infer the medium-run inflation target from information contained in past policy actions and from central bank interest rate projections. The publication of interest rate projections may improve the public's estimate of the medium-run inflation target and thereby improve the public's ability to forecast future policy actions and inflation.

6.4.1   Policy Rule Uncertainty

We first analyze an economy where the public knows the central bank's inflation target but is uncertain about the parameterization of the central bank's policy rule. In this case, the public forms its expectations about future policy and the economy using an estimated policy rule.[22] The assumption that the public is uncertain about the central bank's reaction functions seems realistic in light of the ongoing debate about the specification and parameters of the FOMC's reaction function. More generally, given the limited available data from consistent policy regimes, uncertainty about central bank reaction functions appears to be a pervasive feature of the economic landscape.

One could imagine a central bank publishing its policy rule and eliminating this type of uncertainty. Indeed, Svensson (2005b) has argued that the central bank should publish its objective function and model and thereby provide the public with all the information it needs to form expectations of future policy actions. However, we view a central bank's knowledge and understanding of its own preferences, and by implication its policy strategy, as far too complex and inchoate ever to be explicitly expressed to the public or, indeed, even written down within the halls of the central

22. A similar problem was studied by Orphanides and Williams (2005), but they did not consider the value of interest rate projections in improving the public's estimates of the policy rule.

bank. Not surprisingly, no central bank has yet put Svensson's proposal into practice. Still, based on the experiences discussed earlier in this chapter, we do think that the central bank can provide a potentially useful signal to the private sector of its plans for the future setting of the policy rate.

In the simplified model that we are using, there is only a single free parameter in the policy rule to be estimated: the coefficient in front of the change in the output gap, λ/κ. Assuming (as we do) that the public knows the value of κ, uncertainty about the parameters of the monetary policy rule is equivalent to uncertainty about the central bank's preferences, in particular, the penalty on output gap variability. We assume that private agents know the general formulation of the policy rule and know the true inflation target so that their estimation problem is far simpler than that faced by the public in reality. In this way, our analysis likely understates the effects of publishing interest rate projections on public expectations and macroeconomic performance. Nonetheless, the analysis of this simple problem nicely illustrates the qualitative effects of providing interest rate projections when the public is uncertain how the central bank will react to economic conditions.

Of course, in theory, if a policy regime were fixed for all time, agents would gradually accumulate precise information regarding the policy rule from observed policy actions and the uncertainty regarding the central bank's preferences would vanish. In practice, however, agents must form expectations having gathered only a finite set of observations of any given policy regime. One could explicitly endogenize the choice of the data sample used in policy rule estimation by allowing for time variation in the value of λ, but that would introduce a nonlinearity into the model and significantly complicate the analysis. Instead, for the present purpose, we assume that the policy regime is fixed and simply posit an environment where agents use only n observations in estimating the monetary policy reaction function. We consider two illustrative cases: in one, agents use the past forty observations (ten years of data) in estimating the policy rule; in the second, agents use eighty observations (twenty years of data).

We assume the central bank can choose to augment the public's information regarding the monetary policy rule through communication of its future policy intentions. Specifically, we assume that each period, the central bank can provide a signal, denoted $i^P_{t+1|t}$, of its own internal projection of the next period's interest rate setting, denoted $E_t(i_{t+1}|CB)$, where the conditioning information set is clearly denoted as the central bank's. (In the literature, these are often termed "unconditional" forecasts.)[23]

23. Note that in the simple model that we consider, the central bank could provide "unconditional" projections of inflation or the output gap, meaning projections consistent with the projected future path of interest rates, and the analysis and results would be the same as in the case of interest rate projections. This equivalence obtains because all of these projections are linear combinations of the same state variables. This contrasts with the case of cen-

As discussed in section 6.2, central bank communication of interest rate projections is often verbal and imprecise in practice. Even if the central bank provides a numerical interest rate projection, the manner in which it is constructed, say, by taking a median vote, may create a wedge between the published projection and the true expected path for interest rates. Therefore, in our analysis, we allow for *transmission noise* in conveying the interest rate projection to the public. This noise reflects the fact that the central bank may not be able to, or may not choose to, send a perfectly clear signal of its expectation of future policy. In particular, we assume that the central bank signal of its interest rate projection is given by:

$$(11) \qquad i^P_{t+1|t} = E_t(i_{t+1}|CB) + z_t, \quad z_t \sim N(0, \sigma_z^2),$$

where the transmission noise, z_t, is assumed to be an i.i.d. normally distributed random variable with variance σ_z^2. The limiting case of $\sigma_z = \infty$ corresponds to the central bank providing no useful information to the public regarding the future course of policy. The opposite limiting case of $\sigma_z = 0$ corresponds to the central bank perfectly communicating to the public its expectation of the interest rate path and thereby its policy rule. For intermediate cases, we interpret a highly noisy signal, say, $\sigma_z = 1$, as corresponding to a central bank providing only qualitative hints about the possible direction of future policy. A modestly noisy signal, say, $\sigma_z = 0.1$, suggests a central bank providing fairly detailed, numerical information about its expectations of the future path of policy.

Note that for analytical convenience, we assume that all the information regarding the future course of policy is contained in the central bank's one-step-ahead projection of the interest rate. In practice, a central bank is likely to communicate a forecast that covers several periods. In our model, there is no additional information contained in the two-step-ahead forecast that is not already contained in the one-step-ahead forecast. More generally, though, we view providing a multiperiod forecast as a way to reduce the transmission noise relative to a one step-ahead forecast, so it can be analyzed in this framework as a reduction in the degree of transmission noise.

Given the past history of central bank signals and actions, private agents estimate the value of λ on the basis of the policy equation. In particular, at the end of each period, agents run two regressions using the most recent n observations of data. The first is a regression of the observed inflation gap on the observed change in the output gap. Because we assume the inflation target is known, no intercept or other term is included in the regression. Note that the innovation to this equation is the policy shock, w_t. Because this equation involves endogenous variables on both sides, estimation is

tral bank publication of forecasts of inflation and output conditional on an arbitrary assumed path of policy with no explicit guidance on policy, as is typically done in many central banks. These conditional forecasts yield no useful information regarding the nature of the shocks to the public in our model.

done using instrumental variables, where the lagged output gap is the instrument. The second is a regression of the expected one-period-ahead inflation gap on the expected one-period-ahead change in the output gap consistent with the published central bank interest rate projection. Estimation of this equation is likewise done using instrumental variables. Note that the innovation in this case is the central bank transmission noise, z_t. In both cases, we impose the restriction that the estimated coefficient be positive, consistent with the restriction that the penalty on output gap variability be nonnegative. For symmetry and to avoid an upward bias in the estimates, we also impose the restriction that the estimated coefficient be no larger than twice the true value. Given the assumption that $\lambda = 1$, the estimates are constrained to lie between 0 and 2, inclusive.

Estimation of these two equations yields two point estimates of λ and estimates of the variances of the residuals in the two equations. We assume that agents then form an estimate $\hat{\lambda}_t$ by taking a weighted average of the two point estimates, with the weights equaling the inverse of the respective standard deviations of the regression residuals. In this way, agents take into account the relative amounts of noise observed from the two sources of information regarding the monetary policy rule.[24] In the following period, agents compute expectations of future variables conditional on $\hat{\lambda}_t$. Then, given the realized values of the innovations, the values of all endogenous variables are computed. The process is then continued, with agents reestimating the policy rule equations at the end of each period.[25] We compute the statistics of interest for these experiments using model stochastic simulations. We run each simulation 41,000 periods and drop the first 1,000 periods to minimize the effects of initial conditions.

Central bank publication of interest rate projections improves the public's understanding of the central bank's policy rule. The solid line of figure 6.3 shows the root mean squared error (RMSE) of $\hat{\lambda}_t$ (relative to the true value of $\lambda = 1$) over the simulations for various degrees of transmission noise, as measured by σ_z. As noted in the preceding, the solid line assumes that agents estimate the policy rule using only forty periods of data, but still the average estimation errors for $\hat{\lambda}_t$ are reasonably modest. As seen in figure 6.3, clear communication of interest rate projections facilitates the public's ability to estimate the policy rule. With zero transmission noise, the public's estimate of the policy rule equals the true policy rule at all

24. This method of combining estimates performs very well in terms of the resulting efficiency of the estimates in the model simulations. An alternative approach of having agents apply maximum likelihood would likely yield similar results, but at a much greater computational cost.

25. Technically, each period, we compute the rational expectations equilibrium consistent with the public's estimate of λ. We then compute residuals to the policy rule equation and to the equation describing the policy projection that make the setting of policy and the expectation of policy consistent with the true value of λ and the realized values of w_t and z_t.

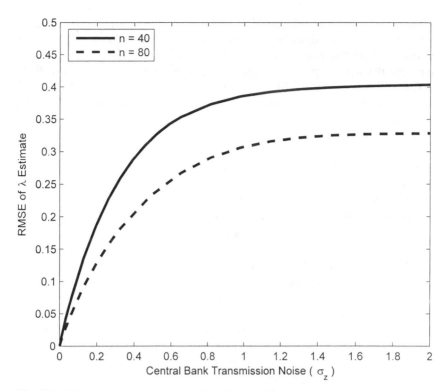

Fig. 6.3   Interest rate projections and estimates of λ

times. But as the degree of transmission noise rises, the accuracy of the public's estimates of the policy rule diminishes.

Publication of interest rate projections is potentially useful at aligning private and central bank expectations even if the public has a relatively long history of observations of policy actions. The dashed line in figure 6.3 shows the RMSE of $\hat{\lambda}_t$, assuming that agents use eighty observations in estimating the policy rule.[26] Not surprisingly, the effect of publishing interest rate projections (for a given transmission noise) is smaller when the public has a longer history of policy actions on which to base their policy rule estimates. Nevertheless, even with twenty years of data, publication of interest rate projections can have a potentially significant effect on the public's understanding of the policy rule.

26. The doubling of the number of observations would, all else equal, lead to a reduction in the RMSE by a factor of $\sqrt{2}$. This is indeed approximately true for the results reported in figure 6.3 when σ_z is 1/2 or smaller. However, the restriction that $\hat{\lambda}_t$ be between 0 and 2 reduces its RMSE, and this effect is larger when the sample size is small and when the magnitude of transmission noise is large. As a result, for values of σ_z above 1/2, the RMSE curve for $n = 40$ lies below what would be expected based on the difference in sample sizes.

This alignment of the public's and the central bank's expectations of monetary policy reduces the magnitude of fluctuations in output and the inflation gap and, therefore, on the central bank loss. The solid line in figure 6.4 shows the central bank loss for various degrees of central bank transmission noise, σ_z, when $n = 40$. For comparison, the loss assuming that the central bank does not publish interest rate projections is about 1.03. The central bank loss is minimized when the transmission noise is zero and rises as σ_z increases. Even a noisy central bank signal of policy intentions yields a noticeable improvement in macroeconomic performance over that which would occur absent central bank publication of interest rate projections.

The benefits of central bank communication of interest rate projections are greatest when the public has relatively little data on which to base their estimates of the policy rule. The dashed line in figure 6.4 shows the corresponding results for $n = 80$. The benefits of communicating policy intentions are only about one-half as large as when $n = 40$. Of course, in the limit as the sample size increases to infinity, central bank interest rate projections would be superfluous because the public would know the exact policy rule based on past observations of policy actions.

These results show that when the public is uncertain about how the cen-

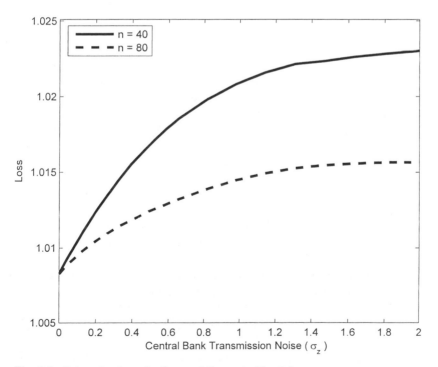

Fig. 6.4   **Interest rate projections and the central bank loss**

tral bank will respond to economic conditions, publishing interest rate projections can help align private and public expectations of future policy actions and thereby improve macroeconomic performance. This finding confirms that of Orphanides and Williams (2005), who, using a simple stylized model, find that the central bank loss is lower when the public knows the monetary policy rule than if they have to estimate the policy rule based on limited data.

6.4.2   Inflation Target Uncertainty

The case of policy rule uncertainty provides a strong case for central bank transparency and the potential value of publishing central bank interest rate projections. We now consider the case where the public is uncertain regarding the true value of the medium-run inflation target.[27] The case of inflation target uncertainty is of particular interest for two reasons. First, this case is of interest on its own merit. As discussed in Woodford (2005) and Williams (2006), a central bank constrained by the zero lower bound on interest rates will want to engineer above-trend inflation for a time, but, if the public has little experience with policy constrained by the zero bound, private agents may not understand the central bank's intentions. Second, this case is well suited for analyzing the issue of the effects of interest rate projections if the public inefficiently uses the information contained in interest rate projections.

In analyzing inflation target uncertainty, we assume as before that the public and the central bank have complete information regarding the other aspects of the economy. We also continue to assume that the central bank communicates in terms of a noisy one-period-ahead internal forecast of the interest rate. And to keep the analysis as simple as possible, we now assume that the public knows the central bank's preference parameter λ. Under these assumptions, the public faces a standard signal extraction problem in order to try to disentangle the realizations of the inflation target and the policy shock. One way to interpret the solution to this problem is to consider what private agents will determine as the most likely value of the true inflation target from realized policy actions and published central bank interest rate projections. We assume that the central bank, but not the public, knows the realized values of the two policy-related innovations, v_t and w_t. The public observes the current interest rate, from which it can infer the sum, $\pi_t^* + w_t$, but it cannot disentangle the current level of the inflation target and the realization of the policy shock w_t. Likewise, from the published interest rate projection, the public can infer the sum, $\delta\pi_t^* + \psi z_t$, where ψ measures the relationship between the inflation target and the interest rate implied by the monetary policy rule, but it cannot disentangle

---

27. For further discussion of target shocks in the context of public uncertainty of future policy actions, see Faust and Svensson (2001) and Geraats (2005).

the expected level of the inflation target and the realization of the transmission noise shock, z_t.[28]

Given the assumptions of independent Gaussian disturbances, the resulting optimal filter estimate of the inflation target at time t, based on information available in period t, denoted by $\hat{\pi}_t^*$, is given by

$$(12) \qquad \hat{\pi}_t^* = \delta\,\hat{\pi}_{t-1}^* + \gamma(\pi_t^* + w_t - \delta\hat{\pi}_{t-1}^*) + \theta(\delta\pi_t^* + \psi z_t - \delta\hat{\pi}_{t-1}^*),$$

where the parameter $\gamma \in [0, 1]$ is the gain associated with the revelation of the policy action, and the parameter $\theta \in [0, 1]$ is the gain associated with the central bank's projection of the interest rate in the next period. As noted in the preceding, we assume that the unconditional mean of the inflation target is 0 and that this is known by the public. We initially assume that agents know the true values of the variances of the different shocks and filter the data optimally. Given that the shocks w_t and z_t are independent, the signal-to-noise ratio of the combined two signals, denoted ϕ, is given by:

$$(13) \qquad\qquad\qquad \phi \equiv \frac{\sigma_v^2}{\sigma_w^2} + \frac{\delta^2\sigma_v^2}{\psi^2\sigma_z^2}.$$

The optimal steady-state filter gains, γ^* and θ^*, are given by the following two equations:

$$(14) \qquad \gamma^* + \theta^* = 1 - \frac{2}{2 - (1 - \delta^2 - \phi)^2 + \sqrt{(1 - \delta^2 - \phi)^2 + 4\phi}},$$

$$(15) \qquad\qquad\qquad \gamma^* = \frac{\gamma^* + \theta^*}{\phi}\,\frac{\sigma_v^2}{\sigma_w^2}.$$

Equation (14) is the standard formula for a problem of two independent Gaussian latent variables, where one follows an AR(1) and the other is serially uncorrelated (see Harvey 1989). Equation (15) parses the sum of the two gains according to the relative signal-to-noise ratios of the two processes.

Private agents form expectations of future variables based on their estimate of the inflation target. Output, inflation, and interest rates are then determined conditional on these expectations. Figure 6.5 displays the optimal filter gains associated with the policy action, γ^*, and with the interest rate projection, θ^*, respectively. Not surprisingly, if the central bank signal of its policy intentions is highly noisy, the public mostly ignores that signal and bases its beliefs primarily on policy actions. As the clarity of the central bank projections improves, the public places greater weight on

---

28. The value of ψ is a function of the other model parameters. In the model simulations, we first obtain the reduced-form solution of the model and then set ψ equal to the inverse of the coefficient on the inflation target in the reduced-form equation for the interest rate.

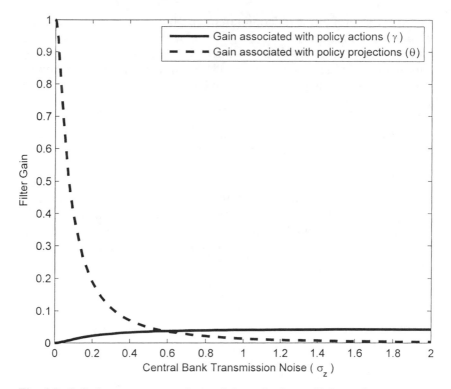

Fig. 6.5   Inflation target uncertainty and the optimal use of information

those projections and less weight on the current policy setting. As the signal-to-noise goes to 0, the public optimally responds only to published interest rate projections and not at all to policy actions.[29]

The public's inaccurate assessments of the medium-run inflation target create persistent discrepancies between the public's estimate of the target and the target's true value, which distort the paths of inflation and the output gap away from those desired by the central bank. Imperfect public information about the inflation target affects the responses to shocks to the policy rule and the inflation target. Given the relatively small variance assumed for the inflation target shocks, sizable persistent shifts in the inflation target are relatively "rare," so the public's view of the inflation target is

29. As in the case of policy rule uncertainty, if the central bank perfectly communicated its expectation of the interest rate in the next period ($\sigma_z = 0$), this information would be sufficient for the public to completely ascertain the inflation target. Additional information from the central bank about its projection of interest rates two, three, or more periods in the future would be superfluous. However, as mentioned in the preceding, we interpret our analysis in terms of providing signals on the projected path of interest rates over a few years.

not very sensitive to a surprising policy action. Indeed, in the absence of interest rate projections, the optimal gain parameter for policy actions, γ, equals 0.043, indicating that the public's estimate of the inflation target initially would rise only by 4.3 *basis points* in the period of a 1 percentage point shock to the actual target.

The public's misperception of the inflation target gradually shrinks over time following a shock to the inflation target, both because the target itself is returning to baseline and the public's estimate is catching up with the target. With imperfect information, following a positive shock to the inflation target, the public wrongly ascribes too much central bank behavior to the transitory policy shock, so output rises more and inflation rises less than if the public knew about the shift in the inflation target. The excessive rise in the output gap continues and eventually causes the inflation rate to persistently overshoot the true target. As a result, the loss associated with a shock to the inflation target is greater when the central bank does not effectively communicate its intentions.

Although central bank communication helps improve the public's understanding of the medium-run inflation target, it also potentially introduces public expectational errors owing to central bank transmission noise that otherwise would be absent. The noise in the interest rate signal distorts the public's expectations of future policy and is a source of aggregate variability. The magnitude of these misperceptions depends on both the variance of the transmission noise shocks and the filter gain applied by the public to central bank communication. We account for this "cost" of noisy transmissions in our calculation of the effects of publishing interest rate projections.

Publishing interest rate projections improves the public's ability to discern the true medium-run inflation target, leading to better macroeconomic outcomes. The solid line in figure 6.6 shows the central bank loss as a function of the degree of central bank communication transmission noise, assuming that the public uses the optimal filter described in the preceding. An increase in transparency achieves a better alignment of public expectations of future policy with those of the central bank. The improved management of expectations better aligns the economy's responses to the inflation target and policy shocks with those in the complete transparency benchmark. On net, the benefits of the public's improved understanding of the inflation target outweigh the costs of extra noise in the system resulting from central bank communication noise, and the loss monotonically decreases as the quality of the signal about the central bank's interest rate projection improves. The benefits of transparency are larger when the inflation target is highly persistent. The smaller benefit of communication when the inflation target is not very persistent reflects the fact that in this situation the responses of the economy to an inflation target shock and a

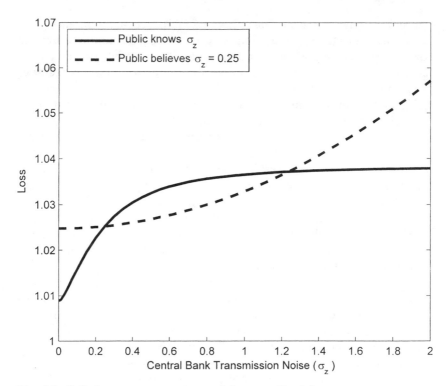

Fig. 6.6   Inflation target uncertainty and the central bank loss

transitory policy shock are quite similar. Thus, the public's parsing of the sources of the shock has little effect on inflation and output and, therefore, on the central bank loss.

6.4.3   Possible Public Confusion Regarding the Interest Rate Projections

One concern about central bank provision of interest rate projections is that private agents may misconstrue the accuracy of these projections or view them as unconditional commitments of future policy actions on the part of the central bank. If private agents systematically underreact to interest rate projections, the effects and usefulness of those projections would be more muted than reported in the preceding. A more significant concern is that private agents might overreact to published statements of central bank intentions and thereby underreact to the information in policy actions, with potentially deleterious effects on the economy. Such misperceptions of the quality of the central bank projections should not persist indefinitely because agents will eventually deduce the true value of central bank information from observed data. Nonetheless, it is conceivable that misperceptions of the noise in the central bank published projections could persist for a significant period of time and, therefore, be a problem during a transition period following the initial publication of interest rate projections. For this reason, we consider the effects of public confusion as to the degree of transmission noise in central bank rate projections.

If the public systematically underestimates the accuracy of the central bank interest rate projections, then the benefits of central bank communication are muted. The dashed line in figure 6.6 shows the central bank losses for different degrees of noise in the central bank projections, where the public filters the incoming information from policy actions and interest rate projections and believes that the central bank is sending a signal with $\sigma_z = 0.25$. The portion of the curve corresponding to values of σ_z between 0 and 0.25 is nearly flat, indicating that achieving the benefits of central bank communication of rate projections depends critically on the public's knowledge of the quality of the signal.

Interestingly, in the intermediate case where the public only moderately overestimates the accuracy of the central bank's signal, the central bank loss is actually lower than if the public had correctly assessed the degrees of transmission noise. Thus, for a given degree of transmission noise, the central bank loss is actually reduced when private agents inefficiently use information in forming expectations. This result reflects the net effects of the effects of target misperceptions on the responses to the different shocks. The overestimate of the accuracy of the central bank signal reduces the loss following a shock to the target because it reduces the misperceptions in that case. The same result holds for the responses to transitory policy shocks, in which case the public's mistaken belief that the shock reflects in small part a shift in the inflation target can lead to a small reduction in the loss associated with the shock. Offsetting these gains is the increase in aggregate variability owing directly to the responses of output and inflation to the noise in the central bank signal. On net, in this model, the gains exceed the costs for moderate degrees of overestimation of the quality of the signal. This finding illustrates the more general point that there does not exist an exact universal correspondence between the alignment of private and public expectations and the minimization of the central bank loss.[30] Under certain conditions, systematic expectational errors can be beneficial to the achievement of the central bank's goals, while in other cases such errors can interfere with the achievement of those goals.

30. It is possible to devise other examples where an improved alignment of private and central bank expectations increases the central bank loss. For example, if one allows for both a transitory shock to the true inflation target that has a significantly higher variance than either the persistent inflation target or the policy shocks, then either partial transparency or even no transparency can be optimal. This occurs because the public sees some probability that any realized shock is highly persistent, which causes inflation to rise more and the output gap to move less than for a transitory shock, both desirable responses if the source of the shock is a transitory disturbance to the inflation target. Such an example is not realistic, but illustrates the general point that has been made repeatedly in the literature: transparency can be a double-edged sword.

Nonetheless, it is worth stressing that in the examples considered here, we find that the central bank loss is minimized when the central bank is perfectly transparent, that is, $\sigma_z = 0$.

If the public severely overestimates the accuracy of central bank signals, then publishing interest rate projections can be counterproductive, until private agents realize their misperception of the accuracy of central bank signals. As the degree of the public's overestimation of the accuracy of the signal increases, the loss associated with aggregate fluctuations resulting from the responses to noise in the central bank's signal rises. As seen in the figure, if the true value of σ_z exceeds about 1.25, while the public believes it to be 0.25, the central bank loss exceeds that which would occur if the central bank did not publish interest rate projections at all. Under this condition, the costs associated with the public's response to the noise generated by the central bank signals outweigh the benefits these signals provide in the responses to the other shocks.

The potential for misperceptions of the accuracy of the interest rate projections suggests that an important part of such communication is to avoid sending highly noisy signals of future policy intentions that confuse markets. Indeed, concern that communication of policy intentions was doing more harm than good appears to have been behind the FOMC's abandonment of policy guidance in 1999, as discussed in the preceding. But in the cases of the Reserve Bank of New Zealand and the Norges Bank, publication of interest rate projections does not appear to have led to excessive or counterproductive market reactions. Moreover, as evidenced by the deviations of market expectations from the RBNZ interest rate projections illustrated in figure 6.1, it is clear that market participants do not view the projections as unconditional commitments, nor do they forsake independent analysis of economic conditions and forecasting of policy.

6.5 Conclusion

Indirect signaling of future policy intentions has been the overwhelming choice of central banks in the past. Recently, however, some central banks, including the Fed, have revealed some information to the public about their future policy intentions. But only two central banks, the RBNZ and the Norges Bank, have gone so far as to provide explicit quantitative forecasts of the policy expectations. The existing theoretical literature has not focused on transparency with regard to interest rate projections, nor has it reached firm conclusions regarding the optimal degree of central bank transparency in general. In our theoretical analysis, we find that central bank communication of interest rate projections can better align the public's and the central bank's expectations, and this better alignment of expectations generally leads to improvements in macroeconomic performance.

Although our results provide some support for the argument that the better alignment of expectations improves performance, our analysis also highlights some of the pitfalls that may accompany publishing interest rate projections. An important concern is that the public would misconstrue the central bank communication as providing an unconditional commitment or may put too much weight on the information from the central bank communication relative to other sources of information. We find that the latter concern, if realized, could be costly in terms of macroeconomic stabilization and could even cause performance to worsen relative to the case of no central bank communication. These results underline the need for a well-developed central bank communications strategy that mitigates such problems by highlighting both the conditionality and uncertainty regarding interest rate projections.

References

Archer, David. 2005. Central bank communication and the publication for interest rate projections. Bank of International Settlements. Unpublished Manuscript.

Bernanke, Ben. 2004. Central bank talk and monetary policy. Remarks at the Japan Society corporate luncheon, New York. http://www.federalreserve.gov/boarddocs/speeches/2004/200410072/default.htm.

Bernanke, Ben, Vincent R. Reinhart, and Brian P. Sack. 2004. Monetary policy alternatives at the zero bound: An empirical assessment. *Brookings Papers on Economic Activity*, Issue no. 2. 1–100. Washington, DC: Brookings Institution.

Blinder, Alan S. 1998. *Central banking in theory and practice.* Cambridge, MA: MIT Press.

———. 2004. *The quiet revolution: Central banking goes modern.* New Haven, CT: Yale University Press.

Bomfim, Antulio, and Glenn D. Rudebusch. 2000. Opportunistic and deliberate disinflation under imperfect credibility. *Journal of Money, Credit, and Banking* 32:707–21.

Carpenter, Seth. 2004. Transparency and monetary policy: What does the academic literature tell policymakers? FRB Finance and Economics Discussion Paper Series no. 2004–35. Washington, DC: Federal Reserve Board. http://www.federalreserve.gov/pubs/feds/2004/200435/200435abs.html.

Cogley, Timothy, and Argia M. Sbordone. 2005. A search for a structural Phillips curve. *Federal Reserve Bank of New York Staff Reports* no. 203. New York: Federal Reserve Bank of New York.

Eggertsson, Gauti B., and Michael Woodford. 2003. The zero bound on interest rates and optimal monetary policy. *Brookings Papers on Economic Activity*, Issue no. 1:193–233. Washington, DC: Brookings Institution.

Erceg, Christopher J., and Andrew T. Levin, 2003. Imperfect credibility and inflation persistence. *Journal of Monetary Economics* 50 (4): 915–44.

Faust, Jon, and Eric M. Leeper. 2005. Forecasts and inflation reports: An evaluation. Paper prepared for the Sveriges Riksbank conference, Inflation Targeting: Implementation, Communication and Effectiveness, Stockholm, Sweden. http://www.riksbank.com/upload/Dokument_riksbank/Kat_foa/FaustLeeper.pdf.

Faust, Jon, and Lars E.O. Svensson. 2001. Transparency and credibility: Monetary policy with unobservable goals. *International Economic Review* 42:369–97.

Federal Reserve Board of Governors. 2000. Modifications to the FOMC's disclosure policies. January 19. http://www.federalreserve.gov/boarddocs/press/general/2000/20000119/attachment.pdf.

———. 2003. Press release. August 12. http://www.federalreserve.gov/boarddocs/press/monetary/2003/20030812/.

Fuhrer, Jeffrey C., and Glenn D. Rudebusch. 2004. Estimating the Euler equation for output. *Journal of Monetary Economics* 51:1133–53.

Geraats, Petra M. 2002. Central bank transparency. *Economic Journal* 112:532–65.

———. 2005. Transparency and reputation: The publication of central bank forecasts. *Topics in Macroeconomics* 5:1–26.

Goodfriend, Marvin. 1986. Monetary mystique: Secrecy and central banking. *Journal of Monetary Economics* 17:63–92.

Goodhart, Charles A. E. 2001. Monetary transmission lags and the formulation of the policy decision on interest rates. *Federal Reserve Bank of St. Louis Review* 83 (July/August): 165–81.

Gürkaynak, Refet S., Brian Sack, and Eric T. Swanson. 2005a. Do actions speak louder than words? The response of asset prices to monetary policy actions and statements. *International Journal of Central Banking* 1:55–93.

———. 2005b. The sensitivity of long-term interest rates: Evidence and implications for macroeconomic models. *American Economic Review* 95 (1): 425–36.

Harvey, Andrew C. 1989. *Forecasting, structural time series models and the Kalman filter*. Cambridge, UK: Cambridge University Press.

Hellwig, Christian. 2005. Heterogeneous information and the welfare effects of public information disclosures. University of California, Los Angeles, Unpublished Manuscript.

Hördahl, Peter, Oreste Tristani, and David Vestin. 2006. A joint econometric model of macroeconomic and term structure dynamics. *Journal of Econometrics* 131:405–44.

King, Mervyn. 2006. Speech presented at the Lord Mayor's banquet for bankers and merchants, London, England. http://www.bankofengland.co.uk/publications/speeches/2006/speech278.pdf.

Kohn, Donald L. 2005. Central bank communication. Remarks at the annual meeting of the American Economic Association, Philadelphia. http://www.federalreserve.gov/boarddocs/speeches/2005/20050109/default.htm.

Kohn, Donald L., and Brian Sack. 2004. Central bank talk: Does it matter and why? In *Macroeconomics, monetary policy, and financial stability*, 175–206. Ottawa, Ontario: Bank of Canada.

Kozicki, Sharon, and Peter A. Tinsley. 2001. Shifting endpoints in the term structure of interest rates. *Journal of Monetary Economics* 47:613–52.

Lange, Joe, Brian Sack, and William Whitesell. 2003. Anticipations of monetary policy in financial markets. *Journal of Money, Credit, and Banking* 35 (6): 889–909.

Leitemo, Kai. 2003. Targeting inflation by constant-interest-rate forecasts. *Journal of Money, Credit and Banking* 35:609–26.

McGough, Bruce, Glenn D. Rudebusch, and John C. Williams. 2005. Using a long-term interest rate as the monetary policy instrument. *Journal of Monetary Economics* 52:855–79.

Miller, Rich. 2005. The Fed may be talking too freely. *Business Week Online*, March 24.

Mishkin, Frederic S. 2004. Can central bank transparency go too far? In *The future of inflation targeting*, ed. Christopher Kent and Simon Guttmann, 48–66. Sydney, Australia: McMillan.

Morris, Stephen, and Hyun S. Shin. 2002. Social value of public information. *American Economic Review* 92 (5): 1521–34.

———. 2005. Central bank transparency and the signal value of prices. *Brookings Papers on Economic Activity*, Issue no. 2. 1–66. Washington, DC: Brookings Institution.

Norges Bank. 2005. *Inflation Report*. November. http://www.norges-bank.no/upload/import/front/rapport/en/ir/2005-03/ir-2005-03-en.pdf.

Oda, Nobuyuki, and Kazuo Ueda. 2005. The effects of the Bank of Japan's zero interest rate commitment and quantitative monetary easing on the yield curve: A macro-finance approach. Bank of Japan Working Paper no. 05-E-6. Tokyo: Bank of Japan.

Orphanides, Athanasios, and John C. Williams. 2005. Imperfect knowledge, inflation expectations, and monetary policy. In *The inflation-targeting debate*, ed. Ben S. Bernanke and Michael Woodford, 201–34. Chicago: University of Chicago Press.

Poole, William. 2005a. Communicating the Fed's policy stance. Speech presented at the HM Treasury/GES conference, Is There a New Concensus in Macroeconomics, London. http://www.stlouisfed.org/news/speeches/2005/11_30_05.htm.

———. 2005b. How should the Fed communicate? Speech presented at Center for Economic Policy symposium, The Future of the Federal Reserve, Princeton, NJ. http://www.stlouisfed.org/news/speeches/2005/4_02_05.htm.

Qvigstad, Jan F. 2005. When does an interest rate path "look good"? Criteria for an appropriate future interest rate path—A practician's approach. Norges Bank Staff Memo no. 2005/6. Oslo, Norway: Norges Bank.

Reifschneider, David, and John C. Williams. 2000. Three lessons for monetary policy in a low inflation era. *Journal of Money, Credit and Banking* 32 (4): 936–66.

Reserve Bank of New Zealand. 2006. *Monetary Policy Statement*. March. http://www.rbnz.govt.nz/monpol/statements/mar06.pdf.

Roca, Mauro. 2005. Transparency and monetary policy with imperfect common knowledge. Columbia University. Unpublished Manuscript.

Rudebusch, Glenn D. 1995. Federal Reserve interest rate targeting, rational expectations, and the term structure. *Journal of Monetary Economics* 24:245–74.

———. 2002. Term structure evidence on interest rate smoothing and monetary policy inertia. *Journal of Monetary Economics* 49:1161–87.

———. 2006. Monetary policy inertia: Fact or fiction? *International Journal of Central Banking* 2 (4): 85–135.

Rudebusch, Glenn D., and Lars E.O. Svensson. 1999. Policy rules for inflation targeting. In *Monetary policy rules*, ed. John B. Taylor, 203–46. Chicago: University of Chicago Press.

Rudebusch, Glenn D., and Tao Wu. 2004. A macro-finance model of the term structure, monetary policy, and the economy. *Economic Journal*, forthcoming.

———. 2007. Accounting for a shift in term structure behavior with no-arbitrage and macro-finance models. *Journal of Money, Credit, and Banking* 39 (2–3): 395–422.

Schlesinger, Jacob M. 2000. Fed replaces "bias" stance with "risks" outlook. *Wall Street Journal*, January 20.

Svensson, Lars E.O. 1997. Inflation forecast targeting: Implementing and monitoring inflation targets. *European Economic Review* 4:1111–46.

———. 2003. What is wrong with Taylor rules? Using judgement in monetary policy through targeting rules. *Journal of Economic Literature* 41:426–77.

———. 2005a. Monetary policy with judgment: Forecast targeting. *International Journal of Central Banking* 1:1–54.

———. 2005b. Optimal inflation targeting: Further developments of inflation targeting. Princeton University. Unpublished Manuscript.

———. 2006a. Social value of public information: Comment: Morris and Shin (2002) is actually pro transparency, not con. *American Economic Review* 96 (1): 448–52.

———. 2006b. The instrument-rate projection under inflation targeting: The Norwegian example. Princeton University. Unpublished Manuscript.

Swanson, Eric. 2006. Have increases in Federal Reserve transparency improved private sector interest rate forecasts? *Journal of Money, Credit and Banking* 38 (3): 791–819.

Thornton, Daniel L., and David C. Wheelock. 2000. A history of the asymmetric policy directive. *Federal Reserve Bank of St. Louis Review* 82 (September/October):1–16.

Trichet, Jean-Claude. 2006. The state of the economy: Overcoming key challenges to sustainable economic growth. Speech presented at Institute of Economic Affairs conference, London.

Walsh, Carl E. 2005. Optimal transparency under flexible inflation targeting. University of California, Santa Cruz. Unpublished Manuscript.

Williams, John C. 2006. Monetary policy in a low inflation economy with learning. Federal Reserve Bank of San Francisco. Unpublished Manuscript.

Woodford, Michael. 2003. *Interest and prices: Foundations of a theory of monetary policy.* Princeton, NJ: Princeton University Press.

———. 2005. Central-bank communication and policy effectiveness. In *The Greenspan era: Lessons for the future*, 399–474. Kansas City, MO: Federal Reserve Bank of Kansas City.

Comment   Marvin Goodfriend

On May 3, 2006, the *Wall Street Journal* carried a front page story and an editorial about Federal Reserve guidance for markets on interest rate policy.[1] Confusion about the Federal Reserve's intentions for interest rates occurs from time to time and this episode is just the latest of many that have occurred in the past. What I would call "rhetoric risk" is an inevitable part of monetary policy accompanied by communications intended to provide markets with guidance about the future direction of short-term interest rates.

This chapter addresses an important practical question that is closely related to rhetoric risk: is it desirable for a central bank to release its projection of the future path of its interest rate policy instrument? Essentially, the chapter investigates whether publishing an interest rate forecast would en-

Marvin Goodfriend is a professor of economics and chairman of The Gailliot Center for Public Policy, Carnegie Mellon University, and a research associate of the National Bureau of Economic Research.

1. See Ip (2006) and Wall Street Journal (2006).

able the public to improve its inference of private central bank information relevant for monetary policy and thereby improve the effectiveness of monetary policy.

The chapter addresses this question in a conventional model of monetary policy in which the forward-looking IS function contains a shock to the natural rate of interest, and the forward-looking aggregate supply function contains a shock to real marginal cost.

The policy function in the model, which is the first-order condition for optimal monetary policy, contains two more shocks. First, there is a first-order autoregressive shock to the medium-run inflation target. The credibility of the central bank's long-run inflation target implicitly is assumed to be fully secure, ruling out the possibility of inflation drift in the model. The public understands that at any point in time the actual inflation target may deviate persistently, though not permanently, from the long-run inflation target. Second, there is a policy shock to current inflation, given the current inflation target and the current output gap in the policy function. In addition, the model allows for the public to be imprecisely aware of the parameter that weights the central bank's concern for inflation relative to output in the first-order condition for optimal policy.

The authors assume that the public and the central bank have accurate, complete, contemporaneous information about the structural parameters of the private economy. Both observe perfectly and contemporaneously the current shock to the natural rate of interest and the current shock to real marginal cost. There is no data processing lag in the model.

The authors use the model to consider the consequences of publication by the central bank each period of a noisy forecast of future short-term interest rates conditional on the central bank's private information and the central bank's optimized policy. They consider two cases. In the first case, the central bank *publicizes* its medium-run inflation target exactly, but *keeps secret* the parameter in its optimal policy rule that governs the cost of inflation relative to output. In the second case, the central bank *keeps secret* its medium-run inflation target, but *publicizes* the parameter in its optimal policy rule relating inflation to output. In both cases, the central bank is presumed to *keep secret* the policy shock to current inflation, given the current inflation target and the current output gap.

In each case, the public in the model is assumed to infer optimally aspects of the policy rule that are kept secret. The main finding of the chapter emphasized by the authors is that the release of a projection for future short-rates can improve macroeconomic performance in both cases.

One can regard the chapter as a study of the extent to which the release of a noisy projected path for short-term interest rates conditioned on the information set of the central bank can substitute productively for transparency about the parameter relating inflation to output in the optimal policy rule or transparency about the medium-run inflation target.

My reactions to the chapter are as follows.

The chapter references research that reports empirical evidence of significant variation in the medium-run inflation target and significant persistence of the medium inflation target. One might question the identification of the statistical process generating an (implicit) inflation target in historical data. In any case, however, it seems reasonable to suppose that going forward, the innovation variance and persistence of the inflation target might be much smaller now that inflation has been stabilized around a relatively low rate. On this basis, the model could be expected to overstate the quantitative improvement in macroeconomic performance that could be yielded by releasing interest rate projections when the medium-run inflation target is kept secret.

Furthermore, the model provides no reason why a central bank should keep its medium-term inflation target secret in the first place. Agents would prefer to have direct knowledge of the central bank's medium-run inflation target in making their decisions. The same goes for the parameter weighting the cost of inflation relative to output in the policy rule. The model gives no reason why these policy variables should not be publicized, especially as publication would improve welfare in the model.

That said, I believe that in practice the public would continue to face a nontrivial signal processing problem with respect to central bank private information, even if policy were made more transparent as in the preceding. In practice, interest rate policy actions depend in part on multiple, imperfectly correlated inputs that the public does not observe. For instance, central banks have networks—regional, financial/supervisory, small business, industrial, and international—that feed information into the policy process. Central banks devote enormous resources to measuring and understanding the evolution of these inputs and a range of other data, aggregate and otherwise. Central banks continually update comprehensive forecasting models through which they process their thinking about the economy in a consistent way.

The preceding factors may do no more than give a central bank a temporary lead over financial markets, academics, other private observers, and the media in recognizing developments in the economy. Yet such considerations plausibly enable central banks to stay enough ahead of outsiders in understanding the economy to maintain an information advantage relative to the public in any given period.

In principle, one can imagine that a central bank might convey directly to the public information from the diverse sources mentioned in the preceding. However, doing so would be difficult and inadvisable. Much information could be acquired only on a confidential basis and might not be provided to the central bank in as much detail or at all if made public. Moreover, a central bank might be inclined not to divulge its views on particular industries so as not to interfere with individual markets. Moreover, a central bank would have to provide the public with sophisticated modeling services for the public to understand how the central bank utilizes much of its detailed information productively. An alternative is for a central bank to make its information available in a package, embodied in regular comprehensive assessments of current economic conditions, involving forecasts and discussion of how outcomes of key macroeconomic variables such as inflation, output, and interest rates are expected to evolve over time.

Reinterpreting the source of central bank private information along the preceding lines, the model suggests that it may make sense for a central bank to publish its interest rate projections. At a minimum, however, the model suggests also that a central bank should publish those parts of its private information that are feasible to publish and that are readily understood and interpreted by the public, such as a medium-run inflation target. Recall that the model implicitly assumes that there is a fixed, known long-run inflation target.

In closing, I would like to emphasize that if a central bank chooses to publicize its interest rate projection, it should present that projection as part of a comprehensive economic forecast that recognizes the interconnectedness of the economy and interest rate policy. In particular, interest rates should be understood to be a forward-looking stabilizing force in the macroeconomy, reacting to and offsetting prospective macroeconomic forces that would otherwise destabilize inflation, employment, and output. Central bank forecasts should give a coherent, consistent reflection of a central bank's overall view of current and prospective macroeconomic conditions. A central bank should be careful to steer clear of statements about particular sectors of the economy that could draw it into partisan disputes about prospects in particular markets. Above all, forecasts in general, and interest rate projections in particular, should be understood to be exceedingly fragile. Interest rates are among the first macroeconomic variables to react to emerging macroeconomic forces. The market's estimates of prospective developments are revised frequently over time with the potential for sizable interest rate adjustments.

References

Ip, Greg. 2006. Fed struggles to convince markets of its own uncertainty on rates. *Wall Street Journal*, May 3, A1.
Wall Street Journal. 2006. Educating Ben. May 3, A14.

Discussion Summary

Glenn D. Rudebusch said that, in principle, the central bank could send a signal of its medium-term inflation target π^* as an alternative to sending a signal of its projection of the next period's interest rate, the case considered in the chapter—however, the fact that there was not a lot of variation in π^* made this a less desirable option.

Peter Westaway said that the Bank of England presented economic forecasts based on the assumption that interest rates will follow the market forward rate path, rather than, say, assuming that interest rates will remain constant. It thereby avoided having to make assumptions about the implications of different paths for asset prices and having to model learning. Lars E.O. Svensson commented that modeling learning is indeed difficult, but central banks are used to modeling sluggish or irrational expectations, and should do so in this case, as they do in others.

Laurence H. Meyer noted that although the chapter discussed secrets of the temple in the sense of secrets between the central bank and public, he thought that, in fact, there were secrets inside the temple. Not all those involved in monetary policy were equally well informed. As a matter of sequencing, he said that central banks tended to make the decision to make announcements of the type considered by Rudebusch and John C. Williams only after making the decision to target inflation. He also said that although the Federal Open Market Committee (FOMC) provided a forecast of future conditions, it did not reveal the policy response that underpinned that forecast. Doing so would be desirable.

There was some discussion of the possibility that a central bank might lose credibility if it projected interest rates in a manner that subsequently turned out to be inaccurate. Rudebusch argued that the experience of Norway was encouraging in this regard. Svensson concurred, saying that he had conducted a review of monetary policy in New Zealand. In the course of preparing that review, he had not encountered any complaints about poor forecasts. The same was true in Norway. Thomas Laubach, however, expressed the view that central banks would not like to deviate from projections that they had previously published, and Charles Engel worried that a less credible central bank than the Fed might get into trouble if the environment changed and the bank did not move interest rates along the previously forecast path.

Donald L. Kohn suggested that the key issue was the correct model of the economy. People wanted to know what the central bank thought was going on and what it thought was going to happen. Communication was more a question of conveying the big picture. Ideally, then, the private sector would weigh central bank information and react to it. Over the last two years, Federal Reserve efforts to provide information had worked better than many expected. But, he said, the last two months showed that as the economy approached an inflexion point, it was hard to convey uncertainty and conditionality appropriately. The FOMC members worried that if they surprised the markets, stability could be negatively affected. Nonetheless, although there was some reticence, FOMC members were generally favorable to the idea of increased communication.

Andrew Levin pointed out that Norwegian data showed an important difference between central bank and private-sector forecasts. Communication of this fact could foster conversation about why the two disagree. Based on work carried out on New Zealand, it appeared that changes in the policy rate path only had a minimal effect on futures prices. This suggested that revealing the policy rate path might have only marginal impact.

Martin Schneider noted that in the interesting case where there was disagreement between the forecasts of the central bank and the private sector, the central bank and private sector apparently had different beliefs about how the world works. Perhaps, he said, this has implications for the central bank loss function.

Brian Sack said that the importance of releasing both macro projections and policy forecasts was that together they helped the private sector to learn about both the central bank's loss function and the state of the economy. He suggested that one might push this further and ask what the central bank's forecasts were for equity prices or for the price of oil. How far should this be taken? One option might be to report a policy rate forecast conditional on a particular macro path. Finally, he thought that the market should be given credit for understanding the difficulties inherent in forecasting.

7

The Effect of Monetary Policy on Real Commodity Prices

Jeffrey A. Frankel

7.1 Introduction

Commodity prices are back, with a vengeance.

In the 1970s, macroeconomic discussions were dominated by the oil price shocks and other rises in agricultural and mineral products that were thought to play a big role in the stagflation of that decade.[1] In the early 1980s, any discussion of alternative monetary regimes was not complete without a consideration of the gold standard and proposals for other commodity-based standards.

Yet the topic of commodity prices fell out of favor in the late 1980s and the 1990s. Commodity prices generally declined during that period; perhaps declining commodity prices are not considered as interesting as rising prices. Nobody seemed to notice how many of the victims of emerging market crises in the 1990s were oil producers that were suffering, among other things, from low oil prices (Mexico, Indonesia, Russia) or others suffering from low agricultural prices (Brazil and Argentina). The favor-

Jeffrey A. Frankel is the James W. Harpel Professor of Capital Formation and Growth at the Kennedy School of Government, Harvard University, and director of the International Finance and Macroeconomics Program at the National Bureau of Economic Research.

The author would like to thank Ellis Connolly, Yun Jung Kim, and Santitarn Sathirathai for exceptionally capable research assistance; John Campbell, Pravin Chandrasekaran, Gunes Asik, and Lars E.O. Svensson for comments; and the Kuwait Program at Harvard University for support.

1. A small dissenting minority viewed the increases in prices of oil and other commodities in the 1970s as the *result* of overly expansionary U.S. monetary policy, rather than as an exogenous inflationary supply shock (the result of the 1973 Arab oil embargo and the 1979 fall of the Shah of Iran). After all, was it just a coincidence that other commodity prices had gone up at the same time, or in the case of agricultural products, had actually preceded the oil shocks?

able effect of low commodity prices on macroeconomic performance—helping deliver lower inflation in the United States in the 1990s than had been thought possible at such high rates of growth and employment—was occasionally remarked. But it was not usually described as a favorable supply shock, the mirror image of the adverse supply shocks of the 1970s. It always received far less attention than the influence of other factors, such as the declining prices of semiconductors and other information technology and communication equipment. Indeed, anyone who talked about sectors where the product was as clunky and mundane as copper, crude petroleum, and soy beans was considered behind the times. In Alan Greenspan's phrase, gross domestic product (GDP) had gotten "lighter." Agriculture and mining no longer constituted a large share of the New Economy and did not matter much in an age dominated by ethereal digital communication, evanescent dot-coms, and externally outsourced services.

Now oil prices and many broader indices of commodity prices are again at or near all-time highs in nominal terms and are very high in real terms as well. Copper, platinum, nickel, zinc, and lead, for example, all hit record highs in 2006, in addition to crude oil. As a result, commodities are once again hot. It turns out that mankind has to live in the physical world after all! Still, the initial reaction in 2003 to 2004 was relaxed, on several grounds: (1) oil was no longer a large share of the economy, it was said; (2) futures markets showed that the "spike" in prices was expected to be only temporary; and (3) monetary policy need focus only on the core Consumer Price Index (CPI) inflation rate and can safely ignore the volatile food and energy component, unless or until it starts to get passed through into the core rate. But by 2005 to 2006, the increase in prices had gone far enough to receive much more serious attention. This was especially true with regard to the perceived permanence of oil prices, largely because the futures price had gone from implying that the rise in the spot price was mostly temporary to implying that it is mostly permanent.

Certain lessons of the past are well-remembered, such as the dangers of the Dutch Disease for countries undergoing a commodity export boom. But others have been forgotten, or were never properly absorbed.

With regard to point (3), it is time to examine more carefully the claim that if an increase in energy or agricultural prices does not appear in the core CPI, then monetary policy can ignore it. *The central argument of this chapter is that high real commodity prices can be a signal that monetary policy is loose.* Thus, they can be a useful monetary indicator (among many others). The analysis is both theoretical and empirical. The empirical work includes the determination of real commodity prices in the United States, the determination of prices in other smaller countries, and the determination of inventories. We find that real interest rates are an important determinant of the demand for inventories and, in turn, of the prices of agricultural and mineral commodities.

The current fashion in monetary policy is inflation targeting, by which is standardly meant targeting the CPI.[2] To be sure, the usual emphasis is on the core inflation rate "excluding the volatile food and energy sector." The leadership of the Federal Reserve has indicated that the appropriate response to the oil-shock component of recent inflation upticks is to ignore it, that is, accommodate it. But just because agricultural and mineral product prices are volatile does not mean that there is no useful information in them. The prices of gold and other minerals used to be considered useful leading indicators of inflationary expectations, precisely because they moved faster than the sluggish prices of manufactured goods and services. Nor does the volatility mean that excluding such products from the price index that guides monetary policy is necessarily appropriate.

In the first place, the "core CPI" is not a concept that is especially well understood among the general population. Thus, the public will not necessarily be reassured when the central bank tells them not to worry about big increases in food and energy prices. Attempts to explain away high numbers for headline inflation make it sound like the authorities are granting themselves an ad hoc self-pardon—like a "dog ate my homework" excuse. This can undermine the public credibility of the central bank. But credibility and transparency is the whole point of announcing an observable target in the first place. Thus, targeting the core CPI may not buy as much credibility as targeting something more easily understood (even if with a wider band).

The many proponents of inflation targeting will argue that the regime, if properly instituted, makes clear from the beginning that it excludes volatile commodity prices so that there is no loss in credibility. But, in the second place, let us ask if it is appropriate for the inflation target to exclude commodity prices. They may be important, on terms of trade grounds, especially in smaller countries. Stabilizing the traded-goods sector is itself an important goal in a world where balance of payments deficits can lead to financial crises, in which the previously declared currency regime is often one among many subsequent casualties. Recent oil price increases have also illustrated the necessity to take into account terms of trade shocks that come on the import side as well as the export side. Does there exist a price index to serve as an intermediate target that is more easily understood by the public than the core CPI, but also more robust with respect to terms of trade shocks than the overall CPI? Candidates include a producer price index (PPI) and an export price index.

***

2. Among many other references, see Bernanke et al (1999), Svensson (1995, 1999), and Truman (2003).

It is a tenet of international economics textbooks that a desirable property of a currency regime is that the exchange rate be allowed to vary with terms of trade shocks: that the currency automatically depreciates when world prices of the import commodity go up (say, oil for the United States or Switzerland, or wheat for Japan or Saudi Arabia) and that it automatically depreciates when world prices of the export commodity go down (say, oil for Saudi Arabia and wheat for Canada). Yet CPI targeting does not have this property. To keep the headline inflation rate constant, one must respond to a rise on world markets in the dollar price of imported oil by tightening monetary policy and *appreciating* the currency against the dollar enough to prevent the domestic price of the importable from rising. This response is the opposite from accommodating the adverse terms of trade shock, which would require a depreciation. It is true that the core inflation rate does not share this unfortunate property with the headline rate (unless the price increase comes in nonenergy commodities like semiconductors that are in the core). But the other half of terms of trade shocks are declines on world markets in the price of a country's export commodity. Theory says that when the dollar price of oil goes down, Saudi Arabia or Norway ought to depreciate against the dollar. But inflation targeting—*either* the headline CPI variety *or* the core CPI variety—does not allow this result. One would need to target a price index that specifically featured prominently the price of the exportable. The fundamental difficulty is that excluding the volatile food and energy components is not sufficient to accommodate the terms of trade, *either* if some imports lie outside those two sectors *or* if some exports lie within those two sectors.

Throughout this chapter, we will adopt the familiar assumption that all goods can be divided into homogeneous agricultural and mineral commodities, on the one hand, and differentiated manufactured goods and services, on the other hand, and that the key distinction is that prices of the former are perfectly flexible so that their markets are always clear and that prices of the latter are sticky in the short run so that their markets do not.[3] The plan is to look at connections between commodities and monetary policy. We begin with the monetary influences on commodity prices—first for a large country, then for a small one. We conclude with a viewpoint based on reverse causality: the possible influence of commodity prices on monetary policy in a consideration of what price index to use for the nominal anchor. Even if one is wedded to, say, a Taylor rule, the question of what price index to use merits discussion. *The author summarizes a proposal made elsewhere, for countries with volatile terms of trade, to use an export price index (or producer price index) in place of the CPI. If one is en-*

---

3. For young readers, I will recall that these distinctions were originally due to Arthur Okun (1975), who called the two sectors auction goods versus customer goods.

amored of a simpler price-targeting regime, then the proposal is to Peg the Export Price Index (PEPI) in place of targeting the CPI.

7.2   The Effect of Monetary Policy on Real Commodity Prices

The central purpose of this chapter is to assert the claim that monetary policy, as reflected in real interest rates, is an important—and usually underappreciated—determinant of the real prices of oil and other mineral and agricultural products, while far from the only determinant.

7.2.1   Effect of U.S. Short-Term Real Interest Rates on Real U.S. Commodity Prices

The argument can be stated in an intuitive way that might appeal to practitioners as follows. High interest rates reduce the demand for storable commodities, or increase the supply, through a variety of channels:

- By increasing the incentive for extraction today rather than tomorrow (think of the rates at which oil is pumped, zinc is mined, forests logged, or livestock herds culled)
- By decreasing firms' desire to carry inventories (think of oil inventories held in tanks)
- By encouraging speculators to shift out of commodity contracts (especially spot contracts) and into treasury bills

All three mechanisms work to reduce the market price of commodities, as happened when real interest rates were high in the early 1980s. A decrease in real interest rates has the opposite effect, lowering the cost of carrying inventories and raising commodity prices, as happened during 2002 to 2004. Call it part of the "carry trade."[4]

Theory: The Overshooting Model

The theoretical model can be summarized as follows. A monetary contraction temporarily raises the real interest rate, whether via a rise in the nominal interest rate, a fall in expected inflation, or both. Real commodity prices fall. How far? Until commodities are widely considered "undervalued"—so undervalued that there is an expectation of future appreciation (together with other advantages of holding inventories, namely the "convenience yield") that is sufficient to offset the higher interest rate (and other costs of carrying inventories: storage costs plus any risk premium). Only then, when expected returns are in balance, are firms willing to hold the inventories despite the high carrying cost. In the long run, the general price level adjusts to the change in the money supply. As a result, the real money

---

4. See Frankel (2005b).

supply, real interest rate, and real commodity price eventually return to where they were.

The theory is the same as Rudiger Dornbusch's (1976) famous theory of exchange rate overshooting, with the price of commodities substituted for the price of foreign exchange—and with convenience yield substituted for the foreign interest rate. The deep reason for the overshooting phenomenon is that prices for agricultural and mineral products adjust rapidly, while most other prices adjust slowly.[5]

The theory can be reduced to its simplest algebraic essence as a claimed relationship between the real interest rate and the spot price of a commodity relative to its expected long-run equilibrium price. This relationship can be derived from two simple assumptions. The first one governs expectations. Let

$s \equiv$ the spot price,
$\bar{s} \equiv$ its long run equilibrium,
$p \equiv$ the economy-wide price index,
$q \equiv s - p$, the real price of the commodity, and
$\bar{q} \equiv$ the long run equilibrium real price of the commodity,

all in log form. Market participants who observe the real price of the commodity today lying above or below its perceived long-run value expect it in the future to regress back to equilibrium over time, at an annual rate that is proportionate to the gap:

$$(1) \qquad E[\Delta(s - p)] \equiv E[\Delta q] = -\theta(q - \bar{q})$$

or

$$(2) \qquad E(\Delta s) = -\theta(q - \bar{q}) + E(\Delta p).$$

Following the classic Dornbusch overshooting paper, we begin by simply asserting the reasonableness of the form of expectations in these equations: a tendency to regress back toward long-run equilibrium. But, as in that paper, it can be shown that regressive expectations are also rational expectations, under certain assumptions regarding the stickiness of other goods prices (manufacturers and services) and certain restrictions on parameter values.[6]

Equation (3) concerns the decision whether to hold the commodity for another period—either leaving it in the ground or on the trees or holding it in inventories—or to sell it at today's price and deposit the proceeds in the bank to earn interest. The arbitrage condition is that the expected rate of return to these two alternative courses of action must be the same:

$$(3) \qquad E\Delta s + c = i,$$

5. See Frankel (1984).
6. See Frankel (1986).

where

$c \equiv cy - sc - rp$

$cy \equiv$ convenience yield from holding the stock (e.g., the insurance value of having an assured supply of some critical input in the event of a disruption, or in the case of gold, the psychic pleasure component of holding it),

$sc \equiv$ storage costs (e.g., costs of security to prevent plundering by others, rental rate on oil tanks or oil tankers, etc.)

$rp \equiv$ risk premium, which is positive if being long in commodities is risky, and

$i \equiv$ the interest rate.[7]

There is no reason why the convenience yield, storage costs, or risk premium should be constant over time. If one is interested in the derivatives markets, the forward discount or slope of the futures curve, $f - s$ in log terms, is given by:

(4) $f - s = i - cy + sc$,   or equivalently by $E\Delta s - rp$.

Parenthetically, the introduction to this chapter noted that conventional wisdom initially regarded the 2003 to 2004 "spike" in oil prices as only temporary, but expectations regarding the long-run oil price were subsequently revised sharply upward. The changes in the perceived transience or permanence of the price increase were standardly based on the futures markets, which did not catch up with the increase in the spot price until after a year or so. It is curious that so many economists and central bankers are ready to accept that the futures price of oil is an unbiased forecast of the future spot price. This proposition, of course, would follow from the two propositions that the futures price is an accurate measure of expectations (no risk premium) and that expectations are rational. Both halves of the joint hypothesis are open to question. Few familiar with the statistics of forward exchange rates claim that they are an unbiased predictor of the future spot exchange rate. Few familiar with the statistics of the interest rate term structure claim that the long-term interest rate contains an unbiased predictor of future short-term interest rates. Why, then, expect the oil futures price to be an unbiased predictor of the future spot price?[8] The convenience yield, storage costs, and risk premium are variable. So the backwardation (forward prices below spot) in oil prices in 2004 was not necessarily a reason to be complacent, and the flattening or contango (for-

7. Working (1949) and Breeden (1980) are classic references on the roles of carrying costs and the risk premium, respectively, in commodity markets. Yang, Bessler, and Leatham (2001) review the literature.

8. Studies of bias in the commodities futures price as a predictor of the spot price include Bessembinder (1993), Brenner and Kroner (1995), Covey and Bessler (1995), Dusak (1973), Fama and French (1987), Fortenbery and Zapata (1997), and Kolb (1992). Most assume that investors' expectations must be unbiased in-sample, and infer a time varying risk premium. The exception, Choe (1990), infers expectations from survey data.

ward prices above spot) in 2005 to 2006 was not necessarily a reason to worry.

Nevertheless, the large increase in the slope of the futures yield curve during the period 2004 to 2006, the same period that the Federal Reserve was steadily raising interest rates, is consistent with the theory that we have just developed: that the slope depends on the interest rate plus storage costs minus convenience yield. Harder to explain is that the move to contango came rather sharply, however, in early April 2005, rather than gradually. Here a rapid revision in expectations may have played a role.

To get our main result, we simply combine equations (2) and (3):

(5) $-\theta(q - \bar{q}) + E(\Delta p) + c = i \quad \rightarrow$

$$q - \bar{q} = -(1/\theta)[i - E(\Delta p) - c].$$

Equation (5) says that the real price of the commodity (measured relative to its long-run equilibrium) is inversely proportional to the real interest rate (measured relative to a constant term that depends on convenience yield). When the real interest rate is high, as in the 1980s, money flows out of commodities, just as it flows out of foreign currencies, emerging markets, and other securities. Only when the prices of these alternative assets are perceived to lie sufficiently below their future equilibriums will the arbitrage condition be met. Conversely, when the real interest rate is low, as in 2001 to 2005, money flows into commodities, just as it flows into foreign currencies, emerging markets, and other securities. Only when the prices of these alternative assets are perceived to lie sufficiently above their future equilibriums will the arbitrage condition be met.

The Simplest Test

One can imagine a number of ways of testing the theory.

One way of isolating the macroeconomic effects on commodity prices is to look at jumps in financial markets that occur in immediate response to government announcements that change perceptions of monetary policy, as was true of Fed money supply announcements in the early 1980s. Money announcements that caused interest rates to jump up would, on average, cause commodity prices to fall, and vice versa. The experiment is interesting because news regarding supply disruptions and so forth is unlikely to have come out during the short time intervals in question.[9]

The relationship between the real commodity price and the real interest rate, equation (5), can also be tested more directly because variables can be measured fairly easily.[10] This is the test we pursue here.

We begin with a look at some plots. Three major price indexes that have

---

9. See Frankel and Hardouvelis (1985).

10. One precedent is Barsky and Summers (1988, part III), who established an inverse relationship between the real interest rate and the real prices of gold and nonferrous metals.

been available since 1950—from Dow Jones, Commodity Resources Board, and Moody's—are used in the first three figures. (In addition, two others, which started later than 1950, are illustrated in appendix A). To compute the real commodity price, we take the log of the commodity price index minus the log of the CPI. To compute the real interest rate, we take the one-year interest rate and subtract off the one-year inflation rate observed over the preceding year.

The negative relationship predicted by the theory seems to hold. We next apply ordinary least squares (OLS) regression to these data.

It would not be reasonable to expect the regression relationship to hold precisely in practice. It would be foolish to think that the equation captures everything. In reality, a lot of other things beyond real interest rates influence commodity prices. There are bound to be fluctuations both in $\bar{q}$, the long-run equilibrium real price, and c, which includes convenience yield, storage costs, and risk premium. These fluctuations are not readily measurable.[11] Such factors as weather, political vicissitudes in producing countries, and so forth, are likely to be very important when looking at individual commodities. Indeed, analysts of oil or coffee or copper pay rather little attention to macroeconomic influences and, instead, spend their time looking at microeconomic determinants. Oil prices have been high in 2004 to 2006 in large part due to booming demand from China and feared supply disruptions in the Middle East, Russia, Nigeria, and Venezuela. There may now be a premium built in to the convenience yield arising from the possibilities of supply disruption related to terrorism, uncertainty in the Persian Gulf, and related risks. Yet another factor concerns the proposition that the world supply of oil may be peaking in this decade, as new discoveries lag behind consumption (Hubbert's Peak[12]). This would imply that $\bar{q}$, the world long-run equilibrium real price of oil has shifted upward. Other factors apply to other commodities. In coffee, the large-scale entry of Vietnam into the market lowered prices sharply a few years ago. Corn, sugar, and cotton are heavily influenced by protectionist measures and subsidies in many countries and so on (see figure 7.1).

Such effects in individual commodities partially average out when looking at a basket average of commodity prices. This is one reason to use aggregate indexes in the tests reported in the following.

Table 7.1 reports regressions of real commodity prices over the period 1950 to 2005. The results are statistically significant at the 5 percent level for all three of the major price indexes that have been available since 1950—from Dow Jones, Commodity Resources Board (CRB), and Moody's—and

11. An extension for future research would be to attempt to control for some influences on c by means of measures of economic activity and risk such as those used in the inventories equation in the next section.

12. See Deffeyes (2005). Notwithstanding that such predictions have in the past been proven wrong.

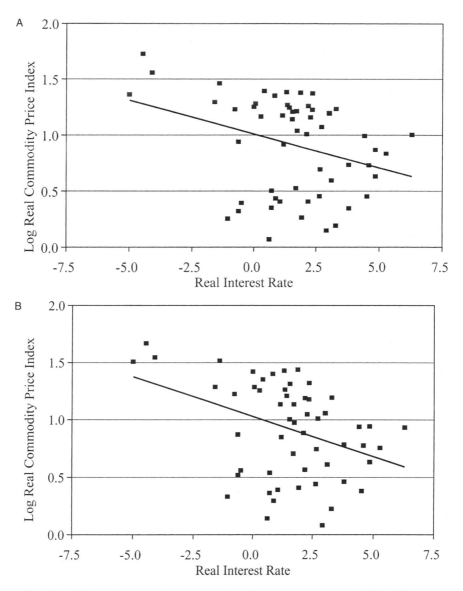

Fig. 7.1   U.S. real commodity prices and real interest rates, annual 1950–2005:
A, **CRB commodity price index versus real interest rate;** *B*, **Dow Jones commodity price index versus real interest rate;** *C*, **Moody's commodity price index versus real interest rate**

Source: Global Financial Data.

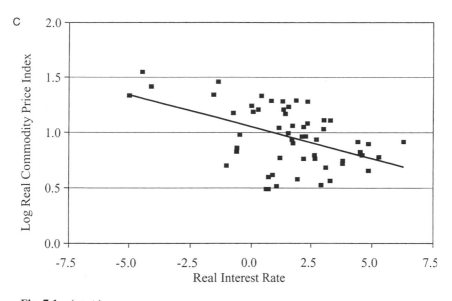

Fig. 7.1   (cont.)

significant for one of the two with a shorter history (Goldman Sachs). All are of the hypothesized negative sign. The estimated coefficient for the CRB, −.06, is typical. It suggests that when the real interest rate goes up 1 percentage point (100 basis points), it lowers the real commodity price by .06, that is, 6 percent. It also suggests that the estimate for $1/\theta = 6$, so $\theta = .16$. In other words, the expected speed of adjustment per year is estimated at 16 percent. The expected half-life is about four years (.84 to the 4th power = .5).

Table 7.1 also reports results for twenty-three individual commodities, presented in order of the size of the estimated coefficient. Despite our fears that sector-specific microeconomic factors swamp the macroeconomic influences for individual commodities, the coefficient is of the hypothesized sign in nineteen out of twenty-three cases and is statistically significant in half (eleven out of twenty-three). Interestingly, oil and gold are the worst of the twenty-three, showing (insignificant) positive coefficients! A fixed effects panel incorporates the information for all the individual commodities with the coefficient constrained to be the same. The coefficient is estimated at −.046 and is highly significant statistically.

The results in table 7.1 suggest that the significant negative relationship between commodity prices and interest rates is reasonably robust across commodity price measures. Is the result as robust over time? It appears that the negative correlation is significant over 1950 to 1979 (see appendix table 7A.1, panel A). However, since 1980, there does not appear to have been a stable relationship between log real commodity prices and the real interest

Table 7.1   Regression of log real commodity prices on real interest rates,
                   1950–2005: results by commodity indices, individual commodities, and
                   fixed effects panel of commodities

	Coefficient	SE
Sample: 1950–2005 (56 annual observations)		
Goldman Sachs (1969–)	−0.080	0.029**
Dow Jones	−0.070	0.023**
CRB	−0.060	0.024**
Moodys	−0.058	0.014**
Reuters (1959–)	−0.009	0.024
Commodities		
Sugar	−0.144	0.035**
Soy bean oil	−0.096	0.030**
Corn	−0.091	0.032**
Rubber	−0.090	0.037**
Wheat	−0.088	0.033**
Lead	−0.071	0.022**
Oats	−0.066	0.029**
Soy beans	−0.064	0.027**
Cocoa	−0.063	0.035
Cotton	−0.061	0.030**
Zinc	−0.050	0.018**
Cattle	−0.048	0.016**
Fixed effects panel	−0.046	0.006**
Nickel	−0.032	0.018
Hogs	−0.031	0.022
Copper	−0.026	0.028
Tin	−0.026	0.032
Aluminium	−0.022	0.017
Coffee	−0.015	0.038
Palladium	−0.012	0.025
Silver	0.002	0.031
Platinum	0.003	0.014
Oil	0.009	0.028
Gold	0.025	0.032

Source: Global Financial Data.
Notes: Real interest rate in percentages and real commodity prices in log units. Commodities are listed by coefficient in ascending order. SE = standard error.
**Significant at the 5 percent level.

rate (see appendix table 7A.1, panel B). The same is true if the sample is divided at 1976 or 1982.

An Effect on Inventories?

Because one of the hypothesized mechanisms of transmission from real interest rates to real commodity prices runs via the demand for inventories, it may be instructive to look at inventory data. Appendixes B and C report regression results for oil inventories (see appendix tables 7B.1 and 7C.1).

The coefficient on the real interest rate is often negative, as hypothesized. It is not always statistically significant, until we control for three other standard determinants of inventory demand, as in table 7.2. The following are the three other determinants:

- Industrial production, representing the transactions demand for inventories. Higher economic activity should have a positive effect on the demand for inventory holdings.
- Risk (political, financial, and economic) among a weighted average of twelve top oil producers. In our measure, a rise in the index represents a decrease in risk, which should have a negative effect on the demand for inventories.
- The spot-futures spread. Intuitively the futures-spot spread reflects the speculative return to holding inventories.[13] A higher spot-futures spread, or lower future-spot spread, signifies a low speculative return and should have a negative effect on inventory demand.

More formally, equation (4) gives us the arbitrage condition relevant for firms deciding whether to incur storage costs:

$$i - cy + sc = E\Delta s - rp.$$

We substitute in the arbitrage condition that comes from the financial speculators,

$$f - s = E\Delta s - rp,$$

and solve for storage costs.

$$sc = f - s + cy - i$$

Storage costs rise with the extent to which inventory holdings strain existing storage capacity:

$$sc = \Phi(inventories).$$

Invert the equation for the supply of inventory storage capacity, and set inventory demand equal to supply:

$$(6) \qquad inventories = \Phi^{-1}(sc)$$

$$= \Phi^{-1}[cy - i - (s - f)].$$

We see from the equation that inventory holdings are positively related to convenience yield (which is, in turn, determined by industrial production and geopolitical risk) and negatively related to the interest rate and the

13. For example, see the discussion of Figure 1.22 in the *World Economic Outlook,* April 2006, Washington, DC, International Monetary Fund; Abosedra and Radchenko (2003); or Balabanoff (1995).

spot-futures spread (two components of the opportunity cost of holding inventories).

Equation (6) is a model of the stock of inventories that firms *desire* to hold. In practice, the actual level of inventories generally deviates from the desired levels. For example, a sudden unexpected acceleration of industrial production will, in the short run, show up as a *fall* in inventories held, even though the desired level of inventories goes up. Only over time are firms able to adjust their actual level of inventories in line with the desired level. This phenomenon is very well known and was the origin of the "stock adjustment" specification in regression equations. For our purposes, it simply means we want to include a lagged endogenous variable and that we should expect its effect on current measured inventories to be very strong.

The results are reported in table 7.2. They show the hypothesized sign on all variables, usually with statistical significance.[14] They, thus, generally support the model.

We have also looked at agricultural inventories, as reported in appendix table 7D.1. Here there is little evidence of an effect of real interest rates. But in this case we were unable to control for risk or other important variables, so perhaps this finding is to be expected.

7.2.2   The Relationship in Other Countries

In the preceding analysis, we have expressed everything—nominal commodity prices, CPI, interest rates—in dollars. But the United States is not the whole world. It is less than 1/3 of Gross World Product, even if its importance in monetary and financial markets is evidently greater than that. In this section, we consider other countries, concentrating on those that currently have floating exchange rates and, thus, are in need of a price target to anchor monetary policy. We will treat them as "small open economies," meaning that they take the world price of commodities as given, even though they range in size up to the United Kingdom.

Adding Exchange Rate Overshooting to Commodity Price Overshooting

We could begin by redoing the previous econometrics with global measures of each of the variables, that is, measuring the commodity price in a GDP-weighted average of the dollar, euro, yen, and so on, measuring the world interest rate as a weighted average of national interest rates and measuring the CPI and inflation rates as the same-weighted average of national CPIs and inflation rates. But we leave this as a possible extension for future research. Instead, we take the U.S. variables to be the global variables, and

---

14. Indeed, these other determinants are sufficiently successful in the inventory equation as to suggest that one include them in the regression estimates of equation (5), where they would serve as determinants of c. Perhaps the addition of such controls would improve the estimates of the macroeconomic influences on the prices of oil and other commodities. This extension is left for future research.

Table 7.2   **Relationship between oil inventories and real interest rates (weekly data; 1,114–1,190 observations depending on data availability)**

Real interest rate	Spot-futures	IP	ΔIP	Risk	Δrisk	Inventories (t – 1)
Nonstationary variables detrended by including quadratic terms in each regression						
−0.394**	−0.821**	0.397**		−0.002**		
(0.089)	(0.041)	(0.062)		(0.001)		
−0.056	−0.079**	0.052**		0.000		0.931**
(0.032)	(0.013)	(0.020)		(0.000)		(0.009)
−0.211**	−0.727**		0.131		−0.005**	
(0.085)	(0.040)		(0.126)		(0.001)	
−0.017	−0.071**		0.009		0.000	0.937**
(0.032)	(0.012)		(0.045)		(0.000)	(0.009)

Note: Standard errors in parenthesis.
**Significant at the 5 percent level.

we proceed directly to look at small countries that by definition take the U.S./global variables as given.

The log spot price of the commodity in terms of currency j is given by

(7) $$s_j = s_{(j/\$)} + s_{(\$/c)},$$

where $s_{(j/\$)}$ is the spot exchange rate in units of currency j per \$ and $s_{(\$/c)}$ is the spot price of commodity c in terms of \$, what has hitherto been called simply s for the dollar case. The real exchange rate between currency j and the dollar is governed by the direct application of the Dornbusch over-shooting model.

(8) $$(s_{(j/\$)} - \bar{s}_{(j/\$)}) - (p_j - \bar{p}_j) + (p_\$ - \bar{p}_\$) = $$
$$-\frac{1}{\upsilon}\{i_j - i_\$ - [E(\Delta p_j) - E(\Delta p_\$)]\}$$

Combining equations (5), (7), and (8),

(9) $$(s_{(j/c)} - \bar{s}_{(j/c)}) = (s_{(j/\$)} - \bar{s}_{(j/\$)}) + (s_{(\$/c)} - \bar{s}_{(\$/c)})$$
$$= (p_j - \bar{p}_j) - \frac{1}{\upsilon}\{i_j - i_\$ - [E(\Delta p_j) - E(\Delta p_\$)]\}$$
$$-\frac{1}{\theta}[i_\$ - E(\Delta p_\$) - c]$$
$$(q_{(j/c)} - \bar{q}_{(j/c)}) = -\frac{1}{\upsilon}(r_j - r_\$) - (1/\theta)(r_\$ - c),$$

where $r_\$$ is the U.S. interest rate, and r_j is the interest rate in country j.

Equation (9) says the real commodity price observed in country j will be high to the extent either that the local real interest rate is low relative to the U.S. real rate or to the extent that the U.S. real interest rate is low. We tested this equation for eight individual countries that currently have independently floating currencies (though they did not all have floating rates throughout the entire sample period).

We computed the real commodity price by converting the commodity price to the currency of the small open economy in question and dividing by the country's price level. We then regressed the log of the real commodity price on the two variables on the right-hand side of equation (9), the U.S. real interest rate and the differential in real interest rates between the small open economy and the United States:

$$\log \frac{CP^{US} \cdot S^{j/\$}}{P^j} = \alpha + \beta_1[(i^j - \pi^j) - (i^{US} - \pi^{US})] + \beta_2(i^{US} - \pi^{US}) + \varepsilon.$$

The results for the eight floating countries are reported in table 7.3, which uses six different commodity price indexes: CRB, Dow Jones, The Economist, Goldman Sachs, Moody's, and Reuters. Monthly data were generally available for the developed countries from 1950.[15] To take full advantage of what data were available, the regressions were estimated separately for the three-month interest rate (three-month Treasury notes or equivalent) and the long-term interest rate with the largest sample (Australia: ten-year bond; Brazil: thirty-year bond; Canada: ten+ year bond; Chile: twenty-year bond; Mexico: three-year bond; New Zealand: ten-year bond; Switzerland: thirty-year bond; United Kingdom: twenty-year bond). The U.S. interest rate for each regression was chosen to match the maturity of the bond from the small open economy.

In general, the evidence appears to support the hypothesis regarding the determination of the log real local-currency index of commodity prices. The estimates show a significant negative coefficient on the real U.S. interest rate, representing global monetary policy, as well as on the real interest differential between the national economy and the United States, representing local variations in monetary stance. Often, significance levels are high. In the case of the three major English-speaking countries, Australia, Canada, and the United Kingdom, both the coefficient on the U.S. real interest rate and the coefficient on the real interest differential are statistically significant and of the hypothesized negative sign in almost every one of the twelve cases, regardless of which of the six commodity price indexes are used and regardless of whether short-term or long-term interest rates are used. The results for New Zealand and Switzerland are almost as strong but for the effect of the short-term U.S. rate, as are the results for Brazil and Chile, except that the coefficient on the long-term real interest differential is not always significant. The only disappointing country is Mexico, where even though the short-term real interest differential always

---

15. For the three Latin American countries, however, it was difficult to find interest rate data preceding their hyperinflations.

Table 7.3 Regressions of log real commodity prices in local currency on real interest rates: monthly observations (over largest possible sample of data since 1950)

	Short rate			Long rate		
	Sample	Real U.S. rate	Real interest differential	Sample	Real U.S. rate	Real interest differential
A. Log real CRB commodity price index in local currency and real interest rates						
Australia	1/1950–8/2005	−0.023** (0.006)	−0.076** (0.003)	1/1950–8/2005	−0.057** (0.005)	−0.067** (0.004)
Brazil	7/1965–2/1989, 1/1995–8/2005	−0.024** (0.007)	−0.006** (0.002)	5/1994–9/2005	−0.161** (0.019)	−0.001 (0.001)
Canada	1/1950–9/2005	−0.047** (0.005)	−0.065** (0.005)	1/1950–9/2005	−0.073** (0.004)	−0.076** (0.006)
Chile	7/1997–9/2005	−0.063** (0.006)	−0.021** (0.004)	2/1993–2/2004	−0.092** (0.014)	−0.018** (0.003)
Mexico	1/1978–9/2005	0.055** (0.013)	−0.017** (0.002)	1/1995–9/2005	0.047** (0.011)	0.000 (0.003)
New Zealand	3/1978–8/2005	0.001 (0.009)	−0.067** (0.004)	1/1950–8/2005	−0.081** (0.006)	−0.075** (0.004)
Switzerland	1/1980–9/2005	0.034** (0.016)	−0.054** (0.009)	5/1953–9/2005	−0.171** (0.013)	−0.095** (0.012)
United Kingdom	1/1950–9/2005	−0.053** (0.010)	−0.086** (0.007)	1/1950–9/2005	−0.106** (0.007)	−0.023** (0.006)
B. Log real Dow Jones commodity price index in local currency and real interest rates						
Australia	1/1950–8/2005	−0.035** (0.005)	−0.071** (0.003)	1/1950–8/2005	−0.061** (0.004)	−0.064** (0.004)
Brazil	7/1965–12/1989, 1/1995–8/2005	−0.036** (0.007)	−0.005** (0.002)	5/1994–9/2005	−0.197** (0.021)	0.000 (0.001)
Canada	1/1950–9/2005	−0.056** (0.004)	−0.059** (0.005)	1/1950–9/2005	−0.076** (0.004)	−0.074** (0.006)

(*continued*)

Table 7.3 (continued)

	Short rate			Long rate		
	Sample	Real U.S. rate	Real interest differential	Sample	Real U.S. rate	Real interest differential
Chile	7/1997–9/2005	−0.084** (0.009)	−0.027** (0.006)	2/1993–2/2004	−0.106** (0.017)	−0.004 (0.004)
Mexico	1/1978–9/2005	0.036** (0.012)	−0.017** (0.002)	1/1995–9/2005	0.015 (0.012)	−0.003 (0.003)
New Zealand	3/1978–8/2005	−0.015 (0.008)	−0.063** (0.004)	1/1950–8/2005	−0.085** (0.005)	−0.071** (0.004)
Switzerland	1/1980–9/2005	0.004 (0.015)	−0.065** (0.009)	5/1953–9/2005	−0.160** (0.012)	−0.076** (0.012)
United Kingdom	1/1950–9/2005	−0.063** (0.009)	−0.081** (0.007)	1/1950–9/2005	−0.108** (0.007)	−0.027** (0.006)
	C. Log real Economist commodity price index in local currency and real interest rates					
Australia	1/1950–8/2005	−0.010** (0.005)	−0.027** (0.002)	1/1950–8/2005	−0.018** (0.004)	−0.031** (0.002)
Brazil	7/1965–12/1989, 1/1995–8/2005	0.005 (0.007)	−0.006** (0.001)	5/1994–9/2005	−0.095** (0.018)	−0.002** (0.001)
Canada	1/1950–9/2005	−0.012** (0.005)	0.004 (0.005)	1/1950–9/2005	−0.018** (0.004)	−0.020** (0.006)
Chile	7/1997–9/2005	−0.049** (0.006)	−0.011** (0.004)	2/1993–2/2004	−0.020 (0.014)	−0.022** (0.003)
Mexico	1/1978–9/2005	0.056** (0.012)	−0.013** (0.002)	1/1995–9/2005	0.093** (0.013)	0.001 (0.004)
New Zealand	3/1978–8/2005	0.011 (0.008)	−0.042** (0.003)	1/1950–8/2005	−0.031** (0.005)	−0.042** (0.002)
Switzerland	1/1980–9/2005	0.061** (0.013)	−0.014 (0.008)	5/1953–9/2005	−0.086** (0.006)	−0.051** (0.006)
United Kingdom	1/1950–9/2005	−0.024** (0.007)	−0.045** (0.004)	1/1950–9/2005	−0.049** (0.005)	−0.021** (0.004)

D. Log real Goldman Sachs commodity price index in local currency and real interest rates

Australia	12/1969–8/2005	−0.054** (0.006)	−0.063** (0.004)	12/1969–8/2005	−0.064** (0.005)	−0.074** (0.004)
Brazil	12/1969–12/1989, 1/1995–8/2005	−0.058** (0.009)	−0.004** (0.002)	5/1994–9/2005	−0.296** (0.025)	−0.001 (0.001)
Canada	12/1969–9/2005	−0.077** (0.007)	−0.060** (0.007)	12/1969–9/2005	−0.096** (0.006)	−0.091** (0.006)
Chile	7/1997–9/2005	−0.098** (0.014)	−0.048** (0.009)	2/1993–2/2004	−0.178** (0.021)	−0.007 (0.005)
Mexico	1/1978–9/2005	0.026** (0.011)	−0.015** (0.002)	1/1995–9/2005	−0.035** (0.013)	−0.002 (0.004)
New Zealand	3/1978–8/2005	−0.030** (0.008)	−0.067** (0.003)	12/1969–8/2005	−0.076** (0.007)	−0.080** (0.003)
Switzerland	1/1980–9/2005	−0.025 (0.015)	−0.077** (0.009)	12/1969–9/2005	−0.219** (0.009)	−0.172** (0.012)
United Kingdom	12/1969–9/2005	−0.051** (0.009)	−0.089** (0.005)	12/1969–9/2005	−0.094** (0.009)	−0.039** (0.007)

E. Log real Moody's commodity price index in local currency and real interest rates

Australia	1/1950–8/2005	−0.031** (0.004)	−0.052** (0.002)	1/1950–8/2005	−0.050** (0.003)	−0.045** (0.003)
Brazil	7/1965–12/1989, 1/1995–8/2005	−0.022** (0.006)	−0.001 (0.001)	5/1994–9/2005	−0.180** (0.023)	−0.001 (0.001)
Canada	1/1950–9/2005	−0.044** (0.003)	−0.040** (0.004)	1/1950–9/2005	−0.056** (0.003)	−0.040** (0.004)
Chile	7/1997–9/2005	−0.096** (0.007)	−0.021** (0.005)	2/1993–2/2004	−0.055** (0.020)	0.004 (0.004)
Mexico	1/1978–9/2005	0.029** (0.008)	−0.011** (0.002)	1/1995–9/2005	0.017 (0.012)	0.000 (0.004)
New Zealand	3/1978–8/2005	−0.021** (0.005)	−0.044** (0.002)	1/1950–8/2005	−0.067** (0.004)	−0.045** (0.003)

(continued)

Table 7.3   (continued)

	Short rate			Long rate		
	Sample	Real U.S. rate	Real interest differential	Sample	Real U.S. rate	Real interest differential
Switzerland	1/1980–9/2005	-0.030** (0.010)	-0.071** (0.006)	5/1953–9/2005	-0.117** (0.009)	-0.046** (0.009)
United Kingdom	1/1950–9/2005	-0.054** (0.007)	-0.059** (0.005)	1/1950–9/2005	-0.084** (0.005)	-0.017** (0.005)
F. Log real Reuters commodity price index in local currency and real interest rates						
Australia	11/1959–8/2005	0.009 (0.006)	-0.042** (0.004)	11/1959–8/2005	-0.008 (0.005)	-0.045** (0.004)
Brazil	7/1965–12/1989, 1/1995–8/2005	0.003 (0.008)	-0.007** (0.001)	5/1994–9/2005	-0.060** (0.015)	-0.003** (0.000)
Canada	11/1959–9/2005	-0.004 (0.007)	-0.004 (0.006)	11/1959–9/2005	-0.024** (0.006)	-0.041** (0.007)
Chile	7/1997–9/2005	-0.029** (0.007)	-0.007 (0.004)	2/1993–2/2004	-0.029** (0.013)	-0.043** (0.003)
Mexico	1/1978–9/2005	0.088** (0.014)	-0.014** (0.002)	1/1995–9/2005	0.128** (0.014)	0.002 (0.005)
New Zealand	3/1978–8/2005	0.041** (0.011)	-0.048** (0.004)	11/1959–8/2005	-0.020** (0.006)	-0.064** (0.003)
Switzerland	1/1980–9/2005	0.102** (0.015)	-0.011 (0.009)	11/1959–9/2005	-0.125** (0.008)	-0.107** (0.009)
United Kingdom	11/1959–9/2005	0.010 (0.009)	-0.070** (0.005)	11/1959–9/2005	-0.037** (0.008)	-0.018** (0.006)

Note: Robust standard errors in parenthesis.
**Significant at the 5 percent level.

appears significantly less than zero, the U.S. interest rate appears significantly greater than zero rather than less.

This seems impressive evidence for what has been the central theme of this chapter so far. The hypothesized effect of the real interest rate on real commodity prices works not only at the U.S. level, but also at the level of local variation among open economies above and beyond the global phenomenon.

7.3   Implications for Monetary Policy

We conclude the chapter with a consideration of some implications for monetary policymakers. The first implication is a reason to add commodity prices to the list of variables that central banks monitor, regardless of their regime—that is, regardless of whether they use discretion or some rule or intermediate target and, in the latter case, regardless of the rule or target that is officially declared. The second implication concerns the possibility, in the case of countries where fluctuations in the terms of trade are important, of giving export prices a larger role in the price index that enters the rule or target than does the CPI (whether headline CPI or core CPI).

7.3.1   Commodity Prices Belong on the List of
Monetary Conditions Indicators

The advice that monetary policymakers should "look at everything" sounds easy to give and hard to reject. But not everyone would consider it obvious that an index of agricultural and mineral commodity prices belongs on a useful list of variables to reveal current monetary conditions, alongside short- and long-term interest rates, the exchange rate, housing prices, and the stock market. The conventional practice is to throw the volatile "food and energy" sector out of the price indexes, concentrating instead on the core CPI if one wants a good indicator of likely future inflation. It is certainly true that if one is looking for the single standard statistic that best predicts future inflation, the core CPI will do better than the headline CPI. But that is not the question. The question is, rather, if one is free to look at lots of information, are agricultural and mineral prices on the list of variables worth paying attention to? This perspective places this chapter on a plane with other chapters that consider the possibility of central banks paying attention to housing prices or the stock market.

The theory and empirical results reported in this chapter suggest that the answer is yes. Real commodity prices reflect monetary ease, more specifically real interest rates, among other factors. We can never be sure what the real interest rate is because we do not directly observe expected inflation. Thus, it is useful to have additional data that are thought to reflect real interest rates.

7.3.2   What Prices Belong in the Inflation Targeters' Target?

The current fashion in monetary policy regimes is inflation targeting. Such countries as the United Kingdom, Sweden, Canada, New Zealand, Australia, Chile, Brazil, Norway, Korea, and South Africa have adopted it, and many monetary economists approve. In part, this is a consequence of the disillusionment with exchange rate targets that arose in the course of ten years of currency crises (from the speculative attack that forced the United Kingdom to drop out of the European Exchange Rate Mechanism in 1992 to the Argentina crisis of 2001). Proponents of inflation targeting point out that if the exchange rate is not to be the anchor for monetary policy, then the ultimate objective of price stability requires that some new nominal variable must be chosen as the anchor. Two old favorite candidates for nominal anchor, the price of gold and the money supply, have long since been discredited in the eyes of many. So that seems to leave inflation targeting. One version of a generalized approach to inflation targeting is a Taylor rule, which puts weight on output in addition to inflation.

But whether it is simple inflation targeting or a Taylor rule, what price index is appropriate? Of the possible price indexes that a central bank could target, the CPI is the usual choice. Indeed, the CPI (whether core or overall CPI) seems to be virtually the only choice that central banks and economists have even considered. But this is not the only possible choice. A proposal made elsewhere is to target an index of export prices.

7.3.3   The Proposal to Peg the Export Price (PEP)

This idea is a more moderate version of an exotic-sounding proposed monetary regime called Peg the Export Price (PEP). The author originally proposed PEP explicitly for those countries that happen to be heavily specialized in the production of a particular mineral or agricultural export commodity. The proposal was to fix the price of that commodity in terms of domestic currency, or, equivalently, set the value of domestic currency in terms of that commodity. For example, African gold producers would peg their currency to gold—in effect returning to the long-abandoned gold standard. Canada and Australia would peg to wheat. Norway would peg to oil. Chile would peg to copper, and so forth. One can even think of exporters of manufactured goods that qualify: standardized semiconductors (that is, commodity chips) are sufficiently important exports in Korea that one could imagine it pegging the won to the price of chips.

How would this work operationally? Conceptually, one can imagine the government holding reserves of gold or oil and intervening whenever necessary to keep the price fixed in terms of local currency. Operationally, a more practical method would be for the central bank each day to announce an exchange rate vis-à-vis the dollar, following the rule that the day's exchange rate target (dollars per local currency unit) moves precisely in proportion to the day's price of gold or oil on the London market or New York market (dollars per commodity). Then the central bank could intervene via the foreign exchange market to achieve the day's target. Either way, the effect would be to stabilize the price of the commodity in terms of local currency. Or perhaps, because these commodity prices are determined on world markets, a better way to express the same policy is "stabilizing the price of local currency in terms of the commodity."[16]

The PEP proposal can be made more moderate and more appropriate for diversified economies, in a number of ways, as explained in the next subsection.[17] One way is to interpret it as targeting a broad index of all export prices, rather than the price of only one or a few export commodities. This moderate form of the proposal is abbreviated PEPI, for Peg the Export Price *Index*.[18]

The argument for the export price targeting proposal, in any of its forms, is stated succinctly: it delivers one of the main advantages that a simple exchange rate peg promises, namely a nominal anchor, while simultaneously delivering one of the main advantages that a floating regime promises, namely automatic adjustment in the face of fluctuations in the prices of the countries' exports on world markets. Textbook theory says that when there is an adverse movement in the terms of trade, it is desirable to accommodate it via a depreciation of the currency. When the dollar price of exports rises, under PEP or PEPI, the currency *per force* appreciates in terms of dollars. When the dollar price of exports falls, the currency depreciates in terms of dollars. Such accommodation of terms of trade shocks is precisely what is wanted. In recent currency crises, countries that suffered a sharp deterioration in their export markets were often eventually forced to give up their exchange rate targets and devalue anyway, but the adjustment was far more painful—in terms of lost reserves, lost credibility, and lost output—than if the depreciation had happened automatically.

But the proposal is not just for countries with volatile commodity exports. The desirability of accommodating terms of trade shocks is a good way to summarize the attractiveness of export price targeting relative to the reigning champion, CPI targeting.[19] Consider the two categories of adverse terms of trade shocks: a fall in the dollar price of the export in world markets and a rise in the dollar price of the import on world markets. In the first case, a fall in the export price, you want the local currency to depreciate against the dollar. As already noted, PEP or PEPI deliver that result automatically; CPI targeting does not. In the second case, a rise in the import price, the terms-of-trade criterion suggests that you again want the local

16. Frankel (2002, 2003) and Frankel and Saiki (2002).

17. Another way to go is to define as the parity a basket that includes the export commodity as well as a weighted average of currencies of major trading partners—for example, 1/3 dollars, 1/3 euros, and 1/3 oil, as the author has proposed for Persian Gulf states.

18. See Frankel (2005a).

19. Among many possible references are Bernanke et al. (1999), Mankiw and Reis (2003), Svensson (1995, 1999), Svennson and Woodford (2005), and Truman (2003).

currency to depreciate.[20] Consumer Price Index targeting actually has the implication that you tighten monetary policy so as to *appreciate* the currency against the dollar, by enough to prevent the local currency price of imports from rising. This implication—reacting to an adverse terms of trade shock by appreciating the currency—seems perverse. It could be expected to exacerbate swings in the trade balance and output.

Few believe that the proper response for an oil-importing country in the event of a large increase in world oil prices is to tighten monetary policy and thereby appreciate the currency sufficiently to prevent an increase in the price of oil in terms of domestic currency. The usual defense of inflation targeting offered by its many proponents is that in the event of such a shock, the central bank can easily deviate from the CPI target and explain the circumstances to the public. But what can be the argument for making such derogations on an ad hoc basis, when it is possible to build them into a simple target rule in the first place? Certainly not a gain in transparency and credibility.

This is not to suggest that this regime would be appropriate for all countries, only that it might have advantages for countries that experience large volatility in their terms of trade. But it has become apparent in this decade that terms of trade volatility is a more serious issue than was believed in the 1980s and 1990s.

To summarize, the argument for PEPI over CPI targeting is twofold. First, CPI targeting requires tightening in the face of an increase in the world price of import commodities, such as oil for an oil importer, while PEPI does not. Second, PEPI allows accommodation of fluctuations in the world price of the export commodities, while CPI targeting does not.

7.3.4   Moderate Version: Peg the Export Price *Index*

The second of the two arguments for the PEPI proposal just given is to eliminate export price variability. The stability in export prices, in turn, would help stabilize the balance of payments. It would, for example, have allowed the Korean won to depreciate automatically in the late 1990s, without the need for a costly failed attempt to defend an exchange rate target before the devaluation.[21] It would have allowed the Malaysian ringgit

20. Neither regime delivers that result. There is a reason for this. In addition to the goal of accommodating terms of trade shocks, there is also the goal of resisting inflation, but to depreciate in the face of an increase in import prices would exacerbate price instability.

21. Earlier research reported simulations of the path of exports over the last three decades if countries had followed the PEP proposal, as compared to hypothetical rigid pegs to a major currency, or as compared to whatever policy the country in fact followed historically: Frankel (2002) focuses primarily on producers of gold, Frankel (2003) on oil exporters, and Frankel and Saiki (2002) on various other agricultural and mineral producers. A typical finding was that developing countries that suffered a deterioration in export markets in the late 1990s, often contributing to a financial crisis, would have adjusted automatically under the PEP regime.

to appreciate automatically in the early 2000s, without the need for the monetary authorities to abandon their nominal anchor, as they did formally in 2005.

How would PEPI be implemented operationally? That is, how would an *index* of export prices be stabilized? As noted, in the simple version of the PEP proposal, there is nothing to prevent a central bank from intervening to fix the price of a single agricultural or mineral product perfectly on a day-to-day basis. Such perfect price fixing is not possible in the case of a broad basket of exports, as called for by PEPI, even if it were desirable. For one thing, such price indexes are not even computed on a daily basis. So it would be, rather, a matter of setting a target zone for the year, with monthly realizations, much as a range for the CPI is declared under the most standard interpretation of inflation targeting.

The declared band could be wide if desired, just as with the targeting of the CPI, money supply, exchange rate, or other nominal variables. Open market operations to keep the export price index inside the band if it threatens to stray outside could be conducted in terms either of foreign exchange or in terms of domestic securities. For some countries, it might help to monitor on a daily or weekly basis the price of a basket of agricultural and mineral commodities that is as highly correlated as possible with the country's overall price index, but whose components are observable on a daily or weekly basis in well-organized markets. The central bank could even announce what the value of the basket index would be one week at a time, by analogy with the Fed funds target in the United States. The weekly targets could be set so as to achieve the medium-term goal of keeping the comprehensive price index inside the preannounced bands, and yet the central bank could hit the weekly targets very closely, if it wanted, for example, by intervening in the foreign exchange market.

A first step for any central bank wishing to dip its toe in these waters would be to compute a monthly index of export prices and publish it. A second step would be to announce that it was "monitoring" the index. The data requirements for computing such an index would not be great. Every country's customs services gathers data on trade volumes and prices; indeed, they tend to do so at earlier stages of development than they gather data on national income or the CPI. For countries that lack fully credible institutions, an added advantage of the PEP proposal is transparency: the components tend to be more readily observable than components of the CPI such as prices of housing or other nontraded services.

A still more moderate, still less exotic-sounding, version of the PEPI proposal would be to target a producer price index (PPI) or the GDP deflator. In practice, it can be difficult to separate production cleanly into the two sectors, nontraded goods and exportables, in which case the two versions of the proposal—targeting an export price index or a producer price index—come down to the same thing. The key point of the PEP proposal is to exclude import prices from the index and to include export prices (as the PPI also does). The problem with CPI targeting is that it does it the other way around.

Appendix A

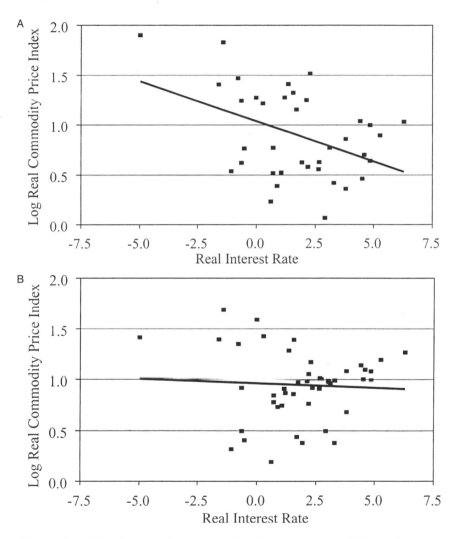

Fig. 7A.1   U.S. real commodity prices and real interest rates: *A*, **Goldman Sachs commodity price index versus real interest rate, annual 1969–2005;** *B*, **Reuters commodity price index versus real interest rate, annual 1959–2005**
Source: Global Financial Data.

Table 7A.1 **Regression of log real commodity prices on real interest rates, 1950–2005: results by commodity indexes, individual commodities, and fixed effects panel.**

	Coefficient	SE
A. 1950–1979 (30 annual observations)		
Reuters (1959–)	−0.080	0.023**
Goldman Sachs (1969–)	−0.078	0.028**
Dow Jones	−0.060	0.015**
Moodys	−0.052	0.013**
CRB	−0.044	0.012**
Commodities		
Sugar	−0.173	0.040**
Gold	−0.117	0.036**
Soy bean oil	−0.093	0.021**
Zinc	−0.090	0.025**
Oil	−0.085	0.032**
Corn	−0.071	0.017**
Cocoa	−0.070	0.037
Silver	−0.068	0.044
Palladium	−0.067	0.023**
Wheat	−0.061	0.024**
Rubber	−0.058	0.041
Fixed effects panel	−0.056	0.006**
Coffee	−0.055	0.028
Oats	−0.053	0.015**
Soy beans	−0.048	0.014**
Tin	−0.048	0.027
Lead	−0.042	0.018**
Cotton	−0.034	0.025
Platinum	−0.030	0.015**
Cattle	−0.026	0.014
Hogs	−0.020	0.024
Nickel	−0.014	0.017
Aluminum	0.000	0.011
Copper	0.029	0.021
B. 1980–2005 (26 annual observations)		
Moodys	0.014	0.018
Goldman Sachs	0.033	0.030
Dow Jones	0.056	0.026**
CRB	0.076	0.026**
Reuters	0.108	0.024**
Commodities		
Nickel	−0.036	0.038
Palladium	0.012	0.051
Lead	0.016	0.029
Cattle	0.020	0.015
Sugar	0.026	0.049
Platinum	0.031	0.029
Oil	0.039	0.044

(*continued*)

Table 7A.1   (continued)

	Coefficient	SE
Zinc	0.044	0.022**
Aluminum	0.049	0.022**
Hogs	0.061	0.030**
Copper	0.068	0.036
Rubber	0.069	0.038
Fixed effects panel	0.072	0.008**
Gold	0.078	0.037**
Soy bean oil	0.079	0.031**
Wheat	0.081	0.034**
Cotton	0.084	0.030**
Corn	0.086	0.034**
Soy beans	0.087	0.032**
Oats	0.090	0.040**
Cocoa	0.120	0.039**
Silver	0.126	0.045**
Tin	0.163	0.045**
Coffee	0.253	0.036**

Source: Global Financial Data.

Notes: Real interest rates in percentages and real commodity prices in log units. Commodities are listed by coefficient in ascending order. SE = standard error.

**Significant at the 5 percent level.

Appendix B
Relationship between Detrended Oil Inventories and Interest Rates

We have used various methods to detrend the inventories series: linear, quadratic and the Hodrick-Prescott (HP) filter. To maximize smoothness, the largest possible smoothness parameter was chosen for the HP filter (1 billion). At this level of smoothness, the HP filter series resembled those generated using the linear or quadratic method.

Graphs show the linear and quadratic detrended series (see figure 7B.1).

Regressions

Six regressions have been estimated to explore this relationship (see table 7B.1).

- In regression 1, there is no detrending.
- In regressions 2 and 3, linear (αt) or quadratic trends ($\alpha t + \beta t^2$) are included as extra regressors.
- Regressions 4 to 6 use a two step procedure, first detrending the inventories series and then estimating the relationship.

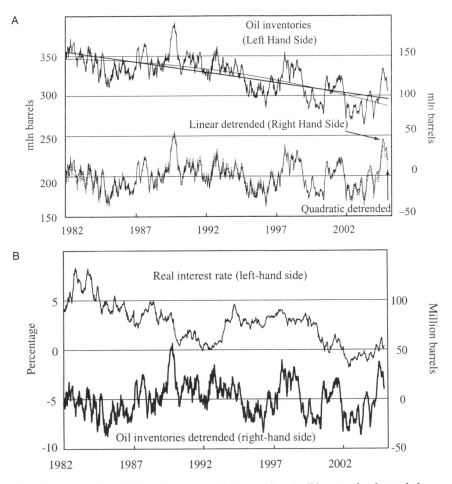

Fig. 7B.1 October 1982 to September 2005, weekly: *A*, oil inventories detrended; *B*, real interest rates and oil inventories

Table 7B.1   Relationship between oil inventories and interest rates

Regressand	Regressors	Real rate coefficient	Standard error
1. Inventories	Real rate	5.96	0.29*
2. Inventories	Real rate and linear trend	−0.69	0.35*
3. Inventories	Real rate and quadratic trend	−0.36	0.35
4. Linear detrended inventories	Real rate	−0.31	0.23
5. Quadratic detrended inventories	Real rate	−0.17	0.23
6. Hodrick-Prescott detrended inventories	Real rate	0.04	0.22

*Significant at the 10 percent level.

When the linear detrending method is used, there is a significant negative relationship between the real rate and inventories. However, this result is not robust to the use of alternative detrending methods if one fails to control for other important influences on inventory demand.

Appendix C

Relationship between Detrended Oil Inventories and Real Interest Rates Controlling for Additional Regressors

This appendix estimates an inventory equation controlling for three regressors, beyond the interest rate: risk in oil exporters, industrial activity in importing countries, and the spot-futures spread.

1: Risk in Oil Exporting Countries (Used As a
   Measure of Risk of Supply Disruptions)

We obtained monthly data from the Political Risk Services (PRS) Group on the "composite risk" for each of the top twelve oil exporting countries. The composite risk ratings cover political risk, economic risk, and financial risk. We have constructed a single measure for the top twelve oil exporters by arithmetically weighting the composite risk rating for each country by the country's share of world oil exports in 2003 and 2004. The countries included are (in descending order of importance): Saudi Arabia, Russia/USSR, Norway, Iran, Venezuela, United Arab Emirates (UAE), Kuwait, Nigeria, Mexico, Algeria, Libya and Iraq. A fall in the index represents an increase in risk. Since the series trends up over time, we have made the series stationary by detrending or differencing. When differencing, we use a relatively tight twelve-week change so there is not a large phase shift (see figure 7C.1).

2: Industrial Countries' Industrial Production
   (a Measure of Changes in Demand)

A monthly series of Industrial Production in Industrial Countries has been obtained from the International Monetary Fund (IMF), International Financial Statistics (IFS) database. Because the data were not seasonally adjusted and displayed a strong seasonal pattern, we seasonally adjusted the data using the X-12-ARIMA algorithm provided in the software Demetra. The series trended up, so detrending or differencing have been used to make the series stationary:

3: Spot—Futures Price Spread

The spot-futures price spread has been calculated by taking the percentage difference between the first futures contract (which is close to the

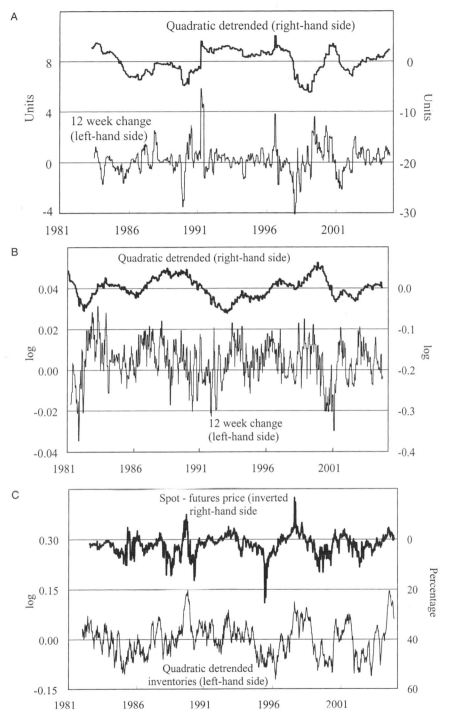

Fig. 7C.1 *A*, Risk in top twelve oil exporters, monthly, weighted by 2003–2004 oil exports; *B*, log industrial countries IP, monthly; *C*, inventories and futures prices, weekly

spot rate) and the third futures contract ($s + i - f$), adjusting for the three-month Treasury rate over the two-month period between the contracts (the maturity is not matched perfectly). There is quite a high correlation between this spread and movements in U.S. oil inventories:

Regression results

The relationship between weekly oil inventories and real interest rates is estimated controlling for the three regressors described in the preceding. When included individually, the **spot-futures price spread** is significant with the expected sign (when the spot price rises relative to the futures price, oil inventories fall). The twelve-week change in **oil exporter risk** is also significant with the expected sign (a negative change in the risk rating leads to an increase in oil inventories). However, **industrial production** is not significant. The real interest rate coefficient is negative in all these regressions but is not significant.

When all the regressors are included simultaneously (either in levels *or* in changes), the spot-futures spread and risk are both significant with the expected sign. The real rate coefficient is negative and significant. When **lagged inventories** are added, the real rate coefficient is no longer significant. When the spot-futures spread is assumed to be endogenous and industrial production (IP) and risk are used as instruments, the real rate coefficient is not significant (see table 7C.1).

The results are reasonably similar when the data are detrended by including quadratic terms in each regression or through a first-stage regression of each non-stationary regressor on a quadratic trend, with the residuals used in the second-stage regression where inventories is the regressand.

Table 7C.1   Relationship between inventories and interest rates (weekly data; 1,114–1,190 observations depending on data availability)

	Real rate	Spot-futures	IP	ΔIP	Risk	Δrisk	Inventories (t − 1)
A. Nonstationary variables detrended by including quadratic terms in each regression							
Real rate only	−0.064						
	0.097						
Spot-futures spread	−0.093	−0.760**					
	0.077	0.039					
IP	−0.057		0.008				
	0.101		0.059				
12 week ΔIP	−0.014			−0.178			
	0.103			0.136			
Oil exporter risk	−0.095				0.000		
	0.103				0.001		
12 week Δoil exporter risk	−0.192					−0.009**	
	0.100					0.001	
Spot-futures, IP, risk	−0.394**	−0.821**	0.397**		−0.002**		
	0.089	0.041	0.062		0.001		
Spot-futures, IP, risk and	−0.056	−0.079**	0.052**		0.000		0.931**
lagged inventories	0.032	0.013	0.020		0.000		0.009
Spot-futures, ΔIP, Δrisk	−0.211**	−0.727**		0.131		−0.005**	
	0.085	0.040		0.126		0.001	
Spot-futures, ΔIP, Δrisk and	−0.017	−0.071**		0.009		0.000	0.937**
lagged inventories	0.032	0.012		0.045		0.000	0.009
Instrumental variables							
Spot-futures; instruments:	−0.068	0.343					
IP and risk	0.124	0.178					
Spot-futures; instruments:	−0.159	−1.313**					
ΔIP and Δrisk	0.102	0.212					
B. Inventories, IP, and oil exporter risk detrended using first stage regressions with quadratic trends							
Real rate only	−0.031						
	0.065						
Spot-futures spread	0.021	−0.754**					
	0.053	0.039					
IP	0.011		−0.003				
	0.065		0.058				
12 week ΔIP	0.043			−0.200			
	0.070			0.133			
Oil exporter risk	−0.154**				0.000		
	0.076				0.001		
12 week Δoil exporter risk	−0.226**					−0.009**	
	0.077					0.001	
Spot-futures, IP, risk	−0.131**	−0.806*	0.304**		−0.002**		
	0.067	0.042	0.062		0.001		
Spot-futures, IP, risk and	−0.027	−0.076**	0.044**		0.000		0.933**
lagged inventories	0.023	0.013	0.019		0.000		0.009
Spot-futures, ΔIP, Δrisk	−0.066	−0.723**		0.089		−0.005**	

(*continued*)

Table 7C.1   (continued)

	Real rate	Spot-futures	IP	ΔIP	Risk	Δrisk	Inventories $(t-1)$
	0.065	0.041		0.127		0.001	
Spot-futures, ΔIP, Δrisk and	−0.003	−0.070**		0.006		0.000	0.937**
lagged inventories	0.024	0.012		0.044		0.000	0.009
Instrumental variables							
Spot-futures; instruments:	−0.145	0.282					
IP and risk	0.086	0.179					
Spot-futures; instruments:	0.076	−1.368**					
ΔIP and Δrisk	0.072	0.231					

**Significant at the 5 percent level.

Appendix D

Relationship between Agricultural Inventories and Real Interest Rates, using Detrended Inventories

Annual inventories data were obtained from the U.S. Department of Agriculture for twelve agricultural commodities. For comparative purposes, we also include results using a series for petroleum inventories from the Energy Department. To make the results easier to compare across commodities, we logged the inventories series, so the coefficients are semielasticities. Quarterly inventories data are available for some commodities, but the seasonal patterns are extremely strong, so we converted all the commodities to a common annual frequency.

We estimated five regressions to explore this relationship for each commodity:

In regression 1, there is no detrending.
- In regressions 2 and 3, linear (αt) or quadratic trends $(\alpha t + \beta t^2)$ are included as extra regressors.
- Regressions 4 and 5 use a two-step procedure, first detrending the inventories series and then estimating the relationship.

The data suggest no systematic negative relationship between real interest rates and agricultural inventories. The different specifications do not appear to have a significant effect on the results. The relationship has also been estimated for the fixed effects panel of the nine commodities with data available from 1950 to 2004. This sample is broken in 1982 to test for any effect from the change in monetary policy regime. The results suggest there is a spurious positive relationship between interest rates and inventories. The results for agricultural inventories are not to be taken too seriously as we were unable to control for risk or other important variables.

Table 7D.1   Relationship between agricultural inventories and interest rates (annual data)

	Log inventories (1)	Log inventories with linear trend (2)	Log inventories with quadratic trend (3)	Linear Detrended Log inventories (4)	Quadratic detrended log inventories (5)
Hay (1950–2004)	0.023**	0.008	0.005	0.007	0.004
	(0.008)	(0.005)	0.005	0.004	0.004
Rice (1956–2004)	0.050	0.029**	0.019**	0.029**	0.018**
	(0.027)	0.013	0.010	0.013	0.009
Barley (1950–2005)	0.050**	0.048**	0.026	0.045**	0.023
	(0.019)	0.020	0.020	0.019	0.018
Sheep (1950–2005)	−0.045	0.016**	0.016**	0.015**	0.014**
	(0.026)	0.007	0.007	0.006	0.006
Hogs (1950–2004)	−0.006	−0.009	−0.010	−0.008	−0.008
	(0.004)	0.005	0.006	0.004	0.004
Cattle (1950–2005)	0.007	0.006	−0.008	0.006	−0.007
	(0.010)	0.010	0.004	0.010	0.004
Wheat (1950–2004)	0.074**	0.069**	0.063**	0.065**	0.053**
	(0.010)	0.010	0.010	0.009	0.009
Soybeans (1950–2004)	0.100**	0.023	−0.011	0.021	−0.010
	(0.041)	0.016	0.009	0.015	0.008
Oats (1950–2005)	−0.031	0.014	−0.013	0.013	−0.011
	(0.020)	0.015	0.011	0.014	0.009
Corn (1950–2004)	0.070**	0.033**	0.027**	0.031**	0.023
	(0.021)	0.011	0.013	0.011	0.012
Wool (1976–2003)	0.020	0.018	−0.013	0.018	−0.008
	(0.014)	0.016	0.028	0.015	0.016
Cotton (1965–2004)	0.004	0.010	0.045	0.010	0.039
	(0.029)	0.032	0.032	0.030	0.030
Petroleum (1973–2004)	0.029**	0.024**	0.001	0.024**	0.000
	(0.010)	0.004	0.003	0.004	0.003
(1950–2004)	0.029**			0.025**	0.010**
	0.009			0.004	0.003
(1950–1981)	0.028**			0.027**	0.016**
	0.010			0.007	0.005
(1982–2004)	0.038**			0.041**	0.004
	0.008			0.007	0.006

Note: Standard errors in parentheses.
**Significant at the 5 percent level.

References

Abosedra, Salah, and Stanislav Radchenko. 2003. Oil stock management and futures prices: An empirical analysis. *Journal of Energy and Development* 28 (2): 173–88.

Balabanoff, Stefan. 1995. Oil futures prices and stock management: A cointegration analysis. *Energy Economics* 17 (3): 205–10.

Barsky, Robert, and Lawrence Summers. 1988. Gibson's paradox and the gold standard. *Journal of Political Economy* 96 (3): 528–50.

Bernanke, Ben, Thomas Laubach, Frederic Mishkin, and Adam Posen. 1999. *Inflation targeting: Lessons from the international experience.* Princeton, NJ: Princeton University Press.

Bessimbinder, Hendrik. 1993. An empirical analysis of risk premia in futures markets. *Journal of Futures Markets* 13 (6): 611–30.

Breeden, Douglas. 1980. Consumption risks in futures markets. *Journal of Finance* 35:503–20.

Brenner, Robin, and Kenneth Kroner. 1995. Arbitrage, cointegration, and testing unbiasedness hypothesis in financial markets. *Journal of Finance and Quantitative Analysis* 30:23–42.

Choe, Boum-Jong. 1990. Rational expectations and commodity price forecasts. Policy Research Working Paper Series no. 435. Washington, DC: World Bank.

Covey, Ted, and David A. Bessler. 1995. Asset storability and the information content of international prices. *Journal of Empirical Finance* 2:103–15.

Deffeyes, Kenneth. 2005. *Beyond oil: The view from Hubbert's Peak.* New York: Hill and Wang.

Dornbusch, Rudiger. 1976. Expectations and exchange rate dynamics. *Journal of Political Economy* 84:1161–76.

Dusak, Katherine. 1973. Futures trading and investor returns: An investigation of commodity market risk premiums. *Journal of Political Economy* 81:1387–1406.

Fama, Eugene, and Kenneth R. French. 1987. Commodity futures prices: Some evidence on forecast power, premiums, and the theory of storage. *Journal of Business* 60:55–73.

Fortenbery, Randall, and Hector Zapata. 1997. An evaluation of price linkages between futures and cash markets for cheddar cheese. *The Journal of Futures Markets* 17:279–301.

Frankel, Jeffrey. 1984. Commodity prices and money: Lessons from international finance. *American Journal of Agricultural Economics* 66: (5): 560–66.

———. 1986. Expectations and commodity price dynamics: The overshooting model. *American Journal of Agricultural Economics* 68(2): 344–48.

———. 2002. Should gold-exporters peg their currencies to gold? *Research Study no. 29.* London: World Gold Council.

———. 2003. A proposed monetary regime for small commodity-exporters: Peg the export price ('PEP'). *International Finance* 6(1): 61–88.

———. 2005a. Peg the export price index: A proposed monetary regime for small countries. *Journal of Policy Modeling* 27(4): 495–508.

———. 2005b. Real interest rates cast a shadow over oil. *Financial Times,* April 15.

Frankel, Jeffrey, and Gikas Hardouvelis. 1985. Commodity prices, money surprises, and Fed credibility. *Journal of Money, Credit and Banking* 17 (14): 427–38.

Frankel, Jeffrey, and Ayako Saiki. 2002. A proposal to anchor monetary policy by the price of the export commodity. *Journal of Economic Integration* 17 (3): 417–48.

Kolb, Robert W. 1992. Is normal backwardation normal? *Journal of Futures Markets* 12:75–91.

Mankiw, N. Gregory, and Ricardo Reis. 2003. What measure of inflation should a central bank target? *Journal of the European Economic Association* 1 (5): 1058–86.

Okun, Arthur. 1975. Inflation: Its mechanics and welfare costs. *Brookings Papers on Economic Activity,* Issue no. 2:351–401. Washington, DC: Brookings Institution.

Svensson, Lars E.O. 1995. The Swedish experience of an inflation target. In *Infla-*

tion targets, ed. Leo Leiderman and Lars E.O. Svensson. London: Centre for Economic Policy Research.

———. 1999. Inflation targeting as a monetary policy rule. *Journal of Monetary Economics* 43:607–54.

Svensson, Lars E.O., and Michael Woodford. 2005. Implementing optimal policy through inflation-forecast targeting. In *The inflation-targeting debate,* ed. Ben Bernanke and Michael Woodford, 19–83. Chicago: University of Chicago Press.

Truman, Edwin. 2003. *Inflation targeting in the world economy.* Washington, DC: Institute for International Economics.

Working, Holbrook. 1949. The theory of price storage. *American Economic Review* 30:1254–62.

Yang, Jian, David Bessler, and David Leatham. 2001. Asset storability and price discovery in commodity futures markets: A new look. *The Journal of Futures Markets* 21 (3): 279–300.

Comment   Lars E.O. Svensson

This chapter makes two main points. The first point is empirical: commodity prices are decreasing in the real interest rate. The second point is a recommendation about monetary policy: central banks should stabilize the domestic price of exports, and such a policy is better than Consumer Price Index (CPI) inflation targeting.

I have no problems with the first point. Frankel provides considerable empirical evidence to support his conclusion. It also makes theoretical sense that commodity prices may be negatively correlated with real interest rates. Commodity prices can, to a large extent, be seen as asset prices. Asset prices are discounted present values of expected future returns. A rise in the real interest rate reduces the discount factors and thereby the present value of any given expected future returns. Hence, unless increases in real interest rates are systematically correlated with increases in expected returns or reductions in risk premiums, the negative effect of the real interest rate on the present value should dominate.

I have serious problems with the second point. Counter to what Frankel argues, stabilizing the price of exports seems to me to be much inferior to inflation targeting. For an oil exporter such as Norway facing the recent doubling in the international oil price, the policy would imply a drastic deflation of the CPI by approximately 50 percent. Such a policy would be truly disastrous.

Regarding the first point, should we expect commodity prices to be decreasing in the real interest rate or not? Let us consider a storable com-

Lars E.O. Svensson is Deputy Governor of Sveriges Riksbank, the central bank of Sweden, professor of economics at Princeton University, and a research associate of the National Bureau of Economic Research.

modity in period t that will be used up in period $t + 1$. Consider its pricing in period t under the simplest possible circumstances and risk neutrality. Then the price in period t, p_t, would be given by

$$p_t = \frac{-c_{t+1|t} + p_{t+1|t}}{1 + r_t},$$

where $p_{t+1|t}$ is the price expected in period t that the commodity can be sold for in period $t + 1$, $c_{t+1|t}$ is the expected storage cost between period t and period $t + 1$ to be paid in period $t + 1$, and r_t is the real interest rate between period t and period $t + 1$. If $p_{t+1|t}$ and $c_{t+1|t}$ are given, we see that p_t is decreasing in r_t. We can make this case more realistic and complex by introducing production of the commodity in each period at increasing marginal cost and use of the commodity in each period at decreasing marginal benefit. As long as marginal cost and marginal benefit are relatively independent of the real interest rate, we would still expect commodity prices to be negatively correlated with the real interest rate.

Of course, in a more realistic and complex model, commodity prices and real interest rates are endogenous variables that are simultaneously determined by the structure of the economy, the economic policies conducted, and the nature of the exogenous shocks in the economy. In particular, the correlation between commodity prices depends on the nature of the shocks that hit the economy and how these affect the variables on the right side of the preceding asset-price equation. Consider the relation between commodity prices and shocks to expected potential growth. From a simple Euler condition for optimal consumption choice, we get the following relation between the neutral (Wicksellian real) interest rate, r_t^*, the rate of time preference, ρ, and expected potential output growth, $g_{t+1|t}$:

$$r_t^* = \rho + \frac{1}{\sigma} g_{t+1|t},$$

where σ is the intertemporal elasticity of substitution. Here, potential output is the hypothetical flexprice level of output in an economy with sticky prices, and the neutral interest rate is the corresponding hypothetical flexprice real interest rate. Furthermore, monetary policy can be seen as determining the real interest rate gap, the gap between the real interest rate and the neutral interest rate, $r_t - r_t^*$. In this setting, treat potential output growth as an exogenous stochastic process, and suppose that expected potential output growth $g_{t+1|t}$ increases. Suppose that monetary policy maintains a relatively stable real interest-rate gap. Then, both r_t^* and r_t increase. Furthermore, the increase in potential output growth might increase $p_{t+1|t}$, due to increasing demand for commodity use. In this case, both the numerator and denominator in the preceding expression for the current commodity price increase, so it is no longer obvious that, for this kind of shock, commodity prices and the real interest rate are negatively correlated.

Thus, Frankel's empirical results can be interpreted as stating that the direct negative effect of the real interest rate on commodity prices dominates in most cases. This is not an obvious result, but it is arguably also not that surprising.

The second main point is the shocking suggestion (to me, at least) that pegging the export price index (PEPI) would be a better monetary policy than the (core or headline) CPI inflation targeting currently pursued in many countries. The reasons for this suggestion are not very well developed. Frankel states that PEPI has the property that an adverse terms-of-trade movement would be associated with a currency depreciation. He seems to take for granted that such a property is desirable. Frankel also states that current CPI inflation targeting has the property that an adverse terms-of-trade movement is associated with a currency *appreciation*, which consequently is considered undesirable. It would have been good to have a simple model where these properties of PEPI and CPI inflation targeting and their desirability could be demonstrated.

Is it true that PEPI has the property that an adverse terms-of-trade effect is associated with a currency depreciation? First, consider a terms-of-trade deterioration for a small open economy caused by a fall in the world price (the foreign-currency price) of exports. At an unchanged exchange rate, the domestic-currency price of exports would fall. Keeping the domestic-currency price of exports stable, as PEPI implies, would, hence, indeed require a currency depreciation. Second, consider a terms-of-trade deterioration caused by a rise in the world price of imports at an unchanged world price of exports. At an unchanged exchange rate, the domestic-currency price of exports would remain the same. Hence, in this case, PEPI requires a constant exchange rate and no currency depreciation. Third, consider a terms-of-trade deterioration associated with a rise in the world prices of both exports and imports (that is, with a larger rise in the price of imports than in the price of exports). At an unchanged exchange rate, the domestic price of exports would rise. Hence, in this case, PEPI requires an appreciation of the home currency. Thus, it is not always the case that PEPI implies that an adverse terms-of-trade effect is associated with a currency depreciation.

The optimal policy for the exchange rate in the face of a terms-of-trade deterioration is not obvious and requires a more elaborate model and analysis than there is room for here. Because that step is crucial for Frankel's argument, there should arguably be room for such a model and analysis in his chapter.

Frankel does not provide any convincing argument that inflation targeting is problematic. To be more specific, consider flexible (core) CPI inflation targeting, which is practiced in many countries. This involves stabilizing both the inflation gap between inflation and an inflation target and the output gap between output and potential output. It seems to work fine in both advanced and emerging-market countries. That it works fine in advanced countries is well known. What is somewhat new is that it seems to work so well in many emerging-market countries. The International Monetary Fund (IMF) *World Economic Outlook* of September 2005 notes that inflation targeting has worked fine in a number of emerging-market countries. No country that has adopted inflation targeting has abandoned it, and no country has even expressed any regrets. In particular, inflation targeting seems to work fine even without a number of so-called preconditions, such as good institutions, well-developed financial markets, responsible fiscal policies, and so forth.

Frankel's PEPI may be interpreted as inflation targeting with the CPI price index being replaced by the export price index. But what price index should inflation targeting ideally refer to? Theoretical work by Kosuke Aoki, Pierpaolo Benigno, and others has emphasized that, from a welfare point of view, monetary policy should stabilize sticky prices rather than flexible prices. This minimizes the distortion caused by the existence of sticky prices and brings the economy closer to a flexprice equilibrium. These results can be interpreted as favoring a core CPI or domestic inflation targeting. In particular, these results suggest that central banks should not try to stabilize flexible commodity prices, in direct contradiction to PEPI. Other often-mentioned reasons for choosing a CPI-related index is that the CPI is the index best known by the general public, that stabilizing it would simplify decisions for the average consumer, that it is frequently published, and that it is usually not revised. Indeed, all inflation targeting central banks have chosen the CPI or a core CPI.

The PEPI would imply riding a tiger. Consider Norway, a major oil exporter. The oil price has approximately doubled in a few years. This is a huge terms-of-trade improvement for Norway. Frankel would prefer that Norges Bank, the central bank of Norway, stabilizes the domestic price of oil. In order to keep the domestic-currency price of oil from rising, Norges Bank would have had to double the value of the Norwegian krone during this time, that is, to have had to induce a 100 percent appreciation of the krone. This would be an extremely contractionary policy. Put differently, under the simplified assumption that the relative price of oil to consumer goods has doubled, achieving this new relative price in Norway at an unchanged domestic-currency price of oil requires that other consumer prices are reduced by 50 percent. Thus, Frankel is suggesting that it would have been better for Norway and the Norwegians if Norges Bank had induced such a huge deflation.

How should the central bank respond to oil-price changes (or any terms-of-trade changes)? This follows from the principles of Good Monetary Policy (Svensson 2002). Indeed, for monetary policy, oil-price changes are not very special: they are just another shock (although potentially large and persistent). Good Monetary Policy is flexible inflation targeting, which can more narrowly be specified as aiming at both stabilizing inflation around an inflation target and stabilizing the output gap around zero. Furthermore, the lags between monetary policy actions on one hand and the effects on inflation and output on the other hand imply that central banks should do "forecast targeting." That is, they should look at forecasts of inflation and set the interest-rate path (or plan) such that forecasts of inflation and the output gap "look good." Here, look good means that the inflation forecast (path) approaches the inflation target and the output gap forecast (path) approaches zero. In other words, look good means a reasonable compromise between stabilizing inflation and stabilizing the output gap. These principles for Good Monetary Policy are very simple to state. The practice of achieving them can be quite difficult, though.

Implementing inflation targeting requires interpreting and understanding the nature of the disturbances hitting the economy. Terms-of-trade movements are movements in the *relative* price between exports and imports. Relative-price movements have both income and substitution effects on aggregate demand that need to be sorted out. Terms-of-trade movements can also be accompanied by movements in world inflation or the world price level. Such movements are movements in *absolute* prices, the effects of which also need to be sorted out. A standard problem for inflation targeting central banks is to assess whether incoming shocks are temporary or persistent, for instance, whether a particular shock corresponds to a one-time price-level shift or a persistent inflation-level shift. Making such assessments is a standard part of the analysis by inflation targeting central banks.

These principles and analysis are routinely applied by central banks to oil-price changes (Svensson 2005). Oil-price changes shift inflation and output-gap forecasts at a given interest rate path (they have both income and substitution effects and lead to shifts in the forecasted inflation, output, and potential-output paths). After such shifts, these forecasts may no longer look good. Then central banks adjust the interest-rate path, so the inflation and output-gap forecasts look good again.

What happens to the exchange rate during these shifts? That depends, since the impact of oil-price changes is quite complex. A short answer is whatever is consistent with the optimal inflation, output-gap, and interest-rate forecasts. In some cases, a depreciation is called for, in other cases, an appreciation. Importantly, under inflation targeting, the exchange rate is not a target variable, and there is no target exchange rate level.

In each *Monetary Policy Report* (available at http://www.norges-bank.no), Norges Bank routinely analyzes these issues and presents its conclusion and decision in the form of informative graphs of an optimal instrument rate, inflation, output-gap, and exchange rate forecast, with fan charts emphasizing the unavoidable uncertainty of the forecasts. This inflation and output-gap forecast represents the bank's best compromise between stabilizing the inflation gap and the output gap. The bank presents a baseline scenario but also alternative scenarios with alternative assumptions about exogenous disturbances and the transmission mechanism. This is an excellent example of current best-practice inflation targeting.

My point with this reference to routine elements of the *Monetary Policy Report* of Norges Bank is that there is absolutely no reason to abandon flexible inflation targeting for PEPI. Flexible inflation targeting is superior in handling all kinds of disturbances. The PEPI would be a disaster.

References

Svensson, Lars E.O. 2002. Monetary policy and real stabilization. In *Rethinking stabilization policy, A symposium sponsored by the Federal Reserve Bank of Kansas City,* 261–312. Kansas City, MO: Federal Reserve Bank of Kansas City http://www.kc.frb.org.
————. 2005. Oil Prices and ECB monetary policy. Briefing Papers for the Committee on Economic and Monetary Affairs (ECON) of the European Parliament for the Dialogue with the European Central Bank (ECB). http://www.princeton.edu/svensson.

Discussion Summary

Jeffrey A. Frankel responded to Lars E.O. Svensson that there is limited popular understanding of the core Consumer Price Index (CPI) which makes this a less suitable price index for inflation targeting than Svensson suggested. Frankel also argued that even those who are unwilling to peg an export price index should place some extra weight on export prices in defining the price index that is to be targeted.

William C. Dudley asked why a commodity price change should demand a monetary policy response if it was merely a relative price change. Frankel responded that he thought of commodity price changes as informative about the natural rate of interest, just as previous discussion had suggested that other asset prices were a useful input in estimating the natural rate.

Donald L. Kohn said that a jump in commodity prices would tell policymakers that the natural interest rate had declined, but that commodity prices would then tend to drift down. It was hard to know how central banks could distinguish initial jumps from subsequent movement.

Martin Schneider pointed out that the effects of interest rates seemed strongest on perishable goods. Frankel agreed that this was surprising.

Andrew Levin said that, judging from the graphs, the results from fifty years of data were being driven by three outlier years. On the topic of interest rates driving commodity prices, he was skeptical in the case of a commodity such as hogs: he wondered whether the relationship was being driven not by intertemporal optimization, but rather by some kind of aggregate demand shift. Frankel argued that farmers should satisfy an intertemporal optimization condition. Simon Gilchrist observed that commodities such as soybeans require large amounts of land; he suggested that this might explain why interest rates were important. Regarding pegging export prices, Levin said that the optimal policy regime should vary from country to country. In the case of Ghana, for example, with a centralized market for cocoa, it was most important to ensure that the currency is stable against the U.S. dollar.

Tommaso Monacelli said that for terms of trade to enter the loss function, all that was required was to have a non-Cobb-Douglas utility function.

Lars E. O. Svensson said that a country with volatile terms of trade may wish to consider other strategies for insuring against the welfare effects of changes in the terms of trade. Norway, for example, saves part of its windfall gain from rising oil prices in a national fund invested in global assets. Other countries should consider emulating this approach.

Noisy Macroeconomic Announcements, Monetary Policy, and Asset Prices

Roberto Rigobon and Brian Sack

8.1 Introduction

The relationship between economic data, on the one hand, and asset prices and monetary policy, on the other, has become a widely studied topic in the academic literature—and for good reason. Macroeconomic conditions are a key factor determining near-term policy expectations, and those expectations reverberate throughout the financial system by influencing the returns expected on all asset classes.

But despite being widely studied, our current knowledge of the interactions between economic news and asset prices has many shortcomings, and the results are puzzling in some dimensions. Perhaps most importantly, the estimated effects of data releases on monetary policy expectations and asset prices are found to be relatively small. This is the case even for those assets that are known to be very sensitive to near-term monetary policy expectations, such as eurodollar futures and short-term Treasury securities.

This finding is surprising. After all, the literature over the past two decades has argued that monetary policy to a large extent responds systematically to economic conditions. Indeed, the literature has made tremendous progress estimating monetary policy rules that account for these systematic responses in terms of low-frequency data (such as quarterly data). If monetary policy is so systematic, one would expect to see evidence of it also in the higher-frequency movements in interest rates and

Roberto Rigobon is an associate professor with tenure at the Sloan School of Management, Massachusetts Institute of Technology, and a research associate of the National Bureau of Economic Research. Brian Sack is vice president of Macroeconomic Advisers, LLC.

We thank John Y. Campbell and Laurence H. Meyer for valuable comments and suggestions, and Mike McMorrow for excellent assistance with the analysis.

asset prices around data releases. That is, the major economic data releases would be expected to explain an extensive amount of the variation in assets sensitive to near-term policy expectations.

In our view, the puzzle of the "detachment" of monetary policy expectations and asset prices from the incoming economic news is partly related to the difficulties associated with measuring the surprise component of that news. Most studies to date compute a "surprise" measure for a given release based on expectations taken from a survey conducted ahead of the release. They then regress changes in an asset price on this surprise measure, which we refer to as the standard "eventstudy" approach. The attempt to isolate the unexpected component of the release was a vast improvement over earlier efforts that could not make such a separation, as only the unexpected component should prompt a market reaction. However, this approach likely falls short of accurately measuring the market effects of the incoming news—perhaps considerably.

A problem with the standard eventstudy approach is that the macroeconomic news is likely to be measured very poorly, for several reasons. First, it is hard to accurately measure what the markets are expecting for a given release at the time it comes out, including the full distribution of risks seen for the release. Second, even if one accurately measured expectations, the actual release may be seen as a noisy indicator of the underlying true fundamental factor that drives market responses. And third, the variable measured is usually only one component of a report. After all, most of these reports are complicated, providing lots of information of varying relevance.

Thus, it is quite likely that the macroeconomic surprise included on the right-hand-side of the eventstudy is only a very rough measure of the true incoming news. This chapter focuses on measuring the reaction of asset prices and monetary policy expectations to the "true" economic news embedded in the major U.S. data releases. Rather than attempting to better measure the data or the expectations, we focus on developing econometric techniques that will adequately deal with the measurement problems associated with the data surprises used in the existing eventstudy literature.

Our efforts take us in two directions. First, we modify the standard eventstudy regression framework to account for the possibility that the measured surprises contain error. The measurement issues considered here lead to a classical error-in-variables problem of a standard regression, one that biases downward the estimated sensitivity of asset prices to the incoming data. We develop a new estimator that allows for measurement error and, hence, eliminates this downward bias. The procedure could be used in other applications to correct for the error-in-variables problem.

Second, we employ a principal components approach that removes the need to even try to measure the data surprises. In effect, the approach uses the observed market reactions to infer what the true data surprises were. Such an approach may have appeal if one regards the incoming data as being complex and having many dimensions that could affect asset prices—conditions that make it difficult to measure the data surprise in the manner of the standard eventstudy exercise.

The results provide us with unbiased estimates of the response of monetary policy expectations and asset prices to the "true" surprise contained in all of the major data releases. They also allow us to recover the importance of those true surprises. An important finding from the chapter is that macroeconomic data releases matter to a much greater extent than found in previous studies—that is, they account for a greater portion of the fluctuations in market interest rates. Moreover, using these estimators, we are able to refine a set of patterns in the responses that should be explained by any model addressing the interactions between economic variables, monetary policy, and asset prices.

8.2 Estimating the Effects of Macroeconomic Announcements: Current Methods

Researchers in both macroeconomic and financial economics are very interested in understanding the linkage between monetary policy and asset prices. To that end, one strand of literature has attempted to measure the response of asset prices to monetary policy "shocks," or the erratic and unpredictable component of monetary policy decisions. But such shocks are limited in size and account for only a very small portion of the variation in asset prices. Instead, most of the movement in short-term interest rates likely represents the systematic response of monetary policy to economic developments. Thus, it may be more relevant to investigate the responses of monetary policy expectations and asset prices to incoming news about the economy.

A sizable literature has taken up this topic and has provided us with some valuable results. The studies to date almost uniformly take an approach that is commonly referred to as "eventstudy."

8.2.1 The Eventstudy Specification

Papers in the eventstudy literature typically proceed in a simple regression framework in which the reaction of a given asset price (or market yield) is regressed on the surprise components of the data release, as in the following specification:

(1) $$\Delta s_t = \gamma \cdot z_t + \varepsilon_t,$$

(1') $$z_t = M_t - E_{t-\tau}[M_t],$$

where M_t is the released value of the macroeconomic announcement, and $E_{t-\tau}[M_t]$ is a measure of the market's expectation ahead of the release. The specification assumes that the only market-moving information is the surprise component of the release z_t, and the parameter γ is the market sensitivity to that surprise—which is the primary interest of this chapter.

The basic approach implicit in specification (1) has not varied much over time, but the empirical implementation of the equation has changed in two dimensions.

First, the measure of expectations has improved. Early papers in this area had to model the market's expectations either as past realized values of the macroeconomic variables or as the outcome of forecasting models that do not necessarily perform very well. More recently, researchers have increasingly relied on surveys to measure expectations and to better isolate the surprise component of data releases. Hence, the measurement of the variable z_t has likely improved over time.

Second, studies have increasingly used a narrower window to measure the market response to the data release. Whereas earlier papers may have used monthly or quarterly data, the eventstudy literature has moved to using changes at a daily frequency (see, for example, McQueen and Roley [1993] and Gürkaynak, Sack, and Swanson [2005]) or even in some cases on an intraday bases (see, for example, Fleming and Remolona [1997] and Balduzzi, Elton, and Green [2001]).[1] The idea of using a narrower window is to reduce the influence of other events that might be affecting the asset price in addition to the data surprise. In terms of the equation (1), it reduces the variance of the error term ε_t, which should improve the accuracy of the estimate of the parameter γ.

The eventstudy approach has importantly contributed to our understanding of the manner in which monetary policy expectations and asset prices react to incoming economic data. Indeed, as we will show in the following, this approach finds that the market reaction to a number of releases is statistically significant. Nevertheless, in our view, the eventstudy approach has some shortcomings that prevent it from recovering the market response to a "true" macroeconomic data surprise.

8.2.2   The Econometric Problem: Noisy Data Surprises

The potential problem that arises with the eventstudy approach is that the results will only be as good as the measure of data surprises included on the right-hand side of the equation. Indeed, the model (1) implicitly assumes that the measured data surprise z_t truly captures the true macroeco-

---

1. Several other papers use intraday data but focus primarily on foreign exchange rates, including Andersen et al. (2003) and Faust et al. (2003). As an example of a paper using low-frequency data, Cutler, Poterba, and Summers (1989) attempt to measure the influence of macroeconomic shocks on equity prices using a monthly vector autoregression (VAR). Stock and Watson (2003) provide a review of other papers that examine the relationship between financial variables and macroeconomic conditions at a monthly or quarterly frequency. Note, however, that the primary interest in that paper is measuring the predictive power of financial variables for economic outcomes rather than the effects of economic outcomes on financial variables.

nomic news arising from the releases. If that is not the case, the estimated parameter γ will be biased.

Even with the improvements noted in the preceding, it is a somewhat dubious assumption that the variable z_t is perfectly measured—or that it is even well measured. Instead, it is more plausible that the variable z_t contains considerable measurement error, from a variety of sources.

First, it is unlikely that the survey measures used accurately capture the market expectations at the time of the release. In the results presented in the following, we collect those expectations from two surveys and splice them together to create a full time series. Before September 2004, we use the median response from the Money Market Services (MMS) survey, which is a survey of professional forecasters taken the Friday before each release. Since then, we instead use the median response from the regular survey taken by Bloomberg. This figure is the most commonly discussed measure of consensus expectations in the financial markets.

But there are a number of reasons to believe that the expectations measured from these surveys are not necessarily appropriate for gauging the market response. The survey respondents are not the relevant market participants whose expectations matter. Moreover, the survey covers a variety of respondents with very different backgrounds and skill sets, raising questions about whether certain individual responses could distort the measures. It is not even clear that the respondents have the correct incentive scheme, as we suspect that they may assign greater utility to having an out-of-consensus call that comes in correct than having a consensus call that comes in correct. And, last, we arbitrarily use the median from the panel, though the argument for using this over the mean or some other measure is not clear-cut.

In addition to concerns about the cross-section of panelists, we also have some concerns about the timing of the surveys. Ideally, we would like to know the market expectations the moment before the data release. The MMS survey is instead taken the Friday before the release, making it somewhat stale. For those releases that come out on a Friday (e.g., the employment report), that leaves an entire week (and all the data released that week) for expectations to evolve and move away from the survey response. And the situation for the Bloomberg expectations is even worse. Those responses are submitted at irregular times. Most respondents enter their estimates about a week before the releases, but many, instead, do it two weeks in advance, while others wait until the week of the release.[2]

Another source of mismeasurement of the macroeconomic surprise is

2. To take an example, consider the employment report that was released on November 5, 2004. Of the seventy-eight responses to the survey, thirteen were submitted more than two weeks in advance. Most of the responses, thirty-nine, came in about one week in advance (with two others coming in earlier that week). And twenty-four respondents waited until the week of the release to submit their views.

the data release itself. The released data can be thought of as a noisy version of the "true" economic fundamental to which the market responds. Researchers usually focus on just one aspect of the release, and often that one aspect can appear anomalous. A recent example was the advance gross domestic product (GDP) report for the fourth quarter of 2005, which came in well below the market's expectations. That surprise owed in large part to a puzzling drop in defense spending that quarter, and, hence, Wall Street analysts generally dismissed the implications of the report.[3]

Overall, we believe that the measured data surprises could be quite noisy. Market expectations are probably not measured particularly well, as the survey used is a random variable that at best can be considered to be unbiased but not measured without error. And the actual release is likely to contain some noise relative to the true macroeconomic news that affects markets.

8.2.3 The Bias in Eventstudy Estimates

We start with the assumption that the macroeconomic surprises used in the eventstudy literature are measured with error for the reasons discussed in the preceding. In this case, the estimates obtained in the standard literature are plagued with error-in-variables bias.

To provide some structure for discussing the problem, we assume the asset price change immediately around the release at time t is denoted by Δs_t. This market reaction is driven by the true macroeconomic news contained in the announcement, which we denote z_t^*, according to the following equation:

$$(2) \qquad \Delta s_t = \gamma \cdot z_t^* + \varepsilon_t.$$

We are interested in measuring the sensitivity of financial markets to the true economic news, captured by the parameter γ. The residual ε_t captures movements in the asset price in that window that are not driven by the data surprise (or at least not under this linear structure).

To estimate equation (2), most researchers attempt to measure the true macroeconomic news z_t^* as the difference between the released data and the expectation of that data, where the expectation is typically determined from a survey taken in advance of the release. But, as previously discussed, there are two potential problems with that measure—that the release may be seen as a noisy version of the true relevance of the news and that the expectations may be measured poorly. Considering this, we should perhaps

3. For example, David Greenlaw from Morgan Stanley summarized the report as follows: "Much weaker than expected report. Both final sales and inventories came in well below expectations in Q4 [2005]. However, we believe that a significant portion of the downside is likely to be recouped in Q1 . . . Defense [spending] plunged 13% in Q4. We suspect that at least some of this drop reflects a timing quirk that will be unwound in Q1." (David Greenlaw and Ted Weisman, *GDP [Q4 Advance]*, Morgan Stanley Economic Data Bulletin, January 27, 2006)

take the measured data surprises to be a noisy representation of the true economic news, as follows:

$$(3) \qquad z_t = z_t^* + \eta_t,$$

where z_t denotes the measured data surprise. In this case, the mismeasurement of the true data surprise is captured in the variable η_t.

Using this proxy for the true macroeconomic news, researchers typically resort to estimating the following equation:

$$(4) \qquad \Delta s_t = \gamma \cdot z_t + \upsilon_t,$$

using an ordinary-least-squares (OLS) regression. However, given the preceding structure, the error term from the estimated equation is

$$(5) \qquad \upsilon_t = \varepsilon_t - \gamma \cdot \eta_t,$$

which is negatively correlated with the right-hand-side variable in the regression. This correlation, of course, results in the bias in the regression estimate of γ.

To quantify the bias, we assume that the true macroeconomic news has a variance of $\sigma_{z^*}^2$ and that the measurement error is mean zero conditional on the true surprise ($E_t[\eta_t|z_t^*]$) and has a variance of σ_η^2. We also assume that the portion of the asset price movement not explained by the macroeconomic surprise (ε_t) is mean zero conditional on the true news and the measurement error ($E_t[\varepsilon_t|\eta_t, z_t^*]$) and has a variance of σ_ε^2. Under these assumptions, the estimate obtained by an OLS regression is:

$$(6) \qquad \hat{\gamma}_{\text{OLS}} = \gamma - \gamma \frac{\sigma_\eta^2}{\sigma_{z^*}^2 + \sigma_\eta^2}.$$

This estimate has the standard downward bias (toward zero), which is the standard result in the presence of an error-in-variables problem. Based on this consideration, we argue that the typical eventstudy estimation may understate the influence of macroeconomic news on asset prices.

At this point, it is useful to note that we have considered two forms of mismeasurement of the macroeconomic news—one based on noise in our reading of the market's expectations, and one based on noise in the release itself. Both forms are captured by equation (3), and, hence, the bias in the OLS estimates applies to both of them. Nevertheless, the interpretation of the results is different depending on which of the two sources predominantly accounts for the mismeasurement. If the mismeasurement is in terms of measuring the market's expectations, then the OLS estimates are actually missing part of the market reaction. If instead the noise is contained in the actual data, then the market is reacting by less, as it is doing the signal extraction problem and discounting the value of the released data. In that case, the OLS estimates are an accurate measure of the true (but limited) market reaction to the released data.

We are interested in discovering the market reaction to the true surprise, adjusting for the measurement error from these two sources. There are several potential solutions. One is to find an instrument, something that is correlated with the true macroeconomic news but uncorrelated with the measurement error. But such instruments do not exist, leaving the problem of estimation unresolved. Another solution is to improve the data itself, for example, by better measuring market expectations. In that regard, the emergence of economic derivatives may be useful in that they may provide a more accurate and timely reading of market expectations. Still, given all of the preceding considerations, it is not clear that we will ever have a fully accurately measure the macroeconomic news.

In this chapter, we take an alternative approach in which we attempt to address the issue through econometric technique. We will ultimately develop two methods that help us resolve some of these issues and allow us to better understand the linkages from economic news to asset prices and monetary policy expectations.

8.3   Identification through Censoring

The problem of error-in-variables that we discuss in the preceding is, in fact, a problem of identification. To see that, consider the case of measuring the effect of a single data release on a single asset price. In that situation, we can compute only three statistics: the variance of the asset price, the variance of the macroeconomic news, and the covariance between them. The problem is that these moments are determined by four underlying parameters: γ, σ_{z*}^2, σ_{η}^2, and σ_{ε}^2. Thus, the solution is not identified, or there is a continuum of solutions.

In the preceding we noted that an instrumental-variables approach is one way of solving the problem, if one were able to find an appropriate instrument. Note that the availability of such an instrument basically solves the identification problem. For a variable ω_t to be a valid instrument, it must be correlated with the true news but uncorrelated with the measurement error, as follows:

$$(7) \qquad z_t^* = \beta \cdot \omega_t + \kappa_t,$$

The availability of this instrument adds three pieces of information (the variance of ω_t, its covariance with the measured news, and its covariance with the asset price response), while only adding two unknown variables (β and the variance of κ). As long as β is different from 0, these additional conditions resolve the identification problem. However, as noted in the preceding, we cannot think of an instrument that is valid in the circumstances studied in this chapter.

In the absence of a valid instrument, the question is whether we can solve the identification problem through some other means. We will do so by developing a new technique that we label "identification through censoring."

8.3.1   The Case of One Macroeconomic Announcement

To demonstrate the methodology, we first assume that there is only one macroeconomic announcement at a given time. One special feature of macroeconomic announcements is that they occur at prespecified days. This is important because it implies that we can find a sample of other days (or times) at which the magnitude of the surprise variable is exactly 0. When the variable is exactly equal to 0, it means that its error-in-variables is 0 as well. This "censoring" of the measurement error will provide the identification.[4]

Formally, this situation can be described by the following equation:

$$(8) \qquad \Delta s_t = \begin{cases} \gamma \cdot z_t + \varepsilon_t & t \in D \\ \varepsilon_t & t + 1 \in D \end{cases}$$

where D is the set of days (or times) on which the announcements take place. We are assuming that no announcements take place the day before those included in D. Under the assumption that the disturbance ε_t is homoskedastic, we can use the variance of the asset price observed at time $t - 1$ as additional information in the identification. In that case, the following equations hold:

$$(9) \qquad var(\Delta s_{t-1}) = \sigma_\varepsilon^2$$

$$var(\Delta s_t) = \gamma^2 \sigma_{z*}^2 + \sigma_\varepsilon^2$$

$$var(z_t) = \sigma_{z*}^2 + \sigma_\eta^2$$

$$cov(\Delta s_t, z_t) = \gamma \sigma_{z*}^2$$

This is a system of four equations and four unknowns that can be solved for the parameters. Most importantly, the sensitivity of the asset price to the incoming news can be solved as follows:

$$(10) \qquad \gamma = \frac{var(\Delta s_t) - var(\Delta s_{t-1})}{cov(\Delta s_t, z_t)}.$$

This estimator is in the spirit of Rigobon and Sack (2004), in which the estimator depended on the change in the variance relative to the change in the covariance. Here, the change in the covariance is just the covariance itself, as the macroeconomic surprise has no variance when it is censored.

The preceding computations rely on the assumption that the structural

---

4. This intuition comes from Goldberger (1991), who argues that the variance of the error-in-variables in survey data depends on the size of the announcement. He used the following example: If you ask how many cigarettes a person smokes in a day, a nonsmoker will answer zero—and that reply has no error-in-variables whatsoever. But someone who smokes a pack and a half a day will probably have a sizable error. In other words, the magnitude of the error depends on the magnitude of the reply, with complete censoring of the error at zero.

shocks in the asset price equation (ε_t) are homoskedastic. This is a fairly strong assumption, and one that is not necessary. To derive an estimator like equation (10), all we need is a prediction of what the variance would have been like in the absence of the macroeconomic news. Thus, we can incorporate heteroskedasticity to the degree that it is predictable. In other words, the identifying assumption is that the variance of ε_t is predictable.

For example, suppose we observe a release at 8:30, and as a "control window" we use a thirty-minute interval from the previous afternoon at 2:30. The preceding assumes that the variance of ε_t around 8:30 is the same as that around 2:30 on the previous day. But even on days of no announcements, this does not seem to be the case. Instead, we require a much weaker assumption—that the shift in the variance of ε_t on announcement days is the same as the shift on nonannouncement days, or

(11) $$\sigma^2_{\varepsilon,t-1,8:30} - \sigma^2_{\varepsilon,t-2,2:30} = \sigma^2_{\varepsilon,t,8:30} - \sigma^2_{\varepsilon,t-1,2:30}.$$

This assumption allows for the data to have heteroskedasticity over our sample, as long as that heteroskedasticity looks the same on announcement and nonannouncement days. In this case, the estimator (10) still works if we replace the variances with the shift in the variances. This is the assumption that we will employ in the empirical results in the following.

This estimator eliminates the bias coming from error-in-variables that affects the typical OLS estimates. However, the estimator is only as good as its identifying assumptions. The two main identification assumptions needed are that the errors-in-variable are classical and that the variance of the asset prices is predictable (so that we can make an accurate judgment of what the variance would have been in the absence of the macroeconomic surprise). Conditional on those identifying assumptions, the coefficients from this procedure are accurate. However, if either of the two main assumptions is violated, the estimates are biased. We will return to these issues in the following.

8.3.2   The Case of Multiple Macroeconomic Announcements

The Bureau of Economic Analysis (BEA), the Bureau of Labor Statistics (BLS), and other government agencies would make our lives easier if they released one statistic at a time. Unfortunately, this is not the case. Because different releases follow different schedules, often multiple important releases will randomly coincide in both the date and time.

If this problem were just limited to coincidence, we could deal with it by simply eliminating those days with multiple releases. Unfortunately, some of the data releases always coincide with one another. This is the case for those reports that include multiple statistics that have market influence. For example, the employment report involves the simultaneous release of nonfarm payrolls, the unemployment rate, and average hourly earnings—each of which are found to have an independent effect on markets.

In the OLS framework, we can deal with this simultaneity by simply putting the multiple releases into a single regression. We can also address this issue in the identification-through-censoring approach. To achieve identification in such circumstances, it turns out that we simply have to incorporate more than one asset price. For simplicity, we will show this point for the case of two announcements. Also, for simplicity let us assume that the structural shock ε_t is homoskedastic. In this case, the model has the following structure:

(12)
$$\Delta s_t = \gamma_1 \cdot z_{1,t}^* + \gamma_2 \cdot z_{2,t}^* + \varepsilon_t$$
$$z_{1,t} = z_{1,t}^* + \eta_{1,t}$$
$$z_{2,t} = z_{2,t}^* + \eta_{2,t},$$

where the errors in measuring the true surprises ($\eta_{1,t}$ and $\eta_{2,t}$) are likely to be correlated.

Note first that the identification is lost. The covariance matrix of the asset price and the two measures of macroeconomic surprises provides six equations, and the variance of the asset price when there are no surprises provides a seventh moment. But the model has nine unknown parameters: γ_1, γ_2, σ_ε^2, $\sigma_{z_1}^2$, $\sigma_{z_2}^2$, $\sigma_{\eta_1}^2$, $\sigma_{\eta_2}^2$, the covariance between z_1^* and z_2^*, and the covariance between η_1 and η_2. The underidentification is even more severe in the case of three simultaneous announcements.

The solution to the problem is to consider additional asset prices. If we consider two asset prices, we have the following system of equations:

(13)
$$\Delta s_{1,t} = \gamma_{1,1} z_{1,t}^* + \gamma_{1,2} z_{2,t}^* + \varepsilon_{1,t}$$
$$\Delta s_{2,t} = \gamma_{2,1} z_{1,t}^* + \gamma_{2,2} z_{2,t}^* + \varepsilon_{2,t}$$
$$z_{1,t} = z_{1,t}^* + \eta_{1,t}$$
$$z_{2,t} = z_{2,t}^* + \eta_{2,t},$$

where the structural shocks $\varepsilon_{1,t}$ and $\varepsilon_{2,t}$ are possibly correlated, and the errors in the macroeconomic surprises are, as before, also correlated. We have now achieved identification. The variance-covariance matrix of the asset prices and the macroeconomic surprises on both announcement and nonannouncement days provides thirteen moment conditions. These are sufficient to solve for the thirteen unknown parameters.[5]

What delivers the identification? It comes from the fact that the noise contained in our measures of the macroeconomic announcements has to

---

5. Adding the second asset price brings six new moment conditions—its variance and its covariance with the other asset price on both announcement days and nonannouncement days, and its covariances with the two measures of surprise on announcement days and its variance on nonannouncement days) while adding only four new parameters ($\gamma_{2,1}$, $\gamma_{2,2}$, $\sigma_{\varepsilon 2}^2$, and the covariance between ε_1 and ε_2).

be the same independent of the asset price we are considering. That restriction allows the incorporation of an additional asset to bring new information for the identification.

8.3.3   Implementation of the Estimator

In the following results, we will include five different asset prices and will allow for as many as three simultaneous releases. (All details are described in the next section.) This set-up implies that our estimator is always over-identified. To estimate the parameter values, we use a generalized method of movements (GMM) estimator that seeks to minimize the squared deviations of the errors for each moment condition.[6] It can be shown that this estimator is consistent and that the estimates are asymptotically normal.

8.4   The Estimated Effects of Macroeconomic Surprises

This section begins by describing the data that we use and some of the specific decisions made in implementing the various approaches. It then provides some results from both the standard eventstudy estimator and the identification-through-censoring approach.

8.4.1   Data

In the results that follow, we measure the reaction of five financial variables to incoming macroeconomic news. The set of financial variables is intended to capture the behavior of near-term policy expectations as well as broader asset prices.

Specifically, we include several near-term interest rates that are very sensitive to monetary policy. Eurodollar futures rates ere probably the most useful, liquid instrument for that purpose. We, therefore, include the rates on the second and fourth eurodollar contracts to expire—which will reflect changes in monetary policy expectations roughly at horizons of six and twelve months ahead.[7] We also include the two-year Treasury yield, which is very sensitive to the expected path of monetary policy beyond the hori-

---

6. So that the relative importance of the moment conditions is not influenced by the unit of measure, we normalize the movements in each asset price by their standard deviation. The results, however, are expressed in terms of basis points for yields and percentage points for equities.

7. The second contract will have between three and six months to expiration (with an average of 4.5). It is tied to the three-month Libor rate, which will be sensitive to the expected average funds rate over those three months (with an average of 1.5). Adding together these averages yields six months. Similar calculations yield twelve months for the fourth contract. We exclude the first and third contracts because we felt that much of their information would be redundant. In addition, we worried that the variation in the expiration of the first contact from zero to three months might be more problematic (given institutional details such as the spacing of meetings).

zon covered by the eurodollar contracts, and the ten-year Treasury yield. Last, we include the S&P 500 index.[8]

For all of these asset prices, we use intraday data. This feature alone provides a sizable improvement over daily eventstudy exercises. As noted in the preceding, with intraday data, we can look at a narrow window around the time of the release—an interval that includes the influence of data releases at a given time but excludes most other market-moving events. In effect, we are shrinking the size of the error term ε_t relative to the influence of the data.

The intraday data slices we consider are thirty-minutes long, beginning five minutes before the time of an announcement to avoid any complications from variation in the precise timing of the quotes or of the releases. The data releases that we consider all take place at either 8:30 a.m. 9:15 a.m., or 10:00 a.m., giving us slices that run from 8:25 to 8:55 a.m., 9:10 to 9:40 a.m., and 9:55 to 10:25 a.m.

For equities, unfortunately, we only have intraday quotes from when the stock market is open, from 9:30 a.m. to 4:00 p.m. Thus, we have to modify our slices accordingly. For the 8:30 a.m. and 9:15 a.m. releases, we use the change in the S&P index from the previous close to 9:55 a.m. For the 10:00 a.m. release, we can use the same slice that we use for the interest rates.

The control window that we use in each case is a thirty-minute window around 2:30 p.m. on the previous afternoon. We use the variance-covariance matrix in that window to predict what the variance-covariance matrix would have been in the event window in the absence of the data release.

The advantage of using the intraday quotes is shown in figure 8.1, which focuses on the response of the two-year Treasury yield to the nonfarm payrolls statistic from the monthly *Employment Situation* report from the BLS. This is the data release that, in recent years at least, has commanded the most attention in financial markets. As can be seen, there is a clear positive relationship between surprises in the payroll release and the movement in the two-year yield. Moreover, this relationship tightens if we use intraday data instead of daily data.

We investigate the market reactions to thirteen different data releases. Those releases are shown in table 8.1, along with some information about the frequency of the release and the sample over which we have a measure of market expectations. We generally begin our sample in 1994, though the sample for the Chicago Purchasing Manufacturers Index (PMI) has a shorter sample because we do not have a measure of market expectations

---

8. We had hoped to include exchange rates as well, but our intraday data did not extend back far enough to make it a useful sample.

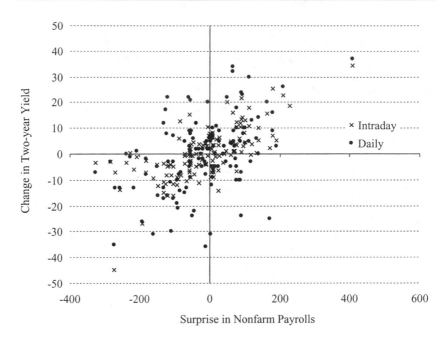

Fig. 8.1   Response of the two-year yield to payroll surprises

Table 8.1   **Macroeconomic data announcements**

Release	Release time	Frequency	Date of first observation	No. of observations
Nonfarm payrolls	8:30	Monthly	7-Jan-94	137
Hourly earnings	8:30	Monthly	4-Feb-94	134
GDP (advance)	8:30	Quarterly	28-Jan-94	46
Retail sales (excl. autos)	8:30	Monthly	13-Jan-94	137
Core Consumer Price Index	8:30	Monthly	13-Jan-94	137
Core Producer Price Index	8:30	Monthly	12-Jan-94	137
Housing starts	8:30	Monthly	20-Jan-94	135
Durable goods	8:30	Monthly	27-Jan-94	135
Capacity utilization	9:15	Monthly	14-Jan-94	137
Institute for Supply Management Manufacturing Index	10:00	Monthly	3-Jan-94	133
Chicago Purchasing Manufacturers Index	10:00	Monthly	31-Dec-99	58
Consumer confidence	10:00	Monthly	25-Jan-94	137
New home sales	10:00	Monthly	2-Feb-94	136

until December 1999. Our list includes nearly all of the major macroeconomic indicators that are generally seen as significant market movers.[9]

8.4.2 Evenstudy Estimates

Even though it may have the shortcomings discussed in the preceding, we still view the standard eventstudy regression as a very useful exercise, one that can tell us a lot about how asset prices and monetary policy expectations are affected by incoming data. The preceding discussion simply cautions that the resulting coefficients may have some downward bias, thus understating the importance of the data. We implement the eventstudy regression per release, using the data described in the preceding. The results are shown in table 8.2.

One of the primary findings from this exercise is that monetary policy expectations react significantly to incoming data. The expected path of the federal funds rate (as captured in eurodollar futures) generally shifts up significantly in response to both strong data on growth (such as retail sales) and high data on inflation (such as core CPI). Overall, we find that twelve of the thirteen macroeconomic variables considered prompt a significant reaction in the eurodollar futures rates.[10]

A second finding is that the effect of the data releases continues to be sizable even as the maturity of the instrument is extended. Indeed, the two-year yield often moves by about the same amount as the eurodollar futures rates, suggesting that any influence on monetary policy is seen as being very persistent.[11] The sensitivity of market yields extends all the way out to the ten-year Treasury note. The magnitude of its reaction is large enough that it suggests that even distant forward rates are reacting to the news, as found by Gürkaynak, Sack, and Swanson (2005).[12]

A final observation from the eventstudy results has to do with the reaction of equity markets. The detachment issue seems particularly problematic for equities, as even the most important data releases (such as nonfarm

9. In all of the results that follow, we discard those days for which we have multiple releases. For the two series from the employment report (nonfarm payrolls and hourly earnings), we always consider their effects together, as discussed in the preceding.

10. Other studies, including Fleming and Remolona (1997), Balduzzi, Elton, and Green (2001), and Gürkaynak, Sack, and Swanson (2005), have found that market interest rates respond significantly to a wide range of macroeconomic data releases.

11. A similar result was found by Kohn and Sack (2003). They noted a similar persistence in the response to Federal Open Market Committee (FOMC) statements and inferred that those statements may be seen as conveying information about the state of the economy in addition to information about the near-term direction of policy.

12. That paper looked explicitly at distant forward rates and found that they often responded to data in the same direction as near-term forward rates. The authors developed the case that this response reflected the fact that long-term inflation expectations in the United States are variable, a case strengthened by the fact that similar sensitivity is not observed in the United Kingdom, perhaps because of its explicit inflation target.

Table 8.2   Effects of macroeconomic data surprises on asset prices: eventstudy approach

	ED2	ED4	Y2	Y10	S&P	Percentage of Y2 explained by data surprise
Nonfarm payrolls	5.74**	8.16**	6.67**	5.34**	−0.03	0.46
	(0.57)	(0.78)	(0.66)	(0.57)	(0.07)	
Hourly earnings	1.72**	2.03**	2.01**	1.84**	−0.23**	—
	(0.79)	(1.11)	(0.92)	(0.76)	(0.07)	
GDP (advance)	1.66**	2.28**	1.84**	1.25**	0.15	0.25
	(0.73)	(0.92)	(0.77)	(0.71)	(0.09)	
Retail sales (excl. autos)	2.27**	3.20**	2.05**	1.91**	0.11	0.23
	(0.57)	(0.78)	(0.55)	(0.43)	(0.07)	
Core Consumer Price Index	1.89**	2.62**	1.96**	1.97**	−0.21**	0.28
	(0.37)	(0.50)	(0.41)	(0.44)	(0.09)	
Core Producer Price Index	1.28**	1.78**	1.39**	1.42**	−0.20**	0.17
	(0.33)	(0.46)	(0.40)	(0.40)	(0.08)	
Housing starts	0.33	0.32	0.23	0.28	−0.07	0.01
	(0.21)	(0.27)	(0.24)	(0.19)	(0.07)	
Durable goods	1.02**	1.37**	1.34**	1.16**	−0.04	0.25
	(0.21)	(0.33)	(0.26)	(0.24)	(0.05)	
Capacity utilization	0.91**	1.36**	1.03**	1.01**	0.05	0.19
	(0.20)	(0.26)	(0.19)	(0.17)	(0.06)	
ISM Manufacturing Index	1.78**	2.56**	2.07**	2.04**	−0.05	0.31
	(0.25)	(0.41)	(0.33)	(0.34)	(0.04)	
Chicago Purchasing Manufacturers Index	1.30**	1.99**	1.55**	1.55**	0.08	0.30
	(0.31)	(0.48)	(0.43)	(0.36)	(0.06)	
Consumer confidence	1.80**	2.15**	1.74**	1.70**	0.08	0.26
	(0.33)	(0.44)	(0.35)	(0.29)	(0.04)	
New home sales	1.02**	1.25**	1.01**	0.85**	−0.05	0.16
	(0.25)	(0.31)	(0.25)	(0.24)	(0.04)	

Notes: The table shows the estimated response of the financial variable (in basis points for rates and percentage points for equities) to a 1 standard deviation surprise in the economic release. ED2 = the rate on the second eurodollar futures contract (a proxy for monetary policy expectations about six months ahead); ED4 = the rate on the fourth eurodollar futures contract (a proxy for policy expectations about twelve months ahead); Y2 = the two-year Treasury yield; Y10 = the ten-year Treasury yield; and S&P = the S&P 500 index. The last column reports the R-squared statistic for the Y2 regression. No statistic is reported for hourly earnings because it is estimated in the same regression as nonfarm payrolls.
**Significant at the 5 percent level.

payrolls) do not prompt a significant market reaction.[13] But looking at the response of equities to all of the releases provides us with an important clue about why that may be the case.

The likely explanation for this finding is that a release such as nonfarm payrolls contains offsetting forces on equity prices. On the one hand, a strong report would suggest more strength in the economy and, hence, bet-

---

13. By contrast, equities do appear to react significantly to monetary policy shocks, as shown by Bernanke and Kuttner (2003).

ter earnings prospects, which should boost equity prices. On the other hand, it also raises long-term interest rates, which should lower equity prices. These two forces offset one another, leaving the net effect on equity prices insignificantly different from 0. A similar story could be told for all of the demand-side indicators, which all have no effect on equities.

If this were in fact the case, then we should more clearly see a negative response of equity prices to data that is directly about inflation. The reason is that there is no offsetting news in that case—higher inflation implies that rates will be higher but not that growth will be higher. Thus, equity prices should fall. Indeed, this is precisely what we find. Indeed, the S&P index reacts negatively and significantly to positive surprises in core CPI, core Producer Price Index (PPI), and hourly earnings—every single inflation measure considered.[14]

Overall, the eventstudy regressions provide an interesting pattern of market responses to different types of incoming news. Nevertheless, the R-squared statistics from the regressions are relatively low, generally ranging from 0.15 to 0.50. In other words, the eventstudy regressions typically account for only a small portion of the variance of the market reactions, even if we focus on the movements in the thirty-minute window bracketing the announcement. This last observation is the area in which we will see some improvement under the new estimator.

8.4.3 Identification-though-Censoring Estimates

Table 8.3 shows the estimated responses under the identification-by-censoring (IC) approach. Broadly speaking, the patterns of the responses are the same as in the eventstudy (ES) exercise: stronger-than-expected readings on growth or higher-than-expected readings on inflation tend to boost market interest rates. The stock market response to incoming data on growth is mixed and often insignificant, while it reacts negatively to incoming data on inflation.

The primary difference between the ES and IC approaches is the magnitude of the market responses. The IC coefficients are often two or three times as large as the ES coefficients. This finding suggests that the problem of detachment is, to a large extent at least, associated with the mismeasurement of macroeconomic news.

For example, a 1 standard deviation upward surprise to core CPI (nearly 0.1 percentage point) is estimated to increase yields 6 to 9 basis points, rather than the response of 2 to 2.5 basis points found under ES. It is worth considering again how to interpret this difference. The IC measure is capturing the market response to a true core CPI surprise, one that market par-

---

14. To our knowledge, this is not an empirical fact that has been emphasized in the literature to date. Fair (2003) finds a positive reaction of equities to inflation news. McQueen and Roley (1993) find a reaction that differs across different states of the business cycle, with negative responses for some variables in some states.

Table 8.3   Effects of macroeconomic data surprises on asset prices: identification-through-censoring approach

	ED2	ED4	Y2	Y10	S&P	Percentage of survey-based surprise due to noise
Nonfarm payrolls	8.65	7.65	10.33	9.62	0.09	0.31
	(0.20)	(0.11)	(0.24)	(0.07)	(0.00)	
Hourly earnings	10.52	4.78	7.57	12.71	−1.16	0.70
	(0.06)	(0.11)	(0.10)	(0.29)	(0.00)	
GDP (advance)	5.71	7.39	5.95	5.15	0.02	0.42
	(0.28)	(0.30)	(0.28)	(0.25)	(0.00)	
Retail sales (excl. autos)	6.00	8.19	5.49	4.25	0.02	0.70
	(0.17)	(0.18)	(0.18)	(0.39)	(0.00)	
Core Consumer Price Index	6.43	8.87	6.61	7.59	−0.94	0.77
	(0.72)	(0.64)	(0.66)	(1.16)	(0.05)	
Core Producer Price Index	4.81	6.30	5.33	5.40	−0.68	0.31
	(1.21)	(1.45)	(1.09)	(1.09)	(0.09)	
Housing starts	1.15	1.08	0.95	0.24	−0.01	0.00
	(0.06)	(0.07)	(0.07)	(1.88)	(0.00)	
Durable goods	1.79	2.76	2.35	1.86	−0.01	0.24
	(0.17)	(0.12)	(0.15)	(0.22)	(0.05)	
Capacity utilization	8.63	11.21	7.99	7.06	1.42	0.92
	(1.57)	(0.81)	(0.93)	(0.81)	(0.00)	
ISM Manufacturing Index	10.92	17.13	13.94	14.06	−1.11	0.94
	(0.62)	(0.50)	(0.57)	(0.59)	(0.01)	
Chicago Purchasing Managers Index	2.42	3.57	3.12	2.94	0.16	0.50
	(2.43)	(1.74)	(8.76)	(2.25)	(0.07)	
Consumer confidence	9.69	12.40	9.67	8.58	0.80	0.90
	(0.72)	(0.75)	(0.77)	(0.69)	(0.03)	
New home sales	8.63	8.19	9.12	8.64	−0.88	0.95
	(1.57)	(1.20)	(1.56)	(1.98)	(0.09)	

Notes: The table shows the estimated response of the financial variable (in basis points for rates and percentage points for equities) to a 1 standard deviation surprise in the "true" economic release (that measured without noise). ED2 − the rate on the second eurodollar futures contract (a proxy for monetary policy expectations about six months ahead); ED4 = the rate on the fourth eurodollar futures contract (a proxy for policy expectations about twelve months ahead); Y2 = the two-year Treasury yield; Y10 = the ten-year Treasury yield; and S&P = the S&P 500 index. The last column reports the fraction of the variation in the survey-based surprise measure that is estimated to be noise.

ticipants are convinced has no measurement error in it and one for which the market expectations are measured perfectly. The true CPI release may be discounted if it is seen as containing measurement error (e.g., a higher-than-expected reading driven by a single component, such as the price of lodging away from home), or its estimated effect under the ES may be downward biased if the market's expectations were measured improperly.

One implication of the results is that monetary policy expectations and asset prices may be more systematically related to incoming data than found under the ES approach. This conclusion accords with our understanding of monetary policy from the (lower-frequency) macroeconomic literature, including the view that one way policy has been effective over the past decade is by systematically responding to changes in economic conditions. Our results provide a high-frequency version of that conclusion.

One issue is that the results appear "too good" in some sense. The estimated amount of noise in the data announcements, a statistic that is also identified in the IC procedure, tends to be very high for many of the releases. (This pattern, of course, is directly related to the fact that the IC coefficients are several times larger than the ES coefficients.) For example, the results suggest that 31 percent of the variation in the nonfarm payrolls surprise is due to noise, while 77 percent of the variation in the core CPI release is due to noise.

It is somewhat hard to grasp just how much noise one would expect relative to some actual "truth" that we never observe. However, some of the readings from table 8.2 are clearly implausible. For example, we doubt that 94 percent of the measured surprise associated with the Institute for Supply Management (ISM) index is actually noise.

The extent of the estimated noise may raise some questions about whether the identification assumptions hold. We might be particularly concerned about our efforts to predict what the variance of the asset prices would have been in the absence of the macroeconomic surprise, as needed in the IC procedure. Note that the estimates of both the sensitivity of the market response (γ) and the amount of noise in the surprises (σ_ε) tend to increase in the shift in the variance of the asset price between nonannouncement days and announcement days. Hence, if we are underestimating the variance that would be present in the absence of a macroeconomic announcement, we would be overestimating both of these parameters.

One reason to suspect this pattern is that the macroeconomic surprises measured on the right-hand side of our equations often coincide with the release of other data that might move markets.[15] For example, the employment report not only includes the current month surprise to nonfarm payrolls, but also revisions to payrolls in the two previous months. Thus, even in the absence of a surprise regarding the current month payroll, one might expect more market volatility than on a nonannouncement day because of the possible market reaction to this other information.

If this were the case, the IC estimates presented in table 8.3 may have some upward bias. But note that this upward bias exists because the data release is actually more meaningful than captured by the surprise measure on the right-hand side of the equation. Thus, it still likely reflects that the

---

15. In addition, the announcement itself (even if it is on expectation) could result in some variance of the asset price because it would presumably reduce uncertainty and cause investors who had different expectations to adjust their positions and views.

macroeconomic news is more important than accounted for by the event-study approach. We might, therefore, want to think of an estimator that can better incorporate that additional information.

8.5   A Principal Components Exercise

This last consideration leads us in the direction of a completely different but complementary approach. The IC estimator was developed out of concern that the macroeconomic surprise variable may be measured poorly, introducing too much variation into that measure. But perhaps the bigger problem is the opposite one—that the right-hand-side variable does not capture *enough* of the surprise in a given data release.

This would be the case if the data release contained market-moving information other than that represented in the surprise measures considered in the preceding. To be sure, most data releases are complicated and convey many pieces of information. It may be difficult to determine a macroeconomic surprise measure that captures all of that information.[16]

An alternative approach that avoids this difficulty is to let the financial market data itself determine the data surprise. Specifically, we again consider the movements of the four interest rates and equity prices in the thirty-minute window around a given release. Our identification assumption is that the primary event driving the markets in those windows is the data release—an assumption that is certainly plausible for the narrow window that we consider around the release. We are not ruling out that other events take place in that window, but if there does appear to be one common event, we will assign its effects to the data release.

The approach that we use to implement this assumption is principal components. For a given release, we stack the market reactions into a matrix with one row per observation and one column for each asset price (the second and fourth eurodollar contracts, the two-year Treasury yield, the ten-year Treasury yield, and the S&P index). The principal components exercise determines a set of orthogonal factors F (same dimensions as X) that are linear combinations of the original data series:

$$(14) \qquad\qquad F = X \cdot A,$$

where $A'A = I$. As a result, the variance-covariance matrix of the responses of the financial variables is given by $F'F = A' \cdot \Sigma \cdot A$, where Σ is a diagonal matrix containing the variances of the factors.

The factors are ordered by the magnitude of their variances (with the factor with the highest variance listed first). In this sense, the first factor ex-

---

16. In the preceding, we have the example of the payrolls release and the relevance of concurrent revisions to past months' payrolls releases. Other examples are quite that retail sales ex-autos coincides with total retail sales (including autos), capacity utilization coincides with industrial production, and so on.

plains as much of the variation across the observable variables as possible, the second factor captures as much additional variation as possible, and so on.[17] The loadings of the financial variables on each of the factors is given by the inverse of the matrix A, or A'.

This approach is more general than the IC estimator. It does not require the two identifying assumptions needed in that case, and it can capture a broader set of information than measured by the surprise variables included in the IC and ES approaches. The potential cost, however, is that it could accidentally include some variation not truly associated with the data release. A finding that there is a strong co-movement in the asset prices over the thirty-minute window around the data release would boost our confidence that the procedure is picking up the effects of that release.

As reported in table 8.4, it turns out that a single factor explains the vast majority of the market reaction to each release. This factor typically accounts for 90 percent to 95 percent of the variation in the asset prices in the thirty-minute window.[18] It is this movement that we associate with the data release, as the release is presumably the dominant market event in the window.[19]

In this case, the first principal component provides a measure of the true data surprise, one that incorporates all of the market-sensitive news included in a given release. As we would expect, these data surprises are somewhat correlated with the survey-based surprises used in the preceding. Table 8.4 shows that the survey-based surprises account for as much as 50 percent of the variation in the first principal component. Thus, clearly the surprises used in the ES exercise are an important component of the total news around a data release. However, they are not a complete measure of the market-sensitive news contained in the release, as suggested by the additional (unexplained) variation in the first principal component.

Figure 8.2 presents the example for ex-auto retail sales. On the horizontal axis is the survey-based surprise used in the preceding, and on the vertical axis is the first principal component (normalized in a way to make it most comparable to the retail sales release). Again, the two measures are clearly related, but they are far from identical. The principal component (PC)-based surprise measure has more variation than can be explained by

17. When we apply this technique to the above data set, we normalize each variable by its standard deviation.

18. The table shows the variance of the first factor relative to all of the other factors. But that statistic is nearly identical to the fraction of the variance of the market interest rates explained by the first factor.

19. For comparison, if we conduct the same exercise in the nonevent window considered in the preceding (the thirty-minute window bracketing 2:30), we find that the first factor explains only 80 percent of the variance of the asset prices. Thus, it does appear that the data release window contains an even event that causes a comovement in the asset prices that is larger than that observed at other times.

Table 8.4   Effects of macroeconomic data surprises on asset prices: principal components approach

	Factor loadings					Variance explained by first factor	Amount explained by survey-based data surprise
	ED2	ED4	Y2	Y10	S&P		
Employment report	8.4	11.9	9.9	8.1	−0.15	0.98	0.55
GDP (advance)	3.8	5.6	4.8	4.8	−0.14	0.95	0.13
Retail sales (excl. autos)	4.0	5.4	4.4	3.7	−0.04	0.96	0.16
Core Consumer Price Index	3.1	4.2	3.6	3.4	−0.23	0.94	0.21
Core Producer Price Index	3.1	4.2	3.6	3.3	−0.14	0.95	0.14
Housing starts	2.1	2.9	2.2	1.9	−0.03	0.91	0.02
Durable goods	2.6	3.7	2.8	2.6	−0.05	0.94	0.19
Capacity utilization	2.3	3.1	2.2	2.0	0.05	0.91	0.20
ISM Manufacturing Index	3.3	5.1	4.1	4.0	−0.02	0.96	0.42
Chicago Purchasing Manufacturers Index	2.1	3.6	2.6	2.3	0.22	0.92	0.34
Consumer confidence	2.9	3.9	3.1	2.8	0.12	0.96	0.24
New home sales	2.3	3.1	2.6	2.4	0.02	0.94	0.15

Notes: The table shows the responses of the financial variable (in basis points for rates and percentage points for equities) to a 1 standard deviation surprise in the first principal component. ED2 = the rate on the second eurodollar futures contract (a proxy for policy monetary expectations about six months ahead); ED4 = the rate on the fourth eurodollar futures contract (a proxy for policy monetary expectations about twelve months ahead); Y2 = the two-year Treasury yield; Y10 = the ten-year Treasury yield; and S&P = the S&P 500 index. The last column reports the R-squared statistic from a regression of the first factor on the particular survey-based data surprise (two surprises in the case of the employment report).

the survey-based surprise measure, presumably capturing the additional information in the release.

Table 8.4 also reports the loadings of the various asset prices on the PC-based surprise measure. For ease of interpretation, we have normalized each PC measure to have a unitary standard deviation, just as we did with the survey-based surprises used in the ES exercise. The coefficients retain many of the interesting patterns observed in the earlier results. The market interest rates considered have a sizable response to the macroeconomic news, suggesting that the news is affecting the expected path of monetary policy. Those responses are typically also observed at longer-term maturities.

One puzzling aspect of the results is that the equity market no longer appears to have as large of a negative reaction to incoming data on inflation. It is true that the first factor explains a larger fraction of equity price movements for the inflation-related data releases than for other releases, but the response relative to the interest-rate response is smaller than in the preceding results. Instead, the factor analysis essentially finds a separate factor that drives much of the movements in equity prices. We wonder whether

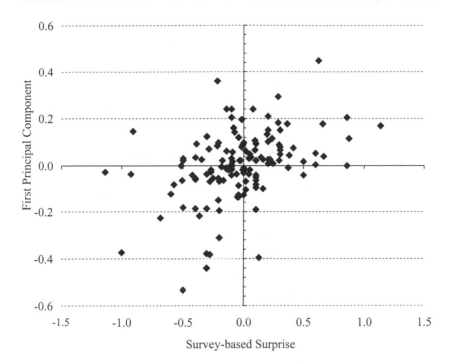

Fig. 8.2   Surprise measures for retail sales: First principal component versus survey-based measure

this finding in part reflects that we are forced to use a wider window for the equity price movements (seventeen and a half hours instead of thirty minutes!), which considerably weakens the identification assumption used in the PC exercise.

Perhaps the most important aspect of the PC exercise is its usefulness for assessing the amount of variation in yields that can be attributed to macroeconomic data. The PC exercise indicates that markets are much more sensitive to macroeconomic data releases than suggested by the ES approach. This is a similar finding as the IC estimator used in the preceding. However, in this case, the reason is not only that we are accounting for the measurement error in the survey-based surprise measure, but also because we are accounting for any other relevant information in the release.

One useful aspect of the PC approach is that, unlike the case for the IC estimator, we recover a time series of the true macroeconomic news, as discussed in the preceding. This allows us to cumulate the effects of each release on a particular asset price. Figure 8.3 shows the cumulative effects of each the data releases on the two-year Treasury yield, where each line represents an individual release. (For example, one line represents the effects of all retail sales releases over our sample.) The point of figure 8.3 is not to

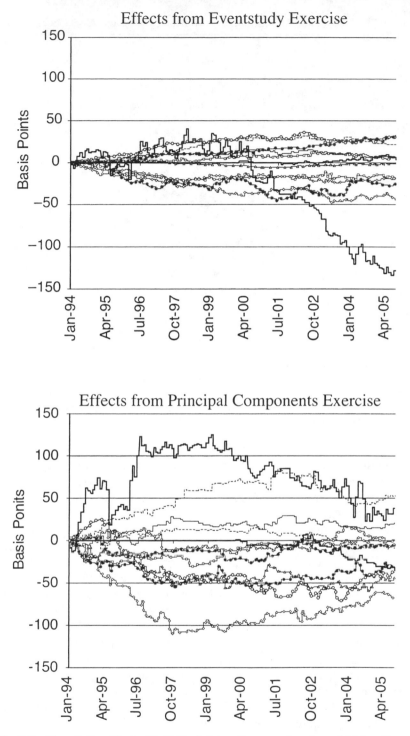

Fig. 8.3   Cumulative effects of individual data releases on two-year yield (one line per release, in basis points)

focus on any particular line, but to get a general sense of the total variation explained under the two approaches. As can be seen, the movements explained by the releases under the ES exercise are much smaller than those under the PC exercise.

Table 8.5 contains some statistics that further quantify the variation explained under the two approaches. It computes the absolute value of the changes attributable to each release, expressed as basis points per year. By this measure, the most influential data release, by far, has been the employment report. Other influential releases include retail sales, the ISM index, the CPI, and the PPI.

More important, the PC measure accounts for much more variation than the standard eventstudy approach. (This, of course, is simply a different way of expressing that the R-squared statistic from the regression increases significantly.) Indeed, this is the case for every single data release considered. We can sum these statistics across all of the releases to obtain a measure of the total variation explained by incoming macroeconomic data (or at least by our releases). By that measure, the PC approach has accounted for nearly twice as much of the variation in the two-year yield than the ES approach. Thus, the new methodology makes an important step toward better understanding the total influence of macroeconomic data on asset prices and monetary policy expectations.

Table 8.5   Variation in the two-year treasury yield explained by macroeconomic surprises

	Sum of absolute changes per year	
Release	Eventstudy approach	Principal component approach
Employment report	66	86
GDP (advance)	6	14
Retail sales (excl. autos)	15	36
Core Consumer Price Index	16	30
Core Producer Price Index	10	31
Housing starts	4	19
Durable goods	12	21
Capacity utilization	10	18
ISM Manufacturing Index	24	34
Chicago Purchasing Manufacturers Index	13	25
Consumer confidence	13	23
New home sales	10	20
Total	199	357

Notes: The table reports the sum of the absolute value of changes in the two-year yield attributable to the economic release under the two approaches. These changes are then summed over the sample for each variable and scaled by the number of releases per year divided by the total number of releases in the sample.

8.6   Implications and Conclusions

We have learned a lot from the standard eventstudy literature. This chapter begins with that approach, implementing it with the benefit of using intraday data and looking across a variety of asset prices. The eventstudy exercise clearly establishes a set of facts that macroeconomists should strive to explain when writing down models of the interactions of macroeconomic developments, monetary policy, and asset prices.

There are three broad observations that derive from the eventstudy exercise. First, policy expectations systematically respond to incoming data, with evidence of stronger-than-expected growth or higher-than-expected inflation leading to an upward revision to the expected federal funds rate path (as reflected in eurodollar futures rates and the two-year Treasury yield). Second, the influence of that data on the yield curve extends to very long maturities (the ten-year yield in our exercise). And third, equities show very mixed reactions to incoming data on growth but negative and significant reactions to data on inflation.

Many of these patterns align well with current macroeconomic models. Those models typically assume that monetary policy is systematically related to incoming data—a relationship that should also be apparent in the high-frequency data. The responsiveness of longer-term Treasury yields is somewhat more challenging to explain in current models, in part due to the difficulty associated with understanding the determination of long-horizon expectations, but it, too, has been taken up in the recent literature. Last, as discussed in the preceding, the lack of response of equities to demand-side indicators could reflect that those releases affect both expected dividend growth and interest rates, with offsetting effects on stock prices.

Nevertheless, the eventstudy estimates leave one significant shortcoming in our understanding of market dynamics—that the measured data surprises explain only a small portion of the variation in asset prices and monetary policy expectations. This chapter argues that this shortcoming likely reflects mismeasurement of the macroeconomic news.

We developed two new approaches to better account for the influence of the macroeconomic news under the assumption that the measured surprises are noisy. The first is a new econometric technique for accounting for error-in-variables, one that has the potential to be used in other applications as well. The second is a principal components approach that takes advantage of our ability (using intraday data) to zero in on the asset price movements right around the release.

The new estimators do not significantly change the patterns of the market responses that we obtain from the standard eventstudy approach. That is, the patterns found under the ES approach (including the three observations noted in the preceding) still represent a set of observations that should be explained by macroeconomic models. However, the two new approaches suggest that incoming news generally has a much bigger impact on asset prices than captured by the eventstudy approach.

In the case of the IC estimator, the results suggest that the noise in the measure of the data surprise causes a downward bias in the measured sensitivity of asset prices to that information. The PC estimator also suggests that this may be the case, and it also allows for the possibility that there is other market-sensitive news in the data release beyond the macroeconomic surprise included in the eventstudy regression.

In sum, we argue that the sensitivity of asset prices and monetary policy expectations to high-frequency information on macroeconomic conditions is likely to be greater than captured in previous studies. This finding accords well with the view that monetary policy systematically responds to economic conditions, and that asset prices more broadly are strongly influenced by the evolution of the economy and policy expectations.

References

Andersen, Torben G., Tim Bollerslev, Francis X. Diebold, and Clara Vega. 2003. Micro effects of macro announcements: Real-time price discovery in foreign exchange. *American Economic Review* 93:38–62.

Balduzzi, Pierluigi, Edwin J. Elton, and T. Clifton Green. 2001. Economic news and bond prices: Evidence from the U.S. Treasury market. *Journal of Financial and Quantitative Analysis* 36:523–43.

Bernanke, Ben, and Kenneth N. Kuttner. 2003. What explains the stock market's reaction to Federal Reserve policy? *Journal of Finance* 60:1221–57.

Cutler, David M., Porterba, and Lawrence H. Summers 1989. "What Moves Stock Prices?" *Journal of Portfolio Management* 15:4–12.

Fair, Ray C. 2003. Shock effects on stocks, bonds, and exchange rates. *Journal of International Money and Finance* 22:307–41.

Faust, John, John H. Rogers, Shing-Yi B. Wang, and Jonathan Wright. 2003. The high frequency response of exchange rates and interest rates to macroeconomic announcements. International Finance Discussion Papers no. 2003-784. Washington, DC: Board of Governors of the Federal Reserve System.

Fleming, Michael, and Eli Remolona. 1997. What moves the bond market? *Federal Reserve Bank of New York Economic Policy Review* 3:31–50.

Goldberger, Arthur S. 1991. *A course in econometrics.* Cambridge, MA: Harvard University Press.

Gürkaynak, Refet, Brian Sack, and Eric Swanson. 2005. The sensitivity of long-term interest rates to economic news: Evidence and implications for macroeconomic models. *American Economic Review* 95:425–36.

Kohn, Donald L., and Brian Sack. 2003. Central bank talk: Does it matter and why? In *Macroeconomics, monetary policy, and financial stability,* 175–206. Ottawa, Ontario: Bank of Canada.

McQueen, Grant, and V. Vance Roley. 1993. Stock prices, news, and business conditions. *The Review of Financial Studies* 6:683–707.

Rigobon, Roberto, and Brian Sack 2004. The impact of monetary policy on asset prices. *Journal of Monetary Economics* 51:1553–75.

Stock, James H., and Mark W. Watson. 2003. Forecasting output and inflation: The role of asset prices. *Journal of Economic Literature* 41:788–829.

Comment   Leonardo Bartolini

Rigobon and Sack's nice chapter rightly points its finger to serious problems with our often-too-eager use of survey-based expectations data and offers a solution for some of these problems. Survey data are likely to capture investors' expectations with large errors. Hence, their use to construct measures of macroeconomic news induces a classic attenuation bias that may explain the weak response of asset prices to news documented in recent studies. For instance, Faust et al. (2003) estimate the ten-year U.S. interest rate to rise by 13 basis points in response to a 1 percent unexpected tightening in the Fed Funds rate—a small and just statistically significant effect. Surely, many scholars of financial markets would maintain that most macroeconomic announcements should *not* be expected to have a large impact on asset prices and would not be surprised by the small size of estimates such as those of Faust et al. (2003). Even so, the debate on whether estimated weak responses of prices to news are puzzling would surely benefit by improved measurement of the news content of macroeconomic announcements, which is Rigobon and Sack's goal in this chapter. For this reason, this chapter makes a useful methodological contribution, also offering estimates of the response of asset prices to news that improve on received wisdom.

Despite such improvement, there are reasons suggesting that the response of asset prices to news estimated by Rigobon and Sack—up to ten times stronger than previously estimated—might overstate the true response of asset prices to macroeconomic announcements, possibly by a substantial amount. To assess this view, let me start by agreeing wholeheartedly with the chapter's key premise: survey-based measures of expectations are marred by such deep problems that special care should be taken to develop methods to address their deficiencies. Among such problems, notable is the fact that such surveys are typically conducted well in advance of data announcements, with leads ranging from a few days to a couple of weeks. Such leads imply that by the time of the announcement, much information on the released series has accumulated, making much of the "measured" news just not news any longer. This sampling-lead problem does not, on its own account, invalidate the rationality of the initial forecast. If forecasters form their expectations rationally, "measured news"

Leonardo Bartolini is senior vice president of the International Research Function at the Federal Reserve Bank of New York.

differs from "true news"—that is, news relative to information available one instant before the announcement—by noise only. Such noise compounds with more traditional measurement errors and can be dealt with by the clever variant of standard error-in-variables estimation methods proposed by Rigobon and Sack.

Sampling leads and measurement errors are not the only problem with forecast data, however. Other problems with such data may lead to biased (conditionally and unconditionally) forecasts that are not readily dealt with by the "censored" estimation method suggested by the authors. For instance, individual forecasts may be biased because of the unusual incentives faced by forecasters to maximize their public recognition. Because the names and affiliation of forecasters participating in the Bloomberg survey used by Rigobon and Sack and in other common surveys are publicly listed, forecasters may have an incentive to forecast in the tail of the forecast distribution, as this increases their chances of being the forecaster that comes closest to the actual release (Laster, Bennett, and Geoum 1999; Lamont, 2002). Some forecasters have also been found to distort forecasts toward realizations that benefit their firm, in a way that Ito (1990) dubs "wishful expectations." Depending on how advanced signals on the eventual data release are distributed among forecasters, a bias in individual forecasts may cause a bias in the consensus (that is, median or mean) forecast as well. Finally, forecast data are often found not to reflect efficiently publicly available information. This feature is hardly surprising, as forecasters have weak monetary incentives to offer best forecasts: the forecasters themselves are seldom investment managers, that is, agents with an incentive to put their money where their mouths are. For instance, forecasters have been documented not to learn quickly from mistakes, leading to serially correlated forecast errors (see, for instance, Mankiw Reis, and Wolfers [2003] and Gürkaynak and Wolfers [2005]). None of these problems is attacked by the methodology of Rigobon and Sack, thus leaving scope for overestimating the response of asset prices to news.

To illustrate this point, let's focus on Rigobon and Sack's neatest contribution—"identification through censoring"—which involves the following: first, to view the estimation of the news content of macroeconomic announcements as a classic error-in-variables problem. Second, to cast such problem as a matter of underidentification. And, finally, to identify the model by adding suitable restrictions to the covariance matrix. In fairness to previous research, I should note that viewing error-in-variables as an issue of underidentification has a time-honored tradition, and equally honored is the tradition of adding restrictions to the covariance matrix to achieve identification.[1] The key novelty in Rigobon and Sack's work is to recognize that the variance of the measured news process and of its noise

---

1. See, for instance, Judge et al. (1982), chapter 19.

component must be zero at all times other than at the time of the announcement. This observation yields a natural restriction to impose on the covariance matrix to achieve full identification.

Take then the authors' basic model of error-in-forecast-measurement:

$$\Delta s_t = \gamma \cdot z_t^* + \varepsilon_t \tag{1}$$

$$z_t = z_t^* + \eta_t, \tag{2}$$

where z_t is "measured news" (that is, data – data expected at $t - 1$) and z_t^* is "true news" (that is, data – data expected at $t - dt$). We are interested in the coefficient γ, for which ordinary least squares (OLS) provides a biased and inconsistent estimator, as in a classic error-in-variables problem. There is no instrument correlated with true news that can be used to address this problem: if there were one such instrument, z_t^* would not be news anymore.

Let us then follow the authors and obtain the additional condition to identify the model by recognizing that the variance of the asset price on nonannouncement days should equal its "structural" variance σ_ε^2, defined as the variance of the asset when $z_t^* = 0$. (This is a critical assumption, which is further discussed in the following.) However, let us drop the assumption that the measurement error has zero mean conditional on the true surprise. That is, let $E[\eta_t \mid z_t^*] \neq 0$, a relaxation that puts us outside the classic error-in-variables model. Consistent with much previous evidence that news derived from survey forecasts is serially correlated, suppose that measured news follows the partial adjustment model

$$z_t = (1 - \rho)z_{t-1}^* + \rho z_{t-1} + \eta_t. \tag{3}$$

In this case, one obtains

$$\mathrm{var}(\Delta s_{t-1}) = \sigma_\varepsilon^2, \tag{4}$$

$$\mathrm{var}(\Delta s_t) = \gamma^2 \sigma_{z^*}^2 + \sigma_\varepsilon^2, \tag{5}$$

$$\mathrm{cov}(\Delta s_t, z_t) = \gamma(1 - \rho)\sigma_{z^*}^2, \tag{6}$$

where equations (4) and (5) are unchanged relative to Rigobon and Sack's analysis, while equation (6) accounts for the sluggish response of measured news. In this case, the estimator γ becomes

$$\gamma = (1 - \rho)\frac{\mathrm{var}(\Delta s_t) - \mathrm{var}(\Delta s_{t-1})}{\mathrm{cov}(\Delta s_t, z_t)}, \tag{7}$$

which differs from Rigobon and Sack's censored estimator $\gamma = [\mathrm{var}(\Delta s_t) - \mathrm{var}(\Delta s_{t-1})]/[\mathrm{cov}(\Delta s_t, z_t)]$ by the term $(1 - \rho)$. Therefore, when news measured from survey data adjusts gradually to true news, Rigobon and Sack's estimator is biased upward.

Is this bias quantitatively significant? Mankiw, Reis, and Wolfers (2003) estimate that about half of the error in inflation expectations from four major surveys remains in the median forecast after one year. So the bias may be significant for some surveys. It may or may not be so for Rigobon and Sack's data, depending on the time series properties of their forecast errors.

Another key feature of forecast data that does not fit neatly into the error-in-variables framework, and which may contribute to an upward bias in Rigobon and Sack's estimated response of asset prices to news, is heterogeneity in forecasters' beliefs. Beliefs heterogeneity, illustrated by the sizable dispersion of individual forecasts in survey data, is a central tenet in the financial analysis of asset trading, from which the macroeconomics literature often abstracts. In the case of Rigobon and Sack's chapter, the cost of such abstraction is that the response of asset prices to news may be overestimated.

To see this point, consider again the censored estimator, $\gamma = [\text{var}(\Delta s_t) - \text{var}(\Delta s_t - 1)]/\text{cov}(\Delta s_t, z_t)$, and note the key identifying assumption that the "structural" (i.e., net-of-news) volatility of asset prices, σ_ε^2, is the same at announcement time (say, 8:30 a.m.) in announcement days, t, and non-announcement days, $t - 1$. This assumption allows attributing the entire rise in volatility at announcement time, $\text{var}(\Delta s_t) - \text{var}(\Delta s_{t-1})$, to the effect of news. The estimator γ then increases linearly with $\text{var}(\Delta s_t) - \text{var}(\Delta s_{t-1})$.

Rigobon and Sack generalize this assumption somewhat, allowing for σ_ε^2 to rise at announcement time *in predictable fashion* over its previous afternoon's level (at 2:30 p.m.) as in

$$(8) \qquad \sigma_{\varepsilon,t-1,8:30}^2 - \sigma_{\varepsilon,t-2,2:30}^2 = \sigma_{\varepsilon,t,8:30}^2 - \sigma_{\varepsilon,t-1,2:30}^2$$

According to equation (8), the increase in σ_ε^2 from its previous afternoon's level in announcement days is the same as the corresponding increase in nonannouncement days. However, rewriting equation (8) as

$$(9) \qquad \sigma_{\varepsilon,t,8:30}^2 - \sigma_{\varepsilon,t-1,8:30}^2 = \sigma_{\varepsilon,t-1,2:30}^2 - \sigma_{\varepsilon,t-2,2:30}^2$$

makes it apparent that equation (8) extends the benchmark assumption $\sigma_{\varepsilon,t,8:30}^2 = \sigma_{\varepsilon,t-1,8:30}^2$ only if σ_ε^2 differs significantly at 2:30 in the two nonannouncement days prior to t. My best guess is that there is *no* systematic difference in 2:30 p.m. volatility between $t - 1$ and $t - 2$ so that equations (8) and (9) effectively reduce to $\sigma_{\varepsilon,t,8:30}^2 = \sigma_{\varepsilon,t-1,8:30}^2$.

While I have no hard data on hand to document this conjecture, indirect evidence seems compelling enough. Consider, for instance, figure 8C.1, which draws data from Fleming and Remolona (1999), the benchmark study of the minute-by-minute behavior of the Treasury market examined by Rigobon and Sack.[2]

Figure 8C.1 plots data on intraday price volatility in the five-year Treasury note market, distinguishing between announcement and nonannouncement days. To assess my conjecture that $\sigma_{\varepsilon,t-1,2:30}^2 = \sigma_{\varepsilon,t-2,2:30}^2$, I would need

2. I thank Michael Fleming for providing me the data needed for figure 8C.1.

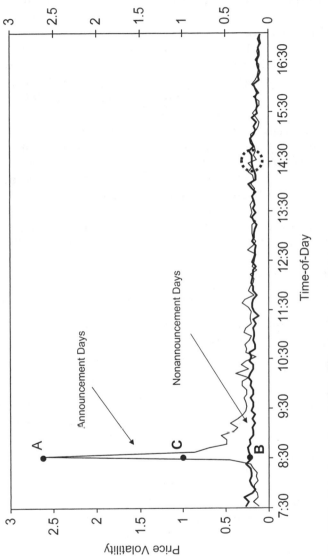

Fig. 8C.1 Intraday price volatility: Five-year treasury notes

Source: Data from figure 1A in Fleming and Remolona (1999). Volatility is measured as standard deviation of log price changes for the five-year note for days with at least one macroeconomic announcements (see Fleming and Remolona [1999] for a complete list of announcements) and days with no announcement, over five-minute intervals starting at the plotted time. Actual values are multiplied by 1,000. The sample period is August 23, 1993 to August 19, 1994.

a breakdown of volatility in the two days prior to announcements. The data I obtained do not offer such breakdown, but figure 8C.1 shows that there is negligible difference in 2:30 p.m. volatility even between announcement and nonannouncement days. I find it hard to believe, then, that there might be a systematic difference in volatility between two (almost random) nonannouncement days. if there is no such gap in volatility, Rigobon and sack's identifying restriction then reduces to assuming that the "structural" price variance at announcement time—that is, the variance when the macroeconomic release comes at its median (or mean) forecast—equals the variance at the same time in nonannouncement days. Rigobon and Sack's censored estimator can then be represented in figure 8C.1 as the distance between point A and point B (scaled by $\text{cov}[\Delta s_t, z_t]$), where point B captures the price volatility that would have been recorded *with no news*.

There are reasons, however, to believe that the volatility at announcement time will be higher in announcement days than in nonannouncement days even when $z_t^* = 0$. The key reason is that in a world with heterogeneous beliefs, $z_t^* = 0$ *is news to all but the median* (or mean) *forecaster*. Almost all investors will want to trade on the announcement, which has come either higher or lower than they individually expected. Much of this trading may reflect private information about the impact of the announcement, inducing price volatility along channels well studied in the finance literature.

While I am not aware of any direct evidence corroborating the view that even announcements at the median forecast generate price volatility, a considerable amount of indirect evidence comes to its support. Fleming and Remolona (1999), for instance, show that bid-ask spreads widen and trading volumes decline in the Treasury market *in advance* of macroeconomic announcements, with both indicators retracing their way *upon* announcements. This evidence suggests that, in a way, trading volume and price volatility might shift from *just before* to *just after* announcement times, irrespective of the actual data release. Other evidence is provided by studies showing that asset price volatility upon announcement rises with the pre-announcement dispersion in beliefs (see, for instance, Green [2004] and Pasquariello and Vega [2006]). Because there is always some dispersion in beliefs about the release in announcement days (while there is none, by definition, in nonannouncement days), structural price volatility is bound to be higher at announcement times even when $z_t^* = 0$. More anecdotally, market participants report opening large positions (long or short, depending on beliefs) in anticipation of releases. These positions get unwound upon announcement, whether the release comes in at its median value or not. As trading volume rises, price volatility is likely to do the same.

In sum, if announcement and nonannouncement days are structurally different in terms of trade dynamics, announcement days are likely associated with higher structural volatility. If properly incorporated, this larger volatility would imply a lower numerator and, hence, a lower value, for Rigobon and Sack's censored estimator γ. Illustratively, in figure 8C.1, news may be responsible for lifting volatility not from point B to point A, but from, say, point C to point A.

Finally, here is a word on the results, which are broadly sensible. The gist of the analysis is that the censored estimates of the impact of news on asset prices are larger than those yielded by event studies that disregard the possibility of attenuation bias. One puzzling aspect of Rigobon and Sack's results is that certain data releases, such as capacity utilization, Institute for Supply Management (ISM), consumer confidence, and new home sales, are estimated to consist almost entirely of noise. These estimates boost the estimated coefficients γ tenfold above the coefficients yielded by earlier event studies. I find the estimated noise component of these indicators to be implausible and view these results as strengthening my belief that the forecast data examined here might not quite fit the classic error-in-variables model.

In sum, this is a nice chapter that offers a considerable improvement in our understanding of the impact of news on asset prices. The methodology offered by the authors may not correct for *all* the shortcomings associated with survey forecast data, but certainly makes a significant advance in correcting for a first-order problem that has been disregarded in previous studies of the impact of news on asset prices.

References

Faust, Jon, John H. Rogers, Shing-Yi B. Wang, and Jonathan H. Wright. 2003. The high-frequency response of exchange rates and interest rates to macroeconomic announcements. Board of Governors of the Federal Reserve System, International Finance Discussion Papers no. 784 October.

Fleming, Michael J., and Eli Remolona. 1999. Price formation and liquidity in the U.S. Treasury market: The response to public information. *Journal of Finance* 54 (5): 1901–15.

Green, T. Clifton. 2004. Economic news and the impact of trading on bond prices. *Journal of Finance* 59 (3): 1201–33.

Gürkaynak, Refet S., and Justin Wolfers. 2005. Macroeconomic derivatives: An initial analysis of market-based macro forecasts, Uncertainty, and Risk. University of Pennsylvania. Unpublished Manuscript.

Ito, Takatoshi. 1990. Foreign exchange rate expectations: Micro survey data. *American Economic Review* 80 (3): 434–49.

Judge, George G., R. Carter Hill, William Griffiths, Helmut Lutkepöhl, and Tsoung-Chao Lee. 1982. *Introduction to the theory and practice of econometrics.* New York: Wiley.

Lamont, Owen A. 2002. Macroeconomic forecasts and microeconomic forecasters. *Journal of Economic Behavior and Organization* 48 (3): 265–80.

Laster, David, Paul Bennett, and In Sun Geoum. 1999. Rational bias in macroeconomic forecasts. *Quarterly Journal of Economics* 114 (1): 293–318.

Mankiw, N. Gregory, Ricardo Reis, and Justin Wolfers. 2003. Disagreement about

inflation expectations. NBER Working Paper no. 9796. Cambridge, MA: National Bureau of Economic Research, June.
Pasquariello, Paolo, and Clara Vega. 2006. Informed and strategic order flow in the bond markets. University of Michigan. Unpublished Manuscript.

Discussion Summary

Richard H. Clarida observed that before announcements of payroll or Consumer Price Index (CPI) numbers, market participants often positioned themselves in volatility trades so that they would do well whether the market moved up or down. In that context, it would be interesting to see what happened when the number came out at consensus.

Drawing a connection with earlier discussions, *Marvin Goodfriend* said that the fact that the authors found a significant announcement effect on long-term interest rates may be a manifestation of classic optimal monetary policy: short rates are expected to be persistent. He also noted that it was interesting that equity prices only tended to respond to inflation news, as optimal monetary policy makes the world behave as much as possible like a flexible price economy.

Thomas Laubach said that news affects asset prices primarily by changing expectations of future policy actions. In that light, it would be interesting to look at time variation, perhaps by splitting into subsamples: for example, in 2001, the CPI was not particularly interesting, but in 2003, when people were worried about inflation, it was probably watched more closely. Sack responded that it was hard to estimate time varying effects but that this could perhaps be achieved using the principal component approach. He also drew attention to the fact that in a separate paper with coauthors, he had found that forward rates ten years out respond strongly to news.

John C. Williams and *Stephen G. Cecchetti* suggested that one could use more information from surveys than just the median forecast. Williams proposed examining the interaction between announcement effects and the dispersion in beliefs in the survey. Cecchetti noted that in principle it should be possible to use an optimal weighting of forecasts.

Clarida commented that Goldman Sachs has economic derivatives contingent on payrolls data. He said that it was surprising how close the first moment was to the Bloomberg consensus. Sack observed that the price history on these assets was still short.

John Y. Campbell said that there was an interesting parallel between the macroeconomic announcements studied in this chapter and the announcements of corporate earnings studied in the finance literature. First, there are private data vendors such as StarMine that reweight individual analysts' earnings forecasts optimally. Second, Andrea Frazzini and Owen

Lamont have found that the average returns on companies making earnings announcements were positive—there is money to be made by buying equities around the times of their earnings announcements. One explanation of this is that risk is concentrated around the earnings announcement. He asked whether the authors had calculated unconditional mean returns around announcements. Sack replied that they had not focused on unconditional means but that the option markets certainly recognized that there was considerable risk surrounding announcements.

9

Is Bad News about Inflation Good News for the Exchange Rate? And, If So, Can That Tell Us Anything about the Conduct of Monetary Policy?

Richard H. Clarida and Daniel Waldman

Dollar Rises as U.S. Consumer Inflation Accelerates in February
March 23, 2005 (Bloomberg)—The dollar rose against the euro after a measure of inflation accelerated last month, bolstering expectations the Federal Reserve will raise its benchmark interest rate at a faster pace.

9.1 Introduction

The interplay between monetary policy and asset prices is a subject of longstanding interest in financial economics. Often, but not always, the focus is directed at trying to understand how monetary policy, or shocks to policy, impacts asset prices—whether these be the prices of equities, bonds, property, or currencies. Less often, the focus is on how, or should, asset prices influence the conduct of monetary policy. This chapter takes a different approach. We ask whether the response of an asset price (in our case the exchange rate) to a nonpolicy shock (in our case a surprise in inflation) can tell us something about how monetary policy is conducted.

This chapter makes a theoretical point and provides some empirical support for this point. We show in a simple, but robust, theoretical monetary exchange rate model that the sign of the covariance between an inflation surprise and the nominal exchange rate can tell us something about how monetary policy is conducted. Specifically, we show that "bad news" about

Richard H. Clarida is the C. Lowell Harriss Professor of Economics at Columbia University and a research associate of the National Bureau of Economic Research. Daniel Waldman is an associate director and senior foreign exchange economist at Barclays Capital.

inflation—that it is higher than expected—can be "good news" for the nominal exchange rate—that it appreciates on this news—if the central bank has an inflation target that it implements with a Taylor Rule. This result at first seemed surprising to us because our model is one of inflation, not price level, targeting so that in the model, a shock to inflation has a permanent effect on the price level. Because purchasing power parity (PPP) holds in the long run of the model, the nominal exchange rate depreciates in the long run to an inflation shock, even though on impact it can appreciate in response to this shock. We show that in a traditional overshooting model in which the central bank sets a growth rate for the money stock, the exchange rate would be expected to depreciate in response to an inflation shock.

The empirical work in this chapter examines point-sampled data on inflation announcements and the reaction of nominal exchange rates in ten-minute windows around these announcements for ten countries and several different inflation measures for the period July 2001, through March 2005. Eight of the countries in our study are inflation targeters, and two are not. When we pool the data, we do in fact find that bad news about inflation is indeed good news for the nominal exchange rate, that the results are statistically significant, and that R-squared is substantial, in excess of 0.25 for core measures of inflation. We also find significant differences comparing the inflation targeting countries and the two noninflation targeting countries. For the noninflation targeting countries, there is no significant impact of inflation announcements on the nominal exchange rate, although the estimated sign is, indeed, in line with our story. For each of the IT countries, the sign is as predicted by the theory and quite significant. Finally, we study two countries, the United Kingdom and Norway, in which there was a clear regime change during a period when we can obtain data. We study the granting of independence to the Bank of England in 1997 and the shift to formal inflation targeting by Norway in 2001. For both countries, the correlation between the exchange rate and the inflation surprise before the regime change reveal that "bad news about inflation was bad news about the exchange rate." After the regime change, we find that, indeed, "bad news about inflation is good news about the exchange rate."

9.2   Optimal Monetary Policy in the Open Economy: Some Results

Before we proceed further, it will be useful to review some of the results from a model of optimal monetary policy and exchange rate determination in the open economy developed in Clarida, Gali, and Gertler (2002). There are two countries, each with staggered price setting and facing cost-push shocks that generate inflation inertia. Home and foreign countries produce differentiated traded goods—the terms of trade is a key relative price. International spillovers arise via a marginal cost/optimal labor supply channel, and these impact inflation dynamics via staggered optimal price setting as in Calvo. The chapter follows Woodford (2003) and derives the central bank welfare function and the optimal monetary policy reaction function in the open economy from taste, technology, and market clearing subject to the Calvo pricing constraint. Solving the model under discretion, there are several results that are relevant to the present discussion.

First, optimal monetary policy in each open economy can be formulated as a Taylor Rule:

$$(1) \qquad i = rr + E\pi_{+1} + b(\pi - \pi^*),$$

where i is the nominal interest rate, rr is the time varying real interest rate, π is inflation, π^* is the inflation target, and E is the expectations operator. Second, under optimal monetary policy, the Taylor Rule is a function of deep parameters:

$$(2) \qquad b = [\sigma + (1 - \sigma)\gamma]\xi(1 - \rho) > 0,$$

where σ is the intertemporal elasticity of substitution, γ is the share of imports in the consumption basket, ξ is the elasticity of substitution across varieties of intermediate inputs to the production of final output, and ρ is the exogenous persistence in shocks to marginal cost. Third, optimal monetary policy features a flexible exchange rate, but the exchange rate itself does not enter the reaction function. Fourth, openness has its effects through the neutral real interest rate and the slope of the Taylor rule. Fifth, the nominal exchange rate under optimal policy has a unit root as does the domestic price level, and they are cointegrated so that PPP holds in the long run.

Clarida, Gali, and Gertler (2002) work out in some detail the symmetric, two-country Nash equilibrium under central bank discretion. They show that in the symmetric equilibrium, bad news about inflation is good news for the exchange rate. That is, a Phillips curve shock that pushes up actual (and expected) inflation triggers under optimal policy an aggressive rise in nominal and real interest rates that actually causes the nominal exchange rate to appreciate. This is so even though in the long run, the nominal exchange rate must depreciate in response to an inflation shock.

There is a tension. Using uncovered interest parity and long-run PPP we have (normalizing foreign interest rates and log price levels to zero):

$$(3) \qquad e = -\Sigma_{j=0,\infty} Ei_j + \Sigma_{j=0,\infty} E\pi_j + p_{-1}.$$

In the long run, the level of the nominal exchange rate must depreciate in line with PPP in response to an inflation shock. Under an inflation targeting monetary policy of the sort derived by Clarida, Gali, and Gertler (2002), after its initial jump, the nominal exchange rate must be depreciating along the adjustment path (because the home nominal interest rate is above the world interest rate when inflation is above target). However, in response to an inflation shock, the domestic price level rises on impact, which will tend to make the exchange rate weaker. In the Clarida, Gali, and Gertler (2002) theoretical model, optimal monetary policy has the property that the rise in interest rates in response to the monetary policy shock is sufficiently large to deliver the association between an adverse inflation shock and a nominal currency appreciation.

9.3   Inflation Shocks in a Dornbusch Style Model

In a Dornbusch style model with a money growth target, a shock that pushes up inflation will, under plausible circumstances, result in a depreciation of the nominal exchange rate Intuitively, in a Dornbusch model with a money growth target—but one that accommodates to some extent an inflation shock so that the price level has a unit root—the long-run PPP anchor tends to make the nominal exchange rate and the price level move in the same direction whether the shock is to the money supply or to the Phillips curve. The analysis is straightforward.

We begin with a money demand equation:

$$(4) \qquad m - p = -\lambda(e^e - e),$$

where λ is the interest semielasticity of money demand. Next is a standard Phillips curve from this literature augmented with an inflation shock term ε.

$$(5) \qquad p = p_{-1} + \mu + \eta(e - p) + \varepsilon$$

Next is a money growth equation, which features the empirically plausible feature that inflation shocks are at least partially accommodated.

$$(6) \qquad m = m_{-1} + \mu + f\varepsilon_{-1}$$

Without this feature, the price level would be stationary in the model, at odds with the vast body of evidence that price levels have a unit root and that central banks tend to accommodate price level shocks. We could easily include a permanent shock to the money supply, in which case bad news about inflation would be bad news about the exchange rate as in the textbook model. Note that the trend rate of growth in the money supply μ anchors the trend depreciation in the exchange rate. Finally, we note for future reference that the ex ante real interest rate satisfies by uncovered interest parity $r = q^e - q$ with $q = e - p$.

We solve the model for the response of e to an inflation shock. To illustrate our point as simply as possible, we assume that the accommodation parameter f is such that policy accommodates the inflation shock with a one-period lag, and the model reaches new steady state in one period with $q^e = 0$. We will solve for the unique f that satisfies this condition, which admits an intuitive interpretation. Interestingly, a more general version of this setup, which allows for gradual accommodation, can feature sunspot equilibriums. Because the subject of sunspot equilibriums with money growth targeting is not the subject of this chapter, we stick with the simple example here.

We can rewrite the model as

(7) $$m - p = -\lambda(q^e - q) - \lambda(p^e - p) = \lambda q - \lambda\mu.$$

We have

(8) $$dp = -\lambda dq.$$

Thus, if an inflation shock causes inflation, the real exchange rate must appreciate under this policy rule. Actual inflation must satisfy

(9) $$dp = \eta dq + d\varepsilon.$$

Collecting terms, under full accommodation (with a lag of one period),

(10) $$\left(1 + \frac{\eta}{\lambda}\right)dp = d\varepsilon.$$

Thus, indeed, an inflation shock causes inflation, so we know the real exchange rate appreciates. The appreciation dampens the impact of the inflation shock so that inflation rises less than one for one with the inflation shock. Even with ex ante full accommodation, in the period of the shock, the money supply is fixed which results in a contraction in demand. Now, what about the nominal exchange rate? Because PPP holds in the long run, and policy fully accommodates the shock with a lag, the price level will be permanently higher and, thus, the exchange rate will be permanently higher (weaker) too.

There is a presumption that the nominal exchange rate will depreciate on impact. And, in fact, it almost certainly will in this textbook model. To see this, note that

(11) $$de = dq + dp = dp\frac{\lambda - 1}{\lambda}.$$

Now λ is the interest semielasticity of money demand, which in empirical studies is usually estimated to be much larger than 1 and in calibration models is often assumed to exceed 5. For example, if the interest elasticity of money demand is 0.5, then starting from an interest rate of 4 percent, a 1 percentage point rise in the interest rate is a 25 percent increase in that rate and will reduce money demand by 12.5 percent for a semielasticity of 12.5 Thus, there is a presumption that that "bad news about inflation is bad news about the exchange rate" in a textbook model, both in the long run and on impact in the very short run. Finally, note that for the expectation of full accommodation to be rational, the central bank must set

(12) $$f = 1 + \frac{\eta}{\lambda}.$$

Thus, while a policy to accommodate may be chosen freely by the central bank, there is a unique value of the feedback parameter f that insures this is a rational expectation equilibrium. Note also that even though this central bank is a money targeter, an inflation shock will induce the ex ante real interest rate to rise since by uncovered interest parity (UIP), in the period of the shock:

$$(13) \qquad\qquad dr = -dq = (\lambda + \eta)^{-1}d\varepsilon.$$

Thus, a rise in nominal and real interest rates in response to an inflation shock, which is a feature of a stable Taylor rule in a wide variety of models, is also true under money growth targeting with partial accommodation.

9.4   Exchange Rate Dynamics under Open Economy Taylor Rules

9.4.1   Overview

In Dornbusch (1976) and Mussa (1982), and in virtually all exchange rate papers written until quite recently—including the "new open economy" contributions of Obstfeld and Rogoff (1996, 2000) and the many other papers recently surveyed and reviewed in Sarno and Taylor (2001)—it is the (stochastic process for) the supply of money that is the key nominal forcing variable for understanding the dynamics of the nominal exchange rate. Although Mussa (1982), in particular, allows for a quite general specification of the stochastic process for the money supply, in practice, theoretical exchange rate models are almost always solved under quite simple—and counterfactual—restrictions on monetary policy, namely, that the instrument of monetary policy is the stock of money. However, for most of the world's major central banks, the empirical evidence in Clarida, Gali, and Gertler (1998) suggests that monetary policy is better described by an *interest* rate rule of the sort first proposed by Henderson and McKibbon (1990) and Taylor (1993). Recent papers by Engel and West (2005, 2006) and by Mark (2004) have begun to explore some of the empirical implications for exchange rates if central banks follow Taylor rules for setting interest rates.

The goal of the next two sections is to characterize exchange rate dynamics in a more or less standard open economy model in which the central bank follows an interest rate rule to implement an inflation targeting strategy. The key to solving the model in closed form is to recognize that—as shown in Campbell and Clarida (1987)—if the *equilibrium* ex ante real interest rate implied by the Taylor rule exhibits first order autoregressive dynamics, then the equilibrium level of the real exchange rate will, period by period, be proportional to the equilibrium ex ante real interest rate. However, the "constant" of proportionality that links the real exchange rate and the ex ante real interest rate is not a free parameter. Instead, it is a fixed point in the space of expectations for the Markov process, which describes the equilibrium inflation process. We show that in this model, conditional on the minimum set of state variables, this fixed point is unique and that the equilibrium is stationary (more precisely, the Blanchard and Kahn [1980] conditions for a unique rational expectations equilibrium are satisfied if the Taylor condition is satisfied).

Some interesting results are obtained. We find that in response to a temporary Phillips curve shock that pushes the inflation rate above target, the nominal exchange rate can either depreciate or appreciate on impact, depending upon how aggressively—as indexed by the Taylor rule slope coefficient on the expected inflation gap—the central bank raises real interest rates to bring inflation back to target. Because of inflation inertia, this adjustment does not happen immediately. We find that the equilibrium half-life of an inflation shock (on inflation, output, and the real interest rate) is inversely related to the Taylor rule coefficient on the inflation gap and is directly related to the Taylor rule coefficient on the output gap. Thus, the more aggressive is the central bank response to an inflation shock, the faster the economy returns to target. However, the more aggressive is the central bank response to the output gap, the slower the economy returns to target.

We also examine the dynamic effect of a once-and-for-all permanent reduction in the central bank inflation target. The announcement of a lower inflation target causes the exchange rate to appreciate on impact, inducing a real appreciation and a recession. Inflation falls on impact, but not all the way to target. Along the adjustment path to the new inflation target, the exchange rate is depreciating. Thus, the exchange rate overshoots in response to a "tightening" of monetary policy.

9.4.2 A Model

To illustrate the idea as clearly as possible, we will work with the simplest model required. It is a simplified version of the model studied in Svensson (2000). It is comprised of four equations: an aggregate demand equation, an aggregate supply equation, a Taylor rule equation, and an uncovered interest parity equation. The economy is small and takes the world interest rate and world inflation as given and equal to 0. The aggregate demand equation is given by

$$(14) \qquad\qquad y = -r + (e - p),$$

where y is log deviation of output from potential, $r = i - E\pi_{+1}$ is the ex ante real interest rate, e is the log nominal exchange rate, and p is the log of the domestic price level. The aggregate supply equation is given by

$$(15) \qquad\qquad \pi = \pi_{-1} + y + \varepsilon,$$

where $\pi = p - p_{-1}$ and ε is a white noise shock to the Phillips curve. Note that we assume a high degree of inflation inertia so that it is the change in inflation that is increasing in output gap. This actually will work against the Clarida, Gali, and Gertler (2002) prediction that under optimal policy "bad news is good news" because inflation inertia will tend to increase the long-run effect on the price level of any given inflation shock. I assume the central bank conducts monetary policy by according to the following Taylor rule:

(16) $$i = E\pi_{+1} + b\{\pi - \pi^*\} + ay,$$

where π^* is the central bank inflation target and b and $a > 0$. Finally, uncovered interest parity implies, in real terms, that

(17) $$e - p = E\{e_{+1} - p_{+1}\} - r.$$

We let $q = e - p$ denote the real exchange rate. Note that $e = \pi + p_{-1} + q$.

We solve equation (17) forward as in Campbell and Clarida (1987) and Svensson (2000) to obtain $q = E\lim_{i \to \infty} q_{+i} - E\Sigma_{k=0,\infty} r_{+k}$. Thus, the log level of the real exchange rate equals the expected long-run equilibrium real exchange rate minus the expected undiscounted sum of short-term real interest rates. In our model, the long-run log real exchange rate is constant and equal to 0, so the level of the real exchange rate is given by

(18) $$q = -E \sum_{k=0,\infty} r_{+k}.$$

We will "guess"—and later verify—that in equilibrium, the ex ante real interest rate follows a zero mean AR(1) process so that $Er_{+j} = d^j r$ with $0 < d < 1$. As shown in Campbell and Clarida (1987), this implies that

(19) $$q = \frac{-r}{(1 - d)}.$$

It is sometimes just assumed in models like this (see Ball [1999], for example) that the real exchange rate is proportional to the short-term real interest rate. Although our model has this feature in equilibrium, d is not a "free" parameter but is, in fact, a fixed point (and as well will see, a function of monetary policy) in the space of expectations for the stochastic process that describes equilibrium inflation.

By substituting equation (19) into the aggregate demand curve, we obtain $y = (2 - d)q$. Substituting the Taylor rule into the real exchange rate equation and using the Phillips curve equation, the system can be written as two equations in two unknowns, q and π:

(20) $$q = \frac{-b(\pi - \pi^*)}{(1 - d)} - \frac{a(2 - d)q}{(1 - d)},$$

(21) $$\pi = \pi_{-1} + (2 - d)q + \varepsilon.$$

From equation (20), we see that $-q[(1-d) + a(2-d)] = r[1 + a(2-d)/(1-d)] = b(\pi - \pi^*)$. Thus, in equilibrium, the ex ante real interest rate is proportional to the inflation gap, even though the central bank also seeks to stabilize output. The dynamics of the system are completely described by the following equation:

$$(22) \qquad \pi = \pi_{-1} - \frac{(2-d)b(\pi - \pi^*)}{(1-d) + a(2-d)} + \varepsilon.$$

Before moving on, it is useful to pause and understand the logic. To obtain equation (22), we guessed that the equilibrium ex ante real interest rate follows an AR(1) process so that $Er_{+j} = d^j r$. Equation (22) shows that if this guess is correct, inflation follows an AR(1) process. But, from the Taylor rule, if inflation follows an AR(1) process, then so does the ex ante real interest rate. Thus, our guess is not logically inconsistent. However, this logic does not prove that there exists a unique fixed point in the space of expectations over the AR(1) process for r. Collecting terms, we can rewrite equation (22) as $(\pi - \pi^*)\{1 + (2-d)b/[(1-d) + a(2-d)]\} = (\pi_{-1} - \pi^*) + \varepsilon$. It follows that any fixed point in the space of expectations for r must satisfy $\{1 + (2-d)b/[(1-d) + a(2-d)]\} = 1/d$. The solutions to this equation are just eigenvalues of the dynamic system when written out in Blanchard-Kahn form. It is easy to show that for any $a > 0$, $b > 0$ is necessary and sufficient for the existent of a unique rational expectations equilibrium. Figure 9.1 presents the determination of this unique equilibrium.

Result 1: A rational expectations equilibrium exists, is unique, and is stationary. The equilibrium persistence $d(b, a)$ in inflation and in deviations from PPP $0 < d(b, a) < 1$ depends upon the parameters of monetary policy. Persistence is strictly decreasing in b—the Taylor rule coefficient on the inflation gap—and strictly increasing in a—the Taylor rule coefficient on the output gap.

Thus, for any given Taylor rule coefficients $a \geq 0$ and $b > 0$, there is a unique, stationary rational expectations equilibrium. The more aggressively the central bank reacts to the inflation gap (as indexed by the parameter b), the faster the economy converges to the long-run equilibrium and the less persistent are deviations from PPP. However, the larger the weight placed on output stabilization (as indexed by the parameter a), the slower the economy converges to the long-run equilibrium. Indeed, it is easy to establish the following three limiting cases: first, for any given a, as $b \to 0$, $d(b, a) \to 1$. That is, as the weight placed on inflation stabilization goes to zero, inflation and the real exchange rate approach a random walk. Second, for any given a, as $b \to \infty$, $d(b, a) \to 0$. That is, as the weight placed on inflation stabilization goes to infinity, the inflation gap and the real exchange rate approach white noise. Third, for any given b, as $a \to \infty$,

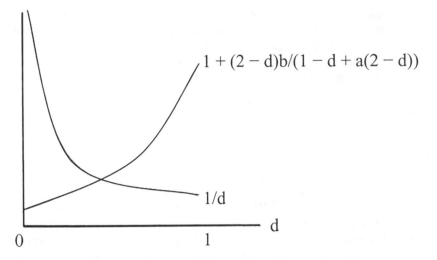

Fig. 9.1 Equilibrium as a function of Taylor rule parameters b and a

$d(b, a) \to 1$. That is, as the weight placed on output stabilization goes to infinity, inflation and the real exchange rate approach a random walk.

An Adverse Inflation Shock

A temporary Phillips curve shock $\varepsilon > 0$ pushes up inflation, but by less than the shock. This is because the central bank reacts to the inflation shock by pushing up the nominal and the ex ante real interest rate. The real exchange rate appreciates on impact. Output contracts. The effect of a Phillips curve shock on the level of the nominal exchange rate depends upon b, the Taylor rule reaction parameter to the inflation gap. The following result is easily verified using equation (20) and the fact that d is decreasing in b.

Result 2: For any given $a \geq 0$, there exists a $b(a)$ such that, for all $b > b(a)$, $\partial e_t / \partial \varepsilon_t < 0$. That is, if the central bank responds sufficiently aggressively to a rise in inflation, the nominal exchange rate *appreciates* on impact in response to an adverse inflation shock. For $b < b(a)$, $\partial e_t / \partial \varepsilon_t > 0$.

Thus, while the real exchange rate must appreciate in response to an adverse inflation shock, the effect on the nominal exchange rate depends upon the Taylor rule reaction function. Interestingly, the "inflation nutter" case $a = 0$ and $b > 0$ is not sufficient to guarantee $\partial e_t / \partial \varepsilon_t < 0$.

The impulse response dynamics to an adverse inflation shock are easy to characterize and are shown in figures 9.2 and 9.3. The nominal interest rate and inflation fall monotonically over time at rate d to π^*, and the output gap and the real exchange rate rise monotonically over time at rate d to 0. Along the adjustment path, the nominal exchange rate is depreciating at

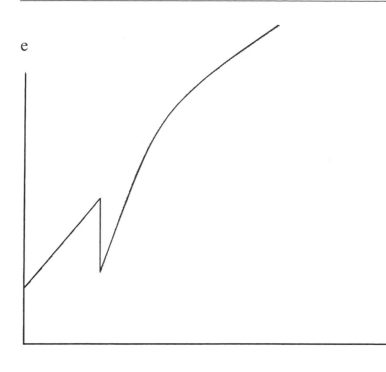

Fig. 9.2 Impulse response to inflation shock: "good news" case $b > b(a)$

the rate equal to the nominal interest rate, until in the steady state it depreciates at the rate π^*.

A Cut in the Inflation Target

We now consider a once-and-for-all cut in the inflation target to $\underline{\pi}^* < \pi^*$. In our model, this is assumed to be immediately credible and to shape expectations on impact. That is, following McCallum (1983), the minimum set of state variables for this model is $s = \{\underline{\pi}^*, \varepsilon, \pi_{-1}\}$. As shown in the preceding, there is a unique rational expectations equilibrium corresponding to this state vector and the parameters a and b, which maps $s \to \{\pi, y, q, i, E\pi_{+1}\}$. Of course, in equilibrium the nominal exchange rate and the price level are non-stationary and are a function of $\{\pi^*, \varepsilon, \varepsilon_{-1}, \varepsilon_{-2}, \ldots\}$.

Assume for concreteness that $\pi_{-1} = \pi^*$ and $\varepsilon = 0$. In the period in which the inflation target is cut, the equation for inflation in the period of the regime change can be written

(23) $$\pi = d\pi^* + \underline{\pi}^*(1 - d).$$

Thus, because of inflation inertia, $0 < \partial\pi/\partial\underline{\pi}^* < 1$ because $d(a, b) < 1$ for b. It follows that the derivative of the inflation gap with respect to the infla-

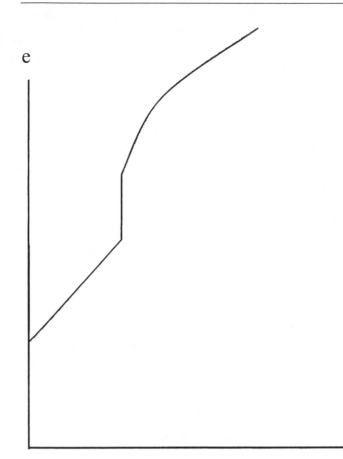

Fig. 9.3 Impulse response to inflation shock: "bad news" case $b < b(a)$

tion target is given by $\partial(\pi - \underline{\pi}^*)/\partial\underline{\pi}^* = -d$. Thus, a cut in the inflation target leads to a rise in the inflation gap. By the Taylor rule, the ex ante real in-
terest rate must rise, and, thus, the real exchange rate must appreciate. As a
result, output declines. Indeed, it is the induced decline in output that reduces inflation part of the way to $\underline{\pi}^*$. Because inflation falls and the real exchange rate appreciates, the nominal exchange rate must appreciate as well.

We now discuss the impulse response dynamics in periods subsequent to
the cut in the inflation target. For concreteness, we focus on the case in
which the new inflation target is zero, $\underline{\pi}^* = 0$. After the regime change, the
nominal interest rate remains above its new steady state level of $i^{SS} = \underline{\pi}^* =
0$. This is because the inflation gap is positive. Thus, along the adjustment
path, the nominal interest rate is everywhere above the world interest rate

of $i^* = 0$ so that the nominal exchange rate must depreciate along the adjustment path.

Result 3: In response to a cut in the inflation target, the nominal exchange rate exhibits overshooting. That is, it appreciates on impact and depreciates over time to its new steady state level.

Thus, if the "surprise" fall in inflation is due to a cut in the inflation target (not a Phillips curve shock), good news for inflation (that it falls) is good news for the exchange rate (it appreciates on impact). Because the model is symmetric, it will also be the case that if a "surprise" rise in inflation is due to an increase in the inflation target (not a Phillips curve shock), bad news for inflation (that it rises) is bad news for the exchange rate (it depreciates on impact).

9.5 Empirical Results

In this section, we use data on inflation announcements and the response of nominal exchange rates around these announcements to empirically test our theoretical model. We focus on three questions: (1) What is the sign of the correlation between inflation surprises and nominal exchange rate changes? (2) Is it significant? (3) Is it different for inflation targeters and noninflation targeters?

Previewing our results, we find that when we pool the data, bad news about inflation is good news for the exchange rate. The sign of the correlation between inflation surprises and exchange rate changes is positive and statistically significant. When we separate the data into inflation targeters and noninflation targeters, we find that these results continue to hold for inflation targeting countries, but the coefficients become insignificant for noninflation targeters.

9.5.1   Data

Our data set consists of high frequency exchange rate and inflation expectation and announcement data. In the following, we describe the construction and properties of our data.

Exchange Rate Data

Our exchange rate data consists of continuously recorded five-minute nominal spot data for nine U.S. dollar crosses: USD-JPY, USD-CAD, USD-NOK, USD-SEK, USD-CHF, EUR-USD, GBP-USD, AUD-USD, and NZD-USD. The data, provided by Olsen Associates and Merrill Lynch, begins in July 2001, and ends in December 2005. For GBP-USD and USD-NOK, we also have high frequency exchange rate data covering the periods 1993 to 1996 and 1997 to 2000, respectively.

Table 9.1   10-minute exchange rate returns (%)

	AUD-USD	NZD-USD	EUR-USD
Mean	0.00	0.00	0.00
Standard deviation	0.07	0.09	0.05
	GBP-USD	USD-JPY	USD-CAD
Mean	0.00	0.00	0.00
Standard deviation	0.05	0.05	0.05
	USD-NOK	USD-SEK	USD-CHF
Mean	0.00	0.00	0.00
Standard deviation	0.07	0.07	0.06

We convert the raw spot data to returns, taking ten-minute percentage changes. Although the spot data is recorded at five-minute intervals, we use ten-minute changes because we are interested in exchange rate behavior during the period beginning five minutes before an inflation announcement and ending five minutes after such an announcement.

Table 9.1 provides summary statistics for our ten-minute exchange rate return data. For all nine U.S. dollar crosses, the mean ten-minute return is 0.00 percent. Although the mean returns are similar across currency pairs, the standard deviations are not, ranging from 0.05 percent to 0.09 percent. The range of standard deviations may be related to the depth and liquidity of markets in different exchange rate crosses. The most liquid currency pairs—USD-JPY, EUR-USD, and USD-CAD—have the lowest standard deviations, and the least liquid crosses—NZD-USD, AUD-USD, USD-NOK, and USD-SEK—have the highest standard deviations.

Inflation Data

We define an *inflation surprise* as the difference between the market expectation for an announcement and the announced value of inflation. We arrange the data so that a positive surprise indicates that inflation was higher than expected, while a negative surprise indicates that inflation was announced lower than expected.

For the 2001 to 2005 period, our inflation expectations data is from the Bloomberg News Service. Bloomberg surveys commercial and investment banks on their expectations for a wide range of macroeconomic announcements, including inflation. We use the median of these expectations as the inflation expectation for a particular announcement.

Our inflation announcement data for 2001 to 2005 is from the Bloomberg News Service as well. Bloomberg records and preserves the announced value of macroeconomic variables, in addition to the revised values. This is an important distinction, as macroeconomic data is often revised in the months following its initial release. Because we are concerned only with the immediate response of the exchange rate to an inflation surprise, we need the actually announced data.

In addition to the 2001 to 2005 data, we have inflation expectation and announcement data for the United Kingdom and Norway for the periods 1993 to 1996 and 1997 to 2000, respectively. Data for both is provided by Money Market Services and is similar to the Bloomberg data.

For all countries except the United Kingdom, where we use retail prices, we use consumer prices as our inflation metric. For most countries in our sample, expectation and announcement data are available for both headline and core inflation, where core inflation is headline inflation minus some of the volatile components, such as food and energy. We have up to four different measures of inflation for each country in our sample: headline inflation measured as month-over-month and year-over-year changes, and core inflation measured as month-over-month and year-over-year changes.

In table 9.2, we present summary statistics for our inflation surprise variables. For most countries in the sample, the mean inflation surprise is slightly less than zero, indicating that forecasters have tended to underestimate inflation. However, across all countries and measures of inflation, the absolute value of mean inflation surprises is never greater than 0.1 percentage points, indicating that any potential bias is small. The standard deviations for the inflation surprises are larger than the means, ranging from 0.1 to 0.3 percentage points.

9.5.2   The Model

We follow the macroeconomic announcement surprise literature, estimating the following equation:

$$(24) \qquad\qquad R_t = \alpha + \beta S_t + u_t.$$

Here R_t is the ten-minute return around the inflation announcement, S_t is the inflation surprise, and u_t is the error term. The exchange rate return is calculated so that a positive value indicates an appreciation of the local currency, and a negative value represents a depreciation of the local currency. In all tables, the coefficient represents the percentage change in the local currency for a 1 percentage point surprise in inflation.

All Countries

Pooling data from all countries in our sample and running a stacked ordinary least squares (OLS) regression on equation (24), we find that bad news about inflation is indeed good news for the nominal exchange rate. For all four specifications (table 9.3), the sign on the inflation surprise variable is positive and statistically significant, indicating that higher than expected inflation results in an immediate currency appreciation and that

Table 9.2   **Inflation surprises**

	Canada				United Kingdom			
	Headline		Core		Headline		Core	
	MoM	YoY	MoM	YoY	MoM	YoY	MoM	YoY
Mean	−0.04	−0.04	−0.03	−0.01	0.00	−0.01	−0.02	−0.02
Standard deviation	0.21	0.23	0.15	0.17	0.13	0.15	0.15	0.14

	Norway				Sweden			
	Headline		Core		Headline		Core	
	MoM	YoY	MoM	YoY	MoM	YoY	MoM	YoY
Mean	−0.07	−0.09	−0.09	−0.10	−0.03	−0.05	−0.03	−0.03
Standard deviation	0.27	0.30	0.22	0.21	0.17	0.17	0.17	0.19

	Japan				United States			
	Headline		Core		Headline		Core	
	MoM	YoY	MoM	YoY	MoM	YoY	MoM	YoY
Mean	0.03	0.02	0.02	0.02	−0.01	0.04	0.00	0.00
Standard deviation	0.13	0.12	0.10	0.08	0.14	0.18	0.10	0.12

	Australia		Euro area		New Zealand	Switzerland	
	Headline		Headline		Headline	Headline	
	QoQ	YoY	MoM	YoY	QoQ	MoM	YoY
Mean	−0.01	0.00	0.00	0.00	−0.04	−0.03	−0.07
Standard deviation	0.18	0.19	0.09	0.07	0.16	0.20	0.23

Table 9.3   **All countries**

	Headline		Core	
	MoM	YoY	MoM	YoY
Coefficient	0.2	0.2	0.5	0.5
T-statistic	5.9	6.2	9.7	9.2
R-squared	0.08	0.09	0.27	0.25
No. of observations	394	387	257	259

Notes: Regression method: stacked OLS. Percentage change in exchange rate results from a 1 percentage point upward surprise in inflation. Positive coefficient indicates appreciation of domestic currency. Countries: Australia, Canada, euro area, Japan, New Zealand, Norway, Sweden, Switzerland, United Kingdom, and United States. Data: July 2001–December 2005. Some countries missing observations.

lower than expected inflation results in an immediate currency depreciation. The R-squares from the regressions are substantial, particularly for the specifications using core inflation, where they exceed 0.25.

Although the signs are positive and significant for all specifications, the results are stronger for the core measures. The coefficients, t-statistics, and R-squares are all larger, with coefficients 2.5 times the size of those in the regressions using headline inflation and R-squares nearly three times greater. Given the tendency of central banks to focus on core inflation, it is not surprising that markets have reacted more strongly to surprises in this measure.

Inflation Targeters versus Noninflation Targeters

Our ten-country sample includes eight inflation targeters and two noninflation targeters—the United States and Japan. Our groupings are similar to those used by the International Monetary Fund (IMF), though the IMF does not include the European Central Bank (ECB) among inflation targeters, as the ECB gives weight to a "reference value" for growth of money supply in the euro area. Despite this dual mandate, we include the ECB in the inflation targeting group, as it has lessened its emphasis on the money supply reference value in recent years. Including the ECB among the noninflation targeters would not significantly alter our results.

For our study, the key question is whether the sign and significance of β are different for inflation targeters and noninflation targeters. Separating and pooling the data into two categories—inflation targeters and noninflation targeters—we find significant differences between the two. For noninflation targeting countries, the impact of inflation surprises is not significant, though the estimated sign is generally positive (table 9.4). For in-

Table 9.4   **Inflation targeters versus noninflation targeters**

| | Inflation targeters | | | | Noninflation targeters | | | |
| | Headline | | Core | | Headline | | Core | |
	MoM	YoY	MoM	YoY	MoM	YoY	MoM	YoY
Coefficient	0.3	0.2	0.6	0.5	0.01	−0.08	0.1	0.1
T-statistic	6.1	6.7	9.4	8.9	0.2	−0.8	1.3	1.1
R-squared	0.11	0.13	0.37	0.31	0.00	0.01	0.02	0.02
No. of observations	286	310	152	182	108	77	105	77

Notes: Regression method: stacked OLS. Percentage change in exchange rate resulting from a 1 percentage point upward surprise in inflation. Positive coefficient indicates appreciation of domestic currency. Inflation targeters include: Australia, Canada, euro area, New Zealand, Norway, Sweden, Switzerland, and United Kingdom. Noninflation targeters include: Japan and United States. Noninflation targeters YoY includes only Japan. Data: July 2001–December 2005. Number of observations may be less than total months due to missing observations.

flation targeters, the estimated coefficients are positive and statistically significant in all four specifications. The R-squares are quite substantial for the inflation targeting regressions, exceeding 0.30 for both core specifications (table 9.4).

Estimating equation (24) separately for each country confirms these results (table 9.5). For the two noninflation targeters, the coefficients are not significant, and for headline inflation in the United States are actually of the opposite sign of what the theory predicts. For all eight inflation targeters, the estimated signs are positive and are statistically significant for six of the countries. These results are particularly strong for the core measures, with R-squares ranging from 0.18 for the United Kingdom to 0.65 for Norway.

Regime Changes

We can also test whether our results hold when there is a clear regime change over time. To test this, we study the granting of independence to the Bank of England in 1997 and the shift to formal inflation targeting in Norway in 2001. For both countries, we have nominal exchange rate and inflation expectation and announcement data prior to and following the regime shifts.

For both countries, the correlation between inflation surprises and nominal exchange rate changes is positive and significant for the 2001 to 2005 period, indicating that when central banks in both countries were inflation targeters, bad news about inflation was good news for the exchange rate. However, prior to the regime changes in both countries, the estimated coefficients were negative (though not statistically significant), implying that bad news about inflation was bad news for the exchange rate (table 9.6).

Sign Effects

Finally, we examine whether the reaction of the nominal exchange rate differs according to the sign of the surprise. We separate the data into three categories: higher than expected inflation, lower than expected inflation, and as expected inflation. We discard observations where inflation was as expected and pool the remaining data for all countries into two groups— positive inflation surprises (bad news) and negative inflation surprises (good news). We then estimate equation (24) for both (table 9.7), though we omit the constant in the regression.

Doing so, we find that although the coefficients are positive and statistically significant across all specifications, the effect is stronger for negative inflation surprises (good news) than it is for positive inflation surprises (bad news). The coefficients, t-statistics, and R-squares are substantially higher for the regressions that use negative inflation surprises. Thus, for equivalent inflation surprises, good news will have a larger impact than will bad news.

Table 9.5   **Individual country results**

	Canada				United Kingdom			
	Headline		Core		Headline		Core	
	MoM	YoY	MoM	YoY	MoM	YoY	MoM	YoY
Coefficient	0.07	0.04	0.5	0.2	0.3	0.2	0.3	0.3
T-statistic								
OLS	1.2	0.8	5.0	3.3	2.9	3.1	3.3	4.0
White	1.4	1.0	6.3	2.8	2.2	2.6	2.8	3.3
Newey-West	1.2	0.9	6.7	2.7	1.9	2.1	2.3	2.7
R-squared	0.02	0.01	0.47	0.19	0.14	0.16	0.18	0.23
No. of observations	54	54	30	50	53	54	50	54

	Norway				Sweden			
	Headline		Core		Headline		Core	
	MoM	YoY	MoM	YoY	MoM	YoY	MoM	YoY
Coefficient	0.5	0.6	1.3	1.3	0.3	0.2	0.2	0.2
T-statistic								
OLS	2.8	3.5	7.5	7.7	3.4	3.3	3.1	3.1
White	2.3	2.4	5.7	5.4	3.6	3.0	3.3	3.2
Newey-West	2.0	2.1	6.6	5.7	3.4	3.1	2.9	2.9
R-squared	0.19	0.27	0.65	0.64	0.23	0.21	0.21	0.20
No. of observations	35	35	32	35	41	42	40	42

	Australia		Euro Area		New Zealand		Switzerland	
	Headline		Headline		Headline		Headline	
	QoQ	YoY	MoM	YoY	QoQ		MoM	YoY
Coefficient	0.1	0.1	0.1	0.1	0.7		0.1	0.1
T-statistic								
OLS	1.0	1.1	1.1	0.9	3.0		2.9	3.1
White	1.0	1.1	1.2	1.0	3.3		2.7	3.0
Newey-West	1.1	1.2	1.1	1.2	3.2		2.7	3.4
R-squared	0.06	0.08	0.02	0.02	0.38		0.16	0.16
No. of observations	18	17	54	54	17		48	53

	Japan				United States			
	Headline		Core		Headline		Core	
	MoM	YoY	MoM	YoY	MoM	YoY	MoM	YoY
Coefficient	0.07	0.1	0.07	0.07	−0.1	−0.2	0.1	0.2
T-statistic								
OLS	1.4	1.8	1.0	0.7	−0.4	−1.1	0.9	0.7
White	1.2	1.9	0.8	0.7	−0.4	−1.1	0.9	0.7
Newey-West	1.3	1.6	0.7	0.7	−0.4	−1.2	0.9	0.8
R-squared	0.04	0.06	0.02	0.01	0.00	0.05	0.01	0.02
No. of observations	54	54	51	52	54	25	54	25

Notes: Percentage change in exchange rate results from a 1 percentage point upward surprise in infla-tion. Positive coefficient indicates appreciation of domestic currency. For U.S. results, currency appreci-ation/depreciation is measured against the euro. Data: July 2001–December 2005. Number of observa-tions may be less than total months due to missing observations. White and Newey-West used to correct for potential heteroscedasticity.

Table 9.6   UK and Norway preinflation targeting

| | UK | | | Norway |
| | Headline | | Core | Headline |
	MoM	YoY	YoY	YoY
Coefficient	0.006	−0.05	−0.06	−0.08
T-statistic				
OLS	0.1	−0.5	−0.7	−1.0
White	0.1	−0.7	−0.8	−1.6
Newey-West	0.1	−1.1	−1.4	−1.6
R-squared	0.00	0.01	0.01	0.02
No. of observations	46	46	46	40

Notes: Percentage change in exchange rate results from a 1 percentage point upward surprise in inflation. Positive coefficient indicates appreciation of domestic currency. Dates: Norway (August 1997–December 2000); United Kingdom (March 1993–December 1996). Number of observations may be less than total months due to missing observations. White and Newey-West used to correct for potential heteroscedasticity.

Table 9.7   Good news versus bad news

| | Headline | | | | Core | | | |
| | MoM | | YoY | | MoM | | YoY | |
	Positive	Negative	Positive	Negative	Positive	Negative	Positive	Negative
Coefficient	0.1	0.3	0.1	0.3	0.4	0.6	0.3	0.6
T-statistic	2.4	5.1	2.5	5.4	4.9	7.1	4.1	7.2
No. of observations	126	164	113	169	80	98	83	102

Notes: Regression method: stacked OLS. Percentage change in exchange rate results from a 1 percentage point upward surprise in inflation. Positive coefficient indicates appreciation of domestic currency. Countries: Australia, Canada, Euro area, Japan, New Zealand, Norway, Sweden, Switzerland, United Kingdom, and United States. Data: July 2001–December 2005. Number of observations may be less than total months due to missing observations. Positive indicates inflation higher than expected—bad news. Negative indicates inflation lower than expected—good news.

9.6   Concluding Remarks

In this chapter, we have presented what is apparently a new empirical regularity—that for inflation targeting countries, bad news for inflation is good news for the exchange rate. There are two antecedents for this empirical finding of which we are aware. The paper by Anderson et al. (2003) who report in their tables but don't discuss, that for some dollar exchange rates during the 1990s, inflation surprises and exchange rates covaried in the way reported in this chapter, but the estimated effects were not significant. In Goldberg and Klein (2006), it is shown that for most of the sample 1999 to

2005, bad news about inflation was bad news for the euro but that bad news about inflation become good news for the euro starting in 2003. They interpret this as consistent with improved ECB credibility during the period. Faust et al. (forthcoming) look at fourteen years of data for the United States and find that bad news about inflation is bad news for the exchange rate. Our findings are also related to but distinct from those in the much cited paper by Engel and Frankel (1984) and the paper of Hardouvelis (1984). They looked at the effect of money supply surprises (not inflation surprises) on the exchange rate. They argued that if a money growth targeting regime were credible, then a surprise increase in the money supply—that pushed money growth above target—would be expected to be reversed and that this would cause the nominal exchange rate to appreciate, which is, in fact, what they found for the Fed and the dollar in the early 1980s. We have presented a simple theoretical model that delivers the prediction that under certain inflation targeting regimes, bad news about inflation can be good news for the exchange rate. This is a workhorse model that does not require the two-country dynamic stochastic general equilibrium framework with optimal monetary policy as featured in Clarida, Gali, and Gertler (2002), and yet it delivers a similar prediction. What can these results tell us about monetary policy? They suggest two conclusions. First, the inflation targeting regimes in the countries featured in our sample are sufficiently credible in that they anchor expectations of inflation and the monetary policy path required to achieve the inflation target to such an extent that the currency becomes *more valuable* upon receipt of news that inflation is surprising high. This credibility effect has to be strong enough to counterbalance the long-run PPP anchor, which would tend to depreciate the currency on the impact of bad inflation news. We note that this is exactly what we find for the Bank of England before independence and for Norway before the adoption of inflation targeting. A second conclusion is that a credible inflation target is not enough for the "bad news is good news" effect to prevail. In other words, we cannot conclude that if bad news about inflation is bad news for the exchange rate, that a central bank is not an inflation targeter. The central bank must raise interest rates sufficiently aggressively to an inflation shock, and not just greater than one for one as required by the Taylor principle. In particular, this observation is important for correctly interpreting the results for the United States and Japan, for which we did not find significant evidence of the "bad news is good news" effect. Especially in the case of the Fed, we do not interpret our results necessarily as evidence against Fed credibility in anchoring inflation expectations. They are also consistent with the Fed's anchoring those expectations in the context of its dual mandate.

References

Anderson, T. G., T. Bollerslev, F. X. Diebold, and C. Vega. 2003. Micro effects of macro announcements: Real-time price discovery in foreign exchange. *American Economic Review* 93:38–62.

Ball, L. 1999. Policy rules for open economies. In *Monetary policy rules*, ed. J. Taylor, 127–44. Chicago: University of Chicago Press.

Blanchard, O., and C. M. Kahn. 1980. The solution of linear difference models under rational expectations. *Econometrica* 48:1305–13.

Campbell, J., and R. H. Clarida. 1987. The dollar and real interest rates. Carnegie-Rochester Conference Series in Public Policy 27.

Clarida, R. H., J. Galí, and M. Gertler. 1998. Monetary policy rules in practice: Some international evidence. *European Economic Review* 42 (6):1033–67.

———. 2002. Simple framework for international monetary policy analysis *Journal of Monetary Economics* 49 (5): 879–904.

Dornbusch, R. 1976. Expectations and exchange rate dynamics. *Journal of Political Economy* 84:1161–76.

Engel, C., and J. Frankel. 1984. Why interest rates react to money announcements: An explanation from the foreign exchange market. *Journal of Monetary Economics* 13:31–39.

Engel, C., and K. West. 2005. Exchange rates and fundamentals. *Journal of Political Economy* 113:485–517.

———. 2006. Taylor rules and the dollar-DM exchange rate. *Journal of Money, Credit, and Banking* 38:1175–94.

Faust, J., J. Rogers, S. Wang, and J. Wright. Forthcoming. The high frequency response of exchange rates and interest rates to macroeconomic announcements. *Journal of Monetary Economics*.

Goldberg, L., and M. Klein. 2006. Establishing credibility: Evolving perceptions of the European Central Bank. Federal Reserve Bank of New York. Mimeograph.

Hardouvelis, G. 1984. Market perception of Federal Reserve policy and the weekly money announcements. *Journal of Monetary Economics* 14:225–40.

Henderson, D. W., and W. J. McKibbin. 1993. A comparison of some basic monetary policy regimes for open economies: Implications of different degrees of instrument adjustment and wage persistence. *Carnegie-Rochester Conference Series on Public Policy* 39:221–317.

McCallum, B. T. 1983. On non-uniqueness in rational expectations models: An attempt at perspective. *Journal of Monetary Economics* 11 (March): 139–68.

Mark, N. 2004. Learning monetary policy rules and exchange-rate dynamics. University of Notre Dame. Mimeograph.

Mussa, M. 1982. A model of exchange rate dynamics. *Journal of Political Economy* 90 (February): 74–104.

Obstfeld, M., and K. Rogoff. 1996. *Foundations of international macroeconomics.* Cambridge, MA: MIT Press.

———. 2000. New directions for stochastic open economy models. *Journal of International Economics* 50 (February): 117–53.

Sarno, L.., and M. P. Taylor. 2001. *Exchange rate economics.* Cambridge, UK: Cambridge University Press.

Svensson, L. E.O. 2000. Open economy inflation targeting. *Journal of International Economics* 50:155–83.

Taylor, J. B. 1993. Discretion versus policy rules in practice. *Carnegie-Rochester Conference Series on Public Policy* 39:195–214.

Woodford, M. 2003. *Interest and prices.* Princeton, NJ: Princeton University Press.

Comment   Charles Engel

This chapter is a very nice contribution, not only to our understanding about monetary policy, but also to our understanding about exchange rates. The key finding of the chapter is that in inflation targeting countries, an announcement of higher inflation leads to a stronger currency. At first this might seem puzzling—doesn't inflation weaken a currency? But clearly markets believe that the central bank in the inflation targeting country will react to news of higher inflation by raising real interest rates. Higher real interest rates strengthen the currency.

The evidence in the chapter is strong—only in inflation targeting countries do we consistently see a relation between announcements of higher inflation and a stronger currency. Indeed, in England and Norway, there is evidence that the effect changed as the countries changed monetary policy to inflation targeting.

The fact that news of higher inflation leads to a stronger currency is not a new result. This is precisely the point that Engel and West (2006) highlighted in their model of exchange rate behavior based on Taylor rules. It is easy to understand the effect using the present value formulation for the real exchange rate as in Engel and West. To see this, simply substitute equation (16) of Clarida and Waldman into their equation (18) to get:

$$(1) \qquad q_t = -E_t \sum_{j=0}^{\infty} [b(\pi_{t+j} - \pi^*) + ay_{t+j}].$$

Here, assuming symmetric Taylor rules in the home and foreign country, π_t is the home inflation rate relative to the foreign inflation rate, and y_t is the home output gap relative to the foreign output gap. The real exchange rate, q_t, is defined in such a way that a decline in the real exchange rate is a home real appreciation.

Denote the exchange rate immediately before the announcement as q_{t-}, and immediately after q_{t+}. Then we have:

$$(2) \qquad q_{t+} - q_{t-} = -(E_{t+} - E_{t-}) \left[\sum_{j=0}^{\infty} (b\pi_{t+j} + ay_{t+j}) \right].$$

If the market learns current inflation is higher, and if there is some persistence to inflation, then q_t must fall.

Engel and West (2006) measure inflation surprises (and output gap surprises) using a vector autoregression (VAR) in inflation, output gap, and interest rates. They construct a "model" real exchange rate by constructing the present value in equation (1) and compare its behavior to the actual real

Charles Engel is a professor of economics and finance at the University of Wisconsin, and a research associate of the National Bureau of Economic Research.

exchange rate.[1] One of the key findings is that, as predicted, positive inflation surprises (in the home relative to the foreign country) lead to a real appreciation.

I very much like the Clarida-Waldman approach. An obvious shortcoming of the Engel-West approach is that the measure of inflation surprise (and our output gap surprise) is inferred from the VAR. What we want to measure is the surprise to the market. Undoubtedly, the market uses much more information in constructing forecasts than is included in the Engel-West VAR. The "event study" approach of Clarida and Waldman gives us a very crisp measure of the surprise—the difference between the actual announced inflation and the expectation of that announcement as collected by Bloomberg News Service from professional forecasters.

Clarida and Waldman mention the relationship of their method to my study with Frankel many years ago (Engel and Frankel 1984.) We looked at the effects of announcements of the money supply in the United States in the early 1980s on the value of the dollar. Like Clarida and Waldman, we related the change in the exchange rate to the difference between the announced value of the money supply and the expected value of the announced money supply as calculated from a survey of forecasters. The flavor of the finding is similar—we found that an unexpectedly high money supply led to an appreciation of the currency. Why? Because it indicated that the central bank was likely to react to this announcement by contracting the money supply. Indeed, we also found that short-term interest rates reacted positively to the money surprise. In the early 1980s, the Fed (supposedly) had a money supply target, so the reaction of the real exchange rate reflected the credibility of Fed policy. Likewise, the exchange rate reaction to news about inflation in the Clarida and Waldman chapter reflects credibility of inflation targeting central banks.

Clarida and Waldman mention three recent studies that have explicitly looked at the exchange rate reaction to announcements about inflation, and the results in those studies tend to support the findings of this chapter. There actually have been many other papers over the years that have examined the reaction of exchange rates to macroeconomic announcements. I will not attempt a survey of them here, but I do want to mention one of the earlier ones, Hardouvelis (1988). Hardouvelis looks at the reaction of interest rates and exchange rates to announcements of a number of economic variables in the October 1979 to August 1984 period. His findings are consistent both with Engel-Frankel and Clarida-Waldman. That is, he finds that the dollar consistently and significantly appreciates in response to positive surprises in the money supply, as in Engel-Frankel, and as we would expect if the Fed were credibly targeting the money stock. But the

---

1. Engel and West (2006) actually construct a discounted present value because the Taylor rule in one country includes a term for the real exchange rate. Mark (2007) considers a model very much like that in equation (1).

reaction of the dollar to announcements of the Consumer Price Index (CPI) and purchasing power parity (PPI) inflation is mixed. Across seven exchange rates, the sign of the response varies and is never statistically significant. As in the Clarida-Waldman chapter, bad news about inflation is not good news for the currency if the central bank is not inflation-targeting.

Although Clarida and Waldman emphasize the usefulness of their findings for interpreting the credibility of inflation targeting central banks, I think another point worth emphasizing is that the chapter provides empirical support for a fairly standard macroeconomic model of exchange rates. The important difference between this and some other empirical models is that the endogeneity of monetary policy is explicit, but otherwise the building blocks are familiar. Elsewhere, Ken West and I (Engel and West 2005) have emphasized that the standard metric for assessing exchange rate models—can they produce a better out-of-sample forecast of the exchange rate than the random walk model?—is not appropriate. Under plausible conditions, the models actually imply that exchange rates should approximately follow a random walk and, therefore, may not be capable of outforecasting the random walk model.

How, then, should we assess exchange rate models? I think the practical problem is that exchange rate changes are primarily driven by changes in expectations. The models pin down which expectations matter—monetary and real fundamentals. But we have a very hard time measuring the market's expectations. Rational expectations imply that the sample distribution of realized ex post values of variables should be the same as the ex ante distribution of agents' expectations. But in practice, when economic fundamentals are very persistent and subject to regime changes, it is difficult to validate rational expectations models using ex post data.

What is needed, instead, is some more direct way to capture the effects of changes in expectations. I think the approach of Clarida and Waldman (and others that use high-frequency responses to announcements) is one excellent way to deal with the problem. The survey data used here are probably a pretty good measure of expectations. The surveys are taken very close to the time of the announcement and are asking about expectations of a very specific number. The "surprise" in inflation measured by Clarida and Waldman is probably very highly correlated with the surprise to the market.

The fact that exchange rates react to news about inflation precisely the way the models predict—bad inflation news is good news for the currency of countries with inflation targeting—is also confirmation of the exchange rate model.

References

Engel, Charles, and Jeffrey A. Frankel. 1984. Why interest rates react to money announcements: An explanation from the foreign exchange market. *Journal of Monetary Economics* 13:31–39.

Engel, Charles, and Kenneth D. West. 2005. Exchange rates and fundamentals. *Journal of Political Economy* 113:485–517.
———. 2006. Taylor rules and the deutschemark-dollar real exchange rate. *Journal of Money, Credit, and Banking* 38:1175–94.
Hardouvelis, Gikas. 1988. Economic news, exchange rates, and interest rates. *Journal of International Money and Finance* 7:23–35.
Mark, Nelson. 2007. Changing monetary policy rules, learning, and real exchange rate dynamics. University of Notre Dame. Unpublished Manuscript.

Discussion Summary

Jordi Galí said that based on reduced-form regressions and structural vector autoregressions (VARs) uncovered interest parity was rejected in the data and that it must, therefore, be the case that the size of the exchange rate response did not match the size of the interest rate response in the way that would be implied by uncovered interest parity.

John C. Williams said that it would be interesting to look further into the uncovered interest parity issue—for example, to look at the movements of interest rates in the two countries and to see whether they also moved as predicted. He also argued that the particular value of the coefficient on surprise inflation in Clarida and Waldman's regressions did not necessarily relate to credibility or lack of credibility, but could reflect the particular loss function of the central bank in question. Clarida agreed that the most that could be inferred was the strength of the central bank's response to inflation.

Marvin Goodfriend recalled that in December 2002, the Fed mentioned deflation for the first time. The ten-year Treasury yield collapsed. He wondered whether this was due to expectations of deflation, or to expectations of a Fed response, and what other asset prices could tell us about this.

Regarding the U.K. evidence, *Peter Westaway* said that he considered that the main policy shift had taken place in 1992, when inflation targeting was adopted, rather than in 1997, when the Bank of England was made independent. Clarida replied that the authors used the 1997 reform because it was as close as possible to an unanticipated regime change. Westaway wondered what results would be obtained with other types of policy rule. Clarida said that in some sense, a Taylor rule could never be disentangled from a sufficiently complicated money rule. Westaway concluded by saying that over long periods, uncovered interest parity did not work well. On the other hand, at the time scale of individual days, it worked well, especially in response to classic monetary shocks.

Remarks

Donald L. Kohn
Laurence H. Meyer
William C. Dudley

Donald L. Kohn

Most fluctuations in stock prices, real estate values, and other asset prices pose no particular challenge to central banks, as they are just some of the usual factors influencing the outlook for real activity and inflation. But many argue that pronounced booms and busts in asset markets are another matter, especially if actual valuations appear to be misaligned with fundamentals. What should a central bank do when it suspects it faces a major speculative event—one that might be large enough to threaten economic stability when it unwinds? To help frame the discussion, I will focus on two different strategies that have been proposed for dealing with market bubbles.[1]

The first approach—which I will label the *conventional strategy*—calls for central banks to focus exclusively on the stability of prices and economic activity over the next several years. Under this policy, a central bank responds to stock prices, home values, and other asset prices only insofar as they have implications for future output and inflation over the medium term. Importantly, the strategy eschews any attempt to influence the speculative component of asset prices, treating any perceived mispricing as, rightly or wrongly, an essentially exogenous process. Following this strategy does not imply that policymakers ignore the expected future evolution of speculative activity. If policymakers suspect that a bubble is likely, say,

Donald L. Kohn is vice chairman of the Board of Governors of the Federal Reserve System.

1. David Reifschneider, of the Federal Reserve Board's staff, contributed substantially to the preparation of these remarks. The views expressed are my own and not necessarily shared by my colleagues on the Federal Open Market Committee.

to expand for a time before collapsing—the implications need to be folded into policy deliberations.

Despite its approach to perceived speculative activity, the conventional strategy does recognize that monetary policy has an important influence on asset prices—indeed, this influence is at the heart of the transmission of policy decisions to real activity and inflation. It occurs through standard arbitrage channels, such as the link between interest rates and the discount factor used to value expected future earnings.

The second strategy, by comparison, is more activist and attempts to damp speculative activity directly. It was described at length in "Asset Price Bubbles and Monetary Policy," an article published by the European Central Bank (ECB) last year. I quote from the article:

> This approach amounts to a cautious policy of "leaning against the wind" of an incipient bubble. The central bank would adopt a somewhat tighter policy stance in the face of an inflating asset market than it would otherwise allow if confronted with a similar macroeconomic outlook under more normal market conditions. . . . It would thus possibly tolerate a certain deviation from its price stability objective in the shorter term in exchange for enhanced prospects of preserving price and economic stability in the future. (ECB 2005, 58)

I am labeling this second approach *extra action,* as it calls for steps that would not be taken in ordinary circumstances.[2]

Compared with the first approach, the extra-action strategy responds to a perceived speculative boom with tighter monetary policy—and thus lower output and inflation in the near term—with the expectation of significantly mitigating the potential fallout from a possible future bursting of the bubble. Thus, the strategy seeks to trade off the near certainty of worse macroeconomic performance today for the chance of disproportionately better performance in the future, on the theory that the repercussions of a major market correction could be highly nonlinear. But the extra-action proposal is by no means a bold call for central banks to prick market bubbles. As the ECB article stresses, such an attempt would be extremely dangerous given the risk that a concerted effort at stamping out a speculative boom would lead to outsized interest rate hikes and recession. Rather, the extra-action strategy is intended only to provide some limited insurance against the possibility of highly adverse events occurring down the road.

I will be talking at length about the differences between the two strategies, but I must stress up front how much they have in common. Both policies aim to achieve the same general objectives of monetary policy, using the same broad analytic framework.

---

2. The article's label for this strategy—leaning against the wind—has been used for many years to describe the standard behavior of central banks. Given this history, I think that using the term *extra action* is less confusing.

At the risk of considerable oversimplification, policymakers can be described as seeking to set policy over time so as to minimize the present value of future deviations of output from potential and inflation from a desired level. Of course, we may not be prepared to write down a specific loss function, but our deliberative processes and our actions seem broadly consistent with that characterization of the general problem. This statement is true whether our institutions have a specific mandate to keep inflation low and stable and output close to potential, as in the United States, or whether our mandate is defined primarily in terms of stabilizing prices, as in the euro area. Stabilizing output complements maintaining price stability in the medium to long run, and often in the short run as well.

We also can agree that asset prices play critical and complicated roles in determining real activity and inflation. These roles involve the wealth effect, the cost of capital, and the relative prices of traded goods, as well as the value of collateral and thus the provision of credit. In sum, asset prices influence the economy in complex and subtle ways over potentially extended periods of time.

Finally, I think it fair to say that most central banks, faced with only a limited understanding of asset prices and their interactions with the full economy, engage in a form of risk management when dealing with market booms and busts. In part, they do this because any particular policy under consideration is never associated with a single forecast for the future paths of output and inflation but, instead, with a large set of possible scenarios with differing odds of coming to pass. Most policymakers engage in at least an informal weighing of these various possibilities and their implications when setting policy.

Now let me turn from areas of agreement to more contentious issues. As I see it, extra action pays only if three tough conditions are met. First, policymakers must be able to identify bubbles in a timely fashion with reasonable confidence. Second, there must be a fairly high probability that a modestly tighter policy will help to check the further expansion of speculative activity. And finally, the expected improvement in future economic performance that would result from a less expansive bubble must be sizable.

For the moment, let me set aside the first condition and assume that central banks can distinguish an emerging bubble from improving fundamentals at an early stage. Should we presume that a limited application of restrictive policy would materially restrain the speculative boom and make its eventual unwinding less disruptive for the overall economy?

Consider the U.S. stock market boom of the mid-to-late 1990s. The boom was fueled by a sustained acceleration of productivity and an accompanying rise in corporate profits—fundamental changes that justified a major rise in equity prices. How high those prices should have risen was difficult to judge in real time because no one, not investors or central bankers, could be sure how fast profits would grow in the future. In the event, share prices increased more than was justified by improved fundamentals. But overly optimistic expectations for long-run earnings growth were not being driven by easy money, and I see no reason to believe that an extra 50 or even 100 basis points on the funds rate would have had much of a damping effect on investor beliefs in the potential profitability of emerging technologies. At present, we just do not have any empirical evidence of a link between interest rates and corporate equity valuation *errors,* as opposed to standard arbitrage effects.

In general, we have a very poor understanding of the forces driving speculative bubbles and the role played by monetary policy. In fact, we cannot rule out perverse effects.[3] When the Federal Open Market Committee (FOMC) tightened in 1999 and early 2000, the trajectory of stock price increases actually steepened, and equity premiums fell—perhaps because investors became more confident that good macroeconomic performance would be sustained. Since mid-2004, we have seen a marked decline in bond term premiums, even as the funds rate has risen steadily, and U.S. central bankers have raised questions about the sustainability of low term premiums. These episodes illustrate that risk premiums often move in mysterious ways, and we should not count on the ability of monetary policy to nudge them in the intended direction.

Perhaps housing markets differ from equity and bond markets. For example, homeowners, who may have a less sophisticated understanding of the economy than professional investors, might mistakenly view a one-time rise in home prices—resulting, professional investors, a say, from a decline in interest rates—as evidence of a more persistent upward trend. If so, a monetary easing directed at stabilizing output and inflation might, conceivably, drive up real estate values by more than fundamentals alone would merit. Still, you would expect any mispricing from these sources to be reversed over time as interest rates returned to normal. In any event, empirical evidence on this issue is scanty. Further research into the causal connections, if any, between policy and bubbles would seem to be needed before we would know enough to act on such linkages with any confidence.[4]

However, let us suppose a situation arises in which we are convinced that tighter policy would check the future expansion of an emerging speculative bubble. Even then, with the second condition now met, the third condition

---

3. From a theoretical standpoint, the "rational bubble" literature demonstrates how a rise in interest rates might lead rational agents to boost the growth rate of asset prices during a speculative episode.

4. Recently, ECB staff economists Carsten Detken and Frank Smets have taken a laudable first step at addressing this issue in a paper that establishes some of the basic empirical facts about the correlations among interest rates, money, credit, asset prices, financial distress, and macroeconomic performance. See Detken and Smets (2004).

might not hold: the expected improvement in future macroeconomic performance from moderating the bubble's expansion may not be enough to more than offset the upfront costs of extra action. To explain this statement, I note again that extra action with *near certainty* weakens the economy and reduces inflation before the bubble bursts in exchange for the *chance* of better macroeconomic performance in the future.

Admittedly, if the worst-outcome scenario associated with an unchecked bubble is judged sufficiently dire and if the scenario is not seen as too improbable, then a risk-averse policymaker might regard the expected return from extra action insurance as worth its upfront cost. However, our confidence in such an assessment would seem to hinge on believing that the effects of market corrections could be markedly nonlinear. Proponents of extra action often cite an increased risk of severe financial distress as a potential source of such effects. However, without the onset of deflation, how large is this risk? In recent history, the health of the U.S. financial system and those of many other industrial countries remained solid after the collapse of the high-tech boom, despite the bankruptcy of dozens of telecom and dot-com firms, the loss of more than $8 trillion in stock market wealth, and stress in the nonfinancial corporate sector.

Of course, the nonlinear risks associated with a collapsing bubble may depend on the initial health of the financial system, and under some circumstances we could be worried about the potential for significant financial distress to accompany the bursting of a bubble, should that bubble expand further. Even in such cases, however, I wonder whether good prudential supervision in advance and prompt action to clean up any lingering structural problems afterward would not be better ways to deal with this possibility.

I do agree that market corrections can have profoundly adverse consequences if they lead to deflation, as illustrated by the United States after the 1929 stock market crash and the more recent experience of Japan. But it does not follow that conventional monetary policy cannot adequately deal with the threat of deflation by expeditiously mopping up after the bubble collapses. In Japan, deflation could probably have been avoided if the initial monetary response to the slump in real estate and stock market values had been more aggressive; in addition, macroeconomic performance would have been better if the government had dealt more promptly with the structural problems of the banking sector (Ahearne et al. 2002). As for the Great Depression, the Federal Reserve actually worsened the situation by allowing the money supply to contract sharply in 1930 and 1931, after unwisely attempting to prick the stock market bubble in the first place. Rather than demonstrating the need for preemptive extra action to restrain emerging bubbles, these examples are object lessons concerning the wisdom of central banks' easing promptly and aggressively following market slumps when inflation is already low, so as to head off the threat posed by the zero lower bound. By doing so, policymakers should be able to avoid the severe nonlinear dynamics of deflation.

Moreover, we should recognize that under some circumstances extra action may exacerbate the problem of deflation and the zero bound. If inflation is already low, and a central bank pushes it even closer to zero in trying to damp an emerging bubble, then extra action may actually increase the odds of monetary policy becoming constrained by the zero bound when the bubble eventually bursts. The only way this is not true is if extra action appreciably moderates the market correction and its expected fallout.

Another purported benefit of extra action is that, by raising the cost of capital to firms and households, it helps reduce overinvestment fostered during speculative booms, thereby making it easier for the economy to recover after the bubble collapses. However, we should be careful not to exaggerate the macroeconomic importance of such capital misallocation. True, the U.S. high-tech boom led to overinvestment in some sectors, wasting resources and creating lingering difficulties while capital overhangs were eliminated. But it is hard to see much of a cost in terms of diminished aggregate productivity, given the robust growth of output per hour over the past few years.

Furthermore, even if tighter monetary policy would have damped the enthusiasm for dot-com firms in the late 1990s, higher interest rates would have also led to less housing and less business investment outside the high-tech sector, where valuations were not obviously out of line with fundamentals. Thus, mitigating capital misallocation in one sector would have created capital misallocations elsewhere, making the assessment of the net gain from extra action difficult. And, as I have been pointing out, extra action would have idled some capital entirely for a time as economic activity fell short of its level consistent with stable inflation.

Now I would like to return to the first condition, the one I sidestepped a few minutes ago—the question of identifying market bubbles in a timely fashion. The ECB article stressed that such identification is a tricky proposition because not all the fundamental factors driving asset prices are directly observable, as the productivity acceleration and stock market boom of the 1990s illustrate. For this reason, any judgment by a central bank that stocks or homes are overpriced is inherently highly uncertain.

Taking extra action against a rise in asset prices mistakenly identified as a bubble has significant costs. By acting to mitigate a nonexistent problem, central banks reduce real economic activity and inflation below their desired levels to no purpose. Admittedly, policymakers, once they recognize their mistake, would presumably want the economy to run hotter for a time to restore the previous rate of inflation and would thereby make up for the initial output losses. But coming to the realization that the original assessment was mistaken and that asset prices were in line with fundamentals is likely to take some time. And, in the meantime, the mistaken call will have reduced welfare by needlessly inducing fluctuations in the macroeconomy.

Timing is also an issue. Let us suppose that the evidence is so compelling that policymakers become fairly confident that valuations are excessively rich. Unfortunately, I suspect that this call would often come so late in the day that, given the lags in the monetary transmission mechanism and uncertainty about the duration of bubbles, raising interest rates might actually risk exacerbating instability. The market correction could occur with policy in a tighter position but before extra action had enough time to materially influence speculative activity.

Notwithstanding the controversial aspects of identifying bubbles, policymakers may still want to warn the public about the possibility of asset price misalignments when the evidence merits. Such talk might do some good by prompting investors to stop and rethink their assumptions. And talk by itself should not do much lasting harm even if valuations turn out to be justified—provided, however, that words are not seen as precursors to action under circumstances in which conventional policy would still be the best approach.

To wrap up this critique, I summarize as follows: if we can identify bubbles quickly and accurately, are reasonably confident that tighter policy would materially check their expansion, and believe that severe market corrections have significant nonlinear adverse effects on the economy, then extra action may well be merited. But if even one of these tough conditions is not met, then extra action would be more likely to lead to worse macroeconomic performance over time than that achievable with conventional policies that deal expeditiously with the effects of the unwinding of the bubbles when they occur. For my part, I am dubious that any central banker knows enough about the economy to overcome these hurdles—at least at this point.

Proponents of extra action have their own bones to pick with the conventional strategy, especially as it relates to the alleged asymmetric nature of the policy's response to asset market booms and busts. In particular, the claim is often made that, based on the FOMC's actions over the past twenty years, the Fed actively works to support the economy in an event of a sharp decline in asset markets but does little or nothing to restrain markets when prices are rising, thereby creating moral hazard problems.

This argument strikes me as a misreading of history. United States monetary policy has responded symmetrically to the implications of asset price movements for actual and projected developments in output and inflation, consistent with its mandate. The most convincing evidence for this statement can be found in the results: interest rates have been consistent with underlying inflation remaining reasonably stable for some time now, accompanied by relatively mild fluctuations in real activity.[5]

Conventional policy as practiced by the Federal Reserve has not insulated investors from downside risk. Whatever might have once been thought about the existence of a "Greenspan put," stock market investors could not have endured the experience of the last five years in the United States and concluded that they were hedged on the downside by asymmetric monetary policy. Nor, for that matter, should they have concluded that the Federal Reserve does not act on the upside: If asset prices had been more closely aligned with fundamentals in the late 1990s, our policy would almost certainly have been easier, all else equal, because aggregate demand would have been weaker and, hence, inflation pressures even more muted than they were. The same considerations apply to homeowners: all else being equal, interest rates are higher now than they would be were real estate valuations less lofty, and if real estate prices begin to erode, homeowners should not expect to see all the gains of recent years preserved by monetary policy actions. Our actions will continue to be keyed to macroeconomic stability, not the stability of asset prices themselves.

Ironically, one can argue that extra action may pose a more significant risk of moral hazard. It is one thing for policymakers to raise questions about the relationship of asset prices to fundamentals and another for a central bank to take action to influence valuations in the direction of some "appropriate" level. How does this strategy play out if a central bank takes extra action and speculative activity continues unabated or even intensifies? Do policymakers raise rates even further above levels consistent with conventional policy and, if so, at what consequences for the economy? And what is the risk that, in taking such steps, a central bank would be seen by investors as taking on partial responsibility for asset prices? If so, would the pressure on central banks to support asset prices in market downturns increase?

References

Ahearne, Alan G., Joseph E. Gagnon, Jane Haltmaier, and Steven B. Kamin. 2002. Preventing deflation: Lessons from Japan's experience in the 1990s. International

5. As evidence of asymmetry, observers often cite Borio and Lowe (2004). The authors purport to show that the federal funds rate was unusually low during the headwinds period of the early 1990s but not correspondingly high before the onset of the 1990 recession. But their assessment is made in relation to the Taylor rule, which is not a particularly good description of monetary policy during this period of opportunistic disinflation. In the event, inflation in the United States came down steadily over the first half of the 1990s, accompanied by significant economic slack—results that seem to belie the claim that policy was overly easy.

Finance Discussion Paper Series no. 2002-729. Washington, DC: Board of Governors of the Federal Reserve System, June.

Borio, Claudio E. V., and Philip Lowe. 2004. Securing sustainable price stability: Should credit come back from the wilderness? BIS Working Paper no. 157. Basel, Switzerland: Bank of International Settlements, July.

Detken, Carsten, and Frank Smets. 2004. Asset price booms and monetary policy. ECB Working Paper Series no. 364. Frankfurt, Germany: European Central Bank, May.

European Central Bank (ECB). 2005. Asset price bubbles and monetary bubbles. *Monthly Bulletin* (April): 47–60.

Laurence H. Meyer

This is a topic of very special interest to me as I served on the Federal Open Market Committee (FOMC) during the period the equity bubble was building. As the bubble was emerging, I was operating along the lines of what I have come to call the "indirect approach" to monetary policy, an approach that Greenspan clearly encouraged at the time and later defended vigorously and an approach that Ben Bernanke provided intellectual support for in a paper written before he became a governor and then chairman of the Fed (Greenspan 2002; Bernanke 2002).

According to the indirect approach, monetary policy should be adjusted only in response to changes in output gaps or inflation—current or prospective—and, therefore, should not directly respond to any other variables, including equity prices, housing prices, or exchange rates.

I have to admit, however, that the experience with the indirect approach in the second half of the 1990s did not turn out entirely well, though the Fed did very effectively execute what Alan Blinder has called the "mopping up" strategy: being alert to the possibility that a possible asset bubble will abruptly correct and quickly adjusting policy in the case of a discontinuous adjustment to maintain aggregate demand (Blinder and Reis 2005).

But with the benefit of hindsight, I look back at that experience and wonder whether monetary policy could have been better managed to mitigate the risks to future macroeconomic performance associated with an emerging equity bubble. I admit that today I still do not know the answer to that question, but my greatest regret about my time on the FOMC is how little time we as a committee devoted to thinking about the appropriate monetary policy response to the suspected equity bubble. So I appreciate

Laurence H. Meyer is vice chairman of Macroeconomic Advisers, LLC, and a director at large of the National Bureau of Economic Research.

The author would like to thank Brian Sack for his helpful comments.

that this conference gives me another opportunity to think about the experience and ask whether there is some approach beyond the indirect one that might have improved macroeconomic outcomes.

I start by identifying the three basic approaches to responding to a suspicion of an emerging equity bubble: the indirect approach, pricking the bubble, and an intermediate approach, sometimes referred to as "leaning against the bubble." I want to explore the meaning and case for the intermediate approach and then consider another way of potentially leaning against an emerging asset bubble—not through the adjustment of the policy rate, but through Fed communication.

Direct and Indirect Approaches

The indirect approach is actually a broader vision for monetary policy that implies policymakers should ignore more than just asset prices in setting policy. This approach, summarized well by the Taylor rule and its successors, holds that monetary policymakers should adjust policy in relation to actual or forecasted changes in output gaps and inflation, period. They should not respond directly to any other variables, be they asset prices or anything else. The beauty of the indirect approach in the context of today's conference is that monetary policy is driven to indirectly lean against asset bubbles by following this strategy, at least to the extent that the rise in asset prices strengthens aggregate demand and, hence, growth; raises output gaps; and increases the risk of higher inflation. But any move to tighter policy in this case should be in proportion to the increase in actual or prospective output gaps and inflation, not calibrated to bring about a given adjustment in asset prices themselves.

An alternative approach that deviates from these restraints is one that involves a direct response of monetary policy to asset prices, on top of the traditional focus on output gaps and inflation. Specifically, it allows for monetary policy to tighten by more than would be justified by output gaps and inflation when asset prices appear to be moving well beyond their fundamental value.

In principle, the direct approach does not call on the Fed to target asset prices, only to respond to asset price movements in the setting of its policy rate. But if we introduce this direct response into a Taylor rule, we would presumably do so by adding a response of the policy rate to the gap between prevailing asset prices and their estimated fair value. From the perspective of the Taylor rule, in this case, it appears that the Fed would be targeting asset prices every bit as much as it would be targeting a preferred inflation rate and the Fed's estimate of the economy's natural rate of unemployment. But perhaps the better way of viewing such an expanded Taylor rule is that it allows for a trade-off between improving the near-term macro performance by responding to changes in prevailing or near-term expected levels of the output gap and inflation and protecting against the possibility of unfavorable macro outcomes later in the event of the abrupt correction of a significant equity bubble.

The direct approach itself comes in two forms. The boldest version calls for the use of monetary policy to prick an equity bubble. One could interpret this as a directive for the central bank to tighten until it appeared that asset prices are moving back to their fundamental value. There appear to be very few, if any, observers of bubbles that argue for this direction. Instead, there is more support for a milder version—and this is what I refer to by "leaning against the bubble"—that calls on monetary policymakers to tighten modestly more than could be justified by movements in output gaps and inflation in the face of a suspected emergence of an equity bubble. This is the approach captured by the modified Taylor rule discussed in the preceding.

Why the Indirect Approach Didn't Work

As I noted in the preceding, the indirect approach itself is intended to lean against equity bubbles. But, in fact, the FOMC, despite following this approach, did not tighten during most of the period in second half of the 1990s when equity prices were soaring and when the wealth effect triggered by rising equity values was powerfully boosting consumer spending. What went wrong?

First, the productivity acceleration was providing a disinflationary impetus to the economy at the same time it was boosting profits and the expected growth rate of earnings. Meeting after meeting, Greenspan would warn that above trend growth and tightening labor markets were signaling possible inflationary pressures ahead, and we should, therefore, be alert to the need to tighten—but not yet, not while core inflation was itself actually declining, especially when we didn't fully understand why.

In effect, even though may of us on the Committee saw ourselves as following an indirect approach, the policy response that otherwise would have been expected from that approach was short-circuited by Chairman Greenspan's perception of a structural break in productivity growth. There is little doubt now that the productivity break did occur and that Greenspan was well out in front of both the Committee and the Fed staff in detecting it. Nevertheless, with the benefit of hindsight, I wonder today whether the resulting policy path was the best for the economy—and, more specifically, whether policy lingered at too low of a funds rate over most of 1999, when equity prices were soaring.

Second, while the FOMC nevertheless thought about tightening on a number of occasions during this period, it was pulled back again and again by some external shock—the Asian financial crisis spreading to Korea, for example, and later the global financial turbulence of the fall of 1998, culminating with the implosion of Long-Term Capital Management (LTCM). Indeed, in the end, the FOMC eased in the fall of 1998 rather than tightened, and perhaps not surprisingly, the equity market really blew out in 1999.

The question this experience raises is whether there are conditions under which the indirect approach is destined to fail to lean against emerging bubbles (for example, during a period of a productivity acceleration) or whether the problem is simply that the indirect approach was not really executed during this period.

The "Leaning against the Bubble" Approach

Maybe, and quite likely, the indirect approach is the best we can do, and we simply have to accept that occasionally we will have periods of speculative excess that will impart some instability to the real economy. But we should at least be open-minded and indeed actively search for a better approach. In that spirit, let me offer a few thoughts on the "leaning against the bubble" approach described in the preceding.

Broadening the Indirect Approach

It seems to me that the indirect approach is often defined too narrowly. The case for leaning against an asset bubble is not some fetish about keeping asset prices close to some measure of fundamental value, but concern with the consequences for broader macroeconomic performance should an asset bubble emerge and then correct discontinuously (as is typically the case for an equity bubble). In a forward-looking approach to monetary policy—one in which monetary policy is set in light of the forecast for output gaps and inflation—the indirect approach in principle is consistent with policymakers taking into account the potential risk to future macroeconomic performance from an emerging equity bubble.

The issue here is that policy response dictated by the indirect view seems to depend importantly on the horizon employed. Consider, for example, monetary policy during a period of rapidly escalating equity prices to levels that the central bank saw as unwarranted by fundamentals. Does the indirect approach consider the effect of equity prices on output today, or in a year, or in two years? Would the magnitude of the policy response increase the longer the horizon considered in the policy rule?

The broader view focuses on the trade-off between less favorable economic performance in the near term from leaning against a bubble and more favorable economic performance later as a result of avoiding or mitigating the adverse effects of the eventual asset market correction. In this sense, leaning against the bubble really should be classified as part of the indirect approach—just one that takes into consideration the entire future path of output and inflation, rather than their values today or in the near-term future.

Risk management and Erring on the Side of Restraint

Another way to think about "leaning against the bubble" is the risk management approach. That is, given the asymmetric downside risks some time in the future associated with a likely correction of an emerging bubble, is there a case for tightening more than would otherwise be appropriate to mitigate the size of the bubble and, therefore, the eventual downside shock to the economy? This seems very much in the spirit of the risk management approach, taking out insurance against some high cost but low probability event. Actually, in this case, at least after some point, it seems like taking out insurance against a high cost and not so low possibility event, but one whose timing and severity is still highly uncertain.

The risk management approach suggests that monetary policy should "err on the side of restraint" when there is a suspicion of an emerging equity bubble. I think back to the experience in the second half of the 1990s. Meeting after meeting we would talk about the possibility of tightening but, most of the time, pull back. In the case of suspicion of an emerging bubble, perhaps the tie should always go to tighter policy.

Bernanke, while ultimately concluding that the indirect approach is the best that central bankers can do in practice, nevertheless has offered a rather sympathetic discussion of the "leaning against the bubble" option (Bernanke 2002). He says that doing so would be analogous to taking out insurance against the destabilizing effects of the emergence and ultimate popping of the bubble. And then he goes on to note that the optimal degree of insurance is rarely zero. However, he concludes that such an approach, while plausible in principle, is not likely to be effective in practice, because a moderate "lean" would have little effect on any asset bubble. That is at least the question, if not the answer.

Bernanke's position on leaning against a bubble quite dramatically highlights the theme of this conference, the two-way relationship between monetary policy and asset prices—that is, not only how monetary policy should respond to asset prices, but also how asset prices respond to monetary policy. Bernanke's argument about the practical limits of leaning against the bubble suggests that the two sides of this interrelation may be importantly related. Specifically, the intermediate approach is more likely to be effective if monetary policy has a relatively large effect on equity prices (or housing prices) relative to its effect on broader aggregate demand. Because Bernanke's reading of the impact of monetary policy on equity prices is that the effect is surprisingly small, this feeds into his conclusion that leaning against a bubble is unlikely to be effective in practice.

The risk management approach, of course, is very much about taking insurance against asymmetric risks. In the case of asset price movements, the risks seem much greater when asset prices are above than when they are below a level consistent with fundamentals. If this is the case, there is a powerful asymmetry in the response to asset price movements that is not captured in the simple expanded Taylor rule discussed in the preceding.

Asset markets seem asymmetric in the sense that asset prices seem more likely to rise smoothly and, beginning from a point of significant overvaluation, to collapse more abruptly. In this case, the risk management approach would be more relevant to a case when asset prices were above fundamentals than when asset prices were below fundamentals.

The risk management approach might also call for a nonlinear response to an emerging asset bubble. When asset prices are only modestly above fair value, given the uncertainty in the estimate of fair value, policymakers might not want to respond at all. But beyond some threshold, a response could be called for and one that gets disproportionately greater in response to the divergence from fair value.

Challenges to Going beyond the Indirect Approach

There are to be sure a number of daunting challenges that confront any strategy that tries to move beyond the narrow indirect approach.

First, there is the so-called identification problem, the difficulty in identifying in real time whether there really is a bubble, given the limits of our knowledge of the determinants of fair value. This may be more relevant, however, to how quickly it makes sense to take an emerging asset bubble into account. But I doubt that this consideration should have made policymakers cautious in concluding that that equities were materially over valued when the price-earnings (P-E) ratio (for the S&P 500, based on lagged earnings) got to 25, and they should have been still less cautious about reaching such a conclusion when the P-E ratio passed 30, and perhaps there should have been no question at all when the P-E ratio surpassed 40. The identification problem sometimes seems to be thrown out as an excuse for not acting, reflecting a false sense of humility about what we know. There really are some things we do know!

Second, and related to the first challenge, if it is difficult to respond early in the process of an emerging bubble, perhaps all the Fed will do if it responds late in the process is put its fingerprints on the inevitable correction. Doing so would appear to put the Fed in the "wealth destruction" business, not a good place for a central bank to be.

Third, as reflected in Bernanke's views, there is some question about the relative effect of a rising policy rate on asset prices (especially at a time when the latter are being driven by speculative frenzy) relative to the effect more broadly on aggregate demand. The argument here is that it would take such a large increase in interest rates to blunt an asset bubble that moving in this direction would almost certainly produce very adverse macroeconomic outcomes. This is a possibility, but the case here is hardly definitive and is worth exploring further.

Fourth, even if we believe there might be an equity bubble and that this might pose a risk to future macro performance, this recognition is not likely to be very helpful in pinpointing when or how discontinuously the bubble might burst. That is, the suspicion of an emerging bubble is simply not very useful for near-term forecasting. The trade-off is, as a result, between the high probability of less favorable performance in the near term against the possibility that there might be more favorable economic performance at some unspecified point in the future, perhaps outside the policy horizon of the central bank.

Fifth, the appropriate policy response has to depend on the assumption about the bubble process going forward. If the bubble were assumed to continue to escalate, then presumably the policy response would be considerably larger even under the indirect approach. If it were assumed to quickly pop, the indirect approach might advocate no response at all, or even an easier policy stance. The lack of understanding of bubble dynamics makes it very difficult to operationalize the broader vision of the indirect approach developed in the preceding.

Sixth, the fact that the emergence of the equity bubble initially strengthens aggregate demand while the ultimate correction will potentially seriously undermine aggregate demand further increases the challenge to monetary policymakers. Indeed, it raises a question about the merits of raising interest rates to mitigate the risks to future macro performance of an emerging equity bubble. If the policy response comes too late in the speculative cycle, it could precipitate and indeed reinforce the adverse effect on aggregate demand of the bursting of the bubble.

Fed Communication: A Tool for Addressing Bubbles

While I have tried to open up the discussion of moving beyond the narrow indirect approach, I have not definitively made the case for doing so. I did the best I could. But given the challenges associated with using the policy rate for combating a bubble, perhaps we should look for other vehicles.

It seems to me that there may also be an important and mostly unexploited role for Fed communication in leaning against emerging bubbles. When we think of Fed communication in the context of suspected bubbles, we usually focus on comments by a Fed chairman directly raising the possibility that asset prices may be overvalued. The most famous of these, of course, was Greenspan's "irrational exuberance" comment in December 1996 (Greenspan 1996). However, such direct verbal interventions tend to be rare.

The question of whether a Fed chairman should ever talk about equity prices reminds me of one of my favorite Fed stories that I included in my book *A Term at the Fed* (Meyer 2004). The incident was about the foreign exchange market rather than the equity market, but could equally well have been about the equity market. Joe Coyne, the Fed's director of public affairs at the time, was imploring then chairman Paul Volcker to say something to calm the foreign exchange market. Volcker was of the school that you did not talk about equity prices or exchange rates, so he resisted. The argument went on as Volcker sat down in the barber's chair. In the middle of a further attempt by Coyne to persuade the chairman, Volcker interrupted Joe and turned to Lenny the barber and asked him what he thought. Lenny responded with a very thoughtful answer supporting the chairman, prompting Volcker to turn to Coyne and ask, "Joe, can you cut hair?" So the point is that Fed chairman have traditionally been reluctant to comment on the reasonableness of equity values or exchange rates.

I would argue that this is the wrong perspective. In fact, the Fed should talk often and forcefully about how it sees asset prices relative to their fair values. Why is this taboo? The two most common explanations are, one, that markets may overreact to such proclamations and, two, that fundamentals are hard to measure. In my view, the second consideration should not stop the central bank. Market participants are aware of the challenges involved here—they do it for a living. The markets will take the information for what it is worth—a reasonable but imperfect measure of the appropriate valuation of asset prices. It gives market participants an additional piece of information to use to the degree that they see fit, and I believe that they will filter it considerably, which should mitigate any concerns about a market overreaction.

It seems likely that market participants would dismiss small deviations from the fair values published by the Fed. After all, it is hard to predict what might happen to a 5 percent over- or undervaluation in the S&P 500. However, the approach would have more bite when asset prices moved well out of line, as in the late 1990s. If the Fed were to publish a deviation of that magnitude, it might make market participants think more clearly about the fundamentals that must be assumed to justify current equity prices. This could have been a useful deterrent to rising equity market values in the late 1990s, in that the assumptions required were quite extreme.

Thus, this approach could effectively lean against bubbles without requiring a response of the short-term interest rate and the economic costs associated with it. It also seems consistent with Bernanke's emphasis on transparency.

Let me offer a specific proposal: the Fed should publish an official report on the determinants of fair value in the equity market (and perhaps in other asset markets) and then provide periodic (perhaps quarterly) updates assessing the value of asset prices relative to fair value. The report, and periodic updates of the measures it includes, would be posted on the Board's Web site.

One advantage of this approach is that the Fed chairman would not have to decide if or when to make verbal interventions in the case of a suspected emergence of an asset bubble. The updates would follow a fixed schedule, and media stories focused on equity valuations would inevitably include the assessment of fair value from the Fed's analysis, increasingly so when there was the suspicion of an emerging equity bubble. The chairman and other FOMC members could reinforce this by explicitly noting any important divergence, but the media would do most of the work. The coverage on the Web site could also include comments and analysis from scholars in the field so that the public had easy access to an academic consensus as well as the Fed's own reading.

This approach could be broadened to apply to a variety of risk spreads as well as equity prices. Indeed, what I am suggesting is very close to what Donald L. Kohn did in a speech delivered last July (Kohn 2005). In that paper, Kohn noted that the Fed routinely monitors risk premiums on equities, corporate bonds, and Treasury securities, in part because these measures are viewed as indicators of economic conditions but also because they can directly affect real economic activity. And they are also important tools for monitoring financial stability.

Kohn followed this speech up with the following comment in a talk earlier this year:

> Notwithstanding the controversial aspects of identifying bubbles, policymakers may still want to warn the public about the possibility of asset price misalignments when the evidence merits. Such talk might do some good by prompting investors to stop and rethink their assumptions. And talk by itself should not do much lasting harm even if valuations turn out to be justified—provided, of course, that words are not seen as precursors to action under circumstances in which conventional policy would still be the best approach. (Kohn 2006)

This approach might take the Fed in the direction of some other central banks in publishing a financial stability report that focuses on financial vulnerabilities.

How would this have worked in the second half of the 1990s? Recall that the P-E ratio (for the S&P 500 based on lagged earnings) at the time that Greenspan uttered his famous irrational exuberance remark was about 18. That was basically in the middle of the range of estimates of fair value for the P-E ratio—from a low of about 14 or 15 that is the longer run historical average for the P-E ratio to the low 20 range that Jeremy Siegel has argued is warranted today (Siegel 2002). In any case, a P-E ratio of around 18 would not really have seemed the critical time to weigh in about the possibility of an equity bubble. So this approach probably would have taken some of the sting out of Greenspan's question—although the fact is that there was not much sting to begin with—less than a 2 percent drop that day. This simply reflects the fact that, in my view, Greenspan was rather precocious at this point.

Still, we wonder if this approach might have had some restraining effect if it had been in play during the subsequent period when the case for a bubble became more compelling. The Fed presumably would have been on record as believing that fair value is somewhere between, say, 14 and, say, 21 for the P-E ratio and would have strongly emphasized the evidence of the mean reverting nature of equity prices. That might itself help. Every time a story was written on whether there was a bubble, the Fed's study would invariably be mentioned and the authority of the Fed would be put behind a presumption that a bubble was emerging.

As I noted earlier, a clear case could have been made that equity valuations were very rich when the P-E ratio surpassed, say, 25, and, by the time it crossed 30, there should have been few doubters that a bubble was emerging, and when it approached and surpassed 40—well, you get the picture.

The emphasis on the fundamental value of asset prices will likely highlight the role of mean reversion. One thing market participants should be confident about is that when equity valuations move dramatically above the fair value range, they will ultimately correct back.

Some will perhaps argue that this approach would not have been very convincing in this episode because the fundamentals of the period were unusually favorable to equity valuations, and it was simply not so obvious that the historical norms applied anymore. We were after all in the "new economy," and the economy did at the time seem to be breaking all the old rules. That is precisely the reasoning that should have been leaned against, I say with the benefit of hindsight.

Still the argument might go, even with the benefit of hindsight, if there was an acceleration of productivity in play at the time and that meant faster growth in output, earnings, and dividends. Plug that into your dividend discount model. Doesn't that justify an increase in the sustainable P-E ratio? The answer is not necessarily and, in any case, not necessarily by much.

The Fed report could point out the difference between arithmetic and economics when it comes to assessing equity valuations. It is arithmetically correct that a persistent increase in the growth rate of earnings, *ceteris paribus,* would raise the value of equities in the dividend discount framework. But *ceteris paribus* is just a fancy Latin name for partial equilibrium. Sound economic analysis is about general equilibrium. In a general equilibrium model, we would have to ask how a productivity acceleration affects other pieces of the dividend discount model. The answer, of course, is that a productivity acceleration, if persistent, would also raise the equilibrium real interest rate, offsetting much if not all the increase in the P-E ratio associated with the faster growth in earnings.

The same logic applies to the argument that soaring equity values was a reasonable response to a plausible decline in the equity premium in a world with less real side volatility and less inflation volatility than previously. A decline in the equity premium, of course, *ceteris paribus,* would raise equity values in the dividend discount model. There is that pesky ceteris paribus again, I know you are thinking. But a decline in the equity premium would also lead, over time, to an increase in the equilibrium real rate, reversing some or all of the earlier rise in equity prices.

So perhaps the message should be that it is hard for changes in economic fundamentals to dramatically alter fair value norms and that asset prices are powerfully mean reverting (relative to fundamentals), and, therefore, attention should always be focused on the fair value norm.

The Bottom Line

The bottom line is that we ought be actively engaged in a discussion about whether monetary policy could improve relative to the narrow interpretation of the indirect approach. I hope I have been able to contribute to that discussion. I do not have much confidence in the leaning against the bubble approach, but I think we have to seriously consider what the risk management approach implies during such periods in the context of a broader vision of the indirect approach and consider whether it would be prudent in such circumstances to at least to err on the side of restraint. I am somewhat more confident that the direction I suggested in terms of Fed communication might at least provide a modest restraining effect during a period of an emerging asset bubble. I think the Fed should consider moving in this direction, and I actually believe they may already have begun to do so.

References

Bernanke, Ben. 2002. Asset-price "bubbles" and monetary policy. Remarks before the New York Chapter of the National Association for Business Economics, New York. http://www.federalreserve.gov/boarddocs/speeches/2002/20021015/default.htm.

Blinder, Alan, and Ricardo Reis. 2005. Understanding the Greenspan standard. Paper presented at Federal Reserve Bank of Kansas City Symposium, The Greenspan Era: Lessons for the Future, Jackson Hole, WY.: http://www.kc.frb.org/PUBLICAT/SYMPOS/2005/pdf/BlinderReis.paper.0804.pdf.

Greenspan, Alan. 1996. The Challenge of Central Banking in a Democratic Society. Remarks at the annual dinner and Francis Boyer lecture of the American Enterprise Institute for Public Policy Research, Washington, DC. http://www.federalreserve.gov/boarddocs/speeches/1996/19961205.htm.

———. 2002. Economic volatility. Speech presented at Federal Reserve Bank of Kansas City symposium, Rethinking Stabilization Policy, Jackson Hole, WY. http://www.federalreserve.gov/boarddocs/speeches/2002/20020830/default.htm.

Kohn, Donald L. 2005. Monetary policy perspectives on risk premiums in financial markets. Paper presented at Federal Reserve Board conference, Financial Market Risk Premiums, Washington, DC. http://www.federalreserve.gov/boarddocs/speeches/2005/20050721/default.htm.

———. 2006. Monetary policy and asset prices. Paper presented at European Central Bank colloquium held in honor of Otmar Issing, Monetary Policy: A Journey from Theory to Practice, Frankfurt, Germany. http://www.federalreserve.gov/boarddocs/speeches/2006/20060316/default.htm.
Meyer, Laurence H. 2004. *A term at the Fed.* New York: HarperCollins.
Siegel, Jeremy. *Stocks for the long run.* 3rd ed. New York: McGraw-Hill.

William C. Dudley

As I see it, a Federal Reserve consensus exists on how monetary policy should respond to asset bubbles. It consists of three major observations:

1. Asset bubbles are hard to identify.
2. Monetary policy is not well-suited to respond to bubbles.
3. The cost/benefit trade-off of "leaning against the wind" against asset bubbles is unfavorable.

From these propositions, two important policy implications directly follow:

1. The central bank should only take asset bubbles into consideration in the conduct of monetary policy to the extent that these asset bubbles affect the growth/inflation outlook.
2. The monetary authorities should be there to "clean up" after bubbles burst, both to prevent systemic problems and undesired downward pressure on economic activity or inflation.

Relative to this consensus, I would argue that:

1. Asset bubbles are not that hard to identify—especially large ones.
2. If one means by monetary policy the instrument of short-term interest rates, then I agree that monetary policy is not well-suited to deal with asset bubbles. But this suggests that central bankers should examine the efficacy of other instruments in their toolbox, rather than simply ignore the development of asset bubbles. Parenthetically, this may require development of additional policy tools if the current tools are deemed inadequate.
3. When the possibility of additional instruments is added to the mix, this may improve the cost/benefit trade-off from addressing asset bubbles early, prior to these bubbles bursting.

William C. Dudley was an advisory director at Goldman Sachs when these comments were presented. He is currently the executive vice president of the Markets Group at the Federal Reserve Bank of New York.
I thank John Y. Campbell and Martin Feldstein for inviting me to participate.

So let's examine in more detail where my views deviate from the Fed consensus.

Turning first to the issue of the difficulty of identifying asset bubbles, I don't think major asset bubbles are hard to identify. What is difficult to determine is how big a bubble will ultimately be and the causes and timing of its demise.

Over the past twenty-five years, for example, I can identify at least five bubbles that one could reasonably have identified in real time:

1. Dollar appreciation in 1984 to 1985
2. Stock market overvaluation in 1987
3. Credit market spread widening in 1998 associated with the failure of Long-Term Capital Management (LTCM)
4. Dotcom and NASDAQ bubble of 1999 to 2000
5. Regional U.S. housing bubbles that are currently in the process of unwinding

I say this with some confidence because I tried to speculate against three of the five bubbles listed in the preceding myself (with limited success I might add, indicating why I remain an economist rather than have transitioned to being a trader). And I probably would have tried to speculate against the other two had good market instruments been available to do so.

As I see it, the development of an asset bubble generally consists of three major stages. First, there is some sort of regime shift that generates an initial rise in valuation that is justified and sustainable. For the U.S. equity market of the later 1990s, this would include factors such as the reduced cyclicality of the economy, benign inflation, or the secular rise in the productivity growth trend. The first two factors could have been expected to lead to a lower equity risk premium and higher equity prices. The latter factor could be expected to lead to a higher earnings growth rate.

For the U.S. housing market of the past five years, the initial impulse to the housing price rise was the fall in long-term interest rates. Only beginning in 2004 did the housing market become a bubble. In some regions, prices continued to rise much faster than income even though mortgage rates were no longer declining.

Second, the rise in valuation leads to a change in perception about the riskiness of investing in the asset class. Rather than the asset being perceived as more risky as the price rises, it is perceived to be less risky because it has not gone down in price. There is a corollary to this. Investors tend to raise their expectations of the prospects for future price appreciation after the asset has gone up in price, when, in fact, rapid price appreciation should lead investors to lower their expectations. If expectations are adaptive rather than fully rational, this can contribute to asset bubbles.

Third, the price appreciation causes the believers in the sustainability of the bubble to forget about the fact that the economy has important self-equilibrating mechanisms. For example, consider what happens when stock prices rise, all else equal. This reduces the cost of capital, which, in turn, stimulates investment. The rise in investment puts downward pressure on profit margins and upward pressure on real interest rates. Both weigh on valuation and undermine the fundamental supports for the initial rise in stock prices.

Oftentimes, the trigger for the collapse of an asset bubble is some event that calls into question a widely held market belief. For example, one trigger for the LTCM debacle was the decision of Russia to default on its ruble debt. This was unexpected because market participants thought the worse-case scenario was that Russia would just print more rubles to service its debt. Another example is the role of portfolio insurance in the 1987 stock market crash. Portfolio insurance works to limit risk if market prices adjust continuously. In 1987, prices gapped lower, and portfolio insurance played an important role in making prices move discontinuously. After the fact, the flaws of portfolio insurance were self-evident. But when it occurred, it was unanticipated.

With respect to the assertion that monetary policy is ill-suited to respond to asset bubbles, I generally agree with this view if, by monetary policy, we are referring to the level of short-term interest rates. I doubt that an additional 50 to 100 basis points of monetary policy tightening in the 1999 to 2000 period would have had a significant impact on the dot-com bubble.

That said, I reach a very different conclusion than the Federal Reserve consensus. Rather than just giving up and saying that monetary policy doesn't work well with respect to asset bubbles, I would argue that the more appropriate conclusion is that this just underscores the need to develop other instruments to use to address such bubbles.

In reaching this conclusion, I would emphasize that the need for new tools has increased. As the role of depository institutions has diminished in the financial system relative to the capital markets, the tools of prudential supervision and regulation of depository institutions most likely has become less effective in preventing or limiting bubbles. This is especially true in cases in which credit standards are determined by the capital markets rather than depository institutions.

Consider, for example, the case for mortgages and credit derivative obligations. The prices for most of these types of obligations are not determined by banks but instead are determined in the capital markets. If bank examiners try to limit the type of mortgage loans that banks make, but the capital markets have a strong appetite for this type of risk, then tough bank supervision would not prevent this business from occurring. Instead, it would simply be forced out of the banking system into the capital markets.

So what tools are available? Unfortunately, not many and not very effective ones at that.

Two major tools come to mind. First, the monetary authorities have the ability to use the "bully pulpit" to influence market participant's views and expectations. For example, with respect to the stock market boom, Federal Reserve officials could have emphasized that higher productivity growth would generate an investment boom that would put pressure on profit margins or that higher productivity growth would lead to higher real interest rates that would put pressure on stock market valuation.

If you look at the evidence from the period, it is quite striking. Corporate profit margins peaked in 1997. But the earnings expectations of equity analysts kept increasing until the stock market bubble collapsed. For example, in the early 1990s, the median long-term earnings growth estimate of equity analysts was 12 percent per year. By 1997, it had climbed to slightly below 14 percent per year. It did not stop climbing until it reached a peak of 17 percent per year in 2000. Clearly, the behavior of profit margins and equity analyst expectations were inconsistent. Federal Reserve officials could have emphasized this disconnect in their speeches and testimony.

In fact, Chairman Greenspan reached a very different conclusion that had a much different implication. He cited the rise in equity analysts' earning growth expectations as evidence that the increase in productivity growth was sustainable. Perhaps, this was not the proper emphasis!

Second, margin requirements could be used to discourage speculative activity. Federal Reserve officials rejected the use of equity margin requirements in response to the stock market bubble because they concluded that such margin rules could be easily circumvented. Although the requirements could be circumvented, an increase in stock market requirements might still have had an impact. The announcement effect alone might have had an impact. We just don't know because Fed officials didn't try to use this instrument. If the Fed had tried and failed, I would be more willing to conclude that margin rules will not work.

Moreover, Fed officials could have pushed for broader authority to make it more difficult for investors to circumvent the margin rules. The margin requirements could have been broadened. Or the margin requirements could have been altered in a way to better target their impact. For example, if the margin requirement had been tied to volatility, this would have implied higher margin requirements on NASDAQ-style equities, precisely the result intended.

Supervision and regulation of depository institutions, the "bully pulpit," and margin requirements—together they do not make a very full or effective tool kit. This suggests that Fed officials and others should explore developing additional instruments to add to the Fed's arsenal.

In addition to broader margin rules, this might include capital adequacy rules and or counterparty risk rules designed to limit leverage and risk. Increased disclosure requirements of portfolio positions by lightly regulated institutions such as hedge funds might also prove useful. Consider the LTCM debacle. Long-Term Capital Management was much more highly leveraged than market participants, and its major counterparties appreciated. Also, many major market participants had market positions similar to LTCM's. Better disclosure might have limited the ability of LTCM to expand its risk positions, and it could also have discouraged market participants from taking similar types of positions.

The disclosure of portfolio positions would enable investors to find out when the "hot money" is all positioned the same way. Such a revelation would change investors' perceptions of risk and could help dampen speculation and incipient asset bubbles.

I clearly don't have the answer with respect to designing new tools for central bankers to use to address asset bubbles. But I think a more fruitful line of inquiry is to move in this direction. In my mind, the issue of whether short-term interest rates should be adjusted to lean against asset bubbles is mostly settled. It is time to move on and explore how central bankers can develop better tools to respond to asset bubbles.

Discussion Summary Donald L. Kohn, Laurence H. Meyer, and William C. Dudley

Martin Feldstein asked *Donald L. Kohn* for his views on Japanese real estate values. When capitalization rates were at 2 percent at a time when Japanese government bonds were yielding at least as much, should the Bank of Japan have responded? Kohn replied that he had been in favor of improving the supervision and regulation of Japanese banks. It had been clear that there was a problem in the banking system. If the Japanese financial system had been reformed earlier, and the Bank of Japan had responded more quickly when the bubble burst, economic outcomes in Japan would have been better. Kohn agreed with Feldstein's suggestion that the government should not have allowed banks to support their balance sheets with equities whose valuations depended on high land values.

Feldstein said that Alan Greenspan's approach had been that the central bank should intervene swiftly following the bursting of a bubble. He suggested that in Japan, however, no amount of monetary easing could have rescued the banks. Kohn responded that a rapid response from the central bank would have helped considerably and that such a response would have ensured that less deflation occurred. Studies at the Fed suggested that although recession could not have been averted, it could have been shorter and less deep.

Feldstein asked *William C. Dudley* what he thought could be done to improve the already impressive resilience of the U.S. financial system. Dudley said that although the mortgage market worked well in stable economic conditions, policymakers should worry about how the subprime market would fare if the economy weakened while house prices declined. Also, the Fed should think about how to expand its span of control. He suggested that further disclosure requirements were needed for creative mortgage products such as negative amortizers and teaser adjustable rate mortgages (ARMs).

Feldstein said that he was intrigued by Laurence H. Meyer's proposal that the Fed should issue quarterly reports on asset prices. But, on the other hand, Graham and Dodd's book recommended that the price-earnings ratio should be around 10. If Feldstein had believed that, he would never have invested in the market. There was a risk that the Fed would wrongly encourage people to sit out of the market. Meyer replied that the Fed should present the conventional wisdom—which may evolve over time. Furthermore, he said, the Fed has the advantage of being seen to have sober judgment. There are, in any case, benefits of airing different points of view. Dudley said that he agreed with this point. In 1999 to 2000, for example, bearish equity analysts were out of a job. It was important to have someone who was still in business at a time like that presenting a dissenting view.

John Y. Campbell pointed out that the Fed has a comparative advantage in helping people to understand the distinction between real and nominal quantities. Feldstein commented that Allan Meltzer's book revealed that even the Fed had only relatively recently understood the distinction. Campbell also mentioned a paper by Federal Reserve Board economists Brian Bucks and Karen Pence that demonstrates that the distribution of self-reported ARM mortgage risks is very different from the true distribution as reported by mortgage lenders. This implies that some mortgage borrowers do not understand their true risk exposures.

Glenn D. Rudebusch said that the Reserve Bank of Australia and the European Central Bank (ECB) had been vocal about house-price bubbles and appeared to have been successful in controlling them. Kohn replied that in the case of Australia, there had also been a change in the tax law so that the treasury and central bank had been working together. Dudley pointed out that there had also been a terms-of-trade shock in Australia's favor, which had strongly underpinned the Australian economy.

Rudebusch asked whether the view of the Fed as a street sweeper cleaning up problems—the so-called Greenspan put—had driven up equity prices as investors felt that they would be protected against price declines. Dudley responded that given that the NASDAQ index went from over 5,000 to less than 1,500, the put had clearly been well out of the money!

Peter Westaway asked Meyer whether he would suggest publishing an unconditional indicator such as a price-earnings ratio, or, on the other hand, something like a risk premium. He also suggested that the Fed's asset price report might be sufficiently complicated that it would require a user guide. Meyer replied that it was important to keep things not too technical. The distinction between conditional and unconditional price indicators was not too important because in equilibrium, increases in the price-earnings ratio are associated with decreases in the risk premium. He said that he liked the simplicity of a measure such as the price-earnings ratio.

Stephen G. Cecchetti said he also agreed with Meyer's proposal. He compared such a report with the numbers produced by the Bureau of Economic Analysis (BEA) or Bureau of Labor Statistics (BLS). Given that industrial production indexes are based on all sorts of imputed statistics, why not do the same in this case? Kohn argued that if there were an academic consensus, the question would be easier. But in 1996, 50 percent of academics thought the market was too high, and 50 percent thought it was too low. Meyer said that that was true when the market price-earnings ratio was 18, but as it rose to 25 or 30, a consensus developed among academics that rationally expected returns on equity had declined.

Brian Sack said that he agreed with Kohn's points about the cost of acting against bubbles that turn out not to be bubbles. He suggested that this was dependent on the particular asset class in question. For example, in the case of equities, a bubble is associated with a low risk premium or high expected earnings growth. In either case, an interest rate increase is called for. But in the case of bonds, a bubble is associated with low risk premiums or low expected inflation. These two scenarios call for different interest rate responses. Kohn responded that he had in mind the cost of sacrificing some short-run output. He agreed that different assets would have different sacrifice ratios.

Contributors

Leonardo Bartolini
International Research Function
Federal Reserve Bank of New York
33 Liberty Street
New York, NY 10045-0001

Markus K. Brunnermeier
Department of Economics
Princeton University
Princeton, NJ 08540

John Y. Campbell
Department of Economics
Littauer Center 213
Harvard University
Cambridge, MA 02138

Stephen G. Cecchetti
International Business School
Brandeis University
P.O. Box 9110
Waltham, MA 02454

Richard H. Clarida
Department of Economics
Columbia University
420 West 118th Street
New York, NY 10027

Hans Dewachter
Economics Department
Catholic University of Leuven
Naamsestraat 69, Bus 3565
3000 Leuven, Belgium

William C. Dudley
Markets Group
Federal Reserve Bank of New York
33 Liberty Street
New York, NY 10045-0001

Charles Engel
Department of Economics
University of Wisconsin
1180 Observatory Drive
Madison, WI 53706-1393

Martin Feldstein
National Bureau of Economic
    Research
1050 Massachusetts Avenue
Cambridge, MA 02138-5398

Jeffrey A. Frankel
Kennedy School of Government
Harvard University
79 John F. Kennedy Street
Cambridge, MA 02138

Jordi Galí
Centre de Recerca en Economia
Internacional (CREI)
Universitat Pompeu Fabra
Ramon Trias Fargas 25
08005 Barcelona Spain

Simon Gilchrist
Department of Economics
Boston University
270 Bay State Road
Boston, MA 02215

Marvin Goodfriend
Tepper School of Business
Carnegie Mellon University
5000 Forbes Avenue
Pittsburgh, PA 15213

Donald L. Kohn
Board of Governors of the Federal
    Reserve System
20th Street and Constitution Avenue,
    NW
Washington, DC 20551

Thomas Laubach
Board of Governors of the Federal
    Reserve Board
20th Street and Constitution Avenue,
    NW
Washington, DC 20551

Andrew Levin
Board of Governors of the Federal
    Reserve System
20th Street and Constitution Avenue,
    NW
Washington, DC 20551

Hanno Lustig
Department of Economics
University of California, Los Angeles
Box 951477
Los Angeles, CA 90095-1477

Marco Lyrio
Finance Group
Warwick Business School
University of Warwick
Coventry CV4 7AL, England

Laurence H. Meyer
Macroeconomic Advisers, LLC
231 South Bemiston Avenue, Suite 900
St. Louis, MO 63105

Tommaso Monacelli
IGIER
Università Bocconi
Via Salasco, 5
20136 Milan, Italy

Monika Piazzesi
Graduate School of Business
University of Chicago
5807 South Woodlawn Avenue
Chicago, IL 60637

Roberto Rigobon
Sloan School of Management
Massachusetts Institute of Technology
50 Memorial Drive
Cambridge, MA 02142-1347

Glenn D. Rudebusch
Economic Research Department
Federal Reserve Bank of San Francisco
101 Market Street
San Francisco, CA 94105

Brian Sack
Macroeconomic Advisers, LLC
231 South Bemiston Avenue, Suite 900
St. Louis, MO 63105

Masashi Saito
Institute for Monetary and Economic
    Studies
Bank of Japan
2-1-1 Nihonbashi Hongokucho
Chuo-ku, Tokyo 103-8660, Japan

Martin Schneider
Department of Economics
New York University
19 West 4th Street
New York, NY 10012

Lars E.O. Svensson
Sveriges Riksbank
SE-103 37 Stockholm, Sweden
and Department of Economics
Princeton University
Princeton, NJ 08544-1021

Daniel Waldman
Barclays Capital
200 Park Avenue
New York, NY 10166

Peter Westaway
Bank of England
Threadneedle Street
London EC2R 8AH, England

John C. Williams
Federal Reserve Bank of San Francisco
101 Market Street
San Francisco, CA 94105

Michael Woodford
Department of Economics
Columbia University
420 West 118th Street
New York, NY 10027

Author Index

Subject Index